Birds of the
HORN OF AFRICA

Ethiopia, Eritrea, Djibouti, Somalia, and Socotra

Dedicated to

John Ash, *ornithologist and pioneer,*
who has done so much to further our knowledge of the Horn of Africa,
and
Christopher Helm, *publisher and friend,*
who dreamed of a field guide to the region.

Birds of the
HORN OF AFRICA

Ethiopia, Eritrea, Djibouti, Somalia, and Socotra

Nigel Redman,
Terry Stevenson, and John Fanshawe

With contributions from
Nik Borrow and Brian Finch

Illustrated by
John Gale and Brian Small

PRINCETON UNIVERSITY PRESS
PRINCETON AND OXFORD

Princeton Field Guides

Rooted in field experience and scientific study, Princeton's guides to animals and plants are the authority for professional scientists and amateur naturalists alike. **Princeton Field Guides** present this information in a compact format carefully designed for easy use in the field. The guides illustrate every species in color and provide detailed information on identification, distribution, and biology.

Related Titles:

Birds of East Africa: Kenya, Tanzania, Uganda, Rwanda, and Burundi, by Terry Stevenson and John Fanshawe
Birds of Kenya and Northern Tanzania: Field Guide Edition, by Dale A. Zimmerman, Donald A. Turner, and David J. Pearson
Birds of Southern Africa, by Ian Sinclair, Phil Hockey, and Warwick Tarboton
Birds of Western Africa, by Nik Borrow and Ron Demey

Published in the United States, Canada, and the Philippine Islands in 2009 by
Princeton University Press, 41 William Street, Princeton, New Jersey 08540

nathist.press.princeton.edu

Published in the United Kingdom and European Union in 2009 by
Christopher Helm, an imprint of A&C Black Publishers Ltd., 36 Soho Square, London, WID 3QY

www.acblack.com

Library of Congress Control Number 2009921681
ISBN 978-0-691-14345-3

Designed by Fluke Art, Cornwall

Printed in China by C & C Offset Printing Co Ltd

10 9 8 7 6 5 4 3 2 1

Illustration credits
John Gale: 1-23, 46-57 (part), 73-81, 93-101, 114-119, 126-128, 133-136, 144 (part)-146 (part), 150-151 (part), 155 (part)-164, 167-173, 179 (part), 181-189, 207-208.
Brian Small: 24-45, 57 (part)-72, 82-92, 102-113, 120-125, 129-132, 137-144 (part), 146 (part)-149, 151 (part)-155 (part), 165-166, 174-179 (part), 180, 190-200, 209-213.
Norman Arlott: 201-206.

CONTENTS

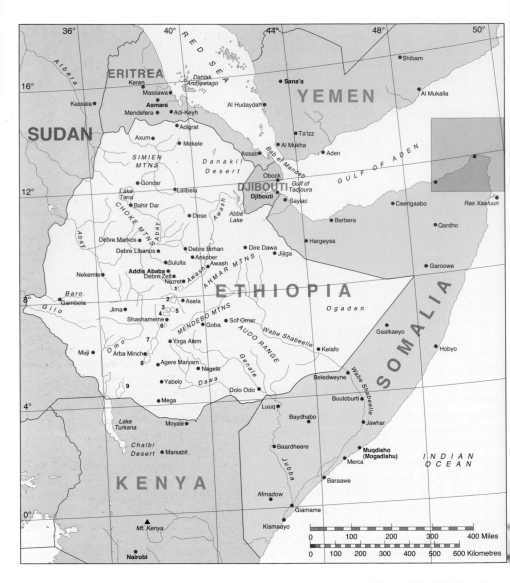

Rift Valley lakes:
1. Koka
2. Zwai
3. Abiata
4. Shalla
5. Langano
6. Awasa
7. Abaya
8. Chamo
9. Chew Bahir

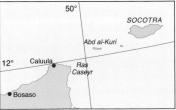

Figure 1: Political map of the Horn of Africa.

INTRODUCTION

The Horn of Africa comprises the countries of Ethiopia, Eritrea, Djibouti and Somalia, together with the Socotra archipelago which is politically part of Yemen. It is a region of high endemism with more than 70 species only (or virtually only) found in this corner of the continent, and also a major migration route for Palearctic species wintering in Africa. The composition of the resident avifauna combines elements of several biomes, including the Sudan-Guinea savanna biome, the Sahel biome, the Sahara-Sindian biome, the Afrotropical Highlands biome, the Somali-Masai biome and the East African Coast biome (Fishpool & Evans 2001). Although parts of the region are currently off-limits to birders (notably Somalia), most of the endemics and near-endemics can be seen in Ethiopia, which has remained the most accessible country within the Horn of Africa. Covering every species ever recorded in the five territories included in the book, the primary aim of this guide is to enable identification to species level of any bird that may be seen in the region, and in many cases to subspecies level if desired.

This book was conceived as a companion to the *Field Guide to the Birds of East Africa* (Stevenson & Fanshawe 2002), and was initiated even before the latter was published. Covering the region lying immediately to the north of East Africa, it is inevitable that there is a considerable overlap in species. Rather than duplicate effort, we have therefore re-used a considerable number of illustrations from the East Africa guide, frequently rearranging them into new plates. Many other images have been digitally manipulated to convert them into the correct subspecies for the Horn of Africa. Nevertheless, a large number of new artworks were prepared for this guide, covering species and subspecies not found in East Africa and, in addition, several groups or plates (e.g. cuckooshrikes, tits, cisticolas and flycatchers) have been re-painted in entirety.

Similarly, the species accounts for overlapping species have been adapted or expanded as necessary (sometimes extensively) to include appropriate information on races and distribution in the Horn of Africa. Despite the strong overlap in the avifauna of the two regions, almost 20% of the species in the Horn of Africa do not occur in East Africa, and new accounts were written for these species. The result is a complete and comprehensive field guide to the birds of this relatively little-known part of Africa. It is worth noting that more than a thousand species have been recorded from the region, which is almost half of the total number of species to be found in sub-Saharan Africa, and a hundred more than in the entire subregion of southern Africa.

Knowledge of bird identification and distribution is constantly evolving, and guides such as this can quickly become out of date. We intend to update the information in future editions of the book, and welcome any comments, corrections or new information to assist us in keeping this field guide as up to date as possible. Please send any contributions to the authors, care of the publishers.

ACKNOWLEDGEMENTS

Most field guides are collaborative efforts, requiring the contributions and assistance of a great number of people. This one is no exception. First, we should once again like to thank all those who contributed to *Birds of East Africa*, the sister-volume on which this book is based. The published literature is also a major source of information, and the principal works consulted in the preparation of this book are listed in the References. In particular, the various publications by John Ash, John Miskell and John Atkins have been invaluable, and the three authors themselves have provided much additional assistance for which we are very grateful. For Djibouti and Socotra respectively, Geoff Welch and Richard Porter have answered numerous queries quickly and comprehensively.

We are deeply indebted to Brian Finch for providing many of the Voice accounts and for commenting on the first drafts of the species texts, and to Nik Borrow for preparing the drafts of the distribution maps which were then expertly redrawn by Marc Dando. Nik also kindly read and commented on the entire text, providing many valuable insights from his considerable knowledge of the region. Large portions of the text were also read by Jason Anderson, John Miskell, János Oláh and Claire Spottiswoode who provided many useful comments and corrections. In particular, Jason Anderson updated information for Eritrea, and John Miskell updated the distribution of birds in Somalia since the publication of his own *Birds of Somalia* (Ash & Miskell 1998). We are also very grateful to Iain Robertson for preparing the original plate list, Philippe Mayaux for the topography and vegetation maps in the introduction, and Mark Balman and Ian May of BirdLife International for the IBAs map.

We would also like to thank the following for answering queries, providing advice or assistance, and for general discussions about African birds: Vasil Ananian, Keith Barnes, David Beadle, Keith Betton, Hugh Buck, John Caddick, Peter Clement, Nigel Collar, Martin Collinson, Tim Crowe, Normand David, Giuseppe De Marchi, Alan Dean, James Dean, Edward Dickinson, Bob Dowsett, Julian Francis, Merid Gabremichael, Floyd Hayes, David Hoddinott, Abdi Jama, Guy Kirwan, Peter Lack, Klaus Malling Olsen, Gerald Mayr, Jaz Miles-Long, Pete Morris, David Pearson, Adrian Pitches, Magnus Robb, Steve Rooke, Hadoram Shirihai, Cheryl Tipp and David Willard. As always, we are very grateful to Robert Prys-Jones and Mark Adams for facilitating access to the magnificent skin collection at the Natural History Museum in Tring and assisting with specific queries.

Most field guides are judged more by the quality of their artwork than by anything else, and we have been fortunate to have our plates painted by two of the world's foremost illustrators. John Gale and Brian Small have done an incredible job in portraying the many birds of the region, and it has been a pleasure and an inspiration to work with them on this book. In the course of preparing and checking the artwork, we are grateful to the many photographers whose work has made our job so much easier, and in particular those whose photographs appear on the African Bird Image Database, which is managed by the African Bird Club. We thank them all.

We are very grateful to Nigel Collar for his diligent editing and much sound advice over the years, but our greatest debt of gratitude is due to Julie and Marc Dando for their considerable work in putting the book together. The digital manipulation of images, production of maps, and design and layout of the plates and text were all executed with professionalism, flair and efficiency. The result is a tribute to their skills.

Finally, but not least, I owe a huge debt of gratitude to my family: my daughter Emily has not seen as much of me as she might have liked in the past two years, and my wife Cheryle Sifontes has cheerfully tolerated the long periods at my desk without complaining and has given me full encouragement in my endeavours.

Nigel Redman
East Sussex, August 2008

HOW TO USE THIS BOOK

The bulk of this book comprises 213 colour plates with text and maps on opposite pages. The design and layout have been executed with field identification in mind. It is our wish to make it as easy as possible to identify birds in the field, irrespective of any previous experience, and this is the primary purpose of any field guide. An explanation of the components and layout of the plate section and species accounts follows.

THE PLATES

In developing the book, we worked closely with the artists to design the plate layouts. Using field notes, museum specimens and a wide range of still and video reference material, they have taken immense care to ensure that the images painted are as accurate as possible. The design of each page has been carefully planned to ensure that the images are reproduced as large as possible, drawn to scale (unless indicated otherwise), and aesthetically laid out. We have tried to show every species recorded in the region in all its major plumages, taking account of sex, age and seasonal and geographical variation, as well as colour morphs if relevant. Thus, most races that are identifiable in the field have been illustrated.

Rather than label plate images by numbers, we have chosen to use English names for species, and the trinomial (subspecific) scientific name, on its own, for races, but a nominate race is usually simply labelled 'nominate'. Where no race is given, the species is either monotypic or racial variation is slight. Males and females are labelled with symbols, and other ages/plumages are given in full. Individual unlabelled images can be assumed to be adult.

Plates are arranged around similar-looking species, often with commoner birds at the top. However, while the family sequence within the plates is largely taxonomic, the species themselves are not always in a recognised taxonomic sequence. Inevitably, closely related species are frequently placed together, but in the case of larger groups, the selection of species for a plate might be linked to habitat, such as dry country plovers, or to a part of the region, such as highland francolins. Sometimes they may be divided according to their geographic distribution, such as African and Palearctic wheatears, or simply by size or colour. Design constraints have meant that a few species appear out of place, on a page with species that are not so closely related; in these cases, the text for the species in question is separated from the rest with a simple line across the page. Partly in order to redress the problem of birds appearing out of sequence, a full checklist of the birds of the region in taxonomic order is given on pages 461-472.

SPECIES ACCOUNTS

Most text pages opposite the plates have a short introduction in italics, highlighting key features common to the group of species on that plate. Sometimes a plate may contain two or more groups of similar species and, space permitting, each group will have a short introduction. Occasionally, complex families may merit a longer introduction to explain identification issues affecting the various subgroups covering several plates. It is intended that this information should be read in conjunction with the species accounts.

The information given in the species accounts comprises the following elements (although only subdivided into two or three subheadings, namely **HH**, **Voice** and **Notes**).

Names Every species is given an English and scientific name (see pages 16-17 for an explanation of the taxonomy and nomenclature used in this book).

Measurements A simple measurement of total length is quoted in both centimetres and inches, taken from authoritative sources. This is the length of the bird measured from bill tip to tail tip, if it was stretched out on its back as a museum specimen. Measurement of length can be quite misleading, as it does not take into account relative bill and tail lengths, or the bulk of the bird, but it is widely used as an indication of the comparative sizes of birds. It is most useful when comparing related species. However, birds vary in size from one individual to another, and many books give a range of length for some species, e.g. 18–20cm. In this book, we have chosen to give a single average figure, as this is usually accurate enough for the estimation of size in the field (which is the purpose of giving the measurement). The only exception is where males and females differ in size significantly, for example in long-tailed species such as widowbirds and whydahs, and in these cases we give measurements for both males (♂) and females (♀). Note that males are often slightly larger than females, although in most raptors females are larger than males (sometimes significantly). For seabirds and raptors, we have additionally given an average wingspan (abbreviated as WS), as these birds are more likely to be seen only in flight.

Identification Each species account typically begins with a sentence summarising one or two key features of the bird, or its general appearance (applicable to all plumages). This is followed by the principal individual plumage characteristics beginning with the adult male, then on to adult female (where sexes differ), and ending with immature and/or juvenile plumages. For most Palearctic species, the account starts with the non-breeding plumage that is most frequently encountered in our area. Birds in flight are also described where necessary. It should be emphasised that these descriptions are not exhaustive, partly owing to constraints of space; it was not our intention to repeat what can be seen on the plates, but to supplement it and highlight the most important information for identification. The text is necessarily terse at times, as we have tried to give as much information as space permitted. For almost every species, the **key identification feature(s) are italicised**. It should be noted that it is always safest to identify a bird from a combination of plumage and other features, not by a single character, even if that character is italicised.

Similar species Distinctions from similar species are given in the Identification section, where relevant, rather than under a separate subheading. We have tried to make sure that similar species are on the same plate. In a few cases this has not been possible, and where such a potential confusion species is mentioned, its plate number is given in brackets.

Geographical variation Many polytypic species are represented by more than one subspecies in our region, and we give details of the racial variation to be found, usually at the end of the Identification section. Races are listed with brief details of their distribution (in brackets) and how they differ from one another, unless variation is very slight. However, although discriminating features are briefly noted for most polytypic species, it is not always possible to identify birds to subspecies in the field without considerable experience or unless two or more forms are side by side (unlikely except in a museum). It may only be possible to identify some races on range or in certain plumages (usually adult or adult male), but the racial information is provided here to inform birders on the extent of geographical variation in the region. Inevitably, some species will be more easily identified to subspecies than others, but readers are advised to exercise caution in claiming a particular subspecies, especially if out of known range or without previous experience. Photographs may help confirm subspecies identifications when access to more reference material is available.

Terminology Although all birders are familiar with the field guide format, it may be helpful to explain some of the terminology as used in this book. A basic understanding of standard ornithological terminology is essential in interpreting the species accounts. Line drawings showing the terms used to describe the parts of perched and flying birds are given in the 'Bird topography' section on pages 21-22.

• When birds are termed **small**, **medium-sized** or **large**, these are relative sizes in comparison to closely related species.

• In order to save space, we have sometimes used a single word to include more than one plumage feature (unless specified otherwise), and this should be obvious when compared to the plates. Thus, **throat** may mean chin and throat, **legs** often include tarsus and feet, **crown** may include forehead and/or nape, and **vent** often includes the undertail-coverts. **Wing-coverts** generally include the lesser, median, greater and primary coverts. **Flight feathers** comprise the primaries and secondaries. More general terms such as **above** and **below** are self-explanatory, and are used as alternatives to upperparts and underparts.

• The use of the terms **breeding** and **non-breeding plumage** is self-explanatory, but in the case of cisticolas, where some populations of a single species have different seasonal plumages and others do not, we have used the term **perennial plumage** to indicate a plumage that is retained throughout the year.

- Without reference to a standard colour chart, the meaningful description of coloration can be somewhat problematic, as understanding of the meaning of names of particular colours can vary from person to person. Consequently, we have deliberately used rather general terms to describe plumage coloration, which should be readily understood by all birders. Words such as buff, rufous, chestnut, olive and horn are used widely, and comparison with the plates will usually elucidate the colour intended. Compound colours are frequently used, such as olive-brown or pinkish-buff. In these cases, the dominant colour is the second word, and the qualifier denotes a tinge or hint of that colour. Thus, olive-brown is brown tinged with olive. The words dusky, dark and pale are used where precise colours are difficult to determine. Where a colour has the suffix -ish, this is used to indicate a dull or weak shade of that colour.
- The terms **winter visitor** and **wintering** have been used widely for Palearctic visitors to the region. These are species that breed in the 'temperate' regions to the north and east of the African continent, during the northern (or boreal) summer. Thus, winter plumage equates to non-breeding plumage.
- We have used the term **immature** quite generally for non-adult birds, but have not dwelt too much on the rather brief **juvenile** plumage. Passerines tend to have this first, non-downy plumage for a few weeks only and, should it be encountered, the bird's parents are invariably close by. For passerines of Palearctic origin wintering in our area, immature is taken to mean **first-winter** plumage.
- Other terms are defined in the Glossary on pages 23-25.

HH (Habitat and habits) Habitat and elevation are important tools in bird identification. Many species are restricted to particular habitats or altitudes, and are unlikely to be found elsewhere, but note that some species may occupy different altitudes at different seasons, and Palearctic migrants may be found in unfamiliar habitats in the non-breeding season. In this section of the species accounts, we outline the principal habitats of the species and, where appropriate, the altitudinal range in metres. These ranges represent known altitudes that the species has been recorded at within the region, but as many species have relatively few records with accurate elevational data their altitude limits must be regarded as provisional. It is likely that some ranges will be extended both higher and lower in the future, as species become better known. We have generally avoided the use of technical terms in the habitat descriptions, but more information can be found in the Habitats section on page 28 and in the Glossary on page 23. Distributions are also summarised, but to save space the five countries/territories and the points of the compass are referred to by abbreviations throughout (see page 15). In a few cases important place names are mentioned (see the endpaper maps). If a species is endemic or almost endemic to the region, this is also stated (and a full list of endemics and near-endemics can be found in Appendix 1). Other relevant information that may aid identification is also given in this section, such as how the birds are likely to be encountered (as pairs, flocks etc), their status and relative abundance in the region, and particular habits or behaviours. Most Palearctic visitors are present from Sep–Nov and/or Mar–May, with some staying throughout the northern (boreal) winter. For non-resident birds, a period in months is often given, e.g. 'Oct–Mar' (meaning the species is present from October to March).

Status The status of birds in the region can be categorised as follows:
    Resident: a species that is present throughout the year and breeds.
    Intra-African migrant: a species that breeds in one part of Africa, and spends the rest of the year in another; such birds may only appear seasonally to or from breeding and non-breeding areas. **Intra-tropical** is sometimes used for shorter-distance African migrants.
    Palearctic migrant: a species that breeds in the Palearctic (during the northern summer), and spends the non-breeding season (the northern winter) in sub-Saharan Africa; such birds may only be passage migrants in our region, but if they remain through the winter, they are frequently referred to as winter visitors.
    Vagrant: a species outside its normal range that is of very irregular occurrence in our region. Some 'vagrants' may prove to be of more regular occurrence with increased observer coverage.

Abundance Relative abundance is somewhat subjective and can vary across the region. For the birder, perceived abundance may also be affected by factors such as knowledge of vocalisations, in the case of shy or skulking species, and effort. However, we have tried to give an indication of average abundance using the following terms, based on the likelihood of a bird being recorded during a visit to an appropriate site (i.e. within geographical and altitudinal range, and in suitable habitat at an appropriate time of year):

Abundant (or *very common*): unlikely to be missed

Common: usually encountered daily in moderate numbers

Frequent (or *fairly common*): likely to be encountered almost daily in small numbers

Uncommon: can easily be missed during a short visit

Scarce: only irregularly encountered, and may not even be seen on longer visits

Rare: very unlikely to be seen, even during a long visit

These terms are sometimes qualified with the word 'locally', where a species has a restricted range in the region or occurs only patchily within its range.

Please note that many species are still poorly known in the region (and many areas are still only rarely visited), and it is likely that their status and abundance within the region may be revised with increased knowledge.

Voice Describing bird songs and calls in a confined space is fraught with problems, and in most cases learning vocalisations is only really achieved through listening to birds in the field or to recordings. For many skulking and look-alike species, however, voice is a vital clue to identity, and a description of the main songs and calls is given for most species in the Voice section.

Songs are generally given in territorial situations or for mate attraction, and they may not necessarily be melodious. They may also be seasonal and can vary geographically. Bear in mind also that many species have a variety of songs and be aware of individual variation, where one bird may sing differently from another in the same location. Calls are usually shorter and are used to maintain contact between individuals and groups, as alarm calls to warn others of danger, or in mobbing situations. Some birds typically call only in flight, while others call more frequently, using different calls for different situations. Some songs are complex versions of typical calls, and it may not be obvious whether the bird is singing or calling. Generally, we describe a bird's song first and then its call, but this may be reversed for species whose calls are more familiar than their songs. Some species typically duet, with both members of the pair performing the 'song'. This is often antiphonal, where one individual's song is immediately followed by the other's, with the resulting sound often seeming to be the product of just one bird. Boubous frequently perform such songs. Asynchronous duets involve both birds singing together in a more haphazard fashion.

Many of our vocal descriptions have been prepared by Brian Finch, based mainly on his own field recordings of birds in East or North-East Africa. In some cases, a description is based on a recording from outside these regions. We have tried to present the most typical vocalisations for all species, and the most appropriate races. Generally, we have not given much detail of the songs of Palearctic visitors if they are unlikely to be heard in the region. Wherever possible, these accounts include transliterations (in italics): Eastern Nicator, for example, is described as extremely vocal, invariably from dense cover, with a loud song that starts hesitantly with a *yu-ik-wit-wer-trrr* and bubbles into a jumbled *cho-chou-choou-chueeee*. Such descriptions are subjective, but we hope give a sense of the sound of the songs and calls. Comparison of transliterations with sound recordings will help to understand our interpretations of bird vocalisations.

Certain conventions have been used in the transliterations (after Borrow & Demey 2004):

Single vowels are pronounced short (e.g. *a* as in apple, *e* as in extra)

ee is pronounced as in 'see'

iiii is higher-pitched than *eeee*

k is pronounced as in 'cat' (*c* is not used for this sound)

ch as in check

sh as in sheep

Stressed syllables are written as capitals, e.g. *CHI*

Pauses are denoted as follows (after Alström et al. 1991):

chuchuchu no discernible pause

ch'wee only the slightest pause between notes

chu-chu-chu short pause, as in ordinary conversation

chu chu chu normal pause
chu, chu, chu longer pause (at least one second)
chu...chu...chu pause of more than 2 seconds
chu... voice continues in the same fashion for a longer period

Note In some cases, a note is included at the end of the species account to draw attention to recent changes in taxonomy or nomenclature, or to alert the reader to possible future changes.

Alternative names '[Alt]' Some alternative English names in widespread or recent use (especially names used in southern Africa or the Western Palearctic) are given at the end of the species accounts. In a few cases, alternative scientific names are also given.

Globally threatened species Those species designated by BirdLife International in 2008 as Globally Threatened are indicated at the end of the species account as follows:

CR = Critically Endangered	Species considered to be facing an extremely high risk of extinction in the wild.
EN = Endangered	Species considered to be facing a very high risk of extinction in the wild.
VU = Vulnerable	Species considered to be facing a high risk of extinction in the wild.

Species considered to be at less risk in 2008 are designated as follows:

NT = Near threatened	Species close to qualifying, or likely to qualify for a threatened category in the near future.
DD = Data Deficient	Species for which there is inadequate information to make an assessment of its risk of extinction at the present time. This is not a category of threat but an acknowledgement that future research may show that threatened classification is appropriate.

For further information, see the BirdLife website: **www.birdlife.org**

ABBREVIATIONS

We have tried to use as few abbreviations as possible, as highly abbreviated text is less easy to read. However, we have used some in the interests of saving space, most notably for the five countries of the region, points of the compass and months of the year.

Species distribution is typically described using the points of the compass and country abbreviations *in combination*, e.g. **WEt** for western Ethiopia and **SSo** for southern Somalia.

A list of our abbreviations is given below:

♂	Male	c.	approximately	N	North
♀	Female	cf.	compare with	S	South
Imm	Immature	sec(s)	second(s)	E	East
Br	Breeding			W	West
Non-br	Non-breeding	Prov.	Province	C	Central
WS	wingspan	NP	National Park		
		NR	Nature Reserve	Er	Eritrea
km	kilometres	Mt	Mount	Et	Ethiopia
sq km	square kilometres	L.	Lake	Dj	Djibouti
m	metres			So	Somalia
cm	centimetres	R.	River	Soc	Socotra
mm	millimetres	I.	Island		
"	inches	Is	Islands	Jan	January, etc.

15

MAPS

Bird distributions in North-East Africa are comparatively well known thanks to pioneering atlases for Somalia (Ash & Miskell 1998) and Ethiopia and Eritrea (Ash & Atkins 2009). Djibouti and Socotra have yet to be atlased comprehensively, but recent surveys have contributed much to our knowledge (e.g. Porter & Martins 1996, Welch & Welch 1999, Porter in prep.).

Our maps are inevitably at a very small scale and are only intended to give a rough idea of range, but we have been fortunate to benefit from the works listed above as well as from the seven volumes of *The Birds of Africa* (Academic Press/Christopher Helm, 1982–2004). Bird distribution in Somalia since the publication of Ash & Miskell (1998) has been updated by John Miskell.

We have tried to keep the maps as simple as possible, distinguishing between resident and migrant populations according to the following categories:

■ Resident

▨ Mainly resident but partially migratory or erratic within range

▨ Breeding visitor (intra-African migrant)

■ Non-breeding visitor, main range (Palearctic or intra-African migrant, or non-breeding range of seabirds)

▨ Non-breeding visitor (sparse occurrence)

X Location of a vagrant or isolated record

? Uncertain record or range

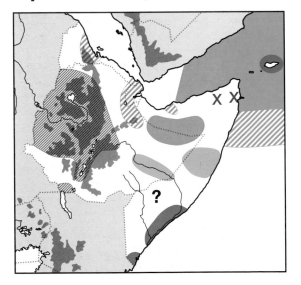

TAXONOMY AND NOMENCLATURE

In our ever-changing taxonomic world, we have the choice of several taxonomies that we could follow for this guide. After much deliberation, we have decided broadly to follow the checklist of African birds as published by the African Bird Club (ABC) on their website (www.africanbirdclub.org). This list is largely based on *The Birds of Africa*, volumes 1–7, updated where necessary. It is commendably conservative with regard to sequence of families (being roughly based on the familiar Voous order, BOU 1977), whilst embracing much of the recent work on taxonomy and nomenclature, particularly at the species level. It also has the advantage of agreeing closely with *Birds of East Africa* (Stevenson & Fanshawe 2002), the sister-volume that forms the basis of this field guide. It is encouraging that the naming of birds in Africa is increasingly stable and less likely to confuse.

In our opinion, a field guide is easier to use if one can quickly find the relevant family or species in question. Most books published in the last three decades broadly follow the Voous order and most birders are familiar with it. New sequences have been proposed, such as the controversial Sibley & Monroe (1990) order and, more recently, the somewhat less radical sequence adopted by the Howard & Moore checklist (Dickinson 2003). The Sibley & Monroe order was swiftly adopted by some books but is now regarded as outdated, and the Howard & Moore order has been followed by others. However, it is now widely accepted that gamebirds and waterfowl are of more ancient lineage than all other birds except tinamous and ratites, and therefore it is becoming customary to place them at the start of any sequence. Thus, for our region, the list should begin with ostriches followed by gamebirds and waterfowl, and then all other families in the old order. Whilst we accept that this may well be correct, we have not felt it necessary to follow this order for a field guide whose primary functions are field identification and ease of use.

English names in the ABC list have not, however, always been followed; preference has been given to names well established in East Africa (especially those used in *Birds of East Africa*) or, for Eurasian migrant species, in the Western Palearctic. Alternative names are also listed where relevant (at the end of a species account). Fortuitously, our choices have broad agreement with the recent global list of IOC-endorsed English names (Gill & Wright 2006), but there are deviations from this list as some of the names chosen for African species in the first edition do not work well in our region.

We are aware that recent genetic studies have shown that some large genera such as *Larus* and *Sterna* should be divided into smaller units, in much the same way as the sunbirds were a few years ago, but we have retained the more familiar larger units pending wider acceptance of these proposals. We have followed the new genera proposed for *Francolinus*, but have not merged *Hieraaetus* into *Aquila*. However, it should be stated that we are not taxonomists and this field guide is not intended to be a taxonomic authority. Further studies will no doubt reveal more generic changes in the future, and we will review our position on all these in subsequent editions of the book.

Perhaps the hardest problem of all has been to decide what splits and lumps to follow. The ABC list is moderately conservative on this subject, choosing not to adopt many of the proposed splits endorsed by, say, Sinclair & Ryan (2003). It is quite likely that some of these will eventually prove to be good species (while others will not), but we agree that we should be cautious until the case has been proven. Genetic studies continue to upset many of our established species limits, and the subject is in constant flux.

In deference to the possibility of further splits, and to facilitate the separation of well-marked forms in the field, we have chosen to treat some taxa separately, with distinct English names, but have indicated their traditional relationships in the (bracketed) presentation of their scientific names. Thus, Coastal and Ethiopian Cisticolas, both of which are usually lumped with Winding Cisticola *Cisticola galactotes*, have been labelled as *C. (galactotes) haematocephala* and *C. (galactotes) lugubris*, rather than as full species, *C. haematocephala* or *C. lugubris*. Therefore, although we do not fully endorse these two taxa as full species, we feel they are sufficiently distinct to merit separate entries in the field guide.

The following forms, contra the ABC checklist (February 2009 version), are treated separately in this field guide, either as full species or as bracketed incipient species: Somali Ostrich, Persian Shearwater, Tropical Shearwater, Yellow-billed Kite, Socotra Buzzard, Somali Courser, Heuglin's Gull, Caspian Gull, Socotra Scops Owl, African Hoopoe, African Stonechat, Siberian Stonechat, Abyssinian Black Wheatear, Kurdish Wheatear, Mountain Thrush, Somali Thrush, Coastal Cisticola, Ethiopian Cisticola, Ethiopian Boubou, Erlanger's Boubou, East Coast Boubou, Four-coloured Bush-shrike, Abd al-Kuri Sparrow, Abyssinian Waxbill, Red-backed Mannikin, Yellow-crowned Canary and Striolated Bunting. Conversely, we have chosen to treat Western Olive Sunbird *Cyanomitra obscura* as conspecific with Eastern Olive Sunbird *C. olivacea*, as there now seems to be little justification for its separation. We have also excluded two other 'species' which were formerly listed in the ABC checklist: Degodi Lark, which is now considered to be a form or synonym of Gillett's Lark (Collar et al. 2009), and Bulo Burti Bush-shrike which has been found to be a morph of Erlanger's Boubou (Nguembock et al. 2008); the same molecular study also recommends that Tropical Boubou is split into four species (three of which occur in our region), and we have followed this in the field guide. For all species whose taxonomic status is uncertain or debatable, brief details are noted in the species accounts.

BIRD IDENTIFICATION

LEARNING TO IDENTIFY BIRDS

Bird identification is a skill best learned from field experience, and preferably lots of it. There is no substitute for watching birds in their natural environment in order to become proficient in being able to distinguish one species from another. Birders in the 21st century are fortunate to have a number of tools to help them do this, such as spectacular optics, astonishing digital cameras, accurate field guides and comprehensive compilations of sound recordings, but the greatest assets of all are patient observation and keen senses. Birding should be fun and instructive. We all learn from our mistakes and become better birders through experience. When confronted with an unfamiliar bird (especially if you are in an unfamiliar location) there are a number of questions that need to be addressed as part of the identification process. Some species will be easily identified, but others will require closer scrutiny. Frequently, a correct identification can be achieved through a process of elimination, by excluding potential confusion species after considering a variety of morphological, behavioural and environmental characters, but it is always best to use a combination of features to clinch an identification. Some basic hints and potential pitfalls are listed below.

- What family does the species belong to? A thorough knowledge of the various bird families and their characteristics is an essential first step.

- Estimate approximate size by comparison with nearby species or other birds you are familiar with, but size-illusion may be a problem when looking through a telescope – in some instances, birds of equal size which are further away may actually appear larger than those in the foreground.

- Note body shape, tail length and shape, bill shape and size, colour of eyes and legs etc.

- Check plumage features for head pattern (eye-stripe, supercilium, crown-stripes, colour of ear-coverts etc); presence or lack of wing-bars; extent of barring, streaks or spots if present; tail pattern etc. Subtle plumage coloration may be the key to identifying some plainer species.

- Note behaviour and habits: does it run or hop, what feeding strategy is employed, does it flick its wings or wag its tail?

- Note flight pattern (direct, undulating, rate of wing-beats, does it glide or soar?) and whether the rump contrasts with the back or tail.

- Consider seasonal plumage variation, age/sex differences, racial variation and effects of moult (see below).

- Consider the possibility that light and background colour can affect how a species is perceived: pale birds can look dark against a bright sky; bright birds can look dull in the gloom of the forest floor; iridescent birds can exhibit different colours in different lights, or even at different angles. Contrast between a bird and its background can affect the impression of its size: a strong contrast can make a bird look larger.

- Note vocalisations, if any, and their circumstances. Many birds are first located by voice, and birders familiar with vocalisations invariably find and see more birds.

- Consider range, altitude and habitat. Many species can be eliminated in this way, but beware of species that may turn up in unfamiliar locations from time to time, especially long-distance migrants.

- Consider time of year. Many species have regular seasonal patterns, but vagrants can turn up at unexpected times.

- Always anticipate a common or widespread species before considering a rarity or a species out of its normal range. Get to know commoner species first.

- Make sure you are familiar with the terminology for the various body parts and feather tracts.

- Make notes and take photographs, especially if you are unsure of an identification.

INDIVIDUAL VARIATION

Almost all individuals of a particular species differ from one another to some degree, mainly in size and/or coloration. This may be slight or considerable, depending on the species. A field guide such as this can only illustrate a few of the more typical plumages and it is therefore helpful to understand the different ways in which individual birds can vary from one another.

Sexual dimorphism Most birds are sexually dimorphic, where males and females have different plumages or differ in size. In some species the sexes are genuinely almost identical while in others the females are simply duller versions of the males, but in a great many the females look completely different, usually lacking the bright colours of the males. However, in a few species (e.g. painted-snipe and phalaropes) it is the females that are more brightly coloured, with the drabber males undertaking most of the breeding duties. Males are usually larger than females, but in raptors the females are generally larger than the males. In most species, size differences between males and females are slight and with considerable overlap. There may also be behavioural differences between the sexes, and in songbirds it is usually only the males that sing.

Seasonal variation Many adult birds exhibit seasonal variation, such as having different breeding and non-breeding plumages (also known as summer and winter plumages in temperate regions), and this is often most apparent in males. It is attained through regular moults, or sometimes through wear (see below).

Age-related variation Most birds undergo a series of plumage changes as they grow older, through a cycle of moults which is usually related to the seasons. In most passerines, an individual will attain its adult plumage within a year, but in some non-passerines (such as large gulls and raptors) a bird will take four or five years to reach adulthood. The terminology for the sequence of plumages for a passerine is: juvenile — first-winter— adult. For a gull taking two years to reach maturity, it would be: juvenile—first-winter—first-summer— second-winter—adult. Terms such as immature, first-year and subadult are less precise, being mainly used where there is some uncertainty regarding the age of the bird or its moult strategy. Definitions of plumage categories are given in the Glossary.

Polymorphism A few species exhibit normal, distinct colour morphs which are unrelated to age, sex or season. Examples of species in our region that have two or more colour morphs include female grey cuckoos, African Scops Owl and Erlanger's Boubou.

Geographical variation Populations of many species differ to a greater or lesser extent across their geographical ranges. This variation may be pronounced with various distinct populations being separated into subspecies (races), or clinal, where the morphological characters of a species change gradually across the range. In addition, populations in colder, northern climates or at higher altitudes tend to be slightly larger than those from warmer regions, and birds in drier, desert areas tend to be paler than those from wetter environments. See page 12 for an explanation of the coverage of geographical variation in this book.

Abrasion and fading Feathers wear out over time, often becoming tatty and faded before they are replaced. This can affect the appearance of a bird in several ways. Fresh feathers with dark centres and pale margins will lose the lighter edges during the course of a few weeks or months, so that a bird that looks scaly in fresh plumage will look uniformly dark when worn; male Pied Wheatears are good examples of this type of abrasion, but many younger birds look spotty or scaly due to pale feather-tips which they gradually lose as the feathers become worn. The sun can bleach feathers making them look paler, and species living in open environments tend to fade more rapidly than those in forests.

Aberrant coloration A very small number of birds may show some form of aberrant coloration. Albinism is perhaps the best known, where a complete absence of pigments results in white plumage and pink bare parts. True albinos are very rare, but partial albinism is not infrequent in some species. Leucism is a condition where loss of pigments results in a much paler plumage then usual. Melanism is a condition where excess dark pigments result in unusually dark individuals. In some species, this is quite frequent and such birds are termed 'dark morphs'.

MOULT

Feathers perform essential functions in waterproofing, heat regulation and flight in birds, and they need to be replaced on a regular basis. This complicated procedure is known as moult. The timing of moult varies from species to species, but is usually linked to an annual cycle. It may take place in a matter of a few weeks in some species, or extend over several months in others. It usually occurs after the breeding season, with many species having a complete moult once per year after their young have fledged and sometimes a second partial moult (of the body feathers) before breeding. Feather growth requires much energy and therefore moult does not usually take place during breeding or migration – flight ability may also be impaired when wing feathers are being renewed. Most adult Palearctic migrants will moult before heading south to Africa, but juveniles are more likely to wait until they arrive on their wintering grounds. Some birds are able to suspend their moult while they migrate and, most intriguingly, a few species break their journey in Ethiopia for two months to moult, before carrying on to eastern and southern Africa.

Wing feathers are usually moulted sequentially, one or two at a time and often fairly quickly, but some larger birds such as seabirds and raptors may take years to complete a single wing-moult. Ducks and geese, however, moult their flight feathers simultaneously, becoming flightless for a number of weeks until the new feathers have grown. This is the 'eclipse' period when the flightless males lose their bright colours and resemble the drabber females in order to be better camouflaged; they are particularly vulnerable at this time and tend to stay hidden in marshes or out at sea. There are many different moult strategies amongst birds, and plenty of 'exceptions to the rule', but whilst it is probably not important to learn all of these, a basic knowledge of moult will allow you to age a bird correctly if seen well. This in turn may also facilitate its identification, as well as enabling you to determine its sex. For example, in some species young males closely resemble adult females, but juveniles and adults usually have different moult strategies, and therefore by discovering if the feathers are worn or fresh the age of the bird can be established. When a young bird fledges, it has fresh flight feathers. Its parents at this time will have worn feathers, having grown them many months earlier. A few weeks or months later, after the adults have moulted, the situation will be reversed. However, juveniles of a few species undertake a post-juvenile moult after only a few months, and are then generally inseparable from recently moulted adults.

There are also differences in the structure and colour of juvenile and adult feathers in many species. Juveniles are often duller than adults and individual feathers may be paler or less glossy; they also tend to be narrower, shorter and more pointed but subtle differences such as this may only be apparent on birds in the hand. In the larger raptors, where moult is extended over a long period, the trailing edge of the wing may appear slightly ragged and uneven due to the feathers being in different stages of moult, whereas in juvenile birds that have grown all their feathers simultaneously, the trailing edge will be smoother.

BIRD TOPOGRAPHY

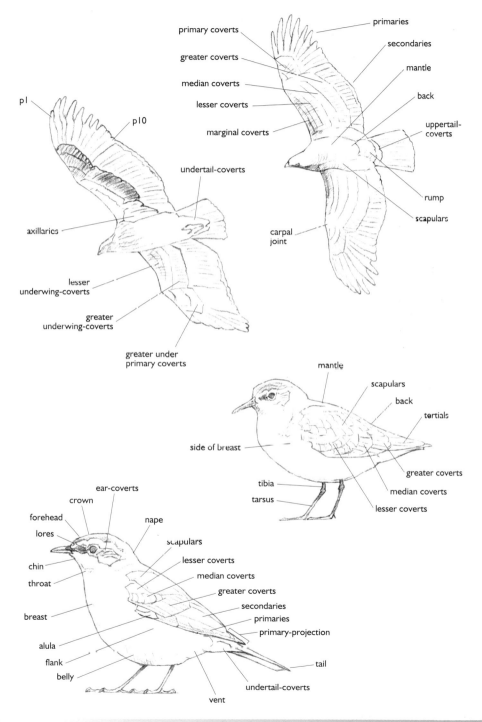

primary coverts

greater coverts

median coverts

pl

p10

lesser coverts

marginal coverts

undertail-coverts

axillaries

lesser underwing-coverts

greater underwing-coverts

greater under primary coverts

primaries

secondaries

mantle

back

uppertail-coverts

rump

scapulars

carpal joint

mantle

scapulars

back

tertials

side of breast

greater coverts

ear-coverts

tibia

median coverts

crown

tarsus

lesser coverts

forehead

nape

lores

scapulars

chin

lesser coverts

throat

median coverts

greater coverts

breast

secondaries

primaries

primary-projection

alula

flank

tail

belly

undertail-coverts

vent

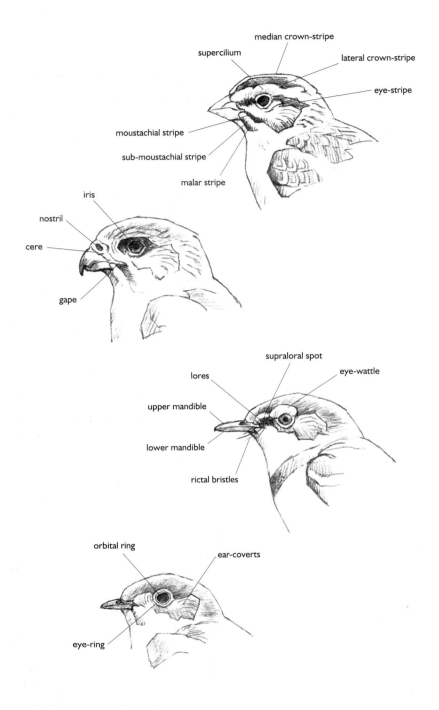

median crown-stripe

supercilium

lateral crown-stripe

eye-stripe

moustachial stripe

sub-moustachial stripe

malar stripe

iris

nostril

cere

gape

supraloral spot

lores

eye-wattle

upper mandible

lower mandible

rictal bristles

orbital ring

ear-coverts

eye-ring

GLOSSARY

Afrotropical The zoogeographical region that comprises Africa south of the Sahara (formerly known as the Ethiopian region).

allopatric Refers to two or more taxa whose breeding ranges do not overlap.

alula A small group of feathers at the carpal joint on the upperwing (also known as the bastard wing).

antiphonal Precisely timed alternating singing by two birds (usually a pair). See also duetting.

arm The inner part of the wing, between the body and the carpal joint.

axillaries The underwing feathers at the base of the wing, at the point where it joins the body (also known as the 'armpit').

bare parts Those parts without feathers, specifically the bill, eyes and legs.

bib A restricted, laterally compressed patch of contrasting feathers on the chin and throat.

biome A major ecological community of flora and fauna, such as desert, savanna or montane forest.

brood-parasite A species that lays its eggs in other species' nests so that the host species will raise its young for it.

burry (used in voice descriptions) A burr is a rough pronunciation of the letter 'r', hence burry is a sound containing burrs; in bird song it is used to denote sounds that are rough around the edges, or a whirring or soft rolling sound.

carpal The wrist area at the bend of the wing (hence 'carpal joint').

carpal bar A contrasting band of feathers on the wing, running diagonally between the carpal joint and the body, usually on the median coverts; notably present on some raptors and immature gulls.

casque An enlargement of the upper mandible on certain hornbills.

cere Bare skin (often brightly coloured or swollen) at the base of the upper mandible on raptors, owls and parrots. The nostrils are within the cere.

cheek An imprecise term for the frontal ear-coverts or the lower side of the face.

cline Gradual change of a species's morphological characters across its geographic range (hence 'clinal variation').

congeneric Belonging to the same genus.

conspecific Belonging to the same species.

coronal bands Stripes on the side of the crown (also called lateral crown-stripes).

crepuscular Active in twilight (at dusk or dawn).

crop Part of the upper food canal, used for temporary storage of food in some birds.

culmen The dorsal ridge on the upper mandible.

dimorphic Having two distinct morphs or colour phases; 'sexually dimorphic' is used to denote that males and females have different plumages or differ in size.

distal Furthest from the body, referring to the tip of the bill or the outer part of the wing or tail.

dorsal The upper surface of the body or a feather (opposite of ventral).

duetting Male and female singing simultaneously or antiphonally in response to each other.

eclipse plumage Dull, female-type plumage exhibited by moulting males of ducks and sunbirds after breeding.

edges/edgings Outer feather margins. Pale edgings on wing feathers can result in a paler wing-panel on the closed wing.

endemic Confined to a particular region.

extralimital Occurring outside the region in question

eye-ring A ring of differently coloured feathers surrounding the orbital ring.

eye-stripe A (usually darker) stripe running from the base of the bill, through the lores and behind the eye (i.e. through the eye; not to be confused with the supercilium). Also called an 'eye-line'.

face A general term for the side of the head which may include the ear-coverts, supercilium, lores and surrounding areas (typically the area from the bill-base to around the eyes).

feral A bird or population breeding in the wild, but descended from domesticated stock (e.g. feral pigeon).

first-winter An immature plumage acquired after the juvenile plumage, usually retaining some worn juvenile feathers, and worn until the following spring; mainly used for Palearctic migrants and gulls.

flight feathers General term for the larger wing feathers, i.e. primaries and secondaries (but not wing-coverts or tail).

form General term for a distinct entity, such as morph, subspecies or species.

fringes Relates to contrasting feather margins, resulting in a scaly appearance to the plumage (see also edgings). When fringes wear off (on older feathers), the scaly appearance disappears to leave a more uniform plumage.

frontal shield An area of bare, fleshy or horny skin on the forehead, usually brightly coloured (e.g. on gallinules and coots).

gape Strictly the mouth, but also applied to the fleshy flange at the base of the mandibles (often yellow in recently fledged birds, and extending back as a line to the eye in some egrets, raptors and cuckooshrikes).

genus (plural **genera**) A taxonomic category between family and species, containing one or more related species. The genus name forms the first part of the binomial scientific name of every species.

gorget A band of distinctly coloured feathers across the throat or upper breast (also sometimes called a 'necklace').

graduated Refers to the tail, when the central feathers are the longest and the outer ones become progressively shorter, resulting in a wedge-shape when the tail is spread.

gular pouch A loose area of skin between the lower mandible and throat (e.g. on pelicans and some storks).

hackles Long, lanceolate feathers on the necks of some pigeons and on Vulturine Guineafowl.

hand The outer part of the wing.

hood General term for different-coloured feathering on the head and neck (cutting off somewhere across the throat), contrasting with the rest of the body plumage.

immature A general term for a non-adult bird.

intergrade Unstable hybrid population (not accorded formal taxonomic status) as a result of interbreeding by two species or subspecies in a zone of overlap.

juvenile The first, non-downy plumage of a bird, worn from fledging until the moult to first-winter. Smaller passerines may only exhibit juvenile plumage for a few weeks, and Palearctic migrants are unlikely to be seen in Africa in this plumage.

jizz A term used to define the overall impression gained of a species from a combination of subtle characters such as size, shape, colour, posture, behaviour and flight action, enabling an identification to be made (with experience) even when a key plumage feature cannot be seen.

lappet A wattle, usually at the base of the bill.

leading edge The front edge of the wing which, when contrastingly marked with pale or dark feathers, is a useful identification feature (e.g. on certain raptors).

lores (adj. **loral**) The area between the bill and the eye, which may be bare or feathered.

malar The area on the side of the jaw, often marked with a stripe bordering the upper edge of the throat.

mandibles The upper and lower parts of the bill (although in the singular it is sometimes used solely for the lower part—see also 'maxilla').

mantle Upper part of the back, between the scapulars.

mask Dark area of plumage around the eye, usually extending from the base of the bill to the ear-coverts.

maxilla The upper mandible.

melanistic Black or blackish, referring to a morph.

mesial stripe A vertical stripe on the centre of the throat.

mirror Non-technical term for a subterminal white spot on the primary tips of some gulls (not usually visible at rest).

monotypic Biological group containing only one taxon. A monotypic species has no subspecies and a monotypic genus has only a single species.

morph A normal but distinct colour variant of a dimorphic or polymorphic species, unrelated to sex, age or season.

morphological Relates to form and structure, i.e. the external characteristics of a bird and therefore including the plumage.

mottled Plumage marked with irregular small spots or blotches.

moustachial stripe A stripe along the lower border of the ear-coverts, bordering the upper edge of malar region (sometimes with a submoustachial stripe inbetween).

nomadic Erratic wandering, usually according to aseasonal weather conditions or food availability.

nominate The first described form of a polytypic species; subsequently described subspecies are given their own trinomial names, but the first-named is designated by repetition of the specific (second) name (e.g. *Nilaus afer afer*). It is usual to refer to the first-named form as the 'nominate' subspecies or race.

notched Term used for a tail where the central feathers are slightly shorter than the rest, forming a shallow fork or notch.

nuchal Relates to the nape or hindneck (e.g. nuchal crest).

orbital ring Ring of bare skin surrounding the eye, not to be confused with the feathered eye-ring outside it.

Palearctic A biogeographical region comprising Europe, North Africa, the Middle East and northern Asia south to the Himalayas and the Yangtze river. It is divided somewhat arbitrarily into Eastern and Western divisions along the Ural mountains in Russia.

parapatric Refers to species whose ranges are adjoining (with a shared border) but do not overlap.

passage migrant A migrant that occurs regularly but briefly whilst on passage between its breeding and wintering grounds (typically twice a year, although some species use different migration routes to and from their breeding grounds).

pectoral tufts Coloured tufts at the sides of the breast (e.g. on sunbirds) used in display but generally concealed under the wings at rest.

pelagic Of the open sea; pelagic species spend most of their lives at sea.

pishing Onomatopoeic term for sounds made with the mouth to attract birds.

polygamous Refers to a breeding strategy where males and/or females have more than one mate during a breeding season.

polymorphic Having two or more distinct morphs or colour phases.

polytypic Biological group having two or more forms within it; usually applied to a species having two or more subspecies.

post-ocular (stripe/spot) A stripe or spot behind the eye, usually the rear part of the eye-stripe.

primary/primaries The outer flight feathers, situated on the hand.

primary projection The portion of the primary tips that are visible beyond the tertials on the closed wing.

proximal Nearest to the body, referring to the base of the bill or the inner part of the wing or tail.

rallid A member of the rail or crake family.

rectrices (singular **rectrix**) Tail feathers.

rictal bristles Stiff feather shafts at the base of the bill in birds that catch insects in flight (e.g. nightjars, swallows and flycatchers).

remiges (singular **remex**) Flight feathers (i.e. primaries and secondaries).

riparian Bordering a river.

Sahel (or **sahelian zone**) Semi-arid zone between the Sahara and the savanna zone.

savanna Grassland with variable tree and scrub cover.

secondary/secondaries The inner flight feathers, situated on the arm.

sedentary A species that remains in the same area throughout the year.

scalloped Patterned with semi-circular markings.

semispecies A taxon that may be regarded as either a subspecies or a species, whose populations hybridise to a substantial but geographically restricted extent.

shaft The central stem of a feather.

shaft-streak Narrow longitudinal mark along the shaft of a feather.

skirl (used in voice descriptions) A high, shrill slightly guttural sound, usually descending in pitch.

spangled Covered with very small bright spots (always lighter than the surrounding plumage).

speculum A brighter, usually iridescent, panel on the secondaries in some ducks (visible only in flight).

subadult An imprecise term referring to an immature plumage that is close to becoming a full adult.

submoustachial stripe A stripe that lies between the moustachial and malar areas.

subterminal Refers to a contrasting band or spot near the end of a feather-tip, usually the tail.

supercilium A contrasting stripe above the lores and eye, usually extending beyond the eye (see also 'eye-stripe' for distinction).

superspecies A group of two or more allopatric species (called 'allospecies') that are more closely related to each other than to other members of the genus.

supraloral (stripe/spot) A short, usually pale, stripe or spot above the lores, and shorter than a supercilium.

sympatric Refers to species whose ranges overlap, though not necessarily in the same habitat (cf. allopatric and parapatric).

tail-streamer Exceptionally long outer or inner tail feathers.

tarsus (plural **tarsi**) Lower part of the leg, below the

'knee'; usually covered with smooth scales but is feathered in some species (e.g. owls and sandgrouse).

taxon (plural **taxa**) Any taxonomic unit, but most commonly applied to a species or subspecies.

tertials The innermost secondaries, sometimes elongated (as in waders and larks) and often contrastingly coloured or tipped.

tibia (plural **tibiae**) Upper part of the leg (the 'drumstick'), partly bare in many birds but often largely feathered (e.g. in most passerines); also loosely known as the 'thigh'.

trailing edge Contrasting band along the rear edge of the wing (cf. leading edge).

trinomial Third part of a species's scientific name, referring to its subspecies (or race).

vent The area around the cloaca, but (for brevity) sometimes used in this book to include the undertail coverts.

ventral The underside of the body or a feather (opposite of dorsal).

vermiculations Fine barring or feather markings that are often only visible at close range.

wattle Fleshy, unfeathered skin, usually brightly coloured, at the base of the bill or on the throat (as in Wattled Plover) or on the face (as in wattle-eyes).

web (of a feather) The flattened vane on either side of the feather shaft; on wing and tail feathers, the web is usually subdivided into 'inner web' and 'outer web'. Web can also refer to the skin between the toes of some birds (e.g. ducks).

window Non-technical term for a contrasting pale panel at the base of the primaries in some birds (e.g. raptors or gulls).

wing-coverts Includes the greater, median and lesser coverts, as well as marginal coverts and primary coverts.

wing-bar A well-defined bar on the upperwing, usually formed by pale tips to the greater and/or median coverts (if both, then it is a double wing-bar).

wing-lining General word for all the underwing-coverts.

wing-panel Usually a contrasting pale area on the closed wing, formed by pale edges to the secondaries and/or tertials (on the outer webs). May also refer to a panel on the base of the flight feathers in flight (cf. window).

wingspan The distance as measured from wing-tip to wing-tip (which may be more useful for size comparison than length for aerial species such as seabirds or raptors).

GEOGRAPHY, CLIMATE AND HABITATS

The Horn of Africa is the easternmost part of the African continent, jutting out into the Arabian Sea (Indian Ocean) to the south of the Arabian peninsula. The region lies immediately to the north of Kenya and east of Sudan, the only two countries that border it. In the north, the Red Sea and the Gulf of Aden form the north-eastern boundary and in the east it is bordered by the Indian Ocean. The Horn of Africa, also some-times known as North-east Africa, lies neatly between the equator and the Tropic of Cancer, approximately within the latitudes of 2°S and 18°N, and extends from west to east between 34°E and 54°E. The region is comprised politically of four countries (Eritrea, Ethiopia, Djibouti and Somalia) covering almost 1.9 million square kilometres; the northern part of Somalia declared independence as Somaliland in 1991, but the country remains internationally unrecognised. The Socotra archipelago, which lies off the north-east tip of Somalia, is also included in the region on zoogeographical grounds, although it is administered by Yemen.

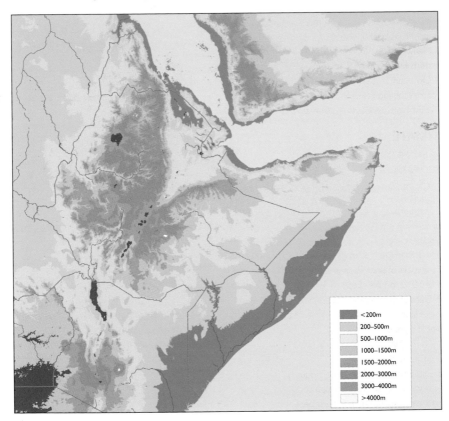

Figure 2: Topography of the Horn of Africa (after Mayaux et al. 2004).

TOPOGRAPHY

The region is dominated by the isolated mountain massif of central Ethiopia and Eritrea (the most extensive highland plateau in Africa), which is bisected by the Rift Valley and its series of important lakes. The highland blocks either side of the Rift are frequently referred to as the Western Highlands (west and north of the Rift Valley) and the South-eastern Highlands (to the east). The plateau of the Western Highlands comprises a con-siderable area of land above 2000m, more than any other country in Africa. There are also many peaks above 4000m and this region includes the Simien Mountains. The South-eastern Highlands are less extensive, but include the Bale Mountains and a number of 4000m peaks. West of the plateau the lowlands of W Ethiopia and W Eritrea extend all along the Sudan border, from the Omo in SW Ethiopia to northern Eritrea. To the east the lowlands are largely arid or semi-arid and dominated by extensive deserts, notably the Ogaden in SE Ethiopia and the Danakil (or Afar) in NE Ethiopia, extending into Eritrea. The southern lowlands of Ethiopia are similar to adjacent northern Kenya. The altitude in the region ranges from 110m below sea-level at Lake Asale in the Danakil Depression to 4620m at Mt Ras Dashen in the Simien Mountains.

Eritrea shares the western lowlands with Ethiopia, and also the northern extension of the highland plateau. Additionally, a broad desert plain extends along the Red Sea coast and offshore there are a number of important islands for seabirds, notably the Dahlak Archipelago. The tiny enclave of Djibouti, a former French colony, is situated at the entrance to the Red Sea. The short sea crossing at Bab el Mandeb is an important migration route between Arabia and NE Africa, especially for raptors. Somalia has the longest coastline of any country in Africa and most of the country comprises semi-arid lowland bushland. In the north, in the semi-autonomous region of Somaliland, an escarpment runs east west, close to the coast and rising to 2400m. This is an extension of the Ahmar Mountains of NE Ethiopia, forming a broken chain of higher ground that extends from the SE Highlands of Ethiopia almost to the north-eastern tip of Somalia.

Many river systems originate in the highlands of Ethiopia and Eritrea. The main rivers flowing out of the Western Highlands are the Tacazze/Setit, the Abay (Blue Nile, whose source is Lake Tana), the Baro/Gilo, the Omo, and the Awash. Two major river systems flow out of the SE Highlands, the Dawa/Genale (which becomes the Jubba in Somalia) and the Wabe Shabeelle. These provide a valuable resource to the arid region of SE Ethiopia and southern Somalia.

CLIMATE

The climate of the Horn of Africa is highly variable and greatly influenced by the highland massif and the prevailing winds. Much of the lowland area in the east is arid or semi-arid, and very hot throughout the year, but the highlands are both cooler and lusher. More detailed information about the climate of the region can be found in Ash & Miskell (1998) and Ash & Atkins (2009).

Temperatures in Somalia do not vary much throughout the year. In the south, the hottest months are March–May, prior to the south-west monsoon, but the coolest months (June–August) average only 3°C less. The difference is more pronounced on the north coast. Here the hottest months (June August) average 9°C warmer than the coolest (December–February). Temperatures on the Red Sea coast of Eritrea are hotter than either coast of Somalia, and this area is famed as one of the hottest regions in the world with temperatures up to 50°C in June–September. In Ethiopia, the western lowlands can also reach 50°C in April–June, and the Danakil Depression has an average monthly figure of 45°C in April–September due to high night-time temperatures. At the other end of the scale, temperatures on the highland plateau can fall below freezing point at night in December, and the lowest mean temperature is 4°C at 3600m in the Simien Mountains.

The highlands of Ethiopia and Eritrea receive regular, seasonal rainfall from the tropical monsoons blowing from the south-west in June–September, but by the time they reach the east of the region the monsoons have little moisture left. In consequence, northern Somalia and eastern Ethiopia are largely dry during the south-west monsoons, although coastal southern Somalia does receive rains from this monsoon. During the north-east monsoon, in December–March, the situation is reversed, with southern Somalia having almost no rain, but the mountains of northern Somalia and the escarpments of the Eritrean highlands facing the Red Sea receiving their principal annual rainfall. In March–May, moist easterly winds from the Indian Ocean blow across the region, producing the main rains for the South-east Highlands and, less reliably, for lowland areas of southern Ethiopia. These winds also cause the 'small spring rains' in the central highlands of Ethiopia and Eritrea. However, there is considerable variation and unreliability in rainfall patterns in the region, especially inland, due to altitude and microclimatic variations; in consequence, many areas are prone to drought on a regular basis.

HABITATS

The Horn of Africa comprises a wide range of habitat types, as a result of its broad range of altitudes and climatic zones, and its position straddling tropical Africa and the borders of the Palearctic region. The summary of major habitats given below is based on Urban & Brown (1971), Ash & Miskell (1998) and Ash & Atkins (2009); more detailed accounts of the habitats and vegetation of the region can be found in these works.

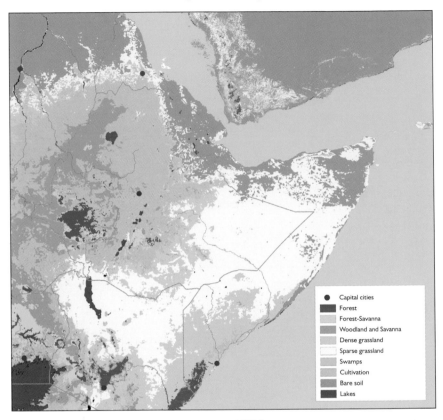

Figure 3: Land-cover in the Horn of Africa (after Mayaux *et al.* 2004).

Desert and semi-desert Deserts in the Horn of Africa comprise open sandy and stony plains, sparse grassland and bare rocky areas. They occur mainly in the east of the region, below 600m, and include coastal areas of Eritrea and the Danakil and Ogaden regions. These arid areas receive sparse rainfall and support little vegetation.

Bushland, grassland and savanna Lowland parts of the entire region are dominated by grassland and savanna at a wide range of altitudes. The flora is largely composed of perennial grasses and succulents, with annual plants after rains and a variable number of bushes and trees, typically less than 6m high. Some areas are quite open with scattered woody plants, notably acacias in the east and south but mixed locally with *Commiphora*. Denser thickets are known as thornbush. In the western lowlands, the typical vegetation is *Combretum–Terminalia* woodland in tall *Hyparrhenia* grassland. Highland grasslands generally occur in valley bottoms, at 1800–2750m.

Woodland Where rainfall is higher, the more wooded areas of bushland and savanna merge into woodland, with trees up to 12m high and a more continuous canopy – but only a single canopy layer. Ground cover is grasses and annuals, where it is not overgrazed. In the Rift Valley and the east of the region, *Acacia–Commiphora* woodland occurs up to 1900m. In the wetter west, the woodlands are dominated by broadleaved *Combretum* and *Terminalia*, mainly at 500–1900m. Riverine woodland (or forest) is an important if fragmented habitat, comprising a variety of species and often including figs (*Ficus*).

Forest Compared to woodland, forest tends to be multi-layered with a denser, more closed canopy. The individual trees are taller, and the ground is heavily shaded and often fairly sparsely vegetated. Forests in the region can be categorised as follows:

- dry evergreen montane forest (on the highland plateau and in N Somalia)
- moist evergreen forest (mainly in SW Ethiopia but also the Harenna Forest south of the Bale mountains and Boni Forest in extreme S Somalia)
- lowland semi-evergreen forest (around Gambela)

On the plateau, the much-reduced natural forest typically comprises olive–*Podocarpus*–juniper, mainly at 1800–2500m, but dry juniper forest extends lower in Sidamo and Bale provinces, and also in Eritrea and N Somalia. Above 2500m, *Juniperus–Podocarpus* is still dominant but at higher levels more open forest includes Giant Heath (*Erica*), *Hypericum*–bamboo (*Arundinaria*) and *Hagenia* forest. Moist evergreen forest occurs up to 2800m and includes species such as *Afrocarpus* and *Pouteria*, with various understorey shrubs. The lowland semi-evergreen forest near Gambela is very restricted and poorly known; it is characterised by a canopy of *Baphia* at around 15–20m high with smaller trees and shrubs below it.

Montane habitats Forest cover in montane areas is described above, but above 3200m the highest slopes are dominated by afroalpine vegetation. Typically this includes Giant Lobelia–*Alchemilla*–tussock grass moorland at 3800–4200m, often with marshy areas where the drainage is poor. Only alpine screes and bare rock occur above this, while the sub-afroalpine belt lower down is dominated by ericaceous scrub (*Erica*). The Sanetti plateau in Ethiopia is a good example of afroalpine vegetation.

Wetlands, lakes and rivers Wetlands are an important habitat in a region where so much of the land is arid or drought-prone. The principal lakes in the region are Lake Tana (1820m) and the series of lakes in the Rift Valley (see map on p. 8). As in East Africa, the latter include freshwater, soda and alkaline lakes; the lakes in the central Rift are situated at around 1600m, while the southern two are at 1250m. The many river systems in the region are also important. Inland swamps occur at Lake Chew Bahir (580m), Lake Tana, Lake Afrera (100m below sea-level) and Lake Abbé (250m), as well as along the shores of Rift Valley lakes and in the Awash valley (900m). The most extensive wetlands in the region are in the Baro–Gilo–Akobo lowlands near Gambela (400m) and along the Wabe Shabeelle river. In Somalia, both the Wabe Shabeelle and the Jubba are critically important wetland habitats.

Coasts and islands The long coastline of the region includes sandy shores, coral beaches, dune systems, deltas and estuaries, and mangroves. The vegetation comprises grasses, salt-tolerant plants, and shrubs such as *Tamarix* and *Suaeda*. Mangrove swamps occur only locally, consisting mainly of *Avicennia marina*. Offshore islands in the Red Sea, off Eritrea, hold internationally important colonies of seabirds, most notably in the Dahlak Archipelago. A few islands off Somalia also hold major seabird colonies including Maydh Island and the Ceebaad islands (off Saylac). Socotra's seabird colonies include the near-endemic Jouanin's Petrel.

Man-made habitats Habitats in this category include urban areas such as gardens and mad-made structures, as well as cultivations and dams.

SOCOTRA

The island of Socotra lies approximately 200km east of Raas Caseyr in NE Somalia, and 380km south of Ras Fartak in Yemen. It is 133km from east to west and 43km from north to south. The archipelago comprises four main islands and two rocky islets. The small islands of Samha and Darsa (collectively known as The Brothers) lie 50km south-west of Socotra, and 60km further west is the larger island of Abd al-Kuri, just 100km off the coast of Somalia. Abd al-Kuri is the second largest island in the archipelago, being 36km from east to west and up to 6km wide.

There are three topographical zones on Socotra: the alluvial coastal plains, the limestone plateau averaging 300–700m, and the Hajhir (or Haggeher) mountains in the north-west of the island, with dramatic granite peaks rising to over 1500m. Vegetation is generally sparse with a high degree of endemism. The dry south-west monsoon brings strong winds in June–September, and is replaced by the wet north-east monsoon in November–March. Lowland areas tend to be semi-arid, dominated by *Croton* scrub with scattered *Euphorbia* and *Ziziphus*. The vegetation in the foothills is richer, often with the distinctive Desert Rose (*Adenium*). In the mountains, vegetation is lushest in sheltered valleys, where it is protected from the winds whilst also benefiting from increased rainfall. Here the habitat is characterised by the presence of the famous Dragon's Blood Trees *Dracaena cinnabari*. Abd al-Kuri has almost no permanent freshwater and a more barren landscape; its mountains are lower, rising to 740m.

IMPORTANT BIRD AREAS

All of the 136 Important Bird Areas (IBAs) in the Horn of Africa are listed and mapped here; protected areas are also marked on the map. These IBAs have been identified against globally agreed criteria by the BirdLife Partnership in the region, and a full directory of Africa's IBAs has already been published (Fishpool & Evans 2001). Although a number of these sites are nationally and internationally renowned protected areas, such as the Bale Mountains National Park and Awash National Park, many are unprotected and vulnerable. For information on the status of these areas, or about the networks of people supporting them, please contact the relevant national NGOs (see Organisations and websites).

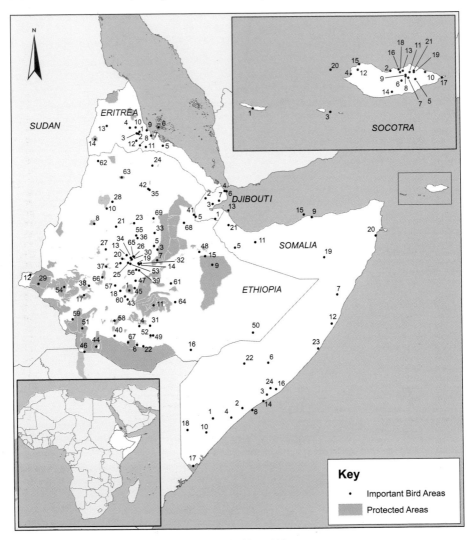

Figure 4: Important Bird Areas and protected areas in the Horn of Africa.

Country	Name	Code	Country	Name	Code
Eritrea	Ghinda	1	Ethiopia	Mount Zuquala	56
Eritrea	Arboroba escarpment	2	Ethiopia	Mugo highlands	57
Eritrea	Asmara escarpment	3	Ethiopia	Nechisar National Park	58
Eritrea	Central Plateau - Keren	4	Ethiopia	Omo National Park	59
Eritrea	Danakil lowlands	5	Ethiopia	Senkele Sanctuary	60
Eritrea	Dahlak Archipelago and offshore islands	6	Ethiopia	Shek Husein	61
Eritrea	Gulf of Zula	7	Ethiopia	Shire lowlands in the Tekeze valley	62
Eritrea	Mareb escarpment	8	Ethiopia	Simien Mountains National Park	63
Eritrea	Massawa coast	9	Ethiopia	Sof Omar	64
Eritrea	Semenawi Bahri	10	Ethiopia	Sululta plain	65
Eritrea	Senafe	11	Ethiopia	Tiro Boter - Becho forest	66
Eritrea	Southern Plateau: Furrus	12	Ethiopia	Yavello Sanctuary	67
Eritrea	Western Plain: Barka river	13	Ethiopia	Yangudi-Rassa National Park	68
Eritrea	Western Plain: Gash - Setit	14	Ethiopia	Yegof forest	69
Ethiopia	Abiata - Shalla Lakes National Park	1	Djibouti	Ali Sabieh - Assâmo	1
Ethiopia	Akaki - Aba-Samuel wetlands	2	Djibouti	Dôda	2
Ethiopia	Aliyu Amba - Dulecha	3	Djibouti	Forêt de Day	3
Ethiopia	Anferara forests	4	Djibouti	Kadda Guéini - Doumêra	4
Ethiopia	Ankober - Debre Sina escarpment	5	Djibouti	Lac Abbé	5
Ethiopia	Arero forest	6	Djibouti	Les Sept Frères	6
Ethiopia	Awash National Park	7	Djibouti	Mabla	7
Ethiopia	Awi Zone	8			
Ethiopia	Babille Elephant Sanctuary	9	Somalia	Aangole - Farblito	1
Ethiopia	Bahir Dar - Lake Tana	10	Somalia	Arbowerow	2
Ethiopia	Bale Mountains National Park	11	Somalia	Balcad Nature Reserve	3
Ethiopia	Baro river	12	Somalia	Boja swamps	4
Ethiopia	Berga floodplain	13	Somalia	Boorama plains	5
Ethiopia	Bishoftu lake	14	Somalia	Buulobarde (Buuloburti)	6
Ethiopia	Bisidimo	15	Somalia	Ceel Hammure	7
Ethiopia	Bogol Manyo - Dolo	16	Somalia	Ceel Munye - Ceel Torre	8
Ethiopia	Bonga forest	17	Somalia	Daalo	9
Ethiopia	Boyo wetland	18	Somalia	Far Waamo	10
Ethiopia	Cheleklcka lake and swamp	19	Somalia	Gacan Libaax	11
Ethiopia	Chilimo forest	20	Somalia	Hobyo	12
Ethiopia	Choke mountains	21	Somalia	Jasiira Ceebaad and Jasiira Sacaada Diin	13
Ethiopia	Dawa - Wachile	22	Somalia	Jasiira lagoon and Muqdisho islets	14
Ethiopia	Denkoro forest	23	Somalia	Jasiira Maydh	15
Ethiopia	Dessa'a forest	24	Somalia	Jowhar - Warshiikh	16
Ethiopia	Dilu Meda (Tefki)	25	Somalia	Laag Badaana	17
Ethiopia	Entoto Natural Park and escarpment	26	Somalia	Laag Dheere	18
Ethiopia	Finchaa and Chomen swamps	27	Somalia	Lascaanod - Taleex - Ceel Chebet	19
Ethiopia	Fogera plains	28	Somalia	Ras Xaafuun - Ras Gumbax	20
Ethiopia	Gambela National Park	29	Somalia	Saylac	21
Ethiopia	Gefersa reservoir	30	Somalia	War Harqaan - isha Dolondole	22
Ethiopia	Genale river	31	Somalia	Xarardheere - Awale Rugno	23
Ethiopia	Green Lake	32	Somalia	Xawaadley reservoir	24
Ethiopia	Guassa (Menz)	33	Socotra	Abd al-Kuri	1
Ethiopia	Gudo plain	34	Socotra	Airport dunes	2
Ethiopia	Hugumburda and Grat-Kahsu forests	35	Socotra	Al-Ikhwan	3
Ethiopia	Jemma and Jara valleys	36	Socotra	Coast of Bindar Di-Sha'b	4
Ethiopia	Jibat forest	37	Socotra	Di-Ishal foothills	5
Ethiopia	Koffe swamp	38	Socotra	Diksam	6
Ethiopia	Koka Dam and Lake Gelila	39	Socotra	Firjih/Central	7
Ethiopia	Konso - Segen	40	Socotra	Firmihin, near Jabal Keseslah	8
Ethiopia	Lake Abe wetland system	41	Socotra	Hajhir mountains	9
Ethiopia	Lake Ashenge	42	Socotra	Hamaderoh plateau and scarp	10
Ethiopia	Lake Awasa	43	Socotra	Jabal Jef	11
Ethiopia	Lake Chew Bahir	44	Socotra	Jabal Ma'lih escarpment/Badiya Qalansiya	12
Ethiopia	Lake Langano	45	Socotra	Muqadrihon pass	13
Ethiopia	Lake Turkana and Omo delta	46	Socotra	Noged plain	14
Ethiopia	Lake Zwai	47	Socotra	Qalansiya lagoon	15
Ethiopia	Lakes Alemaya and Adele	48	Socotra	Ra's Hebaq	16
Ethiopia	Liben plains and Negele woodlands	49	Socotra	Ra's Momi and Fikhah	17
Ethiopia	Lower Wabi Shebelle river and Warder	50	Socotra	Rewgid and Regid plateaus	18
Ethiopia	Mago National Park	51	Socotra	Rookib hills	19
Ethiopia	Mankubsa - Welenso forest	52	Socotra	Sabuniya and Ka'l Fir'awn	20
Ethiopia	Menagesha State Forest	53	Socotra	Shidahah	21
Ethiopia	Metu - Gore - Tepi forests	54	Socotra	Wadi Ayhaft	22
Ethiopia	Mid-Abbay (Blue Nile) river basin	55			

ORGANISATIONS AND WEBSITES

INTERNATIONAL

BIRDLIFE INTERNATIONAL

Wellbrook Court, Girton Road,
Cambridge CB3 0NA, UK
Tel: +44 (0)1223 277318
Fax: +44 (0)1223 277200
Email: birdlife@birdlife.org
Website: www.birdlife.org

The BirdLife Partnership is the global authority on threatened species, co-ordinating research on them and establishing conservation priorities. A network of Important Bird Areas (IBAs) and Endemic Bird Areas (EBAs) has been identified and is promoted through extensive conservation programmes, and a series of national, regional and global publications. The global Secretariat in Cambridge, UK, supports more than a hundred National Partners worldwide. Publications: *World Birdwatch* magazine (quarterly) and, with Cambridge University Press, *Bird Conservation International* (quarterly).

AFRICAN BIRD CLUB (ABC)

c/o Wellbrook Court, Girton Road,
Cambridge CB3 0NA, UK
Email: info@africanbirdclub.org
Website: www.africanbirdclub.org

The ABC aims to provide a worldwide focus for African ornithology and encourage an interest in the conservation of the birds of the region. Its bulletin is a valuable source of information on African birds. Publications: *Bulletin of the African Bird Club* (biannual)

ORNITHOLOGICAL SOCIETY OF THE MIDDLE EAST, CAUCASUS AND CENTRAL ASIA (OSME)

c/o The Lodge, Sandy,
Bedfordshire SG19 2DL, UK
Email: secretary@osme.org
Website: www.osme.org

Although OSME's sphere of interest is the Middle East, the Socotran archipelago is included in their region, and articles and information on Socotra regularly appear in their journal. Publications: *Sandgrouse* (biannual)

NATIONAL

ERITREA

'BIRDWATCHING IN ERITREA'

http://members.tripod.com/kilnsey/
birdwatching_in_eritrea/index.htm

A privately operated website which includes details of where to watch birds in Eritrea and a complete list of Eritrean species.

ETHIOPIA

ETHIOPIAN WILDLIFE AND NATURAL HISTORY SOCIETY (EWNHS)

PO Box 13303, Addis Ababa, Ethiopia.
Email: ewnhs.ble@ethionet.et
Website: http://members.lycos.nl/tigrai/ewnhs.htm

Publications: *Walia* (scientific journal)

SOMALIA (SOMALILAND)

NATURESOMALILAND

c/o Post Office Box 239, Djibouti.
Director: Abdi Jama. Tel: +252 24138813
Email: info@naturesomaliland.com or
abdi.jama@ymail.com
Website: www.naturesomaliland.com

A new organisation, based in Hargeisa, dedicated to conserving the natural environment and safeguarding habitats for birds in Somaliland (northern Somalia). Publications: A quarterly electronic newsletter is planned.

SOCOTRA (YEMEN)

YEMEN SOCIETY FOR THE PROTECTION OF WILDLIFE (YSPW)

29 Alger Street, PO Box 19759, Sana'a, Yemen.
Email: wildlife.yemen@y.net.ye

SOCOTRA CONSERVATION AND DEVELOPMENT PROGRAMME (SCDP)

Ministry of Water and Environment,
PO Box 16494, Sana'a, Yemen.
Email: scdp@socotraisland.org
Website: http://www.socotraisland.org

The SCDP website includes much information about bird conservation on the Socotra archipelago. A complete, up-to-date list of the birds of Socotra can be downloaded from http://www.socotraisland.org/intro/birds.html

EASTERN AFRICA

NATURE KENYA

Box 44486, 00100 GPO, Nairobi, KENYA
Email: office@naturekenya.org
Website: www.naturekenya.org

Publications: The annual journal *Scopus* (hosted by Nature Kenya) publishes papers on the entire eastern African region, including the Horn of Africa. The current editor is Mwangi Githiru: mwangi_githiru@yahoo.co.uk

Species Accounts

OSTRICHES *Endemic to Africa, ostriches are huge flightless birds with small wings, massive legs and two large forward-pointing toes; two species are recognised here. The small wings are mainly used for fanning, dusting and spectacular dancing displays. Ostriches walk at an average of 4 kph, but can sprint at speeds up to 60kph, and act as early warning of predators to a whole range of plains game. They often dust-bathe.*

Common Ostrich *Struthio camelus*   Height 2.2m, 90"

Adult male has blackish body feathering, white wings and tail (often stained with local soil colour), a *small white collar at base of neck* and *pink neck and legs* (brighter in breeding birds); *eyes brown*. Adult female is largely brown with dull pinkish-brown or brown legs. Immature male like adult female, but gains black colour in second year. Immature female similar to adult female. Chicks have striped buff and black heads and necks, and mottled backs. **HH** Uncommon as singles, occasionally in small groups in drier, bushed and wooded grassland, mainly below 2000m. In NE Africa, the nominate race occurs in Er, Dj and N&WEt. Ostriches have a complex breeding system with one major and 5–6 minor hens laying an average of 25 eggs in the same nest (which are incubated by the major hen during the day, and by the male at night). Chicks hatch after around 6 weeks and leave nest after 4 days. They join other young birds to form crèches which can number more than a hundred. Ostriches mature at 3–4 years, but males are unlikely to achieve mating status until 6–7 years. Eggs attract the unique tool-using Egyptian Vulture which uses stones to break them open, as well as other predators like hyaenas. **Voice** Generally silent, but displays a repertoire of roars, booms and hisses during breeding. Male well known for booming call, which is a little like a distant lion's roar: a deep, vibrant *hooo booo hoooomph hooo* (which can be heard over 1 km). Female has a subdued contact *twoo*. [Alt: Ostrich]

Somali Ostrich *Struthio molybdophanes*   Height 2.2m, 90"

Adult male is similar to Common Ostrich, but has cleaner, blacker plumage and a *blue-grey neck and legs*, without the white ring at the base of the neck. In breeding plumage the blue parts are brighter blue, but bill and front of legs become bright pink; *eyes pale grey-brown*. Adult female is similar to nominate race of Common Ostrich, but *always has blue-grey eyes*. Immature browner than adult female, otherwise as Common Ostrich. Chicks similar but plainer. **HH** Locally common and widespread in semi-arid and arid grassland, bush and woodland in Dj, So and S&SEEt. Less social than Common Ostrich, and more often encountered alone or in pairs, and regularly in much denser bush habitat. A browser rather than a grazer. **Voice** Similar to Common Ostrich. **Note** This species is sometimes regarded as conspecific with Common Ostrich.

Common Ostrich

♀

chicks

imm ♂

Common Ostrich

♂ nominate

♂

Somali Ostrich

GIANT PETRELS Large, heavy-bodied petrels, virtually the size of a small albatross. Flight is stiff-winged, only gliding over short distances.

Southern Giant Petrel *Macronectes giganteus*   87cm, 35"; WS c. 195cm, 78"

Has two distinct colour morphs. Adults of the commoner dark morph are grey-brown with a whitish face; immatures are all dark. At all ages they can be identified by a *heavy, pale horn bill with a greenish tip*. The rare white morph (not known in Northern Giant Petrel) is all-white with random small black spots; it has not been reported from our area. **HH** Vagrant. Single found dead on shore of Lac Assal, Dj, in Apr 1991. **Voice** Silent, unless squabbling over food. **Note Northern Giant Petrel** *Macronectes halli* is extremely similar to dark morph Southern Giant Petrel at all ages. In close views shows *heavy, pale horn bill with a dark reddish-brown tip*. No white morph occurs. Not recorded in NE Africa, but could occur. [Alt: Common Giant Petrel] **NT**

ALBATROSSES Spectacular seabirds from the southern oceans, with long narrow wings, short tails, and legendary gliding flight. Only one species recorded in NE Africa.

Shy Albatross *Thalassarche cauta*   98cm, 39"; WS c. 255cm, 102"

Adult shows *narrow black margin to white underwing and black 'thumb-print' where leading edge of wing joins body*. At close range shows dark eyebrow and pale grey cheeks, and a *yellowish-grey bill with a yellow tip*. Sexes alike. Immature has a grey head and grey bill with black tip; underwing pattern same as adult. **HH** Vagrant. Single record 33km off Ras Caseyr, So, in Sep 1986. **Voice** Silent when not breeding; at times gives a low nasal *squark*.

GADFLY PETRELS Medium-sized petrels with relatively long, broad-based wings and tapering wedge-shaped tails. In moderate or strong winds they have a remarkable flight pattern with towering arcs and strong glides.

Atlantic Petrel *Pterodroma incerta*   43cm, 17"; WS 104cm, 42"

A large, long-winged petrel with a *dark head and breast, rest of the underparts white except for dark undertail*; sometimes shows a whitish throat. Underwing all-dark but slightly paler bases of primaries look silvery in strong light. Upperparts entirely dark. **HH** Vagrant. Single record off Dj, Nov 1985. **Voice** Silent at sea. [Alt: Schlegel's Petrel] **EN**

Kerguelen Petrel *Aphrodroma brevirostris*   34cm, 14"; WS 81cm, 32"

A medium-sized, narrow-winged petrel with *head darker than rest of plumage*. Underwing dark with narrow white leading edge on inner wing, and *silvery underside to flight feathers* (but can look entirely dark in poor light). Upperwing all-dark. **HH** Vagrant. One bird found dead in SESo, Sep 1978. **Voice** Silent at sea. **Note** Sometimes placed in *Lugensa*.

Antarctic Prion *Pachyptila desolata*   27cm, 11"; WS 56cm, 22"

Delicate blue-grey seabird with *well-marked, quite broad, black M-pattern on wings and fairly broad black tip to tail*. At close range shows white supercilium and broad dark line through eye. White below *with dusky grey patch on sides of breast*. Sexes alike; immature similar to adult. Buoyant flight, with fast wing-beats and short glides. **HH** Vagrant. A wreck of at least 12 birds occurred in SESo, Aug 1979. **Voice** Silent at sea. **Note** Other prions are possible vagrants from the Southern Ocean; all are rather similar. [Alt: Dove Prion]

Cape Petrel *Daption capense*   39cm, 15.5"; WS 85cm, 34"

Uniquely marked *black and white petrel*. Black upperparts are broken by white patches in wings, and by chequered back and uppertail. Below, white with black wing margins and tail-band. Flight is distinctive, interspersing rapid shallow flaps with longer stiff-winged glides. **HH** Vagrant. One record off SSo, Jan 1957. **Voice** Silent unless feeding. [Alt: Pintado Petrel]

Northern

Southern

Shy Albatross

Southern
Giant Petrel

ad

imm

ad

ad

Atlantic
Petrel

ad

ad

ad

Cape
Petrel

ad

ad

ad

Kerguelen
Petrel

ad

Antarctic
Prion

SHEARWATERS AND PETRELS A varied group of all-dark or black and white seabirds. At close range most are easily identified, but can be difficult at distance, and can also be confused with noddies (plate 79). With experience, some can be identified by flight characteristics. Sexes and immature plumage alike, in all species.

Persian Shearwater *Puffinus (lherminieri) persicus*   33cm, 13"; WS 69cm, 27"

A small compact shearwater with broad rounded wings and relatively long tail; bill long and stout. Very similar to Tropical Shearwater, but *dark brown above with smudgy brown along sides of breast and flanks*, while white on underwing is limited to a *narrower central band, and undertail-coverts are dark*. Tropical is always blacker above (except in very worn birds) and whiter on underwings. Jizz and flight pattern very similar. **HH** Breeding visitor to Soc, and present throughout year in Gulf of Aden; commonly encountered off NSo Apr–Oct. Vagrant Er (once, Jan 1944). **Voice** Silent at sea. **Note** Often considered a race of Audubon's Shearwater *P. lherminieri.*

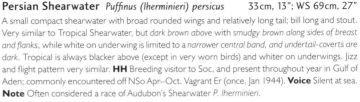

Tropical Shearwater *Puffinus (lherminieri) bailloni*   31cm, 12"; WS 69cm, 27"

A small, rather thickset shearwater with fairly short rounded wings and long slim bill; uniformly *sooty-black or blackish-brown above and white below*. Dark cap stops just below eye-level, *extensive white on underwing with variable brownish markings, and white undertail-coverts*. Rapid fluttering flight, interspersed with short glides, is characteristic of this species and Persian. Feeding birds may rest on sea-surface with slightly raised wings, and then dive and swim underwater. Another taxon described in 1995 as *P. atrodorsalis* (Mascarene Shearwater), blackish above and white below including the vent, is now regarded as the immature *bailloni*. **HH** Apparently a regular visitor off SSo in Nov (presumably from the Mascarenes). **Voice** Silent at sea. **Note** Often considered a race of Audubon's Shearwater *P. lherminieri.*

Wedge-tailed Shearwater *Puffinus pacificus*   46cm, 18"; WS 98cm, 39"

Fairly large all-dark brown shearwater with rather broad secondaries, and a *wedge-shaped tail which looks long and pointed at sea* (cf. Brown Noddy). Bill is dark grey; legs are pale, but hard to see. Wings are well bowed and held forward and slightly above body. Flaps up slowly (but not usually very high) and then glides back towards water, speeding up as wind strengthens, and often progressing forward in low arcs, before rising on wind and gliding down again. Rarer pale morph birds are grey-brown above with a darker cap and tail, and mainly white below; distinctive shape and jizz should clinch identification. **HH** Uncommon visitor to coastal waters off So and Soc, perhaps from the Seychelles, and most records are Apr–Aug. **Voice** Silent at sea.

Flesh-footed Shearwater *Puffinus carneipes*   47cm, 18.5"; WS 115cm, 46"

A large, heavy, all-dark brown shearwater with a leisurely flight pattern, long broad wings, a slightly wedge-shaped tail and stout pale bill (with dark tip). Pinkish feet are diagnostic if seen. Wedge-tailed Shearwater has a lighter build and long pointed tail. Jouanin's Petrel is much smaller with a different flight pattern. **HH** Recorded offshore from Soc, So (twice) and Dj; status uncertain. **Voice** Silent at sea.

Jouanin's Petrel *Bulweria fallax*   31cm, 12"; WS 79cm, 32"

Slender, all-dark petrel with narrow wings and a long, wedge-shaped tail. Significantly smaller than Wedge-tailed Shearwater with a *shorter, heavy-looking bill*, and (in worn individuals) pale bar on upperwing-coverts. Also has very different flight, sweeping over the sea in a series of wide arcs, climbing perhaps 15m above the waves, wings held forward and slightly bowed. **HH** Near-endemic breeding visitor to Soc (some stay all year round); uncommon or rare offshore from Er, Dj and So throughout year. **Voice** Silent at sea. **NT**

Streaked Shearwater *Calonectris leucomelas*   48cm, 19"; WS 122cm, 49"

A large brown and white shearwater with a small head, long neck, broad wings and distinctive flight. Adult is grey-brown above with pale fringes giving a scalloped effect at close range. Head looks *pale-faced with streaking on crown and nape*; bill is horn-coloured with a dark tip. Underparts mainly white, with dark flight feathers and a variable *dark patch on primary coverts*. Flight is lazy in light winds, with long glides on bowed wings between relaxed wing-beats; in strong winds, soars impressively. **HH** Occasionally reported from the Indian Ocean; vagrant Soc (once, Jan 2008) and a probable Dj (Nov 1985). **Voice** Silent at sea.

Persian Shearwater

Tropical Shearwater

persicus

bailloni

Wedge-tailed Shearwater

Flesh-footed Shearwater

Jouanin's Petrel

Streaked Shearwater

STORM-PETRELS Diminutive seabirds with characteristic flight patterns. Small size and usually a white rump means little confusion with other groups, but separating storm-petrels as species can be difficult. Note should be taken of flight and feeding patterns, as well as distribution of white in plumage, and shape and length of wing, tail and legs. Sexes alike; immatures similar to adults.

Wilson's Storm-petrel   Oceanites oceanicus   18cm, 7"; WS 41cm, 16"

Smallest storm-petrel in region, with square-cut or slightly rounded tail beyond which the feet just protrude; upperwing shows paler band across coverts, and extensive white rump-crescent wraps round onto lower flanks. Legs are long and foot-webbing is yellow (but rarely visible). Rather weak flight is distinctive, being dipping and swallow-like, with rapid wing-beats and occasional short glides; sometimes halts to feed, pattering the sea-surface with long legs. **HH** Annual visitor in small numbers from Southern Ocean, occurring off coast of So, Soc, Dj and Er from Apr–Nov; most frequent off east coast of So. **Voice** Silent at sea.

Swinhoe's Storm-petrel   Oceanodroma monorhis   20cm, 8"; WS 46cm, 18"

An all-dark storm-petrel with a forked tail and an indistinct pale band on upperwing-coverts which does not reach forewing. At close range, bill is short and heavy. In flight, wing-beats are deep and tail is usually held closed. Only all-dark species in region, but larger Matsudaira's Storm-petrel *O. matsudairae* could occur; its most distinctive feature is prominent white bases to shafts of primaries. **HH** Vagrant. One record of 3 birds off Raas Caseyr, So, in Aug 1964, and a single off Muscha, Dj, in Apr 1990. **Voice** Silent at sea.

White-faced Storm-petrel   Pelagodroma marina   20cm, 8"; WS 43cm, 17"

An unmistakable species with dark cap and eye-stripe and broad white supercilium; striking face pattern and entirely white underparts prevent confusion with any other storm-petrel. Upperparts are grey, contrasting strongly with black flight feathers and tail, and paler grey rump. In fresh plumage, white tips on coverts form a pale band. Underwing pattern also distinctive, with white underwing-coverts contrasting with black flight feathers. In flight, has long rounded wings, legs extending well beyond square-ended tail (which is frequently spread). When feeding, patters on sea-surface with long dangling legs. Six races worldwide; form in our region is probably dulciae. **HH** Vagrant. One record off Raas Caseyr, So (undated), and another off Soc, Jun 1960. **Voice** Silent at sea.

White-bellied Storm-petrel   Fregetta grallaria   20cm, 8"; WS 46cm, 18"

Very similar to Black-bellied in shape and jizz, with legs barely (or not) projecting beyond tail-tip. Upperparts all-blackish except for white rump. Pale band on upperwing-coverts usually indistinct (unless in worn plumage). Head, throat and breast black, sharply demarcated from white belly (no black line on centre of belly). Undertail black. Underwing with broad white central panel (cleaner than Black-bellied). Flight similar to Black-bellied. **HH** Vagrant from Southern Ocean. Recorded north and south of Soc, Jul 1969. **Voice** Silent at sea.

Black-bellied Storm-petrel   Fregetta tropica   20cm, 8"; WS 46cm, 18"

A stocky storm-petrel with broad-based wings and square-ended tail; legs project slightly beyond tail. Distinctive if seen well, with all-blackish head and upperparts except for white rump; below, breast to belly and underwing-coverts are white but belly bisected by variable black line (sometimes hard to see). Underwing-panel is often smudgy brown at edges and duskier than White-bellied. Undertail black. Throat can show some pale mottling. In flight looks heavy-bodied, swerving and zigzagging low over the ocean; may splash breast first into water, breaking free on long legs and pattering on surface. **HH** Vagrant from Southern Ocean. Two records off SSo, Aug 1964, and another off Soc in 2007. **Voice** Silent at sea.

Wilson's Storm-petrel

Swinhoe's Storm-petrel

White-faced Storm-petrel

Black-bellied Storm-petrel

White-bellied Storm-petrel

TROPICBIRDS *Spectacular, graceful, largely white seabirds, resembling large terns with very long tail-streamers. Often seen 15–30m above sea, mixing fluttery flight with circling and soaring glides, before hovering and plunge-diving to capture food on sea-surface. Sexes similar, but immatures lack tail-streamers. Best identified by amount of black in wings, bill and tail colour.*

Red-billed Tropicbird   *Phaethon aethereus*   81cm, 32"; WS 94cm, 37"

Adult has *black outer primaries*, short, narrow black bar across wing-coverts, *red bill* and long white tail-streamers. At close range, it shows black eye-stripe and fine vermiculations on mantle and lesser upperwing-coverts (looking greyish at distance). White-tailed has different upperwing pattern and lacks vermiculations (so that it looks more strikingly black and white). Immature lacks streamers, has yellowish bill with dark tip, and black terminal tail-band. Race in region is *indicus*. **HH** Breeds in small numbers on islands in Red Sea (e.g. 16 pairs counted off Er in 2001–07), and in Gulf of Aden off So and Soc. Largely pelagic outside breeding season and present offshore throughout year. **Voice** Calls include long harsh chattered trills and scolding rasps, but silent at sea.

White-tailed Tropicbird   *Phaethon lepturus*   81cm, 32"; WS 94cm, 37"

Adult has *long black diagonal bar across wing-coverts, black bases to outer primaries, yellow bill* and long white tail-streamers; at close range shows small black eye-mask. Immature has black patch in outer primaries, and variable black barring from crown to rump and on upperwing-coverts; lacks long tail-streamers and has black-tipped yellowish bill. Immature Red-billed has more black on outer wing. **HH** Hypothetical. Nominate race occurs in Indian Ocean off coast of So, usually far offshore, but no confirmed records for So as yet. **Voice** Silent at sea.

FRIGATEBIRDS *Large aerial seabirds with long narrow wings, deeply forked tails, and hooked bills. Soar and glide easily, often chasing other birds to steal food. Males are easily identified, but all other plumages difficult. Pay attention to pattern of white on underparts and underwing. Immatures distinguishable, but vary considerably through 4–6 years of subadult plumages. Females slightly larger than males.*

Greater Frigatebird   *Fregata minor*   100cm, 39"; WS 208cm, 82"

Adult male *looks all-black* (but has scarlet throat-sac which can be inflated in courtship display). Adult female has grey throat; *white on breast does not extend onto axillaries*. Immature has tawny or white head, separated from white belly by blackish breast-band. As immature ages, all white is lost in male, and breast-band becomes mottled black and white, with less white on belly in female. In flight, *white of underparts never extends onto axillaries* as in Lesser Frigatebird (but can be hard to judge at distance). Race in region is *aldabrensis*. **HH** Rare straggler to NESo (once, Sep 1944), Soc (once, 2007) and SESo (at least 7 records, all Aug–Dec). **Voice** Silent at sea.

Lesser Frigatebird   *Fregata ariel*   80cm, 32", WS 192cm, 76"

Adult male is entirely black *with two small white patches extending from flanks to axillaries* (white armpits). Adult female has *black throat*, and *extensive white on breast extending as collar on neck and onto axillaries*. Immature has russet or whitish head, white breast with or without dark breast-band, and *white axillaries*. Axillaries are important distinguishing feature at all ages, but can be hard to observe accurately at sea or distance. Race in region is *iredalei*. **HH** Extreme vagrant with three records from Er (Gulf of Zula, Dec 1951, Howakil Bay, Aug 2007 and Iddi, Aug 2008), and single records from Dj (off Obock, Mar 1986) and NWSo (Ceebaad Is, Jul). **Voice** Silent at sea.

Red-billed Tropicbird

ad

imm

ad

White-tailed Tropicbird

ad

imm

ad

Greater Frigatebird

imm

♂

♀

Lesser Frigatebird

♂

♀

imm

PLATE 6: BOOBIES

BOOBIES *Striking seabirds with long wings, wedge-shaped tails and long, sharp bills. Extent of black, brown and white in wings and tail aids identification. Transition from immature to adult plumage acquired over 3–4 years. Sexes alike, but females are slightly larger than males. Graceful, slow-flapping and gliding flight, often high over the sea. Make spectacular vertical or angled plunge-dives to capture prey.*

Masked Booby *Sula dactylatra*   92cm, 36"; WS 152cm, 60"

Adult has a white head and body contrasting with *all-black flight feathers and black tail, yellowish bill, small bare black face-patch*, and pale grey legs. No yellow wash on head. Immature is similar to Brown Booby with brown head, throat and upperparts, but has *whitish collar at base of hindneck, and brown at base of neck does not join brown at leading edge of wings*. Immature Masked also has yellow bill and is larger than immature Brown Booby. With age, begins to show *white mottling on back and wing-coverts*. In flight, immature shows *more white on underwing* than other boobies. Race in region is *melanops*. **HH** Breeds Soc and present offshore all year; also breeds Maydh I. off NSo (Nov) and Beilul Is, Er (25 pairs in 2007). Elsewhere, locally common visitor off NSo, Feb–May and Aug–Nov; rare Dj and Er. **Voice** On breeding grounds birds give a nasal barking.

Brown Booby *Sula leucogaster*   74cm, 29"; WS 142cm, 56"

Adult has *upperparts, neck and throat dark chocolate-brown, clearly cut off across upper breast, rest of underparts spotless white*; bill pale yellowish. Separated from similar immature Masked Booby by *lack of white collar on hindneck*, and less clearly defined white on underwing. Immature like adult, but with dull brown feathering below and grey bill. Never shows white spotting above like subadult Masked. At all ages, *brown of lower neck joins brown at leading edge of wing*. Appears lighter on wing and smaller and slenderer than Masked, with comparatively longer tail. Race in region is *plotus*. **HH** Breeds on islands off Er (10,000 pairs on 46 islands in 2007) and Soc, and present offshore all year; less common off NSo with similar distribution to Masked. **Voice** Resting birds give an abrupt, rather rapid nasal barking.

Red-footed Booby *Sula sula*   74cm, 29"; WS 142cm, 56"

Graceful booby. Adults highly variable with white, brown and intermediate morphs: in our area most are white, and brown is very rare. Typical white morph adult resembles adult Masked Booby but is smaller, with narrower black trailing edge to secondaries, *white tail*, and *red feet and legs* (hard to see at distance). Crown may have a slight yellowish wash; *bill blue-grey*. In flight from below, wing shows black trailing edge and diagnostic *black carpal patch* contrasting with white underwing-coverts. Brown morph is entirely dull brown with red feet. Intermediates vary from having white head, body and tail with brown back and wings, to mostly brown with white belly, rump and tail. All adults have pale blue-grey bills and *red feet*. Immatures are largely dull brown with paler brown underparts and all-brown underwings, or with poorly defined rather dirty brown underwing-coverts; bill brownish. Race in region is *rubripes*. **HH** Vagrant Dj (once, Sep 1985) and SESo (3 definite records and 5 probable, all May–Jun and Oct–Nov). **Voice** Silent at sea.

imm

Masked
Booby

imm

ad

imm

Brown
Booby

ad

ad

imm

Red-footed
Booby

ad
white morph

ad
brown morph

PELICANS *Well-known, distinctive bulky birds easily identified both at rest and in flight. Separated from each other by size, colour and behaviour. Soar and glide easily, often in large skeins, and regularly circle at height. Fishing technique is unique, gracefully plunging bill into water from a swimming position to catch prey.*

Great White Pelican *Pelecanus onocrotalus*

140–180cm, 55–70"; WS 250–300cm, 100–120"

Adult is a *massive black and white pelican with yellow bill pouch.* Breeding adult has pinkish hue and short ragged crest; male has purplish facial skin, female orange-yellow. Bill yellow with pink tip and both sexes gain an orange knob where bill joins forehead. Duller non-breeding adult has greyish bill. Immature grey-brown with dull bare parts. Juvenile much darker and browner. In flight shows extensive *black flight feathers contrasting with white coverts above and below.* **HH** Singles to large flocks are widespread in W&CEt and SSo on wide range of fresh, alkaline and (occasionally) coastal salt waters, with concentrations on Rift Valley lakes. Common and gregarious, often fishing together in large flocks. Dispersive resident population is augmented by Palearctic and intra-African migrants. Major colony breeds on Lake Shalla in Et. Rare in NWSo; vagrant Er and Soc. **Voice** Silent, but on breeding grounds gives continuous cacophony of low growling. [Alt: Eastern White Pelican]

Pink-backed Pelican *Pelecanus rufescens*

135–150cm, 54–60"; WS 215–240cm, 84–96"

Adult smaller and duller than Great White Pelican with *overall grey appearance and usually pale bill-pouch.* Small pointed crest gives head a peaked look. Breeding adult develops yellow pouch and brighter pink and yellow facial skin. Immature like dull adult with grey-brown head and back, and paler below. In flight *wings mostly grey with darker flight feathers, but never strongly contrasting black and white as in Great White.* Pink back can be visible in flight but variable and may be absent. **HH** Singles, pairs and small flocks are widespread and common on range of fresh, alkaline and coastal waters throughout most of region except NESo. Much more solitary than Great White and exploits smaller lakes and ponds. Breeds in mangroves on islands off Er (235 pairs in 2005–07), but also inland elsewhere. **Voice** Silent, but in tree-top colonies maintains constant guttural croaking.

GREBES *Low-slung aquatic diving birds with sharp bills, distinctive silhouettes and legs set far back on body. Virtually never seen away from water. Sexes alike.*

Little Grebe *Tachybaptus ruficollis*

28cm, 11"

Small, buoyant, short-necked grebe with short bill, rounded head, and rather square tail. Breeding adult has *chestnut sides to face and neck,* and *swollen creamy gape-spot.* Non-breeding adult has face and neck duller buffy-brown and smaller gape. Immature has greyish-white face and throat and may show some striping on neck. Race in NE Africa is *capensis.* **HH** Pairs and family groups are widespread and common on wide range of fresh and alkaline water from sea-level to 4000m, but generally less common in lowlands. Large flocks occur on Rift Valley lakes in non-breeding season. **Voice** Call is a loud and carrying giggling bray.

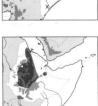

Black-necked Grebe *Podiceps nigricollis*

33cm, 13"

Larger than Little Grebe, with a rather bigger head and *slightly upturned bill.* Breeding adult dark, with *golden tufts behind red eye* and mottled rufous flanks. In African race *gurneyi,* non-breeding birds do not assume black and white non-breeding plumage as in northern nominate race, but lose tufts and become duller in worn plumage. Immature similar to non-breeding adult but browner with buff flanks. At close range, red eye is diagnostic. **HH** Widespread but erratic in small numbers; present throughout year in Et, especially on Rift Valley lakes where it may gather in large non-breeding flocks; vagrant Er and SSo. **Voice** Usually silent, but breeding birds give loud repeated whistles.

Great Crested Grebe *Podiceps cristatus*

56cm, 22"

Large, long-necked slender grebe. Breeding adult has *black crest* and *reddish and black ruff around face.* Non-breeding birds similar, but crest and ruff smaller and paler (race *infuscatus* of tropical Africa lacks drab non-breeding plumage of Eurasian birds). Immature has black and white striping on head and neck. **HH** Singles and pairs, less often groups, are fairly common residents on higher alkaline and freshwater lakes in Er and Et, at 1500–3400m. **Voice** Breeding birds give a goose-like descending growl and nasal bugling.

ad
non-br

imm

ad
non-br

Great White Pelican

imm

ad
non-br

ad
non-br

Pink-backed Pelican

non-br

juv

br

Little Grebe
capensis

imm

br

Black-necked Grebe
gurneyi

br

juv

Great Crested Grebe
infuscatus

br

CORMORANTS *Black or black and white waterbirds with slightly hooked bills. Easily identified by size and plumage. Sexes similar, but male slightly larger than female. Often stand to dry wings after swimming and diving.*

Socotra Cormorant   *Phalacrocorax nigrogularis*   80cm, 32"

Slightly smaller and much slimmer than Great Cormorant, with long slender bill. Breeding adult is sooty-black glossed bronze-green with white streak behind eye and variable white flecks on neck and rump. Non-breeding birds lack gloss, white eye-streak and white flecks. Immature greyish-brown above with pale fringes to wing-coverts, underparts dirty white with brown spotting on breast and belly. **HH** Exclusively marine, non-breeding visitor to NSo and Soc, sometimes in large numbers, and also a coastal breeding resident on Soc. Recently discovered to occur in large numbers in Red Sea, and reported to breed on islands off Er (but not confirmed). **Voice** Unknown. **VU**

Great Cormorant   *Phalacrocorax carbo*   100cm, 40"

Breeding adult glossed dark greenish-black with *white thigh patches* and white throat and neck (majority); some western birds have only a white chin, and others are rarely all-black. Non-breeding adult duller black with no flank-patches. Immature dark brown above with off-white underparts. Appears long-necked, short-tailed and heavy in flight. **HH** Singles to large flocks are common on larger freshwater and alkaline lakes in Rift Valley, preferring more open shores, but disperse in small numbers elsewhere including to coastal wetlands (but rarely on sea). Common in SSo, but largely absent from NSo. Vagrant Er and Soc. **Voice** Silent away from nesting colonies where birds maintain a low reverberant growling. **Note** NE African birds are all considered to be race *lucidus*, which is sometimes treated as a separate species, White-breasted Cormorant *P. lucidus*.

Long-tailed Cormorant   *Phalacrocorax africanus*   53cm, 21"

Much smaller than Great Cormorant *with a shorter neck (and bill)* and *proportionately longer tail*. Breeding adults are black (glossed green) with short crest, red eyes and silvery black-edged wing-coverts and scapulars giving wings scaly appearance. Non-breeding adult lacks crest and is dull brown-black with white chin, dirty white throat and dull off-white underparts. Immature similar to non-breeding adult, but duller brown above, and whiter below. **HH** Singles, small groups and flocks are common on a wider range of waters than Great Cormorant, often dispersing to temporary floods, and preferring waterside vegetation and trees for perches. Largely absent from NSo; vagrant Dj and Soc. **Voice** Breeding birds give a strange, variable high musical barking. [Alt: Reed Cormorant]

DARTER *Similar to cormorants, but slenderer and smaller-headed. Commonly soars or glides in air, unlike cormorants which continually flap. Often called snakebirds on account of swimming with just their slender necks visible above water.*

African Darter   *Anhinga rufa*   79cm, 31"

Large cormorant-like bird with *long thin neck*, *pointed bill* and large tail. Adult male has dark rufous foreneck and thin white line from below eye down sides of neck. Otherwise blackish above with fine white streaks on wing-coverts and elongated scapulars. Adult female is browner above with a less distinct neck-stripe. Immature is much paler brown, lacks neck-stripe, and is whitish-buff below. *Flies and often soars showing distinctive cross-like silhouette.* **HH** Single birds, pairs and less often groups are rather shy on wide range of still or slow-moving fresh and alkaline waters, usually well-fringed with vegetation. Absent from NSo. Vagrant Soc. **Voice** Calls with a series of staccato, gradually descending nasal barks. **Note** Sometimes lumped with Oriental and Australasian birds as Darter *A. melanogaster*.

FINFOOT *Superficially like cormorants and darter, but is reclusive and has bright red bill. Swims low, moving head back and forth, and may partially submerge and slip quietly into dense cover if detected.*

African Finfoot   *Podica senegalensis*   66cm, 26"

Large blackish and brown waterbird, with *bright red bill and legs*. Male is darker with blackish head and brighter bill than female, with an obvious *thin white line from eye down side of neck*, and a more conspicuous white-spangled back. Female is duller with browner head, *whitish eye-ring* and *white throat*. Immature like female, but duller and less spotted. **HH** Singles and pairs are uncommon, secretive and may be overlooked on permanent rivers, streams and pools with overhanging vegetation in W&SEt and SSo (rare) up to 1800m. **Voice** Rarely heard call is a series of sharp cracks, similar to African Darter but sharper.

imm

Socotra Cormorant

ad

ad

non-br

Great Cormorant

br

imm

lucidus

ad

♂

African Darter

br

Long-tailed Cormorant

imm

♂

imm

♂

African Finfoot

♀

BITTERNS *Short-legged herons with comparatively thick necks which are often held upright in freeze position. If seen well identification should not be difficult.*

Dwarf Bittern *Ixobrychus sturmii* 30cm, 12"

Adult is a small dark slate-grey bittern, *strikingly striped black on buff-white below*, with *bright orange-yellow legs*. Sexes alike. Immature is darker with tawny-fringed back and wings, and warm buff below with pale legs. Immature Striated Heron (plate 10) is larger with heavy streaking below. **HH** Singles and loose groups are uncommon to rare intra-African migrants to C&SEt and SSo, mainly Apr–Dec, favouring well-vegetated seasonal waters, including tiny pools; often found in bushes in wetland areas. **Voice** Breeding male gives rhythmical repeated *kwark-a-kwark kwark kwark kwark*, the last three notes being louder.

Little Bittern *Ixobrychus minutus* 38cm, 15"

Distinctive small bittern with conspicuous *cream upperwing-patch*. Two similar races occur: adult male *payesii* has rich chestnut face and neck; slightly larger nominate has face and neck buffy. In both races, adult female browner above with some streaking below. Immature is more heavily streaked below. *All reveal pale upperwing-coverts in flight.* **HH** Singles and small groups can be locally common at permanent or seasonal water where good vegetation cover occurs up to 2400m. Race *payesii* is an intra-African migrant (Mar–Jul in Et, up to Oct in SSo), while nominate birds are Palearctic migrants, Aug–Oct and Apr–May. Vagrant Soc. **Voice** Gives a short *rrah* when flushed, and breeding male gives low long barks at about 2-second intervals.

Yellow Bittern *Ixobrychus sinensis* 38cm, 15"

Similar in size and structure to Little Bittern. Adult male is pinkish-brown above with yellowish-buff wing-coverts. Face and neck are russet and flight feathers (largely obscured at rest) and tail blackish. In flight, *yellowish-buff wing-coverts and pale mantle contrast strongly with dark flight feathers and tail*. Little Bittern has creamier wing-coverts and black back. Female is similar to male but is lightly streaked below. Immature is browner and more heavily streaked. **HH** Vagrant to Soc (first recorded 1999 and several recent records). **Voice** Silent outside breeding season.

Eurasian Bittern *Botaurus stellaris* 75cm, 30"

Adult is a well-camouflaged, large, thick-necked bittern streaked or vermiculated throughout with brown and buff; cap and well-marked moustachial stripes blackish-brown. Sexes alike. Immature less boldly marked than adult with browner crown. **HH** Nominate Palearctic race is rare winter visitor to Er and NEt. **Voice** Breeding birds give far-carrying deep foghorn-like boom, each preceded by soft short bugled *mm-oom*. Silent outside breeding season. [Alt: Great Bittern]

NIGHT HERONS *Large-headed, hunched, stocky crepuscular or nocturnal herons. Flight silhouette is stump-necked and broad-winged. Roost during day, often in trees close to water.*

Black-crowned Night Heron *Nycticorax nycticorax* 61cm, 24"

Adult has black crown and back contrasting with dove-grey wings, whitish face and underparts. At close range has long white neck-plumes. Immature brown and buff with extensive white spots on back and wing-coverts, and well-streaked underparts. Striated Heron (plate 10) is smaller and darker. **HH** Small and sometimes large groups are widespread and may be locally common on permanent water and rivers, generally with fringing vegetation for roosting. Some birds are probably of Palearctic origin. **Voice** Distinctive and far-carrying *kwuk* or *kwark* barked when disturbed and in flight.

White-backed Night Heron *Gorsachius leuconotus* 56cm, 22"

Slightly smaller than Black-crowned Night Heron. Adult has a black head with a *huge reddish eye*, prominent white eye-ring, pale-yellow lores, and rich rufous neck to upper breast. Wings and back blackish-brown, with patch of white plumes on back only easily seen in flight. Immature very like immature Black-crowned, but is smaller with a blackish crown, pale lores, and large red-brown eye. **HH** Singles and pairs are rare and secretive residents of secluded rivers in WEt, where probably overlooked. Crepuscular and nocturnal; likes to roost in dense vegetation during day. **Voice** Quick low barks quite unlike Black-crowned, more like that of an egret *kruk kruk kruk...*

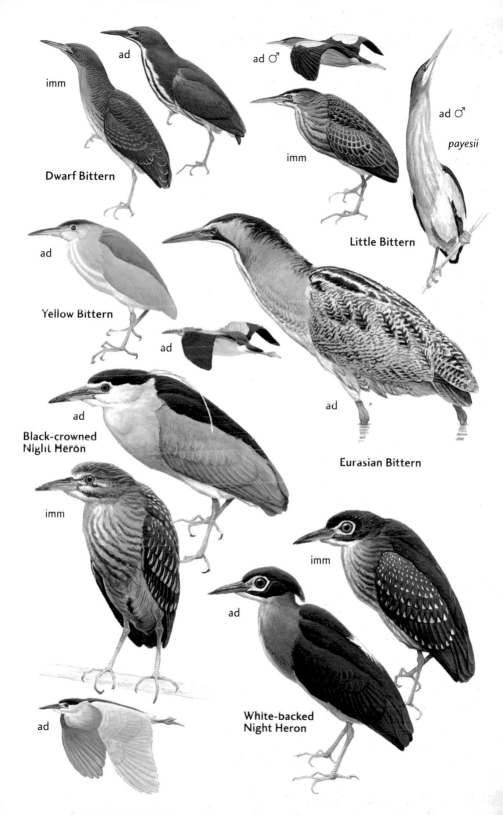

Dwarf Bittern

ad ♂

imm

Little Bittern

ad ♂

payesii

ad

Yellow Bittern

ad

ad

Black-crowned Night Heron

ad

Eurasian Bittern

imm

imm

ad

imm

ad

White-backed Night Heron

SMALLER HERONS Varied group of smaller short-legged herons which, with the exception of the Squacco and the pond herons, are all easily identified. The three Ardeola species all show much white in flight but not at rest; their non-breeding plumages are very similar. Sexes alike; immatures generally similar to non-breeding adults.

Cattle Egret *Bubulcus ibis*   56cm, 22"

Breeding adult is white with a *buff-orange wash on head, back and breast*, short bright red to yellow bill and lores, and short yellow legs (which flush orange in courtship). Non-breeding adult is all white, with paler yellow bill and yellowish-green legs. Immature similar to non-breeding adult, but may have darker legs. **HH** Small to large flocks are abundant and widespread, often with plains game or domestic stock, preferring damper grasslands and cultivation. Flocks often fly in disorderly lines with rapid direct wing-beats. **Voice** Breeding and roosting birds maintain a constant, variable and musical barking. Gives a short bark when disturbed.

Squacco Heron *Ardeola ralloides*   46cm, 18"

Small hunched heron which is *brownish-buff and cryptic at rest*, but reveals *bright white wings and tail in flight*. Breeding adult is rather plain dark buff above and washed apricot on wing-coverts and breast, with some fine dark streaking on head, and dark-tipped blue-grey bill. Non-breeding adult is darker brown above (not as dark as Madagascar and Indian Pond Herons), with brown streaking on buff underparts, and pale greenish-yellow base to bill. Immature is like non-breeding adult, but more heavily streaked below. **HH** Singles and small groups are widespread and common on a range of well-vegetated wetlands from coastal mangroves to small highland freshwater pools. Most birds are Palearctic migrants, but some are breeding residents. **Voice** Disturbed birds call a harsh *skwok*, while breeding birds maintain a constant musical barking and growling.

Indian Pond Heron *Ardeola grayii*   46cm, 18"

Non-breeding adult is very similar to Squacco Heron and not easily separable. It is usually slightly shorter- and heavier-billed, and *darker brown above*, lacking any buff or apricot tones on wing-coverts or breast. Head, neck and breast are evenly and heavily streaked, and mantle is drab brown or grey-brown; *lores usually show dark line*. Non-breeding Madagascar Pond is even darker above with very heavy dark streaks below. Breeding adult has an *unstreaked sandy-buff head, neck and breast, pure white plumes, maroon mantle* and dark-tipped yellow bill. **HH** First recorded Soc in 1999; now a regular straggler there with up to 10 reported (Nov/Dec 2007), including birds in breeding plumage. **Voice** Gives harsh croak when flushed.

Madagascar Pond Heron *Ardeola idae*   48cm, 19"

Non-breeding adult is very similar to non-breeding adult Squacco Heron, but *darker above* (lacking warm buff tones), with *broader blacker streaking below* (contrasting with white lower belly), and a slightly heavier bill. In flight, the distinctive dark back contrasts more than the buffy-brown back of Squacco. Breeding plumage (very unlikely in NE Africa) is pure white with a black-tipped blue bill and orange-red legs. **HH** Very rare non-breeding visitor to coastal and inland waters, with just two records in SSo (in May and Aug). Vagrant Soc. **Voice** The call *krrrrk* is more rattling and reverberant than Squacco Heron. [Alt: Madagascar Squacco Heron] **EN**

Striated Heron *Butorides striata*   40cm, 16"

Small, short and typically crouching heron. Adult is dark grey above with blue-green sheen, black crown (erected when alarmed), and greyish underparts with some rufous streaks. Legs are yellow (orange when breeding). Immature much browner-grey above, with paler crown, light tips to wing-coverts, broad brown and buff-brown streaks below, and duller legs. Two races occur: *atricapilla* (widespread except Red Sea coast) as described; *brevipes* (coastal Er, Dj and NWSo) is darker and more bronzy-green above. **HH** Singles are rather secretive, but widespread and common residents of inland and coastal waters. Typically makes short flights close to water with distinctive jerky wing-beats. **Voice** Flying birds give loud, high-pitched musical bark, single or in series where it drops in tone. [Alt: Green-backed Heron]

Cattle Egret

non-br

br

non-br

br

non-br

Squacco Heron

imm

br

Indian Pond Heron

br

imm

br

imm

ad

ad

Striated Heron

non-br

atricapilla

**Madagascar
Pond Heron**

br

ad

brevipes

EGRETS A confusing group: Little and Western Reef Egrets are hard to identify (and sometimes considered conspecific), but dark morph Little Egret is very rare. Yellow-billed and Great Egrets are more easily identified. Breeding adults have head-, back- and breast-plumes which are lacking in non-breeding birds. Note size and shape of bill, colour of lores, legs and feet (bare parts often flush when breeding but are variable and usually short-lived). Also consider habits and range. Sexes alike; immatures resemble non-breeding adults.

Little Egret *Egretta garzetta*   64cm, 25"

Medium-sized, elegant white egret with *slender black bill, black legs,* and *bright yellow feet*. Lores are usually blue-grey, but may turn yellowish or orange in breeding birds. Dark morph (rare) is similar to Western Reef Egret but the latter has thicker, drooping bill and yellowish-green legs. **HH** Singles to small groups are common and widespread in fresh and alkaline wetlands throughout region, including coast. Mainly resident but migrants pass south along Red Sea coast in Sep–Oct. **Voice** Call is a rather crow-like deep throaty growl, *rrraaahhhh.*

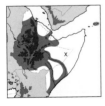

Western Reef Egret *Egretta gularis*   66cm, 26"

Both white and dark morphs differ from Little Egret in having a *slightly decurved and thicker yellowish-brown bill. Yellow foot colour extends halfway up dark green legs;* lores yellow. During courtship, bill and feet briefly become more orange, and lores and legs dark pinkish-red. Dark morph is very dark grey with white throat and variable amount of white on wing-coverts. Immature is variable: grey, grey and white, or all white. Race in NE Africa is *schistacea.* **HH** Common resident on Red Sea and Gulf of Aden coasts, and in SSo (150 breeding pairs counted on 20 islands off Er in 2005–07). Uncommon but regular on Rift Valley lakes in Et, Sep–Mar. Dark and light morphs occur in roughly equal numbers. **Voice** Calls are a short bark, much like Little Egret, and an extended growl.

Black Heron *Egretta ardesiaca*   51cm, 20"

Adult is *smaller* than dark morphs of other egrets and *entirely plain slaty-black* with short crest, black bill, black lores, and black legs with orange-yellow feet. Immature slightly paler blackish-brown and lacks head plumes. Dark morph Western Reef and Little Egrets are larger, paler grey and have white throats. **HH** Singles and small flocks are generally uncommon on Rift Valley lakes in Et, and on freshwater or brackish wetlands in SSo; occasional elsewhere but regular around Djibouti city. Prefers marshy fringes of lakes, but also occurs on open tidal flats. In *unique umbrella feeding action,* birds throw wings forward, creating canopy over water. **Voice** Breeding birds give a long gargling growl, otherwise usually silent. [Alt: Black Egret]

Great Egret *Egretta alba*   92cm, 36"

Adult is largest white heron, with long neck (often held kinked) and *dark gape-line which extends well behind eye.* Long dagger-like bill is yellow in non-breeding and black in breeding birds, while lores turn from yellow to green. Immature is very similar to adult, but has duller black-tipped yellow bill. Race in tropical Africa is *melanorhynchos.* **HH** Singles and groups are widespread and common in wide range of freshwater wetlands throughout region except NSo. **Voice** In flight, commonly gives a repeated drawn-out wooden descending growl. [Alt: Great White Egret/ Heron; *Ardea alba; Casmerodius albus*]

Yellow-billed Egret *Egretta intermedia*   69cm, 27"

Similar to Great Egret, but smaller, with *shorter yellow bill and gape-line which stops below eye.* Neck shorter than Great and not so kinked, but care is needed with singletons. Legs and feet often yellowish, but black in breeding birds. Lores usually yellow, but green when breeding. **HH** Singles and small groups are widespread (except NSo) but never common, favouring marshy grassland and lake fringes. Vagrant Dj and Soc. **Voice** A quiet egret but disturbed birds sometimes give a series of low crow-like short growls. [Alt: Intermediate Egret; *Mesophoyx intermedia*]

Little Egret

br

br

dark morph
non-br

ad

Western
Reef Egret

ad

dark morph br

white
morph
non-br

Black Heron

br

Yellow-billed
Egret

br

Great Egret

non-br

non-br

LARGE HERONS *Classic long-necked, long-legged large herons. Widespread in wetlands (but Black-headed Heron is invariably seen in open grasslands). All are easily identified. Sexes alike. They have loud throaty calls when disturbed, but are otherwise largely silent. Flight is powerful and leisurely, with necks retracted onto shoulders.*

Goliath Heron *Ardea goliath*   150cm, 60"

Massive heron, grey above with heavy spear-like bill, warm chestnut head and hindneck, white foreneck streaked with black, and dark chestnut belly. Immature similar to adult but rather paler grey above with rufous fringes, and paler below with dark streaking; belly washed tawny. In laboured flight, adult shows rich chestnut underparts and underwing-coverts contrasting with grey flight feathers, while immature has less well defined, mottled underwing. **HH** Singles and rarely small groups are widespread, but never common at major lakes, swamps and larger coastal estuaries. Absent from NESo and Soc. **Voice** Disturbed birds give a loud series of descending musical barks, *krrw krowkrowkrowkrowkrow kroww.*

Purple Heron *Ardea purpurea*   84cm, 33"

Slender, elegant and slim-necked heron, dark blue-grey above, with a yellowish bill which is longer and more slender than other large herons; *crown is black, contrasting with striking rich chestnut-rufous face and neck with black stripes on either side;* flanks are chestnut and the belly is black. Flying birds invariably appear dark due to black belly and chestnut flanks. Can be confused with Goliath Heron, but far smaller and paler-billed. Immature similar, but rather duller and brownish above with ochre feather edgings, and lacks chestnut flanks and black belly. **HH** Singles are solitary residents and winter visitors of well-vegetated swamps and lake edges where they tend to feed in cover. Uncommon in open, although often seen flying to communal roosts in evenings. **Voice** Generally silent; flight call is similar to Grey Heron, but sounds more cross and pinched.

Grey Heron *Ardea cinerea*   100cm, 38"

A predominantly grey, black and white heron. Adult is pale grey above with thick black eye-stripe extending as wispy plume, white face and foreneck with black streaks, and grey-white below. In flight, *underwings appear uniform dark grey.* Immature darker and plainer than adult, with overall dingy grey plumage; lacks well-defined black eye-stripe of adult, but crown often dark grey. **HH** Singles are rather solitary but widespread and reasonably common residents and winter visitors in wide range of habitats from coast (including open shores) to soda and freshwater lakes (including temporary water). **Voice** Disturbed and flying birds give a loud sudden nasal *kraahnk,* either singly or in series.

Black-headed Heron *Ardea melanocephala*   92cm, 36"

Similar to Grey Heron, but *black head and hindneck contrast markedly with white throat and foreneck.* Immature is dingy grey above including crown and hindneck, not contrasting strongly with white foreneck as in adult. *In flight all birds show strong contrast of white underwing-coverts and black flight feathers.* **HH** Singles or small flocks are widespread and common residents in wide range of wetlands from coastal lagoons to lakes and rivers inland, but species notable for its preference for drier habitats including cultivation and grassland sites, often far from water. Vagrant Soc. **Voice** Breeding birds maintain a constant noise of various barks and snaps. In flight, call is similar to Grey, but lower-pitched, shorter and not so nasal.

Goliath Heron

imm

ad

imm

ad

Purple Heron

ad

Black-headed Heron

ad

imm

imm

Grey Heron

HAMERKOP *Extraordinary species in monotypic family restricted to Africa, Madagascar and SW Arabia. Easily identified by unique shape. In rather buoyant flight, often soars and may suggest a small eagle. Pairs build several vast nests in trees which they often share with or lose to species like Grey Kestrel, Verreaux's Eagle-owl and Egyptian Goose. Often confiding and unafraid of man. Considered magical or birds of ill omen, but only occasionally persecuted. Hamerkop is derived from the Afrikaans name for hammer-head.*

Hamerkop *Scopus umbretta* 56cm, 22"

Medium-sized, dull-brown waterbird with long crest and flattened bill giving *hammer-headed appearance*. Sexes and immatures all similar, but male may be slightly larger. In distinctive flight appears largely brown, with a slightly darker tail-band. When soaring, may appear rather raptor-like, but long-billed silhouette rules out confusion. **HH** Single birds, pairs and sometimes flocks are common and widespread in a wide range of wetland habitats from tiny temporary roadside pools to the largest Rift Valley lakes. Often nomadic in drier country, responding to local rains. **Voice** Loud distinctive trilling series incorporating dominant *yip pruurr* notes, often several birds calling together; and a sharp, far-carrying *kyip* in flight.

STORKS *Large, long-legged and long-billed birds, usually with black and white plumage, found mainly in wetlands or grasslands. The two species below are mainly white with black flight feathers, and are easily identified by bill colour, habitat and behaviour. White Stork is the classic stork nesting on buildings in Europe, wintering in grasslands throughout sub-Saharan Africa. Yellow-billed Stork is a wetland bird, resident in Africa, but wandering far from breeding grounds.*

White Stork *Ciconia ciconia* 122cm, 48"

Large white stork with black flight feathers, white tail, *red bill and red legs* (which are often splattered with droppings and may appear partially white). Small black line through dark eye visible at close range. Sexes alike. Immature has darker-tipped red bill, duller legs and brownish flight feathers; some birds tinged greyish. Flying birds appear white with long black and white wings and *white tail*. Flocks regularly soar on thermals. **HH** Singles to gatherings of many thousands are widespread and common as winter visitors and passage migrants, Aug–May, preferring moist grasslands up to 2800m; a few remain all year. Uncommon in So, which is east of main migratory route; vagrant Soc. Wintering birds are widely nomadic in response to rains, burning and outbreaks of army worms and locusts. Often associate with other species, such as Abdim's Storks. **Voice** Usually silent on wintering grounds, except for occasional bill-clattering.

Yellow-billed Stork *Mycteria ibis* 108cm, 42"

Large white stork with red face, *slightly decurved yellow bill* and pinkish legs. Adult has pink blush (brighter in breeding birds) to back and wing-coverts. Neck often stained brown from muddy water. Immature greyish-brown with darker flight feathers, dirty brownish-yellow bill, and brownish legs. In flight, appears white with black flight feathers and *black tail*. They also regularly soar on thermals. **HH** Single birds or groups are widespread and common on larger and permanent fresh and alkaline waterbodies throughout region (except NESo). Also visits coastal areas and temporary waters, but rarely stays long. Feeds on fish by standing or walking slowly in water, bill open and partially submerged. **Voice** Breeding birds give squawks and squeals, and also clatter bills.

Hamerkop

ad

ad

imm

White Stork

Yellow-billed Stork

ad

br

non-br

imm

BLACK STORKS *At a distance, black storks need checking for colour of neck, back and belly, but are easily identified at close range. Sexes alike or virtually so.*

Black Stork *Ciconia nigra*   102cm, 40"

Large black stork glossed purple-green with just lower breast to vent white; *long bill, facial skin, eye-ring, and legs all bright red*. Sexes alike, but female slightly smaller. Immature duller brown-black with yellow-green bill-tipped orange, and greenish legs. In flight has white belly extending onto underwing (like Abdim's Stork), but is *entirely black above including rump*. **HH** Singles, pairs and rarely small groups are fairly common Palearctic migrants from Sep–Mar, mainly in west, to habitats fringing lakes and pools; rarely seen far from fresh water, but sometimes in dry open grassland in highland Et. Much more solitary than other migrant storks. **Voice** Silent in region.

Abdim's Stork *Ciconia abdimii*   81cm, 32"

Medium-sized black stork glossed purple-green, with lower back to rump and lower breast to vent white. Rather *small greenish-grey bill*, with *powder-blue facial skin, red lores and eye-ring*, and greenish-grey legs (with reddish knee joint). All bare parts brighten when breeding. Sexes alike, though female slightly smaller. Immature similar but blackish-brown, lacking gloss, with reddish bill and rather darker legs. In flight appears quite small and short-winged, and is mainly black but white belly extends as wedge onto underwing; *shows white rump from above*. **HH** Intra-African migrant, breeding widely in Et in Feb–Jun, and in Er in Apr–Sep (but breeds on Dahlak islands and coastal areas in winter); most winter in southern tropics. Passage through Er, SEt and SSo Oct–Nov and Mar–Apr, but a few remain in Er through the winter. Nomadic and gregarious, with tens of thousands following recent rains, burns and insect emergences. Prefers open grasslands, but visits wide range of habitats including agricultural lands in search of food gluts. **Voice** At breeding sites gives weak whistles and clatters bill.

African Openbill *Anastomus lamelligerus*   81cm, 32"

Medium-sized, shaggy, all-black stork with purple-green gloss and *diagnostic greyish open bill* (gap near tip visible at close quarters). Sexes alike. Immature duller, with some white speckling on hindneck, and straighter, shorter bill. In flight, all black from above and below with strange pterodactyl-like silhouette. **HH** Gregarious intra-tropical migrant of aquatic habitats; mainly a dry-season visitor north of equator (Nov–May). Singles to large groups are widespread and locally common in wetlands below 1500m, mainly in W&SEt and SSo, including freshwater swamps and lakes, inundated grasslands and coastal saltwater creeks and lagoons. Confirmed breeding Lake Tana in WEt (Aug–Sep) and Jubba valley in SSo (Oct). Specialised diet of snails and bivalves. **Voice** Breeding birds call a loud braying; otherwise usually silent. [Alt: African Open-billed Stork]

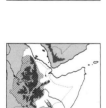

Woolly-necked Stork *Ciconia episcopus*   86cm, 34"

A distinctive black stork with glossy purple-blue and green sheen, *striking white woolly neck and head* with blue-black crown, red-eye, black bill with reddish tip, and grey-black legs. Sexes alike. Immature duller above, with slightly blacker crown, dark eye and dull pinkish legs. In flight, *white head and neck* obvious, but also shows long white undertail-coverts which hide black tail from below. Race in Africa is *microscelis*. **HH** Singles or pairs are widespread in W&CEt and WEr (mainly west of Rift Valley), occurring in marshes, swampy hollows and grasslands, but also in SSo on coastal waters, including lagoons, open shore and saltworks. Both a resident and intra-African migrant, wandering widely and possible throughout region. **Voice** Breeding birds maintain a rhythmical growling and bill-clattering; otherwise silent.

ad

imm

imm

Black Stork

imm

ad

Abdim's Stork

imm

ad

African Openbill

imm

ad

Woolly-necked Stork

GIANT STORKS *Highly distinctive and characterful storks that should not be confused with any other species. Saddle-billed Stork is a solitary bird of large swamps and river valleys, while Marabou is a fearless, widespread, successful, flocking scavenger.*

Saddle-billed Stork *Ephippiorhynchus senegalensis* 42cm, 57"

Very large black and white stork with a very long tricoloured bill (red and black with yellow saddle and two small pendulous yellow or red wattles) and very long grey legs with pink knees and feet. Male has dark eyes, while slightly smaller female has yellow eyes. In flight, wings are mostly white with black wing-coverts. Immature is largely dingy grey-brown with some white patches on back, blackish bill without saddle, and duller legs. **HH** Singles and pairs are uncommon to locally common in suitable permanent freshwater swamps and wetlands, sometimes in midst of dry country, and may occur as high as 3000m. Mainly resident but partially nomadic, mainly in Rift Valley and WEt; uncommon visitor to SSo, Nov–Jul. Hunts with slow walk capturing prey such as frogs from flooded vegetation, often tossing food into air before swallowing it. **Voice** Usually silent, but breeding birds give descending squealing wheezes.

Marabou Stork *Leptoptilos crumeniferus* 152cm, 60"

Huge stork with grey back and wings and white underparts. Naked head and neck pink or reddish showing scabby black spots at close range, and downy white neck-ruff. Birds have two inflatable air-sacs: a bright red one at base of hindneck, and a pinkish pendulous balloon which, variable in size, hangs below neck. Bill massive and horn-coloured. Legs dark grey but often appear white as splattered with droppings. Sexes alike, but female slightly smaller. Breeding adult has light greyish wings, white-edged wing-coverts, and fluffier undertail. Non-breeding adult is darker grey. Immature is duller than adult with brown not grey wings. Massive in flight, soaring on broad wings with neck retracted, but will make short flights with neck extended. **HH** Singles to gatherings of hundreds are common and widespread in range of habitats from city rubbish dumps to lakeshores and also at predator kills. Absent from NESo. Vagrant Dj. **Voice** Silent away from nest, but breeding birds give a wide range of bleating, grunting and squealing noises, as well as bill-clattering.

SHOEBILL *Extraordinary-looking scarce and atypical stork-like bird (which may be related to the pelicans), and the sole member of its family. Nowhere common, preferring remote, secluded and extensive permanent swamps. Walks across floating vegetation or stands silently watching for prey. Usually flies slowly and low with neck retracted, but will soar to very great heights, and occasionally wanders.*

Shoebill *Balaeniceps rex* 124cm, 48"

Giant stork-like *grey bird with a massive, fat, hooked bill.* Adult has a slightly erect crest, pale grey eyes, mottled horn-coloured bill, and grey legs. Sexes alike, but female slightly smaller. Immature fringed with brown. **HH** Rare resident of the Baro-Akobo swamps of WEt, known from just a handful of sites. Singles and pairs are confined to interior of permanent and undisturbed swamps, and are rarely seen in the open. **Voice** Breeding birds make a hollow reverberant hammering sound, donkey-like brays and pig-like squeals. Otherwise silent away from nest. [Alt: Whale-headed Stork] **VU**

Saddle-billed Stork

♀

♂

imm

pouch
inflated

Marabou Stork

ad

imm

ad

Shoebill

IBISES Medium-sized to large terrestrial and wetland birds with long decurved bills. Most are dull or dark brown with green (or purple and green) sheen on wing, best identified by head-shape, calls and range. Sacred Ibis is unique in being black and white. Most have loud diagnostic calls, often given in morning or evening flights to and from roosts. Sexes similar; immatures mainly dull versions of adults.

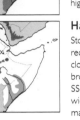

Sacred Ibis *Threskiornis aethiopicus* 80cm, 32"

Largely white ibis with a bare *black head and neck, long black bill* and black legs. Breeding adult grows black plumes from scapulars and inner secondaries, and bare skin on underwing turns bright red. Immature like adult, but rather dull with some white feathering on neck. **HH** Singles, small groups and larger flocks are widespread and common in many habitats, including cultivated lands, often near fresh or salt water from sea-level to 3000m. Vagrant Soc. **Voice** Breeding birds give high squealing yelps and short barks; otherwise silent away from nest.

Hadada Ibis *Bostrychia hagedash* 75cm, 30"

Stocky dark ibis with *greenish-purple glossed wings and short legs*. Bill heavy and downcurved with red culmen (which may brighten in breeding adult). Diagnostic buff-white malar stripe visible at close range. Immature duller than adult without red on bill or gloss on wing. In flight, appears dark, broad-winged and short-tailed; legs do not project beyond tail. Two races occur: *brevirostris* (SEt, SSo) and *nilotica* (W&SWEt), which has a longer bill. **HH** Pairs and small flocks are common and widespread in grasslands, marshy areas and damp forest edges, as well as gardens and cultivation, mainly in highlands below 2400m. **Voice** Very noisy, most often heard at dawn and dusk, calling a varying bugled *haa haa ha-aaa* with last notes downslurred. [Alt: Hadeda Ibis]

Glossy Ibis *Plegadis falcinellus* 65cm, 26"

Similar to Hadada Ibis, but far more *slim and elegant with slender bill and neck and long legs*; always appears dark at distance. Breeding adult largely rich dark chestnut with well-glossed greenish-purple back, wings and tail (close views reveal two cobalt-blue lines on face). Non-breeding adult has head and neck speckled with greyish-white. Immature duller brown. In rather rapid flight, *wings look narrow and feet extend well beyond tail*. **HH** Singles, pairs and small groups are common and widespread, in wetlands of all types including lakes, rivers and coastal lagoons, Aug–May. Many birds probably originate from outside region, possibly including Palearctic. **Voice** Usually silent, but flying parties commonly utter a nasal quack-like growling *ehhk ehhk ehhk...*

Northern Bald Ibis *Geronticus eremita* 75cm, 30"

Stocky, blackish ibis with *shaggy crest, bald reddish face*, and reddish bill and legs. Plumage is dark metallic green with bronze and violet gloss on wing-coverts. In flight legs do not project beyond tail. Immature has head feathered and faintly streaked greyish, much duller plumage, and no elongated feathers on nape; bare parts duller. Second-years have nuchal crest, incipient violet gloss on coverts but head still mainly feathered. Full adult bare-part coloration probably attained in third year. In flight legs do not project beyond tail. Flies in V-formation with shallow wing-beats and short glides. Glossy Ibis has slenderer appearance, longer neck, no bare head and longer legs projecting in flight. Hadada has no bare head and quite different flight action. **HH** Very rare and endangered Palearctic winter visitor, historically recorded from Er and CEt, with single old record from NWSo. In 2006–7 three birds were tracked from Syria to CEt where they wintered. A juvenile was found at Tadjoura, Dj in Dec 2007. Prefers dry rocky areas, often along sides of river valleys; also open fields and coastal lagoons. **Voice** Although unlikely to be heard in region, birds give a strange *yulp* and throaty gulping notes. [Alt: Waldrapp] **CR**

Wattled Ibis *Bostrychia carunculata* 80cm, 32"

A large brownish-black ibis with an *extensive white wing-patch* (formed by mainly white or white-edged wing-coverts; often less white than shown in illustration). Plumage glossed dull green, with dull red bill and legs, and pale eye. Crown has lax crest extending onto neck; small white wattle hangs from throat. Immature duller, with less white in wing and no wattle. In flight legs do not project beyond tail. No other dark ibis has white wing-patch. **HH** ENDEMIC to Er and Et. Common resident in highlands, 1500–4100m. Flocks (sometimes quite large) feed on open grasslands, marshes and moorland. **Voice** Perched birds give an unpleasant, harsh, heron-like growling and deep rattles and gurgles, quite different from other ibises.

imm

ad

Sacred Ibis

ad

Hadada Ibis

imm

ad

imm

br

ad

imm

Glossy Ibis

Northern Bald Ibis

ad

Wattled Ibis

SPOONBILLS *Largely white birds with unique spatulate, spoon-like bills. Adults of the two species are reasonably easily told apart by bill, leg and bare-part colour. Confusion with other species unlikely. Elegant feeders which walk in shallows and scythe water with bills, often in groups.*

African Spoonbill *Platalea alba*   91cm, 36"

Adult is all white with an *extensive bare red face, blue-grey pink-edged bill*, pale blue eyes (in breeding plumage), and *bright pinkish-red legs*. Sexes similar. Non-breeding birds have dark brown eyes. Immature lacks red face, has a dusky yellow bill, dark eyes, dark-tipped primaries and blackish legs and feet. In flight, adult shows all-white plumage, spoon-shaped bill and long red legs; immature has dark tips to primaries. **HH** Singles, pairs and small groups are common in a wide range of freshwater and alkaline wetlands including coastal lagoons from sea-level to 3000m (absent NSo). **Voice** Noisy at nest, giving a crane-like bugling, which is similar but softer when feeding or resting.

Eurasian Spoonbill *Platalea leucorodia*   89cm, 35"

Very similar to African Spoonbill, but adult has a *black bill with yellow spot near tip, black legs* (not red), very small area of yellow (not red) facial skin, and feathering (not bare skin) on forecrown between red eyes. Breeding adult has yellowish crest and wash to centre of breast. Sexes alike. Immature similar to adult, but has black-tipped wings, dull pinkish-grey bill and dark legs. **HH** Usually in small groups, favouring shallow water in coastal, brackish or freshwater habitats. Two similar races occur: nominate is an uncommon to rare Palearctic winter visitor, mainly in Rift Valley and WEt; *archeri* (coastal Er, Dj and NWSo) is smaller and resident on Red Sea coast, breeding in mangroves (284 pairs counted on 18 islands off Er in 2005–07). Vagrant Soc. **Voice** Silent except at breeding colonies.

FLAMINGOS *Tall pink wading birds which mass in thousands on Rift Valley lakes; easily identified by size, plumage and bill colour. Specialist bills allow food to be filtered from lake water and bottom ooze. Greater Flamingo eats a wide variety of minute aquatic animals, while Lesser Flamingo almost always feeds on blue-green algae. Regularly swims and upends, and flies with neck extended.*

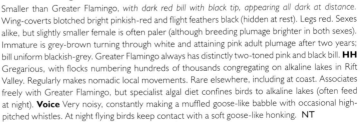

Greater Flamingo *Phoenicopterus ruber*   140cm, 55"

Much larger than Lesser Flamingo (but occasional small individuals can be similar in size); *big bent bill is pink with black tip*. Adult appears largely pale pink or white at distance with line of bright coral-pink on folded wing. Legs are also bright coral-pink. Sexes similar, but female slightly smaller. Immature grey-brown, only attaining adult plumage in second year; bill two-toned (pale grey with black tip). *Lesser has dark, almost concolorous bill at all ages*. In flight, reveals brilliant coral wing-coverts and black flight feathers, contrasting with paler body. Race in Africa is *roseus* which is sometimes split from New World birds as a separate species. **HH** Singles to flocks of thousands are found mainly on muddy-fringed alkaline lakes in Rift Valley and coastal lagoons on Red Sea coast, less often on fresh water. Exploits greater range of habitats than Lesser Flamingo, and benefits more from man-made lakes, dams and sewage ponds. Mainly a non-breeding migrant to region. **Voice** Flocks maintain a constant low, angry, goose-like growling.

Lesser Flamingo *Phoeniconaias minor*   90cm, 36"

Smaller than Greater Flamingo, *with dark red bill with black tip, appearing all dark at distance*. Wing-coverts blotched bright pinkish-red and flight feathers black (hidden at rest). Legs red. Sexes alike, but slightly smaller female is often paler (although breeding plumage brighter in both sexes). Immature is grey-brown turning through white and attaining pink adult plumage after two years; bill uniform blackish-grey. Greater Flamingo always has distinctly two-toned pink and black bill. **HH** Gregarious, with flocks numbering hundreds of thousands congregating on alkaline lakes in Rift Valley. Regularly makes nomadic local movements. Rare elsewhere, including at coast. Associates freely with Greater Flamingo, but specialist algal diet confines birds to alkaline lakes (often feed at night). **Voice** Very noisy, constantly making a muffled goose-like babble with occasional high-pitched whistles. At night flying birds keep contact with a soft goose-like honking. **NT**

Eurasian
Spoonbill

imm

br

imm

br

African Spoonbill

Greater Flamingo

imm

imm

ad

Lesser Flamingo

ad

GEESE AND ALLIES Easily distinguished by size and plumage. Most often seen around or on fresh water, but not restricted to it, and also frequent on marshy grasslands.

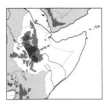

Spur-winged Goose *Plectropterus gambensis* ♂ 100cm, 39"

Adult male is a *massive long-necked goose* with a *bare warty red face* and *iridescent patchy black and white plumage* which shows green reflections in good light. Female is quite similar but smaller and lacks red knob on forecrown. In slow and laboured flight, has *long white bar along leading edge of wing*. Immature similar to female, but duller and browner. **HH** Pairs, family groups and flocks are resident in W&CEt, inhabiting flooded grasslands and swamps below 2000m, but numbers fluctuate and some local movements occur. Frequently perches in trees to roost. **Voice** Male flight call is a repeated variably rapid double wheezy note, almost a hiccup.

Egyptian Goose *Alopochen aegyptiaca* ♂ 73cm, 29"

Bulky brown goose with richer, darker rufous-brown back; *rich brown eye-patches and breast-spot* distinctive. Sexes similar, but female usually slightly smaller. In flight *shows large white oval wing-patches*. Immature is dusky brown, lacking eye-patches and breast-spot. **HH** Pairs, family groups and flocks are common and widespread beside wide range of wetlands including fresh, alkaline and coastal waters up to 3800m. Swims with high posture and upends; also frequently grazes. **Voice** On ground, male gives an agitated nasal, rather high-pitched honking, whilst female accompanies him with low muffled growls. In flight this can be accelerated as birds become excited.

Blue-winged Goose *Cyanochen cyanoptera* ♂ 75cm, 30"

An unmistakable medium-sized grey goose with relatively short legs and small black bill. Wing pattern of *black primaries, glossy green secondaries and pale blue wing-coverts diagnostic*. Head is plain ash-grey with whitish forehead, face and throat; mantle darker grey and underparts mottled grey and white. In flight, shows white underwing-coverts. Sexes similar but female smaller. **HH** ENDEMIC to highlands of Et. Locally common on moorlands, marshes, meadows and grasslands near water, at 2100–4100m, usually in pairs or small groups. Mainly sedentary. **Voice** High-pitched airy whistling is given repeatedly, often breaking into squeals and yelps. **VU**

Knob-billed Duck *Sarkidiornis melanotos* ♂ 75cm, 30"

Adult male is a bulky, boldly marked black and white duck with *large knob (or comb) on top of bill* (smaller in non-breeding birds). In good light back shows green and purple iridescence. Female much smaller, lacks knob on bill, and has head more speckled with black than male. In flight, all-dark wings contrast with white underparts. Immature like female but duller and washed with dingy brown. **HH** Pairs and small flocks are widespread non-breeding Afrotropical migrants on freshwater wetlands, but wander extensively; absent from NSo. Occurs mainly below 1800m, but occasionally up to 2400m. **Voice** Male quite vocal, either on ground or more usually in flight, when he gives a soft burry bark. [Alt: Comb Duck]

Greater White-fronted Goose *Anser albifrons* ♂ 78cm, 31"

A medium-sized, compact goose with grey-brown plumage and orange legs. Adult has fairly long pink bill, *bright white blaze around base of bill* and irregular *black barring on belly*; vent and undertail-coverts white. Juvenile has black tip to bill, and no white blaze or black barring, although black bars begin to develop during first winter. **HH** Siberian species wintering in Europe. Vagrant Soc. **Voice** A high-pitched, musical, disyllabic *kyu-yu* or trisyllabic *kyu-yu-yu*. [Alt: White-fronted Goose]

Spur-winged Goose

♂

♀

♂

Egyptian Goose

ad

Blue-winged
Goose

ad

♀

Knob-billed
Duck

♂

ad

nominate

Greater
White-fronted
Goose

WHISTLING DUCKS *Long-necked, long-legged ducks, giving an about-to-spring-into-the air impression which is distinctive even at distance. Sexes similar; immatures are duller versions of adults.*

White-faced Whistling Duck *Dendrocygna viduata*   48cm, 19"

White-faced dark duck with chestnut neck and breast (face often soiled dirty brown by muddy waters). In flight appears largely dark (except for white face), with limited body-to-wing contrast. **HH** Common and gregarious with small to large flocks gathering together at wide range of waters throughout region, particularly in Rift Valley. Local movements occur, but many birds resident; absent from NSo. **Voice** Calls frequently, often whole flock together, with a whistled *wi wi-wi-yu*, the last three notes descending and slurring into each other. [Alt: White-faced Duck]

Fulvous Whistling Duck *Dendrocygna bicolor*   51cm, 20"

A cinnamon-brown duck with dark brown back and wings. Dark line down hindneck and white flank-stripes are obvious at close range. In flight, shows conspicuous buff-white rump-crescent and strong contrast between body and wings. Immature duller and lacks white flank-streaks. **HH** Small to large flocks are found in wide range of wetlands including shallow inundated grasslands, rice fields and coastal areas, mainly below 2000m, including Rift Valley and Lake Tana (where it has bred). Local movements occur and many birds are non-breeding visitors. **Voice** Call is a repeated, well-spaced explosive double whistle, *wi-whiu*, with second part higher. [Alt: Fulvous Duck]

PYGMY-GEESE *Two species of misleadingly named, very small colourful ducks with short triangular bills; one is reasonably widespread, but rather elusive, the other a vagrant. Birds often hide in dense floating vegetation.*

African Pygmy-goose *Nettapus auritus*   31cm, 12"

Breeding male is easily told from all other ducks by *small size, green and white head, yellow bill, dark green back and mostly chestnut underparts.* Non-breeding or eclipse male, female and immature are more subdued, with grey-brown face-smudges, crown and hindneck. In fast and direct flight it is the only duck showing combination of white face, secondary patches and belly. **HH** Pairs and small groups are widespread but rather local and shy, preferring quiet, well-vegetated waters, invariably with an abundance of water lilies, from sea-level to 1800m. **Voice** A variety of rather irritated whistles and clucks and an occasional explosive *tak*.

Cotton Pygmy-goose *Nettapus coromandelianus*   33cm, 13"

Similar in size and shape to African, but *lacks rufous.* Breeding male has white head with small black cap, *black bill*, green-glossed upperparts and *greenish-black band across breast.* In flight, shows broad white band across wing. Female is duller, with dark line through eye and no breast-band; breast and flanks rather dusky. In flight female lacks male's white band on wing and has narrow white trailing edge instead. **HH** An Indian species, now regular in Oman. Vagrant to Soc (3 records). **Voice** Male gives staccato cackle, *quack, quack-quacky duck*. [Alt: Cotton Teal]

SHELDUCKS *Two species of large, goose-like ducks of Palearctic origin. Sexes show limited sexual dimorphism.*

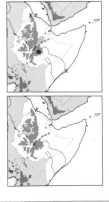

Ruddy Shelduck *Tadorna ferruginea*   70cm, 28"

Large long-necked duck of the highlands. Breeding male is mainly *bright orange-brown with paler whitish head* separated by narrow black collar. Non-breeding male usually lacks collar. Female duller with whitish face and no neck-collar. In flight, wing pattern is like Egyptian Goose, but latter is browner (less orange) with prominent eye-patch. **HH** Uncommon presumed Palearctic migrant to Er (once) and CEt. Breeds on Sanetti Plateau in Bale Mts, SEEt, where resident. Occurs on freshwater pools and lakes, and highland marshes above 3500m. Often grazes on land. **Voice** Repeated honking given by male whilst female accompanies with a quiet whistle; groups give a loud trumpeting chorus.

Common Shelduck *Tadorna tadorna*   65cm, 26"

An unmistakable large duck with mainly white and chestnut plumage, and a dark green head. Breeding male has *bright red bill with large knob.* Female is smaller and lacks knob. Juvenile is grey-brown above, with white face and underparts (no chestnut breast-band) and pink bill. **HH** Palearctic vagrant to Et (once). **Voice** In flight birds give a cackling sound or musical whistling. On ground also utter quacking and growling notes.

White-faced Whistling Duck

ad

Fulvous Whistling Duck

ad

Cotton Pygmy-goose

♀

♂

African Pygmy-goose

♂

♀

Ruddy Shelduck

♀

♂

br ♂

♂

♀

Common Shelduck

RESIDENT DUCKS A mixed group of waterfowl which move about locally, but are mainly considered resident within region. Two are in distinctive genera: Maccoa Duck is the only stifftail, and White-backed Duck is a large-headed species which swims very low in the water. The others are typical dabbling ducks, all easily identified if seen well.

Red-billed Duck *Anas erythrorhyncha* 48cm, 19"

Only *red-billed duck with a dark crown and nape*, contrasting clearly with pale cheeks and foreneck. Rest of plumage largely brown above with pale feather-edges producing scaly effect. Underparts paler and also scaly. Sexes alike. Immature similar to adult, but bill rather pinker. In flight, shows striking white secondaries contrasting with otherwise dark upperwing. **HH** Pairs, family parties and large flocks are common and widespread on shallow freshwater lakes, marshes and pools in Et at 1800–2450m, but down to sea-level in SSo. Less common on alkaline waters, and rare on coast away from major estuaries. **Voice** Male gives a rising, nasal drawn-out *yuuuw*, while female responds with a harsh quacking. [Alt: Red-billed Teal]

Hottentot Teal *Anas hottentota* 36cm, 14"

Small neat duck with dark cap and pale cheeks similar to Red-billed Teal, but easily separated by size, *pale blue sides to bill and dark neck-smudge*. Underparts rich cinnamon. Female duller with less clear-cut head and neck pattern. Immature even duller than female. In flight dark upperwing shows green speculum and white trailing edge to secondaries (much less white than on Red-billed). **HH** Pairs, family parties and small flocks are widespread and fairly common in Et on fresh and alkaline waters of all sizes at 400–2100m; vagrant SSo (one old record). Prefers areas with fringing vegetation and often dabbles close to water's edge. **Voice** Call is similar to Common Moorhen, a nasal series *kekekeke...*, given rapidly.

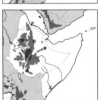

Cape Teal *Anas capensis* 48cm, 19"

Elegant *mottled pale grey duck with pink bill*. Closer views reveal finely speckled head and more boldly mottled underparts. Sexes similar. Immature duller and less clearly spotted. In flight, shows two white bars on secondaries separated by broad dark green bar. **HH** Pairs, family groups and occasionally flocks are typical of shallower Rift Valley soda lakes, occurring more rarely on nearby freshwater, below 2400m. Vagrant Dj. **Voice** Male gives a short whistle followed by a longer upslurred whistle, also a low growling quack. In flight utters a strong but burry quack.

White-backed Duck *Thalassornis leuconotus* 41cm, 16"

A large-headed brown duck which swims very low in water. Close views reveal a *vertical white spot between base of bill and eye* contrasting strongly with dark face and tawny-brown neck; back and flanks tiger-striped rufous-brown and blackish. Sexes alike. Immature duller with less pronounced face-spot. In flight appears dark and short-tailed with white back (a feature which, despite name, is not visible at rest). If disturbed birds prefer to submerge their bodies and swim away partially hidden. **HH** Pairs, family parties and flocks are local and unobtrusive on well-vegetated freshwater lakes of all sizes in Et; vagrant SSo (one old record). **Voice** Generally silent, but male calls a loud, piercing, explosive double whistle, *swit-sweet*.

Maccoa Duck *Oxyura maccoa* 51cm, 20"

Breeding male is an attractive *chestnut stifftail* with a *black head and bright blue bill*. Eclipse male, female and immature are duller brown with a *narrow dark line below eye, broad dark cheek-stripe, and whitish lower cheek and throat*. Silhouette distinctive if tail cocked. Only rarely flies to escape disturbance, preferring to dive or submerge. **HH** Pairs or family groups are common, mainly on highland and Rift Valley lakes in Et at 1600–3000m. Recently discovered in Tigray, Et, and as non-breeding visitor to Er, Mar–Oct. **Voice** Generally quiet, but breeding male gives a low slurred snore that lasts about 3 seconds, gradually falling then rising again. This is repeated at 5–7 second intervals. **NT**

Red-billed Duck

ad

♀

Hottentot Teal

♂

♂

ad

Cape Teal

ad

White-backed Duck

♀

Maccoa Duck

♂

Yellow-billed Duck *Anas undulata* 59cm, 23"

A large dark duck with a *bright yellow bill* (visible even at long distance). Closer views reveal blackish stripe on top of bill, and mostly pale-fringed and scalloped upperparts (except for dark brownish-grey head). Sexes alike. Immature similar, but with broader buff feather-edges. In flight, dark upperwing shows green speculum (narrowly edged with black and white). Two races occur: *rueppelli* is widespread in Et but uncommon in Er; the slightly paler nominate is vagrant to SSo from south (one record). **HH** Pairs, family parties or flocks are common on wide range of wetlands above 1500m. **Voice** Variety of mallard-like quacks, some with a trumpeting quality.

African Black Duck *Anas sparsa* 56cm, 22"

Large blackish duck with variable bold *buffish-white spots on back and rump*, and *pale pink and blackish bill*. Sexes alike. Immature much duller with limited or no spotting above. In flight, upperwing shows blue-green speculum narrowly bordered with black and white. Race in region is *leucostigma*. **HH** Singles, pairs and family parties are shy and elusive on well-wooded streams and fast-flowing rivers (less often ponds) in highlands above 1000m, up to 4250m. **Voice** A harsh, low-pitched, clipped quacking.

PALEARCTIC MIGRANT DUCKS *Large numbers of Palearctic waterfowl winter in region (mainly Oct to Apr), notably on the Rift Valley and highland lakes. All can be identified reasonably easily on water or in flight, by a combination of plumage and silhouette. Note many migrant male ducks wear a dull eclipse plumage, moulting into this before arriving in NE Africa, and remaining in eclipse until at least Dec when they begin to acquire the familiar northern breeding plumage.*

Northern Shoveler *Anas clypeata* 51cm, 20"

Breeding male is a distinctive green-headed, chestnut and white duck with *long spade-like bill*. Female entirely mottled light and dark brown with orange-sided shoveler-bill. Eclipse male similar to female, but darker with more mottled breast and rufous-toned flanks. Immature similar to female but duller. In flight, male has obvious large-billed, rather front-heavy silhouette, and reveals large pale blue shoulder-patches and wide green speculum with white front edge. Female has paler shoulders. **HH** Small to large flocks are very common Palearctic passage migrants and winter visitors to wide range of freshwater and alkaline lakes, mainly Sep–Apr, with concentrations in Rift Valley and highland lakes up to 4000m. They are less common elsewhere. A few birds remain to breed in Et. **Voice** Silent in region.

Northern Pintail *Anas acuta* ♂ 66cm, 26" ♀ 51cm, 20"

Elegant small-billed, slender-necked duck with pointed tail. Breeding male has dark chocolate head, offset by fine white neck-stripe, throat and breast, and very long central tail feathers. Female is all mottled brown with paler, plainer head (and shorter pointed tail). Eclipse male similar to female, but has greyer upperwing. Immature like female. In flight, shows slender neck and pointed tail; male has dark green speculum narrowly bordered with rufous and white; female has brown speculum with white trailing edge. **HH** Flocks are very common Palearctic visitors, Sep–Apr, occurring mainly on highland lakes and tarns up to 4000m, but also wandering to a wide range of other wetlands. **Voice** Silent in region..

Yellow-billed Duck

ad

rueppellii

♀

♂

African Black Duck

♂

Northern Shoveler

♀

♀

Northern Pintail

♂

Eurasian Teal *Anas crecca*   38cm, 15"

Breeding male has *bottle-green (and cream-rimmed) eye-mask, set in rich chestnut head,* horizontal white line along grey body, and yellowish undertail-coverts bordered with black. Female like female Garganey, but has darker brown mottled plumage, *slightly shorter dark bill with orange base, and less distinct face pattern.* Eclipse male and immature are like female, but slightly darker. Rises easily straight from water into flight, revealing green speculum with white borders similar to Garganey, but *more uniform brown-grey upperwings* (including shoulder). **HH** Singles and small groups are common Palearctic winter visitors to shallow and secluded freshwater in highlands of Er and Et up to 2500m, with smaller numbers in So. **Voice** Silent in region. [Alt: Common Teal]

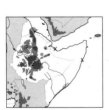

Garganey *Anas querquedula*   41cm, 16"

A small, neat duck; breeding male has *broad bright white stripe which curves from above eye to lower nape,* otherwise mainly mottled brown with silver-grey flanks. Female extremely similar to female Eurasian Teal, but has *slightly longer all-grey bill with more contrasting face pattern* (including paler loral spot). Eclipse male like female, but retains adult male wing. Immature similar to female. In flight, male reveals *pale grey shoulders* and green speculum bordered with white, while female has more uniform grey-brown wing and brownish speculum (also edged white). **HH** Small groups to large flocks are widespread and common Palearctic visitors on pools, lakes and other wetlands, up to 4400m; mainly passage migrant in Er, Aug–Oct and Apr. **Voice** Usually silent in region, but prior to departure male may give a harsh rattling display call, *hrrrroorrrr,* like running a stick rapidly along a fence; a shorter, wooden rattle is given in flight

Eurasian Wigeon *Anas penelope*   51cm, 20"

Breeding male has rounded *rich chestnut head with broad buffy-cream stripe running from base of bill to crown,* neat black-tipped blue-grey bill; otherwise grey with pinkish breast and black vent. Female is mottled brown tinged with silver or rufous, with plainer browner head. Eclipse male is like female but has more rufous tone. Immature is like female. In flight, male has white forewing-patch and green speculum edged with black, while female has duller wing with speculum edged white; both sexes have white bellies. **HH** Common to abundant Palearctic winter visitor to shallow coastal waters and highland freshwater lakes in Er and Et up to 3600m, Oct–Apr; rare in So. **Voice** Silent in region.

Gadwall *Anas strepera*   56cm, 22"

Breeding male is subtle *dusky grey duck,* with mottled breast, finely vermiculated flanks, and *black vent and lower rump.* Female is much browner, with dark eye-line and *yellow-orange sides to bill.* Eclipse male is like female, but retains male wings. Immature is like female. In flight, both sexes show white speculum, with additional black and rufous patches in male. **HH** Uncommon to rare Palearctic passage migrant and winter visitor to Er and Et, up to 2700m, Oct–May. Shyer than other ducks and rarely in large flocks. **Voice** Silent in region.

Mallard *Anas platyrhynchos*   60cm, 23.5"

Breeding male is distinctive with *yellow bill, glossy green head, narrow white neck band and purplish-brown breast.* Female is largely brown with darker brown mottling and streaks, usually darker on crown and through eye; *bill is dull orange with blackish smudge on upper mandible.* Eclipse male is like female but with all-yellow bill and rufous-brown breast. In flight, both sexes reveal *blue speculum conspicuously bordered with white.* **HH** Very rare Palearctic winter visitor to Er and Et. Vagrant Soc. **Voice** Not recorded in region, but elsewhere male calls a soft low raspy *raehb,* female has series of harsh loud quacks.

Eurasian Teal

♀

♂

Garganey

♀

♂

Eurasian Wigeon

♀

♂

Gadwall

♀

♂

Mallard

♀

♂

DIVING DUCKS *A group of diving ducks with longish bills, steep foreheads and white wing-bars. Distinctive breeding males are easily identified, but other plumages require careful observation of face pattern and vent colour. All dive for food, exploiting deeper water than other ducks. Southern Pochard is both a resident and intra-African migrant, while the others are uncommon or rare Palearctic visitors.*

Southern Pochard *Netta erythrophthalma* 51 cm, 20"

A large dark diving duck; male is *blackish-brown, with paler chestnut-brown flanks, red eyes, and blue-grey bill* (no eclipse plumage). Female is more uniform drab brown, but with *well-defined face pattern* (white patch at base of bill and crescent behind eye) and white vent (blackish in male). Immature is like female, but with less white on face. In flight, both sexes show clear white bar across all flight feathers. **HH** Small flocks are locally common on alkaline and freshwater Rift Valley lakes and elsewhere in Er and Et to 3000m; scarce SSo, vagrant Dj. Although small numbers may breed, most are visitors from southern Africa, appearing mainly from Oct–Mar. **Voice** Usually silent, but breeding male calls a loud low churring *prrrrr*, and an explosive wheeze.

Ferruginous Duck *Aythya nyroca* 41 cm, 16"

Breeding male often appears *very dark with white vent*, but at close range shows ferruginous (rust-coloured) head, breast and flanks, and *white eyes*. Female duller and browner than male with dark eyes (but also shows white vent). Eclipse male like female but pale-eyed. Immature is like female, but even duller brown. In flight, both sexes reveal wide white wing-bar, well-defined white belly, and clear white vent. Female Southern Pochard is larger and has prominent pale patches on face. **HH** Uncommon Palearctic winter visitor in small numbers to highland lakes in Er and Et from Oct–Apr at 1850–2300m; also occurs on Soc. **Voice** Silent in region. **NT**

Common Pochard *Aythya ferina* 48 cm, 19"

Distinctive breeding male is *silver-grey, with a chestnut-red head and neck, and black breast and rear-end*; black bill has wide pale grey-blue band. Eclipse male duller than breeding male with browner head, breast and rear. Female has brown head with diffuse pale loral patch, contrasting slightly with greyer-tinged back and flanks; *dark bill with narrower pale band near tip*. Immature like female, but has plainer face and dark bill. In flight, both sexes show largely pale grey upperwings. **HH** Uncommon Palearctic winter visitor in small numbers to freshwater lakes in Er and Et at 500–2700m, Oct–Apr; vagrant Soc. **Voice** Silent in region.

Tufted Duck *Aythya fuligula* 46 cm, 18"

Breeding male is a striking handsome duck, *black with bright white flanks, drooping black crest and yellow eyes*. Eclipse male is duller, with flanks dingy grey-brown and reduced crest. Female is dull dark-brown, with short tuft on rear of crown (not crest), pale belly and yellow eyes; bill is grey with dark tip, and *most birds show variable amount of white around base of bill*. Immature similar to female, but has brown eyes. In flight, both sexes show extensive white wing-bar, white or pale belly, and dark vent. **HH** Singles and small flocks are fairly common Palearctic visitors to freshwater and alkaline lakes in Er and Et, Oct–Apr. Vagrant NSo and Soc. **Voice** Silent in region.

Southern Pochard

Ferruginous Duck

Common Pochard

Tufted Duck

KITES The two black kites are fairly large, long-winged, long-tailed brown birds of prey, often very common, especially in towns and cities. The two grey-and-white kites are smaller and more elegant.

Black Kite *Milvus migrans*   55cm, 22"; WS 135cm, 54"

Fairly large brown raptor with angled wings and *long, slightly forked tail*. Much paler-headed than two races of Yellow-billed Kite, with *black streaking on throat and neck, black bill with yellow cere, and yellow eyes*. Sexes alike; immature may be paler still, even nearly white-headed, and pale-streaked below. In graceful wheeling flight reveals shallow forked tail; most birds show pale bar across upperwing-coverts and variable pale patch in primaries from below. **HH** Nominate *migrans* is common to abundant Palearctic passage migrant and winter visitor, Oct–Apr, to Er, Et and NWSo. Vagrant Soc. It inhabits villages, towns and open country, and frequently with resident Yellow-billed Kites. **Voice** Similar to Yellow-billed Kite, but presumably less vocal on wintering grounds.

Yellow-billed Kite *Milvus (migrans) aegyptius*   50cm, 20"; WS 125cm, 50"

Very similar to Black Kite, with which it is usually considered conspecific, but slightly smaller with a more deeply forked tail. Two races occur, both with *yellow bills and brown eyes*. Widespread resident *parasitus* is mostly brown, with head more rufous-brown (not showing obviously paler head as in Black Kite) and underparts cinnamon-rufous. Tail is more distinctly barred. Race *aegyptius* (breeds Red Sea coasts of Er and NSo) is like adult *parasitus* but browner and less cinnamon below. Sexes are alike, but immature is rather browner, with some dark streaking below and *dark bill*. Some immatures may be indistinguishable from immature Black Kite. **HH** Singles to large groups are common to abundant from sea-level to over 3000m, in villages, towns and open country with trees, often near water. **Voice** Vocal and fairly musical two-part call starts with rising whistle and breaks into downslurred trilling *wi-yrrrrrrrrrrw*. Also a whistled rising *tiew...te te te ti* with explosive opening note.

Black-shouldered Kite *Elanus caeruleus*   33cm, 13"; WS 83cm, 33"

A whitish hawk with grey back and wings, *contrasting black shoulders*, and *short white tail*. Primaries mostly blackish in flight from below. Sexes alike. Immature is browner with heavily scaled back and wings, and buff wash across breast. Flight *soft and elegant*, often beating into wind with head down; soars on raised wings and regularly hovers. **HH** Singles, pairs and occasional small groups are fairly common in wide range of moister open bushed and wooded grassland from sea-level to 2700m in Er and Et; uncommon in Dj and So. Responds rapidly to local insect and rodent plagues. **Voice** Usually an explosive, harsh *w-eeyah*, repeated after brief pauses. [Alt: Black-winged Kite]

African Swallow-tailed Kite *Chelictinia riocourii*   35cm, 14"; WS 70cm, 28"

A rather tern-like waif of a raptor. Adult is *grey above, pure white below*, with *long deeply forked tail*, and usually small black bar on underside of carpal joint (not visible at rest and sometimes absent). Sexes alike. Immature is washed brown above, with buff edges to coverts and back feathers, and *much shorter tail*. Superbly graceful in flight, riding winds with spread tail, wheeling and hovering. **HH** Highly social intra-tropical migrant, breeding in Rift Valley and NEEt; nomadic non-breeding visitor elsewhere, present Nov–Apr in Et. Uncommon migrant to SSo; rare in NSo and Er. Prefers semi-arid and arid bushed and wooded country including coastal lowlands. **Voice** Breeding pairs give an almost tern-like *keek keek*... which breaks into a rapid rising and rattling series. [Alt: Scissor-tailed Kite]

SECRETARYBIRD Extraordinary long-legged raptor, adapted to a specialist terrestrial predatory lifestyle. Walks through grassland hunting prey such as snakes which are stamped to death with small scaled feet.

Secretarybird *Sagittarius serpentarius*   128cm, 51"; WS 200cm, 80"

An unmistakable, large striding grey and black bird with a bare orange-red face, thick eagle-like bill, long crest on nape, long legs with black leggings, and long narrow central tail. Sexes alike but female has duller facial skin. Immature is similar but browner with duller facial skin. If disturbed will often run rather than fly away; flight rather laboured, although soars easily (and not infrequently), presenting very distinctive silhouette. **HH** Singles, pairs and pairs with young are scarce to rare in open bushed and wooded grasslands from near sea-level to 3150m, throughout most of Er and Et (except SE) and NWSo. Vagrant Dj. Usually builds nest in crown of acacia in open savanna. **Voice** At nest pairs make long low burping growls.

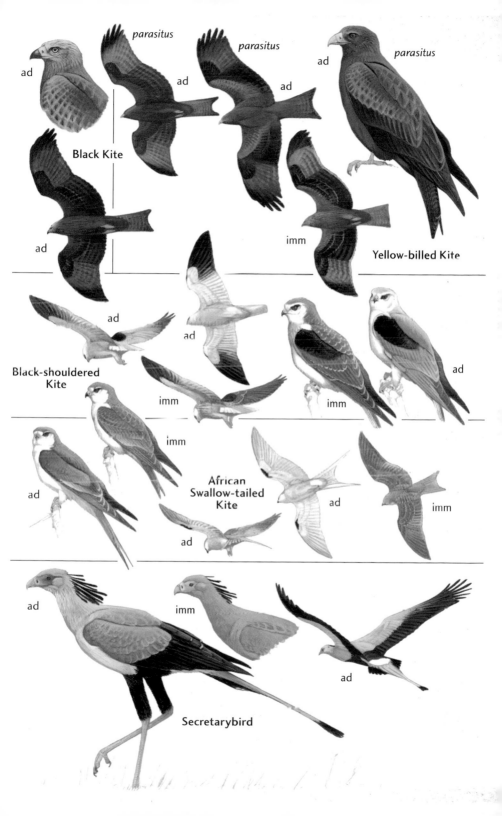

ad

parasitus
ad

parasitus
ad

ad
parasitus

Black Kite

ad

imm

Yellow-billed Kite

ad

ad

Black-shouldered
Kite

imm

imm

ad

ad

imm

African
Swallow-tailed
Kite

ad

ad

imm

ad

imm

ad

Secretarybird

FISH-EATING RAPTORS Two large pied raptors usually associated with water: African Fish-Eagle and Osprey are spectacular fishing birds. Adults are easy to distinguish, but take care with immature birds.

African Fish-Eagle *Haliaeetus vocifer*   68cm, 27"; WS 190cm, 76"

Adult is a striking fishing eagle with gleaming *white head, breast and tail, chestnut shoulders and underparts*, and mostly *black back and wings*. Sexes alike, but female larger than male. Immature scruffy, largely dark brown with dark cap and whitish face, variable dark streaking on nape, throat and breast, and white patches at primary bases on underwings; whitish tail broadly tipped black. Subadult gains whiter head and white underwing-coverts. In flight, appears broad-winged and short-tailed, flapping with shallow beats and soaring on flat wings. **HH** Pairs and pairs with young are common throughout region (except NSo) on wide range of fresh, alkaline and salt waters, from sea-level to 3000m. They can be particularly numerous on Rift Valley lakes and major rivers. **Voice** Very vocal, making familiar waterside sound. Most calls are attractive yodels, *weee........wu wu wu*, with last three notes accelerating and falling. Pairs duet: one calls *wi* and other immediately replies *oo*. Also has a low nasal *ahnk-ank-ank-ank*.

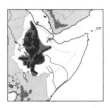

Osprey *Pandion haliaetus*   58cm, 23"; WS 148cm, 59"

A slender brown and white raptor with uniquely shaped, narrow, angled wings. Dark brown above and pearly white below, with rather small flat head, *mainly white crown and broad black band through yellow eyes*. Sexes alike, but female often has fuller chest-band. Immature has less well-defined head pattern, with some narrow dark streaking on crown, and pale fringes to back and wings. In flight appears mainly white below with striking long angled wings and distinctive *black carpal patches, primary tips*, and *dark edges to underwing-coverts*. Often hovers with dangling legs and plunges into water after fish. **HH** Breeds on Red Sea coasts of Er (220 pairs on islands off Er in 2005–07) and NWSo, and common on all coasts in region throughout year. Regular visitor and passage migrant to wide range of freshwater lakes and rivers up to 1900m, especially in Rift Valley and on Lake Tana, from Oct–May. **Voice** Silent in region.

LAMMERGEIER Striking giant scavenger of remote areas and rocky cliffs. Unlikely to be confused with any other species; in distant views may recall immature Egyptian Vulture, but is much bigger.

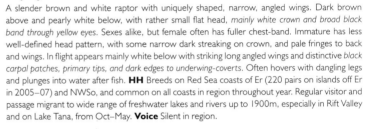

Lammergeier *Gypaetus barbatus*   108cm, 43"; WS 253cm, 101"

Massive *very long-winged black and orange raptor with distinctive diamond-shaped tail*. Face appears whitish at distance, but close-up reveals black lores and beard which hangs below base of bill; underparts are invariably stained russet (with iron oxide during dust-bathing). Sexes are alike. Immature is entirely dark brown, becoming paler on face and underparts with age. Flight silhouette distinct from all raptors except Egyptian Vulture. Race in NE Africa is *meridionalis*. **HH** Singles and pairs are fairly common to scarce in high mountain areas in Er and Et, but wanderers (notably immatures) may turn up unexpectedly elsewhere (e.g. vagrant Dj). Rarely below 1500m, but descends to 300m in Danakil. Requires cliffs for breeding, but ranges considerable distances to scavenge from kills and takes all sorts of carrion. Bones are broken by dropping from heights onto rocky outcrops. Formerly commoner in Et. **Voice** Quite silent, but at nest gives a long, downslurred, wheezy rather burry whistle. [Alt: Bearded Vulture]

African Fish-Eagle

ad

ad

juv

ad

juv

subad

subad

ad

ad

juv

Osprey

ad

ad

imm

ad

Lammergeier

SOLITARY VULTURES *Four vultures which are usually solitary or found in pairs, although Hooded has adapted to feeding in villages and towns where it may be quite numerous. All are attracted to carcasses. Adults are distinctive, but care should be taken in identifying immature birds.*

Egyptian Vulture *Neophron percnopterus*   60cm, 24"; WS 158cm, 63"

Adult is a conspicuous medium-sized *white or buffy-yellow and white vulture, with black flight feathers*, bare orange-yellow face (surrounded by long lax feathers which form shaggy halo), and slender bill with black tip. Sexes are similar, but female is slightly larger. Immature is brown and similar to immature Hooded, but may show some yellow on face, and has *longer feathers on back of head*. In flight, adult has obvious black and white plumage; immature is all brown. All birds have rather long straight wings and *wedge-shaped tail*. **HH** Solitary birds, pairs and family groups are widespread and common throughout most of region, inhabiting arid, semi-arid and bush country from sea-level to 2500m. Resident birds rarely stray far from nesting cliffs, but some birds are migrants from Arabia (arriving Oct–Nov across Bab-el-Mandeb). Attends kills but feeds after more numerous larger vultures. Specialist tool-user, breaking open ostrich eggs by repeatedly dropping stones on them. **Voice** Breeding birds give high-pitched rattled trills and scratchy wheezes. **EN**

Hooded Vulture *Necrosyrtes monachus*   60cm, 24"; WS 163cm, 65"

Size is similar to Egyptian Vulture, but brown with *naked pink head and some sparse whitish-grey down on hindneck*. Slender bill is also pinkish-brown and both bill and head may brighten if excited. Sexes alike. Immature darker, with grey facial skin and dark brown down on head. *In flight, easily told from immature Egyptian by squarer tail*. Race in NE Africa is poorly differentiated *pileatus*. **HH** Singles and small groups are widespread and common in wide range of habitats including arid country, grassland, cultivation and coastal areas from sea-level to 4000m. Much more gregarious than Egyptian Vulture, and occurs in villages and towns, attracted to rubbish dumps. Nests in trees, so not constrained by presence of rocky cliffs. **Voice** Gives a variety of high-pitched complaining *peei-u peei-u peei-u peei-u...* and various scratchy squeals.

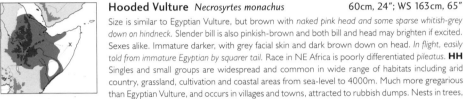

White-headed Vulture *Trigonoceps occipitalis*   75cm, 30"; WS 213cm, 85"

Attractive large blackish vulture with colourful angular head, white crop and white belly. At close quarters adult shows rather peaked triangular-shaped head, with thick white down on crown, bare pink facial skin, and *red bill with pale blue cere*. Immature is duller, with brownish top to head and all-dark underparts. In flight, broad-winged adult shows conspicuous white belly and thighs, extending onto axillaries and as narrow white line along rear of underwing-coverts; *female also has large white patches in secondaries*. Immature in flight is all dark with narrow white line along rear edge of underwing-coverts. **HH** Singles and pairs are most solitary and least common of large vultures, but widespread at low densities from semi-arid open country to wooded grasslands between sea-level and 3000m. Regularly attends kills, but unable to compete with larger species. **Voice** Squeals and chitters when squabbling at carcass, but not as vocal as smaller vultures. **VU**

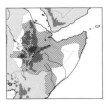

Lappet-faced Vulture *Torgos tracheliotus*   103cm, 41"; WS 265cm, 106"

Thickset squarish head, enormous bill and broad, often spread wings, give this species a massive brooding presence at kills. Adult is largely blackish-brown with extensive whitish streaking on breast, and shaggy white leggings. *Head and neck bare and pink (may flush brightly) with fleshy lappets on sides of face*. Sexes similar. Immature darker, almost black, with duller facial skin and black leggings becoming whiter over six years. In flight looks huge and broad-winged; adult shows conspicuous narrow white crescent on underwing and white leggings. Immature is entirely dark below. Race in NE Africa is *nubicus*. **HH** Singles and pairs are fairly widespread and common residents of open grassland and woodland with plains game from sea-level to 2500m. Densities are generally lower than other large vultures; more than 4–5 together at kills rare, although small groups occasionally gather. **Voice** Quiet, but unusual calls include a low growling *churr* and series of various metallic spitting notes. **VU**

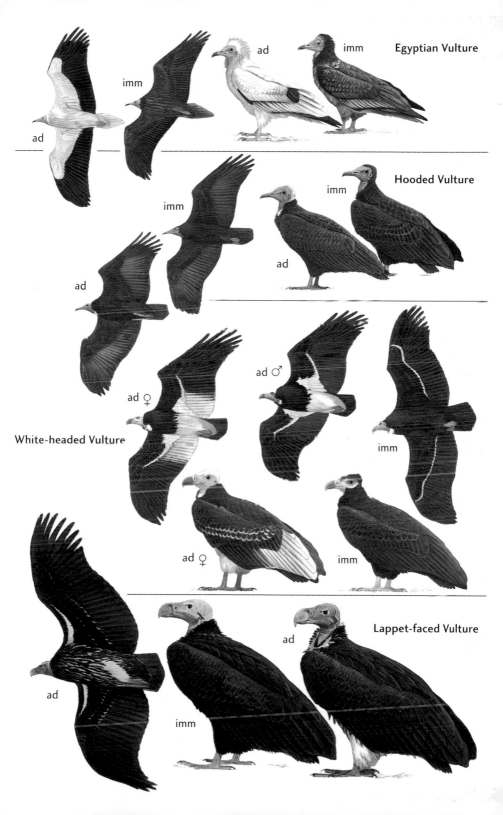

Egyptian Vulture

ad

imm

ad

imm

Hooded Vulture

imm

ad

ad

imm

ad ♀

ad ♂

imm

White-headed Vulture

ad ♀

imm

ad

imm

ad

Lappet-faced Vulture

PLAINS VULTURES Classic plains vultures commonly seen associating together at carcasses (and often with the species on plate 26). All three are easily distinguished on the ground, but immature (and sometimes adult) White-backed and Rüppell's may be difficult on the wing. Immatures are always streaked below. All are resident, but make long-distance movements in search of food.

White-backed Vulture *Gyps africanus* 83cm, 33"; WS 210cm, 84"

Adult is only likely to be confused with Rüppell's, but on ground is easily separated by *entirely blackish bill, darker brown eyes*, and essentially *rather plain body and wings*; white back is usually concealed. Sexes alike. Immature is dark at first, with narrow pale streaking on back and wings (never scalloped), extensive down on neck, and dull brownish ruff. Birds gradually lighten, attaining adult plumage (with white back) in six years. In flight, adult shows *tapering white lower back and rump from above, wholly white underwing-coverts from below*. Underwing of immature shows long thin white crescent just inside leading edge and is thus identical to immature Rüppell's. **HH** Small to large groups are widespread and may be numerous in open grassland and woodland from sea-level to 2500m, usually associating with plains game or domestic animals, and often outnumbering Rüppell's. **Voice** Often silent, but makes an expressive range of hisses, cackles and wheezy rattles at kills. [Alt: African White-backed Vulture] **NT**

Rüppell's Vulture *Gyps rueppellii* 90cm, 36"; WS 238cm, 95"

In close views adult is easily identified from White-backed by *yellowish-horn bill, yellowish eyes, and whitish edges to back feathers and wing-coverts giving a thickly scaled appearance*. Longer- and thicker-necked, slightly heavier-billed and a little larger than White-backed, giving heavier feel when seen together. Sexes alike. Immature is very like immature White-backed with blackish bill, dark eyes, rather plain back and wings and variable pale streaking below. At kills can be separated by slightly larger, heavier appearance; solitary birds should be identified with care and may not be separable. Adult plumage gained over about six years, with scaling, pale bill-tip and yellowish eyes all acquired gradually. In flight from below, adult shows thin white line near leading edge of wing, and may have parallel concentric bars on underwing-covert edges (often hard to see). Mottled belly and pale bill-tip may be visible at distance. Immature is dark below, with single white line on underwing, and cannot be safely separated from immature White-backed. Two races occur: nominate (WEt) as described; *erlangeri* (rest of Et, Er and So) paler with more prominent scaling above. **HH** Groups are widespread, gregarious and sometimes numerous at kills, from sea-level to 3000m. Often associates with domestic animals near colonies on cliffs and rocky outcrops; forages far from nest sites. **Voice** Largely silent, but more vocal than White-backed at kills, uttering an extraordinarily varied range of loud screamed hisses, groans, grunts and low guttural rattles. [Alt: Rüppell's Griffon Vulture] **NT**

Griffon Vulture *Gyps fulvus* 100cm, 40"; WS 248cm, 99"

Larger than Rüppell's and White-backed Vultures, with paler, more contrasting plumage. Adult has *sandy or rufous-brown mantle and wing-coverts* contrasting with blackish flight feathers and tail. Head and neck are whitish, with loose ruff of white feathers. *Bill is yellowish with grey cere*. White-backed is smaller and darker, and Rüppell's has scaly upperparts. Sexes alike. Immature is browner and streakier than adult, with brown ruff and grey bill, becoming paler with age. In flight from below, adult shows pale brown underwing-coverts contrasting with dark flight feathers, with variable white lines on coverts (White-backed has white underwing-coverts; Rüppell's is more uniformly dark). Broad wings are long-fingered with bulging secondaries, and tail is short and rounded. When soaring, wings are held in shallow V. Immature is similar but darker. **HH** Uncommon to rare Palearctic migrant to Er, Dj and Et, Oct–May, from sea-level to 2700m. **Voice** During squabbles and at nest gives loud wheezy hisses and gurgles, barely distinguishable from those of Rüppell's. [Alt: Eurasian Griffon Vulture]

White-backed Vulture

imm

ad

imm

ad

ad

ad

Rüppell's Vulture

imm

ad

ad

ad

imm

ad

imm

Griffon Vulture

ad

ad

imm

SNAKE-EAGLES Six medium-sized eagles with large rounded 'owl-like' heads, striking yellow eyes, bare legs, and (when perched) a rather upright stance. Sexes similar, but immatures often differ, and gain adult plumage over about three years. Underwing, tail patterns and range aid identification. All feed on snakes and other reptiles, and some species intermittently hover when searching for prey.

Black-chested Snake-Eagle *Circaetus pectoralis*   65cm, 26"; WS 170cm, 68"

Adult is blackish-brown above, on head, throat and upper breast, otherwise plain white below. Immature is dark brownish above and paler rufous below. In flight, adult is *all-dark above and on upper breast, contrasting with white belly and underwings*, which show narrow black bars across flight feathers; undertail has three black bands. Immature is brown above and mainly rufous below with rufous underwing-coverts, and indistinctly barred flight feathers, becoming paler and more blotchy with age. Adult Martial Eagle superficially similar but much larger with dark underwings. **HH** Singles are largely resident, widespread and sometimes common in bushed and wooded grassland from sea-level to 3400m; sometimes hovers. **Voice** Usually quiet, but calls a piercing whistled downslurred *peeeu....*, monotone *peee...*, and loud *pee pee pee pee...*

Short-toed Snake-Eagle *Circaetus gallicus*   65cm, 26"; WS 175cm, 70"

Adult is medium-brown above, but very variable below; typically, upper breast brown, rest of underparts white with some crescent-shaped barring. Paler birds may be almost entirely white below, usually with a few brown breast-streaks. Tail has 3–4 narrow dark bars. Immature similar. In flight, *adults can be all white below or show fine brown bars on underwing with contrasting brown breast* (but never as black-and-white as Black-chested). **HH** Fairly common winter visitor from Palearctic (Sep–Apr) to Er and W&CEt, from sea-level to 2000m; no certain records from So. Favours dry bush and wooded savanna. **Voice** Silent in region.

Beaudouin's Snake-Eagle *Circaetus beaudouini*   63cm, 25"; WS 160cm, 64"

Adult is darker above than Short-toed with narrow crescentic barring from breast to vent; shorter wings fall short of tail-tip. Immature has underparts and underwing-coverts rufous-brown (and can resemble Brown Snake-Eagle). In flight, *adult is more finely barred below than most Short-toed, with darker breast and plain white underwing-coverts*; adult Black-chested is completely white below (except for bands on remiges). **HH** Range in West Africa extends west to Sudan in woodland and open plains; several recent records in W&CEt at 1250–4000m, but none fully acceptable and species still hypothetical. **Voice** Silent outside breeding season. VU

Brown Snake-Eagle *Circaetus cinereus*   73cm, 29"; WS 170cm, 68"

Large-headed, dark brown eagle, with conspicuous yellow eyes and pale legs. Immature similar, but may be paler. In flight, appears all-dark above, except for narrow bars on tail. From below, *silver-white greater coverts and flight feathers contrast strongly with brown body and other underwing-coverts*. Tail shows three light bars both above and below, and narrow pale tip. **HH** Singles and pairs are widespread but uncommon in bush and woodland from sea-level to 2000m. **Voice** Gives a drawn-out wheeze and high-pitched metallic *kwink*.

Western Banded Snake-Eagle *Circaetus cinerascens*   53cm, 21"; WS 125cm, 50"

Adult is grey or grey-brown above with extensive brown from throat to belly and *barring restricted to lower belly and lower flanks, single broad white band across tail. Flesh-coloured cere is diagnostic.* Immature much paler and browner with whitish, lightly streaked head. In flight from above a broad white tail-bar is conspicuous at all ages. From below, adult shows *dark chin to belly, mainly white underwing-coverts, and single broad whitish band on tail.* **HH** Singles and pairs are rather uncommon residents of riverine forest, woodland and forest edge in W&SEt, up to 2000m. **Voice** Commonly calls in display over territory, a far-carrying nasal *ayaaah ka-haaa* with first note rising and last falling.

Southern Banded Snake-Eagle *Circaetus fasciolatus*   55cm, 22"; WS 123cm, 49"

Adult is similar to Western Banded Snake-Eagle, *but barring on underparts extends from breast to vent; tail rather longer with four dark and three light bands.* Cere is yellow. Immature similar to immature Western Banded, but often more marked below and has different tail barring. In flight, adult shows *more extensive barring on underparts and underwing-coverts than other snake-eagles.* **HH** Rare resident in riverine forest of lower Jubba in SSo. **Voice** Very vocal far-carrying call as birds display high over canopy (also given from perch): a nasal *woop ta'ta'ta'taaa*, with first note rising and leisurely, last notes rapid, and final note falling. Also a loud clanging *kyan kyan kyan kyan...* sometimes given at end of display. NT

Black-chested
Snake-Eagle

ad

imm

ad

imm

ad

ad

Short-toed
Snake-Eagle

Short-toed
Snake-Eagle

ad

ad

Beaudouin's

ad

ad

imm

ad

ad

Southern
Banded
Snake-Eagle

ad

ad

imm

ad

Brown Snake-Eagle

Western Banded
Snake-Eagle

ad

imm

ad

ad

ad

ad

ad

HARRIERS *Elegant raptors of open country with long tails; all are similar in character and fly with wings held in a shallow V. Females and immatures are hard to identify. Adult female and immature Montagu's and Pallid Harriers are known as ringtails, and are particularly difficult to separate. In all cases, note should be taken of head, rump and wing patterns. With experience, subtle differences in flight action aid identification, even at long distances.*

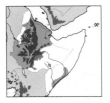

African Marsh Harrier *Circus ranivorus*   45cm, 18"; WS 113cm, 45"

Adult is mostly dark brown above and paler brown below with dark streaking (some are washed rufous on rump, flanks and legs). Extent of pale areas on face and throat varies individually. Immature similar, but darker, with cream-buff nape and throat (not crown), and pale breast-band (again extent varies). In flight, birds are overall slender and dark (without white rump). Adult is brown above with whitish leading edge to wing, *boldly barred underwings and narrowly barred tail*. Immature in flight is darker still, but with buff-white leading edge to wing, pale patch on nape and throat, and often a whitish breast-band. **HH** Vagrant or irregular wanderer to Et and SSo (several recent records in both countries), favouring marshes and swamps, including seasonal wetlands. **Voice** Vocal on breeding grounds, where gives a rough upslurred *weeey*, at intervals of about 4–6 seconds.

Western Marsh Harrier *Circus aeruginosus*   48cm, 19"; WS 128cm, 51"

Heaviest-looking harrier; adult male is dark brown, grey and black, with pale cream crown, nape and throat, variable dark streaking across chest, and rufous-brown lower breast to vent. Adult female largely dark brown, with leading edge of wings and head creamy (face variably brown and some show cream patch across breast). Immature similar, but crown and throat buffier, and cream in wing reduced or absent. In flight, appears sedate, bigger and broader-winged than other harriers. Adult male is brown, grey and black above with grey tail, underwings silvery-grey with black tips, and lower body rufous-brown. Adult female is rich brown with cream cap, forewing and shoulders, and *plain tail*. Rare dark morph adult male is blackish with grey tail and white bases to flight feathers on underwing; adult female lacks cream on forewing, but has white bases to primaries on underwing. **HH** Singles and small groups are fairly common and widespread Palearctic passage migrants and winter visitors to lakes and marshes, flooded grassland and cultivation from Sep–Apr, up to 2400m. Vagrant Soc. **Voice** Silent in region.

Montagu's Harrier *Circus pygargus*   43cm, 17"; WS 112cm, 45"

Adult male has smoky-grey upperparts, head and upper breast, with whiter belly, *chestnut flank-streaking, and short black bar on closed wing*. Adult female is dark brown above, streaked brown on buff-white below. *Close views of face reveal thin stripe through eye, and dark ear-coverts, not prominently edged by whitish collar.* Immature has similar face pattern, but is plain bright rufous below. In flight, slightly heavier and more sedate than Pallid Harrier. Adult male also appears *darker grey, with thin black bar on secondaries, larger black wing-tips, and chestnut-streaked flanks and underwing-coverts*. On underwing adult female shows *two broad pale bars across secondaries, dark-tipped primaries and rufous barring on coverts*. Female and immature have white rumps. **HH** Singles to small groups are fairly regular Palearctic passage migrants and winter visitors to grasslands, especially in highlands, Sep–Apr, up to 4000m. **Voice** Silent in region.

Pallid Harrier *Circus macrourus*   45cm, 18"; WS 110cm, 44"

Very similar to Montagu's Harrier, but of slighter build with longer tail which projects beyond wing-tips at rest. Adult male is an ethereal pale grey above and very white below, with *no black bar across closed wing*. Adult female has *thicker black line through eye and whitish collar around ear-coverts*. Immature similar to immature Montagu's except for more distinctive face pattern. Has buoyant, lithe flight. Adult male is plain ghostly grey with *less black on wing-tips (forming narrow wedge)*, and no secondary bar or chestnut streaking. Adult female has *darker secondaries, and paler primaries, especially towards tips*. Female and immature have white rumps. **HH** Singles and small groups are common Palearctic passage migrants and winter visitors to grasslands Sep–Apr, rarely up to 4500m. Vagrant Soc. **Voice** Silent in region. NT

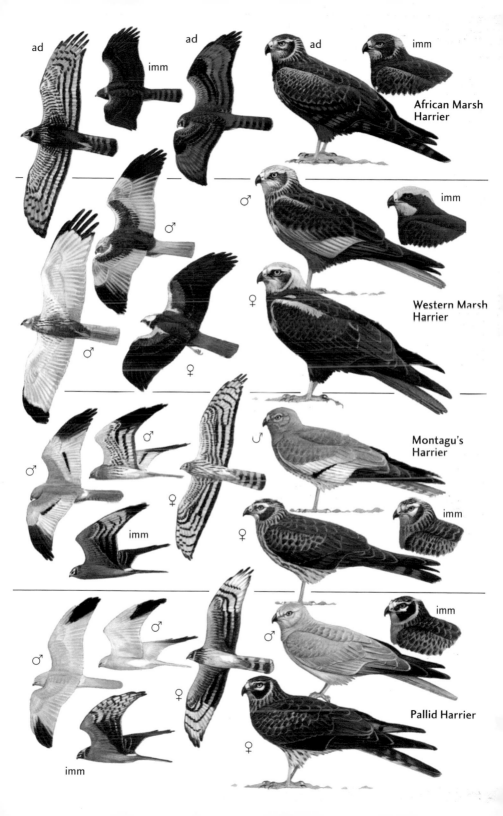

ad

imm

ad

ad

imm

African Marsh Harrier

♂

imm

♂

♀

Western Marsh Harrier

♂

♂

♀

♂

♀

imm

♀

Montagu's Harrier

imm

♂

♂

♀

♂

imm

imm

Pallid Harrier

♀

Four quite similar grey raptors which have a rather upright and bold stance. Adult chanting goshawks are easily told apart by bare parts and rump colour, but immatures can be much more difficult—consider range. Gabar Goshawk and Lizard Buzzard are smaller and should not be confused if seen well.

Eastern Chanting Goshawk *Melierax poliopterus*   50cm, 20"; WS 103cm, 41"

Medium-sized grey raptor which is barred grey and white from breast to vent. Generally paler than Dark Chanting Goshawk (but not always so), and best identified by *yellow cere, long orange-red legs, and white rump*: undertail-coverts usually whiter than Dark Chanting Goshawk. Female similar, but larger than male. Immature is brown above with pale (not dark) eyes, whitish supercilium, and *mainly white rump* (beware: some show narrow barring at sides). Breast brown with variable darker streaking; barred brown and white from lower breast to vent. Cere grey, legs dull yellowish. In character stiff-winged, direct flight adult appears grey above, with black outer primaries and *obvious narrow white rump*. **HH** Singles and pairs are widespread and common in arid and semi-arid bush, dry grasslands and woodland, from sea-level to 1600m in S&EEt and So; occurs almost entirely east of Rift Valley. **Voice** Gives a loud and piercing *pee..peepeepeepeepeepeepeepeepeep,* slowly rising in tone, a rather mewing *peeyuh* and rhythmical *weeu wi-wu-wu-wu-wu* with first note rising, last notes falling and accelerating like bouncing ball.

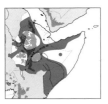

Dark Chanting Goshawk *Melierax metabates*   45cm, 18"; WS 93cm, 37"

Similar to Eastern Chanting Goshawk, but usually slightly darker grey, with *grey-and-white barred rump, and orange-red cere and legs.* Female similar, but larger than male. Immature is very similar to immature Eastern Chanting, but some birds less heavily streaked on breast; best separated by *extensive barring on white rump.* **HH** Singles are common residents of similar but moister habitats to Eastern Chanting, occurring up to 2000m, mainly west of Rift Valley. Like Eastern Chanting typically flies low with stiff beats interspersed with glides, swooping up onto exposed perches. **Voice** Quite vocal, with a gull-like downslurred *peeeyuh* and repeated *whee-pee-pee-pee...*

Gabar Goshawk *Micronisus gabar*   33cm, 13"; WS 60cm, 24"

Superficially like a small chanting goshawk. Typical adult is grey above with bold white rump; head to upper breast also grey, mid-breast to belly barred grey and white, cere and legs orange-red, and eyes dark. Fairly common dark morph adult is mostly black (when perched), with no white rump, and grey-and-black barred tail. Female similar, but larger than male. Immature largely dull brown above with white rump, pale throat and breast streaked warm brown, and mid-breast to belly banded warm brown. Cere, eyes and legs pale yellowish. Dashing and rather accipiter-like flight on short rounded wings; typical adult shows striking *narrow white rump* and heavily barred underwings and tail. Dark morph birds are black above and below with silvery-white bars on underwing and tail. **HH** Singles are widespread and common residents of bush and woodland from sea-level to 2000m, often in drier country; uncommon in NSo. **Voice** Common call is a rising *wi-wi-wi* (rather like Diederik Cuckoo), while a longer series consists of this call but with the last note repeated *wi-wi-wi wiwiwiwiwiwiwi....*

Lizard Buzzard *Kaupifalco monogrammicus*   33cm, 13"; WS 70cm, 28"

Small upright rather stocky and sluggish raptor, grey above and across breast with *vertical black stripe down centre of white throat,* and mid-breast to belly well-barred dark grey and white. Cere and legs red; eyes dark. Sexes alike but female larger. Immature slightly browner version of adult with duller cere and less distinct throat-stripe. Compact and neat on wing, flying low with shallow beats before swooping up onto perches. From above shows mainly grey upperparts contrasting strongly with white rump and *blackish tail with single thin white bar and tip.* From below appears barred, but underwing-coverts quite plain, with barring mainly confined to body and flight feathers. **HH** Pairs are uncommon and local residents of bush, woodland, cultivation and gardens in WEt and SSo, from sea-level to 1500m, often on posts or wires where it can be both unobtrusive and confiding. **Voice** Very vocal, shouting a distinctive *wioo...wu wu wu wu wu wu wu wu wu wu...* with first note rising and then falling and second part slightly lower, and all on same pitch.

Eastern Chanting Goshawk

ad

ad

imm

ad

imm

imm

Dark Chanting Goshawk

imm

ad

ad

ad

imm

imm

dark

imm

ad

Gabar Goshawk

ad

ad

dark
morph

ad

Lizard Buzzard

ad

ad

ad

SPARROWHAWKS *Four similar sparrowhawks of open country. All are built for dashing, manoeuvrable flight. Shikra is a common and widespread resident, Ovampo is rare, the others are vagrants. Best identified by head, cheek and throat pattern, as well as underwing and eye colour; none have obvious white rumps. Adults similar, but female larger than male.*

Shikra *Accipiter badius* 30cm, 12"; WS 58cm, 23"

Small classic sparrowhawk; *grey above* (sometimes with a few white spots on back), with grey cheeks and largely plain grey central tail feathers (may be dark-tipped on female). *Lightly barred pinkish or light rufous-brown below*, except for whitish throat and vent. Male has bright red eyes, female bright orange; cere and legs yellow. Immature dark brown above, whitish below with rufous-brown central mesial stripe, heavily streaked breast, and barred lower breast, flanks and tail. Eyes and bare parts pale yellow. In flight at distance, adult may appear very pale with black wing-tips, similar to Levant Sparrowhawk, but wings slightly more rounded and body more extensively barred below. Tail mostly plain above, but barred below. Race in NE Africa is *sphenurus*. Gabar Goshawk (plate 30) has more rounded wings and white rump. **HH** Singles and pairs are common residents in wide range of woodland and edge habitats from sea-level to 3650m, including towns, gardens and cultivation. **Voice** Various (sometimes woodpecker-like) calls are shrill and querulous, either single upslurs *k-wi* or a chittered series *kwikwikwikwikwi...* [Alt: Little Banded Goshawk]

Ovambo Sparrowhawk *Accipiter ovampensis* 35cm, 14"; WS 68cm, 27"

Graceful, slightly *small-headed* sparrowhawk, with two distinct colour morphs. Normal grey birds are all grey above, *often with a few white marks on rump*, and barred tail with *white streaks on central feather-shafts*. Below *finely barred grey or grey-brown from throat to belly*. Eyes dark wine-red, cere and legs yellowish to red. Rare dark morph is dull black above except for *white streaks on tail-shafts*; in flight, black underwing-coverts contrast with pale bars on flight feathers and tail. At close range both morphs show *exceptionally long middle toes*. Immature rather variable, but all show *white streaks on tail-shafts*. Typical immatures are dark brown above with white supercilium, dark mask on whitish face, plain rusty breast and pale underparts with broad dark banding, or *chestnut-brown below* with streaked breast and barred belly and flanks; others are whiter on crown and underparts. Eyes brown, cere orange-yellow and legs deep yellow. **HH** Very scarce resident of riverine and open woodland in C&SEt at 1300–1700m, with scattered records suggesting that birds may wander. **Voice** Calls 7–12 rapidly delivered notes, a wader-like *kwehkwehkwehkweh....* with nasal upslur.

Eurasian Sparrowhawk *Accipiter nisus* 33cm, 13"; WS 65cm, 26"

Adult male is slate-grey above (sometimes with slight white supercilium), with *buff-orange sides to face*, and barred rusty-orange underparts. Adult female is often much larger, grey-brown above with more prominent supercilium with dark cap, and barred dark brown below. Eyes, cere and legs yellow. Immature like adult female, but browner-grey above, and dark barring below much more mottled and broken. In compact dashing flight, adult male is dark grey above with barred rusty-orange body and leading edge to underwing; longish tail shows 4–5 bars both above and below. Adult female has looser flight, is grey-brown above and well barred below. **HH** Very scarce Palearctic visitor to Er, Et and SSo (once), Sep–Feb, with scattered records typically from wooded country. **Voice** Silent in region.

Levant Sparrowhawk *Accipiter brevipes* 33cm, 13"; WS 65cm, 26"

Adult male similar to Shikra, with grey cheeks and plain upperside to central tail feathers. Best separated by darker upperparts, dark red eyes (not bright red), and richer chestnut barring below. In flight, *wings more pointed and whiter below with blacker tips*. Slightly larger adult female is browner above, and in flight shows more barring on underwing-coverts. Immature browner above than female, with *dark stripe on throat and heavily spotted underparts*. **HH** Vagrant from Palearctic to woodland and bush, with the few widely scattered records in Er, Et and Dj occurring Nov–Mar. **Voice** Silent in region.

Shikra

ad

imm

ad

ad

imm

ad

imm

Ovambo Sparrowhawk

ad

imm

ad

ad

dark morph

dark morph

imm

ad ♂

♀

♂

♂

Eurasian Sparrowhawk

ad ♀

♂

♀

imm

ad ♂

Levant Sparrowhawk

imm ♀

ad ♀

SPARROWHAWKS *Four sparrowhawks of woodland and forest (Great Sparrowhawk is on plate 33). Their secretive nature, similarity in plumages and (in some) different races and morphs make separating then difficult. Size (beware females are larger), markings on underparts and tails, and range all help identification.*

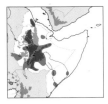

African Goshawk *Accipiter tachiro* 38cm, 15"; WS 68cm, 27"

Commonest large accipiter in region with highly variable plumage. Typical adult male is very dark grey above, with whitish throat and finely barred rufous and white underparts, tail indistinctly barred black and dark grey above (occasionally with small white spots), greyish and lightly barred below. Larger adult female is dark brown above and more heavily barred black-brown on white below. Melanistic birds are blackish with dark grey bands in tails and contrasting flight feathers on underwing. Typical immature is dark brown above with rufous fringes, whitish supercilium, heavy spots on breast and barred flanks (often has pale nape and some have dark mesial stripe). All adults have yellowish eyes and feet (immatures are dark-eyed). In flight, typical adult male is dark above, with rufous-barred body and wing-coverts. Adult female is more heavily barred on body and underwings. Immature is also heavily marked, but with spots not bars. Three races occur: *sparsimfasciatus* (SEEt, SSo) as described; endemic *unduliventer* (highland Er and N&CEt) is smaller and sexually monomorphic, with heavy rufous barring below, plain rufous flanks and *large white spots on tail forming 3 distinct bars*, small yellow pre-ocular patch, grey throat, plain grey back and orange-yellow legs; *croizati* (WEt) poorly marked (possibly synonymous with *unduliventer*), slightly darker and browner. **HH** Singles are widespread but uncommon in wide range of forest, woodland and gardens, from sea-level to 3300m; absent from SEEt and most of So except in Jubba and Shabeelle valleys. **Voice** Gives a sharp snappy *chutt* like smacking of lips, often in high aerial circling display at dawn.

Rufous-breasted Sparrowhawk *Accipiter rufiventris* 33cm, 13"; WS 65cm, 26"

Adult is dark slate-grey above, with tail barred dark grey and black. throat buffy, *cheeks to belly plain rich rufous,* and vent white; eyes, cere and legs yellow. Immature dark brown above with pale supercilium and some rufous feather edges, breast and flanks streaked and barred rufous, plain rufous on thighs. In flight, adult shows *striking contrast between dark-slate upperparts and plain rufous body and underwing-coverts*; immature has rufous plumage streaked and barred, not plain. Race in region is endemic *perspicillaris*. **HH** Widespread but uncommon resident (usually singly) of highland forest and forest edge in Er (rare) and Et, hunting into open country, mainly at 2000–3000m. **Voice** Gives a loud downslurrred *kiu-kiu-kiu-kiu...* [Alt: Red-breasted Sparrowhawk; Rufous-chested Sparrowhawk]

Little Sparrowhawk *Accipiter minullus* 23cm, 9"; WS 45cm, 18"

Very small woodland sparrowhawk; adult is slate-grey above with white rump and white spots on black tail. Grey head and cheeks contrast with white throat, rest of underparts white with fine brown barring, and variable rufous wash on sides of breast and flanks. Eyes orange-yellow; cere and legs yellow. Immature brown above, with some white on rump and white tail-spots, extensive dark brown spots on breast variably becoming bars on flanks. *Strikingly small,* compact and agile on wing. From above, *adult shows white rump and two white spots in centre of very black tail*. From below, barring of body and wings contrast with pale rufous underwing-coverts. Immature has white spots in centre of uppertail but lacks rufous underwing-coverts. Usually monoypic, but paler birds in coastal So sometimes separated as *tropicalis*. **HH** Singles and pairs are widespread in Er, Et and SSo, but usually local and uncommon; rather secretive resident of forest, dense woodland and woodland edge, as well as gardens and plantations, from sea-level to 3000m. **Voice** Has 8–10 rather full sounding and hurried *tiu-tiu-tiu-tiu...*, low-pitched for size of bird. [Alt: African Little Sparrowhawk]

African Goshawk

♂

imm

sparsimfasciatus

♀

ad ♀

dark
morph

ad ♂

♂

dark

ad

ad

ad

unduliventer

Rufous-breasted Sparrowhawk

ad

ad

imm

ad ♂

imm ♀

Little Sparrowhawk

imm

ad

ad

imm ♂

ad ♀

Great Sparrowhawk *Accipiter melanoleucus*   48cm, 19"; WS 90cm, 36"

Very large black and white sparrowhawk; adult *charcoal black above and white below, with conspicuous heavy black barring from sides of breast to flanks.* Rare melanistic form is all black with white throat and contrasting barred flight feathers on underwing. Eyes red to brown; cere and legs yellow. Immature browner above, and *heavily streaked blackish-brown below on either white or rich rufous-brown.* Flying birds show huge but typical accipiter shape. Adult black above, with faint greyer bars on tail; *largely white below, with black flank-patches,* and barring on flight feathers and tail. Immature dark brown above, with *dark streaking on white or rufous underparts* and either whitish or rufous underwing-coverts (immature African Goshawk is spotted and smaller). **HH** Singles of nominate race are widespread but uncommon in wide range of forest, woodland and woodland edge in Er and Et, including stands of exotics and well-wooded towns, from sea-level to 3300m; only four records from So. **Voice** Gives a single loud rising and then falling buzzard-like slur, *seeeuur,* and repeated sharp *keek-keek-keek-...* [Alt: Black Sparrowhawk]

African Cuckoo-Hawk *Aviceda cuculoides*   40cm, 16"; WS 88cm, 35"

Odd, short-crested, weak-billed, slender raptor, with *long wings reaching almost to tail-tip at rest.* Adult male dark grey-brown above, with grey head, throat and upper breast, small rufous patch on nape, and *bold broad rufous barring on white mid-breast to belly.* Large eyes are red-brown or yellow; cere and legs yellow. Sexes similar, but female warm brown above with lighter barring below. Immature dark brown above, with buff fringes and distinct white supercilium; white below with variable dark spotting; eyes grey-brown, cere and legs pale yellow. In flight looks long-winged and rather cuckoo-like. Adult is dark above with pale bands on tail and *barred rufous below and on underwing-coverts.* Immature has variable spotting on body, and black and white barred underwing-coverts. Race in region is *verreauxi* (nominate has solid rufous underwing-coverts). **HH** Singles and pairs are uncommon and secretive, in forest edge, woodland and wooded bushland in W&SEt, up to 3000m. **Voice** Gives a slowly repeated downslurred squealed, *peeuu.* Also duets: one bird whistles a series of rising downslurs, *pek-t-wioo k-t-wioo k-t-wioo...,* the other answers with a rapid rising *pipipipipipi...* [Alt: African Cuckoo-Falcon]

Bat Hawk *Macheiramphus alcinus*   45cm, 18"; WS 105cm, 42"

Atypical, crepuscular, *large falcon-like raptor* with slightly crested head, long narrow pointed wings and long tail. Wings almost reach tail-tip at rest. Adult is mostly sooty-black with white throat bisected by thin black line (but variably also has white on nape, breast and vent). At close range shows *white lines above and below large yellow eyes;* cere and legs grey. Immature is similar, but has much more white on throat and lower belly. In flight appears languid and easy-going, but swift and dashing when hunting. Adult appears all black at distance, but immature often shows some white below. Race in Africa is *anderssoni.* **HH** Singles are rather uncommon residents of forest edge (including riverine forest), woodland and cliffs in SEt and SSo up to 1600m; in Et, mainly in Rift Valley. Birds emerge alongside bat prey at dusk, but occasionally kill small birds and may be active during day. **Voice** Breeding birds call a slow piercing *wii wii wii wii....*

Great Sparrowhawk

imm

imm

ad

ad

dark

ad ♀

imm ♀

African
Cuckoo-Hawk

ad

ad

imm

imm

ad

Bat Hawk

ad

ad

imm

ad

African Harrier-Hawk *Polyboroides typus* 58cm, 23″; WS 133cm, 53″

Large floppy grey raptor with *rather small slim head and bare yellow facial skin* (which turns red if excited). Adult is grey above, with long lax nape feathers and single broad white band across black tail. Head and upper breast also grey, but rest of underparts densely barred black on white; long yellow legs (tibio-tarsal joint can bend backwards). Female slightly larger. Immature highly variable, from dark to light brown above, with pale feather edges, and from dark to light brown below, either mottled or plain. Facial skin grey-green. In flight, wings and tail appear broad and long. Adult is *grey with black band along trailing edge of wing, black wing-tips, and white-banded black tail.* Immature has barred flight and tail feathers, and brown underwing-coverts which contrast with pale primary bases. *Best feature overall is slow, measured flight.* **HH** Singles and pairs are widespread but local residents of forest edge, riverine woodland, well-wooded grassland and cultivation, from sea-level to 3000m, but absent from much of EEt and NSo. Regularly steals young from cavity nests like those of swifts and weavers, using long flexible legs to probe for and grab nestlings. **Voice** Gives a high-pitched upslurred whistle with accent on second half *piiiii'iii;* also a monotonous *piiii* on one note. [Alt: Gymnogene]

European Honey-buzzard *Pernis apivorus* 55cm, 22″; WS 130cm, 52″

Highly variable plumage can cause considerable confusion. Adults are typically grey-brown above with *obvious yellow eyes;* all morphs have *distinctive tail with broad band near tip and two narrow bands near base.* Underparts are often heavily barred, but may also be lightly barred, all white, rufous or blackish. Immatures are even more confusing, as in addition to varied morphs they have 4–5 tail-bars, and dark eyes. In flight, has slow deep wing-beats, but soars with wings flat, and glides with wings slightly lowered. Adult in flight is like *small-headed, long-tailed buzzard,* with dark carpal patches, blackish trailing edge to wing, and distinctive barred tail. Immature has more barring on underwing and shorter, more barred tail, but protruding head and flight action useful with experience. **HH** Uncommon but regular Palearctic passage migrant, with rather few records in Er, Dj and Et, mainly Aug–Nov and Mar–Apr; some probably overwinter. Only a single record in SSo. **Voice** Silent in region.

Grasshopper Buzzard *Butastur rufipennis* 40cm, 16″; WS 98cm, 39″

Perched adult looks slender and falcon-like, largely grey-brown above and light rufous with narrow black streaking below. At close range shows white throat bisected by black stripe and yellow eyes, cere and legs. Sexes alike. Immature is browner above, with pale chestnut-brown head and underparts, and brownish or white throat bordered by dark stripes. In low buoyant gliding flight *reveals unmistakable bright orange-rufous patches on upperwings.* From below, pale chestnut body contrasts with dark-tipped whitish underwings. **HH** Mainly a non-breeding visitor from northern tropics to open dry bush country, and bushed and wooded grassland in SEt and upper Rift Valley mainly below 1650m; also in NWSo (Sep–Oct) and SSo (Nov–Jul). Has bred in SEt, and records in Er and WEt are on edge of breeding range. Groups may gather near fires, perching in open, and dropping to forage for insects on ground. **Voice** Generally silent in region, but gives a loud *ki-ki-ki-ki-kee* when breeding.

BUTEO BUZZARDS *Medium-sized true buzzards with broad wings and short or medium-length tails; plumage often variable. Sexes alike, but females are slightly larger. See also plate 35.*

Red-necked Buzzard *Buteo auguralis* 45cm, 18″; WS 115cm, 46″

Adult has *reddish-brown sides of head and nape and rufous tail with black subterminal band.* Variable below, but usually shows white throat, dark breast-band, and black spots on rest of white underparts. Whole head, neck and breast occasionally rufous. Immature is boldly fringed rufous above, with greyer tail, paler underparts, and less distinct or no breast-band. **HH** Locally common intra-tropical breeding visitor to broad-leaved woodlands of lowland WEt, Dec–May; also recorded in Rift Valley (old records). **Voice** A loud, mewing *peeee-ah,* rather like Common Buzzard.

African
Harrier-Hawk

ad

ad

imm

ad

imm

European
Honey-buzzard

imm

imm

ad

imm

imm

ad

ad

ad

ad

ad

imm

imm

ad

ad

Grasshopper
Buzzard

ad

Red-necked Buzzard

imm

ad

ad

Augur Buzzard *Buteo augur*   53cm, 21"; WS 133cm, 53"

Stocky, red-tailed buzzard with two distinct colour morphs. Pale adult is black above with chequered panel across flight feathers, and white below with brick-red tail. Dark morph adult similar but entirely blackish below. Pale immature is brown above, with heavy streaking on throat, and narrowly dark-barred brown or dull rufous tail, while dark immature is darker overall including underparts. *In flight, highly characteristic silhouette shows broad wings, bulging secondaries and short tail.* Pale birds have white body and underwings with black wing-tips and trailing edge. Dark birds show contrasting black body and underwing-coverts. **HH** Singles and pairs are common residents of open country, rocky outcrops and cultivation, from 1500–4500m. May be confiding; often seen on roadside poles and trees. **Voice** Gives a repeated barking *k'wenk k'wenk k'wenk k'wenk...*, usually in flight.

Archer's Buzzard *Buteo (augur) archeri*   51cm, 20"; WS 130cm, 52"

Very like Augur Buzzard but slightly smaller and *entirely rich chestnut below* except for white throat and black at sides of neck. Upperparts blotched chestnut. No melanistic morph. Immature browner above, white or pale rufous below with variable black markings on sides of neck; tail dark chestnut with faint barring. In flight, adult is like Augur Buzzard but with *chestnut underbody and underwing-coverts*; immature similar but chestnut replaced with white or pale rufous. **HH** ENDEMIC. Fairly common resident in highlands of NSo. **Voice** Call described as a penetrating mewing. **Note** This localised form is usually lumped with Augur Buzzard *B. augur*.

Mountain Buzzard *Buteo oreophilus*   45cm, 18"; WS 108cm, 43"

Small, well-marked buzzard; adult is brown above, with narrow bars on tail and broader dark band near tip; below, heavily blotched dark brown on white; *thighs and vent barred*. Sexes alike, but some individual variation. Immature is softer brown above, buff-tinged below with lighter blotching. In flight, *heavily spotted body and underwing-coverts contrast with flight feathers*, thus very similar to some morphs of Common Buzzard, but never shows warm rufous tones or rufous tail. **HH** Singles and pairs are uncommon over montane forest in CEt at 2500–3600m. **Voice** Noisy pairs indulge in display flights giving a short descending *peeu* repeated by both birds.

Common Buzzard *Buteo buteo*   45cm, 18"; WS 120cm, 48"

Race *vulpinus* (Steppe Buzzard) is highly variable small buzzard with grey-brown, rufous and dark morphs. Typical birds are brown or warm brown, with some barring below, and usually a pale band across lower breast. In flight, typical adults have brown or rufous underwing-coverts, *dark smudged or thin comma-like carpal patch*, and pale flight feathers with black tips and trailing edges, tail grey-brown or rufous (often finely barred and may show dark subterminal band). Immature has less distinct trailing edge to wings. Scarce dark morphs are blackish-brown on body and underwing-coverts. **HH** Singles to large flocks are common diurnal Palearctic passage migrants, Sep–Nov and Mar–Apr; some birds overwinter. Occurs across wide range of open, bushed and wooded habitats in Er, Dj and Et; vagrant So and Soc. **Voice** Silent in region.

Socotra Buzzard *Buteo sp.*   c. 45cm, 18"

The resident buzzard on Socotra, which is not yet formally described, has long been considered to be an isolated form of Common Buzzard, but is closer genetically to Long-legged and may in fact be a separate species. Adult is mainly brown above and in flight from below shows prominent dark carpal patches, extensive white bases to the primaries, and *variable dark streaking and blotching on the underwing-coverts, flanks, breast and belly*. **HH** ENDEMIC. Fairly widespread on Socotra, breeding Oct–Apr. **Voice** A high-pitched *mew*, similar to Common Buzzard.

Long-legged Buzzard *Buteo rufinus*   53cm, 21"; WS 135cm, 54"

Large, long-winged buzzard with variable pale, rufous and dark morphs. Typical birds have *pale cream head and breast* blending to *dark rufous belly*, and *plain orange-white tail*. In flight from above, adult shows contrasting *white primary bases, rufous or pale wing-coverts*, and plain pale orange tail; from below, note rufous body and underwing-coverts (darker on belly), *large black carpal patches*, and black trailing edge to wings. Soars with wings raised in shallow V. Rufous and rare dark morphs, and all immatures, very similar to corresponding morphs of Common Buzzard; best separated by *larger size, longer wings, and larger black carpal patches*. **HH** Nominate birds are uncommon winter migrants from Palearctic, with scattered records in Er, Dj and Et, Sep–Apr; vagrant NWSo (once). Usually solitary. **Voice** Silent in region.

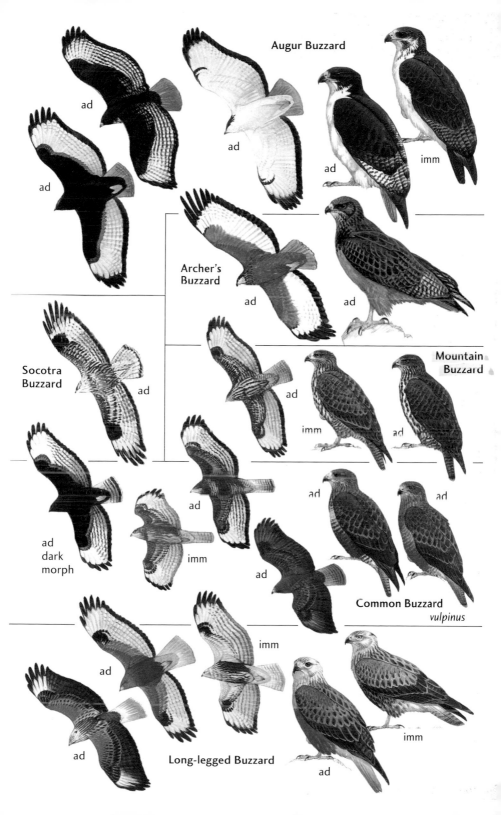

Augur Buzzard

ad

ad

ad

ad

imm

Archer's
Buzzard

ad

ad

Mountain
Buzzard

Socotra
Buzzard

ad

ad

imm

ad

ad
dark
morph

ad

imm

ad

ad

ad

Common Buzzard
vulpinus

ad

imm

ad

ad

imm

Long-legged Buzzard

ad

AQUILA EAGLES *Seven similar large brown eagles (four on plate 37) with long broad wings, broad rounded tails (mostly), and feathered legs. Most adults are rather plain; immatures can have distinctive wing patterns. Overall shape and silhouette also help with identification. Females slightly larger than males. Tawny Eagle is the most common and widespread; familiarity with it, from immature to adult, and its range of browns—from buff to dark—form good basis for comparison with less well-known birds. Four are migrants from the Palearctic.*

Lesser Spotted Eagle *Aquila pomarina*   60cm, 24"; WS 155cm, 62"

Adult is medium-sized brown eagle with darker wings and tail; close perched birds show *narrow feathering on lower legs (and round nostrils, distinctive of spotted eagles)*. Immature is darker than adult, with white spots across wings (those on coverts often worn away) and usually a small golden or white nape-patch. In gliding and soaring flight, wings arch slightly downwards. Compared to Greater Spotted Eagle adult has *head, body and wing-coverts paler than flight feathers* on both wing surfaces, small white flash in primaries on upperwing, often two pale commas at carpal joint on underwing, and variable white crescent on rump. Immature from above shows white rump crescent and usually a *pale spot on back*; a white wing-flash is often strong on inner primaries. Below, wing-coverts may be paler than flight feathers or almost as dark; whitish tips to wing-coverts and trailing edge quickly wear off. **HH** Regular passage migrant from Palearctic through WEt and winter visitor in small numbers to Rift Valley, Sep–Apr. Occurs as singles or in small groups, often near lakes in high country. **Voice** Silent in region.

Greater Spotted Eagle *Aquila clanga*   65cm, 26"; WS 165cm, 66"

Adult *dark and plain-looking*; close perched birds reveal *narrow feathering on lower legs* and round nostrils. Immature also dark, with prominent white spots on wings, often including (but not always) large white spots on coverts. Like Lesser Spotted Eagle glides with wings arched slightly downwards, but looks *broader-winged and shorter-tailed*. In flight, adult looks all-dark above, with *coverts not contrasting strongly with flight feathers*, and just a hint of pale in primaries; rump-crescent indistinct, but some may show white. Below, *wing-coverts similar to or darker than flight feathers*, with usually a single whitish comma at carpal joint. Immature is dark above with white rump-crescent and may show distinctive heavy spotting on wing-coverts. Below, *underwing-coverts are darker than flight feathers*. Rare pale morph, often known as 'fulvescens', could occur; it is most like a pale Tawny Eagle but differs in having narrow feathering on lower legs, round nostrils, broader wings and shorter tail. **HH** Uncommon winter visitor from Palearctic, mainly to Er and CEt, Oct–Mar. **Voice** Silent in region. **VU**

Eastern Imperial Eagle *Aquila heliaca*   75cm, 30"; WS 193cm, 77"

Largest *Aquila*. Adult is very dark with *extensive yellowish-brown nape* (paler than Golden Eagle) and *white shoulders*. Immature is like large pale morph Tawny Eagle, but with numerous *dark streaks on body and large pale spots on wing-coverts*. In flight, adult looks massive, with *white shoulders* and *greyish tail broadly tipped black; underwing-coverts darker than flight feathers*. Immature has pale, streaked body and wing-coverts strongly contrasting with blackish flight feathers, *conspicuous pale wedge on inner primaries*, and creamy-buff rump. Soars on flat wings with tail held slightly closed, appearing longish and square-ended. Golden Eagle soars with wings slightly raised and looks longer-tailed. **HH** Scarce to rare Palearctic winter visitor to Er, Dj and CEt, Oct–Mar. **Voice** Silent in region. **VU**

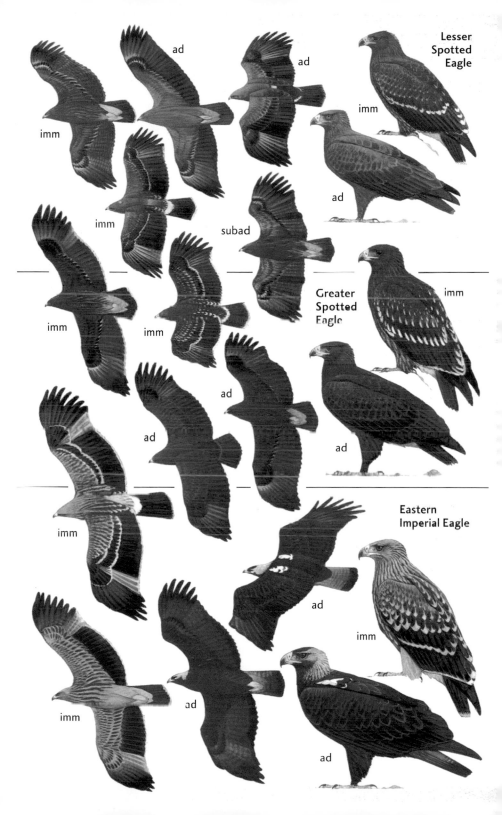

imm

ad

ad

Lesser Spotted Eagle

imm

imm

subad

ad

imm

imm

imm

Greater Spotted Eagle

imm

ad

ad

ad

imm

ad

Eastern Imperial Eagle

imm

ad

imm

ad

ad

Tawny Eagle *Aquila rapax*   65cm, 26"; WS 168cm, 67"

Overall colour varies from dark to very pale brown or creamy-buff; some are vaguely streaky and present a rather scruffy appearance, and a few show random rufous blotches; flight feathers and (plain-looking) tail always darker. At close range, gape is short, only extending back to below middle of eye. Eyes yellowish-brown on adult, dark on immature. Perched immature shows two very narrow bars (pale fringes) across closed wing. In soaring flight wings held flat, and tail broad and rounded. Adult shows browner or paler wing-coverts, contrasting with flight feathers on both wing surfaces (never as plain and dark as adult Steppe Eagle). Immature, from above, shows narrow bands across coverts and along trailing edge of wing, small whitish flash on inner primaries, and pale buffy rump-crescent. From below, shows narrow white trailing edge; pale line between coverts and flight feathers is obscure. Two races occur in Africa: larger and browner *belisarius* is found throughout most of NE Africa, and more rufous nominate occurs in south. **HH** Singles, pairs and small groups are most frequently encountered large brown eagle. Occurs throughout region; often feeds on road kills. **Voice** Vocal, especially near nest and when scavenging at kills. Calls consist of deep barks and growls, and series of quite varied *rrooh*, *kwo*, *kwow* and *uh-uh*.

Steppe Eagle *Aquila nipalensis*   70cm, 28"; WS 188cm, 75"

Adult is slightly larger and darker than Tawny Eagle, *often with buff nape-patch and, at close range, gape extends back to rear edge of dark eyes*; tail can show even even-spaced barring. Immature paler with *two conspicuous bars across closed wing*. In flight, silhouette like Tawny, with flat wings and broad rounded tail. Adult often looks all dark, but closer birds may show small flashes at primary bases on upperwing, small pale back spot, and barred flight feathers with dark trailing edge to underwing. Paler immature has white band along upperwing-coverts, *broad white trailing edges*, small whitish flash on inner primaries, and white rump-crescent. *From below, shows very conspicuous broad white band along centre of wing and broad white trailing edge*. Subspecies concerned is *orientalis*. **HH** Common passage migrant and winter visitor from Palearctic, Oct–Apr; heavy autumn passage in Er and Dj, but very few in spring. Only three records from So. Can occur in flocks on migration, but more frequently found as singles, or in small groups in variety of open country, farmland and grassland. **Voice** Occasionally gives deep growl or bark, lower-pitched than Tawny.

Golden Eagle *Aquila chrysaetos*   78cm, 31"; WS 203cm, 81"

Very large, long-winged eagle with relatively long tail. Adult is mainly dark brown with tawny or greyish wing-panels and *conspicuous golden-brown shawl over head and nape*. Immature similar but without pale wing-panels. In flight, adult is all dark above and below. Immature shows *prominent white flashes in wing above and below, and white base to tail*. Wings are held in shallow V when soaring or gliding, and bulging secondaries give S-shaped trailing edge to wings. **HH** A small resident population was discovered recently in Bale Mts, Et (race unknown); a few records elsewhere in Et and Dj (once) are presumably wanderers. **Voice** Gives a series of barked squeaky yelps at nest, and at times in flight, quite unlike the low dry barks of Tawny Eagle.

Wahlberg's Eagle *Aquila wahlbergi*   55cm, 22"; WS 135cm, 54"

Smaller than other brown eagles with *small pointed crest on back of head*. In flight, dark morph (common) differs from similar plain brown eagles in having *longish narrow, square-ended tail (often held closed)*; wings long, straight and flat. Intermediate and pale (rare) morphs occur, with buffy or white underparts and underwing-coverts; white birds also have black flight feathers. Immature like adult. Confusable with either pale or dark morphs of Booted Eagle, but always lacks latter's pale rump and band across upperwing-coverts (Booted frequently spreads tail in flight). **HH** Widespread but uncommon throughout much of Er and Et in wide variety of open country, but scarce in So; most birds are intra-tropical migrants, but some may be resident and species recorded in every month. **Voice** Breeding birds give a long series of sharp chittering *chitchitchit*, sometimes rising in pitch, and loud whistled downslurred *seeeeeee...* in display.

Tawny Eagle

imm
ad
imm
ad
imm
ad
ad

Steppe Eagle

imm
ad
imm
ad
ad
imm

Golden Eagle

imm
imm
ad
ad
ad

Wahlberg's Eagle

ad
ad
ad
ad
ad

HAWK-EAGLES Varied group of medium-sized eagles, best identified by colour and markings on underparts and underwings, although habitat and range should also be taken into account. All have feathered legs, and females are slightly larger than males. These four species are sometimes placed in the genus Aquila.

African Hawk-Eagle *Hieraaetus spilogaster*   58cm, 23"; WS 140cm, 56"

Black and white open-country eagle with streaked underparts. Close views of adult reveal black and grey banding on secondaries and tail, and *long white feathered legs*. Immature is dark brown above including sides of face, and rufous below with narrow streaking across breast. In flight, tail looks rather long and wings are pinched-in at base. From above, adult shows *large white patches on primaries*, and black and grey barring on secondaries and tail; below, body and wing-coverts are streaked black, *flight feathers mostly white with narrow black tips and trailing edge*, and tail broadly tipped black. Immature like immature Ayres's Hawk-Eagle, but richer rufous below; may show hint of white patches at primary bases. **HH** Pairs are fairly common and widespread throughout most of region in open woodland, bush and semi-arid country, from near sea-level to c.1800m. **Voice** Loud, punctuated repeated upslurs or downslurs *kwee kwee kwee...* often ending on lower note.

Bonelli's Eagle *Hieraaetus fasciatus*   60cm, 24"; WS 155cm, 62"

Similar to African Hawk-Eagle and formerly considered conspecific. Adult is dark brown above (African Hawk-Eagle is blackish above) with *small white patch on back* and plain grey tail with broad black terminal band; underparts white with narrow black streaks. Immature paler above with streaked crown and barred tail, pale rufous below with thin black streaks. In flight, adult is very dark above with capped appearance; white patch on back and two-tone tail are distinctive; from below, black carpal bar contrasts with paler lesser coverts and flight feathers, but *at distance gives impression of whitish body contrasting with dark underwings*. Immature is pale rufous-buff on body and underwing-coverts with dark tips to primary coverts and black wing-tips. Soars on flat wings. **HH** Widespread Palearctic species extending south to Arabia. Recently discovered to breed in Dj. **Voice** Breeders give a haunting *weeeeooo* and other piercing *piu* notes.

Booted Eagle *Hieraaetus pennatus*   45cm, 18"; WS 123cm, 49"

Small, variable eagle with two distinct morphs, plus intermediates and rufous variant of dark birds. Typical pale morph has brownish head, streaked upperparts, often a pale band across wing-coverts, and white underparts with narrow dark streaking. Dark morph has darker head and all-brown underparts. More easily identified in flight, when *both morphs show broad buffy band across upperwing-coverts, buffy scapulars, and pale crescent on rump*. From below, pale morph has largely white body and underwing-coverts (some lightly streaked), contrasting with black flight feathers and greyish tail. Dark morph is quite uniform brown below, except for paler tail and slightly paler inner primaries (rufous birds have body and leading edge of underwing-coverts rufous-brown). Both morphs usually show *white spot at base of leading edge of each wing*—the so-called 'landing lights'. Immature pale morph has pale rufous wash to underparts. Most confusable with Wahlberg's Eagle (plate 37), but Booted often spreads tail in flight, and Wahlberg's always lacks pale band on upperwing-coverts and pale rump. **HH** Fairly common and widespread Palearctic passage migrant and winter visitor (except NSo), occurring in variety of open country, Sep–Apr, up to 4000m. **Voice** Silent in region.

Ayres's Hawk-Eagle *Hieraaetus ayresii*   50cm, 20"; WS 120cm, 48"

A black and white forest eagle with variably spotted underparts. Close views of adult reveal short crest on rear of crown (male also usually has white forehead and narrow white supercilium, and sometimes all-white head), *black-and-grey barred tail*, and *heavily spotted feathering on legs*. Immature is brown above with extensive pale fringes, and tawny-buff on forecrown, sides of face and underparts. In flight, adult differs from larger African Hawk-Eagle in *all-dark upperwings*, and from below, in *spotted (not streaked) underparts and well-barred flight feathers*. Shows white spot at base of leading edge of wing. Immature has pale tawny-buff underparts and underwing-coverts, and extensively barred flight feathers. **HH** Singles and pairs are rather local and uncommon in forest and riverine woodland from sea-level to 2800m; rare in So (only 3 records). **Voice** Breeding birds call loud squealed notes that rise and fall, *weeyah weeyah weeyah...*

imm

imm

ad

ad

African Hawk-Eagle

ad

imm

imm

ad

ad

Bonelli's Eagle

ad

ad
pale

Booted Eagle

ad
dark

ad
dark

ad
pale

ad
pale

ad

imm

imm

ad

ad

Ayres's Hawk-Eagle

Bateleur *Terathopius ecaudatus*   63cm, 25"; WS 175cm, 70"

Stocky, cowl-headed and short-tailed eagle. Adult is largely black with extensive bright red facial skin and cere, grey wing-coverts, and very short chestnut tail (hidden by wings at rest); legs bright red-orange. Most have chestnut backs, but minority are creamy-white or light brown, commoner in arid areas. Perched adult male shows all-black flight feathers; slightly larger adult female has pale grey panel across closed wing. Immature is dark brown with variable paler brown areas on head and underparts, dull blue-grey or greenish facial skin and cere, pale legs and longer tail. Change from immature to full adult plumage takes 6–7 years. Flight is direct and sailing with a few flaps (after take-off) and tilting action of tightrope-walker. From below, both sexes have black and white underwings, but adult male shows broad black trailing edge (all flight feathers except outer primaries), and adult female shows narrow black trailing edge. Orange-red legs project beyond chestnut tail. Immature has similar silhouette, but is brown and may have slightly longer tail. Immature male shows wider dark trailing edge to wing than immature female, presaging adult pattern. **HH** Singles, pairs and, more rarely, small groups are widespread and often common in wide variety of open grassland, bushland and woodland, including arid and semi-arid country, from sea-level to 3000m. Individuals range over wide areas, seeking out carcasses, as well as hunting, and often patrol over roads for kills. May make local seasonal movements. Flight action distinctive and unique. **Voice** Quite vocal: a loud explosive *yaaaow* often followed by sound of beating wings. Also a high-pitched squealed and slightly downslurred *wee weeye weeye weeye...*

Long-crested Eagle *Lophaetus occipitalis*   53cm, 21"; WS 118cm, 47"

Striking, *small blackish eagle with long lax crest and bright yellow eyes.* At rest, adult appears largely black with pale-feathered legs (whiter in male, browner or brown and white in female); long crest often waves in wind. Female slightly larger than male. Immature browner, with shorter crest and dull brown eyes. In rather stiff-winged flight, shows *large white patches in primaries* (both above and below). Underwing also boldly barred black and grey across secondaries; tail shows three pale bands. Told from superficially similar but massive Verreaux's Eagle (see plate 40) by small size, straight wings, dark rump and barred tail. Immature very similar in flight, but dark brown and white not black and white. **HH** Singles are widespread and common residents of moister wooded country in Er and Et (except SE), from sea-level to 2400m; rare in So. Inhabits forest edge and settled areas with fields and isolated trees. Commonly perches on roadside poles and trees, swooping to pounce on rodents. **Voice** Gives a single downslurred *wiiyuu* in flight. This note is repeated at nest in long series.

imm

♀

ad ♂

imm

Bateleur

♂

♀

ad ♀

♂ white-backed
form

Long-crested Eagle

imm

imm

ad

ad

ad

Verreaux's Eagle *Aquila verreauxii* 83cm, 33"; WS 198cm, 79"

Massive black eagle with white back and rump extending as white V around upper back; bright yellow eye-ring, cere and feet. Sexes similar but female larger. Immature has buff-cream crown and nape, and variable blackish-brown back and wings with much pale fringing, especially on wing-coverts; face, neck and breast blackish, browner on belly with large dark streaks and spots; acquires adult plumage over 4 years. In leisurely gliding and soaring flight (rarely flapping) shows distinctive *broad wings narrowing markedly towards body*, and flies on upswept wings. From above, black adult shows *bright white back and rump*, and prominent white patches at base of primaries; from below, birds are entirely black, except for white primary patches (and yellow feet). Long-crested Eagle is similar but smaller, lacks white back and rump, and from below shows barred secondaries and tail. Immature is dark with white primary patches and distinctive wing-shape. **HH** Pairs are local and rather uncommon residents in wide range of rocky, mountainous country up to 4200m, often in drier areas, near inaccessible cliff nesting sites, associated with main prey, rock hyrax *Procavia* spp. **Voice** Displaying birds give a far-carrying, loud upslurred and high-pitched scream *iiy'iii*, interspersed with low barking notes *auw auw auw…* [Alt: Black Eagle]

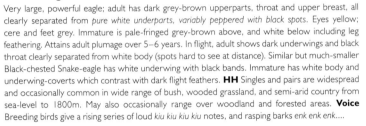

Martial Eagle *Polemaetus bellicosus* 85cm, 34"; WS 205cm, 82"

Very large, powerful eagle; adult has dark grey-brown upperparts, throat and upper breast, all clearly separated from *pure white underparts, variably peppered with black spots*. Eyes yellow; cere and feet grey. Immature is pale-fringed grey-brown above, and white below including leg feathering. Attains adult plumage over 5–6 years. In flight, adult shows dark underwings and black throat clearly separated from white body (spots hard to see at distance). Similar but much-smaller Black-chested Snake-eagle has white underwing with black bands. Immature has white body and underwing-coverts which contrast with dark flight feathers. **HH** Singles and pairs are widespread and occasionally common in wide range of bush, wooded grassland, and semi-arid country from sea-level to 1800m. May also occasionally range over woodland and forested areas. **Voice** Breeding birds give a rising series of loud *kiu kiu kiu kiu* notes, and rasping barks *enk enk enk….*

African Crowned Eagle *Stephanoaetus coronatus* 85cm, 34"; WS 163cm, 65"

Massive, heavily marked eagle with rough crest. Adult is blackish-brown above, with brown head and throat, and *heavily barred and blotched rufous, black and white below*; feathered legs boldly marked black and white; cere, eyes and feet yellow. Immature is *white-headed except for dark-tipped crest*, with heavily scaled grey-brown back and wings; largely white below (with variable pale buff-orange wash across upper breast), with bold blackish spots on legs. In flight, appears massive, broad-winged and quite long-tailed. Adult is dark above, with grey bands on wings and tail, and heavily barred below, with *chestnut underwing-coverts*, broad black trailing edge to wing, and strongly barred undertail. Immature has pale rufous underwing-coverts, more prominently barred flight feathers, and largely white body. **HH** Singles and pairs are rather uncommon and local residents of dense forest and woodland, including riverine and isolated patches, from sea-level to 3300m. **Voice** Unique, loud and far-carrying call is familiar sound of forests. Pairs or single birds engage in aerial tumbling displays (often in middle of day) whilst giving loud ringing calls that rise and fall in waves, *phewee-phewee-phewee-phewee-phewee…* (much-loved by mimicking robin-chats!). [Alt: Crowned Eagle]

Verreaux's Eagle

imm

ad

imm

ad

ad

ad

Martial Eagle

imm

imm

ad

ad

African
Crowned Eagle

imm

imm

ad

ad

ad

KESTRELS *Slim attractive falcons of open country which, though lacking the spectacular flight of some falcons, are still adept at riding the wind, and frequently hover. These four species are predominantly brown, though some have grey heads. Back, tail and underwing markings aid identification. Females are slightly larger than males.*

Common Kestrel *Falco tinnunculus*   30cm, 12"; WS 68cm, 27"

Four distinctive races occur. In resident *rufescens* (highland Et), adult male has grey head, *rufous upperparts well-spotted with black*, lightly barred blue-grey tail with broad black subterminal band, and strongly washed rufous underparts streaked with black. Adult female is largely brown, with pale face, more obvious moustachial stripes, rufous-brown upperparts heavily spotted and barred black, and rufous underparts boldly streaked blackish. Immature is like adult female. Nominate Palearctic wintering race is similar, but much paler. Race *rupicolaeformis* (winter migrant to Er from Egypt) is slightly darker rufous than nominate and more richly coloured. Coastal resident race *archeri* (NEEt, NWSo, Soc) is smaller and brighter rufous with heavier barring above. In all races, eyes are dark, cere and legs yellow, *claws black*. Immature has browner head and tail. In flight, adult male resembles Lesser Kestrel but lacks blue-grey on upperwing, and underwing usually more heavily marked. **HH** Singles and pairs of race *rufescens* are fairly common residents, often in rocky areas, up to 3500m; *archeri* replaces it to east. Nominate race is common and widespread winter visitor, often in flocks, in variety of open country, Oct–Apr. **Voice** Race *rufescens* gives a penetrating *ki-ki-ki-ki...* often followed by a burry squeal. Nominate birds are silent in region. [Alt: Rock Kestrel]

Lesser Kestrel *Falco naumanni*   28cm, 11"; WS 68cm, 27"

Very like Common Kestrel, but adult male has *paler blue-grey head, plain chestnut back, blue-grey greater coverts, and warm chestnut-buff underparts* with discrete dark spotting. Perched adult female and immature only reliably told from nominate adult female Common by *white (not black) claws*. In flight, both sexes show rather wedge-shaped tail, with central tail feathers slightly protruding and, from below, paler silver-grey underwings with limited speckling; from above adult male has *blue-grey bar on greater coverts*. **HH** Small groups to large flocks are widespread and common Palearctic migrants and winter visitors (in smaller numbers) to open bushed and wooded grassland up to 3000m, as well as fields and pastures, Oct–May, though commoner on northward passage. **Voice** Usually silent in region, but may give sharp chatter at roosts. **VU**

Greater Kestrel *Falco rupicoloides*   33cm, 13"; WS 75cm, 30"

Rather thickset warm-brown kestrel, with dark streaks on head and breast, *heavily barred back, wings and flanks, and grey tail broadly barred black*. Adult has *creamy-white eyes* and yellow cere and legs. Immature similar but more rufous, with brown and black barred tail, streaked underparts, and brown eyes. In slightly heavy flight, shows obvious *grey-and-black barred rump and tail from above*, and largely white underwings which contrast with warm-brown underparts and barred undertail. Two races occur: *arthuri* (SWEt) as described; *fieldi* (Er, N&EEt, So) is much paler. **HH** Singles and pairs are uncommon to scarce in semi-arid country with scattered trees, and in dry bushed grasslands below 1800m; rather patchily distributed and some birds are nomadic. **Voice** Gives loud squeals and barking notes, unlike Common Kestrel. [Alt: White-eyed Kestrel]

Fox Kestrel *Falco alopex*   35cm, 14"; WS 80cm, 32"

Large bright chestnut kestrel with long, rather tapering tail. Adult *all chestnut-red, finely streaked with black both above and below*. Eyes brownish-yellow; eye-ring, cere and legs yellow. Immature similar, but has more heavily barred tail and blue-grey eye-ring. In flight appears long-winged with long, slightly graduated tail. From above, looks strikingly rich chestnut with black flight feathers, but from below chestnut body contrasts with paler chestnut underwing-coverts, and silvery-white flight feathers. **HH** Pairs are uncommon and local residents of arid and semi-arid cliff and rocky country in Er and WEt, mainly west of Rift Valley, up to 2900m. Vagrant Dj. **Voice** breeding birds give a high-pitched rasping screech *kreee-kreee-kree*, similar to Common Kestrel.

nominate

♂

♂

♂

♀

Common Kestrel

ad ♂

ad ♀

♀

rufescens

♂

♂

♀

♂

Lesser Kestrel

ad ♂

ad ♀

ad

ad

imm

ad

arthuri

Greater Kestrel

ad

ad

Fox Kestrel

ad

Grey Kestrel *Falco ardosiaceus*   30cm, 12"; WS 65cm, 26"

Stocky, rather large-headed *all-grey kestrel with yellow skin around eyes*, yellow cere and legs; eyes dark brown. Appears all slate-grey at distance, but close views reveal fine black streaking, particularly on head and breast. *Wing-tips do not reach tail-tip at rest.* Female slightly larger than male. Immature similar to adult, but tinged brownish. Eye-ring and cere bluish-green on juvenile, but quickly turn yellow. Often flies rather slowly on stiff wings, but can be dashing, and sometimes hovers. Appears all grey in flight, but in good light primaries look blacker, and may show slightly barred flight feathers and tail from below. Similar Sooty Falcon (scarce passage migrant) has uniform longer, slimmer, more pointed wings, which extend beyond tail-tip at rest. **HH** Singles and pairs are rather uncommon residents of bushed and wooded grassland in Er and Et, mainly west of Rift Valley below 1800m. Breeds in Hamerkop nests. **Voice** Gives a harsh burry downslurred scream, and muffled *keek-keek-keeek…*

Sooty Falcon *Falco concolor*   35cm, 14"; WS 80cm, 32"

Slim all-grey falcon with *long wings reaching to or beyond tail-tip* at rest (much shorter in similar Grey Kestrel). Adult has yellow eye-ring, cere and feet. Immature dark grey above (pale-fringed), with hobby-like face pattern, creamy-buff below with variable blackish streaking; eye-ring and cere pale bluish. Adult in flight looks very long-winged (sometimes with slightly protruding central tail feathers), and often appears all dark grey, but outer wing and end of tail darker in good light. Immature differs from similar immatures in having dark band near tip of undertail. **HH** Common breeding visitor to rocky areas and cliffs along Red Sea coastal region of Er and Dj, May–Oct. 230 pairs counted on islands off Er in 2005–07, mainly in Dahlak archipelago. Spring passage migrant in NSo, but only rarely recorded in Et (all in autumn). Winters in Madagascar and southern Africa. **Voice** Silent in region. **NT**

Pygmy Falcon *Polihierax semitorquatus*   20cm, 8"; WS 38cm, 15"

Tiny, attractive little raptor with *white face and underparts*. Adult male is pale-grey above with blacker wings and short, rather conspicuous black-and-white barred tail; eye-ring, cere and legs reddish-pink; eyes brown. Adult female similar, but with chestnut-brown back. Immature duller than adult, with buff wash across breast and variable dark grey-brown streaking; sexes also distinguished by back colour. Birds have direct rapid undulating flight, revealing *bright white rump, white-spotted black wings, and a black-and-white barred tail*. Race in NE Africa is *castanotus*. **HH** Pairs and family groups are common residents of semi-arid bush and dry acacia grasslands of S&EEt (east of Rift Valley) and So, from near sea-level to 1500m. Often seen conspicuously perching on tops of small bushes. Breeds in White-headed Buffalo Weaver nests. **Voice** Breeding birds give discordant, rather loud screaming squeal, recalling woodpecker.

ad

ad

ad

imm

Grey Kestrel

ad

ad

imm

ad

imm

Sooty Falcon

imm ♀

imm ♂

imm

ad ♀

Pygmy Falcon

ad

ad ♂

♀

MEDIUM-SIZED FALCONS *Dark dashing falcons with rather long sickle-shaped wings, although Red-footed and Amur also have leisurely kestrel-like hunting behaviour (including hovering). Head and underwing markings aid identification. Migrant species often associate with storm fronts and may gather to feed at termite emergences. Most have females slightly larger than males.*

African Hobby *Falco cuvierii* 28cm, 11"; WS 65cm, 26"

Small neat falcon; adult dark grey-black above and *rufous-chestnut below* with fine blackish breast-streaks at close range. Beware some adults have small patch of chestnut on nape and have whitish cheek patches and throat, looking superficially similar to Taita Falcon. Immature similar, but duller and browner above, with paler throat and *more heavily streaked underparts*; some younger birds may lack rufous on underparts. In flight appears dashing, slender and rather short-tailed. Adult has rufous underparts extending onto underwing-coverts; flight feathers and tail paler buffy-rufous with much barring. Immature similar but more heavily streaked below. **HH** Singles and pairs are uncommon residents and local wanderers in woodland and forest edge in Et (except SE), typically in highlands but lower in SSo, from sea-level to 4100m. **Voice** Breeding birds give a screaming and shrill *ki ki ki ki...* and burry *kree kree kree...*

Eurasian Hobby *Falco subbuteo* 30cm, 12"; WS 75cm, 30"

Adult is dark grey above and whitish below, heavily streaked with black; *legs and vent chestnut*. Neat face pattern with white cheeks curving round ear-coverts like inverted comma. Immature similar, but browner above with buff fringes, and mostly buff below with heavy dark streaking. Agile in flight, like giant swift, with long slender wings, and can appear all dark at distance with white throat. Closer birds show heavily streaked underparts, densely barred underwing, and *chestnut vent*. Immature paler without vent colour of adult. **HH** Singles or small groups are common passage migrants from Palearctic throughout region, Sep–Nov and Mar–May, occurring in wide variety of habitats up to 2700m. Vagrant Soc. **Voice** Silent in region. [Alt: European Hobby]

Eleonora's Falcon *Falco eleonorae* 38cm, 15"; WS 93cm, 37"

Medium-large, long-winged, long-tailed falcon with two distinct colour morphs. Pale morph is all dark above with hobby-like face pattern (but more rounded cheek-patch), and breast to vent strongly washed rufous with black streaking. Dark morph looks all brownish-black. Immature dark above with pale fringing, heavily blotched and streaked on buff below. Flight varies from soaring to relaxed with elastic wing-beats, agile and dashing when hunting. Long wings and tail always apparent. On both morphs *blackish underwing-coverts* distinctive, contrasting with paler flight feathers. Immature differs from immature Eurasian Hobby in longer wings and tail, and pale bases to flight feathers. **HH** Rare passage migrant in Er, Dj, Et and NSo, but probably overlooked. Can occur over any habitat on passage, southwards in Oct–Nov, northwards in May. **Voice** Silent in region.

Taita Falcon *Falco fasciinucha* 28cm, 11"; WS 65cm, 26"

Adult is dark slate above with *rufous nape-patches divided by blackish line*. Below, *white throat contrasts with rest of rich rufous underparts*. Immature browner above with pale fringes and streaked below. Often flies with stiff wings, but also makes spectacular diving stoops; looks short-tailed and pale-rumped; shape recalls small Peregrine. From below adult shows mainly *rich rufous underparts and underwing-coverts*. Immature has evenly barred underwing. Confusion only likely with African Hobby, but latter is smaller and slimmer with narrower wings and longer tail; usually lacks white throat and cheeks of Taita (though throat can be paler than rest of underparts). Barbary Falcon is larger and paler, lacking rufous on underparts. **HH** A very rare presumed resident in SEt, usually found on high cliffs. Known from 3 old records near Yabelo (1800m) and one recent sight record south of Agere Maryam. **Voice** Breeding birds give a low-pitched, slightly slurred *krieer-krieer-krieer.* **NT**

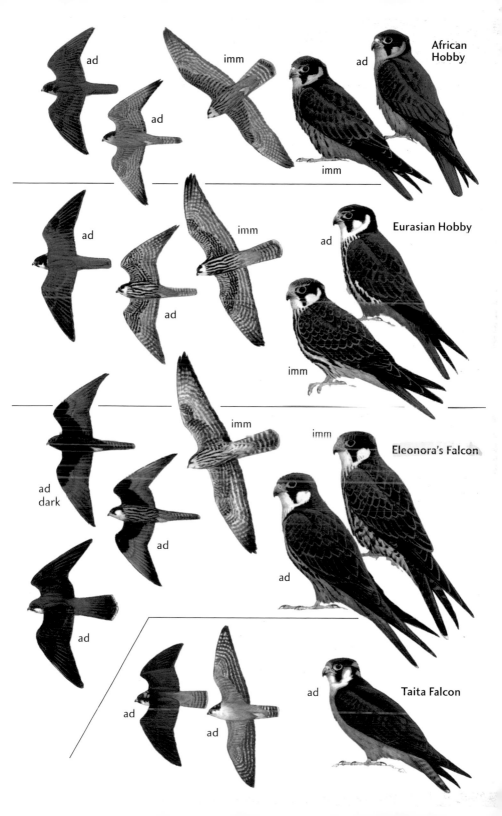

African
Hobby

ad

ad

imm

ad

imm

Eurasian Hobby

ad

imm

ad

ad

imm

Eleonora's Falcon

imm

ad
dark

ad

ad

ad

Taita Falcon

ad

ad

ad

ad

Amur Falcon *Falco amurensis*   28cm, 11"; WS 65cm, 26"

Perched adult male appears all slate-grey with chestnut vent and leg feathering; eye-ring, cere and legs orange-red. Adult female is grey above with black barring, and white forehead, cheeks and throat; rest of underparts whitish-buff with black streaks and barring, and plain buff vent. Immature like adult female, but paler above with brown fringes and streaked dark below on white (without barring). In flight, adult male shows *striking white underwing-coverts contrasting with dark flight feathers*, and chestnut vent. Adult female also has *largely white underwing-coverts*, but flight feathers and tail barred with black from below. Immature has darker crown and whiter underparts than immature Red-footed Falcon. Second-year male has mixed immature/adult plumage like Red-footed Falcon, but with white on underwing-coverts. **HH** Singles, small groups and, less often, large flocks are passage migrants from Eastern Palearctic, moving south through So and (rarely) SEt in Nov–Dec, and returning north on wider front Mar–Apr. **Voice** Mainly silent in region but roosting birds maintain burry squeals. [Alt: Eastern Red-footed Falcon]

Red-footed Falcon *Falco vespertinus*   30cm, 12"; WS 70cm, 28"

Perched adult male identical to perched adult male Amur Falcon. Adult female has *blackish eye-mask, white cheeks and throat, and orange-buff crown, nape and underparts*; back, wings and tail grey barred blackish. In immature, dark eye-mask stands out against whiter face, underparts buffy with blackish streaking. In flight from above, adult male is dark grey with silvery-grey flight feathers; below shows *black underwing-coverts* and chestnut vent. Adult female is orange-buff below and on underwing-coverts, contrasting with heavily barred flight feathers. Immature usually more buff below than immature Amur Falcon. Second-year male shows mixture of immature and adult plumage. **HH** Vagrant from Palearctic, passing mainly to west of our area (Oct–May), with records from Er, NEEt, Dj and SSo. **Voice** Silent in region. [Alt: Western Red-footed Falcon] **NT**

Red-necked Falcon *Falco chicquera*   33cm, 13"; WS 63cm, 25"

Adult is distinctive if seen well: only falcon with *rich rufous crown and nape and black-and-white barred underparts*. Close views reveal dark brown moustache-stripes, black barring on upperparts, and rufous band across upper breast. Immature is dull on crown and browner above, with buffy or pale rufous underparts, narrowly streaked on breast, with heavier blackish barring on flanks and belly. Flight is fast and dashing. From above, adult shows rufous crown, dark outer wings and black subterminal tail-bar; from below, pale throat and chest contrast with well-barred body and wings. Immature has pale rufous body and underwing-coverts largely barred, not streaked as on other mid-sized falcons. Race in region is *ruficollis*. **HH** Singles are widespread but rather local, occurring mainly in WEt and Rift Valley below 1200m; vagrant So (once). Shows marked preference for palm country, especially *Borassus*. **Voice** Breeding birds give a burry downslur and more barking *kikikiki...* [Alt: Red-headed Falcon]

Saker Falcon *Falco cherrug*   50cm, 20"; WS 110cm, 44"

Very large brown and white falcon with *whitish crown* (very narrowly streaked black). Underparts white, variably streaked brown (but usually broadly); *leg feathering heavily blotched with brown*. Can be almost identical to some (pale crowned) immature Lanner Falcons (plate 45), but at close range Saker lacks dark band across forecrown, and has less well-defined face pattern; Lanner also usually has paler leg feathering; Saker has spots in outer tail, and incomplete bars on upperside of central tail feathers, suggesting centre of tail is plain (all barred on adult Lanner). In flight, long wings are broad-based, and *show whitish bases to flight feathers from below*. **HH** Scarce winter visitor from Palearctic to Er and Et (mainly in central areas), Oct–May; vagrant Dj and NSo. Often found close to water at lower altitudes, but up to 2700m. **Voice** Silent in region. **EN**

Amur Falcon

♂ ♂ imm ad ♀ imm ♀ ad ♂

Red-footed Falcon

imm ♂ subad ♂ imm ♀ ad ♂ ♀ ♂ ad ♀

Red-necked Falcon

imm ad ad ad ad imm

Saker Falcon

ad ad ad imm ad

LARGE FALCONS *The three falcons on this plate, together with Saker Falcon (plate 44), are a confusing group of large powerful falcons which often soar but chase prey with diving stoops or fast low flight. Best identified by head, body and underwing markings. Females are larger than males.*

Lanner Falcon *Falco biarmicus*   43cm, 17"; WS 100cm, 40"

Adult has *rufous crown and nape, relatively narrow moustache-streaks*, grey upperparts (variably mottled) and barred tail. Mostly plain buff or pinkish-buff below, with streaks and bars on flanks and thighs. Immature much browner above with pale brown crown, buffy below with heavy dark streaking. Beware some immatures have rather pale crowns and look like rare Saker Falcon, but Saker usually has *darker leg feathering*; also, all-barred tail distinctive from most Sakers, but some Lanners have plain central tail. In flight, wings narrower than Saker but have similar rather blunt tips. From below, adult has quite plain underwings and lightly marked underparts. Immature is very heavily streaked below and on underwing-coverts. Two races occur: *abyssinicus* (Er Et, NSo) as described; *tanypterus* (migrant to Er and NEt from N Africa) is paler with buff crown. **HH** By far the commonest large falcon in region, inhabiting semi-arid bush, open rocky hill country, vicinity of cliffs, and woodlands, from near sea-level to 4250m. **Voice** Breeding birds give a deep harsh *kak-kak-kak...* and loud quivering squeals and barks.

Peregrine Falcon *Falco peregrinus*   43cm, 17"; WS 100cm, 40"

Adult has *black crown, nape, and broad moustache-stripes*. Resident race *minor* is dark grey above with extensive *black-and-white barring below*, while slightly larger Palearctic migrant races *calidus* and nominate *peregrinus* are paler above, less barred below (*calidus* is slightly paler and larger than nominate). Immature *minor* is dark grey-brown above, buffy below, with streaking on breast becoming more blotched and barred on flanks and vent. Immature *calidus* and nominate *peregrinus* are paler brown above (including crown) and buff below with narrow dark streaking. In flight appears compact and broad-chested, wings look broad at base and pointed at tips; tail rather short. Adult shows very black and white head, and barred underparts. Immature has underwing-coverts and flight feathers evenly dark-barred, not contrasting. **HH** Resident *minor* is uncommon but widespread throughout region, usually in vicinity of cliffs or tall buildings, while *calidus* occurs Oct–Apr, including at coastal sites. No confirmed records for nominate *peregrinus*. **Voice** Race *minor* gives a loud slow and deliberate series of barked gull-like downslurs, *kew-kew-kew....* Migrant birds are silent in region.

Barbary Falcon *Falco pelegrinoides*   38cm, 15"; WS 88cm, 35"

Suggests a Peregrine × Lanner hybrid, but compact shape is much more like Peregrine in flight. Close views reveal *rufous hindcrown and nape* (with two dark smudges) and slightly narrower moustache-stripes than Peregrine. Paler above than Peregrine and *buffier below, with a few small spots on breast and fine bars on flanks and leg feathers*. Taita Falcon is smaller and darker with rufous underparts. Immature has paler nape-patch and browner upperparts, with darker crown than Lanner. Underparts less boldly streaked than either Lanner or Peregrine. In flight, adult often shows dark 'comma' on greater underwing-coverts. Immature separated from immature Lanner by evenly barred underwing. **HH** A rather local presumed resident in Er, CEt, Dj and NSo, inhabiting arid areas with cliffs, often associated with sea, from sea-level to 4000m. **Voice** Calls similar to Peregrine but higher-pitched. **Note** May be conspecific with Peregrine Falcon.

Lanner Falcon

abyssinicus

imm

imm

ad

ad

ad

Peregrine Falcon

minor

imm

ad

ad

imm

ad

Barbary Falcon

imm

ad

imm

ad

ad

GUINEAFOWL Endemic to Africa, guineafowl are distinctive spotted gamebirds of forest and bush. All are highly gregarious, foraging, chasing and dust-bathing together. They respond to danger with loud far-carrying rattling and trilling calls. Sexes are alike.

Helmeted Guineafowl *Numida meleagris* 61cm, 24"

Adults are easily identified by upright *bony casque on top of head*. Races vary mainly in shape and colour of casque and gape-wattles, and length of bristles on cere. Nominate birds (Er and Et west of Rift Valley) have variable-sized casque and rounded blue gape-wattles. East of Rift Valley and in So, *somaliensis* has pointed blue wattles with red tips, and prominent tuft of bristles extending from bill-base. Immatures duller than adults with smaller casques and wattles; juveniles spotted and barred with rufous, buff and black. **HH** Family groups to large flocks are widespread and sometimes very common in wide range of grassland, bush country, woodland and cultivation from sea-level to 2500m. **Voice** Gives a trumpeted loud rattling *kruh-kruh-kruh-krahhhhh krr krr krr...*, and piping squeaky *pi-pi'oo*, the first two notes identical, the last falling.

Crested Guineafowl *Guttera pucherani* 54cm, 21"

A *shaggy-crested forest guineafowl* which is spotted with pale blue. The nominate race (also known as Kenya Crested Guineafowl) has bright red skin around the eyes and on the throat, and entirely spotted neck feathering. Immatures are much duller with extensive rusty, buff and black bars, spots and mottling. **HH** Family groups and small flocks of the nominate race occur in riverine forest and dense thickets along the lower Jubba and Boni Forest in SSo, but this population is greatly threatened from habitat destruction. **Voice** Gives a very harsh rhythmical clucking with descending churrs.

Vulturine Guineafowl *Acryllium vulturinum* 71cm, 28"

A tall and elegant guineafowl with a *long pointed tail*, a bare blue-grey head and neck with a bristly russet nape, and a *bright cobalt-blue breast covered by long lanceolate black and white feathers*. Immature is largely dull grey-brown with rufous and buff mottling. **HH** Small groups to large flocks are locally common in arid and semi-arid bush country and grassland in S&EEt and So, from sea-level to 1400m. **Voice** Rattled call is faster and higher-pitched than Helmeted Guineafowl, a piped *wi-yi-wi-yi-wi-yi-wii*, the *yi* notes being slightly higher, creating a see-saw effect; also gives a downslurred growl.

SMALLER GAMEBIRDS The francolins and allies are a large group of predominantly brown gamebirds occupying a variety of habitats (see also plates 47 and 48). Most are shy and difficult to observe.

Stone Partridge *Ptilopachus petrosus* 28cm, 11"

A *dark bantam-like gamebird which frequently cocks its tail*. At close quarters shows a slightly scaly head, faint barring on the flanks, and red facial skin. Sexes similar, but female may be paler on the breast. Immature similar to adult but rather more barred. Two races occur: *florentiae* (SW&WEt) as described; *major* (WEr, NWEt) is paler and larger with broader chestnut streaks on the flanks. Crested Francolin could be confused when its tail is cocked, but it always shows a prominent white supercilium. **HH** Pairs and small groups are locally common on rocky hillsides, at 600–1400m. If disturbed usually runs over rocks to cover. **Voice** A well orchestrated duet, rising and falling like a whistled wave *oo-wirr'oo-wirr'oo-wirr...*, while other birds utter soft trilled churrs.

Crested Francolin *Dendroperdix sephaena* 30cm, 12"

A small brown francolin with a long white supercilium and some white streaking on the upperparts; *often cocks tail and raises crown feathers when agitated or alarmed* (does not look crested if relaxed). Race *grantii* (C&SEt) has small bold dark brown spots across the breast, while *spilogaster* (SEEt, So) is more finely streaked brown below. Females and immatures are slightly more barred above. *In flight mostly black tail is conspicuous*. Stone Partridge may look superficially similar but lacks the white supercilium. **HH** Pairs and family groups are widespread and often common in a wide range of bush country, wooded grasslands and thickets from sea-level to 1500m, mainly east of the Rift Valley. **Voice** Calls are monotonous repeated and very rapid short rising squeals followed by descending scratchy notes *kik-kera'ra kik-kera'ra kik-kera'ra...* **Note** Formerly in genus *Francolinus*.

nominate

somaliensis

imm

Helmeted Guineafowl

Vulturine Guineafowl

Crested Guineafowl

nominate

Stone Partridge

florentiae

♀

♂

grantii

Crested Francolin

MONTANE FRANCOLINS *These rather dark francolins are typical of highland forests or scrub, but some descend to lowlands; most are shy and difficult to observe. They draw attention to themselves with their loud calls (notably in the morning and evening) when they may also appear at forest edge or on trails. The red-winged francolins on plate 48 are also montane. All the species on this page were formerly in the genus Francolinus, and are sometimes called spurfowl.*

Harwood's Francolin *Pternistis harwoodi* 34cm, 13.5"

A medium-sized, grey-brown francolin with red bill and red legs, and *bare red skin around the eyes.* Upperparts are finely vermiculated, and neck and breast are heavily scaled. Sexes are very similar, but female is paler and with more extensive buff belly. Scaly Francolin lacks the red eye-patch, but ranges do not overlap. Within Harwood's small range, Clapperton's Francolin (Plate 48) also has a red eye-patch, but differs in having a white throat and heavily blotched underparts. Erckel's Francolin is larger and has a chestnut crown and yellow legs. **HH** ENDEMIC to highlands of CEt, notably the Jemmu valley, at 1300–2500m. Inhabits scrubby hillsides, patches of native thick scrub and sometimes dense *Typha* beds alongside streams; locally common within very restricted range. **Voice** A loud carrying *keriik keriik keriik*, usually given in sets of three well-spaced calls, very rasping and unpleasant. **VU**

Scaly Francolin *Pternistis squamatus* 31cm, 12"

A medium-sized, olive-brown francolin with variable pale buff-brown feather-edges giving a scaly effect. Bill red, and legs red or orange-red. Male may have one or two spurs. Immature has a duller bill than adult, is warmer rufous-brown flecked with black above and lightly barred black and white below. There is much clinal variation within the species; the form in SWEt is *schuetti*. **HH** Pairs and small groups are widespread and locally common in dense undergrowth of forest, bamboo and secondary areas in Et, at 800–2700m. **Voice** Crescendo call begins with soft, rising and grating churrs that get louder *k-rrrk k-rrrrk...* and end in a set of hysterical screamed and rasping *kereeeek kereeeek kereeeek.*

Erckel's Francolin *Pternistis erckelii* 41cm, 16"

A large francolin of highland scrub and remnant forest patches, with a black face, chestnut crown and nape, short white stripe behind the eye and white ear-coverts. *Most of upperparts and underparts streaked with chestnut.* Bill black and legs yellow. Sexes alike but female is smaller. Djibouti Francolin is similar but allopatric. **HH** Near-endemic to highlands of Er and Et, at 900–3000m (only other population is in hills of Red Sea Prov, Sudan). Pairs are rather shy, usually remaining within cover. **Voice** An insane cackled laughter, speeding towards the end with a bouncing ball pattern. This series is repeated at regular intervals for long periods.

Chestnut-naped Francolin *Pternistis castaneicollis* 41cm, 16"

A large red-billed francolin with a *black forehead and short black supercilium.* Two well-marked races occur: nominate *castaneicollis* (entire range except SEt) is grey-brown above, boldly marked with black, white and chestnut; *crown, nape and ear-coverts are ginger-rufous.* Underparts heavily scaled, with bold chestnut striping on the flanks. There is much variation within *castaneicollis*, but it is clinal and other described races are not recognised here: *ogoensis* (NSo) is much paler and *kaffanus* (SWEt) is darker and greyer. The distinct race *atrifrons* (SEt) is largely dull brown above with pale feather shafts and fringes, and little or no chestnut on the nape or back; underparts are largely buffy with some darker speckling across the upper breast. In all forms, sexes are similar but legs spurred in male. **HH** ENDEMIC to Et and NWSo. Inhabits forest edges and clearings, at 1750–3150m, including moorland above the tree line. In NSo, in scrub and juniper forest at 1200–2100m. **Voice** Birds from the Bale Mountains give a soft *kewek-kewek-kewek*; alarm call on the ground is a growling *krr-krr-krr-krr...*, which sometimes precedes the main call. In flight a loud cackling *kraak kraak kraak...* is given, reminiscent of a louder version of a Common Snipe.

Djibouti Francolin *Pternistis ochropectus* 35cm, 14"

A large dark francolin, similar to Erckel's, with a black face and short white supercilium behind the eye, but ear-coverts grey (not white). *Underparts heavily streaked blackish (not chestnut).* Female is similar to male but smaller and duller. No other francolin occurs within its range. **HH** ENDEMIC to Dj. Locally common, but declining, in undergrowth of dry woodland and juniper forest in Foret du Day and Mabla Mts, at 700–1800m. **Voice** Call is a loud *Erk* followed by an accelerating series of *kak* notes and ending in a chuckle. **CR**

Harwood's
Francolin

♂

♀

Scaly Francolin

ad

Erckel's
Francolin

ad

ad
atrifrons

Chestnut-naped
Francolin

♀

Djibouti
Francolin

ad
nominate

♂

RED-WINGED FRANCOLINS Both have rather strong head patterns and pale throats, but their ranges barely overlap. Sexes alike, but males have a single spur. Immatures are duller versions of adults. Formerly in the genus Francolinus.

Orange River Francolin *Scleroptila levaillantoides*   34cm, 13.5"

A cryptic, medium-sized francolin with grey-brown upperparts with rufous barring and buff shaft-streaks; *all forms have an unmarked white throat*. Underparts variable cream-buff heavily blotched with chestnut on the breast and flanks. In flight shows *rufous patches in wings*, but primary tips are grey-brown. Moorland Francolin has finely-spotted buff throat and more rufous in the wings in flight. Three races occur: *lorti* (NEEt, NSo) is the palest race, creamy below with a *scaly necklace across the upper breast*; similar *archeri* (SWEt) is buff below; *gutturalis* (Er, NEt) *lacks the mottled black-and-white necklace* (or shows only an indistinct necklace) and has heavier black streaking below. **HH** Frequent to locally common in grassland and wooded grassland: *gutturalis* at 1800–2500m and *archeri* at 1500–1800m; in So, *lorti* occurs on scrub-covered hillsides at 1200–2000m. Generally shy and elusive. **Voice** Call is an urgent, high-pitched, repeated *ki-keet ki-kit*. **Note** The three races in NE Africa were formerly lumped in Greywing Francolin *S. africanus* of southern Africa; they are sometimes split from disjunct southern races of Orange River as a separate species: Archer's Francolin *S. gutturalis*.

Moorland Francolin *Scleroptila psilolaemus*   34cm, 13.5"

Similar to Orange River Francolin but browner above and *buff throat is finely spotted*. Stripes on head are pale buff. Underparts buff with small black spots across the upper breast; rest of underparts heavily marked with chestnut spots and barring on the flanks. *In flight, shows much rufous in the wings*. Race in Et is nominate. Orange River Francolin has a pure white throat and less rufous in the wings. **HH** Locally frequent to common, but shy, in moorland and grassland in C&SEEt, generally at 2400–4000m. Feeds in damp grassy areas, sometimes near pools. **Voice** Gives a repeated short and unhurried *tirich-chi-che'e*. **Note** Formerly lumped in Greywing Francolin *S. africanus*.

SAVANNA FRANCOLINS These three species are typical of bushland or grassland habitats, although sometimes at moderate altitudes in highland areas. All were formerly in the genus Francolinus.

Coqui Francolin *Peliperdix coqui*   24cm, 9.5"

A small well-marked francolin. In race *maharao* the adult male has a *chestnut-rufous head and neck*, with black and white barring on the underparts confined to the breast and flanks; the belly is plain buff. Adult female has a buff-chestnut head, a black line above and behind the eye, and another around the throat; the entire underparts are buff with fine barring on the flanks. Immature is similar to female but paler. In flight, all plumages show reddish-brown sides to the tail. **HH** Pairs and family parties are rather local in wooded and bushed grassland in SEt, mainly at 1200–1350m. **Voice** Two very different calls are heard mainly at dawn and dusk, an onomatopoeic and repeated see-sawing *co-kee co-kee co-kee...* which is delivered leisurely and increases in volume, and a growled burry *ke-ke-ke-kekeke kuh* which falls away gradually.

Clapperton's Francolin *Pternistis clappertoni*   34cm, 13.5"

A medium-sized francolin with a red-based blackish bill, *bare red skin around the eyes and a white throat*. Underparts are heavily marked with black. Sexes alike but adult female is smaller. Immature is like female but duller. Two races sometimes recognised: *nigrosquamatus* (W&CEt) and *sharpii* (WEr, NWEt); the latter lacks a dark moustachial. Harwood's Francolin is darker and lacks a white throat. **HH** Pairs and family parties are widespread in bushed grassland in Er and Et, mainly west of the Rift Valley, at 500–2100m. **Voice** Gives a loud grating *kerak...* repeated in a series of 4–6 times.

Yellow-necked Spurfowl *Pternistis leucoscepus*   40cm, 16"

Large francolin with blackish bill, distinctive *bare yellow throat* and red-orange skin around eyes. Brown upperparts have some narrow buff streaking, underparts more heavily streaked brown and white. Females are generally smaller than males and lack leg spurs. Immature is similar, but generally greyer with narrow black barring above and paler yellow throat. In flight reveals large pale patch in primaries. **HH** Pairs and family parties are common residents in drier bushland, bushed and wooded grassland and cultivation in Er and Et (mainly east of Rift Valley), from sea-level to 1600m. **Voice** Gives a loud grating series of up to seven descending, scratchy upslurs that fade away: *k-wirrrk... k-wirrrrrrk... k'wirrrrrrkk'wirrrrrrkk'wirrrrrrk*. [Alt: Yellow-necked Francolin]

ad

lorti

ad

gutturalis

Orange River Francolin

Moorland Francolin

ad

nominate

♀

♂

Coqui Francolin

maharao

ad

Clapperton's Francolin

sharpii

ad

Yellow-necked Spurfowl

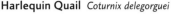

QUAILS Small rotund grassland birds, rarely seen unless flushed when they tend to fly low and straight before dropping into cover and hiding. Most often encountered in pairs, although Harlequin Quail may occur in large numbers on migration.

Harlequin Quail *Coturnix delegorguei*　　　　　　　　　　18cm, 7"

Adult male is dark brown quail with *bold black and white face* pattern *and long white supercilium*. Underparts are rich-rufous and black, with black streaking extending onto flanks. Adult female and immature are very similar to Common Quail but generally darker and less streaked on flanks. **HH** Common and widespread nomadic intra-tropical migrant in grassland and cultivation, mainly in lowlands below 1300m; often appears in large numbers during rains. Present in Et Feb–Aug, and in So May–Jan. Status uncertain on Soc. **Voice** Gives a sharp but rather quiet, rhythmical and insect-like *swit-wit-wit wit-wit-wit wit-wit...*

Common Quail *Coturnix coturnix*　　　　　　　　　　　19cm, 7.5"

Very difficult to tell from female Harlequin Quail, particularly as usually only seen in flight. In breeding race *erlangeri* (highlands of Et) adult male is distinctive with dark chestnut face, but female differs from female Harlequin in being paler overall with heavier streaking on flanks. Both sexes of nominate Palearctic race are also similar, and are paler than Harlequin, especially on cheeks. Adult male may show black throat-patch. **HH** Sometimes common in moist grassland and cultivation up to 2700m, usually at higher altitude than Harlequin Quail. Afrotropical migrant *erlangeri* is present Apr–Oct; nominate Palearctic birds visit Sep–Apr (rare in So). **Voice** Male has a three-part soft but far-carrying *twi twi'wit, twi twi'wit, twi twi'wit...*, female answering with a soft nasal *nrah*.

Blue Quail *Coturnix adansonii*　　　　　　　　　　　　14cm, 5.5"

Adult male is *small dark quail without white supercilium*. Black and white throat contrasts with *dark slate-blue body plumage and rufous wing-patches*. Adult female is generally dark brown with much mottling, paler throat and *strongly barred underparts*. Appears very small and dark on wing. **HH** Uncommon nomadic species of W and C Africa; 5 records reported in W&CEt but none fully acceptable. **Voice** Gives a trisyllabic whistled piping *kew kew yew*, descending in half-tones, first note slightly louder.

BUTTONQUAILS Tiny secretive quail-like birds usually only seen when flushed (and hard to flush a second time). With experience, small size and whirring flight identify them as buttonquails. Often appear slimmer than quails, with longer bill. Male is responsible for incubation and rearing the young.

Common Buttonquail *Turnix sylvaticus*　　　　　　　　14cm, 5.5"

If seen well, adult shows *pale eyes*, very scaly upperparts, *rufous-orange wash across breast, and black spots on sides of breast and flanks*. Adult female is brighter than male. Immature is like male but more spotted across breast. In flight, *pale upperwing-coverts contrast with darker flight feathers*; rump and tail barred brown. More round-winged and hesitant flight than true quails. Race in Africa is *lepuranus*. **HH** Uncommon resident and intra-tropical migrant to dry and moist grassland, and rough cultivation, from sea-level to 2000m. Absent from much of W&EEt and NSo. Single birds and pairs are most often seen; can be more numerous during influxes. **Voice** Female has a soft resonant fog-horn-like bugle that increases in volume, *whooooooooooo*. [Alt: Kurrichane Buttonquail, Little Buttonquail]

Quail-plover *Ortyxelos meiffrenii*　　　　　　　　　　13cm, 5"

Very small strange bird which may suggest a tiny courser or even a lark. Standing birds are well camouflaged but show *unique bold black and white wing pattern in flight*. Female brighter than male, and immature paler. **HH** Rare in semi-arid grasslands in SEt, and perhaps partially migratory. One record on Sudanese side of border with WEr. Recorded at 900–1800m. Disturbed birds run, freeze, or may rock forwards in slow walk. **Voice** Reported to give a soft low whistle, but silent when flushed. [Alt: Lark Buttonquail]

Harlequin Quail

♀

♂

Blue Quail

♂

♀

Common Quail

nominate

erlangeri

Common Buttonquail

♀

Quail-plover

♀

FLUFFTAILS Tiny secretive rails which are extremely difficult to see. Usually only located by call. All males have chestnut on the head, but colour of tail and presence of spots or streaking on the body and wings aid identification. Females are even harder to observe and identify, and are described below.

Buff-spotted Flufftail *Sarothrura elegans*   16cm, 6.5"

Adult male has bright chestnut-red head and breast, blackish-brown back and wings *heavily spotted with buff* (sometimes appearing very dense and mottled), and rufous-and-black banded tail. Adult female is brown above, spangled with pale buff and black, largely dingy olive-brown below with whitish throat and extensive darker brown-and-buff barring. Immature is like adult female but plainer and duller. Race in NE Africa is nominate. **HH** Rare elusive resident of forest, juniper and dense thickets (not necessarily near water), mainly in highlands of S&WEt at 1250–2200m, notably at Bulcha Forest. Also occurs as erratic wanderer, turning up in unexpected places like city gardens. Vagrant NSo (once). **Voice** Often heard after rain and sometimes throughout night; distinctive far-carrying fog-horn note grows in volume, each call lasting c.3 seconds and is given roughly every 10 seconds.

Red-chested Flufftail *Sarothrura rufa*   16cm, 6.5"

Adult male has deep chestnut-red head, upper back and breast; rest of plumage is black with narrow white streaks, and *small white spots on tail*. Adult female is dark brown above, spotted or lightly barred buff, brown below scaled and barred buff, with whitish throat and belly. Immature like female but plainer and darker. Race in Et is *elizabethae*. Both other flufftails in region have banded tails. **HH** Secretive breeding visitor (or resident) of bogs, swamps and marshes in W&CEt, at 1200–2600m, recorded May–Oct. **Voice** Calls all year with long series of accelerating *e-wump...* notes, and also a nasal upslurred *wiiwiiwiiwii*.

White-winged Flufftail *Sarothrura ayresi*   14cm, 5.5"

Slightly smaller than other flufftails. Adult male has head, upper back and breast mainly chestnut, with darker crown, lores and cheeks; chin and throat whitish. Rest of upperparts blackish-brown with narrow white streaks; tail barred black and rufous. Flanks streaked black and white, *rest of underparts white*. Adult female is similar but rufous restricted to neck and sides of breast. Upperparts and flanks tend to be spotted rather than streaked. Immature is browner with some barring on breast. *In flight, both sexes show prominent white secondaries.* **HH** Rare breeding visitor (Jun–Sep) to wet grasslands and marshes at 1800–2600m on CEt plateau north of Addis Ababa; currently known from just three sites including Weserbi on Sululta Plain and Berga. Absent in dry season; non-breeding grounds of Et population unknown, possibly SWEt (or even South Africa). **Voice** A deep, low *oooh oooh*. **EN**

Black Crake *Amaurornis flavirostra*   21cm, 8"

Small distinctive *black crake with yellow-green bill and red eyes and legs*. Sexes alike. Immature is browner above and greyer below with whitish throat and duller bill and legs. **HH** Pairs and small groups are widespread and often common in Et on virtually any lake or small pool with fringing and floating vegetation, especially in Rift Valley; locally fairly common in SSo but only one record in NSo. Occurs from sea-level to 1800m. Often walks in open at any time of day. **Voice** Call is a frequently heard and noisy duet: one bird makes a complex and musical bubbling while the other responds with low growls.

Buff-spotted Flufftail

Red-chested Flufftail

White-winged Flufftail

Black Crake

CRAKES A varied and mostly secretive group of terrestrial birds inhabiting moist grasslands, rank vegetation, and temporary and permanent swamps. Invariably brief views hinder identification. With similar species look for bill and leg colour, extent of spots and streaks above, and barring (if any) on flanks.

African Crake Crex egregia   22cm, 8.5″

Adult is like several other crakes with mottled brown upperparts, grey face and breast, and black-and-white barred flanks and belly. Best identified by yellow-green or grey bill with pinkish-red base, *narrow white supercilium and no white streaking or spots on upperparts*. Sexes similar. Immature duller, with fainter supercilium and brown bill, brownish face and throat, and less distinct barring on flanks. **HH** Shy and very rare intra-African migrant to marsh and swamp edges, rank and wet grass. Only a few records in C&SWEt, at 700–2500m, but has bred. **Voice** Gives a dry *krik-krik-krik-krik...*, also a quiet francolin-like *chi-co* with second note lower and rather questioning.

Corncrake Crex crex   28cm, 11″

Larger than African Crake, but overall tone much more buffy-brown, with pale pinkish-brown bill, broad grey supercilium, greyish throat and breast, and rest of the underparts pale and barred russet on flanks. *Striking bright rufous wing-coverts obvious in flight.* Sexes similar, but female may show less grey on foreneck. Immature duller and less heavily patterned. **HH** Uncommon Palearctic passage migrant to both dry and wet grasslands in Sep–Oct and Mar–May, from sea-level to 2700m; rare in So; vagrant Soc. **Voice** Silent in Africa, but male utters repeated advertising *crek-crek* when breeding. **NT**

Spotted Crake Porzana porzana   23cm, 9″

Small dark brown crake *with extensive white spots and flecks above and below*, barred flanks, and *plain buff undertail-coverts*. Adult male has grey face and throat well spotted with white and short thick yellow-green bill with red base. Female has less grey on face and throat. Immature is browner including sides of face and breast. **HH** Very scarce Palearctic passage migrant to swamps, marshes and wet grasslands from sea-level to 2400m, with scattered records throughout, Sep–Oct and Apr–May; more frequent in Er and very rare in NWSo (three old records) and Dj (once, Jan). **Voice** Silent in region.

Baillon's Crake Porzana pusilla   18cm, 7″

Very small brown and grey crake; adult male best told from Little Crake by *plain greenish bill, slightly heavier white streaks, rings and squiggles on back and wing-coverts, and more strongly barred flanks*; also has shorter primaries. Adult female is similar but paler on throat and breast. Immature is buff-brown below, with pale throat, and buff-brown barred flanks. **HH** Resident race *obscura* is rare in marshes and dense lakeside vegetation at 1500–2400m in CEt; known to wander locally and probably joined by migrant Palearctic race *intermedia* from Nov–Apr; one old record in NWSo and vagrant on Soc. **Voice** Gives a frequent very sharp *tik*, various rasping noises, a loud wooden rattling, and other calls with a laughing quality.

Little Crake Porzana parva   19cm, 7.5″

Very like Baillon's Crake, but adult has *red base to pale green bill*. Adult male is duller above with fewer solid white streaks, *almost plain brown wing-coverts*, longer primaries, and *less distinct barring confined to lower flanks, vent and undertail-coverts*. Adult female is *buff-brown below* with whiter throat and breast. Immature is like female, but whiter below, more spotted above, and with more extensive barred flanks. **HH** Rare Palearctic migrant and probable winter visitor with records from Er (Sep–Dec), NWEt (Sep–Oct and Apr) and NWSo (Sep–Oct). Vagrant Soc. **Voice** Silent in region.

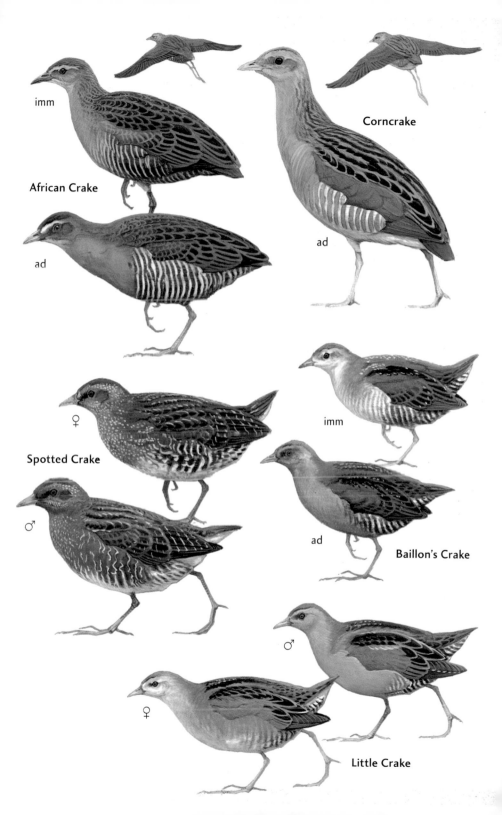

imm

African Crake

ad

Corncrake

ad

Spotted Crake

♀

♂

imm

ad

Baillon's Crake

♂

♀

Little Crake

GALLINULES *Two bulky rallids, similar to moorhens in structure (plate 53), but rather secretive inhabitants of dense reedbeds and swamps; adapted to walk on floating vegetation and readily climbs Typha stems to feed or roost.*

Allen's Gallinule *Porphyrio alleni* 26cm, 10"

Similar to Purple Swamphen, but *much smaller with red bill and greenish-blue frontal shield.* Sexes alike but frontal shield apple-green in breeding female. Immature largely brown with buff fringes to back and wings, whiter throat and belly, and rich buff undertail-coverts; in good light shows *blue-green centres to some wing-coverts and flight feathers.* Bill is dark with red base, legs dull olive or red-brown. **HH** Widespread but generally scarce in most of Et, Jun–Nov, although in years of good rains large influxes may occur; scarce in SSo with one breeding record, and only one old record from Er. Inhabits well-vegetated swamps, marshes and lakes from sea-level to 1800m. **Voice** Vocal, calling a loud clucking *kuk kuk kuk...* and nasal moans. [Alt: Lesser Gallinule]

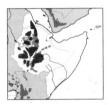

Purple Swamphen *Porphyrio porphyrio* 46cm, 18"

Enormous purplish-blue and green rallid with white undertail-coverts, *heavy red bill and frontal shield, thick red legs and long toes.* Sexes alike. Immature is duller grey-blue, especially pale on belly, with browner not bronzy-green back and innerwings: bill, frontal shield and legs are duller. Race in tropical Africa is *madagascariensis.* **HH** Pairs and small groups are widespread in Et, but uncommon to rare, in larger marshes and swamps up to 1800m; vagrant So (twice). Generally shy and retiring, but feeds in open where not disturbed. **Voice** Loud and varied repertoire, consisting of strong trumpeting and bugling calls. **Note** The various forms worldwide are sometimes considered separate species, with birds in tropical Africa known as African Swamphen *P. madagascariensis.* [Alt: Purple Gallinule]

RAILS *Somewhat longer-billed than crakes, but similarly secretive inhabitants of dense vegetation and swamps. Note bill colour, markings on flanks and colour of undertail-coverts.*

Rouget's Rail *Rougetius rougetii* 30cm, 12"

Adult is unmistakable, with *plain olive-brown upperparts, and cinnamon-rufous underparts contrasting with gleaming white undertail-coverts.* Chin whitish and lower flanks olive-brown. Rather long bill is dark red, as are legs. Sexes alike. Immature is paler than adult with brownish bill. **HH** ENDEMIC to Er and Et; widespread and fairly common in montane grasslands and moorlands, at 1700–4100m. Inhabits lush habitats by pools and streams, as well as marshes and bogs; sometimes in dry habitats. Often less shy than other rails and may be seen in open at any time of day. Flicks tail when walking revealing prominent white undertail-coverts. **Voice** Calls after or during wet periods; long series starts with loud piercing rapid *wi-hi-hi-hi-hi-hi-hi* breaking into rasping duet of *kurrrick kreeeeek*, first note rising, second on same pitch. **NT**

African Rail *Rallus caerulescens* 28cm, 11"

Dark brown and grey rail with *long red bill, red legs*, and black-and-white barred flanks. Only other rail in region with long bill (apart from vagrant Water Rail) is Rouget's, which is rufous below with extensive white undertail-coverts. *Upperparts are plain dark brown*, underparts mainly slate-grey; chin and lateral undertail-coverts white. Sexes alike. Immature similar but browner on head and breast, with diffuse bars on flanks and duller bill and legs. **HH** Widespread presumed resident in highlands of C&WEt, but generally uncommon to rare, in wide range of swamps and marshes at 1350–2000m. **Voice** Gives a forced series of squealed notes that break into a long trilled and descending *pipipipipipipipi....pi pi pi*, last notes slower and downslurred. [Alt: African Water Rail]

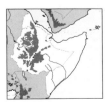

Water Rail *Rallus aquaticus* 26cm, 10"

Similar to African Rail, but slightly smaller with *olive-brown upperparts boldly streaked blackish.* Adult has face, neck and chin to upper belly slate-blue (African Rail has whitish chin). Barring on flanks and belly is less extensive than on African Rail, *undertail-coverts wholly white and legs fleshy.* Sexes alike. Immature duller and browner with dark cap, brownish face, whitish chin, and brown-and-white barred flanks; adult's grey underparts are replaced by buffy-white and undertail-coverts are buff; bill duller than adult's and less red. **HH** Palearctic vagrant to Soc; generally inhabits dense reedbeds. **Voice** Gives a variety of squeals from cover, reminiscent of piglet, but likely to be silent in region.

imm

ad

Allen's Gallinule

Purple Swamphen

imm

ad

Rouget's Rail

ad

imm

imm

ad

African Rail

imm

ad

Water Rail

COOTS AND MOORHENS Bulky-bodied, small-headed, blackish rallids which are widespread and familiar. Colour of bill and head-shield easily identifies adults, but care is needed with immature plumages. Sexes are alike.

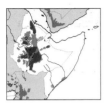

Red-knobbed Coot *Fulica cristata*   40cm, 16"

Very dark grey-black rallid with striking white bill and frontal shield. Breeding adult has *two swollen red knobs above frontal shield*, but hard to see at distance and quickly reduced and darker after breeding. At close range, *feathering in front of eye is rounded* (ends in point in Eurasian Coot), and top of frontal shield is straighter and more squared-off. White bill is often tinged bluish. In flight wings are all dark. Immature lacks frontal shield and is more brownish-grey above, with paler grey underparts and variable white on face and throat. **HH** Small flocks are common on lakes and pools in Er and Et up to 3300m (though rare in So). Non-breeding flocks of hundreds may gather on freshwater lakes in Rift Valley and nearby highlands. **Voice** Varied single calls include a nasal *krrk*, reverberating *iuenk*, and deeper *ernh,* also an occasional metallic chinking. [Alt: Crested Coot]

Eurasian Coot *Fulica atra*   42cm, 17"

Very like Red-knobbed Coot but *lacks red knobs* at all times. At close range, *feathering in front of eye ends in point at base of frontal shield* (rounded in Red-knobbed Coot), and top of frontal shield more rounded; bill is creamy-white, often tinged pinkish. In flight, *shows narrow white trailing edge to secondaries* (lacking in Red-knobbed Coot). Immature is grey-brown, darker on crown and nape, with foreneck and breast mainly whitish, and bill grey. Race in Africa is nominate. **HH** Palearctic vagrant to Dj and Soc. **Voice** Silent in region, but calls are higher-pitched than Red-knobbed; has strident metallic chink given as contact and alarm calls. [Alt: Common Coot]

Common Moorhen *Gallinula chloropus*   35cm, 14"

Blackish rallid with *yellow-tipped red bill and rounded red frontal shield*, white stripes along flanks and white undertail-coverts (with black central stripe). Mantle and wings browner than rest of plumage. *Legs yellow-green with red garter above 'knee'.* Immature generally all dull brown above with dark olive bill and no frontal shield, paler below with whitish throat and buffy flank-stripes; legs dull greenish. **HH** Singles, pairs and family groups are fairly common up to 2400m in Er and Et, but local in So and an uncommon visitor on Soc. Resident race is *meridionalis*; nominate birds from Palearctic may reach region in winter. Prefers well-vegetated fresh water, and frequently swims in open. **Voice** Highly vocal and quarrelsome. Calls are nasal, loud and explosive, either single notes or rattled series.

Lesser Moorhen *Gallinula angulata*   23cm, 9"

Smaller than Common Moorhen with a *mostly bright yellow bill* (red only along top) and *small pointed red frontal shield*; legs greenish-yellow, lacking red garter. Adult male otherwise similar in plumage to Common Moorhen, but female paler and browner above with pale grey face and underparts, and smaller frontal shield. Immature is dull brown above with paler underparts and yellowish bill (immature Common has dark bill and darker flanks). **HH** Very uncommon intra-African breeding migrant in Et, May–Nov; two old records SSo and one recent record in Er. Much shyer than Common Moorhen, keeping to cover in well-vegetated wetlands and seasonal pools. **Voice** Calls are similar to Common Moorhen, but more bubbly and querulous.

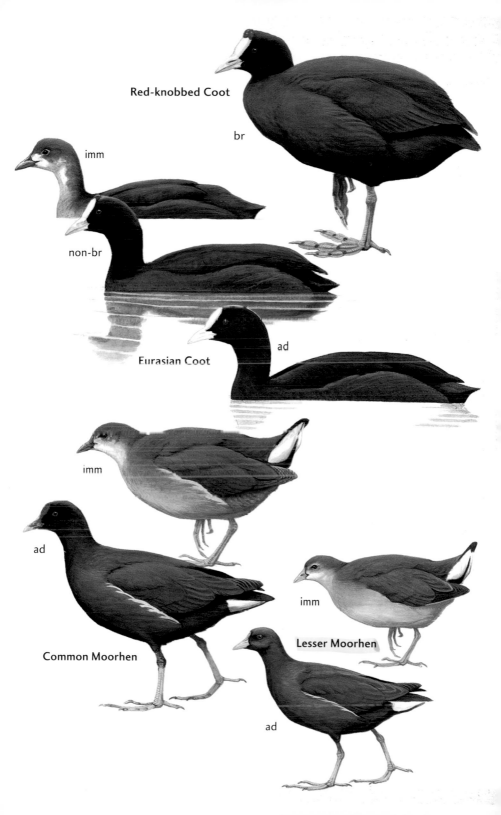

Red-knobbed Coot

br

imm

non-br

Eurasian Coot

ad

imm

ad

Common Moorhen

imm

Lesser Moorhen

ad

CRANES *Attractive tall birds of wetlands and moist agricultural land, all easily identified if seen well. Crowned and Wattled Cranes are unmistakable; Common and Demoiselle Cranes are separated by head and neck pattern, and by size. Sexes very similar, but females slightly smaller. Immature birds tend to be duller than adults. Resident cranes perform elaborate courtship dances. Flight is slow and majestic, with neck and legs outstretched.*

Black Crowned Crane *Balearica pavonina*   100cm, 40"

Adult is *largely blackish* with dark chestnut, black and white wings, *bristly golden crown, mostly red cheeks edged above with white, and small red wattle on throat.* In flight looks hunched and laboured with lowered neck and bowed wings revealing extensive white on upperwing contrasting with black and chestnut flight feathers. Immature is smaller with shorter crest, rufous head and neck, and rufous-fringed body plumage. Race in Et is *ceciliae.* **HH** Pairs, family groups and larger flocks are widespread in W&CEt up to 2000m in wide range of wetter habitats, including swamps, inundated grasslands and moister agricultural land, but will range well away from wetter areas to feed. Makes local seasonal movements. **Voice** Gives a loud atmospheric bugling *ooh-eyannh* or *oh-wang*; also a single *wonk*, or *ka-wonk.* **NT**

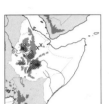

Wattled Crane *Bugeranus carunculatus*   120cm, 48"

Very large stately grey and white crane with dark cap, *bare red face and feathered white wattles*; largely white face and *gleaming white neck* visible even at great distance. Rest of plumage black and grey, with elongated inner secondaries drooping over tail. In flight, white neck contrasts with dark wings and body. Immature is duller and rather browner, with pale (not dark grey) crown, duller face and smaller wattles. **HH** Pairs, family groups and sometimes larger flocks are resident on permanent swamps, rivers and wet grasslands in W&CEt at 1700–4000m. **Voice** A high-pitched burry bugling. **VU**

Common Crane *Grus grus*   115cm, 46"

Adult is mainly grey with black head and upper neck and *broad white stripe on sides of neck.* Small red patch on crown hard to see at distance. Elongated inner secondaries droop over tail and are tipped blackish, appearing much bushier than sleek feathers of Demoiselle and Wattled Cranes. Grey upperparts sometimes stained brown. In flight, grey wing-coverts contrast with black flight feathers. Immature is smaller and duller, with less bulky inner secondaries and without striking adult head and neck pattern; instead head is variably washed with buff or pale rufous. **HH** Occasional Palearctic winter visitor to Er and N&CEt at 1650–2950m, mainly Oct–Mar. Vagrant Dj and Soc. Gregarious in winter, often in large flocks. Feeds in wet and dry areas, roosting near water. Pairs regularly perform dancing behaviour on wintering grounds. **Voice** Groups of migrants give muffled bugling whilst feeding and in flight.

Demoiselle Crane *Anthropoides virgo*   95cm, 38"

Distinctly smaller and slimmer than Common Crane. Adult is black-necked grey or dark grey crane with *long black breast feathers, white plumes extending from eye to hindneck* and sleek elongated inner secondaries drooping over tail. Common Crane has black and white neck and bulkier inner secondaries. In flight appears mainly blackish and grey, lacking contrast of other cranes, but shows more black on neck than Common. Immature much duller than adult, with less well-defined plumes behind eyes and only a hint of black foreneck. **HH** Rare Palearctic winter visitor to Er and N&WEt, Oct–Mar. Vagrant Dj. Inhabits savannas, cultivation and marshes, mainly below 2000m. Gregarious in winter, sometimes mixing with Common Cranes. **Voice** Migrating birds call *grro.* Other calls similar to Common Crane.

Wattled Crane

ad

imm

ad

imm

Black Crowned Crane

ad

imm

Common Crane

imm

imm

Demoiselle Crane

ad

ad

LARGE BUSTARDS *Stately birds which prefer to walk purposefully, only taking wing when disturbed. Males have spectacular balloon displays, visible over long distances, and are larger than females. All are easily identified if seen well.*

Denham's Bustard *Neotis denhami* ♂ 115cm, 46"

Male is large with *extensive triangular chestnut-rufous patch on hindneck*, black-and-white striped crown and face, pale grey neck, extensive black and white coverts, and white belly. Female is smaller with brown crown-centre and slightly paler rufous hindneck. Immature is like female. Race in Et is nominate. **HH** Very rare intra-African migrant in open and lightly bushed or wooded grassland in WEt, at 400-1750m (at eastern edge of range). Displaying male inflates white throat and chest hugely and expands chestnut nape, either striding with tail raised or standing tall with tail lowered. **Voice** Usually silent, but breeding male gives low resonant booms; also a barked *kaa-kaa* in alarm. [Alt: Stanley's Bustard] **NT**

Heuglin's Bustard *Neotis heuglinii* ♂ 88cm, 35"

Large black-faced bustard; male has *black crown, mask and chin*, blue-grey neck, and chestnut band on lower breast separated from white belly by narrow black line. Female is smaller, more subdued, face striped not black. Immature like female. In flight, reveals white primary wedge in dark upperwing. **HH** Singles and pairs are fairly common and widespread in arid and semi-arid country, including desert edge, in lowland areas of S&EEt and So (except SE) from sea-level to 700m. Very rare in Er. **Voice** Not known—probably mostly silent.

Kori Bustard *Ardeotis kori* ♂ 125cm, 50"

Largest bustard; crested head, black collar and extensive *black and white patterning at bend of closed wing* distinctive. Sexes similar, but adult female smaller and more lightly built. Immature is like a less clearly marked female. Prefers to walk, but will fly; adult male is world's heaviest flying bird. Race in NE Africa is *struthiunculus*. **HH** Singles and small groups are widespread and sometimes common in open grassland up to 1600m in S&EEt and NWSo (plus two old records in SSo). Displaying male inflates throat-ruff and chest, lowers wings, and lifts tail to reveal mass of soft white undertail-coverts. **Voice** Male gives a low resonant *voomp* at intervals of up to 10 seconds and both sexes may utter harsh *craark* when disturbed.

Arabian Bustard *Ardeotis arabs* ♂ 90cm, 36"

Significantly smaller, more elegant version of Kori Bustard, with *white-chequered wing-covert pattern at bend of wing* (not black and white). Sexes similar, but adult female smaller and rather greyer. Immature is similar to adult, but much duller, lacking contrast in wing. Three races occur: *stieberi* (NWEr, NWEt) has orange-brown upperparts; nominate *arabs* (coastal Er, Dj, NEEt, NWSo) is greyer above with reduced spotting on coverts; *butleri* (WEt) is slightly darker above, with greyer neck. **HH** Singles and pairs are locally fairly common residents in arid and desert country up to 900m (but uncommon in So). **Voice** Rasping or honking croaked *pah pah* when displaying.

MacQueen's Bustard *Chlamydotis macqueenii* ♂ 65cm, 26"

Pale, medium-sized bustard with sandy upperparts finely vermiculated with brown. Adult has *blue-grey neck with black stripe on side of neck*, and white crown-tuft with black centre. Sexes similar but female smaller, greyer and less boldly marked. Immature lacks black neck-stripe. In flight shows striking wing pattern with black flight feathers contrasting with white primary flash and sandy-brown upperwing-coverts; underwing largely white with black trailing edge and wing-tips. Flight action distinctive, with slow wing-beats and jerky upstroke. **HH** Vagrant Soc (once), from Arabia or Central Asia. **Voice** Silent in region. **Note** Formerly treated as conspecific with Houbara Bustard *C. undulata* of North Africa. **VU**

♀

♂ Denham's Bustard

♀ Heuglin's Bustard

♂

♀

♂

imm Kori Bustard

♂

stieberi Arabian Bustard

♂ MacQueen's Bustard

SMALLER BUSTARDS *Males can easily be identified on plumage and call, while females and similar immatures present more of a challenge. Most call and perform aerial displays which are strikingly different from the ground-based displays of larger bustards (plate 55).*

Buff-crested Bustard *Lophotis gindiana*   53cm, 21"

Small, relatively short-legged bustard; male has warm buff-brown back marked with darker brown spots and bars, *pale rufous crown and cheeks, black throat-line and belly*, and unbarred tail. Crest only visible in ground display. Female is similar, but crown mottled and buff neck well barred, with black confined to belly. Immature is like female. From above, flying birds show well-patterned flight feathers and small white wedge on coverts. **HH** Singles and pairs are common in arid and semi-arid bushland up to 1700m in Et (east of Rift Valley) and So. Adult male has rocket display, flying up and tumbling on closed wings, to stall and land at last minute. **Voice** Loud shrill calls may lead to an aerial display in which male calls an accelerating series *kri-kri-kri*, slowing down towards end.

White-bellied Bustard *Eupodotis senegalensis*   60cm, 24"

Male has rather plain brown back and wings, blue-grey neck, and *black and white face pattern with pinkish-red base to bill*, and white belly. Female is similar, but browner and more washed out, with blue-grey confined to hindneck. Immature is browner, lacking blue-grey tones. In flight, shows mainly white underwings and belly. Two races occur, but precise distribution not known: canicollis (S&EEt, So) has narrow black line from base of bill to below and behind eye; nominate senegalensis (Er, NWEt) is smaller with white chin and lacking black eye-line. **HH** Pairs and family groups are common in wide range of open grassland and semi-desert below 1450m, usually with bush or tree cover. Adult male has subdued display, walking near female, raising crest, craning neck, and puffing up throat. **Voice** Has a loud, far-carrying, rather goose-like cackling duet: male gives *ah-nghaa-nghaa*, female replies *eh-e-e-er*.

Little Brown Bustard *Eupodotis humilis*   45cm, 18"

Small pale bustard with white belly. Male has *black throat finely spotted with white, and black tuft on nape*. Female is much plainer; *breast and upperparts heavily spotted buff*. Female White-bellied is darker with grey hindneck and vermiculations rather than spots on upperparts. Both sexes show blackish flight feathers. In flight, shows long narrow white wing-bar separating dark flight feathers from sandy wing-coverts. **HH** ENDEMIC. Singles or pairs are fairly common in SEEt and N&CSo, usually on red sandy soils in open areas with thick scrub from near sea-level to 1500m. **Voice** Call described as high-pitched rattle, *we-we-we*, given with head thrown backwards. **NT**

Black-bellied Bustard *Lissotis melanogaster*   63cm, 25"

Male is medium-sized, black-bellied bustard. Distinguished from very similar Hartlaub's by *less black on face, greyer-brown cheeks, very slender brown-backed neck*, and brown and buff rump and tail barred dark brown. Female separated by slender *plain brown neck*. Immature like adult female. In flight, male is black below with large white patch in primaries and *black trailing edge to secondaries* on upperwing. **HH** Singles and pairs are widespread and fairly common in lusher open, bushed and wooded grassland up to 3000m in Et, but rare in Er and SSo. In display flight climbs with exaggerated wing-beats and glides to ground. **Voice** Displaying male starts with intake of breath, makes loud nasal upslur (followed by pause of up to 10 seconds) before short low growl and explosive pop.

Hartlaub's Bustard *Lissotis hartlaubii*   70cm, 28"

Male is more thickset and crisply marked than Black-bellied Bustard. Identified by *white 'thumb print' over ear-coverts which contrasts with blacker face, thicker silvery-grey-backed neck*, and black rump and barred dark brown tail. Female is separated from extremely similar Black-bellied by *rather darker tones, cream line down foreneck, and speckled (not plain) brown hindneck*. Immature similar but duller. In flight, male shows blackish rump and tail, and *only inner secondaries have black trailing edge*. **HH** Pairs and family parties are patchily distributed in C&SEt in drier bushed grassland and open plains up to 1800m; rare in S&NWSo. Tends to prefer shorter grass and less dense vegetation than Black-bellied. Male has striking parachute display similar to Black-bellied. **Voice** Displaying male has quiet click, then slightly louder *pop* (like cork from bottle) followed by quiet deep drawn-out moaning *booooom*.

Buff-crested
Bustard

White-bellied
Bustard

canicollis

nominate

Little Brown
Bustard

Black-bellied
Bustard

Hartlaub's
Bustard

JACANAS are striking, long-legged, long-toed waterbirds which walk and feed on floating vegetation. Adults are easily identified, but beware confusion between Lesser and half-grown immature African. PAINTED-SNIPE is a somewhat crepuscular dumpy snipe-like bird which often hides in dense vegetation during the day. Duller male is responsible for nest building, incubation and raising young. PHALAROPES are slender graceful waders that habitually swim, spinning in circles and picking food items from surface of water. Like painted-snipe they exhibit reversed sexual roles.

African Jacana *Actophilornis africanus*　　　　　31 cm, 12"

Adult is striking chestnut and white waterbird, with *powder-blue bill and frontal shield*, black hindneck, and *dark chestnut from lower breast to vent*. Sexes similar but female slightly larger than male. In rather weak flight wings are *chestnut and black*. Immature is paler and duller brown above, with white supercilium and small greyish frontal shield (hard to see); underparts mostly white washed yellowish at sides of breast. **HH** Widespread and common resident of freshwater ponds and lakes with good surface cover, from sea-level to 2000m. **Voice** Noisy, calling a series of rapid repeated rattling notes, shrill squeals and aggressive trills.

Lesser Jacana *Microparra capensis*　　　　　16 cm, 6.5"

Very small jacana which looks brown above and white below at distance. Close birds show rufous crown and nape (some are black on forecrown), white supercilium, narrow rufous eye-stripe, and golden-yellow and rufous patches at sides of breast. Sexes alike. In flight reveals conspicuous *white trailing edge to most of wing, and rufous rump and tail*. Immature is paler and duller than adult, with black rump. **HH** Rare resident in Et at 1650–1800m, on vegetated lakes and pools in Rift Valley and Lake Tana. **Voice** Gives a simple series of rattled chitters that rise and fall in tone.

Pheasant-tailed Jacana *Hydrophasianus chirurgus*　　　Non-br. 31 cm, 12"

Non-breeding adult is mainly brownish above and white below with prominent *dark line down sides of neck, extending into band across breast*. Breeding adult (not likely in region) unmistakable, with white head, golden-yellow hindneck, dark chestnut plumage with white wing-coverts, and *long downcurved tail*. In flight, has white wings with dark tips. Immature like non-breeding adult but has rufous cap and often lacks breast-band. **HH** Vagrant from Indian subcontinent to Soc (twice). **Voice** Silent in region.

Greater Painted-snipe *Rostratula benghalensis*　　　24 cm, 9.5"

Unmistakable if seen well, with *long, slightly drooping bill, rotund tail-less appearance, and pronounced stripe around and behind eye*. Noticeable light saddle-like ring separates fore and hind body. Male much duller than female, but with more conspicuous buff-gold spots on wing-coverts; lacks her rich chestnut head, neck and upper breast. Immature like male, but paler and less spotted. Flies weakly on rounded wings, often with dangling legs. Race in Africa is nominate. **HH** Uncommon resident and erratic wanderer in Et and SSo up to 1650m, inhabiting well-vegetated fresh and alkaline water margins; most frequent in Rift Valley. Skulking habits and cryptic plumage render it easy to overlook. **Voice** Female has a long call during rains, starting with series of dove-like slurred *oo-o*, rising then falling in tone, followed by series of hiccups.

Red-necked Phalarope *Phalaropus lobatus*　　　18 cm, 7"

Small-headed, slender-necked shorebird with *needle-thin black bill*. Non-breeding adult is grey above, white below with black smudge behind eye. Breeding female has dark grey face, upperparts and breast, with white chin, *rufous sides to neck*, and buffy stripes on back. Breeding male is similar but duller. **HH** Common Palearctic passage migrant and winter visitor on coast of So (especially NE and SE) and offshore, including Soc, sometimes in large numbers, Sep–May. Vagrant Dj. Rare inland, mainly on Rift Valley lakes. **Voice** Flying birds utter a low, churred trill of four identical notes *trrt-trrt-trrt-trrt*. [Alt: Northern Phalarope]

Grey Phalarope *Phalaropus fulicarius*　　　20 cm, 8"

Non-breeding adult is very like Red-necked Phalarope but larger, with *heavier, broader bill*, and paler, plainer mantle. Breeding female has black-tipped yellow bill, black cap, white cheeks and brick-red underparts. Breeding male similar, but duller. **HH** Vagrant to Et (once, Jan 1973). **Voice** Rarely gives a simple *chit* in flight. [Alt: Red Phalarope]

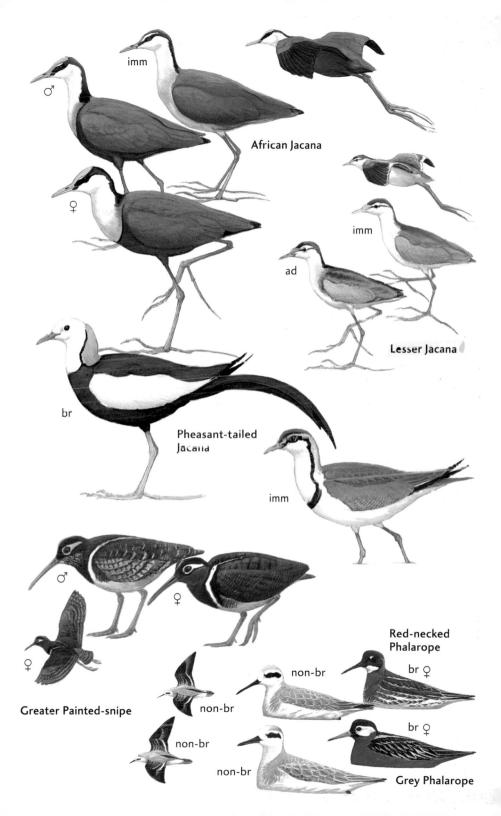

imm

♂

African Jacana

♀

imm

ad

Lesser Jacana

br

Pheasant-tailed Jacana

imm

♂

♀

♀

Greater Painted-snipe

Red-necked Phalarope

non-br

non-br

br ♀

non-br

non-br

br ♀

Grey Phalarope

Four unmistakable, boldly marked, large black and white shorebirds in three different families which can be identified by plumage pattern, shape of bill, and leg colour. All have distinct flight calls.

Black-winged Stilt *Himantopus himantopus*   38 cm, 15"

Tall elegant black and white wader with *thin bill and very long pinkish-red legs.* In adult, crown and hindneck vary from pure white to white with variable amounts of dark-grey. Female differs from male by browner back. Immature is duller with pale fringes to brownish back and wings. In flight, *stiff black wings contrast with white body and long trailing pink legs.* **HH** Common at wide range of waters, including alkaline and freshwater lakes, flooded fields and coastal lagoons up to 3300m. Breeds regularly in Et and Soc. Numbers increase from Aug–Apr, presumably Palearctic migrants. **Voice** Sharp distinct pinking call, based around *kek-kek-kek…* or *kik-kik-kik-…*

Pied Avocet *Recurvirostra avosetta*   43 cm, 17"

Distinct black and white shorebird with *slender upcurved black bill, black cap and hindneck, and long blue-grey legs.* Sexes similar, but male has longer bill than female. Immature has browner markings with some grey-brown mottling to back and wings. In stiff-winged flight, shows distinct black and white pattern and long trailing legs. **HH** Local but widespread non-breeding intra-tropical migrant on range of alkaline and freshwater lakes up to 2500m, especially on alkaline lakes in Rift Valley, and present throughout year. Rare in Er and So, all Sep–May. Has distinct feeding action, walking in shallow water and sweeping bill from side to side. **Voice** Quite vocal; a metallic sharp *ink-ink-ink…*

Crab-plover *Dromas ardeola*   41 cm, 16"

Rather large-headed black and white shorebird with *heavy black bill and blue-grey legs.* Sexes alike. Immature has some dark streaking on crown and mantle, and wings washed grey. In slow heavy flight, large bill is distinctive. **HH** Singles and flocks are present all year on coastal flats in Er, Dj and So, but mainly Mar–Nov at regular sites. Breeds colonially in burrows, at just a handful of locations worldwide; at least 8000 pairs counted on Eritrean coastal islands in 2005–07, representing largest population in world. Vagrant Soc. Feeds plover-like, with a stalk, short run, stop and stab. **Voice** Noisy; has a musical and mournful *kerrui* or *kirruerk,* either singly or in long series.

Eurasian Oystercatcher *Haematopus ostralegus*   43 cm, 17"

Thickset black and white shorebird with *bright orange-red bill and pinkish-orange legs.* Sexes similar. Non-breeding adult has white bar across throat. Immature dirtier than non-breeding adult with brown-tinged upperparts; bill and legs less bright. In flight, bold white wing-bar and bright orange-red bill highly distinctive. Race concerned is *longipes* from central Palearctic. **HH** Singles and small groups are fairly common to uncommon passage migrants to coasts of Er, Dj and So, mainly Jul–Nov and Mar–May. Some birds oversummer. Vagrant Soc. **Voice** Gives an occasional high-pitched piping.

Black-winged Stilt

ad

imm

ad

Pied Avocet

ad

imm

ad

imm

ad

Crab-plover

ad

br

Eurasian
Oystercatcher

non-br

THICK-KNEES Also known as dikkops or stone curlews, this family is easily identified as a group by well-camouflaged brown plumage, large yellow eyes, and long thick yellowish legs (hence name). Mainly nocturnal, they seek shade and stand hunched and inactive during most of the day, freezing or squatting if disturbed. Identification of streaked species can be difficult: note markings on wing-coverts, extent of yellow on bill, as well as habitat and range. Sexes and immatures are all very similar. Loud, far-carrying calls are often heard at night.

Spotted Thick-knee *Burhinus capensis* 43cm, 17"

Only spotted species: *bold black spots over most of upperparts and wings, no bar across wing-coverts*. Ground colour varies from buff-brown in paler *dodsoni* (coastal Er, Dj, NSo), to brighter warm tawny in *maculosus* (rest of region). In flight, shows limited white in upperwings and no wing-bar. **HH** Pairs or family groups are widespread at low densities, but may also be locally numerous. Inhabits dry open bushed and wooded grassland from near sea-level to 1800m, and regularly seen on dirt roads at night. **Voice** Call is a long series of identical notes (not rising and falling) that break into a punctuated series *pipipipipi.....pi pi pi pi pi pi pi...* [Alt: Spotted Dikkop]

Water Thick-knee *Burhinus vermiculatus* 41cm, 16"

Typical thick-knee with streaked brown-grey plumage; closed wing usually shows *wide grey panel bordered above by narrow white bar and above that by thicker blackish bar*; no second black bar immediately below white (unlike Stone-curlew). At close range shows diagnostic *fine vermiculations to upperparts (not present in other thick-knees)*. Bill has small dull yellowish-green patches at base and black culmen. Eyes and legs often more greenish-yellow than similar species. Beware some birds have narrow white bar indistinct or even lacking, but can be told from Senegal Thick-knee by greener bill and legs. **HH** Pairs and small groups are fairly uncommon in SEEt and SSo near water of all types, including lake shores, river sandbanks, coastal creeks and lagoons. **Voice** Call is a long rising then falling series of shrill notes; unlike Senegal they are unhurried and slur together *wi-wi-wi-wi-wi-wi-wi-wi-wi... wii wii wii.* [Alt: Water Dikkop]

Senegal Thick-knee *Burhinus senegalensis* 38cm, 15"

Very like Water Thick-knee but wide *grey wing-panel is bordered above by black bar only (no narrow white band)*. Bill as in Water Thick-knee with black culmen, but slightly longer and heavier, with more extensive and often brighter yellow patches near base; eyes and legs also usually brighter yellow. **HH** Singles, pairs and small groups associate with water in WEr and N&WEt (mainly west of Rift Valley) up to 1900m; no overlap with Water Thick-knee. **Voice** Calls like Water Thick-knee, but all notes shriller, distinctly separate and hurried (not slurred together) *pi-pi-pi-pi-pi-pi-pi-pi,* with no slower terminal notes.

Stone-curlew *Burhinus oedicnemus* 43cm, 17"

Most similar to Water Thick-knee, but *narrow white wing-bar bordered both above and below with black bars*. Senegal Thick-knee lacks white bar on coverts. Bill comparatively small with *extensive yellow base*, including basal half of culmen. **HH** Nominate *oedicnemus* is uncommon or locally common Palearctic winter visitor to Er and Et, Oct–Mar. Race *saharae*, mainly resident in N Africa, recorded in So and probably sometimes reaches Er in winter; paler and less streaked than nominate. Occurs in open country, including grasslands and recently burnt areas up to 2300m. **Voice** Silent in region. [Alt: Eurasian Thick-knee]

Spotted Thick-knee

Water Thick-knee

Senegal
Thick-knee

Stone-curlew

COURSERS *Delicate, subdued-plumaged birds of open country. All are crepuscular to some extent, but vary from near-diurnal Temminck's to near-nocturnal Bronze-winged. All have upright stance especially when alarmed and prefer to run to cover rather than fly. Often exploit burned areas. Reasonably easily separated by head, breast and underwing markings. Sexes similar; immatures have pale fringes to wing-coverts and back.*

Temminck's Courser *Cursorius temminckii*   21 cm, 8"

Slightly smaller than similar species with *rufous cap. Lower breast dull rufous, with a blackish smudge in centre of belly* (can be hard to see). Pale lores, dark eye-line and whitish superciliary stripe give neat 'capped' head pattern. Somali and Cream-coloured Coursers are much paler. Easily flushed into rather jerky flight, when shows dark underwing with no white trailing edge. **HH** Pairs and small groups are widespread and fairly common in Et (but scarce in Er) in wide range of drier open bushed and occasionally wooded grassland, up to 2450m; recently found breeding in NWSo, and often nomadic. **Voice** Repeated, strange, rather mournful nasal *peeu*, some notes with reverberating quality.

Somali Courser *Cursorius somalensis*   22 cm, 8.5"

Larger, longer-legged and paler than Temminck's Courser, with white lower belly. Whitish superciliary stripes and black eye-lines join to form clear V on back of head; cap is sandy on forecrown and blue-grey on hindcrown. In flight, *underwing is black on outer half, and pale sandy on innerwing with white trailing edge.* Two races occur: nominate (E&SEEt, Dj, most of So) as described; *littoralis* (SEt, coastal SSo) darker and greyer. **HH** Pairs and small groups are common and widespread in arid and semi-arid desert, grassland and scrub, mainly below 1000m. Most are resident but some local movements occur. Vagrant Er (once, Mar, at 2400m). **Voice** Scratchy descending slurred *pyau* and muffled *pip*, often with several birds calling together. **Note** Formerly conspecific with Cream-coloured Courser.

Cream-coloured Courser *Cursorius cursor*   24 cm, 9.5"

Very like Somali Courser but slightly larger and more *sandy-buff or pinkish-buff* with slightly shorter, straighter bill, shorter legs and proportionately longer wings. In flight, shows *entirely black underwing* in contrast with sandy body. **HH** Uncommon to rare winter visitor to Er and NWSo, Sep–Mar, in arid short grassland and desert or semi-desert plains below 600m. Vagrant NEt and SSo. Resident population on Soc. **Voice** May call *quett* or *kritt* when disturbed.

Double-banded Courser *Rhinoptilus africanus*   24 cm, 9.5"

Distinctive, with heavily scaled upperparts and *two clear narrow black breast-bands.* In flight, shows rufous band across secondaries and inner primaries. Two races occur: *raffertyi* (CEt) is dark grey-brown above; *hartingi* (SEEt, So) is more cinnamon-rufous above with cream fringes. **HH** Singles and pairs are uncommon in semi-arid open habitats, often in bare stony areas, below 1000m (occasionally up to 1500m). Vagrant Dj. **Voice** Rapid shrill trill that rises and falls (rather like Water Thick-knee) and continues with sharp, often paired *keek-eek* notes. [Alt: Two-banded Courser]

Heuglin's Courser *Rhinoptilus cinctus*   27 cm, 10.5"

Cryptic beautiful courser, with *unique pattern of black, white and chestnut bands running above and below broad mottled brown breast-band.* In flight, underwing largely white with black tips to outer primaries. Three similar races occur: *mayaudi* (C&EEt, NWSo); *balsaci* (SSo); *cinctus* (SEt). **HH** Singles and pairs may be locally common in semi-arid bush and wooded country, from near sea-level to 1700m. **Voice** Spectacular call which starts with sharp *keek-keek*, then breaks into an accelerating rising then falling wave of sharp *kik* notes. [Alt: Three-banded Courser]

Bronze-winged Courser *Rhinoptilus chalcopterus*   28 cm, 11"

Largest courser which may suggest Crowned Lapwing, but told by *bold face pattern around large dark eyes*, two breast-bands, (upper broad, lower narrow) and dull purple-red legs. Violet tips to primaries rarely visible in field. In flight, reveals broad white band across underwing, with creamy coverts and black primaries and trailing edge. **HH** Uncommon to rare in WEr and WEt, in bushed and wooded country below 2200m. Wanders widely, but exact status as intra-African migrant poorly known. Strictly nocturnal, but found in shade during day. **Voice** Mournful, rather thick-knee-like call starting with downslur, then three notes slurring into each other, *oo oo-wa-woo.* [Alt: Violet-tipped Courser]

Temminck's
Courser

Somali Courser

somalensis full sp.

Double-banded
Courser

raffertyi

Cream-coloured
Courser

Bronze-winged
Courser

Heuglin's
Courser

cinctus

PRATINCOLES Graceful, rather tern-like on the wing, but squat and short-legged on the ground. Best identified by throat and underwing markings, but also consider range. Sexes alike.

Collared Pratincole *Glareola pratincola* 26cm, 10"

Breeding adult has pale buff throat surrounded by narrow black line (streaks in non-breeding birds); at rest, wing-tips and tail are roughly same length. In flight, shows white rump, deeply forked tail, and dark underwing with *chestnut-red underwing-coverts*. Secondaries have very narrow white edges, but these may wear off. Immature is heavily mottled above, with less well-defined throat and shorter tail. Two (or three) races occur; resident African birds are slightly smaller, darker and with less chestnut on underwing-coverts than Palearctic migrants. **HH** Nominate birds are widespread Palearctic migrants to Er, Et and NWSo, Aug–May, on flat, sparsely vegetated land around lakes, rivers and at coast, up to 2350m (and once at 2900m). Resident breeding birds in Rift Valley and SSo are *fuelleborni* (SSo birds sometimes considered separate race *erlangeri*). Vagrant Dj and Soc. **Voice** Utters a wide range of sharp creaky high-pitched and rather tern-like *krik* and *keek* calls. [Alt: Red-winged Pratincole, Common Pratincole]

Madagascar Pratincole *Glareola ocularis* 25cm, 10"

Stocky dark pratincole with white streak below and behind eye (giving capped and masked appearance), pale chestnut patch on belly and short tail. Immature browner, lacking white streak on face, and less bright below. In flight shows *short, shallow forked tail, orange-chestnut underwing-coverts*, and clear white lower belly. From above, smaller crescent-shaped rump-patch is useful distinction from Collared. **HH** Non-breeding migrant from Madagascar which flocks in large numbers from May–Sep on coasts and river systems of SSo; very rare further inland, with just one record from Et. **Voice** Gives a short sharp *twik twik twik*, and a whinnying rising and falling series of *kik* notes. **VU**

Black-winged Pratincole *Glareola nordmanni* 25cm, 10"

Very like Collared Pratincole, but has *black underwing-coverts*, no white trailing edge to wing, shallower, shorter forked tail and, at rest, wings extend well beyond tail-tip. Overall darker than Collared with more extensive black loral patch and less red at base of bill (not reaching nostrils). Immature is also dark, with ill-defined throat-patch and *black underwing-coverts*. **HH** Rare Palearctic passage migrant in Rift Valley Sep–Oct, and apparently overwintering in WEt with several records of large flocks close to Sudan border. Main migration route is to west of region. Two old records from NWSo. **Voice** Calls are very like Collared Pratincole, but with more bubbling quality. **NT**

Rock Pratincole *Glareola nuchalis* 19cm, 7.5"

Small and dark with *neat white stripe from behind eyes and across hindneck*; legs bright red. In flight, *dark underwing shows white central line*. Immature is buff-fringed above and lacks collar on hindneck. **HH** Nominate race is presumed to be a rare breeding resident in WEt, notably on Didessa river, but may be an intra-African migrant to region. Invariably in pairs on rocks in fast-flowing rivers. **Voice** A rapid sharp series of tern-like *kik-kik-kik...* notes, and softer *kip-kip*. [Alt: White-collared Pratincole]

Egyptian Plover *Pluvianus aegyptius* 21cm, 8"

Chunky attractive shorebird, largely black and white and blue-grey above, with bold head markings, black and white breast-band, and orange-buff washed underparts. Sexes similar; immature duller with brown mottling on wing-coverts. In flight reveals *striking white and grey wings with diagonal black band and tips*. **HH** Pairs and small groups are locally common on sandbanks along larger rivers in WEr and WEt, but less common in Rift Valley, up to 1150m. Generally sedentary, but responds to water level changes with local movements. Sometimes noted around lakes. **Voice** Noisy; has a loud *cherk cherk...* or *chee-chee-chee...*in flight.

ad

imm

ad

Collared Pratincole

br

ad

ad

Madagascar
Pratincole

imm

ad

ad

Black-winged
Pratincole

imm

ad

ad

Rock Pratincole

imm

ad

ad

Egyptian Plover

SMALLER PLOVERS These plovers are mainly resident in our area. The three smaller species run incredibly fast, almost floating over the ground. Caspian Plover is not associated with wetlands. All can be confiding and may allow close approach; they are best identified by head and breast markings.

Kittlitz's Plover *Charadrius pecuarius* 15cm, 6"

Breeding adult is slightly long-legged *buff-breasted* plover with *black stripes extending across forecrown, through eyes and meeting on hindneck*. Non-breeding adult is duller, and may lose black head-stripes and breast colour. Immature as non-breeding adult, but buffier on face and hindneck-collar; upperparts buff-fringed, and some show dark breast-patches. In flight, adult shows limited white wing-bar and *toes project beyond tail*. **HH** Locally common and widespread resident on short grass and muddy fringes of wide range of inland waters below 2700m. Most frequent in Rift Valley but also on temporary pools and coastal saltpans; rare in Er and NSo. **Voice** Calls are rather variable; commonest is a loud harsh downslurred trill, *trit-tri-rit-rit*.

White-fronted Plover *Charadrius marginatus* 17cm, 6.5"

Similar to Kittlitz's Plover, but generally paler, with *bright white forecrown giving peak-headed look*. Breeding adult has blackish frontal bar and eye-stripes, and short white supercilium. Breast and hindneck often with tawny-buff wash (sometimes restricted to patches at sides of breast). Non-breeding adult (especially female) may lack black head markings. Immature lacks any black on head, has buff-fringed upperparts and is whiter below. Tail projects beyond wing-tips at rest, and *toes do not extend beyond longish tail in flight*. Kentish Plover (plate 63) is more compact and browner, with darker patches at sides of breast. Race in NE Africa is *tenellus* (some authors regard it as *mechowi*, restricting *tenellus* to Madagascar). **HH** Pairs and loose groups are locally common residents on coast in SSo, sometimes extending inland along major rivers. Also recorded in coastal Er and NSo. **Voice** Gives a low muted *chut*, with loud dry churred trill in flight.

Three-banded Plover *Charadrius tricollaris* 18cm, 7"

Slightly misleadingly named plover, with *two black breast-bands separated by third white band, and broad white forehead and supercilium*; sides of face grey with obvious red orbital ring and pale eyes; bill red with black tip, legs orange-red. Sexes alike. Immature is more weakly marked with pale-fringed upperparts and duller legs; some show disproportionally long tail. Flies with irregular stiff wing-beats on longish dark wings, revealing *thin white wing-bar* and white trailing edge to secondaries. **HH** Pairs are common and widespread in Er, Et (except SE) and NWSo, beside wide range of fresh and alkaline water from sea-level to 2800m, often on soft muddy margins with some cover. **Voice** In flight utters rising *phiuu-eet*, and displaying birds give long rising and falling series of rapid spitting notes that decelerate and become gravelly in quality.

Caspian Plover *Charadrius asiaticus* 21cm, 8"

Medium-sized, fine-billed, rather elegant plover. Non-breeding adult has *broad white supercilium, white lores and broad grey-brown breast-band*. Breeding male has white-faced look, with smart chestnut breast-band narrowly bordered black below. Breeding female similar to non-breeding adult; immature has buff-fringed upperparts, and more mottled breast-band. *Wing-tips extend beyond tail at rest*. Non-breeding adults differ from non-breeding sand plovers (plate 63) by finer bill, more prominent supercilium, broader and complete breast-band, and dry-country habitat. **HH** Locally common Palearctic passage migrant and winter visitor, Aug–Apr, invariably in flocks on short grasslands; moves like courser, preferring to run than fly. Mainly an autumn passage migrant in Er, Et and NWSo; in coastal SSo common on passage in autumn and spring, but small numbers also overwinter on dry ground and coastal dunes (main wintering grounds are in S Kenya/N Tanzania, and southern Africa). Vagrant Dj and Soc. **Voice** Repeated dry *chip* or *tchup* as birds fly in compact flocks.

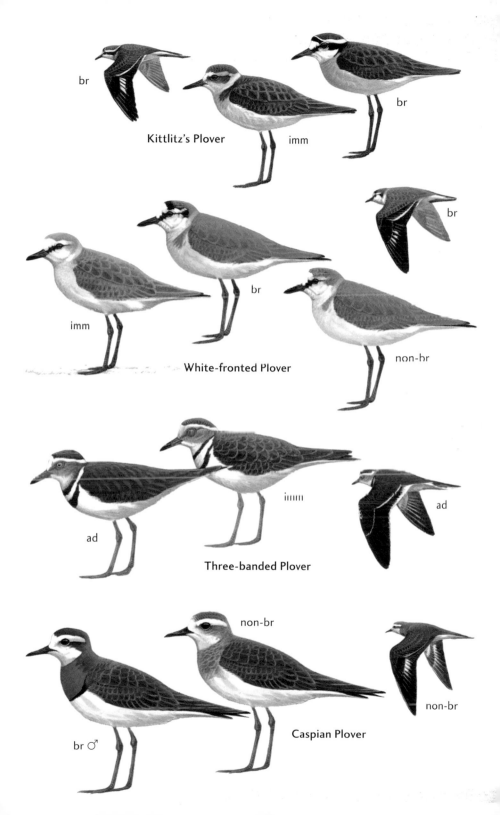

br

Kittlitz's Plover

imm

br

White-fronted Plover

imm

br

br

non-br

Three-banded Plover

ad

imm

ad

br ♂

non-br

Caspian Plover

non-br

MIGRANT PLOVERS These plovers visit North-east Africa from their Palearctic breeding grounds, mainly Oct–Apr, but a few are present all year. All are easily identified in breeding plumage, but need care otherwise: note head, breast and wing markings.

Common Ringed Plover *Charadrius hiaticula*   19cm, 7.5"

Non-breeding adult is brown above, with single blackish breast-band and dull white forehead; bill dark, legs dull orange. Breeding adult is crisper, with jet-black breast-band, bright white forehead, brighter *orange bill-base (with black tip) and orange legs*. Immature like dull non-breeding adult, with reduced or broken breast-band. In flight shows *prominent white wing-bar*. **HH** Race *tundrae* is common passage migrant and winter visitor, mainly to coast and major lakes (up to 2900m), Sep–May; a few remain all year. **Voice** Gives a sad rising then falling *pweoo*, usually in flight. [Alt: Ringed Plover]

Little Ringed Plover *Charadrius dubius*   17cm, 6.5"

Very like Common Ringed Plover but smaller and slimmer with dark bill, *narrow yellow orbital ring* and *pale pinkish or yellowish legs* proportionally longer than Common Ringed Plover. Breeding adult has dark forecrown-stripe separated from brown crown by narrow white band. Immature duller with broken breast-band and less distinct eye-ring. In flight, *wing is entirely dark* (without white bar). **HH** Race *curonicus* is not uncommon but fairly solitary passage migrant and winter visitor to fringes of mainly inland waters, much less often to coast, Sep–Apr. Favours grasslands near lakeshores, up to 2900m. **Voice** Gives a short downslurred *peeu* in flight, not rising and falling as in Common Ringed Plover.

Kentish Plover *Charadrius alexandrinus*   16cm, 6"

Small plover with *dark patches at sides of breast* (never a full band) *and blackish legs*. Non-breeding adult confusable with White-fronted Plover (plate 62) but differs in whiter hindneck and underparts, wings extend slightly beyond tail. Breeding male has black frontal bar, eye-stripe and chest-patches, and may show rufous wash on nape (variable). Breeding female as non-breeding adult, immature slightly buffier. In flight shows narrow white wing-bar and white outer tail. Ringed and Little Ringed Plovers are darker above with paler legs and (usually) complete breast-bands. **HH** Locally common breeding resident on coasts of Er, Dj and NSo; numbers increase Sep–Mar with Palearctic migrants. Mainly coastal, on sand- or mudflats, but also inland especially beside saline lakes in Rift Valley, and recorded up to 2900m. **Voice** Call is a soft *tu-it* and rolling *prrr*. Flying birds may give scratchy upslurred *bipip*.

Lesser Sand Plover *Charadrius mongolus*   19cm, 7.5"

Non-breeding adult is very like Greater Sand Plover, but *smaller, slenderer, with rounder head, shorter bill and shorter, blacker legs*. Shows neat compact outline, lacking ranginess of Greater. Breeding adult has mostly *black forecrown* and eye-patch, and broad chestnut breast-band. Immature like non-breeding adult, but slightly washed buff on head. In flight *toes hardly show beyond tail-tip*. Non-breeding Kentish Plover is smaller with neater breast-patches and white collar. Caspian Plover has finer bill, white lores and different habitat. **HH** Race *pamirensis* is common passage migrant and winter visitor to coasts of Er, Dj and So, Sep–Apr, with some throughout year. Rare inland, mainly in Rift Valley but once at L. Arakit (2900m). Favours mud- and sandflats; usually in flocks. **Voice** Flight call is a hard, short dry trill on one note *trreet*. [Alt: Mongolian Plover]

Greater Sand Plover *Charadrius leschenaultii*   23cm, 9"

Non-breeding adult is told from very similar Lesser Sand Plover by *larger size, more angular head, longer, heavier bill and longer grey-green legs*. Breeding adult has *white forecrown* and usually narrower, clearer-cut chestnut breast-band. In flight *toes project well beyond tail*. **HH** Very common passage migrant and winter visitor along coast, Sep–May, with some all year; rare inland, in Rift Valley. Favours mudflats and tidal lagoons; usually in flocks. Most birds are race *columbinus*; heavier-billed *crassirostris* occurs on passage in So (and once in Et). **Voice** Flight call very like Lesser Sand Plover, but may be slightly softer and more rolling.

non-br

**Common
Ringed Plover**

br   *tundrae*

non-br

br

Little Ringed Plover

br ♂

non-br

Kentish Plover

non-br

non-br

br

Lesser Sand Plover

non-br

br

Greater Sand Plover

WETLAND PLOVERS *The plovers below are usually associated with wetlands and are all easily identified if seen well. Noisy and conspicuous (calling both day and night), they are often seen in aggressive territorial encounters. Sexes alike. Immatures have similar basic pattern to adults, but are often browner, with less clear-cut markings and pale-fringed upperparts (only described below if markedly different).*

Spur-winged Plover *Vanellus spinosus*   28cm 11″

A familiar black, white and brown plover with *white cheeks and sides of neck contrasting with black crown, throat and breast.* Bill and legs black. Curved carpal spur is hard to see. In flight, shows white bar across upperwing-coverts. **HH** Common and widespread in variety of habitats across region up to 2900m, beside both fresh and alkaline waters; absent from most of NSo. **Voice** Calls are piercing *keek* notes that become scratchy as bird gets more excited.

Long-toed Plover *Vanellus crassirostris*   31 cm 12″

Large upright plover with *white face and foreneck* standing out clearly against black nape and breast-band; bill pinkish with black tip, legs dull red. In flight, large white shoulders contrast strongly with black flight feathers. Race in region is nominate. **HH** Very localised in extreme WEt in extensive swamps and marshes, and sometimes on rivers. **Voice** Noisy; call is metallic and spitting, starting slowly then speeding up, almost sounding like a rattle, *kik kik kik kik-kik-kik kikikikikik...*

African Wattled Plover *Vanellus senegallus*   34cm 13.5″

A large brown plover with *black-tipped yellow bill, bright yellow legs*, pin-stripe streaks on throat and neck, small white forehead-patch, and *prominent yellow wattles at sides of bill.* The nominate birds in our region are brown-bellied (sometimes separated as race *major*). In flight, shows white bar across upperwing-coverts, similar to Spur-winged. Immature has smaller wattles and brown forecrown. **HH** Pairs and small groups are fairly common and widespread in Er and Et west of 40°E in damp grasslands and marsh edges up to 2100m; one old record from NWSo. **Voice** Gives a pinched, non-metallic *kip-kip-kip...*, repeated for long periods.

Spot-breasted Plover *Vanellus melanocephalus*   34cm, 13.5″

Large brown plover with black cap, white supercilium behind eye, and black chin and throat. Sides of head grey and *breast finely spotted black.* Adults have small yellow pre-ocular wattle. In flight, shows white bar across upperwing-coverts, similar to Spur-winged. Only likely to overlap with Black-winged (plate 65) which has unspotted breast and red legs. **HH** ENDEMIC. Pairs or small flocks are locally frequent to common in highland grasslands and moorland in Et, often in damper areas or near pools, at 2400–3800m. **Voice** An unpleasant rasping, rather like Crowned Plover.

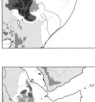

White-tailed Plover *Vanellus leucurus*   28cm, 11″

An elegant, long-legged plover with rather plain face. Adult is uniformly greyish-brown above, often with lilac wash on mantle. Below, pale chin contrasts with pale brownish upper breast and pale grey lower breast. *Long legs yellow.* Black bill often noticeably longer than other plovers. In flight shows striking wing pattern and *all-white tail.* Immature has darker crown and heavily scaled upperparts. **HH** Rare Palearctic winter visitor to Er and NEt, with several recent records, Oct–Feb; also two recent records on Rift Valley lakes in CEt. **Voice** Can be very noisy, giving querulous *kiu* repeated by individuals or small parties. In flight, also gives series of *kik* notes.

Spur-winged
Plover

Long-toed
Plover

imm

ad

ad

African Wattled
Plover

Spot-breasted
Plover

ad

ad

nominate

ad

White-tailed Plover

DRY COUNTRY PLOVERS Generally associated with dry country and grasslands, and best identified by head, breast and wing markings. Sexes alike; immatures are generally duller with paler fringes on upperparts.

Black-headed Plover *Vanellus tectus*　　　　　　26cm, 10"

Attractive *spike-crested* plover, with white chin, forehead and nape-patch. In front view appears to have *narrow black 'tie' from throat to breast*. Bill is red with black tip; small loral wattles and legs also red. In flight shows extensive white on primary and greater coverts. Two races occur: nominate (Er, Et west of Rift Valley) and *latifrons* (extreme SEEt, SSo), which has larger white patch on forecrown. **HH** Resident and often approachable and tame in semi-arid and arid open and bushed plains from sea-level to 1900m. Widespread but patchily distributed. Largely crepuscular or nocturnal, often standing in shade during day. **Voice** Quite vocal, more so in flight: call is a burry, muffled, tinny series that develops into a loud rattle *kreek-kreek...krkrkrkrkrkr...*

Crowned Plover *Vanellus coronatus*　　　　　　31cm, 12"

Smart head pattern of *black cap and white crown-ring* stands out at long distance; ring accentuates flat head and steep forehead. Alert and upright, with yellow eyes and bright red legs. Immature similar, but head pattern less well-defined and upperparts fringed buff; eyes, bill and legs dull. Two races occur: nominate (Et except SE, plus SSo) as described; *demissus* (SEEt, N&CSo) paler and sandier. **HH** Pairs, small parties and flocks are common residents (and local wanderers) in wide range of drier grasslands, including bushed and wooded areas, from sea-level to 2000m, mainly east of Rift Valley. **Voice** Noisy and aggressive, calls consisting of scratchy upslurs, *kir, kiree, kree*, etc., either singly or in series.

Northern Lapwing *Vanellus vanellus*　　　　　　30cm, 12"

Palearctic species with *long curving crest, dark green upperparts*, broad black breast-band, and white belly. Breeding adult has black face, non-breeding shows paler face and narrow buff fringes to upperparts. Immature duller, more heavily scalloped above with shorter crest. In flight, reveals *very broad wings*, appearing all dark above and black and white below. **HH** Palearctic vagrant to Soc. **Voice** Flight and alarm call is a strange, high-pitched, slurred *wee'yu* or *pee-wit*, given singly.

Black-winged Plover *Vanellus melanopterus*　　　　　　27cm, 10.5"

Very like Senegal Plover, but more thickset and shorter-legged; hard to tell at distance (but ranges do not overlap in NE Africa). At close range typically shows slightly broader white forehead and wider black breast-band, but this is not consistent. *Reddish eye-ring* is good field mark at close quarters. In flight, upperwing shows *diagonal white bar fully across coverts, and black trailing edge to secondaries*. Race in NE Africa is nominate. **HH** Flocks may be common in higher-altitude grasslands and cultivation in Er and Et, at 1350–3000m; uncommon in NWSo (breeding). **Voice** Gives a harsh, strident, staccato upslurred *ki-ki-ki-ki-krrrrrri*.

Senegal Plover *Vanellus lugubris*　　　　　　26cm, 10"

Slightly smaller, slenderer and longer-legged than Black-winged Plover, often with clearer-cut but smaller white patch on forecrown; black breast-band usually narrower, yellowish eye-ring indistinct. In flight, shows *white trailing edge to secondaries*. **HH** Small groups and flocks are regular non-breeding visitors to SSo, Apr–Jul, preferring open grassy areas, bushland and coastal dunes. **Voice** Gives a fluty attractive *tyu-u* or *tyu*, repeated singly, never in series. [Alt: Lesser Black-winged Plover]

Sociable Plover *Vanellus gregarius*　　　　　　30cm, 12"

Breeding adult has striking head pattern with prominent white forehead and supercilium and black crown, delicate pinkish-grey body and wings with *black and dark chestnut belly*; bill and legs black. Non-breeding birds are duller with some pale fringes and white belly. At all ages, prominent supercilium separates from all other plovers except very different Crowned and Spot-breasted. *In flight, shows striking tricoloured wing pattern*, recalling Sabine's Gull *Larus sabini*. **HH** Rare Palearctic winter visitor to Er and CEt, Oct–Mar (but only one recent record), mainly on dry plains but also in grassland and savanna from sea-level to 2800m. One old record NWSo. Endangered, with much of population recently found to winter in Sudan. **Voice** Silent in region. **CR**

Black-headed
Plover

ad

Crowned
Plover

imm

ad

Northern
Lapwing

ad

Black-winged
Plover

imm

ad

Senegal Plover

ad

imm

non-br

br

Sociable Plover

Grey Plover *Pluvialis squatarola* 31cm, 12"

Large, stocky, heavy-billed plover. Non-breeding adult is silvery grey-brown above, and grey-mottled below, with broad but weak supercilium, and often with a dusky face- or eye-patch. Breeding adult is black from face to belly, and brightly spangled silver, grey and black above. Sexes alike. Immature like non-breeding adult, but with slightly stronger buffy-yellow wash. In flight, *black axillaries, white rump and obvious wing-bar* are diagnostic. **HH** Very common Palearctic passage migrant and winter visitor to coast, mainly Sep–May, but some oversummer. Much less common inland, up to 2900m. **Voice** Very vocal, atmospheric and mournful slurred whistle that rises and falls *pee-yu-eeee*. [Alt: Black-bellied Plover]

Pacific Golden Plover *Pluvialis fulva* 26cm, 10"

Slimmer and smaller than Grey Plover. Non-breeding adult always shows some golden-yellow above, *stronger buff-yellow supercilium*, and mottled dusky brownish-yellow underparts. Breeding adult is *spangled black and gold above*, with black face to belly. Sexes alike. Immature like non-breeding adult, but with stronger buffy-yellow wash. In flight, *grey underwing and axillaries* are diagnostic, along with *mottled golden (not white) rump*, and *indistinct wing-bar*. **HH** Uncommon to fairly common Palearctic winter visitor to the Er and So coast, Sep–May, invariably in flocks. Regular inland up to 1600m, especially to grassy areas and mud beside lakes in Rift Valley. **Voice** In flight, gives a loud shrill spaced *tu-whi'yu*.

SANDPIPERS AND ALLIES *A highly varied group of (mainly) Palearctic shorebirds which occur during the period Aug–May, although smaller numbers remain throughout the year (also includes plates 67–72). Species vary in size from small stints (plate 69) to curlews (plate 71). Sandpipers exploit a wide range of wetland and coastal habitats, often in large numbers. Many moult into striking breeding plumages towards the end of their stay in NE Africa. The two species below are somewhat atypical.*

Ruff *Philomachus pugnax* ♂ 30cm, 12", ♀ 23cm, 9"

Highly variable, *small-headed, short-billed, scaly-backed* shorebird; adults have bright orange legs. Usual non-breeding male and female brown or grey-brown, scaly above, with lightly mottled head to breast. Female is smaller. Some males are extensively white on head, back and underparts. Breeding males gain exotic ruffs after leaving Africa. Immature is boldly scaled above with bright buffy fringes. In rather powerful long-winged flight, shows narrow white wing-bar and *white oval patches at sides of tail*. **HH** Very common Palearctic winter visitor and passage migrant to both fresh and alkaline waters (especially with muddy fringes) up to 2900m, Aug–May. A few stay all year. **Voice** Unlike most shorebirds, Ruffs are almost totally silent.

Ruddy Turnstone *Arenaria interpres* 23cm, 9"

Stout shorebird with *short orange legs* and short, broad-based, slightly upswept bill. Non-breeding adult is dark brown and black above, with dark breast-band contrasting with white throat and belly. Breeding adult is striking mix of black, white and chestnut. Immature is like non-breeding adult, but with pale feather edges above and duller legs. In flight, reveals *obvious bold triangular pattern of white bars on wings, back and tail*. **HH** Common passage migrant and winter visitor to coast from Aug–May, with small number oversummering; regular but much less numerous inland, up to 2000m. **Voice** Flight call is a hurried *tuk'a'tuk*; also gives a low throaty musical churred trill. [Alt: Turnstone]

non-br

Grey Plover

br

non-br

br

non-br

non-br

Pacific Golden Plover

imm

imm

ad

♂

Ruff

Ruddy Turnstone

non-br

br

non-br

MEDIUM-SIZED SANDPIPERS *Three similar species of sandpiper closely related to the larger species on plate 67. Note structure and colour of upperparts and legs. The distinctive Terek Sandpiper poses few problems if seen well.*

Common Sandpiper *Actitis hypoleucos* 20cm, 8"

Short-legged, *rather plain brown and white* sandpiper with obvious horizontal stance; *white underparts peak to form white wedge at shoulder,* and tail is noticeably longer than wing-tips. Non-breeding adult has whitish throat and centre of breast. Legs variably greenish to yellowish-olive. Breeding adult has some black streaking above and fuller breast-band. Immature has buff-barred wing-coverts. Flight diagnostic, with jerky shallow beats and glides on bowed wings, showing clear white wing-bar. **HH** Very common winter visitor and passage migrant to lakes, rivers and coast up to 2900m, Aug–May, with a few all year. Ever-bobbing tail is good feature even at distance. **Voice** Noisy, calling a piercing series of rapid, virtually identical notes which run together *pipipipipipipipipipipi…,* as well as a plaintive long *siiuuu.*

Wood Sandpiper *Tringa glareola* 20cm, 8"

Similar to Green Sandpiper, but more graceful and longer-legged; *browner above with more prominent white supercilium, spotted back and yellowish legs.* Breeding adult is more mottled above, with *streaked neck and sides to breast which fade gradually into white underparts.* Immature is warmer brown above with buff speckles. Flying birds reveal small squarish white rump and *pale underwings;* feet extend well beyond tail-tip. **HH** Common passage migrant and winter visitor to wide range of inland waters from sea-level to 4100m, Jul–May (only inshore at coast). Some birds present all year. **Voice.** Noisy; a loud piercing *chiff-iff-iff…* on one tone. Flushed birds call for long periods, often in towering flight.

Green Sandpiper *Tringa ochropus* 23cm, 9"

Dumpier and *much darker than Wood Sandpiper with finer spotting on upperparts* (non-breeding adult appears almost plain above), supercilium confined to front of eye, and *eye-ring more obvious. Dark mottling on breast always ends in clear-cut line.* Legs grey-green. Breeding adult similar but head and breast with stronger streaking. In flight *blackish wings and underwing contrast with brilliant white rump and underparts;* toes only just project beyond tail-tip. **HH** Single birds common on passage and as winter visitors between late Jul and Apr. Commonest inland on fresh water, from extensive marshy lakeshores to temporary pools and puddles, from sea-level to 2700m; only inshore at coast. Shyer than Wood Sandpiper, bursting into erratic zigzagging flight when flushed. **Voice** Noisy; call is a distinctive ringing *tiuyiu-yiu-yiu…*

Terek Sandpiper *Xenus cinereus* 25cm, 10"

Striking and unusual with *long orange-based upswept bill, short orange legs.* Non-breeding adult is mainly grey-brown above and white below. Often appears to show blackish shoulders at distance. Breeding adult is similar but greyer with blackish scapular lines and brighter legs. In flight, wings reveal broad white trailing edge to secondaries. **HH** Common passage migrant and winter visitor to coasts of Er and So, Aug–May, with a few all year; regular but less common inland, on lakeshores up to 1500m. Vagrant Soc. Feeding birds rush around in horizontal posture, often switching direction. **Voice** Flight call is a rapid rather dry monotone *tu-yer'yer.*

Common Sandpiper

non-br

br

Wood Sandpiper

imm

br

Green Sandpiper

non-br

br

Terek Sandpiper

br

non-br

LARGER* TRINGA *SANDPIPERS *Four species of larger sandpiper, usually readily identified by leg colour and bill structure, as well as upperpart markings in flight.*

Common Greenshank *Tringa nebularia* 32cm, 13"

Large grey-brown and white sandpiper with *long, slightly upturned bill tapering from heavy base*, and long greenish or grey-green legs. Non-breeding adult has crown and sides of neck lightly streaked grey, rest of underparts white. Breeding adult is more heavily streaked on head, neck and breast, with white-fringed blackish and grey scapulars giving rather spangled appearance. Immature browner above with buff feather-edges. In flight, dark wings contrast with *long white wedge up back*, and toes just project from tail-tip. **HH** Common on wide range of both inland and coastal waters up to 2900m, mainly Aug–May, but some are present in all months. Alarmist, towering up and calling when flushed. **Voice** Gives a memorable loud, ringing and clear downslurred *tiu* variously repeated 2–6 times, often *tiu-tiu-tiu*.

Marsh Sandpiper *Tringa stagnatilis* 25cm, 10"

Smaller, slimmer and more delicate than Common Greenshank, with *fine straight bill* and proportionally *longer legs*. Non-breeding adult is grey-brown above, with light streaking from crown to sides to breast; face, supercilium and underparts white, legs greenish-yellow. Breeding adult shows black streaking on head and neck, and some black spotting on back and flanks; legs brighter yellow. Immature is browner above, with pale feather-edges. In flight shows contrast between dark wings and paler body, with *long white wedge on back, and toes extending well beyond tail*. **HH** Common inland on wide range of waters up to 2900m, from large Rift Valley lakes to small pools, mainly Aug–May but some present throughout year. At coast, more confined to estuaries and brackish pools. Vagrant Soc. Often feeds very actively, pecking at water surface and rushing about. **Voice** Noisy; call is a squealed unmusical sharp patternless *kiu kiu kiu...*, lacking ringing quality of Common Greenshank.

Spotted Redshank *Tringa erythropus* 32cm, 13"

Tall attractive wader with long legs and *long straight bill with striking red base*. Non-breeding adult is mostly grey above and whitish below with prominent supercilium, *notably white in front of eye*, and *red legs*. Breeding adult is largely black, with fine white spotting above, showing white bars below as plumage changes; legs black in breeding plumage. Immature like non-breeding adult, but finely spotted and rather browner above, lightly barred brown-grey below. In powerful rising flight, shows dark upperwing, *white wedge on back and trailing red feet*. **HH** Singles and small groups are regular visitors to wide range of inland waters up to 2900m, Sep–May, but very uncommon at coast (and rare in Dj and So). Birds are alert and shy, often feeding in small groups, swimming and upending. **Voice** Call is a loud questioning and rising double *tch'wit*.

Common Redshank *Tringa totanus* 28cm, 11"

Smaller and slightly dumpier than Spotted Redshank with browner upperparts, *shorter bill* (with more extensive red at base), and striking *orange-red legs*. Non-breeding adult has short white supercilium and grey-brown head and breast. Breeding adult is extensively mottled, streaked and barred with brown. Immature is like non-breeding adult but streakier below with paler yellow-orange legs. Terek Sandpiper (plate 67) is superficially similar, but has upturned bill, shorter legs and more horizontal stance. In rather jerky flight, shows *broad white trailing edge to most of wing*, and white wedge up back; red feet partially exposed beyond tail-tip. Three races occur: paler and greyer *ussuriensis* is most frequent, with smaller numbers of nominate. Race *eurhinus* is known from single record in Er (Dec). **HH** Common in small numbers on coast, Aug–May. Less common inland, but not infrequent, at freshwater and alkaline lakes, and marshes up to 2900m. Some birds oversummer in Er and NSo. **Voice** Gives a loud ringing *teu-uu-uu* all on same pitch.

Common Greenshank

br

non-br

br

non-br

Marsh Sandpiper

br

non-br

Spotted Redshank

br

non-br

Common Redshank

STINTS AND SMALLER SANDPIPERS (including species on plate 70). Best identified by careful attention to markings on head, upperparts, rump and tail, and by leg colour (but beware of mud on legs).

Little Stint *Calidris minuta*   15cm, 6"

Non-breeding adult is grey above with dark feather-shafts, pale below with mottled greyish breast-patches (which may form a band); bill and legs black. Breeding adult has much rufous on head and upperparts (may extend onto sides of breast, but throat always white), *creamy-buff stripes at sides of mantle* (forming a V), and chestnut and buff feather-edges with blackish centres giving strong scaly effect. Immature also boldly mottled above with black and rufous, stripes on back, whiter forecrown and supercilium. In flight, shows narrow white wing-bar, white sides to rump, and *grey outer tail.* **HH** Very common Palearctic migrant and winter visitor, Aug–May, occurring in flocks on wide variety of fresh and alkaline waters inland up to 2900m, as well as on coast, but some birds oversummer. **Voice** Gives a dry *chit,* either singly or running into a trill.

Temminck's Stint *Calidris temminckii*   15cm, 6"

Similar to Little Stint, but *plainer grey-brown above,* with fairly *clear-cut grey-brown breast* and *shorter yellow-green legs* (resembles mini Common Sandpiper). Breeding adult has some rufous-fringed, black-centred feathers on back and scapulars. Immature has scaly buff-fringed wing-coverts. At take-off and landing may show white outer tail, hard to see in typical towering flight. **HH** Locally common Palearctic winter visitor Sep–Apr; occurs singly or in small loose associations, especially at freshwater lakes and pools with muddy fringes and some cover, up to 2400m; always in smaller numbers than Little Stint and never on shores at coast. **Voice** Gives 4–5 rather high dry notes in rapid insect-like trill *trrrrrrt.*

Broad-billed Sandpiper *Limicola falcinellus*   17cm, 6.5"

Non-breeding adult suggests large stint with *longish broad-based bill drooping at tip.* Grey upperparts show darker shaft-streaks, with some faint streaking on breast. *Diagnostic double or forked supercilium* varies, may not be so obvious on non-breeding birds. Breeding adult is dark above with golden-buff and white fringes, prominent V on mantle, and *white below with strong black arrows on breast and flanks.* Immature similar but brighter. In flight shows dark leading edge to wing and narrow white wing-bar. **HH** Uncommon to rare Palearctic migrant to coastal mudflats of Er, Dj and So, Sep–May. Rare inland (only two confirmed records in Et). Vagrant Soc. **Voice** Not very vocal; calls in flight with a dry *chut chut...* that can run into a brittle *churr.*

Long-toed Stint *Calidris subminuta*   15cm, 6"

Scaly upperparts may suggest Little Stint, but *more upright, with longer neck, longer yellow-brown legs, and very long middle toe* (hard to see in field). Prominent whitish supercilium highlights capped effect. Non-breeding adult is grey-brown above with dark feather-centres. Breeding adult has broad rufous fringes above. In flight looks very like Little, but *toes project slightly beyond tail* (flight action often more erratic and may tower). **HH** Eastern Palearctic vagrant to marshy fringes of Rift Valley lakes in Et (three records), Dj (twice), and Soc (once). **Voice** Flight call is a deep trill, much deeper than Temminck's Stint.

Red-necked Stint *Calidris ruficollis*   15cm, 6"

Non-breeding adult is virtually identical to Little Stint, but may have slightly broader-based bill, shorter legs, and longer wings and tail. Breeding adult, however, is very distinctive with *bright rufous head, throat and breast (without streaks), bordered below with short black streaks.* Breeding adult Little Stint shows white chin and streaked rufous throat and breast. **HH** Eastern Palearctic vagrant to coastal So: three records in spring (early May) and two in autumn (Aug–Sep). **Voice** Gives a slow, fairly deep *chit chit,* similar to but stronger and slower than Little Stint.

br

non-br

Little Stint

ad
moulting

Temminck's
Stint

non-br

non-br

br

Broad-billed
Sandpiper

non-br

br

Long-toed Stint

ad
moulting

br

Red-necked Stint

Sanderling *Calidris alba*   21cm, 8"

Small sandpiper, confusable with Little Stint and Broad-billed Sandpiper. Non-breeding adult is usually *pale grey above and very white below*, often with black smudge at bend of folded wing; bill and legs black; bill slightly shorter and thicker than Little Stint. Breeding adult (rare in region) is spangled black, silver and chestnut above with rufous head and breast. Immature is mottled silvery and black above with buff wash at sides of breast. In flight shows *much black in wing with strong white wing-bar*; centre of tail black. **HH** Common passage migrant and winter visitor to coast, mainly Aug–May; rare inland with a few records in Rift Valley. Small numbers oversummer. Hyperactive, constantly running and foraging along water's edge. **Voice** Flying and feeding birds give a rhythmical sharp *twik twik twik...*

Curlew Sandpiper *Calidris ferruginea*   22cm, 8.5"

Slender medium-sized sandpiper with *long, evenly decurved bill.* Non-breeding adult has distinct white supercilium, and is grey-brown above variably extending onto upper breast. Breeding adult gains chestnut head and underparts in Mar–May, many showing mottled intermediate plumage. Immature more like non-breeding adult, but browner above with pale feather-fringes, and buffy wash on sides of breast. In flight clearly shows *white rump* and wing-bar. **HH** Flocks are widespread winter visitors and passage migrants from sea-level to 2900m, Aug–May; very common at coast and inland, with some oversummering. **Voice** Very noisy in flight, where birds call with frequent cheerful trilled *chrrut...*

Dunlin *Calidris alpina*   21cm, 8"

Non-breeding adult similar to Curlew Sandpiper, but *slightly smaller and dumpier, with shorter legs, darker breast, and decurved bill curving only towards tip.* Breeding adult is largely black and rufous above, with streaked breast and *black belly-patch.* Immature is more streaky and gingery-brown above than non-breeding adult, with streaks on breast extending onto flanks as small black spots. In flight shows *black centre to rump and tail*, and white wing-bar. Two similar races could occur: nominate and *centralis.* **HH** Uncommon Palearctic winter visitor to Er, Aug–Mar, but a few oversummer. Rare on coasts of So and inland in Et. **Voice** Flight call is a dry trill *kreeee* falling in tone at end.

Pectoral Sandpiper *Calidris melanotos*   23cm, 9"

Medium-sized sandpiper, at all ages with *short, slightly decurved bill*, streaky brown upperparts, and *well-defined band of dark streaks across breast*; no other small shorebird has such a clear-cut breast-band. *Legs and feet dull yellowish.* In alarm looks long-necked with upright stance suggesting Ruff. In flight also Ruff-like, with black centre of tail and white ovals on sides of rump. **HH** Holarctic vagrant with only one confirmed record in Et, Mar 1971. **Voice** Gives a harsh, low scraping and dry trill *krrt* in flight.

Red Knot *Calidris canutus*   25cm, 10"

Thickset sandpiper with rather short, straight bill, and short neck and legs. Non-breeding adult is largely grey and faintly scaled above with prominent pale supercilium, whitish below streaked grey on breast and flanks; legs grey-green. Breeding adult is *mottled black, chestnut and grey above and bright chestnut below*; bill and legs black. In flight shows narrow white wing-bar and *pale grey rump.* Non-breeding Dunlin and Curlew Sandpiper are smaller and slimmer, with proportionately longer, finer bills. **HH** Palearctic vagrant to So (three records in Jun and Aug), and Soc; also an unconfirmed record in Et. **Voice** Gives a regularly spaced, paired nasal *kiu-kiu.*

Great Knot *Calidris tenuirostris*   27cm, 11"

Slightly larger than Red Knot, with longer neck and *longer wings (extending beyond tail); bill longer and slightly decurved.* Non-breeding adult similar to Red Knot, but slightly darker above and *more spotted on breast.* Breeding adult is heavily blotched black above with *chestnut spots on scapulars*; breast is heavily spotted with black, extending onto flanks as chevrons. Immature similar to non-breeding adult but has darker feather-centres above and buff suffusion on spotted breast. In flight shows narrow white wing-bar and *white rump.* **HH** E Palearctic vagrant to Dj (once, Feb 2001). **Voice** Silent in region.

Sanderling

non-br

br

non-br

br ♀

br ♂

Curlew Sandpiper

br

non-br

Dunlin

non-br

Pectoral Sandpiper

non-br

Red Knot

br

br

Great Knot

non-br

GODWITS *Two species of large Palearctic migrant shorebirds, best identified by size and shape of bill, head, wing and tail markings, and distinctive calls.*

Black-tailed Godwit *Limosa limosa* 40cm, 16″

Tall elegant wader, with striking *long straight bill* (extensive pink base) and very long legs. Non-breeding adult has *uniform, fairly dark grey-brown back, head, neck and breast*, gradually fading to white belly. Breeding male has rust-red from sides of face to breast, black-and-white barred lower breast, and white belly. Breeding female variable, usually with less rufous. In flight, shows *broad white wing-stripe, white rump and wide black tail-bar*; long legs and toes trail markedly. **HH** Small and large flocks are sometimes common on larger lakes and wetlands in Er and Et up to 2900m (especially in Rift Valley), Aug–May, with some oversummering; rare in Dj and So; vagrant Soc. Occasional at coast. **Voice** Flying birds call *wika-wika-wik*.

Bar-tailed Godwit *Limosa lapponica* 38cm, 15″

Similar to Black-tailed Godwit but with noticeably *shorter upper leg* and shorter, *slightly upcurved bill* (which also has striking pink base in non-breeding birds). Non-breeding adult has pale grey-brown *mottled and streaked upperparts, throat and sides of breast*, and more extensive white underparts. Breeding male has mostly dark bill and *deep chestnut-red head, neck and underparts*. Breeding female and immature are rather like non-breeding adult, but with variable buff wash to neck and breast. In flight, reveals *plain upperwing*, white rump extending as wedge onto back, and *narrowly barred tail*, feet barely extending beyond it. **HH** Small numbers occur regularly on passage and as wintering birds, exclusively on coast, Sep–May; no confirmed records inland. **Voice** Flying birds give a nasal *kweek-eek*.

CURLEWS *Large Palearctic migrant shorebirds with very long bills. Best identified by size and shape of bill, head, wing and tail markings, and by distinctive calls.*

Slender-billed Curlew *Numenius tenuirostris* 41cm, 16″

Small, pale curlew with *short, slim, evenly downcurved bill, tapering to fine point*. Adult has whiter underparts than other curlews, with *large bold black spots on breast and flanks*, usually rounded or heart-shaped. Indistinct supercilium accentuates capped appearance, but lacks bold head pattern of Whimbrel. Immature is similar, but has streaks on flanks instead of spots. In flight, paler inner wing contrasts with dark outer wing; also shows white rump and paler tail than other curlews. From below, *white underwing-coverts contrast* with darker wing-tips. Some Eurasian Curlews can be small and have shorter bills, but shape of bill and overall proportions help separate them. **HH** Palearctic vagrant, with one old record from Er (Aug 1858). **Voice** Call is a wavering, rising *kwereree* or variants of it. **CR**

Whimbrel *Numenius phaeopus* 45cm, 18″

Smaller than Eurasian Curlew with long bill (but still relatively short) that decurves suddenly towards tip, and *bold striped head with prominent pale central crown-stripe*. Sexes and immature are all similar. In rather fast-winged flight, shows white wedge extending from base of tail to centre of back. **HH** Common Palearctic passage migrant and winter visitor to estuaries, mudflats and reefs, etc., mainly Sep–May, but some birds oversummer. Rare inland, mainly to large Rift Valley lakes. **Voice** Very noisy, both on ground and in flight. Distinctive tittering whistle of 7–12 notes, *bi'bi'bi'bi'bi...*, is typical sound of coast Also has an attractive curlew-like bubbling of rising and falling slurs.

Eurasian Curlew *Numenius arquata* 57cm, 23″

Much larger and generally a warmer brown than Whimbrel, with *much longer, more evenly decurved bill, and plainer unstriped head*. Considerable range in size of both body and bill length, from larger female to smaller male. Sexes similar, but immature more streaked below with buffier wash on neck and breast. In flight shows similar white wedge on back as Whimbrel, but wing-beats slower, stronger and more even. Two races occur: nominate, and slightly paler, larger *orientalis*, with more streaking on flanks and whiter underwing-coverts in flight. **HH** Fairly common winter visitor and passage migrant mainly to coast, Aug–May, with occasional birds oversummering. Most frequent on larger estuaries and creeks; uncommon or scarce on larger lakes inland, up to 1800m. **Voice** In flight, call is a distinctive, very loud *cour-lii*, and a bubbling call is occasionally heard.

Black-tailed Godwit

non-br

br

non-br

br

Bar-tailed Godwit

ad

Slender-billed
Curlew

ad

Whimbrel

ad

Eurasian Curlew

SNIPES *Well-camouflaged, long-billed cryptic birds of marshes and swamps. Because of their often skulking behaviour, all five can be hard to see well. Note back, underwing and tail patterns, as well as behaviour, habitat and calls, to aid identification. Sexes and immature plumages are all similar.*

Common Snipe *Gallinago gallinago* 26cm, 10.5"

Classic snipe, with long bill, striking buff-yellow and black-brown striped head and back, brown-and-buff striped breast, darkly barred flanks, and white belly. In towering and twisting flight, shows *white trailing edge to secondaries and broad rufous tips to tail feathers with limited white at sides.* Race in Africa is nominate. **HH** Locally common to uncommon Palearctic winter visitor and passage migrant, occurring in large marshes and swamps, smaller ponds and seasonally flooded grasslands up to 2900m, Sep–May. **Voice** Gives a harsh *schhp* with upslur at end, less dry than other snipes.

African Snipe *Gallinago nigripennis* 30cm, 12"

Similar to Common Snipe, but *longer-billed, much darker above,* with *more contrast between dark breast and white belly.* Flushed birds tower less than Common Snipe, often flying closer to ground, revealing *darker, more rounded wings* (with white trailing edge to secondaries), *whiter belly,* and *much more white in outer tail.* Race in NE Africa is *aequatorialis.* **HH** Reasonably common and widespread but local resident in highland and montane wetlands in Et, mainly 1300–3800m, although non-breeding birds may wander to lower altitudes; uncommon in Er. **Voice** Call is similar to Common Snipe, but harsher and drier, and longer than Pintail Snipe. When breeding, gives aerial drumming display like Common Snipe, but lower-pitched (latter does not breed in region). [Alt: Ethiopian Snipe]

Pintail Snipe *Gallinago stenura* 25cm, 10"

Very like Common Snipe, but has slightly shorter bill and shorter tail barely projecting beyond folded wings. If preening, unique *pin-like outer tail feathers* may be visible. In flight shows *rather pale wing-coverts contrasting with darker flight feathers, no obvious white trailing edge to secondaries, and well-barred dark underwing.* Birds take off more slowly than Common Snipe, towering and zigzagging less. **HH** Vagrant from Asia to So (two records, Dec–Mar) and Soc. **Voice** Gives a short harsh *schht,* similar to but drier than Common Snipe.

Great Snipe *Gallinago media* 28cm, 11"

Plumper, darker and shorter-billed than Common Snipe, with *rows of white spots on wing-coverts, and more strongly barred flanks and belly* (other snipes have unbarred white belly). Immature has less obvious wing-covert spots. Appears *heavy and rather pot-bellied* in flight, flushing at close range and usually flying low and direct over short distance before dropping back into cover (superficially reminiscent of African Snipe). *Upperwing shows white bars across coverts and* very limited white trailing edge to secondaries; *underwing and belly are dark and closely barred; white outer tail is* diagnostic, but often hard to see. **HH** Locally common (but rarely reported) Palearctic autumn migrant to highland flooded grassland, swamps and marshes at 1500–2700m in Er and Et, mainly Aug–Oct; only two spring records (Mar–Apr). Vagrant Dj and So. **Voice** When flushed gives a low *etch,* followed by a deep distinct *crork crork…* **NT**

Jack Snipe *Lymnocryptes minimus* 19cm, 7.5"

Small dark snipe with short bill, broad buff supercilium which splits above eye, no central crown-stripe, and yellowish lines on dark, green-glossed back. Breast and flanks are streaked not barred. Hard to flush, rising quietly from near feet, and only flying short distance before dropping into cover; appears short-billed in flight, with narrow wings and wedge-shaped dark tail. **HH** Scarce and occasional (perhaps overlooked) Palearctic winter visitor to marshes and wetlands in Et, Nov–Feb, up to 2750m; rare in Er, So and Soc. When feeding, body bounces rhythmically as if on springs. **Voice** Usually silent.

Common Snipe

African Snipe

Pintail Snipe

Great Snipe

Jack Snipe

SKUAS *Two genera of fierce gull-like seabirds which regularly steal food (often from gulls and terns) by forcing them to regurgitate or drop items. All are difficult to identify, with both light and dark morphs and intermediates. Careful note should be made of overall shape and proportions, shape and length of tail-streamers (if present), and extent of white in the primaries. All are very uncommon in NE Africa,* Stercorarius *visiting from the Arctic and* Catharacta *from the Southern Ocean.*

Arctic Skua *Stercorarius parasiticus*   41cm, 16″ (+ br tail 8cm, 3″)

Neat, rather elegant and slighter than Pomarine Skua. In both morphs breeding adult has *elongated, pointed central tail feathers,* and *prominent white wing-flashes.* Light morph also has dark cap and pale underparts, and may have breast-band. Dark morph is entirely dark grey-brown (with white wing-flashes). Intermediates occur. Non-breeding adult may lack tail-streamers and show barring on back and uppertail-coverts. Immature (also with light and dark morphs) has variable barring above and below, and on underwing-coverts. With experience can be identified by proportions, and if seen well shows *short pointed projections to centre of tail.* Juvenile usually warmer brown than juvenile Pomarine, with pale rufous feather-edges. Flight is very *falcon-like,* chasing other seabirds on rapid wings. **HH** Rare passage migrant off So, Oct–Nov and Apr–May. Vagrant Er (twice, Nov–Dec) and Soc. Two inland records in Rift Valley, Et (Jul and Nov). **Voice** Silent in region. [Alt: Parasitic Jaeger]

Pomarine Skua *Stercorarius pomarinus*   46cm, 18″ (+ br tail 9cm, 3.5″)

Bulky and deep-chested with heavier bill than Arctic Skua. Breeding adult has *long spatulate central tail feathers* (may be worn or lost) and *prominent white wing-flashes.* Commoner pale morph usually (but not always) has dark breast-band and barring on flanks and undertail. Dark morph is all blackish-brown, except for white wing-flashes. Immature barred and varied as Arctic, but looks bulkier; tail looks square-ended or with slight blunt projections. Non-breeding adult is like immature, but with plain dark underwing-coverts. Flight *steadier, heavier and slower* than Arctic Skua. **HH** Probably a regular passage migrant in southern Red Sea off Er and Dj, possibly wintering, and occasionally in large numbers. Very rare passage migrant off So, Nov–Dec and Feb–Apr. **Voice** Silent in region. [Alt: Pomarine Jaeger]

South Polar Skua *Catharacta maccormicki*   53cm, 21″

Heavier and shorter-tailed than Pomarine Skua, but smaller and slimmer than Subantarctic Skua, with less heavy bill and usually showing *paler hindneck contrasting with dark hood.* Adults have three colour morphs: dark, intermediate and light. All show prominent white wing-flashes in flight. Dark morph is mainly blackish-brown with paler collar, and sometimes has narrow pale band at base of bill. Intermediate morph has dark brown upperparts and paler brown underparts, with pale collar (sometimes extending onto mantle) and pale forehead. Light morph has *head and underparts creamy or pale greyish-brown, contrasting with dark upperparts and underwing.* Immature similar to intermediate adult, but greyer and with bicoloured bill. **HH** Vagrant to SSo, with two records (both May 1981). **Voice** Silent in region.

Subantarctic Skua *Catharacta antarctica*   62cm, 25″

A large, bulky, powerful brown skua with thick bill, broad wings and comparatively short broad tail. Shows extensive white wing-flashes in flight. Adult is uniformly dark brown with fine pale streaks on hindneck and upper mantle. Dark or intermediate South Polar Skuas are slimmer and smaller-billed, less streaked above. Immature is like adult but has bicoloured bill, paler legs, smaller white wing-flashes. Birds in our area are most likely race *lonnbergi* which is numerous in South African waters. **HH** Vagrant, with only one confirmed record: a freshly dead bird, race *lonnbergi,* in SSo (Jun). **Voice** Silent in region. [Alt: Brown Skua]

imm

br
pale morph

br
dark morph

Arctic Skua

imm

br
dark morph

Pomarine Skua

br
pale morph

South Polar Skua

ad
pale morph

ad
dark morph

ad

ad

Subantarctic Skua

lonnbergi

SMALLER GULLS *One Afrotropical and two Palearctic migrant gulls which are easily identified in breeding plumage, but are otherwise more difficult. Note head and eye colour and, in flight, wing markings. Sexes alike. Plumage changes from immature to adult in just over one year.*

Grey-headed Gull *Larus cirrocephalus* 41 cm, 16"

Breeding adult is a neat *grey-headed gull*, with *pale yellow eyes surrounded by pink-red orbital ring*, thickish dark red bill and red legs. At close range pale grey hood shows darker grey edge, and underparts may have pale pink wash. Non-breeding adult has much paler, poorly defined hood or whitish head with smudge behind eye. First-year is similar to first-year Black-headed Gull, with smudges on crown and behind *dark eyes*, and narrow black tail-band, but slightly larger, with more black in primaries and darker underwing. Bill is pinkish with dark tip; legs dirty orange-brown. In flight, upperwing of adult shows black outer primaries (with two white spots) and *dark grey underwing*. Race in Africa is *poiocephalus*. **HH** Flocks are common and widespread on fresh and alkaline waters in Rift Valley of Et, mostly as non-breeding visitors from south, Sep–May. Occasional records elsewhere including Lake Tana (1800m). Only a single record in So, in NW. **Voice** Utters a loud rasping downslurred *graarr*, typical of smaller gulls. [Alt: Grey-hooded Gull]

Black-headed Gull *Larus ridibundus* 38cm, 15"

Slightly slenderer and smaller than Grey-headed Gull, with *dark brown eyes at all ages*. Breeding adult has neat *dark brown hood and partial white eye-ring*, dark red bill and red legs. Non-breeding adult has white head with *dark spot behind eye*, and paler red bill with dark tip. In flight from above, adult shows white leading edge to outer wing; from below, darker inner primaries contrast with mostly light grey underwing. First-year is very like first-year Slender-billed Gull, but latter has longer bill and slender-necked appearance. Separated in flight from first-year Grey-headed by more white in primaries and paler underwing. **HH** Common Palearctic winter visitor and passage migrant to wide range of waters up to 2900m, particularly in coastal Er and inland in Rift Valley of Et, mainly Sep–Apr with a few oversummering. Less common in So. **Voice** Gives a shrill but low-pitched raspy downslurred *kreeeeaa*. [Alt: Common Black-headed Gull]

Slender-billed Gull *Larus genei* 40cm, 16"

Most similar to Black-headed Gull, but has *long-necked look, with gently sloping forehead and long bill*. Breeding adult has pure white head, and may have pink-washed underparts; bill varies from dark blood-red to paler orange-red; legs bright red. Eyes appear small, and are usually pale yellowish-white (but dark in very young birds) with small reddish orbital ring. Non-breeding adult may have light grey smudge behind eye. First-year has paler yellowish-brown bill and legs. In flight best told from similar plumages of Black-headed by overall shape, especially long-billed, long-necked look. **HH** Fairly common Palearctic migrant to coastal Er and Dj, Nov–Apr. Four inland records on Rift Valley lakes in Et and Lake Tana; vagrant Soc. **Voice** Gives a deep throaty *rraaaa*..

1st-year

br

Grey-headed Gull

1st-year

br

non-br

non-br

1st-year

br

Black-headed Gull

br

br

non-br

br

1st-year

br

non-br

br

Slender-billed Gull

LARGE WHITE-HEADED GULLS *The taxonomy of large white-headed gulls is highly complex, contentious and liable to change. All moult through a confusing range of plumages from immature to adult in 3–4 years, being very brown and dark-tailed in 1st year, greyer or blacker above in 2nd, tail mostly white and wing-tips gaining adult pattern in 3rd, followed by adult plumage (non-breeding and breeding) after that. All have black bills in 1st year, becoming yellow with a red spot as adults; leg colour varies and is described below. Familiarisation with the common Lesser Black-backed Gull forms a good basis for comparison; note overall size and shape, wing markings, and back and leg colour. All three species are visitors from the Palearctic.*

Lesser Black-backed Gull *Larus fuscus*   56cm, 22"

Slightly smaller and slimmer than other black-backed gulls, and standing birds often have drawn-out attenuated look. Breeding adult of common nominate race is *black-backed*, with white head, fairly slender yellow bill with red spot, and yellowish legs. Non-breeding adult is very similar (including white head). Immature passes through age groups as described above in introduction, but note legs are pinkish until second year. Best identified from similar-aged large gulls by smaller, slenderer appearance. In flight, appears *slimmer-winged* than others, adult showing small white tips to primaries, and single white spot on outermost feather. **HH** Common Palearctic visitor, mainly Oct–Apr, with a few present throughout year. Most numerous on coasts of Er and So, but also on larger Rift Valley lakes in Et, occasionally up to 2900m. **Voice** Usually silent in region, but a penetrating *keow* is used throughout the year.

Heuglin's Gull *Larus (fuscus) heuglini*   63cm, 25"

Large, bulky, dark-backed gull, currently considered a race of Lesser Black-backed. Immature and adult very like Lesser Black-backed, but always look *bigger*, especially if seen together, and also slightly larger-billed. Situation further confused by possible presence of two races, *heuglini* and '*taimyrensis*' (rare). Breeding adult *heuglini* is *dark grey above* with white head (non-breeding has *head streaked grey*), bill yellow with red spot (or yellow with red spot and narrow blackish band on subadult), eyes pale yellow, and legs yellow. Immature has pinkish legs. Adult '*taimyrensis*' has paler grey back, more streaking on head in non-breeding plumage, and either yellow or pinkish legs. **HH** Nominate *heuglini* is fairly common Palearctic winter visitor to coasts of Er and So, Oct–Apr, a few oversummering; less common inland on Rift Valley lakes in Et. **Voice** Usually silent in region, but calls are slightly deeper than Lesser Black-backed Gull. **Note** Paler birds from east of range, often separated as *taimyrensis*, may be hybrids between *L. heuglini* and extralimital Vega Gull *L. vegae*.

Caspian Gull *Larus cachinnans*   63cm, 25"

Large, lanky gull, *slender and long-legged*, with *smallish head, slender bill and gently sloping forehead*. Eyes quite small, often dark, set higher and more forward on head than other white-headed gulls. Breeding adult nominate *cachinnans* has pale grey upperparts, noticeably paler than either race of Heuglin's and closer to colour of extralimital Herring Gull *L. argentatus*, bill yellow with red spot and legs pale yellow or pale pink; non-breeding birds similar but show some light streaking on hindneck. Race *barabensis* ('Steppe Gull', sometimes regarded as a race of Heuglin's Gull) has darker upperparts, close to '*taimyrensis*' of Heuglin's Gull, and *bright yellow legs*; bill yellow with red and black subterminal markings and pale tip; eyes often pale. Non-breeding birds are similar but with light streaking on hindneck. Jizz is often best way to identify Caspian Gulls, especially race *barabensis*. **HH** Nominate *cachinnans* is rare winter visitor to Soc, probably also to coasts of Er and Dj, but true status clouded by identification and taxonomic issues. Race *barabensis* is rare visitor to Er and Soc, and may occur elsewhere in region. **Voice** Calls are similar to other members of complex. Generally higher-pitched and faster than Lesser Black-backed and Heuglin's Gulls. **Note** Sometimes treated as conspecific with *L. michahellis* of S Europe and Mediterranean, under name Yellow-legged Gull. **Armenian Gull** *L. armenicus*, formerly included within the *cachinnans* group, winters in northern Red Sea and may occur in Er. Winter adult is very similar to *barabensis* but is slightly smaller with a more rounded head and a heavier, more blunt-tipped bill; eyes usually dark.

1st-year

ad

2nd-year

br

Lesser Black-backed Gull

nominate

1st-winter

1st-year

ad

1st-winter

br
heuglini

Heuglin's Gull

2nd-year

br
taimyrensis

br

1st-winter

ad

Caspian Gull

nominate

DARK-HOODED GULLS Sooty and White-eyed are both similar, and identification (particularly of immatures) requires careful attention to size, shape and colour of bills. They attain adult plumage in just over two years. The massive Pallas's is distinctive in all plumages, changing from immature to adult in just over three years.

Sooty Gull *Larus hemprichii*   47cm, 18.5"

Breeding adult is *dark brownish-grey above and across breast*, with *sooty-brown head* and *white hind-collar*; breast to vent white. At close range shows *white mark above eye* (a second faint mark below eye may also be present), *greenish-yellow bill with narrow black band and red tip*, yellowish legs. Non-breeding adult has generally less well-defined markings and duller bill and legs. First-year is paler, plainer and browner above with pale fringes to wing-coverts, and no white hind-collar; *bill pale grey with black tip*; legs dull grey-green. In rather slow laboured flight, adult appears dark above with white trailing edge to wing; dark head and breast contrast strongly with white underparts and tail. Immature shows similar (but duller) pattern, with wide black band across tail. **HH** Flocks are very common on coasts of Er, Dj, So and Soc all year, breeding on offshore islands; recent survey found 1,067 pairs on 67 Eritrean coastal islands. **Voice** Single birds are rather quiet, but flocks are very noisy, with all members calling a nasal downslurred *weeooo...weeooo...* and creating a loud chorus.

White-eyed Gull *Larus leucophthalmus*   43cm, 17"

Breeding adult is similar to Sooty Gull, but slightly smaller and slenderer with *black head, white crescents above and below eye*, slender, slightly drooping red bill with black tip, paler *grey upperparts and breast*, yellow legs. Non-breeding adult is similar, but duller with some pale flecking on head. First-year is similar to first-year Sooty, but darker and browner (lacking extensive pale fringes to wing-coverts); *slender bill is all dark* (at all ages, bill of Sooty Gull looks two-toned). In light and buoyant flight basic pattern is similar to Sooty at all corresponding ages, but wings appear narrower and more pointed. **HH** Common resident along coasts of Er, Dj and NSo, breeding on offshore islands; recent survey found 5,900 pairs on 49 Eritrean coastal islands. Rare visitor to Soc, and absent south of 10°N in So. **Voice** Similar to Sooty Gull but less harsh. **NT**

Pallas's Gull *Larus ichthyaetus*   66cm, 26"

Breeding adult is *spectacular massive gull* with *black hood and large yellow bill with black and red bands near tip*; white crescents above and below eye visible at close range. In non-breeding adult, hood is reduced to dark smudges around and behind eye. First-year differs from other first-year large gulls (like Heuglin's) by *dark smudge behind eye, dark-tipped pale bill, white underparts and clear-cut black tail-band*. In flight, adult appears very large and pale, with *black on wings restricted to primary tips*. First-year shows *grey panel across wing-coverts* and solid black tail-band. **HH** Regular Palearctic winter visitor (usually in small numbers), Nov–Apr, to inland lakes in Et, notably Lakes Abiata, Langano and Tana. Rare in Er and Soc; vagrant to Dj and So. **Voice** Silent in region. [Alt: Great Black-headed Gull]

Sabine's Gull *Xema sabini*   36cm, 14"

Distinctive gull, slightly smaller and shorter-legged than Black-headed. Breeding adult has *blackish-grey hood and yellow-tipped black bill*. Primary tips show prominent white spots at rest; legs dark. Non-breeding adult loses hood, but has dark nape and hindneck. First-year is *grey-brown above with whitish fringes giving scaly effect*. In flight, adult has diagnostic *tricoloured wing pattern and shallow tail-fork*. First-year has similar pattern, but is black, white and brown rather than black, white and grey, forked tail tipped black. **HH** Breeds in high Arctic and winters off SW Africa. Highly pelagic outside breeding season. Vagrant SESo (once, May 1981). **Voice** Silent in region.

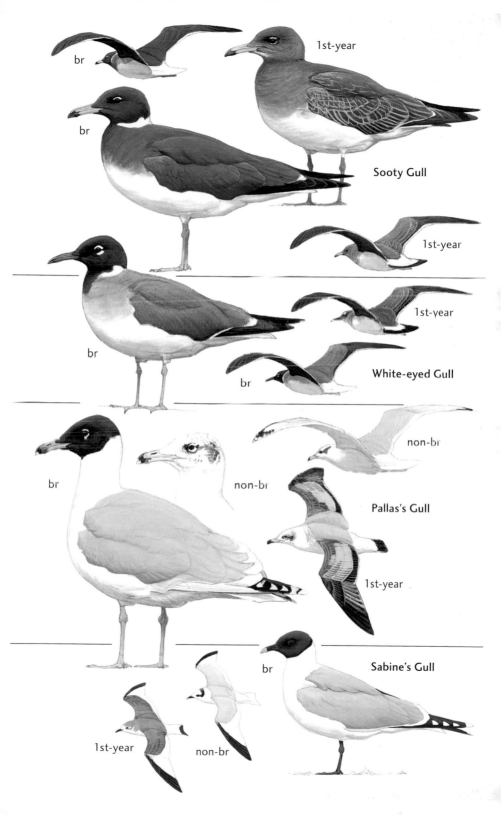

br

1st-year

br

Sooty Gull

1st-year

br

1st-year

1st-year

br

White-eyed Gull

br

non-br

non-br

Pallas's Gull

1st-year

br

Sabine's Gull

1st-year

non-br

TERNS Most are grey above and white below, with black caps in breeding plumage (see also plate 78). Some can be identified by size and bill colour, but medium-sized terns are difficult to identify in non-breeding plumage. Sexes alike.

Lesser Crested Tern *Sterna bengalensis*   39cm, 15.5"

Smaller and slimmer than Great Crested Tern with *straight, rich orange-yellow bill*. Breeding adult has *black cap stretching from bill to nape* and forming short crest. Non-breeding adult has white forecrown with black confined to above and behind eye, and on nape. Immature has duller bill and dark outer flight feathers. Flight lighter, more dipping and buoyant than Great Crested, with slightly darker outer primaries (notably darker in immature) and uniform pale grey back, rump and central tail. **HH** Very common resident and intra-African migrant on coast all year. Breeds Jun–Sep on islands off Er (63,000 pairs in 2005–07), Dj and NWSo, when there are fewer in SSo; numbers lower Dec–Feb in Er. Occurs as singles or in small to large flocks, both offshore and in creeks and estuaries. **Voice** Quite noisy, with feeding parties giving a high descending *krreek*.

Greater Crested Tern *Sterna bergii*   49cm, 19"

Larger than Lesser Crested Tern, with *heavier pale yellow bill*, decurved at tip. Breeding adult has crested black cap *separated from bill by narrow white forehead*. Non-breeding adult has black confined to behind eye and around nape. Two races occur: *velox* is distinctly darker grey above with paler grey rump and tail; *thalassina* is like Lesser Crested but obviously larger, with longer, paler bill. First-year has speckled blackish-brown crown, grey-brown back and wings with much pale fringing, and dark carpal bar. Flight is more forceful and shallower than Lesser Crested. **HH** Race *velox* is common resident or non-breeding visitor on all coasts. Breeds on islands off Er (2,200 pairs in 2005–07), Dj and NWSo, Jun–Nov. Race *thalassina* breeds on islands off Tanzania, with a few records of non-breeders in SSo, Jun–Jul. **Voice** Gives low, slightly descending scrapy rasps, *krrekk* or *krreerrk*. [Alt: Swift Tern]

Caspian Tern *Sterna caspia*   54cm, 21"

Largest tern with *massive red bill* tipped black. Breeding adult has short crested black cap, pale grey back and wings, and rather short forked tail. Non-breeding adult has white-streaked forecrown. First-year is like non-breeding adult but has duller orange bill. Flight is strong and steady, showing distinct *blackish ends to underwings* in all plumages. **HH** Singles and small groups of non-breeding birds are regular Palearctic or Afrotropical migrants along coast and on Rift Valley lakes all year, but mainly Sep–May. Small numbers breed on islands off Er, Nov–Feb. **Voice** Gives a variable high-pitched *sqeeweeweoo* and harsh *krre-ahk*.

Sandwich Tern *Sterna sandvicensis*   41cm, 16"

Similar proportions to Lesser Crested Tern with pale grey upperparts, *long slender black bill* with yellow tip, white rump and shallow tail-fork. Breeding adult has black cap with short crest and well-marked bill; black confined to nape and behind eye in non-breeding birds. First-year has virtually all-dark bill, some brownish fringes on wing-coverts, and darker tail. Flight is powerful and deep, showing variable darker grey wedge in primaries. **HH** Rare Palearctic visitor to coasts of Er, Dj and So, Dec–May; vagrant inland, with just one record in Rift Valley of Et. More frequent passage migrant around Soc. **Voice** Utters a high-pitched scratchy, slightly wavering *kirrireek*.

Gull-billed Tern *Sterna nilotica*   38cm, 15"

Solid, medium-sized tern with *short heavy gull-like black bill*, pale grey back, wings and rump, short shallow-forked tail, and longish dark legs. Breeding adult has neat glossy black cap and no crest; non-breeding adult has *black smudge just behind eye*. First-year is like non-breeding adult but with some brown scaling on wing-coverts. In buoyant lithe flight, wings often reveal narrow dark trailing edge to primaries. **HH** Singles and flocks are common Palearctic winter visitors and passage migrants, mainly Aug–May, but some oversummer. Occurs around major inland lakes (especially in Rift Valley up to 2100m), at coast (mainly Er and SSo), and also often over grasslands. Does not plunge-dive but swoops and picks food from surface. **Voice** Call is a loud raspy *crr-aarp* with accent on second syllable.

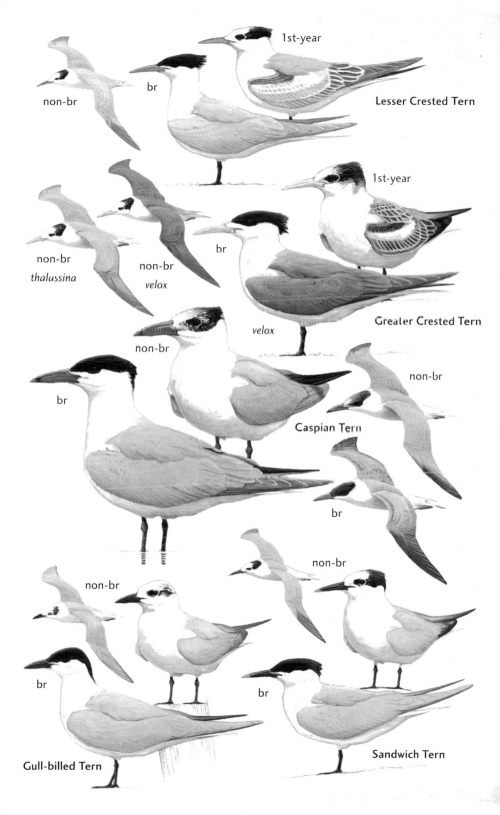

non-br

br

1st-year

Lesser Crested Tern

non-br
thalussina

non-br
velox

br

1st-year

velox

Greater Crested Tern

non-br

br

non-br

Caspian Tern

br

non-br

br

non-br

br

br

Gull-billed Tern

Sandwich Tern

Common Tern *Sterna hirundo* 36cm, 14"

Breeding adult has black cap and pale grey upperparts contrasting with whiter rump and tail, latter having elongated but not very long outermost feathers; underparts *washed pale grey. Bill usually black* in NE Africa, but may be red with black tip. Non-breeding adult has white forecrown, less contrast between back and rump, and blackish bar across lesser wing-coverts. First-year similar but may show a few brown fringes above, darker primaries, and dark bar across secondaries. In flight breeding adult shows mostly *white underwing with dark grey trailing edge to primaries*, dark wedge on upper primaries, and medium-length forked tail. Non-breeding adult has paler rump than very similar White-cheeked Tern. **HH** Flocks are very common along coast of So, Mar–Nov, with some recorded all year. Large numbers may occur in offshore mixed-species feeding flocks and at estuarine roosts. Uncommon winter visitor and passage migrant to Er, Oct–May; rare inland in Et. **Voice** Gives a descending *skreeoo* with accent on first syllable.

Arctic Tern *Sterna paradisaea* 38cm, 15"

Very like Common Tern, but slightly smaller with longer tail. *Bill shorter than Common and legs very short.* Breeding adult has *dark red bill without black tip, and greyer underparts*, contrasting slightly with whiter cheeks At rest, tail-streamers extend well beyond wing-tips. Non-breeding adult has white forecrown and short black bill. First-year is similar but paler and with faint dark carpal bar (darker on Common). In flight, upperwing more uniform, lacking dark wedge on primaries of Common Tern, and all flight feathers look translucent from below. First-year has whiter secondaries than Common. **HH** Rare Palearctic migrant to coastal So, with records of adults in Apr–May and Oct and first-year birds in May–Jul. One inland record (May). **Voice** Silent in region.

White-cheeked Tern *Sterna repressa* 33cm, 13"

Breeding adult is *dark grey above and below* with black cap and obvious *contrasting white cheeks*; back, wings and forked tail are uniform dark grey. Bill is red with black tip (like Common Tern). Non-breeding adult is very like non-breeding Common Tern with white forehead and underparts and dark carpal bar, but *rump and tail always greyer than on Common*, and more grey on underwing. First-year is like non-breeding adult but with paler silvery-grey primaries. In flight, outer wing is paler than inner wing. Diffuse grey trailing edge on underwing contrasts with paler underwing-coverts. See also Whiskered Tern (plate 80). **HH** Very common resident on all coasts, but fewer birds Dec–Mar. Breeds on islands off Er (18,000 pairs in 2005–07) and NW&SESo. Often feeds offshore. **Voice** Gives a harsh *kee-errr*, similar to Common Tern.

Roseate Tern *Sterna dougallii* 35cm, 14"

Breeding adult is similar to Common Tern but appears *much whiter with very long tail-streamers and long slender bill* which varies from bright red to black or a mixture of both; *underparts often washed pink.* Non-breeding adult and first-year have less distinct carpal bar and longer bill than similar Common Tern. In flight shows narrow dark leading edge on primaries from above, but *underwing is always very white.* **HH** Race *bangsi* is locally common breeding visitor to islands off SSo, present Apr–Oct. Vagrant NSo and Soc. **Voice** Gives a distinctive, scratchy almost wader-like *kirurit*.

Saunders's Tern *Sterna saundersi* 23cm, 9"

Very small tern which flies with rapid wing-beats. Breeding adult has *white forehead-patch that does not extend behind eye*, and 3–4 black outer primaries appearing as slightly larger dark wedge than on Little Tern. Black-tipped yellow bill is similar to Little, but legs are brownish or olive. In field non-breeding adult and immature cannot be separated from Little Tern. **HH** Very common along coast of ESo and Soc, present throughout year, and breeding May–Jun. Fairly common on coast of Er, Dj and NSo and may breed. Occasional non-breeding records on Rift Valley lakes, Oct–Nov and Feb–May. **Voice** Gives a frequent *plik plik...*, not obviously different from Little Tern.

Little Tern *Sterna albifrons* 23cm, 9"

Very like Saunders's Tern but breeding adult has *white forehead-patch that extends just behind eye*, with only 2–3 black outer primaries and brighter orange-yellow legs. Other plumages cannot be distinguished in field. **HH** Status uncertain, but probably a scarce Palearctic migrant with only a few confirmed records from Er, Dj and So, Oct–Apr. Likely to be overlooked due to identification problems. **Voice** Not recorded in region.

non-br

non-br

br

Common Tern

non-br

br

non-br

Arctic Tern

non-br

White-cheeked Tern

br

non-br

non-br

non-br

Roseate Tern

br

bangsi

br

br

non-br

non-br

br

br

non-br

non-br

Little Tern

br

Saunders's Tern

DARK-BACKED TERNS *Two dark-backed, fork-tailed sea terns which can be hard to identify at distance. Note extent of white on forecrown, nape and back contrast, and overall colour of upperparts. Sexes alike, but immature plumage is quite different.*

Bridled Tern *Sterna anaethetus* 35cm, 14"

Slightly smaller than Sooty Tern, with dark grey-brown upperparts, narrow white forehead and, at close range, *thin white supercilium which invariably extends behind eye. Dark crown contrasts with paler back*, and often a paler grey hindneck. In buoyant flight, underwing may show less contrast than Sooty, with grey-white coverts grading into dark wing-tip. Immature has greyish forecrown, pale fringes to back and wing-coverts, and mostly white underparts with grey wash to flanks. Race in NE Africa is *antarctica*. **HH** Singles and flocks occur offshore all along coast, with breeding on islands off Er (30,000–35,000 pairs in 2005–07), Dj, N&SESo and Soc, Apr–Sep. **Voice** Noisy on breeding grounds where birds give an almost gull-like barking.

Sooty Tern *Sterna fuscata* 43cm, 17"

Larger than Bridled Tern with *uniform sooty-black upperparts*, no paler hindneck or contrast between crown and back. *Brilliant white forehead does not extend behind eye*. In flight, underwing white and black, coverts contrasting with wing-tip. Immature is largely dark-brown flecked with white above, and with off-white belly. Race in NE Africa is *nubilosa*. **HH** Singles to very large flocks (many hundreds) are usually encountered well offshore off So, often feeding over active fish shoals, Apr–Nov. Irregular breeder at three sites on islands off N&SESo coast. Single record in Er and occasional inland. **Voice** Breeding birds give a strange three-part wavering *waa-a-aa* (entire colony making considerable din!).

NODDIES *All-brown sea terns with pale caps, well-angled wings and broad, slightly forked tails (when spread). If seen together should not present identification problems, but solitary birds more difficult; note extent of pale cap, bill size and any contrasting pale areas on the upperwing. Sexes and immature plumages are similar.*

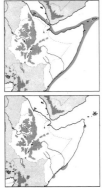

Brown Noddy *Anous stolidus* 41cm, 16"

Larger, browner and altogether heavier than Lesser Noddy, with pale cap clearly demarcated from blackish lores, and thicker bill. In flight *upperwing looks two-toned*, paler brown band contrasting with darker brown coverts and flight feathers. Race in region is *plumbeigularis* (usually lumped in Indian Ocean race *pileatus*). **HH** Locally common off coast, Apr–Dec, usually feeding well offshore and not seen from mainland. Breeds on Maydh Is, off NSo (20,000 birds in 1979), and islands off Er (11,000 pairs in 2005–07). **Voice** Breeding birds have a rather unmusical rasp. [Alt: Common Noddy]

Lesser Noddy *Anous tenuirostris* 33cm, 13"

Darker, smaller and more elegant than Brown Noddy, with thinner bill and silver-grey cap which grades into pale lores. In flight appears *very dark brown-black without contrast on upperwing*. Looks narrower-winged, with more rapid wing-beats and lighter feel than Brown Noddy. **HH** Common non-breeding visitor off SSo, mainly May–Aug, with smaller numbers to Dec; vagrant NSo and Soc. **Voice** Silent in region.

SKIMMER *Black and white tern-like bird, with graceful, elastic, measured flight. Feeds in calm water, skimming surface with its flexible thin lower mandible partially submerged, and snapping up small prey with stunning accuracy.*

African Skimmer *Rynchops flavirostris* 41cm, 16"

Attractive long-winged, short-tailed tern-like bird most noted for its laterally compressed red bill (with pale tip), lower mandible longer than upper. Breeding adult is all black-brown above and white below. Non-breeding adult is duller with greyish-brown collar across hindneck. Immature is paler brown above, with shorter blackish bill and dull yellow legs. **HH** Singles to small flocks occur sporadically in S&WEt, but are only regular on Rift Valley lakes, sometimes in large numbers. Also occurs on coast, but rare in Er and So. **Voice** Often silent, but groups give a high-pitched quavering contact *kreek kreek kreek*.

1st-year

Bridled Tern

ad

ad

1st-year

Sooty Tern

ad

ad

1st-year

ad

ad

ad

ad

Brown Noddy

ad

Lesser Noddy

non-br

br

br

African Skimmer

MARSH TERNS Three closely related small, slight terns which are mainly found over inland lakes and marshes. All are easily identified in breeding plumage, but much more difficult in variable non-breeding and immature plumages. Key features to note are extent of black on crown, rump and tail colour, presence of a shoulder 'peg', and, at close range, bill size. Sexes alike. White-winged Tern vastly outnumbers the others throughout the region.

White-winged Tern *Chlidonias leucopterus*   23cm, 9"

Breeding adult is stunning, boldly patterned tern with *black head, body and underwing-coverts* contrasting strongly with *mainly white wings, rump, tail and vent*. Non-breeding adult varies, but is largely grey and white with some blackish markings on hindcrown and behind eyes, giving appearance of wearing ear-muffs or headphones. *Rump and tail whitish contrasting with pale grey back and wings*; primaries may show darker grey wedge, and some show distinctive *black feathering on underwing-coverts*, but no small black peg at sides of breast. Shorter-billed than either Whiskered or Black Terns. Immature like non-breeding adult, but may have slightly more extensive dark cap, and darker grey-brown back. In flight looks light and bouncy. **HH** Very common passage migrant and winter visitor to inland lakes and dams up to 2900m, Aug–May, although a good number oversummer. Highly gregarious and may occur in flocks of thousands, especially on larger Rift Valley lakes. Much rarer at coast apart from on fresh water just inland. Vagrant Soc. **Voice** Feeding parties utter *short plik plik...* calls. [Alt: White-winged Black Tern]

Whiskered Tern *Chlidonias hybrida*   26cm, 10"

Slightly larger and stronger-billed than White-winged and Black Terns. Breeding adult has black cap, white sides to face and dark grey underparts. Non-breeding adult has black patch behind eye and fine black streaking on rear-crown (suggesting *Sterna* tern): *rump, tail and back uniform pale grey*. Beware confusing *Sterna*-like birds which lose grey underparts before moulting black cap. Immature like immature White-winged, but back is more boldly spangled brown and buff and rump is grey not white. Flight action stronger and steadier than White-winged. White-cheeked Tern (plate 78) is similar but larger with deeply forked tail, and exclusively maritime. Two races may occur: nominate (Palearctic migrant south to equator) as described; breeding adult *delalandei* (Africa south of equator) is darker than nominate, with white cheeks reduced to narrow stripe (non-breeding plumages indistinguishable). **HH** Locally common, but not numerous, on wide range of fresh and alkaline inland waters up to 2900m, mainly in Rift Valley, Oct–May. Scarce in So and Dj; vagrant Soc. Race *delalandei* not confirmed for region, but may occur. **Voice** Vocal; gives unpleasant low rasps and churrs, unlike most terns.

Black Tern *Chlidonias niger*   23cm, 9"

Breeding adult has largely black head and underparts, with grey wings and whitish underwing-coverts (black in White-winged Tern), uniform grey back, rump and tail. Non-breeding adult is like non-breeding White-winged, but with more extensive, solid black on crown and diagnostic *dark peg at sides of breast*; rump, tail and back uniform grey. Rather longer-billed and shorter-legged than White-winged. Immature best told from similar immatures by dark breast-patches. Flight action light and buoyant. **HH** Rare Palearctic migrant with very few confirmed records, but recorded in most months of year and in all countries except Soc. **Voice** Silent in region.

Black-naped Tern *Sterna sumatrana*   30cm, 12"

Distinctive, handsome, very white tern with slender black bill and well-defined *black band running through eyes and across nape*. Crown and underparts pure white, back and wings pale grey except for black outer web of outermost primary. Tail deeply forked. Non-breeding plumage similar to breeding. First-year similar but has dark carpal bar and primary tips. **HH** Hypothetical vagrant; an Indian Ocean species reported to occur in Somali waters, but no confirmed records. **Voice** A short raspy low *kirit*.

White-winged Tern

br

non-br

non-br

br

Whiskered Tern

non-br

br

delalandei

non-br

nominate

non-br

non-br

br

Black Tern

br

1st-year

br

br

Black-naped Tern

SANDGROUSE *Well-camouflaged, rather dove-like ground birds of dry country. Most active in the early morning and evening when small to large flocks congregate at waterholes.*

Chestnut-bellied Sandgrouse *Pterocles exustus* ♂ 33cm, 13"

Adult male has *yellow-buff head, neck and breast, dark chestnut belly* (may look black at distance) and long pointed tail. Adult female is largely mottled and streaked except for yellowish-buff sides to head and throat, and broad buffy breast-band. In flight shows *dark underwing and belly and pointed tail.* Three races occur: nominate *exustus* (NEr) is brownish-sandy above with dark chestnut belly; *olivascens* (SEt and SWSo) is more olive above, female more heavily barred; *ellioti* (Er except N, Et except S, N&CSo) is paler and brighter, and more rufous on belly. **HH** Often common in dry open country and dry bushed grassland from sea-level to 1500m. Drinks during the day. **Voice** Flight call vaguely resembles gobbling turkeys: a mixed set of musical pops and gurgles, *etchup-ga-googooliga...*

Black-faced Sandgrouse *Pterocles decoratus* 23cm, 9"

Adult male has neat face pattern with vertical *black stripe from forecrown to throat,* and *narrow black and white stripes curving above and behind eye.* Underparts have a *narrow black breast-band above broader white band.* Adult female is almost entirely barred, mottled and streaked except for plain yellowish-buff lower face and breast-band. In flight shows grey-buff underwings contrasting with dark belly. Race in region is paler *ellenbecki.* **HH** Pairs and small flocks are locally common in areas of dry open and bushed grassland from near sea-level to 1100m in S&SEEt and SSo. Drinks during the day. **Voice** Flight call is an explosive *wop'dela wiiiii,* last note being a fading whistle.

Spotted Sandgrouse *Pterocles senegallus* ♂ 35cm, 14"

Pale yellowish-buff sandgrouse with *long pointed tail.* Adult male has *chin, throat and sides of neck orange-yellow,* contrasting with *pale grey head and breast.* Adult female is mainly buff with duller orange face, *finely spotted black* above and on breast. In flight shows black secondaries contrasting with paler primaries and buff underwing-coverts, black line down mid-belly. **HH** Locally common in Er and adjacent Et on dry open plains below 600m; scarce non-breeding visitor to NSo, mainly Mar–May. Drinks in early morning. **Voice** Flight call is a simple *twikoo,* repeated frequently.

Lichtenstein's Sandgrouse *Pterocles lichtensteinii* 28cm, 11"

Rather stout sandgrouse with extensive barring above and below. Adult male has *black and white bands on forecrown,* small white spot behind eye, and *broad buff-brown breast-band traversed by two narrow black bands* (one centrally, one below). Adult female is entirely barred with narrow blackish lines. In flight looks bulky, the pale innerwing contrasting with darker flight feathers. Two races occur: nominate *lichtensteinii* (Er, NEt, NSo, Soc) is yellowish-buff heavily barred with black; *sukensis* (SEt, SSo) is darker with heavier barring. **HH** Fairly common in Et and So, preferring stony and sparsely bushed country from near sea-level to 1750m. Drinks before dawn or just after dusk. **Voice** Flight call is a high-pitched whistled bubbling *wicky-wi-wheo-wickiwicki-weeo...;* also a low churr.

Four-banded Sandgrouse *Pterocles quadricinctus* 28cm, 11"

Adult male is like Lichtenstein's Sandgrouse with black and white bands on forecrown, and best told by *bands of chestnut, white and black across breast* and *plain buff-brown neck and upper breast.* Adult female is extensively barred, except for face, throat and upper breast which are plain rich buffy-brown. In flight shows pale underwing. **HH** Pairs and flocks are locally common residents and wanderers in Er and Et west of Rift Valley, inhabiting open and bushed grasslands at 500–1800m. Drinks before dawn and after dusk. **Voice** Flight call is a repeated piercing rhythmic whistle *wi-ti-wi'wrreee,* last note tremulous.

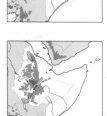

Yellow-throated Sandgrouse *Pterocles gutturalis* 31cm, 12"

Large, bulky sandgrouse. Adult male has *pale yellow face and throat encircled by black band.* Rest of upperparts rather plain grey-brown, with some dark spotting on scapulars and *broad rufous fringes to wing-coverts;* belly dark chestnut. Adult female is heavily mottled black, brown and buff, with paler yellowish face and throat, and dark chestnut belly. In flight, looks large and heavy with dark underwings and belly. Race in Et is *saturatior.* **HH** Uncommon resident and wanderer in Et on open short grasslands and highland plains, at 600–2200m, mainly in Rift Valley. No recent records from Er or NEt. Drinks in mid-morning. **Voice** Flight call is a strange musical cawing, *ah-oo-op-oo-ah-er-aap....*

olivascens

♂

♂

♀

Chestnut-bellied
Sandgrouse

♀

♂

Black-faced
Sandgrouse

ellenbecki

♂

♀

Spotted Sandgrouse

♂

sukensis

♀

Lichtenstein's Sandgrouse

♂

♀

♂

Four-banded
Sandgrouse

♀

♂

Yellow-throated
Sandgrouse

saturatior

GREEN PIGEONS *Tree-dwelling fruit-eating pigeons whose coloration makes them very hard to see. Often first located by their yapping, rather un-pigeon-like calls. Point-winged appearance and fast, direct flight can suggest parrots. Sexes alike.*

African Green Pigeon *Treron calvus* 27cm, 10.5"

Rather stout pigeon, usually encountered in small groups. Adult has *yellow-green head, neck and breast*, purple shoulder-patch on green wings, and yellow belly with dark centres to undertail-coverts; thighs bright yellow. Outer wing-coverts and secondaries broadly edged pale yellow, forming conspicuous wing-panel. Grey-green tail with little contrast from above, but from below blackish with broad silvery terminal band. Long undertail-coverts chestnut with pale tips. Immature duller than adult, and lacks purple shoulder-patch. Race in Et is *uellensis*. **HH** Uncommon in WEt, in woodland, forest edge, open country and cultivation at fruiting trees, 1200–2000m. **Voice** Very complex and un-pigeon-like call which usually begins with series of rising crackling notes, and continues with varied whinnying notes and lower musical growls. Often several birds call together.

Bruce's Green Pigeon *Treron waalia* 28cm, 11"

Differs from African Green Pigeon in having *greyish head, neck and upper breast sharply separated from striking yellow lower breast and belly*; large purple shoulder-patches, and chestnut central undertail. *In flight clearly shows yellow breast and belly*; undertail like African Green. Duller immature lacks purple patch on wing. **HH** Small flocks are common and widespread in Er, Et, Dj, NSo and Soc, in wooded valleys and semi-arid grassland where typically found in fruiting figs, from near sea-level to 1900m. **Voice** Similar to African Green but notes crisper and more crackling, with an insane churring and laughing quality.

BRONZE-NAPED PIGEON *Very dark arboreal pigeon of forested areas. Difficult to locate when high in canopy, but draws attention to itself with frequent calls.*

Eastern Bronze-naped Pigeon *Columba delegorguei* 27cm, 10.5"

Adult male appears all dark slate-grey with *striking white half-collar on lower nape*. If seen well shows iridescent green, purplish-pink and bronze sheen to hindneck. Adult female is duller, lacks collar, and is washed rufous-bronze on crown and nape. Immature like female, but darker greyish-brown above and dark rufous below. In all plumages bill is dark with whitish tip. Race in Et is assumed to be *sharpei*. Lemon Dove (plate 86) is cinnamon-brown below with pale face. **HH** Recently discovered in forest near Tepi in WEt at 1200m; status unknown; may be vagrant. **Voice** Complex call, *oo-oo-oo oo-oo-oo-oo-oo-oo-ah'ah'ah*; after three see-sawing notes, a descending series of *oos* is followed by a faster series of deeper notes with peculiar effect like voice breaking. [Alt: Delegorgue's Pigeon]

ad

African Green Pigeon

ad

Bruce's Green Pigeon

imm

Eastern
Bronze-naped
Pigeon

sharpei

♂

♀

♂

COLUMBA PIGEONS *Large pigeons with a small-headed, large-bodied appearance. Flight is swift and direct and birds often take to the air with loud wing-claps. Sexes similar; immatures are like dull versions of adults.*

Speckled Pigeon *Columba guinea* 34cm, 13.5″

Unmistakable, robust grey and maroon-brown pigeon with *conspicuous white spots on wing-coverts, bare red skin around* eyes, and pink-and-white striated neck. In flight, reveals distinct *pale grey rump* and broad black end to tail. Immature is duller grey-brown with greyish eye-patch. **HH** Widespread and common in Er and Et from near sea-level to 3000m, and spreading rapidly through Somalia. Occurs in open country with cliffs and in many towns. **Voice** Two main calls, a throaty *woopor...woooo*, first note rising then falling, last note falling and fading; and a monotonous sustained *woo-woo-woo-woo...*. [Alt: Rock Pigeon]

White-collared Pigeon *Columba albitorques* 32cm, 12.5″

Large, dark grey highland pigeon with prominent *white collar on hindneck* and broad band of iridescent green-tinged hackles below it. Dark tips on wing-coverts form two incomplete rows of black spots. Bill is black with *whitish cere*. In flight, shows prominent white patch on primary coverts. **HH** ENDEMIC to Er and Et. Pairs and small flocks are common in towns, villages and rocky areas, feeding in open grasslands and cultivation, at 1800–4200m. **Voice** A soft *coo-oo*, but rarely heard in wild and probably largely silent.

Somali Pigeon *Columba oliviae* 30cm, 12″

Pale grey pigeon with brownish-grey wings, *pale vinous-grey head with pale rufous nape, yellowish eye with red orbital ring*. Bill black with whitish cere; legs pinkish. In flight, pale tail has broad black terminal band and pale wings have contrasting dark trailing edge. **HH** ENDEMIC. Pairs and small flocks are locally common in bare rocky hills in coastal areas of N&NESo, from near sea-level to 750m (and once at 1425m). **Voice** Described as *wuk-wuk-wuk-oh, wuk-ow*, not unlike other pigeons in quality. [Alt: Somali Stock Dove]

African Olive Pigeon *Columba arquatrix* 38cm, 15″

Very large dark grey pigeon with *bright yellow bill, orbital ring and feet.* Boldly spotted white on wing-coverts and across breast. Pale grey hindcrown and nape contrast with dark purplish forecrown on male. Female is slightly duller and immature rather browner. In flight simply appears very dark and bulky with yellow bill and feet. **HH** Pairs and small flocks are locally common in canopy of highland forest and woodland in S&WEt and NWSo, and in adjacent country with isolated fruiting trees, at 700–3400m. Recently found in Dj and Er, where presumably isolated resident populations exist. **Voice** A deep vibrating *churr* is followed by rising *oo* notes. [Alt: Rameron Pigeon]

Rock Dove *Columba livia* 33cm, 13″

Wild Rock Doves are stocky blue-grey pigeons with *pale grey wings and two broad black wing-bars,* hackles on neck tinged with iridescent green and purple. In flight shows *prominent white rump,* black terminal tail-band, black trailing edge on wings, and two short black bars on secondaries; *underwing largely white.* Feral populations are highly variable, from birds resembling wild types (usually with dark rumps) through to brown-and-white and sooty-black individuals. **HH** Feral birds ('*domestica*') are widespread but generally rather uncommon in cities, towns and larger villages in region, nesting on buildings. Wild birds of race *schimperi* breed in Red Sea hills of Sudan, perhaps south to NEr, but no reliable records. **Voice** Bubbling rising and falling *churr*, interspersed with wing-clapping. [Alt: Rock Pigeon; Feral Pigeon]

Speckled Pigeon

ad

White-collared Pigeon

ad

Somali Pigeon

ad

African Olive Pigeon

ad

Rock Dove
schimperi

ad

Feral Pigeon
'domestica'

WOOD DOVES Small, delicate grey-brown doves, with banded rumps, rufous wing-patches, and iridescent spots on their wings. Characterised by attractive long cooing songs which die away (and can be hard to distinguish). Sexes alike (except in Tambourine). Immatures have much duller wing-spots and lightly barred upperparts.

Emerald-spotted Wood Dove *Turtur chalcospilos* 20cm, 8"

Typical wood dove, grey-brown above, paler below with pinkish breast, and *iridescent green spots on wings*. Bill varies from blackish to dark red with black tip. Flaps noisily into flight, showing warm rufous panel in wing, two bold black bars across lower back, and broad black terminal tail-band. **HH** Singles and pairs are widespread and common in Et (mainly E of Rift Valley) and So, in dry bush, scrub, woodland and farmland from sea-level to c.1500m. **Voice** Slow long call of muffled *poo* notes lasts c.10 secs: 2–3 hesitant upslurs, then three see-sawing notes, and long slow series of 15 descending notes, accelerating and fading. [Alt: Green-spotted Dove]

Blue-spotted Wood Dove *Turtur afer* 20cm, 8"

Very like Emerald-spotted Wood Dove, but rather darker brown above and warmer deep buff below, with *dark purplish-blue wing-spots* (may appear blackish) and *purplish-red bill with yellow tip*. In flight, overall tone browner than Emerald-spotted. **HH** Singles and pairs are common in Er and Et (except SE), generally in moister habitat than Emerald-spotted, e.g. forest edge, woodland, gardens and secondary areas, from sea-level to 1800m. **Voice** Like Emerald-spotted, but final notes all on one pitch, not descending. [Alt: Blue-spotted Dove]

Black-billed Wood Dove *Turtur abyssinicus* 20cm, 8"

Very like other wood doves, but paler and cleaner-looking, with *black bill and purplish-blue iridescent wing-spots*. Upperparts greyer than Blue-spotted, and underparts tinged pale lilac. Similar in flight to others, but appears greyer and colder-toned. **HH** Singles and pairs are locally common in WEr and WEt, occurring in woodland, thick scrub and forest up to 1500m (Emerald-spotted prefers dry bush). Overlaps in range with Blue-spotted, but probably not with more similar Emerald-spotted. **Voice** Like Emerald-spotted but slightly higher-pitched and often repeats three faster rhythmic notes amongst descending *poos*.

Tambourine Dove *Turtur tympanistria* 22cm, 8.5"

Adult male is rich dark rufous-brown above with *brilliant white face and underparts* and blue-black wing-spots (very hard to see). Adult female is duller with whitish sides to face, mostly grey underparts, and white in mid-belly. Immature has dull head pattern like female but is barred above, lacking wing-spots, and brownish below. In flight male appears dark brown above with rufous wings, white below. **HH** Singles and pairs are fairly common in wide range of forest, dense woodland, bush and thickets in SWEt and SSo from sea-level to 2150m. **Voice** Like Emerald-spotted Wood Dove but typically lacks slurred notes of introduction and all final *poo* notes are on same pitch, not descending.

Namaqua Dove *Oena capensis* 25cm, 10"

Delicate small dove with *long pointed graduated tail*. Adult male is *black on face and upper breast* with yellow-tipped purplish bill, two black bands across lower back, and dark purple-black spots on wings. Rest of underparts white, contrasting with black undertail-coverts. Adult female lacks black mask, and has pale buff-grey or whitish face and dark grey bill. Immature is like female, but back and wing-coverts are spotted and edged with pale rufous, grey, black and white. Flight is swift and direct, revealing rufous wings and long, slender tail. **HH** Widespread and common throughout Er, Et, Dj and So, in drier bush and cultivated areas from sea-level to 2400m, but wanders widely. Vagrant Soc. Frequently occurs in sizeable flocks. **Voice** Gives a plaintive descending *oooo* at around two-second intervals.

Emerald-spotted Wood Dove

ad

Emerald-spotted   Black-billed

Blue-spotted

Black-billed Wood Dove

ad

ad   **Blue-spotted Wood Dove**

♀   ♂

♂   Tambourine Dove

imm   ♀   ♂

♂   **Namaqua Dove**

RING-NECKED DOVES Grey-brown and pinkish-grey medium-sized doves with black half-collars on their hindnecks. Best identified by eye colour and voice. All have distinctive songs and calls on alighting, and spend considerable time feeding on the ground. Sexes are alike. Immatures similar with buffy fringes above.

Ring-necked Dove *Streptopelia capicola* 26cm, 10″

Most common and widespread ring-necked dove. Basic appearance is *brownish-grey with small but prominent black eyes* (obvious even at distance). Three similar races probably occur: widespread *somalica* (S&SEEt, So) is palest; *tropica* (SWEt, Rift Valley) is browner above and more pinkish below; *electa* (WEt) is darker, with greyer face and belly. **HH** Pairs and flocks are widespread (mainly east of Rift Valley) and may be very common at forest edge, in open woodland, dry acacia bush and cultivation, from sea-level to 1500m. **Voice** A three-note call *oo-oo-rrooo* repeated fairly rapidly (saying "work harder" over and over), as well as other *coos* and growling calls, and a nasal crooning *err-waaaa* on alighting. [Alt: Cape Turtle Dove]

African Collared Dove *Streptopelia roseogrisea* 28cm, 11″

Very pale pinkish-grey, dry-country dove with *delicate pale pinkish-grey head, neck and breast*, and *sandy-brown upperparts. Wine-coloured eye has narrow white orbital ring.* Wing-tips are browner and paler than other ring-necked doves. Most like Vinaceous Dove, but latter usually has dark loral line, broader black neck-collar and darker primary tips. Ring-necked has greyer head, without pinkish tinge; neither has dark red eyes, but call is best distinction. Two races occur: nominate (WEt) as described; *arabica* (Er, N&NEEt, NSo) darker with greyish underwing-coverts. **HH** Flocks are common in northern part of region, mainly below 300m, in variety of habitats including thornbush, semi-deserts, wadis and farmland. **Voice** Call is a distinctive musical rolling *hoo krrrrrrooo-oo*, emphasis on first note, very different from other ring-necked doves. [Alt: Pink-headed Dove]

Red-eyed Dove *Streptopelia semitorquata* 32cm, 12.5″

Larger and darker than Ring-necked Dove with *dark red eyes surrounded by narrow diamond-shaped ring of dull maroon skin.* Steep pale grey forehead contrasts with otherwise mainly plain brown upperparts and *dark pinkish underparts.* In flight rather dark and uniform above with *wide grey band across end of tail* (lacking white). Immature has brown eyes, rufous-fringed upperparts, and rather obscure hind-collar. **HH** Solitary birds and pairs, less often flocks, are widespread and common in moist forest, woodland and gardens from sea-level to 2500m in Er, Et (except SE) and N&SSo; absent from much of So. **Voice** Call varies slightly, but is typically a very rhythmical *oo-oo oo-oo-oo oo* which sounds like "I-am-a-red-eyed-dove!" (with third and fifth notes lower). Also has various other growling calls, and a single or double moan *uu-raaow.*

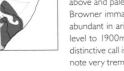

African Mourning Dove *Streptopelia decipiens* 29cm, 11.5″

Grey-brown ring-necked dove with *whitish or pale yellow eye and narrow red orbital ring.* Two races occur, varying in overall tone: nominate *decipiens* (Er, Et except SE, NWSo) is grey-brown above and pale pink below; rather bleached *elegans* (SEEt, SSo) is grey above and whitish below. Browner immatures have dull brown eyes. **HH** Pairs and flocks are widespread and sometimes abundant in arid and semi-arid bush and wooded country, typically including acacias, from sea-level to 1900m. Often found near water, and particularly numerous in Rift Valley. **Voice** Most distinctive call is a cheerful descending rolling *churr rrrrrrroooooooo*, and an *oo-rrrrrrr* on landing, last note very tremulous and throaty.

Vinaceous Dove *Streptopelia vinacea* 25cm, 10″

Small, pale, pinkish-grey dove, very like Ring-necked (race *tropica*) but with little overlap in range. Usually has *pale pinkish (not grey) forehead*, and is variably washed pink below, but can only be safely separated on call. Also very like African Collared Dove, but latter is paler, especially on flight feathers, and has dark red eye. Calls are distinctive. **HH** Singles and pairs are common in dry wooded and bushed grassland below 1800m in Er and Et, almost entirely west of Rift Valley. **Voice** Gives a rapid monotonous four-note *oo-oo-o'oo* with third note higher and all notes clear, lacking tremulous quality of Ring-necked. Also a three-note *oo'o-oo* with third note lower.

Ring-necked Dove

ad

ad

arabica

African Collared Dove

ad

Red-eyed Dove

ad

nominate

African Mourning
Dove

ad

Vinaceous Dove

African White-winged Dove *Streptopelia reichenowi* 25cm, 10"

Grey-toned ring-necked dove with brownish back; *pale yellow or honey-coloured eye surrounded by white eye-ring* is obvious at close range. In flight shows distinctive *white bar across upperwing-coverts*; less obvious at rest, but usually shows white on edge of closed wing. Female like male, but slightly browner below. **HH** Locally common near-endemic in SEEt and SSo below 1500m, in riverine woodland, palm stands and adjacent scrub, usually near water. In So, restricted to Jubba and Shabeelle valleys. **Voice** Gives a very monotonous rising and rolling *churr rrrooke'rrrooke'rrrooke'*... sometimes followed by a long series of descending short *oo* notes that may rise to form rolling call again. **NT**

LAUGHING AND TURTLE DOVES Three doves with rufous scalloping on the upperparts or wings. Laughing Dove has a mottled breast, the turtle doves have characteristic dark neck-smudges; none has a black hind-collar. Sexes similar; immatures duller than adults.

Laughing Dove *Streptopelia senegalensis* 23cm, 9"

Fairly small slender pinkish dove, pale rufous above with *pink and black mottling across upper breast and steel-blue wing-coverts* (no black collar or neck-smudges). Female is slightly paler below. Appears slender in flight revealing *blue band across wings* and white corners to tail. Immature significantly duller and plain below (lacks black breast mottling). Nominate race occurs throughout; marginally smaller *sokotrae* on Soc is not now considered valid. **HH** Pairs and flocks are very common throughout region in wide range of habitats, from sea-level to 2400m, including gardens, villages and towns. **Voice** Gives a strange laughing 5–6-note refrain, *oo-oo-oo-oo-oo* with fourth note highest and fifth lowest.

Dusky Turtle Dove *Streptopelia lugens* 30cm, 12"

Very dark grey dove with slightly paler grey face and *distinct black patches on sides of neck. Broad rich rufous edges to some wing-coverts and tertials* give scaly effect. In flight appears very dark with dull grey corners to tail. Immature is paler with more extensive rufous feather-edges. **HH** Singles, pairs and small flocks are widespread and sometimes common in highlands of Et at 900–2700m (but down to 250m in Er); only three old records in NSo. Occurs in forest edge, wooded areas, farmland and gardens. Birds wander widely, sometimes to lower altitudes. **Voice** Gives a very deep gargling and scraping *oo-oo orrrrr-orrrrrr* with all notes descending.

European Turtle Dove *Streptopelia turtur* 28cm, 11"

Much paler and slightly smaller than Dusky Turtle Dove with distinctive *black and white patch on neck, broad and extensive rufous edges to wing-coverts*, and blue-grey edge to closed wing. In flight suggests Laughing Dove but cleaner, brighter and longer-winged. Three similar races occur: nominate *turtur*, paler *arenicola*, and *rufescens* with broader rufous edges on wing-coverts. **HH** Uncommon Palearctic passage migrant and winter visitor to Er and Et, up to 2750m. Passage birds recorded Sep–Nov and Mar–Apr, with a few overwintering. Rare in Dj and So. **Voice** Song is a monotonous purring *prrrrrr prrrrrr prrrrrr*, repeated 3–4 times, and occasionally heard in region.

Lemon Dove *Aplopelia larvata* 24cm, 9.5"

Plump brown dove with *greyish-white face and cinnamon-brown underparts*. If seen well shows green and purple sheen to nape and back. Sexes alike. Immature similar, but duller below with some rufous edgings to breast feathers. Eastern Bronze-naped Pigeon (plate 82) is blackish-grey above and lives in canopy. Race in region is *bronzina*. **HH** Singles and pairs are shy and uncommon (except locally), often walking on ground in shade of forest undergrowth and exploding into noisy flight when disturbed. Occurs mainly in areas of dense highland forest in Er and Et, from 1200 to 3000m. **Voice** Calls with very low notes, either a pulsating *poopoopoopoopoo...* or a slow rising moan *ooooo*. [Alt: Cinnamon Dove; formerly in genus *Columba*]

African
White-winged
Dove

ad

nominate

Laughing Dove

ad

Dusky Turtle Dove

ad

nominate

European
Turtle Dove

ad

Lemon Dove

ad

bronzina

PARROTS *The three medium-sized, mainly brown and green parrots are best identified by presence or absence of yellow on head, and colour of underwing-coverts and belly, but their ranges barely overlap. All attract attention with loud calls, but are often hard to find in the canopy. Lovebirds are small bright green parrots with distinctive head or rump markings.*

Meyer's Parrot *Poicephalus meyeri*   23cm, 9"

Adult is mainly grey-brown on head and upperparts with green (or bluish-green) rump and lower breast to vent, *bright yellow band on forecrown, shoulders and underwing-coverts*. Close views reveal wholly dark bill and brown-red eyes. In flight clearly shows yellow underwing-coverts. Immature duller than adult and lacks yellow crown and thighs. Two races occur: nominate (WEr, NWEt) as described; *saturatus* (SWEt) is darker. **HH** Pairs and small parties are locally common in riparian woodland below 2200m; associated with baobab and tamarind in Er. **Voice** Loud high-pitched screeches interspersed with slurred chattering. [Alt: Brown Parrot]

African Orange-bellied Parrot *Poicephalus rufiventris*   25cm, 10"

Adult male is rather striking with *broad bright orange band across breast*, grey-brown head and blue-green rump and vent. In flight, adult male shows orange underwing-coverts. Adult female is very like immature Meyer's Parrot, but lacks yellow on shoulder and has brown underwing-coverts. At close quarters, bill is black and eyes deep orange-red. Immature is slightly paler than adult female. Two races occur: nominate *rufiventris* (C&SEt) as described; *pallidus* (SEEt, So) is paler on head and breast. **HH** Pairs and small groups are locally common in wide range of semi-arid and arid bushed and wooded grassland below 1700m, often in fig trees. **Voice** Intermingles quiet chattering with rather muffled screeches.

Yellow-fronted Parrot *Poicephalus flavifrons*   25cm, 10"

Bright green parrot with yellow head (sometimes tinged orange on male) and *bicoloured bill*: upper mandible blackish, lower whitish. Eyes orange-red. Sexes alike but female may have less yellow on head. Immature is dull yellowish-green on head, appearing all-green at distance. **HH** ENDEMIC to Et. Uncommon or locally common widespread resident, mainly in W&CEt, at 1150–3200m. Occurs in variety of woodland including acacia bush, fig trees and, at higher elevations, juniper and *Hagenia* woodland. **Voice** Calls are typical of genus, comprising high-pitched, slurred but strangely musical notes, lacking grating stridence of other parrots.

Red-headed Lovebird *Agapornis pullarius*   13cm, 5"

Vivid green lovebird with *pale blue rump* and striking red, black and white tail feathers (best seen in display). Adult male has *cherry-red face and black underwing-coverts*. Adult female has orange face and green underwing. In flight clearly reveals bright red or orange face and dark underwings. Immature like adult female, but face all-greenish and bill duller red. Race in Et is *ugandae*, but nominate *pullarius* may occur. **HH** Uncommon in woodlands in SWEt at 500–950m, perhaps only a visitor (records all Nov–May). **Voice** Call is different from all other lovebirds, a rapid-fire high-pitched metallic chinking *tink tinktink tink tink...*

Black-winged Lovebird *Agapornis taranta*   15cm, 6"

Bright green lovebird with *green rump and black flight feathers*. Adult male has *red band on forehead* (not extending onto chin). Adult female lacks red on forehead. In flight, male has black underwing-coverts, female green. Immature is like adult female but underwing-coverts are black, bill yellowish. **HH** ENDEMIC to Er and Et. Pairs and small groups are common residents in woodland and forest in highlands up to 2750m. **Voice** Much drier rattled notes than other members of genus. Explosive *tatt-tatt* notes are interspersed with unmusical squeaks and hisses.

Rose-ringed Parakeet *Psittacula krameri*   ♂ 41cm, 16"; ♀ 33cm, 13"

All emerald-green parrot with diagnostic *long graduated tail*. Adult male has black throat and rose-pink collar narrowly bordered above with blue. Adult female is largely bright green. In flight shows long pointed tail and blackish flight feathers contrasting with bright yellow-green underwing-coverts. Immature like adult female. Race in region is *parvirostris*. **HH** An uncommon resident in WEr and NWEt, in a variety of woodlands (especially *Hyphaene* palms and baobabs), mainly at 650–1950m. Also in Dj, and recorded once in NWSo. **Voice** Gives a variety of metallic churrs and chatters. [Alt: Ring-necked Parakeet]

ad

Meyer's Parrot

imm

ad

nominate

African Orange-
bellied Parrot

nominate

♂

♀

♂

ad

imm

♂

Rose-ringed
Parakeet

parvirostris

♂

ad

♀

Yellow-fronted
Parrot

♀

♂

♂

ugandae

imm

♂

Black-winged
Lovebird

Red-headed Lovebird

TURACOS *The three turacos are mainly bottle-green and dark blue, but reveal scarlet wing-patches in flight. Identification is based on the colour and pattern of head markings. Within wooded and forested habitat birds run and bound through the canopy, often with their tails raised, before swooping to trees nearby. Their raucous calls are characteristic sounds of the forest.* **GO-AWAY-BIRDS** *and* **PLANTAIN-EATERS** *are the striking but less colourful open-country relatives of turacos. In all, sexes are similar and immatures are like subdued adults.*

Fischer's Turaco *Tauraco fischeri* 40cm, 16"

A green turaco with *peaked crest edged dull red and thinly fringed white* (red of crest extends onto nape). Has bright red bill and white lines above and below red orbital ring. Wings green-blue and tail dark blue-green. **HH** Singles and pairs are very local and uncommon in riverine woodland and remnant forest patches in lower Jubba valley in SSo. **Voice** Call is a burry series of loud growls, the rising notes commencing slowly and progressing as a rapid series of up to 12 identical notes. **NT**

White-cheeked Turaco *Tauraco leucotis* 43cm, 17"

Green and blue turaco with *rounded crest*, red bill and red orbital ring. Told from other green turacos by *small white patch in front of eye and larger white patch on side of neck* (population in Sidamo region has smaller or vestigial neck-patch). Two races occur: nominate (Er, N&WEt) has crest tipped dark blue; *donaldsoni* (SCEt, east of Rift Valley) has crest tipped dull crimson. **HH** Near-endemic (small range extension into SE Sudan). Pairs or small parties are locally common in forests and woodlands, 900–3600m. **Voice** Growling call similar to other green turacos: *whoi-whoiwhoi whwhwhwhwhwhwh wher-wher-wher-wher-wher-wher*, introductory notes rising gradually, followed by short rattling series, then a slower deliberate rising set of notes, stopping abruptly. **Note** Race *donaldsoni* may be parapatric with nominate *leucotis*.

Prince Ruspoli's Turaco *Tauraco ruspolii* 40cm, 16"

Distinctive turaco, easily told from White-cheeked by *bushy pinkish-cream crest, and lack of white patch in front of eye*; also lacks white patch on side of neck. **HH** ENDEMIC to SEt. Uncommon resident in small patches of forest near Genale river, Wadera, Negele and Arero, favouring mixed broadleaved woodland at 1100–1800m; also found in degenerated habitats. Likely to be found in vicinity of fruiting trees. Hybridisation with White-cheeked recorded. **Voice** A very versatile turaco with wide range of calls. Main song consists of subdued introductory growled notes followed by long rising series that does not speed up: *wher, woh-woh-woh* (middle notes higher) *wirr-wirr-wirr* (rapid) *woh-woh-woh-woh-woh* (usually a series of five identical notes). **VU**

White-bellied Go-away-bird *Corythaixoides leucogaster* 50cm, 20"

Large slender grey and white go-away-bird with tall grey crest. *Grey upperparts, throat and breast are sharply separated from white lower breast to vent*; long tail is grey, black and white. Sexes largely alike, but bill black in adult male and green in adult female. Immature is duller than adult with plainer wings. In ragged undulating flight reveals white bars in wings and broad white band in tail. **HH** Pairs and family groups are common, widespread and often confiding in arid and semi-arid wooded and bush country up to 1500m. **Voice** Call is a repeated *waah*, and a more rapid high hollow *wop-wop-wop...*

Bare-faced Go-away-bird *Corythaixoides personatus* 48cm, 19"

Black-faced go-away-bird with long green-tinged greyish crest, *breast pale green*, belly pinkish. Sexes are alike, but immature has duller face, brownish crest, and no green on breast. Nominate race is almost endemic to Et. **HH** Pairs and small groups are uncommon in open woodland, acacia bush and riverine scrub, mainly near Rift Valley at 1350–1850m. **Voice** Usual call is a rather surprised *corr!* and less often heard is a loud, insane cackling duet.

Eastern Grey Plantain-eater *Crinifer zonurus* 50cm, 20"

Thickset grey-brown turaco with ashy head and shaggy white-tipped crest. Conspicuous bill varies from pale greenish-yellow to yellow. In rather ragged flight, reveals white bar in primaries and bold grey, black and white tail pattern. Immature like adult. **HH** Pairs and groups are sometimes common in wide range of open woodland and bushed grassland in Er and N&WEt (mainly west of Rift Valley), including cultivation and gardens, at 450–2500m. **Voice** Calls with loud querulous nasal notes which build up into maniacal laughter.

Fischer's Turaco

ad

nominate

ad

ad

donaldsoni

White-cheeked Turaco

♂

♀

ad

Prince Ruspoli's Turaco

White-bellied Go-away-bird

ad

Bare-faced Go-away-bird

nominate

ad

Eastern Grey Plantain-eater

CRESTED CUCKOOS Large, long-tailed, long-winged crested cuckoos with loud, stirring calls. All are at least partially migratory, mainly within the Afrotropics, but their movements are not well understood. Sexes alike, and two have light and black morphs. All are brood parasites: Great Spotted on starlings and crows; Levaillant's on babblers; and Jacobin on bulbuls and babblers.

Great Spotted Cuckoo *Clamator glandarius*   38cm, 15"

Largest crested cuckoo; adult has *shaggy pale grey crest*, dark grey-brown upperparts with *bold white spotting across wings*, pale cream underparts with buff-orange throat, and long dark graduated white-tipped tail. Strikingly different immature has black crown and cheeks, and reveals clear *chestnut primary patch* in flight. **HH** Widespread breeding resident (but breeding only confirmed for So) and Afrotropical migrant in woodland, bushed and wooded grassland, and cultivation from sea-level to 3000m. Movements poorly understood and population presumably augmented with Palearctic migrants in Oct–Mar, but some birds present all year. Vagrant Dj. **Voice** Migrants are silent, but breeding birds give loud woodpecker-like rattling *chhhtrtrtrtrrr-titititititit.*

Jacobin Cuckoo *Clamator jacobinus*   33cm, 13"

Similar to but smaller and shorter-tailed than Levaillant's. Two races occur: widespread *pica* is *black above and entirely white below (or hair-streaked)*, with white wing-patch and white-tipped tail. Light morph of southern *serratus* is similar, but washed pale grey and finely streaked below. Dark morph *serratus* is jet-black (*including tail*) except for white wing-patch (dark morph Levaillant's is larger with white tips to tail). Immature is brownish-black above and washed buff below. **HH** Sometimes common in bush, wooded grassland, scrub and cultivation at 200–2700m. Breeds sporadically across region. Migrations not well known. One population of *pica* breeds in Et and So (once) in Mar–Aug, later moving south; other birds of race *pica* visit NE Africa from NW India (Dec–Apr). Southern *serratus* moves north in non-breeding season, and is present in Er, Et and So in Mar–Sep. Vagrant Dj and Soc. **Voice** Migrants are silent, but breeding birds give squealed double and single notes *kwir'kik kwir'kik kwir kwir...* [Alt: Black-and-white Cuckoo; Pied Cuckoo; formerly *Oxylophus*]

Levaillant's Cuckoo *Clamator levaillantii*   40cm, 16"

Large, crested black and white cuckoo with two distinct morphs: widespread light morph is black (glossed green) above and white below with *heavy black streaking on throat and breast*. Coastal dark morph is entirely black except for white patch at base of primaries and *tips to tail*. In flight, white wing-patches and tail-spots are conspicuous on both forms. Immature is duller brownish above, with throat and underparts washed buff. **HH** Uncommon resident in Er and Et, breeding sporadically, and perhaps an intra-African migrant in some areas; scarce in So. Favours moist woodland, bush and forest edge from sea-level to 2100m, shunning drier areas. Usually seen singly and keeps to dense cover. **Voice** Calls are loud single-spaced squealed and rattled notes *tttttttttttt kweer kweer kweer tttttttt tttttt...* [Alt: Striped Cuckoo; formerly *Oxylophus*]

Asian Koel *Eudynamys scolopaceus*   43cm, 17"

A large, long-tailed cuckoo from Asia with *red eyes*. Adult male is *all glossy black and uncrested*, with broad, rounded tail and stout *pale greenish bill*. Adult female is dark brown above, heavily spotted and streaked white, and whitish below, with streaks on throat and coarse brown barring on rest of underparts; *tail is strongly barred brown and whitish*. Juvenile is blackish with pale tips to coverts, and variable barring below; tail faintly barred. **HH** Vagrant to Soc, with two males and female in Feb 2004. **Voice** Unlikely to be heard in region. On breeding grounds, birds give a loud series of *ko-ell* notes, gradually increasing in volume and pitch. [Alt: Common Koel]

imm

Great Spotted Cuckoo

imm

ad

ad

Jacobin Cuckoo

imm

ad

dark
morph

serratus

ad

ad

Levaillant's Cuckoo

ad

imm

ad

dark
morph

pica

♂

♀

Asian Koel

ad

GREY CUCKOOS Very similar-looking grey and barred cuckoos; all are hard to distinguish. Females of some species have a rufous 'hepatic' morph. Careful note should be taken of size, tail pattern, extent of yellow on the bill, barring and rufous colours, and calls. In dashing flight often resemble small raptors and may flush other birds. Three are long-distance migrants; while one, African, is a partial intra-African migrant.

African Cuckoo *Cuculus gularis*   33cm, 13"

Large grey cuckoo, adult male grey above and on throat and breast, and thinly barred black and white below. From Common Cuckoo by *more yellow-orange on bill (usually almost all basal half)* and by complete white bars (usually very hard to see) on two outer feathers of proportionately shorter tail. Adult female is brown-grey above, with paler barred breast (often with buff wash), but can be very similar to adult female Common. Immature is barred throughout including rump. **HH** Widespread and fairly common to uncommon intra-African migrant to drier woodland, wooded and bushed grassland below 1350m; recorded Mar–Jun in Et and May–Sep in So (mainly in NW). Parasitises Fork-tailed Drongo, but there is no evidence of breeding in region, and birds may be overlooked when silent. **Voice** Gives a quiet repeated *pooh-pooh*, very similar to African Hoopoe, but slightly slower. **Note** Formerly considered to be a race of Common Cuckoo.

Common Cuckoo *Cuculus canorus*   33cm, 13"

Extremely similar to African Cuckoo but wings and tail considerably longer; adult male best told by *yellow-orange confined to base of bill* and outer tail feathers spotted not barred (very hard to see). Adult female has two distinct colour morphs: either grey-brown (normal) or brick-rufous (uncommon; not illustrated); both are barred below with strong rufous wash to sides of breast. Immature strongly barred like African, but crown and rump plain (not barred). Two races occur: nominate as described; *subtelephonus* is smaller and duller, with paler throat and more lightly barred underparts. **HH** Widespread and common Palearctic migrant to forest edge, woodland, wooded and bushed grassland from sea-level to 2300m; recorded on southward passage Aug–Nov, and moving north Mar–May. Most birds probably nominate; the few *subtelephonus* are all Sep–Nov (but this race probably overlooked). **Voice** The familiar *cuc-koo* call is occasionally heard in spring. [Alt: European Cuckoo]

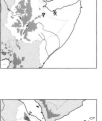

Asian Lesser Cuckoo *Cuculus poliocephalus*   28cm, 11"

Smaller and more distinctly marked than larger grey cuckoos, and extremely similar to Madagascar Lesser Cuckoo *C. rochii* (not recorded in region). Adult male is grey above, on throat and breast, and *barred black on white below*. Adult female has two distinct colour morphs: one is grey-brown with buff tinge to breast and flanks, the other is bright brick-red. Immature is grey-brown barred white and buff above, and is barred dark below. **HH** Vagrant from South Asia to NWSo (two records, Nov). Usually winters further south in eastern Africa. Two birds in SEt in Apr 1993 were either this species or Madagascar Lesser Cuckoo. **Voice** Normally silent in region, but flushed birds may utter a loud staccato rattle. [Alt: Lesser Cuckoo]

Red-chested Cuckoo *Cuculus solitarius*   30cm, 12"

Adult male is dark grey above (sometimes lighter on head), with *grey throat, broad rufous band across breast,* and black and white banding from upper breast to belly. Adult female is similar but has whitish-buff throat. Immature is charcoal black above (with scaly pale fringes in fresh birds) and with black throat and black-and-white barring below. **HH** Common and widespread resident in forest edge, woodlands and gardens in Et (especially in SW), at 400–2500m, wandering widely in rains. Although recorded in most months, most records are Mar–Aug. Vagrant SSo (once). Parasitises scrub robins and robin-chats (which regularly mimic their calls). **Voice** Call is a familiar seasonal sound, a three-note whistle, each note descending a half-tone, *fwi-fwi-few* (often rendered "it-will-rain!"); also has rising bubbling call, often partly in duet.

♂

♀

imm

♂

African Cuckoo

♀

♂

♂

Common Cuckoo

imm

♀ hepatic

♂

Asian Lesser Cuckoo

♂

♂

imm

♂

Red-chested Cuckoo

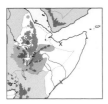

Black Cuckoo *Cuculus clamosus*   30cm, 12"

Variable dark cuckoo with two races in region: more easterly and widespread nominate is often entirely black (blue-black in good light), but may show some pale barring below, especially on vent. Western *gabonensis* is black above and rather dingy black and buff below, with strong wash of rufous across breast and throat. Similar Red-chested Cuckoo (plate 90) has plain grey or whitish-buff throat and yellow orbital ring. An intermediate form ('*jacksoni*') also occurs in SEt. Sexes alike, and immatures duller. **HH** Nominate is a common and widespread intra-African migrant (Apr–Sep) to forest edge, woodland, wooded grassland and thickets, at 500–1800m; *gabonensis* (WEt) inhabits forest (May–Jul). Rare in So (two records). Parasitises bush-shrikes. **Voice** Usual call is a three-note rising whistle, first two identical, third an upslur starting a half-tone higher *for for-fier*, sometimes leading into a cheerful rising bubbling call.

SHINING CUCKOOS Small, slender cuckoos with distinctive, partially iridescent male plumages, but rather confusing barred females and immatures. Extent of green and brown in plumage and colour of outer tail aid identification. Females are secretive, but males are vocal; females also have distinctive calls. Diederik Cuckoo largely parasitises weavers; Klaas's parasitises warblers and sunbirds; African Emerald parasitises robins and smaller thrushes.

Diederik Cuckoo *Chrysococcyx caprius*   19cm, 7.5"

Adult male is metallic bronze-green above, with *bold green and white face pattern, obvious red eye, and white spots on wing-coverts*. White below with barred flanks and *outer tail-spotted black and white*. In flight, shows spotted outer tail and entirely barred underwing. Adult female more brown and green above, with russet throat and upper breast, and thickly barred flanks: eyes dull brown. Immature has two colour morphs: commonest is like adult female, but with rufous barring on upperparts and heavily streaked throat; rarer form is largely rufous above and below. Both have bright red bills. **HH** Common intra-African migrant in wide range of bushed and wooded grassland, and cultivation from sea-level to 2500m, often appearing during rains. In Er and Et, present from Apr–Oct. In So, mainly a passage bird but, as in Et, almost entirely absent Nov–Mar. **Voice** Memorable onomatopoeic *dee-dee-dee-dee-derik* which can be clear, but often wildly accelerated and slurred.

Klaas's Cuckoo *Chrysococcyx klaas*   18cm, 7"

Adult male is *iridescent bright green above with plain wings, small white bar behind dark eye*; snow-white below with *dark green patches on sides of breast*. Adult female bronze-green above with fine russet barring below; eyes pale brown. In flight, adult male shows white underwing-coverts and largely white outertail; female and immature also show white outertail. Immature like adult female, but more heavily barred above and below, with subdued bar behind eye, and dark bill. **HH** Common and widespread resident and partial intra-African migrant in moister and often denser habitats than Diederik Cuckoo, including woodland, forest edges, bush and gardens, from sea-level to 2300m. Rather rare in Er and absent from NSo. In SSo, recorded Feb–Nov with most in Apr and Nov. **Voice** Gives a repeated high-pitched slurred whistle *fwiii-fi, fwiii-fi.*

African Emerald Cuckoo *Chrysococcyx cupreus*   23cm, 9"

Adult male is stunning gaudy *emerald-green and yellow cuckoo* unlike any other bird. In flight shows black and white underwing-coverts, and dark unbarred flight feathers. Adult female is barred rufous and green above, and barred green and white below; may show whitish flecks or barring on crown and nape, but never has white flash behind eye of Klaas's. Immature very similar to adult female. **HH** Solitary, but widespread and locally common resident of moist forest, dense woodland and thickets at 500–2900m, mainly in W&SEt; uncommon in Er and absent from So. May be partial intra-African migrant as numbers higher in Mar–Jun. Males call regularly from high canopy and are surprisingly hard to see despite bright colours. **Voice** Very distinctive set of four whistles *whi'twau wor-wee* (often translated as 'hel-lo geor-gie'), with first two notes descending, a short pause, and then two accentuated rising slurs.

ad

gabonensis

ad

imm

nominate

Black Cuckoo

ad

imm

Diederik Cuckoo

♂

♂

♀

♂

♀

imm

♂

♂

Klaas's Cuckoo

♀

♂

African Emerald Cuckoo

YELLOWBILL *Medium-sized, non-parasitic cuckoo with short, rounded wings and long graduated tail. Has weak flight and inhabits dense vegetation. Closely related to Asian malkohas (genus* Phaenicophaeus).

Yellowbill *Ceuthmochares aereus* 33cm, 13"

Odd cuckoo with *bright yellow bill* and pale blue skin around red eyes. Two races occur: nominate (SWEt) is dark grey above with bluish sheen, and paler grey below; *australis* (SSo) is generally greener-toned with pale throat. Both appear dark at distance. Sexes alike; immature duller with brownish throat, pale horn bill, and brown eyes. **HH** Elusive and perhaps scarce resident, inhabiting dense thickets, forest patches and edges from sea-level to 2000m. Poorly known in Et with few confirmed records; in So also only known from handful of records from Jubba and Shabeelle valleys. **Voice** Call typically starts with paired clicking notes accelerating into rapid series of descending *tics*, terminating in long rattle. Also has loud rising whistle with accent on last part *weee-eeeeeee*. **Note** Racial identity of Et birds uncertain; presumed nominate. [Alt: Green Coucal]

COUCALS *Cumbersome non-parasitic cuckoos easily identified as a group but difficult to separate as species. All are bulky with short rufous or chestnut wings, long tails, red eyes (except Black Coucal), weak flight, and loud bubbling calls. Note range, size, head and tail colour. Sexes alike, but immatures vary.*

White-browed Coucal *Centropus superciliosus* 41cm, 16"

Adult has *dark crown and face separated by long white eyebrow*, with *fine pale streaking* extending onto brown-rufous back. Pale below, streaked and barred darker. Immature similar, but supercilium, streaking on upperparts and entire underparts suffused with buff. Nominate race occurs throughout region; birds from Soc described as *socotrae*, supposedly with paler crown and underparts and green-glossed tail, but not now considered valid. **HH** Pairs are widespread and common in wide range of rank vegetation, thickets and bushed and wooded grassland, often near water, from sea-level to 1800m; generally absent from most arid areas. **Voice** Much more hurried series of descending hollow notes than other coucals. Also has variety of harsh *kak* notes.

Black Coucal *Centropus grillii* 38cm, 15"

Smallest coucal. Breeding adult is highly distinctive, *all-black with chestnut wings*. Non-breeding adult is dark brown, heavily streaked with buff on head and upper back, with barred rufous-and-black wings and tail, and buffish below with fine pale streaks on breast; undertail-coverts barred brown and buff; bill pale brown or horn. Immature like non-breeding adult, but has more extensive barring over crown and forehead (resembles White-browed but smaller and always lacks white eyebrow). **HH** Rare and localised in swamps, river valleys and flooded grasslands in SWEt, and perhaps overlooked. Known to wander widely during rains. **Voice** Gives a regular, rather hollow-sounding *kuk-uk kuk-uk kuk-uk...*, both notes identical and rhythmic; also a subdued descending series of notes, typical of coucals.

Senegal Coucal *Centropus senegalensis* 41cm, 16"

Very like Blue-headed Coucal but *distinctly smaller with less heavy bill*. Head and nape glossed green (often looks black in field). Separation from Blue-headed requires caution. Immature like White-browed Coucal, but has browner crown, only a faint buff supercilium, and buffy not greyish-white underparts. Race in region is nominate. **HH** Locally common resident of drier habitats such as forest clearings, thickets and bushed grassland (the least water-dependent coucal). Occurs mainly in WEt, and absent from Er. **Voice** Call varies locally, but is typically descending after an initial two-note introduction, rather minor-key, and ending on higher series of identical notes.

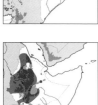

Blue-headed Coucal *Centropus monachus* 46cm, 18"

Large, robust coucal with glossy blue-black crown extending over nape (may look black in field); off-white to buff below, with long black tail slightly glossed green. Immature like adult, but has dull, faintly streaked crown, barred primaries, buffy underparts, and blackish-brown tail. Two races occur: nominate (WEr, C&WEt, mainly west of Rift Valley) as described; *fischeri* (extreme WEt) has inner secondaries and wing-coverts more olive-brown. **HH** Common resident (but rare in Er) close to water in marshes, papyrus swamps and other dense wet areas at 500–2700m. **Voice** Call is typical of coucals, a descending series of hollow notes, lower and slower than White-browed.

Yellowbill
nominate

ad

imm

White-browed Coucal

ad

nominate

non-br

**Black
Coucal**

imm

Senegal Coucal
nominate

ad

br

imm

ad

Blue-headed Coucal
nominate

BARN OWLS *Two distinctive species with heart-shaped faces that belong to a different family to all other owls in Africa.*

African Grass Owl *Tyto capensis*   38cm, 15"

Similar to Barn Owl, but larger and with much *darker brown back and wings*, which contrast with paler buff underparts. Flying birds are dark brown above with small buff patch at base of primaries (much smaller than in Marsh Owl). **HH** Very rare resident of highland grassland and moorland, with only two records in CEt (perhaps only vagrant to region). Rarely seen in daylight unless flushed. **Voice** Usual call is a harsh but short raspy scream *kreee*; also gives various dry rasps and chitterings near nest.

Barn Owl *Tyto alba*   35cm, 14"

Ghostly owl, patterned golden-buff and pale grey above (finely speckled black and white), with small dark eyes set in pale heart-shaped facial disc, and white to creamy-buff underparts. In buoyant flight appears largely pale golden-buff and white. Race in sub-Saharan Africa is *affinis*. **HH** Pairs are uncommon but widespread residents from sea-level to 2400m, often near settlements, and in buildings, old wells and Hamerkop nests, but tends to be absent from forest and arid country. Rare or absent from much of Er, SE&SWEt and So (except SE). **Voice** Calls frequently, although bird usually unseen, a high-pitched screamed *chrirrrr,* given singly or in series.

MEDIUM-SIZED OWLS *A mixed group of owls that can be identified by a combination of plumage, habitat and calls. Sexes are alike, but females may be larger than males. Immatures tend to be similar to but a little darker than adults.*

Marsh Owl *Asio capensis*   35cm, 14"

Warm uniform brown above and on breast, and buff-brown below, *with penetrating dark eyes set in paler facial disc*. Short ear-tufts sometimes visible at rest. In flight, resembles African Grass Owl but longer-winged and shows *obvious, larger rich buff patch at base of primaries*. Short-eared Owl is larger and paler, with yellow eyes. **HH** Probably a rare resident but status uncertain with only a few records for Et, centred around Lake Tana and Rift Valley, at 700–2700m. Generally found singly, but sometimes in small groups, in open wetlands as well as grassland and moorland. Birds are often active just before dusk and flush easily in daylight. **Voice** Usual call is a rising rasp *krrrik* or series of rasps.

Short-eared Owl *Asio flammeus*   38cm, 15"

Extensively streaked and mottled owl with rounded head and *yellow eyes*. Ear-tufts rarely visible. In buoyant flight, looks long-winged (with black tips) and flies with distinctive 'slow motion' wing-beats interspersed with frequent glides; can look very like smaller Marsh Owl, but appears more patterned above and has yellow (not obviously dark) eyes. **HH** Irregular Palearctic winter visitor to open grasslands and marshes in coastal Er and scattered localities in Et, Oct–Apr, from sea-level to 2400m. Vagrant Dj (twice) and Soc (once, 2007). **Voice** Silent in region.

Abyssinian Owl *Asio abyssinicus*   43cm, 17"

Heavily mottled and streaked dark brown owl, with *fierce orange-yellow eyes, and conspicuous long ear-tufts*. Perches with upright stance. Much slimmer and smaller than eagle owls, and ear-tufts more vertical. **HH** Nominate race is an uncommon resident of montane forest in N&CEt at 1800–3900m, but sometimes found in open on ground. **Voice** Call is drawn-out deep *who-woohm* or a single inquisitive *who*, repeated at intervals of several seconds. Female has a similar, softer call. Young birds give drawn-out, high-pitched *pee-eh*, reminiscent of extralimital Long-eared Owl. **Note** Formerly conspecific with Long-eared Owl *A. otus*. [Alt: African Long-eared Owl]

African Wood Owl *Strix woodfordii*   34cm, 13.5"

Attractive *round-headed owl (no ear-tufts)*, with pale, lightly barred facial disc, dark brown eyes, underparts heavily barred rufous-brown and white. Two races occur: browner *umbrina* (Et) and more blackish *nigricantior* (SSo). **HH** Uncommon or scarce resident in Et, in wide range of highland and lowland forest, woodland and mature gardens, at 800–2600m. Rare in SSo, in Boni Forest and lower Jubba valley. **Voice** Male gives a rhythmic *oo-hoo-oohu-hu-hu-hu*, female often replying with identical series on lower tone. Male also gives a long rising then falling slurred *oo-ooooooo*.

Barn Owl

affinis

African Grass Owl

Marsh Owl

Abyssinian Owl

nominate

Short-eared Owl

African Wood Owl

umbrina

African Scops Owl *Otus senegalensis* 17cm, 6.5"

Well-camouflaged scops owl entirely streaked and mottled grey-brown, but some individuals are lightly washed warmer brown or pale rufous. Bright yellow eyes are set in narrowly black edged grey facial disk, underparts boldly marked, giving marbled effect. **HH** Pairs are common and widespread in dry bush and woodland in Et, including large trees along rivers, from sea-level to 2,000m; uncommon in Er (no recent records) and So. **Voice** Calls for long periods, a musical *krrrou* given at varying regular intervals of 4–8 seconds.

Socotra Scops Owl *Otus (sunia) socotranus* 15cm, 6"

Similar to African Scops Owl but *smaller, more compact and greyer*; throat and breast finely vermiculated greyish, *belly and vent white*, with prominent long dark streaks on entire underparts (finer than on African and Eurasian). Eurasian is browner above and below, African has more marbled effect below; neither is as white below as Socotra Scops. **HH** ENDEMIC. Widespread resident on Soc in wooded areas up to 850m. **Voice** Song is a 3–4 note series *tuk tuk t-rrooo*, very similar to Oriental Scops *O. sunia*. **Note** Formerly treated as race of African Scops or Striated Scops *O. brucei*, but better considered as race of Oriental Scops or as separate species.

Eurasian Scops Owl *Otus scops* 18cm, 7"

Very slightly larger than African Scops Owl with a longer primary projection, and often a little browner and plainer, but otherwise very similar and probably not separable in field when silent. **HH** Singles are uncommon Palearctic winter visitors in Er and Et, Oct–Apr, but almost certainly overlooked. Very rare in So and vagrant Dj. Most are nominate, but at least one *pulchellus* has been recorded (NEEt). Occurs in wooded habitats and forest edge, especially in riverine woodland and near lakes, at 250–2100m. **Voice** Silent in region, but call is a familiar *hoo* repeated at regular intervals for long periods.

Northern White-faced Owl *Ptilopsis leucotis* 26cm, 10"

Larger, paler and greyer than other scops owls with variable yellow to red eyes and *white face mask with black borders*. **HH** Pairs are uncommon residents in Er and Et (uncommon in So) from sea-level to 2100m, preferring dry woodland, bushed and wooded grassland, often in acacias. **Voice** Gives a hollow dove-like *kuk-koo'ooh* with last note descending. **Note** Southern form *P. granti* (south of equator) was formerly lumped in this species, but has a different voice.

Pearl-spotted Owlet *Glaucidium perlatum* 19cm, 7.5"

Brown above with *small white spots on crown and back*, larger white spots on scapulars (forming white line), *two dark eye-spots (false eyes) on nape*, and intimidating yellow eyes. Underparts variably streaked and spotted rufous-brown with broad streaking extending to lower flanks. Race in NE Africa is *licua*. **HH** Singles and pairs are widespread and fairly common in bushed and wooded grasslands, preferring drier areas with acacias, from near sea-level to 2400m; scarce in NW&SSo. Partially diurnal and often mobbed by small birds. **Voice** Call starts with long series of short piped *fwoo-fwoo-fwoo…* notes that gradually rise in pitch and volume and, after a pause, a shorter sequence of whistled downslurs *fweeu-fweeu-fweeu…* often given in see-sawing duet.

African Barred Owlet *Glaucidium capense* 22cm, 8.5"

Larger than Pearl-spotted Owlet with *narrowly barred crown and nape, and well barred and spotted underparts*; back is lightly barred or plain. Pearl-spotted has spotted crown and streaked underparts. **HH** Race *scheffleri* is local and uncommon in coastal forest and woodlands in SSo, especially riverine forest on the Jubba. **Voice** Long series commences with regular identical piped downslurs then, after a pause, a set of peculiar vibrato downslurs that seesaw towards end.

Little Owl *Athene noctua* 20cm, 8"

Pale, compact and fairly long-legged owl of open country. Appears flatter-headed than owlets, with poorly defined face-mask. Crown lightly spotted and underparts faintly streaked with whitish belly. Legs thinly feathered. Two races occur: *spilogastra* (Red Sea coast of NEr), and *somaliensis* (Dj, NSo and SEEt), smaller and darker with less spotting on crown. **HH** Fairly common, relatively diurnal resident in thornbush and semi-desert, often perching on rocks, from sea-level to 1950m. **Voice** Calls of NE African birds are unknown, but European birds utter a far-carrying, rather mournful *keeeeer* as well as various squeals. **Note** Race *spilogastra* is sometimes split as Ethiopian Little Owl *A. spilogastra*.

African
Scops Owl

Eurasian
Scops Owl

nominate

Socotra
Scops Owl

nominate

Northern
White-faced
Owl

Pearl-spotted Owlet

licua

nominate

African Barred
Owl

Little Owl

somaliensis

scheffleri

EAGLE-OWLS *A striking group of large, heavily built owls. Verreaux's Eagle-Owl is distinct, but the other three are more similar; general colour, range and calls aid identification. Sexes similar, but females are larger than males. Immatures resemble adults unless described.*

Greyish Eagle-Owl *Bubo cinerascens* 43cm, 17"

Dull grey-brown eagle-owl, heavily spotted brown, buff and cream above, lightly barred below with slightly darker, rather misshapen blotches on upper breast; ear-tufts often prominent, *eyes dark brown*, orbital ring pink. Immature is browner than adult. **HH** Pairs are widespread and fairly common throughout, from sea-level to 2500m in wide variety of bushed and wooded country, often with cliffs and rocky hills. **Voice** Gives single low hoot. **Note** Formerly conspecific with extralimital Spotted Eagle-Owl *B. africanus* (which has yellow eyes). [Alt: Vermiculated Eagle-Owl]

Verreaux's Eagle-Owl *Bubo lacteus* 66cm, 26"

Massive finely barred pale grey-brown eagle-owl with paler face broadly edged black and dark brown eyes with *pink eyelids* (only visible when eyes closed). Smallish ear-tufts are often laid flat and inconspicuous. Immature has duller face with narrower black borders and shorter ear-tufts. **HH** Pairs and family groups are fairly common in wooded grassland and woodland, including riverine acacia groves, from sea-level to 1800m. Occurs widely, but is largely absent from NESo and SEEt. **Voice** Very deep grunted *huh-huh, huhhu, huh*, which is far-carrying, but often absent-mindedly halting. Immature gives a loud piercing scream that rises then falls and fades. [Alt: Giant Eagle-Owl]

Cape Eagle-Owl *Bubo capensis* 58cm, 23"

A large dark eagle-owl, blotched buff and dark brown above, and heavily marked *dark brown and orange-buff on breast*, and distinctly barred on belly. *Intense orange eyes* set in grey-brown facial mask with narrow black edges; ear-tufts pronounced. Race in Er and Et is *dillonii*. Greyish Eagle-Owl is much smaller, with dark eyes and less heavily marked breast; Desert Eagle-Owl is much paler. **HH** Pairs are uncommon residents in Er and N&CEt at 2400–4200m in rocky moorland and montane country. **Voice** Call of Et birds not recorded, but extralimital *mackinderi* has a deep repeated *oooo...oo*, second note lower.

Desert Eagle-Owl *Bubo ascalaphus* 50cm, 20"

Large, pale eagle-owl with comparatively short ear-tufts and bright yellow or orange eyes. Plumage variable, but generally sandy-ochre with creamy or pale tawny facial mask edged black, throat white, upper breast spotted black, rest of underparts finely barred dark. Race in region is nominate (sometimes separated as '*desertorum*'). **HH** Presumably rare resident of rocky desert areas in Er, but only two confirmed records; also recorded on Sudan side of Eritrean border. **Voice** Loud call is distinctive *whoo-oo*, which can sound like a single note, given at intervals of 4–8 secs. Often female answers with deep falling *woooo*. **Note** Formerly conspecific with much larger, darker Eurasian Eagle-Owl *B. bubo*. [Alt: Pharaoh Eagle-Owl]

Pel's Fishing Owl *Scotopelia peli* 61cm, 24"

Huge owl, unlikely to be confused with any other bird. Bright orange-rufous and heavily barred dusky above, and a little paler below with variable dark spots and bars (usually more concentrated on flanks). Sexes similar; female slightly less rufous, but considerable individual variation. Immature much paler orange-rufous; head may be almost white. **HH** Singles and pairs are uncommon in Et beside well-wooded slow-flowing larger rivers, as well as lakes, at 400–1900m. In SSo, a rare threatened resident in mid-Jubba riverine forest. **Voice** Common call is a deep booming *oom... oom...oom...* given at 4–5 sec intervals; also an eerie downslurred scream.

Greyish Eagle-Owl

Verreaux's Eagle-Owl

Cape Eagle-Owl

dillonii

Pel's Fishing Owl

Desert Eagle-Owl

desertorum

Nightjars are notoriously difficult identify; not only do the species look alike, several have different colour morphs, and they are most frequently encountered at night. Many are best told by call, although the amount of white in the wings and tail, range and habitat, all help identification. Many also have white throat markings, but these are variable. Most females have a similar wing and tail pattern to males, but these areas are coloured buff rather than white. Immatures resemble adults. During the day, nightjars are inactive and perfectly camouflaged, hiding in the shade along branches or on the ground in leaf-litter.

NIGHTJARS WITH WHITE SIDES TO THE TAIL *Four species with outer tail feathers entirely white or with white outer webs (buff in females). Two species have elongated central tail feathers.*

Slender-tailed Nightjar *Caprimulgus clarus*   ♂ 28cm, 11″

Typical *Caprimulgus* nightjar, with white spots on primaries (6–7 feathers), white bar across lesser wing-coverts, narrow white outer tail, and white tips to secondaries forming white bar across trailing edge of wing. Both sexes have *slightly elongated central tail feathers* (typically male 2cm, female 1cm), but often hard to see in female. Female has wing-spots and outer tail buff. **HH** Common and widespread resident in dry bush country, coastal scrub and untended cultivation, often near water, in S&EEt (especially Rift Valley) and SSo, from sea-level to 1500m. **Voice** Gives a slow steady churr, typically about 8 notes per sec, *kwoikwoikwoikwoi…* (like pulsating of generator), and also a rapid *kwip-kwip* or *kwip-kwip-kwip* in flight. **Note** Longer-tailed birds in our region are sometimes separated as race '*apatelius*'.

Long-tailed Nightjar *Caprimulgus climacurus*   ♂ 43 cm, 17″

Similar to Slender-tailed Nightjar with white spots on primaries (5 feathers), white bar across lesser wing-coverts, narrow white outer tail, and white tips to secondaries forming white bar along trailing edge of wing. *Both sexes have very long central tail feathers (entire tail is up to 34cm in male),* but moulting birds have shorter tails and are like Slender-tailed. Female has wing-spots and outer tail buff. Race *nigricans* in our region is much darker bird than Slender-tailed, with strongly banded tail. **HH** Fairly common resident or Afrotropical migrant (no records Jun–Aug) in WEr and WEt, preferring bushed grasslands and semi-arid country at 500–750m (once at 1850m). **Voice** Calls with very fast and constant, almost reeling, churr of 40+ notes per sec (much faster than other churring species); also a nasal *chyaw* flight call.

Swamp Nightjar *Caprimulgus natalensis*   23cm, 9″

Adult male has *broad white outer tail* with no white bars on lesser wing-coverts or trailing edge of wing. Looks short-tailed in flight when male also shows white spots on primaries (4–5 feathers). Female has wing-spots and outer tail buff. With good views both sexes reveal *dark cheeks* and buff collar but overall coloration is golden or buffy. Montane Nightjar is similar but darker, with more obvious tawny collar and more easterly distribution. Only nominate race occurs in NE Africa. **HH** Rare Afrotropical migrant to WEt (three records, Feb–Jun) with preference for wet grasslands and marshy areas. **Voice** Gives a repeated simple monotonous *chok-chok-chok…* and melodious laughing *whip hululululu* in flight. [Alt: African White-tailed Nightjar, Natal Nightjar]

Montane Nightjar *Caprimulgus poliocephalus*   23cm, 9″

Rather dark nightjar with *rufous collar*, looking blackish or chocolate overall. Male has white spots on primaries (4 feathers) and *all-white outer tail*. Female has buffy wing-spots and less white on outer tail. Male has similar tail pattern to Swamp Nightjar, but latter paler overall, with no rufous collar, different habitat and more westerly range. **HH** Uncommon resident in highland areas of Et, usually near forest, but also in nearby farmland and well-wooded urban areas, mainly 1350–3000m. Recently discovered in Er. **Voice** A nasal *ank-ank-ank* often precedes a haunting, high-pitched whistled *piiiyu-pirrrrr* (first note a falling and then rising upslur, last note slightly falling and tremulous). [Alt: Abyssinian Nightjar; Mountain Nightjar]

Slender-tailed Nightjar

Long-tailed Nightjar

nigricans

Swamp Nightjar

nominate

Montane Nightjar

NIGHTJARS WITH WHITE TAIL-CORNERS A large group of nightjars with white on the outer tail restricted to the distal half or less (includes species on plate 98). Call, range and exact amount of white in tail aid identification.

Dusky Nightjar *Caprimulgus fraenatus* 24cm, 9.5"

Rather dark nightjar (including ear-coverts), with broad rufous hindneck and large creamy-buff spots on wing-coverts – similar to Montane Nightjar but buff-fringed scapulars. In flight, male shows white spots on primaries (3–4 feathers) and fairly large white tail-corners. Female has spots on wings and tail smaller and washed brownish. **HH** Locally common resident in C&SEt and NWSo at 500–2300m, most often found in grasslands and on rocky slopes, always with some cover; only a few records in NEt and Er (May–Sep), where it may be intra-African migrant. Recorded once in SSo. **Voice** Gives a long series of deep hollow-sounding churrs, lacking any rising or falling inflections, and often commences with a pair of hurried hiccup-like notes, *kwi-kuk kwi-kuk*. [Alt: Sombre Nightjar]

Nubian Nightjar *Caprimulgus nubicus* 22cm, 8.5"

Variation in general colour complicates identification even more than usual. Typical male resembles Dusky Nightjar, but with *smaller white tail-corners*. In daylight appears *paler, more grey-brown*, and *in flight shows more rufous in wings, notably inner primaries and secondaries*. Central tail feathers typically silvery-grey. Female has wing-patches washed buffy, and tail-spots slightly smaller. Four races described for region, but only two currently recognised: *torridus* (C&SEt, So, Soc) is brownish-grey above with well-spotted wing-coverts and scapulars; *tamaricis* (Palearctic winter visitor to Er, and once to NSo) is buffish-grey with narrow black streaking on crown. Birds on Soc and SSo formerly separated as '*jonesi*' and '*taruensis*' respectively. **HH** Occurs in dry bush and semi-desert from sea-level to 900m. Status uncertain: *tamaricis* is common winter visitor in Er, Aug–May; *torridus* is resident, but Et birds may be intra-tropical migrants; widespread but thinly distributed throughout breeding range. **Voice** Call is a barking, paired *wow-wow*, very like Freckled Nightjar but less musical, more rushed.

Plain Nightjar *Caprimulgus inornatus* 23cm, 9"

Rather uniform nightjar with grey-brown, brown and rufous morphs. All males have white spots on primaries (4 feathers), *large white corners to tail*, and *no white on throat* (may show small black spots on crown and scapulars like Star-spotted Nightjar). Females have buffy-brown wing-spots, and no white in tail. **HH** Uncommon resident in Er, Et (except SE) and NWSo, but may be partially migratory in Er. Recorded from wide variety of bush country and grassland from sea-level to 1500m. **Voice** Breeding birds call with a long mechanical churr similar to but higher-pitched than Dusky Nightjar; gives a *chuck* when flushed.

Star-spotted Nightjar *Caprimulgus stellatus* 23cm, 9"

Very like Plain Nightjar, with similar uniform appearance, with brown, grey-brown, rufous and buff morphs. Best told from Plain by voice and *smaller white corners to tail* on both sexes. Day-roosting birds show white patches on either side of throat, and very small black spots on crown and scapulars. **HH** Uncommon resident in CEt (mainly in Rift Valley) with single record from NWSo. Favours bare stony areas with little ground cover, up to 1600m. **Voice** Gives a steady yelping *pweu, pweu, pweu*.

Donaldson Smith's Nightjar *Caprimulgus donaldsoni* 19cm, 7.5"

Small, boldly patterned species with grey-brown and rufous morphs. In flight, shows white spots on primaries (4 feathers), and small white corners to tail on both sexes (slightly tinged buff on female). Birds seen in daylight often show *large white throat-patch and broadly-edged creamy-buff scapulars*. **HH** Locally common and widely scattered resident in dry bush country in SEt and NW&SSo, from sea-level to 1950m. Perches in bushes. **Voice** Gives a monotonous whistled, rather tremulous *t-weer-tweeu* (first note a rising upslur, last notes descending).

Dusky Nightjar

torridus

Nubian Nightjar

♂ ♀

♂ ♀

Star-spotted Nightjar

♂ ♀

Plain Nightjar

Donaldson Smith's Nightjar

♂ ♀

European Nightjar *Caprimulgus europaeus* 27cm, 10.5"

Large migratory nightjar; in flight male shows white spots on primaries (3–4 feathers) and white tail-corners. Three races occur, varying in overall tone from dark grey-brown (nominate) to paler grey-brown (*unwini*) and cinnamon-buff (*plumipes*), but difficult to judge in dark. In daylight, shows narrow black streaks on crown, blackish mottled shoulders, heavy black streaks on back, and *pale bar on lesser wing-coverts*; lacks rufous hindneck of many nightjars. Female lacks white (or buff) in wings and tail. **HH** Uncommon or rare Palearctic passage migrant occurring in wide range of more open habitats, Sep–Nov and Mar–Apr; tends to roost on branches during day. Mostly nominate birds in Er and Et; mostly *unwini* in So, with single record of *plumipes* in NSo (Oct). A major passage was noted off Raas Caseyr (NESo) in May 1980, heading towards Oman. **Voice** Usually silent in NE Africa, but may call *quoik* when flushed. [Alt: Eurasian Nightjar]

Freckled Nightjar *Caprimulgus tristigma* 27cm, 10.5"

Large, dark grey-brown nightjar, mottled all over with fine greyish or buffy speckles; sometimes shows whitish throat markings. No rufous hindneck. In flight male shows white spots on primaries (4 feathers) and small white tail-corners. Female has white wing-spots but tail is barred dark brown on brown (no paler corners). Race in NE Africa is nominate. **HH** Uncommon resident on *rocky hills and escarpments* in Et, at 350–2000m; usually seen singly. **Voice** Paired, musical and whiplashed *kow-wow kow-wow...* often interspersed with irregular nasal upslurs *wup-wup-wup...*

Egyptian Nightjar *Caprimulgus aegyptius* 25cm, 10"

Slightly smaller and shorter-tailed than European Nightjar, but *much paler and rather sandy-coloured*, lacking heavy streaking on upperparts. In flight, male shows only *very small white spots on primaries* (often invisible at distance), and small white tail-corners; *underside of primaries noticeably pale*. Female lacks white in wings and tail. Pale race *unwini* of European Nightjar has darker, barred underside of primaries, streaks on upperparts. Two races occur: nominate (Er and Et) is darker and greyer than extralimital *saharae* of N Africa; *arenicola* (NWSo, once) is similar but larger. **HH** Rare Palearctic winter visitor, Nov–Mar, with only a few records (but may be regular). **Voice** Song is a slowly repeated hollow-sounding *tok-tok-tok-tok-tok...*, sometimes given in paired notes that evolve into single notes.

Nechisar Nightjar *Caprimulgus solala* c. 28cm, 11"

Large reddish-brown nightjar known only from a single unsexed specimen. Wings show *large white patch (tinged pale buff) in primaries, but much closer to base of primaries than all other African nightjars* (except Pennant-winged); also has white tail-corners. **HH** ENDEMIC. A single road-kill was found in Nechisar NP, SEt, in Sep 1990, but subsequent searches have been unsuccessful. The species may be rare or only a visitor to Nechisar. **Voice** Unknown. **VU**

Standard-winged Nightjar *Macrodipteryx longipennis* 20cm, 8"

Breeding male unique and spectacular with large flags at ends of long wires (elongated shafts of second primary). In flight looks like a nightjar being chased by two smaller birds. Non-breeding male and female are more like typical female nightjars, but without white wing-spots or tail-corners. In good light, rufous hindneck and strongly barred blackish and rufous flight feathers and tail distinguish it from all except larger female Pennant-winged. **HH** Intra-tropical migrant to CEr and W&CEt, Dec–Jun. Vagrant NWSo (once, Jun). Inhabits bushed grasslands and marshy lakeshores at 750–2000m. **Voice** A very high-pitched rapid insect-like *titititititit...*

Pennant-winged Nightjar *Macrodipteryx vexillarius* 28cm, 11"

Breeding male is unmistakable with broad white flash right across wing and long white wing-streamers (elongated second primaries). Non-breeding male loses long pennants, but still distinctive with broad white flash and black ends to wings. Female has rufous hindneck and strongly barred blackish and rufous flight feathers and tail (no white); like non-breeding male and female Standard-winged Nightjar, but larger. **HH** Trans-equatorial migrant breeding south of equator and 'wintering' to north; vagrant SESo (once, Aug). **Voice** Breeding birds utter a rapid insect-like *chitchitchitchit...*, similar to but slower than Standard-winged.

nominate

♂

♂

♀

European Nightjar

♂

♀

Freckled Nightjar

♂

♂

Egyptian Nightjar

nominate

♂

nominate

wing

Nechisar Nightjar

Standard-winged Nightjar

br ♂

♀

non-br
♂/♀

br ♂

♀

non-br
♂/♀

Pennant-winged Nightjar

WHITE-RUMPED SWIFTS *Three similar white-rumped black swifts which mainly differ in tail shape. Sexes and immatures are similar.*

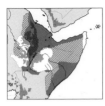

Little Swift *Apus affinis*   14cm, 5.5"

Small swift with rectangular white rump-patch (extending onto lower flanks), *square-ended tail*, and obvious white throat-patch. Seems stocky in flight, with fairly broad wings, interspersing rather fluttery wing-beats with short glides. Three similar races occur: *galilejensis* (Er, NWSo) has largest white rump-patch; *affinis* (SSo) has slightly smaller white rump; *aerobates* (most of Et, NSo) has darker wings and tail. **HH** Small to large flocks are common and widespread from coasts to 2500m. Nests under bridges, in villages and towns, as well as in natural sites like cliffs and gorges. Vagrant Soc. **Voice** A very noisy swift which frequently calls with musical twittering downslurs.

Horus Swift *Apus horus*   15cm, 6"

Stocky dark swift with *shallow forked tail*, broad white band on rump (wrapping round flanks like Little Swift) and large white throat (may extend onto upper breast). Flying birds are shorter-tailed than White-rumped Swift, and spread tail may appear only slightly notched. Race in region is nominate. **HH** Pairs and small flocks are locally common residents in Et (especially in Rift Valley), usually in open country at 900–1900m; breeds in banks near lakes and rivers. **Voice** Low-pitched, burry, downslurred screams have unique nasal pinched quality.

White-rumped Swift *Apus caffer*   15cm, 6"

Slender and slightly longer than Little Swift, with *forked tail and narrow crescent-shaped white rump* (which hardly wraps onto lower flanks), throat clearly white. In fluid flight looks slim-winged with pointed tail that only appears forked when spread (often while banking). **HH** More solitary than Little, but pairs and small flocks are locally common in Er and Et at 400–2300m in villages and towns, as well as near rocky cliffs and gorges. Resident in Er, but apparently an intra-tropical migrant in Et, present Mar–Oct; rare in So. Nests in crevices and often in old mud swallow nests. **Voice** Breeding birds give rapid short burry, buzzy rattled churrs, lower-pitched than most other swifts.

LARGE SWIFTS *Outsize swifts with broad wings and thickset bodies, and deep powerful flight (noisy at close quarters). Single Mottled Swifts can be hard to judge for size and both species wander far from nest sites. Sexes and immatures are very similar. Both species were formerly in the genus Apus.*

Alpine Swift *Tachymarptis melba*   22cm, 8.5"

Distinctly patterned huge swift: uniform brown above and *largely white below with well-defined brown breast-band*. Powerful in flight, with deep wing-beats. Three races probably occur: *africanus* is darkest with small white throat-patch; nominate *melba* is larger and paler brown with larger throat-patch; *archeri* is paler than *melba* with shorter wings. **HH** Singles or small groups are locally common in Er and Et, often in mixed flocks with other swifts; breeding birds are *africanus*, which may be partially migratory as fewer birds Oct–Jan. In NSo, *archeri* is (presumably) resident at 600–1800m. Vagrant Dj and Soc. Nominate *melba* probably a Palearctic migrant to region but no confirmed records. **Voice** At breeding colonies, gives a twittered trill and soft trilled scream.

Mottled Swift *Tachymarptis aequatorialis*   21cm, 8"

Very large grey-brown swift with mottled underparts (only visible at close range and in good light) and small dingy white throat. When nearby, striking and impressive on long wings with rather pointed forked tail. Race in NE Africa is nominate. **HH** Single birds to large flocks are common and widespread in Er and Et, often with other swifts. Probably breeds on cliffs in highlands but birds wander widely, often feeding over wetlands, and may be encountered anywhere. **Voice** Around breeding colonies gives dry twittered trills, almost screamed in excited aerial chases.

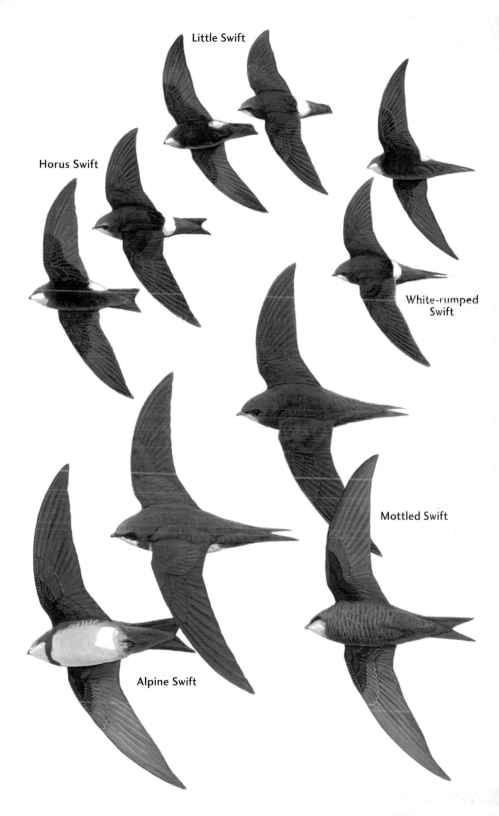

Little Swift

Horus Swift

White-rumped
Swift

Mottled Swift

Alpine Swift

PLAIN SWIFTS *Similar-sized largely plain blackish or dark brown swifts presenting serious identification problems. Subtle plumage differences are often muddled by light conditions and some, particularly lone, birds cannot be identified with confidence. Mixed-species flocks allowing comparisons help. Try to watch swifts against dark backgrounds and avoid strong backlighting. Particular attention is needed to presence or absence of contrasts on upperwing and underwing, extent of white on throat and forehead, and location and season. All species have short, well-forked tails. Sexes and immatures are similar.*

African Black Swift *Apus barbatus*   18cm, 7"

Dark *blackish swift with slightly paler blackish-brown patch on inner upperwing* (secondaries and greater coverts) that contrasts with darker body and rest of wing. Birds always have dark forehead, with variable white or whitish-grey throat. **HH** Hypothetical: 3 birds at 2900m near Goba in Dec 2006 were considered to be this species; confirmation required. Nearest population is central Kenya where race is *roehli*. **Voice** Calls an excited rasped trill that lacks any musical quality. [Alt: Black Swift]

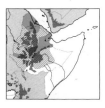

Nyanza Swift *Apus niansae*   17cm, 6.5"

Nominate race is a dark brown swift and in good light *always obviously brown* (not black); also shows *contrasting lighter innerwing-patch* on flight feathers from above (slightly more extensive than on African Black Swift); also visible from below, often appearing translucent. Forehead is dark brown, with variable but usually poorly defined whitish throat. Paler race *somalicus* (NEEt, NSo) has well-defined white throat. **HH** Small and sometimes large flocks are locally common, often in drier country, breeding in rocky cliffs and gorges from sea-level to 2700m; also occurs in towns. Nominate race is widespread in Er and Et; *somalicus* is fairly common in NSo (extending across border into extreme NEEt); occasionally wanders. **Voice** In flight gives short dry rasping trilled downslurs and high-pitched twittering notes. **Note** Race *somalicus* was formerly a race of Pallid Swift.

Common Swift *Apus apus*   18cm, 7"

Nominate race is an entirely sooty black-brown swift, lacking contrast in wings of Nyanza and African Black Swifts, with small but prominent white throat-patch. Forehead is dark (paler in immature). Eastern race *pekinensis* is paler and browner, with slightly larger brighter throat-patch. **HH** Common Palearctic passage migrant in Er, Dj and Et, sometimes in huge flocks, but confusion with other species disguises its true status. Main passage is Aug–Nov (south) and Mar–May (north), but occurs in other months. Both races recorded, but most birds not identified to race. Only two confirmed records in NWSo (including Sep record of *pekinensis*). **Voice** Usually silent in NE Africa, but may call with harsh, high-pitched screams. [Alt: Eurasian Swift]

Pallid Swift *Apus pallidus*   18cm, 7"

All-brown swift with *prominent white throat, pale forehead, and dark eye-patch*. Upperwing shows paler secondaries contrasting with darker outer primaries and mantle (Common Swift is more uniform above). From below, pale inner wing feathers also contrast with darker wing-tip, and good views may reveal *light scaling on body*. Identification poses extreme problems: can be very like Nyanza Swift (race *somalicus*), Common Swift (race *pekinensis*) and even Forbes-Watson's Swift. **HH** Extreme Palearctic vagrant: three records Dj (Oct–Mar), plus several unconfirmed records in Er and Et. In Africa occurs mainly further west, but also widespread in Arabia. **Voice** Likely to be silent in region, but call is a downslurred scream, slightly lower-pitched than Common Swift.

Forbes-Watson's Swift *Apus berliozi*   18cm, 7"

Very like Common Swift (especially paler race *pekinensis*), being uniform sooty-brown with prominent white throat. *Upperwing shows oily iridescent sheen* in good light. Very close views may reveal pale fringes on upperparts and faint scaly underparts. Dark-headed birds may be indistinguishable from *pekinensis* (except on call), but some have obvious whitish forehead (when only confusion is with blacker immature nominate Common). Larger and darker than Nyanza Swift (race *somalicus*), but also confusable with Pallid Swift. Two very similar races described: nominate (Soc), and slightly darker *bensoni* (coastal So), but validity requires confirmation. **HH** Near-endemic. Small to large flocks are common breeding visitors on Soc (Apr–Nov), but non-breeding movements unknown. In So considered a common resident and partial migrant, some birds moving south to winter in coastal East Africa. Breeds in fissures on cliffs in mountains on Soc, mainly at 600–1200m (probably also in NSo), but favours sea caves in coastal So. **Voice** In flight birds give musical trilled downslurs.

African Black Swift

roehli

Nyanza Swift

nominate

Common
Swift

somalicus

pekinensis

nominate

bensoni

Pallid Swift

Forbes-Watson's
Swift

SLIM SWIFTS Two slender swifts (in different genera) which are relatively easy to identify from all other swifts and from each other. Note slender pointed tail and rather uniform plumage. Sexes alike; immatures similar to adults with slightly shorter tail.

African Palm Swift *Cypsiurus parvus* 18cm, 7"

Very slim uniform mouse-brown swift, with long scimitar wings, and long, very deeply forked tail. Highly characteristic flickering flight, with tail invariably held closed and needle-like. Three weakly differentiated races probably occur (but racial identity in CEt uncertain): nominate *parvus* (WEr, NWEt) is palest; *laemostigma* (SEEt, SSo) is darker with mottled throat and greenish gloss to flight and tail feathers; *myochrous* (?SWEt) is larger with stronger gloss and less mottled throat. **HH** More solitary than other swifts, but pairs and small flocks are common and widespread residents from sea-level to 1350m, invariably associating with palm trees, but wandering widely. Absent from EEt and NSo. **Voice** Breeding birds utter thin high-pitched twittering and rattled trills.

Scarce Swift *Schoutedenapus myoptilus* 17cm, 6.5"

Slender dark brown (or grey-brown) swift with slightly paler throat (beware birds often looking very dark against bright sky). Rather long tail is often held closed and appears narrow and pointed, only showing deep fork when spread. Race in Et is nominate. **HH** Rare intra-tropical migrant to CEt, Jun–Sep, mainly in Rift Valley, feeding over forest at 1300–3000m; only 5 confirmed records for Et. **Voice** Does not scream like other dark swifts, but flocks chitter like spinetails during aerial chases and near to breeding colonies.

SPINETAILS Atypical swifts with distinctive wing-shape (broad with curved wing-tips and pinched-in near body) and short tails; usually in pairs or small groups. Fairly easy to identify; special note should be taken of extent of white in plumage, range and habitat. Sexes and immatures are similar.

Mottled Spinetail *Telacanthura ussheri* 14cm, 5.5"

Blackish, medium-sized spinetail, closely resembling Little Swift (plate 99), but *white rump extends as narrow whitish band across lower belly* (can be hard to see), and white throat is less well defined. Indistinct mottling across throat and breast is also obscure in field. Wings and tail are strongly glossed blue; tail is square-ended. Flight is swift-like, without fluttering of other spinetails. Differs further from Little Swift by longer, broader wings with more rounded wing-tips. **HH** Resident in woodland, open forest and edges in East Africa (often associating with baobabs); vagrant to NE Africa with single old record (race *stictilaema*) in extreme SSo (Aug). **Voice** Flying birds give a variety of rhythmic chitters and squeaks.

Böhm's Spinetail *Neafrapus boehmi* 10cm, 4"

Extremely short-tailed spinetail with broad black wings (narrowing close to body), extensive white belly and narrow white rump contrasting with blackish-brown throat and upper flanks. Uncertain fluttering bat-like flight with much slow wheeling and chasing, often low over canopy; looks tail-less in flight. **HH** Resident in forest and woodland in coastal lowlands of East and SE Africa (inland on major rivers); vagrant to NE Africa with single old record (race *sheppardi*) in extreme SSo (Aug). **Voice** Distinctive musical twittering. [Alt: Bat-like Spinetail]

Himalayan Swiftlet *Aerodramus brevirostris* 14cm, 5.5"

A medium-sized plain swiftlet with a fluttering flight. Brown above with paler grey-brown underparts and a prominent, *broad greyish rump-band.* At close range top of head and wing-linings appear darker. *Tail distinctly notched.* **HH** Vagrant Soc; 6 birds seen and photographed Nov 2007 (first record for Africa). The species is an altitudinal migrant in the Himalayas, perhaps occasionally reaching the Maldives (after storms). **Voice** Rapid twittering and buzzy single notes given in display, but likely to be silent at other times. **Note** Sometimes placed in genus *Collocalia*.

African Palm Swift

Scarce Swift

nominate

laemostigma

Mottled Spinetail

stictilaema

Böhm's Spinetail

sheppardi

Himalayan Swiftlet

MOUSEBIRDS *Endemic to Africa. Social, crested and long-tailed, mousebirds scramble through bushes and trees using both their feet and bills. All call regularly to maintain contact.* Colius *have rather weak floppy flight, while* Urocolius *fly strongly, fast and direct. Sexes alike; immature duller than adult.*

Speckled Mousebird *Colius striatus* 33cm, 13"

Adult is a scruffy, long-tailed, buff and brown bird with *brown crest*, whitish cheeks, blackish patch around eye, and fine dark barring on throat and breast. *Bill black above and pink below.* Similar immature has shorter crest and paler duller bill. Much geographical variation in Africa; three races occur in Horn: *leucotis* (most of Er and Et, except SE) is palest, with bluish-white eye; *mombassicus* (SEEr, SSo) is darker with brown eye; *hilgerti* (NEEt, Dj, NWSo) has browner ear-coverts. **HH** Small flocks are widespread and common in variety of moister bush from thickets to forest edge, including gardens, from sea-level to 2400m. **Voice** Scratchy and unpleasant raspy churrs given perched and in flight.

White-headed Mousebird *Colius leucocephalus* 31cm, 12"

Adult has *white crest* and face, obvious *small blackish eye-mask*, finely barred throat, hindneck and mantle, and grey-brown tail. *Bill is pale with dark tip.* Immature has duller crest and less pronounced barring. Race in region is nominate. **HH** Flocks are fairly common in arid and semi-arid bush in SSo. One record for Et. More localised than other mousebirds. **Voice** Calls rapid, spitting metallic notes *titititititititit...*

Blue-naped Mousebird *Urocolius macrourus* 35cm, 14"

Slender, thin-tailed, crested adult is mainly grey with *red mask, black-tipped red bill, and blue nape-patch*. Immature duller, with less distinct blue nape, greenish facial skin and pale bill. Four similar races occur: nominate (Er, NEt) is brownish-grey above and pinkish-buff below; *pulcher* (extreme SEt, SSo) greyer with aubergine tinge on breast; *abyssinicus* (C&SEt, NSo) has whiter throat and darker breast; *griseogularis* (WEt) darker and greyer. **HH** Widespread and common in arid and semi-arid bushland, woodland and sparsely bushed grassland from sea-level to 2000m (once at 2400m). Invariably in flocks and flies fast between bushes, often flying considerable distance if flushed. **Voice** Gives a single loud, rather mournful *piiiyew* and softer short nasal slurred notes, rather wader-like in quality.

TROGONS *Spectacular, long-tailed birds which, despite bright green and red plumage, can be elusive and hard to see. They make short silent undulating flights, but are unobtrusive and sit still for long periods, often high in the canopy, on horizontal branch in characteristic hunched posture, often with back towards observer. Only one species in NE Africa.*

Narina Trogon *Apaloderma narina* 30cm, 12"

Adult male is *vivid green above* with green throat and upper breast, red belly and blue-green tail with white outer tail feathers (tail looks all white from underneath). Adult female duller and has cinnamon-brown (not green) forecrown, throat and breast. Immature like adult female, but has white tips to wing-coverts. In flight, flash of white outer tail feathers is distinctive. Two races occur: nominate male (Er, Et, NSo) as described; male *littorale* (SSo) is bronzier-green on upperparts and breast, duller red below, with bright green bare skin on cheeks (not blue); female has paler breast. **HH** Singles and pairs are widespread and fairly common residents of forest and richer woodland in Er and Et from sea-level to 3400m; in NSo (rare) occurs in wooded hills with junipers; in SSo confined to riverine forest in Jubba valley and Boni Forest. **Voice** Gives a repeated, pulsating, crooned *krooo-krrrou*, with strong accent on second note. Each long series commences with short purred notes and increases in volume.

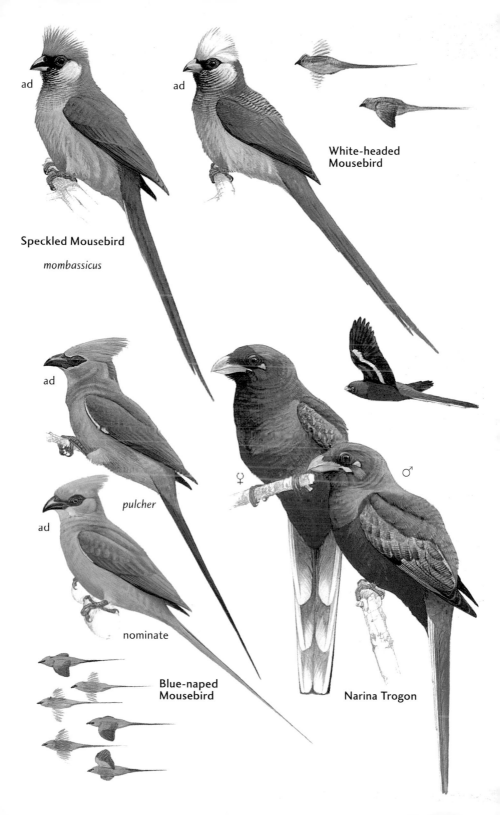

ad

ad

White-headed
Mousebird

Speckled Mousebird

mombassicus

ad

ad

pulcher

♀

♂

nominate

Blue-naped
Mousebird

Narina Trogon

KINGFISHERS Stocky, dagger-billed, colourful birds. Despite the family name, only a few species catch fish and many are not dependent on water, inhabiting bush country, woodland and forest. Displays and calls make some species conspicuous, but forest birds are shy and cryptic despite their bright colours. The four species below are invariably or often found in waterside or wetland habitats, but Grey-headed and Brown-hooded are better grouped with the 'woodland kingfishers' (see plate 104).

Pied Kingfisher *Ceryle rudis*   25cm, 10″

Striking large *crested black and white kingfisher*. Adult male has two complete breast-bands; adult female has single broken band. Immature similar to adult female, but has brown fringing to face and throat, and duller breast-band. Fishes from hovering flight, thereby exploiting open water. **HH** Highly social: singles and groups are widespread and common residents and partial migrants in Er, Et and SSo beside all types of water, from sea-level to 2400m, including coastal shallows. Largely absent from NSo. Occurs in fewer numbers May–Jul, and is much rarer east of Rift Valley. **Voice** Has explosive and rather tern-like *chit-chit..*, which often breaks into a metallic, musical, rhythmic chittering with many birds joining in excitedly.

Grey-headed Kingfisher *Halcyon leucocephala*   21cm, 8″

Adult has pale grey head, neck and breast, black upper back and bright blue lower back, wings and tail, with red bill and *chestnut belly*. Sexes similar, immature duller with dusky barring on head and breast, very pale chestnut belly, and dark-tipped red bill. Two races occur: nominate (Er, Et, NWSo) as described; *hyacinthina* (SSo) has violet-tinged wings and tail. **HH** Pairs are common and widespread in wide range of woodland, bush and cultivation from sea-level to 2300m, often near water; absent from NESo. Mainly resident, but also partially migratory; large numbers in Et in Mar–Apr and Sep–Oct, and absent from Er in winter. **Voice** Song is a rising, falling, then rising wave of notes that become very strident. Call is a series of identical sharp notes, *tchk, tchk, tchk…* [Alt: Grey-hooded Kingfisher; Chestnut-bellied Kingfisher]

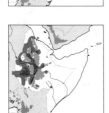

Brown-hooded Kingfisher *Halcyon albiventris*   21cm, 8″

Similar to Grey-headed Kingfisher, but adult has *pale brownish crown* and is plain below with buffish flanks; bill bright red. Sexes differ: male's back is black, female's dark brown. Darker-billed immature has browner crown and light barring on breast. In flight shows *warm rufous-chestnut underwing*. Race in coastal So is *orientalis*. **HH** Pairs are locally common along Jubba and lower Shabeelle valleys in SSo, where may be partially migratory as no records Nov–Feb. **Voice** Call is a repeated monotonous whistled sequence of four descending notes with emphasis on first note, next three gradually fading.

Giant Kingfisher *Megaceryle maxima*   43cm, 17″

Spectacular *massive* kingfisher, blackish above with *fine white speckles and bars*. Adult male has broad chestnut breast-band and black-and-white barred belly; adult female has breast streaked black and white, and entire belly and vent chestnut. In flight, underwing-coverts white on male, chestnut on female. Immature resembles adult, but chestnut bands are speckled and broken. Race in region is nominate. **HH** Single birds (or occasionally pairs) are shy but widespread in Er and Et on highland lakes, rivers and streams, at 750–1800m. Uncommon in Er, but fairly common in WEt and Rift Valley; few records east of Rift Valley and absent from So. **Voice** Loud, far-carrying, raucous laugh followed by single notes *kiau-kiau-kee-ee-ee-ee-ee-ee- kiau-kiau-kiau-kiau…*, often given in flight.

Pied Kingfisher

♀

♂

Grey-headed Kingfisher

imm

ad

nominate

Brown-hooded Kingfisher

imm

♂

orientalis

Giant Kingfisher

♂

♀

WOODLAND KINGFISHERS A group of woodland and forest kingfishers which includes Grey-headed and Brown-hooded on plate 103, and Striped on plate 105. Often found well away from water, they feed on insects, lizards and occasionally small birds. All have loud trilling calls and striking displays. Sexes are similar; immatures tend to be duller than adults and often scaled on the breast.

Woodland Kingfisher *Halcyon senegalensis* 22cm, 8.5"

Rather thickset kingfisher: adult of nominate race is dove-grey, black and bright blue with striking *red and black bill, and no blue on breast*. Migrant southern race *cyanoleuca* has grey head washed blue, and black extends slightly behind eye. Immature is similar to adult, but has buff wash on head, lightly scaled breast and flanks, and dark bill. **HH** Singles and pairs are widespread and common in variety of woodland, bushed grassland, cultivation and gardens at 400–1500m, almost entirely in and west of Rift Valley; nominate birds are resident in Et, but apparently only breeding visitors to Er. Southern race *cyanoleuca* migrates north after breeding, and in our region is only known from extreme WEt. **Voice** Song is a descending rattled series introduced by an isolated explosive note: *chit chtchtchtchttitititchrrrrrrr*; also calls with a repeated musical rattled upslur.

Mangrove Kingfisher *Halcyon senegaloides* 23cm, 9"

Very like Woodland Kingfisher, but has slightly darker grey head and *bright all-red bill*. Immature duller than adult with buff-brown wash on head, breast and flanks, and dark bill. Flying birds reveal a *black carpal crescent on underwing*. **HH** Uncommon presumed resident in SSo, mainly along lower Shabeelle and Jubba valleys in range of bush and forest; although in mangroves elsewhere, not found in them yet in Somalia. **Voice** Song is similar in structure to Woodland Kingfisher, but after an introductory isolated *chink* the series is much slower and more emphatic: *chink trrt trrt trrt trrt trrt trrt trrt trt trtt trtrtrtrtrtrtrtrt.*

Blue-breasted Kingfisher *Halcyon malimbica* 26cm, 10"

Larger than similar Woodland Kingfisher, with *blacker wings, blue breast-band* (which contrasts with white throat and belly) and blue hindcrown and neck; *bill red and black*. Immature is duller, with buff underparts and dark red-brown bill. **HH** Rare presumed resident in three areas of WEt, in forest and dense riverine woodland at 950–1400m. Birds in Et are isolated but presumed to be nominate race. **Voice** Song is a loud whistled series of rising then falling notes, usually finishing on same pitch as opening note *fih fi fi fi fifififififi fi fi fi.*

Collared Kingfisher *Todirhamphus chloris* 24cm, 9.5"

A blue-green kingfisher with pure white underparts and broad, well-defined white collar, separated from blue-green head by dark band of greenish-black. Prominent short white supercilium extends only as far as eye. Bill black with pale base to lower mandible. Immature like adult but with dusky mottling on collar and underparts. Race in NE Africa is endemic *abyssinicus*. **HH** Confined to coastal mangroves off Er, where probably resident (perhaps breeding visitor). Rather rare and elusive, found mainly near Massawa, on Dahlak Is and in Assab area. Very rare in So, with two records in NWSo and one in SESo. **Voice** Song is a loud ringing *kek-kek-kek-kek-kek*. [Alt: White-collared Kingfisher]

imm

ad

nominate

**Woodland
Kingfisher**

imm

**Mangrove
Kingfisher**

ad

imm

**Blue-breasted
Kingfisher**

ad

nominate

**Collared
Kingfisher**

abyssinicus

SMALLER KINGFISHERS All (except Striped) are essentially dark blue and rufous with white throats and neck-spots. Head pattern, colour of bill and underparts, habitat and range aid identification. Sexes alike; immatures are duller with black bills, some scaling on the breast and dark legs.

Striped Kingfisher *Halcyon chelicuti* 17cm, 6.5"

Small, dumpy, rather drab brown and white kingfisher with dark eye-stripe, pale throat and collar, and variably streaked crown, lower breast and flanks. Bill is black with red lower mandible. Sexes similar, although male has black band on underwing (seen when flashes open wings in display), and greyer crown than female. In rapid direct flight shows turquoise-blue back, rump and tail. Immature has dull reddish bill, is less streaked and can be dark-scaled below. Race in NE Africa is nominate. **HH** Singles and pairs are common and widespread in Et (except SE) and SSo, from sea-level to 2100m in wide range of bushed grassland and open woodland, often far from water; rather rare in Er and NWSo. Avoids very arid areas. **Voice** Regularly repeated call is a emphatic isolated first note followed by a descending series of trills, *fi-frrrrrrr ...fi-frrrrrrr ...fi-frrrrrrr ...*

Half-collared Kingfisher *Alcedo semitorquata* 18cm, 7"

Black-billed, short-tailed kingfisher; blue-green above and pale rufous-orange below with white throat and spot on side of neck; *dark blue patches at sides of breast* diagnostic. Sexes alike; immature similar but paler below with dark scaling across breast, dark legs. Immature Malachite Kingfisher is also dark-billed, but smaller, and lacks blue breast-patches. **HH** Singles and pairs are shy and uncommon on well-wooded or open streams and rivers in Er and Et, at 750–2300m, mainly in and west of Rift Valley. **Voice** In flight or while perched gives a simple single or repeated metallic *chink.*

Common Kingfisher *Alcedo atthis* 18cm, 7"

Similar to Half-collared Kingfisher, with greenish-blue crown and wings, pale rufous-orange underparts and black bill. Back and tail bright turquoise-blue, most noticeable in flight. Differs from Half-collared in having pale *rufous-orange ear-coverts* and no blue breast-patches. Sexes alike, but female has reddish base to lower mandible. Immature similar but duller with dark legs. **HH** Widespread Palearctic species; vagrant to Soc (once, 2007). **Voice** Call is a single short whistle, *zii*, usually given in flight.

Malachite Kingfisher *Alcedo cristata* 12cm, 5"

Adult is blue above, rufous below, with *slightly shaggy crown barred blue-green and black extending down to eye*, and bright red bill. Immature is similar, with shorter black bill, brownish-rufous underparts and whitish belly. Two races occur: *galerita* (most of Et except SE, SSo) as described; *stuartkeithi* (Er NEt) is slightly paler on rump and vent. **HH** Pairs and singles are common and widespread from sea-level to 2700m, occurring beside all types of water where fringed with vegetation. Most frequent in Rift Valley and west of it; some local movements appear to occur, but are not well known. Vagrant Dj and NESo. **Voice** Gives a short sharp rather unmusical *chht* that may run into a dry chitter.

African Pygmy Kingfisher *Ceyx pictus* 11cm, 4.5"

Similar to Malachite Kingfisher but slightly smaller; adult has *small dark blue crown not extending down to eye* and orange cheeks with purplish-pink wash to ear-coverts. Immature like adult but duller, with darker face, breast-scaling and shorter blackish bill. Race in region is nominate. **HH** Widespread, often far from water, in forest and denser thickets in bushed and wooded grassland and riverine woodland, from sea-level to 1500m. Most frequent in Rift Valley and west of it; also fairly common in SSo, mainly along Shabeelle and Jubba valleys. **Voice** Gives a high-pitched *tsi-tsi....* and squeaky chittering. **Note** Sometimes placed in genus *Ispidina.*

imm

ad

Half-collared Kingfisher

imm

♂

Common Kingfisher

Striped Kingfisher

♂

imm

imm

ad

galerita

ad

Malachite Kingfisher

African Pygmy Kingfisher

nominate

RESIDENT BEE-EATERS A group of largely green and cinnamon bee-eaters usually encountered in pairs or small groups in open country (except for forest Blue-breasted). Colour of underparts, face pattern and tail shape aid identification, along with limited range overlap. Sexes are similar; immatures resemble adults but are duller. Sit fairly upright with slowly wagging tails, leaving perches to sally out after insects, and snapping them up with an audible click. Often associate with bush fires and termite emergences.

Little Bee-eater *Merops pusillus*   15cm, 6"

Small neat bee-eater: adult is green above with yellow throat, well-defined black gorget, and dull cinnamon-rufous underparts. Two races intergrade in highlands: *ocularis* (WEr, WEt) has narrow ultramarine stripe just over eye-mask and sometimes a blue-white top edge to gorget; *cyanostictus* (Et east of Rift Valley, NW&SSo) has longer blue superciliary stripes joining over bill, and thin purplish-blue top edge to gorget. Immature is duller and paler than adult, washed variably pale green below. Larger Blue-breasted Bee-eater has white edge to yellow cheeks and narrow blue forehead. **HH** Pairs or family groups are common and widespread in bushed and wooded grassland, and more open woodland, from sea-level to 1600m. **Voice** Gives a sharp high-pitched *tsip tsip...*, and when excited these break into a long metallic sequence interspersed with some quite musical nasal skirls.

Blue-breasted Bee-eater *Merops (variegatus) lafresnayii*   20cm, 8"

Similar to Little Bee-eater, but distinctly larger: adult has *white wedge on cheeks*, separating yellow throat from black eye-mask, and *deep blue forehead and short supercilium*. 'Blue-breasted' is confusing name, since gorget varies from very dark purplish-blue to blackish, and often appears black in field; rufous-cinnamon band below it extends to belly. Immature lacks gorget, is duller green below, and has less well-defined white cheek. **HH** Near-endemic. Common in wide range of wooded and bushed habitats in Er and Et at 500–2500m. Birds in SEt sometimes mistaken for extralimital Cinnamon-chested Bee-eater *M. oreobates* (common in E Africa). **Voice** Calls with short dry deep throaty trills suggestive of small plover. **Note** Race *lafresnayii* in Er and Et is larger than other (lowland) races of Blue-breasted, and has blue forehead and more rufous on underparts, so perhaps better treated as separate species, or even as a race of Cinnamon-chested Bee-eater.

Somali Bee-eater *Merops revoilii*   17cm, 6.5"

A washed-out, slightly unkempt bee-eater. Adult is pale blue-green above, with white throat, and *pale apricot underparts*. Immature is duller version of adult. In flight, reveals *silvery-blue rump and undertail-coverts*. **HH** Singles and pairs are shy, solitary and sedentary residents in SEEt and So up to 600m, in arid and semi-arid bushland and grassland; also occurs in extreme SWEt. **Voice** Rarely heard call consists of long ramble of musical, excitable but rather mournful *chits* and whistled slurs.

Little Green Bee-eater *Merops orientalis*   24cm, 9.5"

Adult is a slender, *very bright green, streamer-tailed bee-eater*, with a narrow eye-mask and *very narrow black gorget*. At close range shows a narrow blue line below eye-mask; throat and cheeks often brighter and paler. Upperparts usually show bronzy tone, especially on crown and nape. Immature is similar, but paler, lacking gorget and tail-streamers. Swallow-tailed Bee-eater has forked tail in all plumages and Blue-cheeked Bee-eater is much larger; neither has green throat. Race in region is *viridissimus*. **HH** Singles and small groups are common residents in WEr in arid and semi-arid bushland and desert up to 1200m. In WEt it is apparently a non-breeding visitor Dec–Apr, usually below 750m. **Voice** Calls an uninteresting ramble of scratchy metallic notes with little variation. [Alt: Green Bee-eater].

ad

imm

ocularis

ad

cyanostictus

Little Bee-eater

ad

imm

lafresnayii

Blue-breasted Bee-eater

ad

imm

Somali Bee-eater

ad

imm

Little Green Bee-eater

viridissimus

White-throated Bee-eater *Merops albicollis*   28cm, 11″

Adult is pale blue-green bee-eater with *striking black and white head pattern*, tawny nape, and long central tail feathers. Sexes are similar, but male has slightly longer tail-streamers. Immature is similar to adult, but has yellow wash over throat, is duller with many buff-edged feathers, and lacks tail-streamers. **HH** Common intra-African migrant, breeding Apr–Aug in open bushland and semi-desert in Er, Dj, NWSo and N&CEt. More widespread as migrant, dispersing to woodland, bush and grassland, as well as more open forest and gardens, from sea-level to 1700m. Highly gregarious and vocal on migration; southward passage mainly Sep–Nov, northward Apr–Jun. **Voice** Gives a rather harsh throaty *chep*, which often breaks into musical slurs with several birds taking part in excitable wader-like chorus.

Swallow-tailed Bee-eater *Merops hirundineus*   22cm, 8.5″

Elegant blue-green bee-eater. Adult has yellow throat, bright blue forehead and supercilium, narrow blue gorget and *long, deeply forked blue tail*. Sexes are similar, but female is paler with narrower gorget and shallower forked tail. Immature is also similar, but has whitish throat, no gorget and less forked tail. Race *heuglini* in Et has slightly darker blue gorget than southern races. **HH** Pairs and small groups are uncommon in drier bushed grassland and woodland in W&SWEt at 500–750m, mainly around Gambela and the Omo river. There are no records Aug–Nov, which suggests some local movements. **Voice** Sweet musical slurs and trills with rather wader-like quality are given randomly for long periods.

European Bee-eater *Merops apiaster*   28cm, 11″

Striking *chestnut and golden bee-eater with yellow throat and pale blue underparts*. In fresh plumage, adult male has broad golden sides to chestnut back; non-breeding male and female are much duller and greener above. At rest or in flight, adults show projecting central tail feathers (slightly shorter in female), absent in young birds. Immature is greenish above, with brown-washed crown, dull green sides to back, pale yellow throat and blue underparts. **HH** Small to large flocks on passage are harbingers of Palearctic migration with main southward movement in Aug–Oct and more sporadic northward passage Mar–May. Some birds overwinter in Et. Prefers open country, especially wetlands, from sea-level to 3000m. **Voice** Far-carrying, loud and attractive calls are very fluid and deep throaty trills and churrs, *prrutt, prrutt prrutt*, often with many birds calling together.

Blue-cheeked Bee-eater *Merops persicus*   30cm, 12″

Slender vivid emerald-green bee-eater. Adult has *green crown, blue borders to eye-mask*, and yellow chin blending into orange-brown throat. Female has shorter tail-streamers. Immature is duller with less blue around eye and no tail-streamers. Shows particularly obvious *cinnamon underwings* in banking flight. Race in region is nominate *persicus*. **HH** Small parties are regular Palearctic passage migrants and winter visitors throughout region Sep–May, preferring bushed and wooded grassland below 1500m, often near water. Main southward passage is Aug–Nov and northward in Feb–May. Overwintering birds remain in south of region. A few pairs recently bred in Dj in Mar–Apr. **Voice** Has an attractive fluid trill, *preepp, preepp, preepp*, repeated for long periods with slight changes in tone.

Madagascar Bee-eater *Merops superciliosus*   30cm, 12″

Overall slightly duller than similar Blue-cheeked Bee-eater, with *smoky olive-brown cap, white borders to eye-mask* and dull brick-red throat. Female has shorter tail-streamers. Immature is much duller than adult and lacks bold head pattern. Very similar to immature Blue-cheeked, but less green with more uniform throat. In flight, shows *plain cinnamon underwings* like Blue-cheeked. Race in region is nominate. **HH** Common intra-tropical breeding visitor from south to Er (rare), Et and So (except NE), mainly Apr–Sep below 1500m (but up to 1800m) in bushed and wooded country, often near water. Some birds present all year, especially in So, but fewer Dec–Mar. Usually seen in small flocks. **Voice** Very like Blue-cheeked , but slightly higher-pitched and less fluid. [Alt: Olive Bee-eater]

ad

imm

imm

White-throated
Bee-eater

imm

ad

heuglini

Swallow-tailed
Bee-eater

European
Bee-eater

imm

ad

imm

ad

persicus

Blue-cheeked
Bee-eater

imm

ad

superciliosus

Madagascar Bee-eater

Red-throated Bee-eater *Merops bulocki*   23cm, 9"

Colourful, rather upright bee-eater. Adult has *entirely red throat, blue-green forecrown*, green upperparts, warm buff-cinnamon underparts with *deep cobalt-blue vent*. Immature is duller with red-orange throat and green stripe below eye-mask. Race in region is *frenatus*. **HH** Pairs and flocks are locally common in WEt up to 750m, in bushed and wooded grassland, near lakes and rivers. Although presumed resident, no records Sep–Nov, and may be intra-topical migrant. Recorded WEr (once). **Voice** Calls with variety of short musical yaps, churls and trills.

Northern Carmine Bee-eater *Merops nubicus*   38cm, 15"

Spectacular large long-tailed bee-eater with powerful wheeling flight. Adult is bright carmine (vivid crimson) above with turquoise-blue rump, lower belly and vent, *well-defined green-blue crown and throat*, and long central tail feathers. Sexes similar. Immature much duller with strong olive-brown wash, mottled head and throat, and short tail-streamers. **HH** Widespread and often very common in much of Er, Et (especially Rift Valley) and So (except NE), up to 2500m in bushed and wooded grassland, as well as cultivation and wetlands. Frequently uses large animals and birds as perches and 'beaters'. Present all year and presumed resident, but may be partial migrant. **Voice** Song is series of unattractive loud skirls, chitters and complaining notes, lacking sweetness or variation of smaller bee-eaters. **Note** Sometimes lumped with extralimital Southern Carmine Bee-eater *M. nubicoides* as Carmine Bee-eater *M. nubicus*.

BROAD-BILLED ROLLER *Compact bright chestnut roller (which appears dark at distance) with broad bright yellow bill. Acrobatic, agile and slender in flight, often appearing rather falcon-like; unlike Coracias rollers, pursues aerial insect prey. Always chooses to perch conspicuously at the top of tallest trees. Sexes alike.*

Broad-billed Roller *Eurystomus glaucurus*   28cm, 11"

Adult is *bright chestnut roller* (variably washed lilac below) with *broad yellow bill*. Immature is much duller brown above with dusky yellow bill, and pale blue below. In flight, birds show strong contrast between chestnut back and deep azure-blue outerwing and tail. Race in Et is *afer* (sometimes separated as *aethiopicus*). **HH** Singles, pairs or small groups are fairly common intra-African breeding migrants in bushed and wooded grassland, woodland and forest edge, mainly in WEr, WEt and SSo, from sea-level to 1900m. **Voice** Gives a deep and raspy single *ahk* or *wak*, and a *uh-uh-uh-uhuhuhuhuh* in rapid sequence.

ROLLERS *Colourful, robust birds with large heads and strong black bills. Most perch prominently in open country or in woodland. Noted for their agile flight and rolling aerial displays. Sexes alike. Most species have blue and chestnut plumage (see also plate 109).*

Rufous-crowned Roller *Coracias naevius*   35cm, 14"

Large-headed thickset roller which *lacks blue underparts of other species*. Adult has *rufous crown with broad white supercilium* and rufous-purple underparts broadly streaked white. In flight, dark purple-blue flight feathers contrast with rufous wing-coverts and greenish-brown back. Immature similar, but duller and greener above and below. Race in region is nominate. **HH** Singles and pairs are locally common but never numerous, often associating with rocky areas and large trees in drier woodland and bushed grassland up to 2100m. Widespread in most of region except WEt. Vagrant Dj. **Voice** Gives a loud, harsh and throaty *ouw*, and in display flight a strident *ak-ak-ak-aka-aka-aka-aka...kiau-kiau-kiau....* [Alt: Purple Roller]

Red-throated Bee-eater

ad

imm

frenatus

imm

ad

Northern Carmine Bee-eater

imm

imm

ad

Rufous-crowned Roller

afer

Broad-billed Roller

imm

ad

BLUE AND CHESTNUT ROLLERS Striking rollers, best identified by presence or absence of lilac on throat and by tail shape and length. Bold and confiding, they drop onto prey on the ground from prominent perches such as roadside posts. All have raucous calls and perform rolling display flights. Sexes alike.

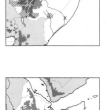

Abyssinian Roller *Coracias abyssinicus*   41 cm, 16″

Slender vivid blue roller with whitish face, rufous-brown back and *very long outer tail-streamers*. Appears bluer than other species, and like slim long-tailed European Roller. In flight, told from latter by whiter face and dark blue (not blackish) flight feathers. In worn plumage, tail-streamers may be broken or missing. Immature is duller than adult, with olive-brown tinge to back, and squared tail without streamers. **HH** Singles and less often small groups are locally common residents (and perhaps intra-tropical migrants) in semi-arid bush and woodland in Er and Et, mainly west of Rift Valley, at 200–2400m. Vagrant SSo (once), Dj (once) and Soc. **Voice** Calls are very harsh and unpleasant variable loud rasps.

Lilac-breasted Roller *Coracias caudatus*   38 cm, 15″

Striking blue and chestnut roller with *lilac throat heavily streaked white*. Adult has white forehead, supercilium and chin, light olive-chestnut back, dark blue wing-coverts, and deep blue underparts. Outer tail-streamers are slender and straight. Race in region is *lorti*; extralimital races have more extensive lilac on throat and breast. Immature is much duller and greener above, with brownish wash to throat and breast, no tail-streamers. **HH** Pairs are widespread and common intra-tropical breeding migrants and presumed residents in open bush country, wooded grassland, woodland and cultivation from sea-level to 1700m. In Et, occurs mainly in Rift Valley and to east. Vagrant Er (once). Some birds remain in SEt all year, but mainly present in Et and So in Mar–Oct. **Voice** Displaying birds give loud dry rasps breaking into a long series that develops into a harsh nasal rattle.

European Roller *Coracias garrulus*   31 cm, 12″

Robust, thickset roller with blue head, chestnut-brown back, blue underparts and *rather short square-cut tail* (without streamers). On arrival in Oct, non-breeding adults and first-year birds are very pale with washed-out greenish-blue heads and underparts, and muddy-brown backs. Prior to departure in Apr, adults are striking blue, with bright chestnut backs, and purplish-blue wing-coverts and rumps. **HH** Singles (often moving together in loose associations) are locally common Palearctic passage migrants, typically in bushed and wooded grassland up to 1400m. Birds appear to undertake a loop migration, with large southward passage in Er and NSo in autumn, Aug–Nov, and very heavy northward spring passage through SSo in Apr. Some birds overwinter in SEt and SSo, Dec–Feb. **Voice** Usually silent in region, but may occasionally utter a deep croak. **NT**

Indian Roller *Coracias benghalensis*   33 cm, 13″

Large chunky roller with square-cut tail. Adult has whitish forehead, turquoise-blue crown, rufous-brown nape and *greenish-brown back*. Ear-coverts, throat and breast are washed lilac and finely streaked with white; belly turquoise-blue. At close range note *narrow ring of bare yellow skin around eye*. Although not as bright as some species at rest, in flight wings and tail reveal stunning pattern of deep blue and turquoise. Readily told from all African rollers by *broad band of turquoise across outer primaries and deep blue terminal tail-band*, contrasting with turquoise base. Immature is duller but retains diagnostic wing pattern. **HH** Vagrant from Indian subcontinent to Soc (once, Dec 1998). **Voice** Silent in region.

Lilac-breasted Roller

lorti

imm

ad

imm

ad

Abyssinian Roller

imm

ad

imm

Indian Roller

ad

imm

ad

European Roller

WOOD-HOOPOES *Endemic to Africa, and until recently considered closely related to the scimitarbills (see plate 111). They are a homogeneous group of clumsy-looking, glossy, long-tailed social birds, and species are best identified by careful attention to the exact colour of head, back and bill, as well as range and habitat— extreme caution should always be exercised, especially when identifying out-of-range species. Sexes similar, but males are slightly larger than females with longer, more decurved bills. The taxonomy of this group is in urgent need of revision, and it is possible that all three species below may represent a single variable species.*

Green Wood-hoopoe *Phoeniculus purpureus*   37cm, 14.5"

Adult is a large red-billed iridescent bird with white spot and bar in wing, and long graduated white-tipped tail. Two races occur: *marwitzi* (extreme SSo) is relatively easy to identify with *green head and back* (although wings may shine violet and blue), while *niloticus* (WEt) is generally more violet-blue and very like Violet Wood-hoopoe, but will always shows *some green on head* (if watched for several minutes). Immature is dull blackish, with brownish throat-patch, straighter, shorter black bill, and dark legs. **HH** Singles or extended family groups are uncommon in a wide range of wooded and bushed habitats in WEt at 500–800m. In SSo, only found in Boni Forest (two records) where presumed resident. **Voice** Nasal, bubbling and maniacal cackling in which group members engage in noisy displays (calls probably indistinguishable from Violet and Black-billed Wood-hoopoes). [Alt: Red-billed Wood-hoopoe]

Violet Wood-hoopoe *Phoeniculus damarensis*   37cm, 14.5"

Adult is very like race *niloticus* of Green Wood-hoopoe, but head, nape and back shine violet-blue, with *green restricted to throat*. Immature is duller with brown-buff streaked throat and shorter black bill. **HH** Family groups inhabit semi-arid and arid bush and woodland, often associating with rivers and doum palms. Despite records from extreme SW&SEt, presence in Et requires confirmation. **Voice** Probably not distinguishable from Green. **Note** Isolated E African race *granti* has been proposed as separate species (Grant's Wood-hoopoe) from nominate *damarensis* in SW Africa, but both may prove to be conspecific with Green Wood-hoopoe.

Black-billed Wood-hoopoe *Phoeniculus somaliensis*   37cm, 14.5"

Very like Green Wood-hoopoe (formerly considered a race), but has more violet and blue gloss, and black bill (sometimes with limited red at base and occasionally mostly red). Bill said to be more slender and decurved than other wood-hoopoes, but varies with sex and age, males having longer bills, young birds shorter, straighter ones. Immature duller with some buff on throat and black bill and legs. Three similar races occur, but their precise distribution is uncertain: nominate (SEEt, So) as described; *neglectus* (CEt) greener above with brown or buff chin and shorter bill; *abyssinicus* (Er, NEt) with deeper green-violet crown, greener breast and more red at base of bill, some birds showing all-red bill. **HH** Singles, pairs or family groups are common and widespread throughout region, occupying semi-arid bushed and wooded areas, often in larger acacias and riverine woodland, from sea-level up to 2100m. **Voice** Probably not distinguishable from Green Wood-hoopoe.

ad

imm

Green Wood-hoopoe

marwitzi

imm

imm

ad

ad

**Black-billed
Wood-hoopoe**

nominate

Violet Wood-hoopoe

granti

HOOPOES Bizarre crested rufous-cinnamon and black-and-white birds. Often seen in buoyant butterfly-like flight, or walking on the ground where they dig for food with long, slightly decurved bills. The crest is usually depressed, projecting behind the head to give a unique head-shape; it is often raised momentarily on landing, but otherwise only when alarmed or in display. Their name is derived from their distinctive calls.

African Hoopoe *Upupa (epops) africana*   28cm, 11″

Adult is most easily separated from Eurasian Hoopoe in flight when it reveals *all-black primaries*, but also differs in being *darker and more richly rufous-cinnamon*, and having *plain black tips to crest* (not black and white, or black and buff of Eurasian). Sexes very similar. Immature also similar to adult, but darker and rather browner. **HH** Common and widespread in a wide range of bushed grassland and open woodland south of the equator and partially migratory; in NE Africa known only from extreme SSo (twice, Jan and Sep) and CEt (once, Oct). **Voice** A double *pooh-pooh* given at about three-second intervals (very similar to African Cuckoo). **Note** Often treated as conspecific with Eurasian Hoopoe.

Eurasian Hoopoe *Upupa epops*   28cm, 11″

Three races may occur: all are quite similar to African Hoopoe, but have *bold white band across primaries* and narrow band of white (nominate) or pale buff *(waibeli and senegalensis)* below black tips of crest. These races differ from each other in overall tones of back, head and underparts: *waibeli* darkest, *senegalensis* intermediate, and nominate palest. Immatures are duller versions of adults. **HH** Race *senegalensis* is a common intra-tropical migrant and possible resident throughout most of region; nominate birds are common Palearctic passage migrants and winter visitors throughout region, Sep–Apr; *waibeli* has not been recorded but may occur in SW. Occurs in a wide range of woodland and bush, from sea-level to 3000m, avoiding most arid areas. **Voice** Calls may be indistinguishable from African Hoopoe.

SCIMITARBILLS Like small slim woodhoopoes (plate 110), but recent evidence suggests they are not related. They can be identified by bill colour, presence or absence of white in the wings and tail, and range. Females are slightly duller than males, and often washed brown on the throat and breast.

Abyssinian Scimitarbill *Rhinopomastus minor*   24cm, 9.5″

Small and neat, adult with a sharply decurved bright *orange-red bill and all-black glossed blue-purple plumage*, lacking white in tail. Immature similar, but all brownish below with dull brownish-red bill. Two races occur: nominate (C&SEEt, So) has white wing-bar across primaries; *cabanisi* (SEt) is larger and lacks white bar. **HH** Pairs are fairly common and widespread in drier bushed and wooded grassland including acacia scrub, from sea-level up to 1800m. Prefers more arid and open areas than Common Scimitarbill. Occurs mainly east of Rift Valley. **Voice** Usual call is a hollow rattle of identical notes, terminating on a single or double lower note: *k-k—k-k-k-k-k-k-kiow*, and also a *kreekreekreekree…* given as piercing burry scream

Common Scimitarbill *Rhinopomastus cyanomelas*   30cm, 12″

Larger than Abyssinian Scimitarbill, but with slight violet gloss. Adult has *strongly decurved black bill*, white wing-bar across primaries, and white tips to tail (may also show a little white on coverts). Immature similar, but has shorter, straighter bill and less violet gloss. Race in region is *schalowi*. **HH** Singles and pairs are uncommon in bush and woodland along Shabeelle and Jubba rivers and in Boni Forest in SSo. **Voice** Normal call is a loud repeated downslurred sequence *quee-quee-quee-kirr-kirr-quee…*; also a hollow wooden rattle and high-pitched *sisisisisisi* while foraging.

Black Scimitarbill *Rhinopomastus aterrimus*   27cm, 10.5″

Similar to Common Scimitarbill, but in our area race *notatus* is *glossed blue*, with *shorter, less decurved black bill* (sometimes with creamy sides), white band across primaries, *variable small white spot on primary coverts*, and less graduated tail with white tips on outermost feathers. Sexes similar but female lacks iridescence below. Immature like adult but duller and less glossy. **HH** Pairs are uncommon in woodland and bushland in Er and Et (except SE) from sea-level to 1900m. Most frequent in Er and Rift Valley; also in NWSo (twice). **Voice** Call is a carrying, fluty but mournful *kwee-kwee-kwee…* given as descending sequence with muffled short last note. [Alt: Black Woodhoopoe]

African Hoopoe

Eurasian Hoopoe

senegalensis

nominate

senegalensis

cabanisi

ad

ad

schalowi

imm

Abyssinian Scimitarbill

imm

notatus

imm

ad

Common Scimitarbill

Black Scimitarbill

Hornbills are noisy and characterful birds of many habitats from semi-arid bush to lowland forest. Most are black and white, varying in size from diminutive bush species to the giant casqued forms. Unique breeding behaviour involves the female being encased within a cavity and fed by her mate while she incubates the eggs and rears the young.

DRY BUSH HORNBILLS *These smaller hornbills are widespread and characteristic birds of the African bush. Colour of bill and wing markings aid identification.*

Eastern Yellow-billed Hornbill *Tockus flavirostris*   51cm, 20"

Typical bush hornbill easily identified by combination of *banana-yellow bill* and white-spotted wing-coverts. Male has slightly larger bill with thicker casque than female, and rich rose-pink rather than black bare throat-patches. Immature has smaller dusky yellow bill and is less clearly marked. **HH** Pairs and family groups are widespread at low densities in semi-arid bush country and drier wooded grassland up to 1700m in Er, Et and So, mainly east of Rift Valley. Associates with groups of Dwarf Mongoose *Helogale parvula*, acting as lookouts for birds of prey, and benefiting from the insects flushed. **Voice** Regularly calls a gently rising and falling series of very low-pitched, throaty rasping notes, *kruk-kruk-krukrukrukruk-krakrakrark-kerkrukrukruk...* **Note** Formerly conspecific with Southern Yellow-billed Hornbill *T. leucomelas* of southern Africa.

Red-billed Hornbill *Tockus erythrorhynchus*   45cm, 18"

Much smaller than similar Yellow-billed Hornbill with *slender, more decurved red bill* and whiter face and neck. Male has slightly heavier bill than female, often with blacker base to lower mandible. Eyes dark with pale pink orbital ring. Immature duller, with buff spots on wing-coverts and smaller dull red bill. Race in region is nominate. Male Jackson's has thicker bill with yellowish tip and black face. **HH** Pairs, family parties and sometimes larger flocks are common and widespread residents in dry bush and woodland up to 2100m throughout most of region except WEt. **Voice** Gives a rather urgent rising and falling series of nasal *kankankankankankank-kik-hahaha-kik-hahaha...*, rather higher-pitched than other similar hornbills. **Note** The various forms of Red-billed Hornbill in Africa are sometimes split into several species. The nominate birds in our region would then become Northern Red-billed Hornbill.

Von der Decken's Hornbill *Tockus deckeni*   48cm, 19"

Striking black-faced pied hornbill, like Jackson's but with *unspotted black wing-coverts*. Male has large red-orange bill with well-defined creamy-yellow tip, and female has all-black bill. Immature resembles female, but has duller bill and indistinct white spotting on wing-coverts. **HH** Pairs and family parties are widespread and common in dry bushed and wooded grassland in Et (mainly in and east of Rift Valley) and SSo, from sea-level to 1500m. **Voice** Gives a long series of low-pitched *kuk-kuk-kukukukukukukuk-kuk...*, all on same pitch.

Jackson's Hornbill *Tockus jacksoni*   48cm, 19"

Like Von der Decken's Hornbill but has *boldly spotted wing-coverts*. Male also has red bill, but with smaller, less well-defined creamy tip; female has all-black bill. Immature duller than adult. **HH** Known only from four old specimens and several recent unconfirmed sight records in SWEt; possibly a rare resident but may be a casual visitor. **Voice** Gives a long sequence of low rasping *krukrukrukrukruk...*, all on much the same pitch. **Note** Formerly considered conspecific with Von der Decken's Hornbill.

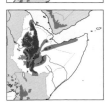

Hemprich's Hornbill *Tockus hemprichii*   59cm, 23"

Relatively large, scruffy bush hornbill, blackish above with pale fringes to wings and *dusky red bill* (brighter lower mandible in male, dusky-based in female). Immature like female. In buoyant undulating flight appears dark above and white below with much white in outer tail (although outer edge of tail is black). **HH** Pairs and family groups are common in dry bush and woodland with rocky outcrops and cliffs in Er, Et (except W and SE) and NSo (uncommon), mainly at 1600–3900m, but sometimes as low as 400m. Birds wander, even visiting towns and plantations, but depend on rock crevices in cliff and gorges for nesting. **Voice** Gives a dramatic long series of loud whistled *kek-kek-kek...* notes that start slowly and accelerate into a frantic piping *pip-pip-pip-pipipipipipipipi...* before fading away.

Eastern
Yellow-billed
Hornbill

Red-billed
Hornbill

Von der Decken's
Hornbill

Jackson's
Hornbill

Hemprich's
Hornbill

WOODLAND HORNBILLS *Largely woodland species with loud piping calls and dramatic courtship displays in which they rock on perches, point their bills skywards, and flick open their wings. Primarily arboreal, but agile, and will drop to the ground to feed.*

African Grey Hornbill *Tockus nasutus* 51 cm, 20"

Dull grey-brown hornbill with pale fringes to wing feathers and *long pale supercilium extending down side of grey-brown neck to nape*. In nominate race, male has dark bill with slender flat casque and striking creamy-white wedge at base. Female has no casque, purplish-red bill-tip and larger yellow-white wedge. Immature like adults, but duller with buff feather-edges and smaller blackish bill. In undulating flight, reveals *white corners to long grey-brown tail*. **HH** Pairs and groups are widespread and common residents in woodland and bushed grassland (especially with acacias) in Er, Et (except SE) and SSo, from sea-level to 1500m. **Voice** Gives a sharp *pi pi pi…* that accelerates and develops into a descending, rather sad piping *pipipipipipi pieu pieu*. In flight, also often gives a single far-carrying *pieu*. [Alt: Grey Hornbill]

Crowned Hornbill *Tockus alboterminatus* 55 cm, 21.5"

Slender dark hornbill with *bright red bill and long black tail with white corners*. Two races occur: eastern paler-backed *suahelicus* (SSo) and more western black-backed *geloensis* (WEt). Despite name, no obvious crown or crest, but white streaks behind eyes create dark-capped effect. Male slightly larger than female with heavier casque. Immature like female but duller, with dull yellowish bill. In rather floppy undulating flight birds show obvious white tips to outer tail. **HH** Pairs and family groups are fairly common in woodland and forest edges in WEt at 700–2750m. In SSo, rather uncommon and restricted to riverine forest in Jubba valley. **Voice** Gives very sharp high-pitched *kip-kip-kip* and long, piercing, rising and falling refrain, *kwi-kwi-kwikwikwi*.

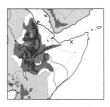

Silvery-cheeked Hornbill *Bycanistes brevis* 74 cm, 29"

A very large dark hornbill with *white underparts confined to lower belly and vent*. Face and ear-coverts tipped silvery in adults, but often hard to see at distance. Adult male has *massive bill and pale cream casque*, which may extend beyond bill-tip, and blue-grey eye-ring; adult female has duller, smaller casque confined to basal half of bill, and pinkish eye-ring. Immature duller with smaller bill, brownish face and dull, not brownish-red, eyes. In flight reveals *all-black upperwing* and white carpal patch on underwing. **HH** Family parties are widespread and locally common in highland forests, woodlands and mature gardens in W&CEt at 500–2400m; status in Er uncertain with only two records. **Voice** Strident loud goat-like braying, *wa-wa-wa-wa-wa*, and longer rising and falling *aah-aaaah-aaaah-aaah-aah-ah*.

GROUND-HORNBILLS *Atypical pedestrian hornbills, now placed in separate family (Bucorvidae), and amongst Africa's most engaging birds. They live in closely knit co-operative family groups and do not seal their nests. Walking large distances to feed, they only take to trees in defence, and to roost or breed. They enjoy a catholic diet from termites to hares (and even young eaglets from nests!), and indulge in a wide range of social chasing, preening and sunbathing.*

Abyssinian Ground-hornbill *Bucorvus abyssinicus* 110 cm, 43"

Huge shaggy-looking black bird with long heavy decurved bill and stout black legs. Adult male has large bill topped with *open casque*, pale yellowish patch at base of upper mandible, *blue skin around eye, and red and blue skin on throat*. Slightly smaller adult female has reduced casque, and entirely blue eye skin and wattles. Immature is brownish-black, has poorly formed casque and smaller greyish wattles. In flight, reveals *striking white primary feathers*. **HH** Pairs and family groups are fairly common in open grassland with scattered trees at 200–2000m (occasionally up to 2400m) in Er and Et (except SE); rather rare in NWSo. **Voice** A very deep reverberant booming, delivered as a rather bouncy *w'rump-rah-rah-rah* and given at well-spaced intervals. Often calls at dawn when the air is cool and still; calls can carry over long distances.

imm

♂ ♀

African Grey Hornbill

nominate

♀ ♂

Crowned Hornbill

suahelicus

imm

Silvery-cheeked Hornbill

♂ ♀

Abyssinian Ground-hornbill

♂ ♀

TINKERBIRDS AND BUSH BARBETS A seemingly homogeneous group of barbets with boldly striped heads and blackish upperparts spotted or streaked yellow. They are best identified by the presence or absence of red on the forecrown and markings on the underparts. Smaller tinkerbirds have different-coloured forecrowns. Sexes similar.

Yellow-fronted Tinkerbird *Pogoniulus chrysoconus* 10cm, 4"

Very like Red-fronted Tinkerbird but with *yellow-orange forecrown-spot and much stronger yellow wash on underparts*. Immature birds have black not yellow spot on forecrown. Two races occur: nominate (NWEt) as described; *xanthostictus* (W&CEt) tinged greenish-yellow below, with smaller forecrown-spot and blacker hindcrown. **HH** Singles and pairs are uncommon in moister habitats than Red-fronted including forest edge, riverine woodland, thickets and mature gardens, at 750–2400m. **Voice** Some calls doubtfully distinguishable from Red-fronted Tinkerbird, but possibly faster and lower-pitched. Also utters a very fast trill when excited. [Alt: Yellow-fronted Tinker Barbet]

Red-fronted Tinkerbird *Pogoniulus pusillus* 10cm, 4"

Small confiding tinkerbird with *red spot above bill*; much smaller than Red-fronted Barbet with short malar stripe. Streaked whitish on black above with yellowish rump, buffy-yellow below. Immature similar but with black not red spot over bill. Two races occur: *affinis* (C&SEt, SSo) as described; *uropygialis* (Er, NEt, NSo) has yellowish (not white) streaks above and yellower fringes on wings. **HH** Singles and pairs are common and widespread in dry bush and woodland from sea-level to 2500m. In NSo, it is montane, often in junipers, while in SSo it occurs in lowlands, especially along Jubba and Shabeelle valleys. **Voice** Common call is a fairly rapid continuous series of metallic *ponk-ponk-ponk...* notes; also has a repeated double *po-ponk*, and fast, rather nasal trill when excited. [Alt: Red-fronted Tinker Barbet]

Red-fronted Barbet *Tricholaema diademata* 17cm, 6.5"

Stocky, robust barbet with *long yellow-white supercilium and red forecrown-spot*. Nominate race is white below with spots on lower flanks. Immature duller with just a little red over paler bill. Red-fronted Tinkerbird is superficially similar but is much smaller and has short malar stripe. Black-throated Barbet has black throat, no red forecrown-spot. **HH** Uncommon in Et, mainly in Rift Valley, in dry bush and acacia woodland at 600–1700m. **Voice** Wide vocabulary; usually gives a rapid descending hollow *pooh-pooh-pooh-pooh...*, and a slow, nasal, pinched *wah wah wah....*

Black-throated Barbet *Tricholaema melanocephala* 14cm, 5.5"

Similar to Red-fronted Barbet with *boldly striped black-and-white head* (no red forecrown) *and long black bib tapering to sharp point in centre of whitish belly* (no spots on flanks). Immature rather duller with pale bill. Three races occur: nominate (Er, NEEt, NWSo) as described; *stigmatothorax* (SEt, SSo) browner with blackish-brown head-stripes and bib; *blandi* (SEEt, NSo) paler brown with buffy or cream spots on forehead and breast. **HH** Singles and pairs are fairly common in semi-arid bush and thorn-scrub country from sea-level to 1350m; rather uncommon in NESo. **Voice** Gives a throaty *hiau-hiau-hiau...*, sometimes breaking into descending musical churrs, often in duet.

Black-billed Barbet *Lybius guifsobalito* 17cm, 6.5"

Stocky black barbet with *bright red face, throat and upper breast*, black bill, flight feathers edged pale yellow and upperwing-coverts edged whitish. Immature duller with brownish-black head and mottled red face and throat. **HH** Pairs and small parties are common and widespread in Er and Et (except E and SE) in wide range of bush and woodland with fruiting trees, at 400–2400m. **Voice** Call is a mechanical rolling *ki-twop ki-twop ki-twop...*, first note of each series higher.

ad

imm

**Yellow-fronted
Tinkerbird**

nominate

affinis

ad

imm

**Red-fronted
Tinkerbird**

imm

ad

Red-fronted Barbet

nominate

ad

stigmatothorax

ad

imm

ad

nominate

Black-throated Barbet

Black-billed Barbet

WOODLAND BARBETS *A varied group of medium-sized to large barbets found mainly in woodland and forest; several have extensive areas of black in the plumage and red on the head, and one is boldly patterned black and white. Sexes alike.*

Brown-breasted Barbet *Lybius melanopterus*   19cm, 7.5"

Large eastern barbet with red head (streaked black on nape), *broad brown breast-band*, white belly and vent, and pale bill. Immature similar, but has much less red in face, grey-brown breast and darker bill. **HH** Singles and pairs (occasionally small groups) are uncommon in woodland and forest edge, as well as fragmented groups of large trees, along Shabeelle and Jubba rivers in SSo. **Voice** Call is a repeated nasal and very pinched *wek*.

Vieillot's Barbet *Lybius vieilloti*   17cm, 6.5"

Stocky barbet with *red face* (like Black-billed on plate 114), dark upperparts finely spotted white, *mainly lemon-yellowish underparts and rump, breast whitish with red spots*, bill blackish with tooth. Immature similar but paler yellow below with less red on face, throat and breast. Race in region is nominate. **HH** Uncommon resident in Er, with one record in NEt, inhabiting acacia woodland and scrub from sea-level to 1350m. **Voice** Song consists of slowly repeated bell-like notes with strange mournful quality. Sometimes a lower note is injected into song.

Double-toothed Barbet *Lybius bidentatus*   23cm, 9"

Impressive longer-tailed, *ivory-billed* barbet, black above (with white centre to back) and *extensively bright red below with white crescent patches on lower flanks*; creamy-white eyes ringed by bare yellow skin; double notch on each side of upper mandible. Female like male, but has a few black streaks on red flanks. Immature duller, showing much less red below, and greyish skin around dull brown eyes. Race in Et is *aequatorialis*. **HH** Pairs and family groups are uncommon residents in W&SWEt in range of woodland, wooded grassland, gardens and cultivation with scattered fig trees at 600–1800m. **Voice** Loud song is a nightjar-like churring, but much raspier, and call is a dry frog-like rasp, *erk*.

Banded Barbet *Lybius undatus*   18cm, 7"

Variable barbet with red forecrown and (usually) black throat, *readily told from all other barbets in region by barred plumage*. Eyes yellow or creamy-white. Red-fronted Barbet (plate 114) also has red forecrown but is spotted rather than barred, and lacks black throat. Four races occur: nominate (NW&CEt) has mainly black head and breast with short white supercilium behind eye, and is only faintly washed yellow below; *squamatus* (EEt) similar but with white flecking on head-sides and less well-defined black throat; *leucogenys* (W&SWEt) quite variable, some birds showing much white on head and throat, underparts more strongly tinged yellow; *thiogaster* (WEr, NEt) paler, with mottled throat and more spotting below. **HH** ENDEMIC. Fairly common and widespread in variety of wooded habitats in Er and Et (except SE), at 450–2750m. **Voice** Frog-like contact *week* notes are very like Double-toothed Barbet. Main call is a long series of unmusical rapid *wek-wek* notes, given singly or as duet, with female accompanying with rapid dry rasps. **Note** Race *salvadorii* is a synonym of *squamatus*.

Brown-breasted Barbet

ad

imm

Vieillot's Barbet
nominate

ad

imm

♂

Double-toothed Barbet

aequatorialis

leucogenys
white phase

thiogaster

nominate

Banded Barbet

leucogenys

GROUND BARBETS *Colourful, largely ground-dwelling barbets with narrow tails, and brightly patterned black, yellow, white and red plumage. All have rather mechanical songs and some duet. Easily identified by head and breast patterns. Sexes are similar.*

d'Arnaud's Barbet *Trachyphonus darnaudii* 18cm, 7"

Heavily spotted barbet with *pinkish bill, pale yellowish-orange head*, broken black-and-white breast-band, variable but small black bib and *orange-red vent*. Two races occur, varying in extent of black on crown. Nominate (SWEt) has crown speckled black; *boehmi* (SEEt, SSo) has all-black crown. Immature similar but rather duller, with browner crown. Red-and-yellow Barbet is larger and more colourful with red and white on face. **HH** Pairs and family groups are fairly common in semi-arid bushed and wooded grassland from sea-level to 1500m; frequently seen on ground near termite hills, or moving through bush with rather weak low flight, and breed in holes in open ground. **Voice** Song is a mechanical duetting accompanied by cocked and frantically waving tails; it comprises a set of two rising and two falling notes repeated for long periods *kee-ta-ti-tootle kee-ta-ti-tootle…*

Red-and-yellow Barbet *Trachyphonus erythrocephalus* 23cm, 9"

Stunning red, black and yellow barbet, with white-spotted upperparts, *long reddish bill, and striking white comma on ear-coverts surrounded by red*. Two intergrading races occur: adult male *versicolor* (S&SWEt, SWSo) has red confined around white comma, yellow throat with small black bib and plain orange-yellow breast; *shelleyi* (EEt, So except SW) is smaller and paler, especially on belly. Female similar to male in both races, but has orange crown speckled with black, browner back, and no black throat. Immature like adult, but with less orange. **HH** Pairs and family parties are widespread and locally common (mainly east of Rift Valley) in dry bush and woodland with termite mounds, up to 1500m. **Voice** Performs spectacular loud rolling duets, with a musical and reverberant series of three descending notes repeated endlessly, weedle-kwau teedle-kwau teedle-kwau…

Yellow-breasted Barbet *Trachyphonus margaritatus* 23cm, 9"

Large conspicuous barbet, like Red-and-yellow but barely overlapping in range, *head and breast much yellower*, lacking latter's orange tones, *no white patch on ear-coverts or red on face*. Sexes similar, but female lacks black throat-patch. Both sexes have black crown (only male Red-and-yellow has black crown). Two similar races occur: nominate (Er, N&CEt) as described; *somalicus* (NEEt, NSo) paler below. **HH** Singles or pairs are common in dry thornbush and wooded grassland with termite mounds, from sea-level to 2400m. **Voice** Loud song is similar to Red-and-yellow Barbet but faster, higher-pitched and less musical.

ad

nominate

d'Arnaud's Barbet

ad

boehmi

♂

♀

♂

versicolor

Red-and-yellow Barbet

shelleyi

Yellow-breasted Barbet

♂

♀

nominate

HONEYGUIDES *Solitary, dull-plumaged birds with conspicuous white outertails. They form two distinct groups: large or medium-sized with stout, rather swollen bills (genus* Indicator*); and small, active and rather warbler-like with slender bills (genus* Prodotiscus*). Sexes alike, unless otherwise described. All are brood-parasites:* Indicator *lay their eggs in the nests of hole-nesting species, while* Prodotiscus *parasitise species with globular nests.*

Greater Honeyguide *Indicator indicator*   19cm, 7.5"

Adult male has *pale pinkish bill, black throat and white ear-patch*. Rest of plumage is dull brown with small yellowish shoulders (usually concealed); when worn, may show small whitish area on rump. White outertail noticeable in undulating flight or when landing. Female mostly dull brown above with paler, greyer underparts and grey-brown bill. Immature is more olive-brown above than adults, with *creamy-yellow throat and breast* and small white area on lower rump. **HH** Uncommon to fairly common and widespread in riverine and open woodland, bush country and farmland with scattered large trees, from sea-level to 2400m. Sits upright in canopy, calling repeatedly, often from well-established song-posts. Will lead people and ratels to bee nests. **Voice** Song is a far-carrying repeated explosive *wi-chew wi-chew wi-chew...*, first note high, second lower, and also a rather complaining nasal chattering. [Alt: Black-throated Honeyguide]

Scaly-throated Honeyguide *Indicator variegatus*   19cm, 7.5"

Mostly dull olive-green above with browner wash to head; *forecrown, throat and breast are mixed dark grey and white giving scaly or mottled appearance.* Mid-breast to vent plain dirty white, sometimes tinged yellowish. Immature similar but washed greenish on head and breast. **HH** Locally common, but never numerous in wide variety of woodland and forest habitats in SEt at 1300–3000m, but lower in SSo along Jubba valley and in Boni Forest. Rather sluggish and shy; presence often first revealed by its distinctive call. **Voice** Call is a long, rather purred rising trill *trrrreeeeeeeeeeeee*; also a complaining *tew-tew-tew...*

Lesser Honeyguide *Indicator minor*   14cm, 5.5"

Classic common honeyguide: medium-sized, with grey head and underparts, and indistinctly streaked olive-green back and wings. Adult has *medium grey underparts, small pale loral spot, and dark grey malar stripes*. Immature has head uniform grey, lacking both loral spots and malar stripes. Two similar races: *teitensis* (SEEt, SSo) as described; *diadematus* (Er, W&CEt, NSo) darker and browner. **HH** A rather active, fairly common and widespread species (but rare in Er and NSo), inhabiting forest edge, open woodland, bush country and trees within cultivated areas, from sea-level to 2600m; usually avoids forest interiors. **Voice** Song starts with short downslur and then, after brief pause, continues as series of dry chips at about two per sec, *tew chet-chet-chet-chet-chet-chet...*; also a nasal chittering.

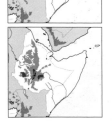

Wahlberg's Honeybird *Prodotiscus regulus*   12cm, 5"

Brown and white honeybird with *dull brown head, back and wings, tail with black centre and terminal bar.* Breast brownish-grey, throat and belly paler dirty white. Immature similar, but slightly paler above washed yellowish below, with all-white outer tail. **HH** Local and uncommon in open wooded areas and bush country at 900–2000m, mainly in Rift Valley. Vagrant NSo (once). **Voice** Song is a long, very dry rattle. [Alt: Sharp-billed Honeyguide]

Green-backed Honeybird *Prodotiscus zambesiae*   11cm, 4.5"

In areas of overlap with Wahlberg's Honeybird easily separated by olive-green back and wings (not brown). Outer tail plain white on adult, underparts greyish with paler belly. Immature similar, but paler and buffier with small dark tips to outer tail feathers. Race in Et is *ellenbecki*. **HH** Rather rare at forest edge and in mixed woodlands in C&SWEt, at 1750–2000m. **Voice** Displaying birds fly low over treetops giving a chittering high-pitched rattle and nasal *zhwink*. [Alt: Eastern Honeybird; Slender-billed Honeyguide]

Greater Honeyguide

♂

♀

imm

Scaly-throated Honeyguide

imm

ad

Wahlberg's Honeybird

nominate

imm

ad

Lesser Honeyguide

teitensis

ad

ad

Green-backed Honeybird

ellenbecki

ad

ad

imm

WRYNECKS *Curious cryptically patterned woodpecker relatives, although their appearance and behaviour is quite different, often suggesting a large warbler or thrush at first glance. They are frequently seen on the ground where they feed on ants, but fly into trees if disturbed. Sexes are alike.*

Red-throated Wryneck *Jynx ruficollis* 19cm, 7.5"

Adult has upperparts all finely mottled, barred and speckled with brown, grey and black, with series of darker spots forming streak on nape and back. *Throat and breast rufous*, rest of underparts buffy-white, with fine brown streaks and bars and cinnamon wash to vent. Immature darker than adult with more barred upperparts; rufous on throat and breast less extensive and finely barred. Race in region is *aequatorialis*. **HH** Widespread, but only locally common resident in Et, in open woodland, remnant forest edges and highland grassland with scattered trees, at 1500–3300m. **Voice** Call is a raptor-like and piercing *cor-quee-quee-quee-quee-quee*, and a chittering when excited. [Alt: Red-breasted Wryneck]

Eurasian Wryneck *Jynx torquilla* 18cm, 7"

Similar to Red-throated Wryneck, being mottled, barred and speckled grey and brown with blackish stripe down nape and back, but has dark streak through eye and *no rufous on throat or breast*. **HH** Fairly common Palearctic passage migrant and winter visitor to open woodland and bush country in Er, Dj and Et, from Sep–Apr. Occurs singly, mainly in and west of Rift Valley, from sea-level to 2400m. Rare in So (four records). **Voice** Silent in region.

LARGER WOODPECKERS *Three woodpeckers of woodland and bush country: careful attention to face markings and range aid identification. Males all have a red cap and females have a black forecrown peppered with white. All have golden-yellow tail-shafts. Immatures tend to be similar to females but darker and more boldly marked.*

Nubian Woodpecker *Campethera nubica* 20cm, 8"

Medium-sized woodpecker, barred above and *boldly spotted below*. Adult male has red malar, narrowly streaked black-and-white ear-coverts, and white throat. Adult female has similar streaked ear-coverts and white throat, but malar stripe is black speckled with white. Immature is darker, lacks red on crown and can be quite streaky below. Two races occur: nominate (Er, Et except extreme SE, NW&SWSo) as described; *pallida* (NE&SESo, SEEt) paler above, less spotted below. **HH** Common and widespread in dry bush, acacia and wooded grasslands from sea-level to 2100m (once at 2750m in Er). **Voice** Gives a long series of repeated, hardly varying metallic *tinkh-tinkh-tinkh-tinkh-tinkh...* notes which speed up and slow down with levels of excitement and are frequently given in duet.

Mombasa Woodpecker *Campethera mombassica* 20cm, 8"

Like Nubian Woodpecker but with *streaked underparts and lightly speckled upperparts* (may appear plain in field). Both sexes have plain whitish throats. **HH** Uncommon in forest and woodland along lower Jubba river and in Boni Forest in SSo. **Voice** Call is a rising burry dry trill *whirrrrrr-whirrrrrr-whirrrrrr-whirrrrrr*. **Note** Formerly conspecific with larger extralimital Golden-tailed Woodpecker *C. abingoni*.

Bearded Woodpecker *Dendropicos namaquus* 23cm, 9"

Large woodpecker with *bold black and white face pattern*, finely barred dark olive back and wings, and paler, *tightly barred olive-brown and buff underparts*. Adult male has black forecrown (with tiny white speckles) and red hindcrown. Adult female has entire crown black (also with white speckles on forecrown). Immature is speckled red, black and white on crown in both sexes. In race *schoensis* in NE Africa, black eye-stripe connects with moustachial stripe. **HH** Widespread but rather local in Et (especially in Rift Valley), in variety of woodland and bush country with large trees, often favouring mature acacias, from sea-level to 1600m. Uncommon in So, in NW and in Jubba valley. **Voice** Call is a long descending series of yelps, *kree-kree-kree-kreekreekree*, accelerating towards end.

Red-throated Wryneck

ad

aequatorialis

Eurasian Wryneck

ad

Nubian Woodpecker

nominate

♂

♂

♀

Mombasa Woodpecker

♀

♂

♀

Bearded Woodpecker
schoensis

SMALLER WOODPECKERS *A mixed group of smaller woodpeckers. They inhabit an equally varied range of habitats, from forest to dry bush. All are reasonably easily identified if seen well.*

Green-backed Woodpecker   *Campethera cailliautii*   17cm, 6.5"

Small woodpecker with greenish upperparts finely streaked buff, heavily spotted below; *spots become bars on flanks*. Adult male has all-red crown. Adult female has black forecrown (finely spotted white) and red hindcrown. *Both sexes lack malar stripe* (cf larger Nubian Woopecker on plate 118). Two races occur: *nyansae* (WEt) as described; nominate (SSo) more yellow-green above with spots rather than streaks, and entirely spotted below (no barring on flanks). **HH** Isolated race *nyansae* is rare in WEt in mixed woodland, at 750–1200m; nominate race rare in SSo, along Jubba valley and in Boni Forest. **Voice** Call is an irregular, rather lazy upslurred *ke-wiu* or *kiu-week*. [Alt: Little Spotted Woodpecker]

Cardinal Woodpecker   *Dendropicos fuscescens*   14cm, 5.5"

Small woodpecker with *lightly streaked sides to face, well-streaked underparts, and spotted wings*. Three races occur, with some intergradation: *hemprichii* (Er, most of Et and So), and darker *massaicus* (extreme SEt) both have *distinctly barred backs* on blackish-brown background, and are only faintly tinged yellow below. In WEt, race *lepidus* has olive-green back with darker olive barring (often looking plain in field), and is yellowish below. In all races cap is largely red in adult male and blackish-brown in adult female; both sexes have *black malar* and golden-yellow shafts on tail. **HH** Common and widespread, inhabiting forest edge and clearings, open woodland, dry bush and cultivation, from sea-level to 2450m. **Voice** Gives a very cross-sounding series of dry high-pitched and tuneless rattled churrs that change slightly in tone.

Abyssinian Woodpecker   *Dendropicos abyssinicus*   16cm, 6.5"

Small woodpecker with *golden-green back, boldly spotted wings and red rump*, underparts yellowish-white, broadly streaked blackish-brown. Crown in adult male largely red, brown in adult female; both sexes have brown ear-coverts and submoustachial stripe. Cardinal Woodpecker is smaller and less golden above, usually with barring. **HH** ENDEMIC to Er and Et. Uncommon resident in variety of woodlands at 1300–3250m; absent from SEEt. **Voice** Call is like Cardinal Woodpecker, but higher-pitched, more musical and less of a dry rattle; most frequently given by pairs, but not very vocal and best located by rapid tapping. [Alt: Golden-backed Woodpecker]

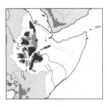

Brown-backed Woodpecker   *Picoides obsoletus*   14cm, 5.5"

Like Cardinal Woodpecker but easily separated by *dark brown ear-coverts encircled with white, and brown tail with small white spots*. Adult male has red restricted to rear of crown; adult female has crown and nape entirely brown. Two races occur: *heuglini* (Er, NEt) is brown above and lightly streaked below with little spotting on wing-coverts; *ingens* (NW&WEt) is darker above and more streaked below, with well-spotted wing-coverts. **HH** Uncommon and inconspicuous in variety of woodland, forest edge and cultivated areas with large scattered trees, at 1200–1800m. **Voice** Usual call is a rattled musical *chreetchee-chree-chee* or variants, and also a series of upslurred squeals, rather like a small raptor.

Grey Woodpecker   *Dendropicos goertae*   19cm, 7.5"

Plain olive-green and grey woodpecker with red rump. Adult male has red crown, *no or very little red/orange on belly, faint barring on flanks, and pale yellowish bars on wings and tail (mainly on underside)*; similar adult female lacks red on head. Immature duller than adult, with stronger barring on underparts. Race in region is *abessinicus*. **HH** Fairly common in WEr and NWEt in wide range of woodland, forest edge, bush country and farmland with trees, at 400–1800m. **Voice** Common call is a descending series of squealed *kwikwikwi...*, but also gives an upslurred musical churr, *trrree't'ri'tree*. **Note** Sometimes placed in genus *Thripias*.

Grey-headed Woodpecker   *Dendropicos spodocephalus*   19cm, 7.5"

Very similar to Grey Woodpecker but *darker grey on head and underparts*, slightly more golden above, and plainer (less barred) wings; tail is proportionately shorter than Grey and *unbarred*. Adult male has *large red belly-patch*; similar adult female has no red on crown. Immature duller than adult with less intense red areas. **HH** Fairly common in wooded habitats in highlands of Et (except NW and SE) up to at least 2500m. **Voice** Similar to Grey Woodpecker. **Note** Formerly conspecific with Grey Woodpecker *D. goertae*.

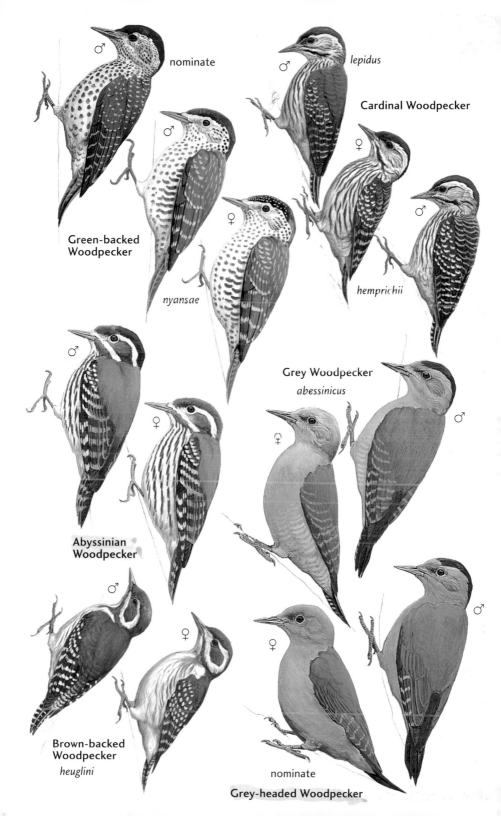

nominate

♂

lepidus

♂

Cardinal Woodpecker

♀

Green-backed
Woodpecker

♂

♀

nyansae

hemprichii

♂

Grey Woodpecker
abessinicus

♂

♀

♂

♀

Abyssinian
Woodpecker

♂

♀

Brown-backed
Woodpecker
heuglini

♀

nominate

Grey-headed Woodpecker

Larks are a difficult group to identify without comparative experience of the commoner species; this is further complicated by racial variation and the existence of different colour morphs in some species. In addition, there is considerable sexual size dimorphism in some species. Pay careful attention to presence or lack of rufous in wings, colour of outer tail, face pattern and habitat. Sexes alike. Immatures similar to adults unless otherwise described.

BUSH LARKS Mirafra *is a large genus of larks of grassland and bush, variable in size and plumage. Most have stout bills, short hind claw, and short, rounded wings with rufous patches (most visible in flight).*

Red-winged Lark *Mirafra hypermetra*   23cm, 9"

A large bulky lark with a long tail and *black spots at sides of breast usually forming two small blackish patches* (may not be visible on worn birds or immatures). Long heavy bill, rufous wings (particularly noticeable in flight), buffy supercilium, slight shaggy appearance to crown, and brown tail are all generally similar to Rufous-naped, but upperparts are less rufous. Three races occur: nominate (SSo) has brownish upperparts; *gallarum* (E&SEt) is much greyer above with less buff below; *kathangorensis* (SWEt) is darker than other races with pale underwing-coverts. **HH** Occurs from near sea-level to 950m, preferring open grassy areas with bushes and small trees. Often perches on and sings from tops of small bushes, but also has very distinctive laboured song-flight. **Voice** Very fluty, rather chat-like song, with short varied phrases repeated monotonously. [Alt: Red-winged Bush Lark]

Rufous-naped Lark *Mirafra africana*   17cm, 7"

Quite large and short-tailed with heavy bill, obvious pale buffy supercilium, crown feathers often raised giving shaggy-headed appearance, and non-contrasting *buffy outer tail*. Race in our area is one of the most distinctive, and may be a separate species, Sharpe's Lark M. *sharpii*: *Upperparts bright rufous with prominent pale fringes*, underparts cinnamon-buff with neat rufous streaking on breast. Somali Lark is larger, with longer bill and tail and white outer tail. **HH** Race *sharpii* is virtually endemic to NWSo (one record NEEt), where fairly common on open grassy plains in areas of broken dry woodland. Sings from tops of bushes, and perches on tussocks of grass, but prefers to run between tussocks rather than take flight. **Voice** Normal song is *sii-su-eeeee* with middle falling and last part gently rising to fade. Many local variations based on this; also a monotonous piping.

Somali Lark *Mirafra somalica*   20cm, 8"

Distinctive large lark with *reddish plumage and very long bill*; tail is dark brown with rufous central and *white-edged outer feathers*. Two races occur: nominate *somalica* (N&CSo) is bright rufous above and mainly buff below with white throat and streaking on breast; race *rochei* (coastal plains of C&SSo) is darker and browner, especially on crown and wings, breast washed cinnamon with heavier streaking. Nominate overlaps with Rufous-naped (race *sharpii*) in NWSo but latter has shorter, heavier bill and buffy outer tail. Race *rochei* is more like Red-winged Bush Lark but latter is larger with more robust bill, darker plumage and blackish spots at sides of breast. **HH** ENDEMIC. Fairly common and widespread in So (except S). Inhabits open grassy plains with some shrubs. **Voice** Unknown. **Note** Sometimes placed in *Certhilauda*, but *rochei* has display behaviour typical of *Mirafra* (although not observed in nominate). [Alt: Somali Long-billed Lark]

Flappet Lark *Mirafra rufocinnamomea*   14cm, 5.5"

Fairly small with four races in our area. Generally *very brown (or rufous-brown) above and warm buff or fulvous below*, with buffy-rufous outer tail. Breast-spotting varies from rufous to blackish. Races *rufocinnamomea* (NW & CEt) and *torrida* (SEt) are rufous above, heavily marked blackish; *omoensis* (SWEt) blacker above; *fischeri* (SSo) warm earthy-brown above without bold markings. **HH** Often first encountered in display flight when it makes loud far-carrying *prrrrrrrr-rrrp* sound with wings. On ground rather shy, often crouching and keeping near cover. Inhabits grasslands with or without scattered trees, bushes or rocks, from sea-level to 2300m. Frequent to common in Et, but rare in So. **Voice** Rarely heard song from top of bush is a loud, piercing, serin-like rising-and-falling *si-uu-si-si-uu..*

nominate

Rufous-naped Lark

sharpii

Red-winged Lark

gallarum

Somali Lark

rochei

nominate

torrida

Flappet Lark

fischeri

Foxy Lark *Mirafra alopex* 16cm, 6"

Medium-sized, slim and variable; generally paler in arid areas, more rufous on red soils and darker in highlands. All are quite heavily streaked above with *bold white (or buff) supercilium* and rufous wing-patches, visible in flight. Underparts whitish with short blackish (or rufous-brown) streaks across breast. Three races occur: widespread *intercedens* (S&SEEt and SWSo) has variable, heavily streaked upperparts and well-marked breast; *macdonaldi* (SEt) is brighter above and less heavily streaked; nominate *alopex* (SEEt and NWSo) is the most distinctive, with *bright rufous upperparts*, only lightly streaked, buff supercilium and no black streaks on breast. Slightly smaller Flappet Lark has indistinct supercilium and is more fulvous below. **HH** Solitary birds and pairs are locally common or uncommon at 200–1800m, inhabiting semi-arid and bush country with or without some grass cover. **Voice** Scratchy serin-like song is usually a short and hurried series, given from bush-top or in flight. **Note** Until recently, conspecific with Fawn-coloured Lark *M. africanoides* of southern Africa, but within NE Africa, *alopex* may be distinct from *intercedens* and *macdonaldi*. Sometimes placed in genus *Calendulauda*. [Alt: Abyssinian Lark]

Gillett's Lark *Mirafra gilletti* 17cm, 6.5"

Similar to Foxy Lark with long whitish supercilium, but differs in having pinkish-rufous crown and ear-coverts, *greyish rump, rufous-brown streaking across breast* (usually blackish on Foxy) and *no rufous wing-patches*. Two poorly marked races: nominate (EEt and NWSo) as described; *arorihensis* (SEEt and So except NW) paler and more reddish with finer streaking. **HH** Near-endemic (range just creeps into extreme NE Kenya). Singles and pairs are fairly common to uncommon in arid bush country on sandy or stony soils at 200–1350m. **Voice** Usual song from a low shrub or in flight is a monotonous, rapid *sii-sii-sii-seeu-seu*, first three notes identical, latter two lower, falling and ending rather abruptly; lacks scratchiness of Foxy Lark. **Note Degodi Lark** *Mirafra degodiensis*, described as a good species in 1975 from two birds collected near Bogol Manyo in SEt, is now considered to be synonymous with Gillett's Lark (Collar *et al.* 2009).

Singing Bush Lark *Mirafra cantillans* 13cm, 5"

Fairly small lark with short stout bill; *upperparts grey-brown* with dark streaking, *buffy supercilium* accentuates dark ear-coverts; bill dark above, pinkish below. Underparts buffy with small streaks on sides of breast; throat white. In distinctive hesitant moth-like flight (shared with White-tailed and Friedmann's Larks) shows rufous wing-patches and obvious *pure white outer tail feathers*. Two races occur: *marginata* (Er, N&SEt and So) as described; *chadensis* (WEr) paler and sandier with less heavy streaking. **HH** Locally common but patchily distributed in bush country with sparse grass cover from sea-level to 1800m. Also appears in flocks in seasonal grasslands during rains. Flies and dives into cover when flushed, hovering briefly before plunging to ground. **Voice** Song, from high circling flight or prominent perch, is a continuous, rather monotonous series of repeated notes preceded by slower, slightly lower notes.

White-tailed Lark *Mirafra albicauda* 13cm, 5"

Like Singing Bush Lark but *upperparts very heavily streaked blackish* giving much darker impression. Rufous patches on wings and *white outer tail obvious in hesitant flight*. Underparts buffy with short blackish breast-streaks; throat white. Flappet Lark is more fulvous below. **HH** Rare presumed resident on Nechisar plain in SEt at 1300m, in grasslands on black cotton soil. **Voice** Sings a complex rambling of harsh and sweet notes, plus much mimicry, from perch or in sustained fluttering song-flight. [Alt: White-tailed Bush Lark]

Friedmann's Lark *Mirafra pulpa* 14cm, 5.5"

Very like Singing Bush Lark, but overall tones *more rufous* and bill slightly larger. Best identified by voice; has puffy white-throated appearance when calling. Singing Bush Lark is slightly smaller and much greyer, with no rufous on wing-coverts and tertials. **HH** Apparently nomadic or migratory, but movements poorly known. In our region known only from type locality in SEt. Likes open bush country with short grass cover at 600m. **Voice** Calls from tops of bushes and in flight, a rising and falling reedy whistled *whooyu*, repeated at about two-second intevals. **DD**

intercedens

grey form

rufous form

Foxy Lark

alopex

Gillett's Lark

nominate

arorihensis

Singing Bush Lark
marginata

White-tailed Lark

Friedmann's Lark

Ash's Lark *Mirafra ashi* 15cm, 6"

Medium-sized bush lark, rather greyish above and *heavily scalloped with pale fringes*; whitish supercilium poorly defined. Underparts buffy-white, finely streaked rufous-brown on breast; sides of breast and flanks suffused with pinkish-brown. Outer tail feathers white, but extent varies. **HH** ENDEMIC. A poorly known species, discovered in 1981, and restricted to single locality in Somalia, where locally common in open grassland with small scattered bushes on coastal plain north of Mogadishu. Occurs with Somali Lark (race *rochei*), which is larger with long bill and more rufous plumage. Both species share habit of running across open ground between tussocks. **Voice** Unknown. **EN**

Collared Lark *Mirafra collaris* 15cm, 6"

An attractive and distinctive species, mostly *bright cinnamon-rufous above*, with a lightly streaked black and white hindneck. *Black band across base of neck separates white throat from red mottling across upper breast.* In flight rufous upperparts and wing-coverts contrast with *blackish flight feathers and tail*. **HH** Widespread and locally common near-endemic in So and SEEt, inhabiting arid bush country on red sandy soils up to 1000m. **Voice** Song is poorly known, but reported as a plaintive rising whistle; also has an aerial display like Flappet Lark where wings produce an audible *burrr*.

Pink-breasted Lark *Mirafra poecilosterna* 16cm, 6.5"

Slim appearance and bill give a rather pipit-like impression. Upperparts grey-brown and lightly streaked, with greyer crown; *supercilium and face pinkish-cinnamon, and breast and flanks mottled with same colour*, like no other lark or pipit. No white in tail and no rufous in wings. **HH** Common in bush country with little ground cover up to 900m, where frequently perches on bush tops with horizontal stance. **Voice** Monotonous descending hissed song is given from small trees or in flight. Also utters an occasional single squeaked *tseet* from ground. **Note** Sometimes placed in genus *Calendulauda*.

LONG-CLAWED LARKS *Two species of medium-sized, short-tailed larks with robust legs and very long hindclaws; they appear large-headed with an upright stance.*

Sidamo Lark *Heteromirafra sidamoensis* 14cm, 5.5"

Short-billed lark with a rather long and distinctly thin neck, shortish tail, relatively long legs and very long hindclaw. Crown is finely streaked, with *indistinct pale median stripe*; prominent creamy supercilium and pale buff hindcrown and nape, *upperparts richly patterned with heavy scalloped effect*, primaries rufous-brown, most visible in flight. Underparts whitish with small blackish streaks on breast and buffy flanks. Outer tail feathers white. Race *torrida* of Flappet Lark is superficially similar. **HH** ENDEMIC. Restricted to tiny area of grassland at c.1450m east of Negele in SEt. Discovered in 1968 and still very poorly known. Rather shy and unobtrusive, running rapidly through long grass like rodent, but stands upright when still. **Voice** Song is a loud, rather formless squeaky series of rising and falling notes with typical lark-like quality, usually given in rather low hovering song-flight before parachuting to ground. When flushed, utters a soft *tswee-ee-eep* or *twi-twi-twi* (up to 9 notes) before dropping back into cover. **Note** Recent unpublished studies suggest this taxon may be conspecific with Archer's Lark. **EN**

Archer's Lark *Heteromirafra archeri* 14cm, 5.5"

Very like Sidamo Lark in shape and proportions, with stout bill, long, thin neck, short tail and very long hindclaw. Crown finely streaked, with *indistinct pale median stripe*. Face buffy with dark border at rear of ear-coverts; nape and sides of neck buffy-brown. Upperparts strongly patterned with pale fringes giving scalloped effect. Underparts buff with dark streaking on breast. Differs from Sidamo Lark by having *brown wings (lacking rufous patch) and white outer tail feathers* (pinkish-buff on Sidamo). Singing Bush Lark (plate 121) is longer-tailed and has rufous wing-patches. **HH** ENDEMIC. Known only from two small sites in NWSo, close to the Ethiopian border, at 1500m. No recent confirmed records. Inhabits open short grasslands, but very secretive, preferring to creep away through grass; flies only when flushed. **Voice** Unknown. **Note** Several *Heteromirafra* larks found recently near Jijiga, EEt, close to original site for Archer's Lark in NWSo, may have been Archer's, although their song was similar to Sidamo Lark. **CR**

Collared Lark

Ash's Lark

Pink-breasted Lark

Sidamo Lark

Archer's Lark

SHORT-TOED LARKS More pointed wings than Mirafra *(lacking rufous wing-patches) and dark square tails with white (or buff) outer feathers. Bills are strong and short. Blandford's and Erlanger's were formerly included in Red-capped Lark C.* cinerea.

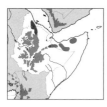

Blanford's Lark *Calandrella blanfordi*   15cm, 6"

Similar in size and shape to Erlanger's Lark, but *much sandier and paler* with reduced streaking on upperparts. *Crown is pale rufous,* without black forehead, nape pale sandy and only faintly streaked, *blackish patch at side of breast smaller* and less obvious than in Erlanger's. Two races occur: nominate *blanfordi* (Er, NEt) as described; *daroodensis* (NEEt, NSo) paler with less rufous on crown, and underparts white with pinkish wash. (A third race occurs in SW Arabia.) **HH** Fairly common on open short grasslands and dry stony plains from 600–1800m, sometimes gathering in large flocks. **Voice** Song similar to Erlanger's. Single liquid chirrups given in flight.

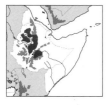

Erlanger's Lark *Calandrella erlangeri*   15cm, 6"

Distinctive species with *deep rufous cap* (sometimes raised) *and large black patch on side of breast. Blackish forehead and black streaking on hindcrown* contrast with bold white supercilium. Upperparts heavily streaked black; unstreaked underparts pinkish-apricot. Shows very dark white-edged tail when flushed. Immature very different with dark brown upperparts, finely spotted white on crown, and white fringes to mantle; underparts with some brown spots. **HH** ENDEMIC to CEt, inhabiting short dry grasslands and fallow fields in highlands at 1900–3600m. Usually in flocks outside breeding season. **Voice** Main song is a deliberate series of five or so rapid rising-and-falling notes rather than a long musical series. Single liquid chirrups given when flushed.

Somali Short-toed Lark *Calandrella somalica*   14cm, 5.5"

Smallish lark with moderate streaking on upperparts, lacking rufous cap of previous two species. Three races occur: *perconfusa* (NWSo and NEEt) is dark brown above with buffy fringes, tail dark with buffy-white edges, breast to vent washed pale brown with short heavy dark streaks across breast; throat whitish; *pale supercilium and eye-ring and pale pinkish bill* distinctive at close range. Race *megaensis* (SEt) similar, but more heavily streaked above and slightly reddish; *somalica* (NCSo and EEt) much more reddish above with underparts washed pinkish. Flappet is more fulvous below; Singing has obvious white outer tail and rufous wing-patches. **HH** Near-endemic. Occurs in flocks on open ground with short grass cover at 600–1650m. **Voice** Song complex, rising and falling notes incorporating mimicry. Call is a dry *chirrup.* [Alt: Rufous Short-toed Lark]

Greater Short-toed Lark *Calandrella brachydactyla*   14cm, 5.5"

Similar to other short-toed larks in shape, and best told by *pale greyish-brown coloration* with *small pale yellowish-horn bill* and dark tail with white on outermost feathers; also shows creamy-buff supercilium and small light streaks at sides of upper breast sometimes appearing as distinctive small dark patch. **HH** Common Palearctic winter visitor, Sep–Apr, to Er and NEt, less common So and Soc. Mainly nominate birds in north of region, but eastern *longipennis* also recorded in SSo. Usually in small flocks, in variety of habitats from sea-level to 2400m. **Voice** Song not heard in region. Call is a dry *chirrup.* [Alt: Short-toed Lark]

Greater Hoopoe-Lark *Alaemon alaudipes*   19–23cm, 7.5–9"

Large, slim, long-legged lark with *long, decurved bill.* Adult is unmistakable with striking head pattern and dense black blotches on white breast. Upperparts largely grey in NE African race *desertorum.* In flight shows unique *black and white wings and tail.* Sexes alike but female smaller. Immature less well-marked. **HH** Common resident in arid coastal plains of Er, NEEt, Dj and NSo, from sea-level to 400m. Usually singly or in pairs; prefers to run rather than fly. **Voice** Song is a series of thin, melancholy, far-carrying notes which accelerate as the bird begins its spectacular song-flight, and then slow down again as it parachutes back to earth. [Alt: Hoopoe Lark]

Lesser Hoopoe-Lark *Alaemon hamertoni*   18–20cm, 7–8"

Smaller and plainer than Greater Hoopoe-Lark, and somewhat reminiscent of pipit. Lacks striking head pattern of Greater and also *lacks black and white wings* in flight. Three races occur, varying in shade of upperparts: nominate (CSo) is grey (like *desertorum* Greater); *altera* (NSo) is sandy-brown; *tertia* (NWSo) is like *altera* but more rufescent. **HH** ENDEMIC. Common resident on open tussocky grasslands, from sea-level to 1600m. No overlap with Greater Hoopoe-Lark. **Voice** Unknown.

Blanford's Lark

blanfordi

Erlanger's Lark

daroodensis

perconfusa

Greater
Short-toed
Lark

somalica

Somali
Short-toed
Lark

megaensis

tertia

Lesser
Hoopoe-Lark

altera

Greater
Hoopoe-Lark

desertorum

These larks do not fit easily into previously mentioned groups. They are not specifically related or similar looking, and are included here purely for convenience.

Bimaculated Lark *Melanocorypha bimaculata*   17cm, 7"

Large chunky lark with heavy yellowish-brown bill and well-marked head pattern. Readily identified by long white supercilium, conspicuous *black patch at sides of breast* and *short tail with prominent white tips* (but not sides). Race *rufescens* (in NE Africa) has greyish olive-brown upperparts, and sides of breast and flanks washed rufous. Greater Short-toed Lark is much smaller and has white sides to tail. **HH** Uncommon to rare Palearctic winter visitor to Er, NEEt; vagrant Dj (once). Frequents cultivation, grassy plains and stony hills from sea-level to 2275m. Usually in flocks. **Voice** Flight call is a dry trilling *prrp* or *tchup-turrup*. Song not heard in Africa.

Short-tailed Lark *Pseudalaemon fremantlii*   14cm, 5.5"

Boldly marked, rather long-billed, short-tailed lark, with distinctive *black crescent below eye and vertical bar down cheek*. Prominent streaking on breast, often showing as dark patch at sides. In flight, short square tail has white outer feathers. Two races occur: nominate (So and SEEt) is rather buffish above and pale rufous below; darker *megaensis* (SEt) is more heavily streaked blackish above with rufous edges, and with reddish-brown on sides of breast and flanks. **HH** Fairly common and widespread resident, usually in small flocks on dry soils with short grass, and on burnt grassland, from sea-level to 1800m. **Voice** Distinctive song is an attractive jumble of rising and falling notes with minor-key intrusions. On ground it calls with chips and explosive downslurs.

Desert Lark *Ammomanes deserti*   16cm, 6.5"

Medium-sized plain lark with considerable racial variation but *always unstreaked on upperparts* with whitish throat and diffuse streaking on breast. Fairly heavy bill is yellowish-brown. In flight, dark brown tail shows pale pinkish-rufous at base and flight feathers are edged rufous. Three races occur: *samharensis* (Er) has grey-brown upperparts and pinkish-buff underparts; *assabensis* (NEEt and NWSo) is darker above and slightly darker below; *akeleyi* (NSo) is sandy-grey above and pale pinkish-buff below. **HH** Common and widespread resident in wide variety of sparsely vegetated habitats in stony or sandy areas, from sea-level to 1800m. **Voice** Song is a strong series of rising-and-falling throaty trilled notes. Call is strident, more to be expected from small plover rather than lark.

Crested Lark *Galerida cristata*   18cm, 7"

Sandy grey-brown lark with *long pointed crest*, often raised or blown up by wind but not always immediately obvious. *Bill fairly long and strong*. Underparts very pale sandy with dark brown streaks across breast. Sides of tail and *underwing-coverts pinkish-cinnamon* (conspicuous in flight). In flight, wings appear heavier and broader than similar Thekla Lark. Two races occur: *altirostris* (Er and NEt) is sandy-brown above; *somaliensis* (NWSo and SEEt) duller and greyer. Race *isabellina*, with more cinnamon upperparts, may occur in NWEt. Very similar Thekla Lark is darker above with heavier spots across breast, and has shorter, stouter bill. **HH** Common within range, particularly in sandy desert with sparse cover and coastal plains, up to 750m. Usually in pairs, but more may gather at water holes. **Voice** Long rambling song usually from ground or low perch consists of many randomly introduced, rather scratchy notes.

Thekla Lark *Galerida theklae*   16cm, 6.5"

Very like Crested Lark but slightly smaller with less spiky crest, and *darker above with shorter, heavier spots across breast*. Underwing-coverts greyish or pinkish-grey. Combination of dark-toned upperparts and breast-spotting accentuates whiteness of throat. Usually has *shorter, stouter bill* than Crested. Six races occur, differing in tone of upperparts and underparts, and intensity of streaking: *praetermissa* (highlands of Er and Et), *huei* (Bale Mts), *huriensis* (SEt), *harrarensis* (EEt), *ellioti* (SEEt, So), *mallablensis* (coastal SSo). Race *huriensis* has a longer, spiky crest; eastern races are paler and sandier. **HH** Widespread (but patchy) in NE Africa; frequent to abundant in Er, Et and So, occurring in pairs and loose flocks *in rockier areas* than Crested Lark, but will use cultivation, lightly bushed grassland and stony acacia steppe. Ranges barely overlap, but where they meet in Er and NWSo they are separated altitudinally: Thekla is montane in Er, Et and NSo, up to 4100m, but occurs down to sea-level in SSo. **Voice** Sings from rocky ground, a short series of sweet notes recalling a bunting. More complex series with mimicry in flight. **Note** The highland races in our region may represent a separate species. [Alt: Short-crested Lark]

Bimaculated Lark

nominate

rufescens

Short-tailed Lark

megaensis

Desert Lark

assabensis

akeleyi

Crested Lark

Thekla Lark

somaliensis

praetermissa

Obbia Lark *Spizocorys obbiensis*   13 cm, 5"

Small, short-legged lark with stout bill and pink legs. Rather greyish overall with heavy streaking above. Distinctive face pattern includes dark line through eye, another below eye, and *dark moustachial streak*. Underparts whitish with strong *brown streaking on breast and flanks*. Tail dark brown with white outer edges. Sexes alike. No confusion species in limited range. **HH** ENDEMIC to a 570km coastal strip of So, often abundant and usually in flocks. Inhabits short-grass plains and sand-dunes; very active, foraging with hunched posture. **Voice** Flight call is described as *tip-tip*. **DD**

Masked Lark *Spizocorys personata*   15 cm, 6"

Distinctive lark with grey-brown upperparts, *black face mask and pale pinkish or horn-coloured bill*. Underparts unstreaked with small whitish throat blending to greyish breast and rufous belly. Tail dark brown with buff outer feathers. Sexes alike. Two races occur: nominate (EEt) as described; *yavelloensis* (SEt) darker and greyer. **HH** Rare breeding resident in S&EEt, inhabiting bare gound with sparse grass cover or lava boulders, at 200–1700m. **Voice** Various calls described in flight and on ground include a rolling *tew-tew-tutew-tew* and high-pitched *treeeeeeee*, but no proper song has been reported.

SPARROW-LARKS *Small chunky sparrow-like larks with heavy conical bills, usually found in flocks. Sexually dimorphic: males are boldly marked on the head and underparts; females and immatures are much drabber. Also known as finchlarks.*

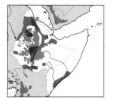

Chestnut-headed Sparrow-Lark *Eremopterix signatus*   11 cm, 4.5"

Male is unmistakable. *Black and dark chestnut facial markings encircle white patch on crown.* Cheek-patch very white. Facial pattern extends as *broad black vertical stripe from chin to vent*, sides of breast and flanks white. Back and wings pale grey-brown, narrow white tail-edges. Some males lack chestnut on head, and show black and white head pattern. Female has indication of male-like facial pattern but crown brown, *supercilium rufous*, cheeks buffy-white. Immature is like a poorly marked female. Race *harrisoni* (SWEt?) is greyer above. **HH** Nominate race is common in variety of arid and semi-arid habitats in S&EEt and So, including lava and sandy desert, open stony areas with some bush cover, and short dry grasslands from sea-level to 1400m. **Voice** Call consists of spaced piping notes, some similar to Lesser Striped Swallow. Song is a series of repeated rising mournful notes.

Chestnut-backed Sparrow-Lark *Eremopterix leucotis*   12 cm, 5"

Male is distinctive, with *rich chestnut back and wings*, bold black and white head pattern and mostly black underparts (with *white vent*). White on ear-coverts and nape, but not on crown. Shows *pale rump* and white on outer tail in flight. Female duller with variable (but usually extensive) black mottling on head and underparts, and *chestnut wing-coverts*. Immature is like male female. Two races occur: male nominate (Er, Et and NWSo) has black shoulder, female is generally dark; male *madaraszi* (SSo) is more reddish above and female has more black on underparts. **HH** Widespread and common, subject to erratic wanderings. Can occur in large numbers in grassy areas, cultivation and recently burnt grasslands, between sea-level and 1800m. **Voice** Song is more complex than other sparrow-larks, a mournful series of slurs and chips delivered both in flight and from ground.

Black-crowned Sparrow-Lark *Eremopterix nigriceps*   11 cm, 4.5"

Male is similar in pattern to Chestnut-backed, but *upperparts largely grey-brown, underparts entirely black*. White on ear-coverts and nape; white patch on forehead variable in size. Race in region is *melanauchen*. Birds on Soc described as race *forbeswatsoni* on basis of more extensive white forehead, but this now considered invalid. Female very plain, pale rufous-buff above with fine streaking, and *buffish-white below*. In both sexes tail is blackish-brown with pale edges and brown central feathers, giving distinctive pattern in flight. Immature similar to female. **HH** Common and widespread in Er, NEt, So and Soc in dry open country with sparse vegetation and semi-desert, most commonly in coastal areas, from sea-level to 1400m; invariably in flocks. **Voice** Song mainly consists of a loud, short, squeaky *swi-chi-tchi*, usually delivered in flight. This sometimes breaks into other, more complex series of high-pitched squeaky notes.

Obbia Lark

Masked Lark

yavelloensis

Chestnut-headed
Sparrow-Lark

♂

♀

nominate

Chestnut-backed
Sparrow-Lark

♂

♀

nominate

Black-crowned
Sparrow-Lark

♂

♀

melanauchen

MARTINS Highly aerial birds that prefer open areas; some often occur together in mixed-species flocks. Most martins are brown and white with short, only slightly forked tails. Sexes alike; immatures similar to adults.

Rock Martin *Ptyonoprogne fuligula*   12cm, 5"

Variable brown martin associated with rocks and cliffs. In flight, fanned tail shows small white spots near end of each feather. Dark southern races are unmistakable; paler northern races (*arabica* and *obsoleta*) sometimes considered a separate species, Pale Crag Martin *P. obsoleta*, and can be confused with larger Crag Martin. Four races occur: *fusciventris* (W&CEt) is *dark brown above and below, showing contrasting pale cinnamon throat; pusilla* (WEr, N&CEt) is paler brown with pinkish-grey breast; *arabica* (coastal Er, Dj, NEEt, NSo, Soc) is grey-brown above and has pale grey-brown breast with pale pinkish throat; *obsoleta* (?Et, NSo) is even paler and greyer, and *almost white below.* **HH** Common and widespread from sea-level to 4000m, occurring in pairs and small loose flocks wherever there are cliffs, but also breeds on buildings in towns. Race *obsoleta* may only be non-breeding Palearctic visitor, Nov–May. **Voice** Utters short monotonous phrases, each terminating in a buzzy churr.

Crag Martin *Ptyonoprogne rupestris*   14cm, 6"

Chunky, uniform martin, larger than Rock Martin but confusingly similar to paler races of it. Grey-brown above (rump concolorous with mantle), paler below with *darker vent; whitish throat is finely streaked* at close range. In flight, white tail-spots are prominent, and silvery-grey underside of wings contrast with *blackish-brown underwing-coverts.* Rather broad wings and powerful, graceful flight is distinctive. Pale northern races of Rock Martin are slightly smaller and paler above and below, with unmarked pale throat and paler undertail-coverts; dark underwing-coverts are less extensive and less contrasting than on Crag Martin, and paler rump often contrasts with mantle. **HH** Uncommon Palearctic winter visitor to Et, Dec–Apr, south to Rift Valley; usually in flocks, at higher altitudes (2000–3600m); one old record from Er. **Voice** Call is a series of loud chips and squeaks, higher-pitched and more strident than Rock Martin.

Sand Martin *Riparia riparia*   12cm, 5"

Plain brown above, white below with brown breast-band, *uniform brown underwing,* and slightly forked tail. Similar Banded Martin is much larger with white underwing-coverts. Plain Martin is similar in size but has dusky chin and throat. **HH** Common Palearctic passage migrant and winter visitor, Aug–May, from sea-level to 2400m. Sometimes appears in migrating flocks of thousands moving rapidly and directly. Most birds are nominate *riparia,* but paler *shelleyi* is winter visitor to Er. **Voice** Series of churrs on different notes resulting in a formless twittering song.

Plain Martin *Riparia paludicola*   11cm, 4.5"

Upperparts, throat and breast are brown; *belly is white.* Three races occur, differing in tone and size: *paludibula* (NEt) is small and fairly dark; *schoensis* (highlands of Et) is larger and darker; *ducis* (vagrant to So) is even darker with little or no white on the belly. **HH** Common and widespread species, often in large flocks, occurring at 400–2400m over rivers, lakes and wetlands. **Voice** Continuous harsh rasping *churr* from perch and single notes in flight. [Alt: Brown-throated Sand Martin]

Banded Martin *Riparia cincta*   15cm, 6"

Similar to Sand Martin but *much larger,* with *short white stripe in front of eyes, white underwing-coverts* and square-ended tail. Race *erlangeri* (Er and Et) has breast-band extending to point in centre; *suahelica* (vagrant to So) is darker with broader breast-band. **HH** Locally common resident or intra-tropical migrant over grasslands and moorland at 750–3000m. Only three records in SSo, Jan–Feb. Flight is powerful, low and slow; glides frequently. **Voice** Musical notes are given in descending series, with twangy, nasal, rather lark-like quality. Calls in flight, but song is usually delivered from top of low vegetation.

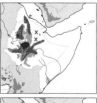

Common House Martin *Delichon urbicum*   14cm, 5.5"

Rather stocky blue-black martin with *white rump and underparts;* tail forked, but not elongated as with some pale-rumped swallows. Immature and non-breeding adult duller and browner with grey-tinged rump. No other hirundine has pure white rump, but beware white-rumped swifts (plate 99). **HH** Common Palearctic passage migrant and winter visitor, Aug–Apr. **Voice** In flight gives pleasant, short, buzzy chirp, with many calling at same time.

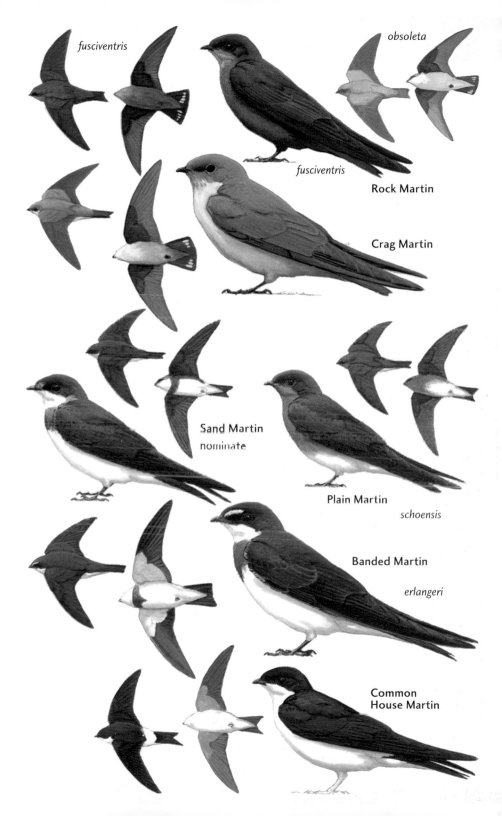

fusciventris

obsoleta

fusciventris

Rock Martin

Crag Martin

Sand Martin
nominate

Plain Martin

schoensis

Banded Martin

erlangeri

**Common
House Martin**

Colour of ear-coverts, underwing-coverts and underparts aid identification. Sexes are similar, but females may have shorter outer tail-streamers. Immatures are even shorter-tailed, and are duller above and paler below.

Red-rumped Swallow *Cecropsis daurica* 18cm, 7"

Blue-black cap with variable narrow rufous supercilium and collar; *ear-coverts rufous*. All pale rufous below with *black undertail-coverts*, pale rufous underwing-coverts, and dark tail (without tail-spots); tail-streamers may appear to curve inwards in flight. Rump and underparts vary from buffy-cream to dark rufous. Non-breeding birds often have paler rumps and shorter tails. At least three races occur: migrant *rufula* (Er, NEt and ?NSo) has rufous forehead and two-toned rufous rump; resident *melanocrissus* (highlands of Et) has dark blue forehead (like crown), narrow rufous supercilium and uniform rump; *domicella* of N tropics (WEt) has white underparts and underwing-coverts and may be a separate species. Racial identity of NSo birds uncertain; single Feb record in SSo may have been Afrotropical *emini*. **HH** Winter visitor to northern areas, Oct–Apr; common and widespread resident in open country at 500–3600m, often in towns. **Voice** Flight call consists of a pinched, nasal *zwink-zwink*. Song is a quiet rambling of soft nasal squeaks.

(D) = domicella (caption within map)

Mosque Swallow *Cecropsis senegalensis* 21cm, 8"

Larger and bulkier than Red-rumped Swallow, but similar with blue-black cap descending to eye and rufous ear-coverts. *Pale throat contrasts with richer rufous breast* and rufous (not black) undertail coverts. Easily identified in flight by *white underwing-coverts* contrasting with blackish flight feathers. Race *monteiri* (vagrant SSo) has white spots on tail; *saturatior* (Et) has all-dark tail. **HH** Pairs or small loose flocks are widespread and locally common at 1100–2700m, occurring in all but the most arid areas; few records in Sep–Nov, suggesting partial migration. **Voice** Song is loud and rambling, given either perched or in flight. Notes are drawn-out nasal slurs, similar in quality to Grey-backed Fiscal.

Lesser Striped Swallow *Cecropsis abyssinica* 17cm, 6.5"

Strongly marked, richly coloured swallow with extensive *bright rufous head* and rump, and *heavy black streaking on white underparts*. Two races occur: nominate (Er, Et) and *unitatis* (SEt, SSo) which is more heavily streaked below. **HH** Pairs and small groups are widespread and common from sea-level to 2400m, occurring in wide range of habitats apart from very arid country. Present all year but probably some seasonal movements. **Voice** Cheerful ramble of rising and falling nasal chips and twitters, terminating in a louder and deliberate well-spaced series of descending nasal notes. Usually given from perch, but will sing in flight.

Grey-rumped Swallow *Pseudhirundo griseopyga* 15cm, 6"

Slim swallow with *pale grey rump and grey-brown crown*; underparts white. Sexes alike. Immature duller with browner rump and no elongated outer tail feathers. **HH** Commonly seen in flocks, but rather local, at 1600–2500m over open grassland and burnt areas in W&CEt, Sep–May; occurs lower when not breeding. Uniquely breeds in rodent burrows. **Voice** Calls are harsh and burry, more like Sand Martin than other swallows, and flocks utter low churrs while feeding.

Red Sea Cliff Swallow *Petrochelidon perdita* 15cm, 6"

Small swallow with *square-ended tail*. Upperparts glossy blue-black with *grey rump; white chin-spot contrasts with blue-black throat and upper breast*; rest of underparts white with pale rufous wash on undertail-coverts. In flight, underwing-coverts white with a little rufous on axillaries, extending across breast in narrow band. **HH** Known from a single adult found dead near Port Sudan in May 1984 (outside our region). Unidentified cliff swallows (mapped) in Awash NP and the Rift Valley in Et in 1988 (and subsequently) differed from adult Red Sea in several respects (see illustrations, based on field descriptions), but may have been this species. **Voice** Unknown. **DD**

White-tailed Swallow *Hirundo megaensis* 13cm, 5"

Small, blue and white swallow with diagnostic *white tail* (but with dark sides). Female is duller with less white in tail. Immature browner. Ethiopian Swallow is longer-tailed with chestnut forehead, buffy throat and incomplete dark breast-band; the only white in its tail is a row of spots. **HH** ENDEMIC to SEt, around Yabelo and Mega (Sidamo Prov.), but fairly common within very small range; inhabits open acacia savanna with termite mounds, at 1000–1700m; also recently recorded further east, near Negele, and once near Moyale. **Voice**. No complex song has yet been identified. **VU**

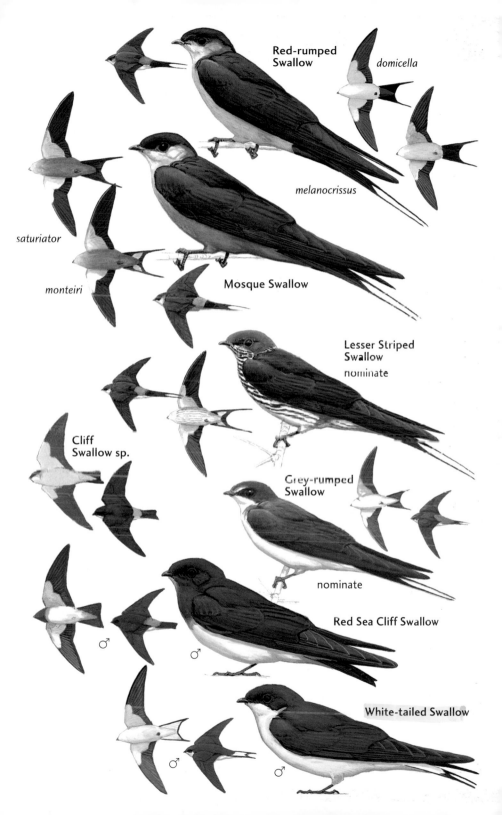

Red-rumped Swallow

domicella

melanocrissus

saturiator

monteiri

Mosque Swallow

Lesser Striped Swallow
nominate

Cliff Swallow sp.

Grey-rumped Swallow

nominate

Red Sea Cliff Swallow

♂

♂

White-tailed Swallow

♂

♂

Four similar species with uniform upperparts. Chestnut head and throat markings and the presence or absence of breast-bands aid identification.

Barn Swallow *Hirundo rustica*   19cm, 7.5"

Adult has blue-black upperparts and breast-band, *chestnut forecrown and throat*, and white or buffish underparts. Tail is deeply forked with white spots on shorter central feathers. Immature is variable, duller and browner above, with less chestnut on head and throat and shorter tail. **HH** Very common Palearctic visitor Jul–May, occurring throughout region from sea-level to 3600m. Sometimes migrates and roosts in huge flocks. **Voice** Song delivered in flight or perched is a continuous rambling and cheerful twitter, with finch-like quality.

Red-chested Swallow *Hirundo lucida*   15cm, 6"

Very like Barn Swallow but smaller with shorter tail-streamers; other differences include smaller chestnut band on forehead, *more extensive chestnut throat, narrower blue breast-band* (sometimes incomplete), and larger white spots on tail. Race *rothschildi* (Et) has *white underwing-coverts*, not dusky as in nominate of W Africa. **HH** Common resident over grassland and marshes in highlands of Et at 1200–3300m (occasionally down to 750m). **Voice** Song is much like Barn Swallow but notes are harsher. Call is a harsh squeaking and chipping.

Ethiopian Swallow *Hirundo aethiopica*   14cm, 5.5"

Similar to Barn Swallow with chestnut forecrown, but has *white or very pale buff throat*, and an *incomplete blackish breast-band*. In good light looks blue above and very white below. Forked tail has large white spots and is similar in length to Red-chested Swallow. Two races: widespread nominate as described; *amadoni* (EEt, So) has white throat and upper breast. **HH** Locally common in wide variety of open country throughout region up to 3000m. **Voice** Most calls are nasal and harsh, but infrequently heard song given in flight consists of many sweet cadences and trills.

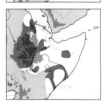

Wire-tailed Swallow *Hirundo smithii*   18cm, 7"

Adult is shiny blue above, very white below with *neat chestnut cap*. In good plumage the white-spotted tail has *long, very thin wires*, but hard to see at any distance, and are sometimes broken off. Immature has dull brown crown and no tail-wires. **HH** A fast-flying, common and widespread swallow, usually in pairs and often near water, from sea-level to 2500m; scarce in Er and absent from much of So. **Voice** Rather quiet; song is a subdued twittering similar to Barn Swallow, but shorter in duration.

SAW-WINGS *Black or black-and-white swallows with a variable purplish or green gloss which is difficult to see in the field. Male has a broad-based, deeply forked tail that is shorter in female and immature.*

Black Saw-wing *Psalidoprocne pristoptera*   15cm, 6"

All-black swallow with deeply forked tail. Four races occur: a) nominate [Blue Saw-wing] (Er, NEt) has purplish-blue gloss; b) *oleaginea* [Ethiopian Saw-wing] (SWEt) has rich oily-green gloss; c) *blanfordi* [Blanford's Saw-wing] (CEt) has greenish wash; d) *antinorii* [Brown Saw-wing] (C&SEt) has purplish-bronze gloss (but all hard to see in field). All show *white underwing-coverts*. Immature is duller and browner. **HH** Pairs and small flocks are common, mainly in highlands at 500–3100m, often in clearings in forest or over riverine woodland, and frequently perching on treetops. Blue Saw-wings in Er may be partially migratory, moving south to winter in Et highlands. **Voice** Frequently utters seemingly random soft nasal squeaks, *weeu, see*, in flight and when perched. **Note** The various forms are sometimes treated as separate species.

White-headed Saw-wing *Psalidoprocne albiceps*   14cm, 5.5"

Adult male is very distinctive with *pure white head and narrow black eye-stripe*. Adult female has dark ashy grey-brown head and white throat. Immature is dull dark brown with slightly paler throat (hard to see in field). **HH** Hypothetical: four recent records in SWEt, none fully acceptable. Occurs in wider variety of habitats than other saw-wings including forest clearings, open woodland, bushed grassland and cultivation. **Voice** Similar to Black Saw-wing but is more hissing and breaks into a quiet chatter.

Barn Swallow
nominate

ad

imm

ad

ad

Red-chested Swallow

ad

rothschildi

ad

Ethiopian Swallow
nominate

imm

ad

ad

ad

Wire-tailed Swallow

antinorii

ad

imm

ad

antinorii

Black Saw-wing

♀

nom

♂

oleaginea

blanfordi

♂

White-headed Saw-wing

WAGTAILS *Slim birds with long tails and legs, often seen walking on the ground constantly bobbing their tails. The Palearctic migrant species begin arriving during Sep–Oct. They are mostly drab non-breeding and first-year birds, but breeding adult males can be seen from Feb until they migrate north again, mainly from Mar–May.*

Yellow Wagtail *Motacilla flava*   19cm, 7.5"

On arrival in NE Africa the plumage of Yellow Wagtails is highly varied and for many birds racial separation is not possible. Typical individuals are brownish above with variable yellow below, often strongest on belly and flanks. Adult males have most extensive yellow below, but not their distinctive breeding head patterns. Female and first-year birds have olive-brown or plain brown upperparts and usually show some yellow on belly, but may have entirely white underparts. From Jan, males (and some females) acquire distinctive head patterns and become greener above and entirely yellow below (except for whitish throats on females). Six races and four named intergrades occur; males described below:

M. f. feldegg (Er, Et, Dj, So, Soc) has completely black top to head (some eastern birds show white stripe on sides of throat and are named '*melanogrisea*'). [Alt: Black-headed Wagtail]

M. f. thunbergi (Er, Et, Dj, So) has dark grey crown blending into blackish face. [Alt: Grey-headed Wagtail]

M. f. flava (Er, Et, Dj, So, Soc) has blue-grey crown and darker cheeks separated by distinct white supercilium. [Alt: Blue-headed Wagtail]

M. f. beema (Er, Et, Dj, So) has pale grey crown and cheeks separated by white supercilium. [Alt: Sykes's Wagtail]

M. f. lutea (Er, Et, Dj, So, Soc) has head mostly yellow, variably washed green on crown and ear-coverts. [Alt: Yellow-headed Wagtail]

M. f. leucocephala (Et, twice) has almost entirely white head. [Alt: White-headed Wagtail]

Intergrades between *feldegg* and *flava* come in two forms:

M. f. 'superciliaris' (Er, Et) has black head (like *feldegg*) with white supercilium.

M. f. 'dombrowskii' (Er, Et, So) is more like *flava* but has blackish ear-coverts. Another intergrade is presumed to be hybrid between *flava* and *flavissima*:

M. f. 'perconfuscus' (Et, So) has head like *flava* but a yellow supercilium.

Since hybrids are not uncommon, some individuals can never be racially assigned. Differs from larger Grey Wagtail in all plumages by never having grey mantle. **HH** Very common Palearctic migrant from Sep–May, with several different races often occurring together, sometimes in flocks of thousands. Birds favour lake shores, swampy land, short grasslands and open cultivation, frequently associating with cattle and plains game, from sea-level to 2700m. **Voice** Very vocal; call given in flight and on ground is a rising *sweeep*, softer than other wagtails in region. Race *feldegg* sounds considerably harsher.

Citrine Wagtail *Motacilla citreola*   17cm, 7"

Like Yellow Wagtail but *upperparts clean grey with two broad white wing-bars* in all plumages. Breeding male has *lemon-yellow head with black band on nape*. Underparts yellow with greyish flanks and white undertail-coverts. Female and adult winter duller, with grey or olive-grey crown and ear-coverts, and pale yellow supercilium and underparts. First-winter birds usually show no yellow at all, being entirely grey and white, with black and white remiges; can be distinguished from first-winter Yellow by greyer upperparts with broader wing-bars, pale lores and *all-dark bill* (lower mandible pale in all forms of Yellow). First-winter White has black breast-band. **HH** Nominate *citreola* is a scarce Palearctic passage migrant to Soc; vagrant Dj and Et. **Voice** Contact call is a harsh, loud *sreep*, like Yellow Wagtail

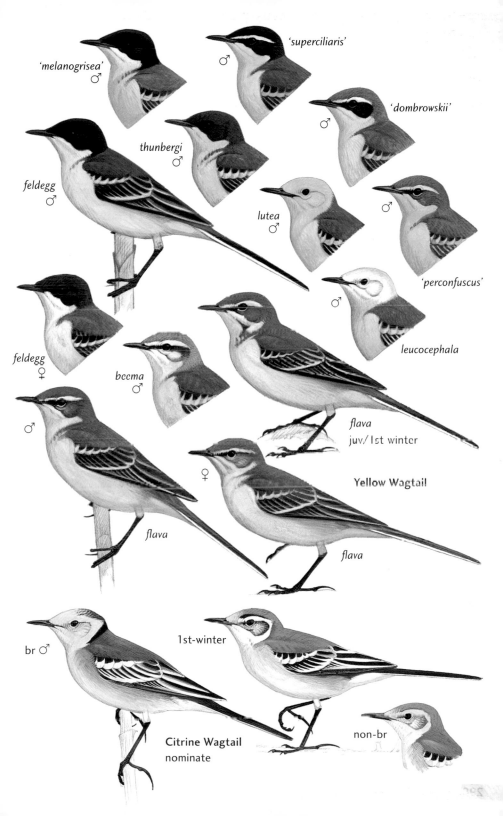

'melanogrisea'
♂

'superciliaris'
♂

'dombrowskii'
♂

thunbergi
♂

feldegg
♂

lutea
♂

'perconfuscus'
♂

leucocephala

feldegg
♀

beema
♂

flava
juv/1st winter

♂

♀

Yellow Wagtail

flava

flava

br ♂

1st-winter

Citrine Wagtail
nominate

non-br

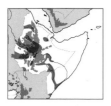

African Pied Wagtail *Motacilla aguimp*   20cm, 8"

Only very black and white wagtail in region: *adult without grey or brown in plumage*, and comparatively broad breast-band. Immature brownish-grey above. All ages separated from White Wagtail by *black forehead and extensive white wing-patches*. Race in region is *vidua*. **HH** Most widespread resident wagtail, occurring from sea-level to 1900m along riverbanks, lakeshores, in cultivated areas and forest glades, as well as in towns. Scarce in highlands in Et, commoner at low elevations in S; uncommon in SSo. **Voice** Sweet calls are frequently paired notes, which break into an attractive complex and warbled song.

White Wagtail *Motacilla alba*   19cm, 7.5"

Non-breeding male has crown, nape and breast-band black, giving *white-faced appearance*, even more obvious in breeding plumage when throat is also black. Non-breeding female and first-winter are rather dingy: crown to rump grey, face washed pale olivaceous, and dark narrow breast-band. Breeding female like breeding male, but not quite so clean-looking with some grey on crown. Most birds in region are nominate *alba*, but eastern form '*dukhunensis*' has occurred in Et (once) and on Soc: has broader wing-bars, sometimes forming white panel. **HH** Common Palearctic winter visitor Oct–Apr to most of Er and Et; less common in NW&SSo. Frequents lakes and rivers, marshes, cultivation and villages from sea-level to 3000m. **Voice** Does not sing in region, but often calls with an urgent dry paired *chh-tit* in flight or on ground.

Mountain Wagtail *Motacilla clara*   19cm, 7.5"

Elegant and proportionately longer-tailed than other wagtails. Adult is largely clear grey above and white below with *neat narrow black breast-band*. Immature is similar, but washed brown above, with indistinct breast-band. **HH** Pairs of nominate *clara* are widespread residents in Et, at 900–2700m, along rocky, fast-flowing rivers and at forest edges. Recently recorded in Er. **Voice** Very vocal: one simple song is usually three notes *siiiii seee-uu* (first rising, then last notes falling to fade). Alarm and contact calls are a strange metallic explosive *chit*, which can break into complex whistles and descending trills with buzzing quality. [Alt: Long-tailed Wagtail]

Grey Wagtail *Motacilla cinerea*   20cm, 8"

Slim, graceful wagtail with long tail. Non-breeding plumage variable but typefied by *grey upperparts with yellow rump, yellow underparts (may be restricted to vent)*, whitish throat and no breast-band. Breeding male has yellow underparts and black throat. Female has white throat and yellow breast to vent. **HH** Frequent to common Palearctic winter visitor, Aug–Apr, along rocky streams, rivers and forest trails in highlands of Et and NSo, mainly at 1200–3000m; occurs at lower elevations in Er and SSo, sometimes to sea-level. Constantly wags long tail. **Voice** Call is a loud, harsh and explosive *ti-titt*. Infrequently heard song is the call interspersed with a loud *siiii*

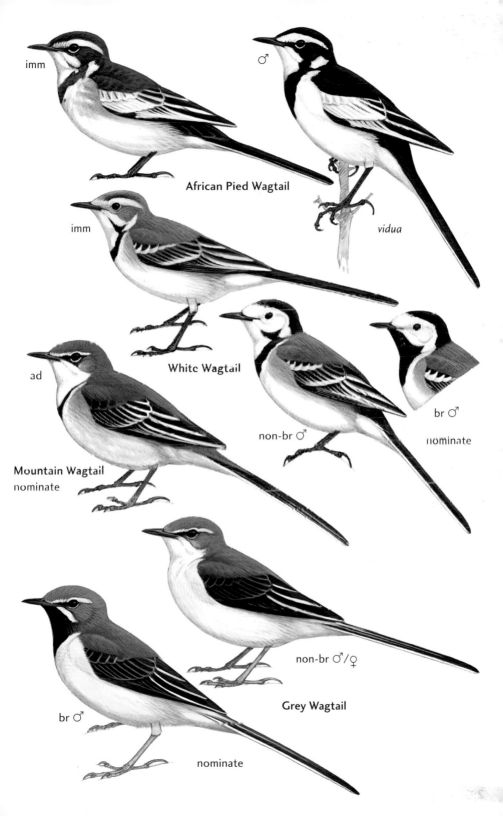

imm

♂

African Pied Wagtail

vidua

imm

White Wagtail

ad

non-br ♂

br ♂

nominate

Mountain Wagtail
nominate

non-br ♂/♀

Grey Wagtail

br ♂

nominate

LONGCLAWS *Ground-dwelling birds which are streaky brown above, with variable amounts of yellow or orange below. Distinctive jerky flight of stiff wing-beats alternating with glides.*

Abyssinian Longclaw *Macronyx flavicollis* 20cm, 8″

Adult is brownish-black above with buff fringes giving a heavy mottled appearance. Prominent supercilum is saffron-yellow in front of eye and buff behind. *Throat is also saffron-yellow, bordered with broad black necklace.* Rest of underparts deep buff with variable black streaks at sides of breast. In flight shows large white corners on tail. Sexes alike. Immature similar, but darker above, with buff throat and narrower, browner necklace of spots. No other longclaw occurs in range. **HH** ENDEMIC to Et. Singles or pairs are common in highland grassland and moorland at 1200–4100m. **Voice** Calls are typical of genus, with long slurred whistles given by perched birds. **NT**

Pangani Longclaw *Macronyx aurantiigula* 20cm, 8″

Adult is similar to Abyssinian Longclaw, but throat is usually orange or orange-yellow (female and older immatures may have yellow throats), bordered with *narrow black necklace. Centre of breast to belly bright yellow with extensive black streaking, extending onto tawny-buff flanks.* Undertail-coverts paler and lightly streaked. In flight tail has white corners and tips to most feathers. Immature has ill-defined breast-band and mainly buff underparts with some yellow on breast. **HH** Uncommon in dry bushed grasslands and open areas in SSo. **Voice** Not so vocal; call is a varied, drawn-out, whistled *siuuweeeee* rising then falling and rising to fade. **Note** The sole record of Yellow-throated Longclaw *M. croceus* in region (from SSo) is now known to have been a Pangani Longclaw.

Golden Pipit *Tmetothylacus tenellus* 16cm, 6″

Adult male in breeding plumage is streaked and mottled dark brown, olive-yellow and buff above, and brilliant yellow with a neat black breast-band below. In flight, striking *bright yellow wings with black tips and bright yellow outer tail* are distinctive. Adult female is more like typical pipit, but has dull yellow edges to primaries and outer tail, and is mainly plain buff below with pale yellow restricted to belly; underwing-coverts are pale yellow. Non-breeding male resembles female but is tinged brighter yellow. Immature is browner and even more like a typical pipit with streaking across breast, but may show yellowish wing-edgings. **HH** Pairs and small groups are uncommon to locally common nomads of bushed and wooded grassland in dry country from sea-level to 900m. Local movements are often in response to rains when aerial displays make the birds' presence very obvious. Forages on ground, but often perches on bushes wagging tail like wagtail. **Voice** Usually silent, but can be very vocal after rains. Complex whistled song, given both perched and in song-flight, has weaver-like quality.

PIPITS *A difficult group of slim brown birds with slender bills and longish tails. Density of streaking on mantle and breast, presence or lack of white in the tail, habitat and calls all aid identification.*

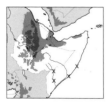

Tawny Pipit *Anthus campestris* 17cm, 6.5″

Adult is pale, slim and rather plain-looking except for *pale-fringed blackish median coverts* which form band across wing. Upperparts uniform sandy-brown, almost unstreaked, underparts unstreaked. *Outer tail white.* Immature streaked both above and across breast. *Dark lores* and *short hindclaw* are subtle but useful distinctions from Grassland in all plumages. Race in region is nominate, but *griseus* may also occur. **HH** Common to fairly common Palearctic winter visitor in short dry grassland up to 2900m, Sep–Apr, in Er, Et and NSo; less common in SSo. Has bred in NSo and possibly in EEt. Rather wagtail-like, running around and frequently bobbing tail. **Voice** Calls given in flight and on ground are *seeep*, softer than other large pipits, and chirpy *tsuc..*

Grassland Pipit *Anthus cinnamomeus* 17cm, 6.5″

The most common and widespread pipit. Medium brown above with darker streaks on crown and mantle, facial pattern strong with obvious buffy supercilium, *pale lores* and dark malar stripe. Lower mandible yellowish, legs pinkish, with *long hindclaw.* Buffy-white below with short dark streaks across breast; flanks usually plain. In flight shows *extensive whitish in outer tail.* Two races occur: *annae* (Er, Dj, N&SSo) is fairly pale with greyish tinge; nominate *cinnamomeus* (highlands of Et) is warmer above with cinnamon feather-edges, and buff below. **HH** Very common in open country from sea-level up to 3000m, except for desert areas; rather localised in Er. **Voice** Varies regionally: typical song is a repeated *trrlit-trrlit-trrlit*, flight call a repeated *trit*. [Alt: African Pipit, Grassveld Pipit]

imm

ad

Abyssinian Longclaw

imm

ad

Pangani Longclaw

♂

♂

Golden Pipit

♀

Grassland Pipit
cinnamomeus

annae

ad

Tawny Pipit

Long-billed Pipit *Anthus similis* 17cm, 7"

Large, comparatively uniform species, generally less streaked than Grassland. Birds often appear dark in worn plumage. Bill is long but not obviously so. In flight, bird appears heavy and tail looks long with *buffy-white outer feathers*. Four races occur: *hararensis* (highlands of Er and Et) is fairly dark above with prominent streaking, cinnamon-buff below; *nivescens* (NEEt, Dj, N&SSo) paler above with less streaking, and paler below; *sokotrae* (Soc) like *nivescens* but with blacker streaking above; *arabicus* (coastal Er) has cinnamon-buff underparts and cinnamon-grey outer tail feathers. **HH** Widespread but never numerous, usually solitary or in pairs, in highland rocky country with light grass cover and/or trees, at 1300–3000m. **Voice** Song is a lazy series of four notes repeated randomly *chrit swit chweep chreer...*, flight call a muffled *trrit-tip*.

Plain-backed Pipit *Anthus leucophrys* 16cm, 6.5"

Plainer than Grassland Pipit with *unstreaked or only lightly marked back* and sandy wing edgings; pale buffy or cinnamon-buff below with indistinct streaks on breast; lacks obvious malar stripe, lower mandible yellowish-pink. In flight, *tail looks uniform dark brown with buff edges*. Two distinctive races occur: *saphiroi* (SEEt, NWSo) as described; *omoensis* (Er, N&WEt) is darker above and richer cinnamon below with heavier breast-streaking. **HH** Locally common, preferring short grass with or without trees, mainly at low altitudes but up to 2200m. **Voice** Song rather monotonous, like Long-billed Pipit, but notes scratchier and less distinct. **Note** Race *saphiroi* is sometimes included in extralimital Buffy Pipit *A. vaalensis* of E&S Africa.

Malindi Pipit *Anthus melindae* 15cm, 6"

Similar to Grassland Pipit but longer-legged, darker, greyer and more mottled above. Streaking on underparts bolder and more extensive, reaching onto flanks. Non-breeding birds more mottled above (less uniform) with more blurry streaking below, *obvious yellow base to lower mandible and rich orange-yellow legs*. Shows white outer tail in flight. Two races occur: nominate (SSo) is earth-brown above; *mallablensis* (coastal SESo) is paler above with paler edges to wings, and whiter below with finer, less extensive streaking. Long-billed Pipit (race *nivescens*) is larger and longer-billed with less streaking below and buff outer tail. **HH** Common near-endemic to coastal SSo in open lowland areas, including dunes, cultivation and edges of wetlands; often in small groups. **Voice** Song is a rapidly delivered continuous series, softer than other large pipits; flight call is *shreep*. **NT**

Bush Pipit *Anthus caffer* 13cm, 5"

Small, rather plain-faced pipit with indistinct supercilium and no malar stripe; resembles small cisticola more than typical pipit. Warm brown above with darker streaking, and whitish below finely streaked with dark brown across breast and flanks; white outer-tail tinged buff. All other small pipits in region are larger with dark malar stripe and heavier streaking below. **HH** In NE Africa, race *australoabyssinicus* is rare in bushed and wooded grassland in SEt, in Yabelo–Mega area, at 1400–1700m. Feeds on ground and often flies into trees when disturbed. **Voice** Quite silent for pipit. Song is a nasal monotonous *wii-zhweep* given from top of small bush, effect being rather see-saw-like. [Alt: Bushveld Pipit]

Red-throated Pipit *Anthus cervinus* 15cm, 6"

Heavily streaked both above and below including rump and flanks, with white outer-tail. Adult has *brick-red on face, supercilium and upper breast*, but extent and intensity varies; this plumage can be seen in all months. First-winter and some females lack red and can be distinguished from Tree Pipit by whiter underparts with heavier black streaking, and *whitish stripes on darker mantle*. **HH** Common Palearctic passage migrant and winter visitor to marshy areas, lakeshores and highland grasslands from sea-level to 3950m, Sep–May; mainly spring migrant in So, Mar–May. **Voice** Invariably calls a single high-pitched, sharp *zeeez*, more drawn-out than Tree Pipit and usually given in flight.

Tree Pipit *Anthus trivialis* 15cm, 6"

Olive-brown and heavily streaked above with *plain rump*, buff supercilium and narrow dark malar stripes. *Warm buff on breast and flanks* (but whiter on belly) with long dark streaks across breast (less distinct on flanks). White on outer tail feathers. Non-breeding Red-throated is darker above and whiter below with heavier streaking. **HH** Common Palearctic passage migrant and winter visitor, Sep–May, from sea-level to 4100m, favouring wide variety of open wooded areas; in So, mainly a passage migrant, Sep–Oct and Apr–May. Vagrant Soc. **Voice** Commonly calls a distinctive nasal *eeez*, easily separated from Red-throated with experience.

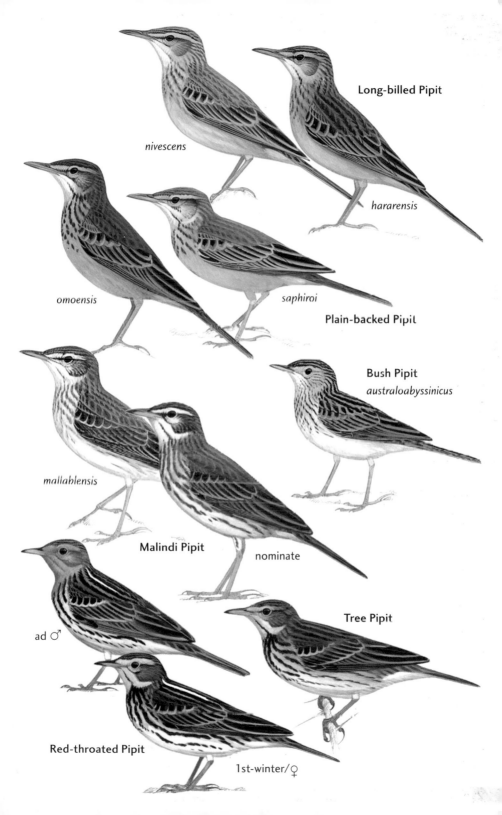

Long-billed Pipit

nivescens

hararensis

omoensis

saphiroi

Plain-backed Pipit

Bush Pipit
australoabyssinicus

mallablensis

Malindi Pipit

nominate

Tree Pipit

ad ♂

Red-throated Pipit

1st-winter/♀

CUCKOOSHRIKES *Found alone, in pairs, or as members of mixed-species flocks, cuckooshrikes are medium-sized, rather quiet birds which tend to keep a horizontal posture as they move actively, but slowly through cover. Male* Campephaga *are blue-black with orange-yellow gapes, and could be confused with several other species such as drongos or black flycatchers (but those species sit upright). Black boubous lack the blue-black gloss and have heavy bush-shrike bills. Females are distinctively marked with yellow, grey, white and black. The grey* Coracina *cuckooshrikes behave similarly, but the sexes are more alike.*

Black Cuckooshrike *Campephaga flava*   20cm, 8"

Adult male is wholly glossy blue-black with *small orange-yellow gape*; some have yellow shoulder-patches (beware confusion with Red-shouldered Cuckooshrikes with yellow shoulders). Adult female is olive-brown above with blackish barring, and obviously yellow-edged wings and tail. White below washed yellow on sides of breast and barred all over with small black crescents; much yellow on undertail. Immature like female but with very heavy barring. **HH** Uncommon to scarce in SEt and SSo, in woodlands, forest edge and scrub, at 1200–1800m in Et but down to sea-level in So. Mainly a breeding resident in Et, but some birds in Et and most in So are probably intra-tropical migrants from south (Jun–Oct). **Voice** Rather quiet unless breeding: commonest call is a repeated insect-like trill lasting 2 secs; a louder descending *shree-shree-shree* is given less frequently.

Red-shouldered Cuckooshrike *Campephaga phoenicea*   20cm, 8"

Adult male is glossy blue-black with *brilliant red shoulders* (some morphs have orange-yellow shoulders, when confusable with some Black Cuckooshrikes). Adult female is very like female Black, but more *grey-brown above*, with *mostly black undertail* (except for yellow tips). Immature is like female, but more densely barred and spotted. **HH** Fairly common but elusive resident in west of region, occurring in forest edge, open woodlands and overgrown cultivation, at 750–1900m. **Voice** Quiet, only occasionally giving high-pitched sibilant hissing and soft *tit-tit-tit-tit-tit...*

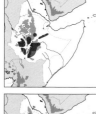

Grey Cuckooshrike *Coracina caesia*   22cm, 8.5"

Adult male is almost uniform medium grey (wings slightly darker), with blackish lores and chin, conspicuous large dark eyes and pale eye-rings. Adult female is similar but lacks dark lores and chin. Immature finely barred greyish-brown and white with darker tail. **HH** Pairs or small groups are locally fairly common in canopy of highland forest in C&SEt, at 1800–2900m. Race in Et is *pura*. **Voice** Contact call is a high-pitched hissing, and song a high-pitched complex jumble of twitters and squeaks.

White-breasted Cuckooshrike *Coracina pectoralis*   25cm, 10"

Adult male is distinctive: grey above with darker wings and tail, throat to upper breast grey with rest of underparts snowy-white. Adult female like male but all white below or with pale grey wash across breast. Immature finely barred grey, brown and white above, with dark spotting on white below; white fringes on remiges. **HH** Singles or pairs are uncommon residents of savanna woodland and forest edge in W&SEt, at 500–2400m. Very restless behaviour; never stays around for long. **Voice** Usual call is a high-pitched upslurred burry *swit*, the song a rather rhythmical mixture of similar burry upslurs and downslurs interspersed with chattering.

HYPOCOLIUS *A unique bird, usually placed in its own subfamily within the waxwings (Bombycillidae) or as a separate family,* Hypocoliidae. *Rather like a slim, long-tailed Southern Grey Shrike in shape.*

Grey Hypocolius *Hypocolius ampelinus*   23cm, 9"

Adult male is mainly grey above, paler below, with prominent *black mask* from lores and across nape, *primaries black with white tips*, conspicuous in flight. Long grey tail is black-tipped. Female mostly grey-buff without black mask, primaries tipped black and white, tail tipped brownish-black. Immature like female but duller. **HH** Winters sparsely in Arabian peninsula; vagrant Er (once, in 1850). Frequents palm groves, oases, scrub and gardens; gregarious but unobtrusive, often silent in dense cover, emerging rather late to bask in sunlight. **Voice** Quiet in winter, but sometimes gives plaintive mewing or trilling notes.

Black Cuckooshrike

Red-shouldered
Cuckooshrike

Grey
Cuckooshrike

pura

White-breasted
Cuckooshrike

Grey Hypocolius

PITTAS *Ground-dwelling, colourful birds with strong straight bills, long legs and short tails. Breeding birds call and display in the canopy, but otherwise are usually found in leaf-litter on the forest floor.*

African Pitta *Pitta angolensis*   18cm, 7"

Very attractive and distinctive with boldly marked head, green back, blue shoulders, *tawny-buff breast* and red belly. In flight black wings show obvious white patch at base of primaries; bright blue shoulders and rump conspicuous. Sexes alike. Immature duller with buffy-pink vent. **HH** Intra-African migrant; breeds in SE Tanzania Dec–Apr, moving northwards to Kenya, May–Sep. Vagrant Et (Addis Ababa, once in Jul). Extremely shy, often on ground within dense cover, standing motionless for long periods. **Voice** Gives a loud far-carrying explosive *quoip* from lateral branch in mid-canopy, coinciding with a jump. Notes are identical and spaced every few seconds. On migration makes a low croaking sound. [Alt: Angola Pitta]

BULBULS, GREENBULS AND BROWNBULS *With only a few exceptions, most bulbuls are extremely hard to identify, but relatively few species in NE Africa representing five genera. Consider the characteristics of different genera, preference for any particular forest level, range and voice. Check for small eye-rings, eye colour and traits such as tail-raising, wing-flicking and throat-puffing. Sexes are alike or very similar.*

Pycnonotus bulbuls are ubiquitous birds of non-forest habitats. To separate races/species, check neck and breast markings, and colour of undertail-coverts.

Common Bulbul *Pycnonotus barbatus*   18–21cm, 7–8"

Slim brownish bird with almost black head (may show slight crest), brown breast, pale belly and *white or yellow undertail-coverts*. Many races described, some well marked, but intermediates occur where populations meet. Ten races are currently recognised in Africa, tentatively divided into four species by some authors. The four races in our region conveniently represent all four 'species' as follows, but intergrades in areas of overlap can pose identification pitfall.

A. Common Bulbul *P. barbatus schoanus* (Er and highlands of Et except SE): Black head, *dark brown breast* grading into pale belly and *white undertail-coverts*. Indistinct white on side of neck (sometimes absent) and no scaling on breast. Presumed *schoanus* × *somaliensis* hybrids occur in arid areas.

B. Dark-capped Bulbul *P. tricolor spurius* (SCEt): Similar to *schoanus* but has *yellow undertail-coverts*, breast paler brown and ends more abruptly, contrasting with white belly. [Alt: Black-eyed Bulbul]

C. Somali Bulbul *P. somaliensis* (Dj, NEEt, NWSo): Conspicuous small *white patch on side of neck* and *scaly breast* (formed by white fringes to breast feathers). *White undertail-coverts*.

D. Dodson's Bulbul *P. dodsoni* (So except NW, SEEt): Like *somaliensis*, with conspicuous smudgy white patch on side of neck, but has *yellow undertail-coverts*. *Scaly breast more pronounced*, extending to upper belly. Upperparts also lightly scaled. Broad pale tips to tail feathers. Smaller than *schoanus*. Presumed *schoanus* × *dodsoni* hybrids can look like out of range *somaliensis*.

HH Extremely common and widespread in virtually all habitats throughout region from sea-level to 4400m. Race *dodsoni* occurs in more arid country. Usually bold, noisy and conspicuous. **Voice** Sings a fairly slow deliberate set of descending notes, accelerating as birds become excitable. Also a variety of chatters given at all times. Race *dodsoni* is similar, but faster and more shrill.

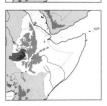

Yellow-throated Leaflove *Chlorocichla flavicollis*   22cm, 8.5"

Large, dull and olive-grey-brown above with *contrasting white throat*, with only a tinge of yellow in race *soror*. Frequently puffs out white throat. Rest of underparts pale greyish-olive. Eyes are pale grey in males, whitish in females. Often looks rather dishevelled. **HH** Pairs and small groups are uncommon and elusive but noisy in WEt in variety of thick undergrowth in woodland and forest edge, including wooded streams, thickets and overgrown cultivation, at 500–2000m; isolated population in WEt is presumed to be *soror*. **Voice** Typically sings a rather excitable babbler-like chattering, commonly in flight. [Alt: Yellow-throated Greenbul]

African Pitta

ad

imm

Common Bulbul

spurius

schoanus

somaliensis

dodsoni

Yellow-throated Leaflove

soror

Phyllastrephus are slim-looking greenbuls with slender bills; some are brown above with red-brown tails. They live mostly in the undergrowth or middle levels of forest interiors, so a slender-billed bird in undergrowth may well be a Phyllastrephus *greenbul, which habitually slowly raises and lowers the tail or flicks it nervously, while a shorter-billed bird in mid-stratum vines is more likely to be an* Andropadus *greenbul, which has sharper, more agitated movements.* Chlorocichla *are rather bulky, strong-billed, noisy greenbuls which prefer forest edge and clearings, secondary growth, thickets and overgrown cultivation (see also plate 134).*

Fischer's Greenbul *Phyllastrephus fischeri*   18cm, 7"

Plain olive-brown above with dull reddish tail. Below, very white throat contrasts with olive-brown breast and flanks. Only member of genus in coastal forests with *creamy-white eyes*. **HH** Inhabits forest undergrowth and thick bush in coastal lowlands; formerly recorded from lower Jubba in SSo (four old records), but not recently. Shy and hard to see but presence announced by frequent noisy contact calls. **Voice** Foraging groups utter a constant deep, throaty, descending and chattering *cheee-cha-cha-cha-cha-cha* that accelerates and fades.

Northern Brownbul *Phyllastrephus strepitans*   17cm, 6.5"

Very like Terrestrial Brownbul but smaller and lighter in build; more russet above, with *russet-brown rump and tail*, and greyish-brown below, often with buffy wash, and with less contrasting whiter throat; undertail-coverts cinnamon. Eyes are brown or slightly red-brown; Fischer's Greenbul has pale eyes. Bill blackish, legs bluish-black or grey. **HH** Small flocks are common in thickets in coastal lowlands in SSo and in thicker scrub within semi-arid areas in S&SEEt, up to 1800m. **Voice** Parties maintain a continuous, rather nasal pinched chatter from mid-canopy (which recalls larger babblers), whilst slowly pumping tails.

Terrestrial Brownbul *Phyllastrephus terrestris*   19cm, 7.5"

Very like Fischer's Greenbul but with *wine-red eyes* (not creamy-white) and less olive above (if seen well). From smaller Northern Brownbul by *more earth-brown upperparts* without russet overtones on rump and tail. *White throat* also contrasts more with greyish-brown breast and flanks. Bill blackish-horn, with paler lower mandible. Legs blue-grey. **HH** Inhabits dense undergrowth of coastal and riverine forest; in our region known only from lower Jubba in SSo (race *suahelicus*). Presumed to be very rare, with only two old records and one recent. **Voice** From near ground it delivers a babbler-like chattering, lower-pitched than Northern Brownbul, and lacks harshness and laughing quality of Fischer's Greenbul. [Alt: Terrestrial Bulbul]

Sombre Greenbul *Andropadus importunus*   18cm, 7"

Rather plain greenbul of thickets and scrub. Race *insularis* is uniform olive-brown above, yellowish-olive below (slightly browner on throat and flanks), with *creamy-white eye*. Immature similar, but with dark eye and small yellowish eye-ring. **HH** Locally common in wide variety of thick undergrowth in SSo, especially in riverine areas and coastal scrub; also reaches extreme SEt (Dolo and Ramu). **Voice** Calls from bush tops or telephone wires, a fast rising-and-falling series of cheerful notes with quality of Common Bulbul. Sings throughout heat of day. [Alt: Zanzibar Sombre Greenbul]

Yellow-bellied Greenbul *Chlorocichla flaviventris*   22cm 8.5"

Large, thickset greenbul of eastern lowlands. Race *centralis* is dark olive-brown above, with ruffled crown often raised as shaggy crest, obvious *white crescent above red-brown eye, and sulphur-yellow underparts* (paler on throat). Sombre Greenbul is smaller, less yellow below, and has brown throat and staring white eye. **HH** Inhabits dense forest undergrowth, thickets and bush; locally very common in SSo, especially along lower Jubba and in Boni Forest. **Voice** Basic song is five slow, rather halting nasal notes, *eh eh uh eeh eh* (first two and final note identical, third lower, fourth higher than first), often initiated with rather angry slurred churrs. [Alt: Yellow-bellied Bulbul]

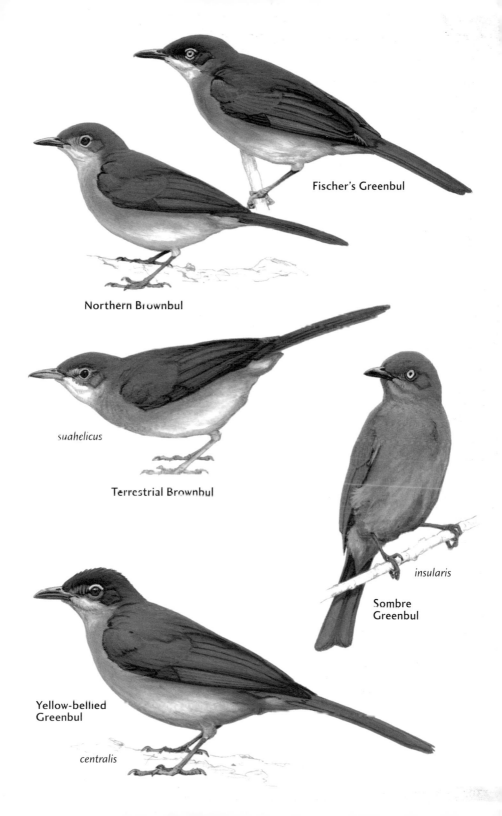

Fischer's Greenbul

Northern Brownbul

suahelicus

Terrestrial Brownbul

insularis

Sombre
Greenbul

Yellow-bellied
Greenbul

centralis

ROBIN-CHATS *Small or medium-sized chats with orange underparts, a white supercilium and a dark centre to the rufous tail. Sexes alike; spotted and scaly juvenile plumage is quickly lost and not often seen in the field (as with many other juvenile thrushes and chats). All are usually solitary or in pairs. Fabulous songsters with much variation and mimicry.*

Rüppell's Robin-Chat *Cossypha semirufa* 18cm, 7"

Boldly marked and entirely bright rufous-orange below. Crown and sides of face black with long white supercilium. *Tail reddish-orange with blackish central feathers.* Immature heavily spotted, with less pronounced supercilium, and rufous-brown below with dark scaling. Two races occur: nominate (most of Er and Et except SE) as described; *donaldsoni* (SEEt) has almost complete rufous collar and darker upperparts. **HH** A common highland forest bird, including juniper and *Podocarpus*, but also in overgrown gardens and thickets, at 1200–3100m. **Voice** The most accomplished songster; basic song is musical warbled, thrush-like refrain given in short bursts or continuously. Often mimics birds in vicinity plus other small animal noises and human whistles. Sings from cover, particularly before dawn and at dusk.

White-browed Robin-Chat *Cossypha heuglini* 20cm, 8"

Very like Rüppell's Robin-Chat, but *tail rufous-orange with olive-brown central feathers.* White supercilium flares more behind eye than Rüppell's. Immature like immature Rüppell's. Two races occur: nominate (SWEt) as described; coastal *intermedia* (SSo) is slightly smaller. **HH** Prefers lower altitudes and more open habitats than Rüppell's. Uncommon resident in two disjunct populations in undergrowth, thickets and woodland edge from sea-level to 1650m. **Voice** Song, most commonly given pre-dawn and at dusk, is a simple refrain of three high notes and two lower notes, each sequence increasing in volume, speed and urgency. Alarm call is a loud but wooden *takata-kata-kata.* Does not mimic other species. [Alt: Heuglin's Robin]

Red-capped Robin-Chat *Cossypha natalensis* 17cm, 7"

Only robin-chat with *rufous-orange head* (sometimes browner on crown); if seen well beady black eyes are conspicuous. Mantle and wings blue-grey, tail rufous with black centre. Immature mottled black and rufous above, paler below with dark scaling. **HH** Shy bird of forest undergrowth and thickets from sea-level to 1600m. Patchy occurrence in our region; presumed to be intra-African migrant (race *intensa*) but movements poorly understood. Uncommon visitor to C&WEt, mainly Nov–Mar. Common non-breeding visitor to SSo, mainly Jun–Oct when birds absent from Et. **Voice** An accomplished mimic; bouts of singing can last many minutes. Quality is drunken or lazy compared to other robin-chats, notes slurred and not too pure. Commonest call is monotonous, distinct and endlessly repeated *preeep-prooop.* [Alt: Natal Robin]

Snowy-headed Robin-Chat *Cossypha niveicapilla* 22cm, 8.5"

Large robin-chat with *white stripe over top of crown* (can be hard to see); large black patches on sides of head and rufous collar are often more obvious. Mantle and wings slate-grey with olive wash; centre of tail black. Immature like other immature robin-chats but larger. **HH** Not uncommon but shy in lowland deciduous woodland in WEt at 750–1200m. **Voice** Usually heard at dusk; rapidly delivered, strong, varied song has fluty quality, with much mimicry. Common call is a repeated mournful piping *fweeeeo…* [Alt: Snowy-crowned Robin-Chat]

White-crowned Robin-Chat *Cossypha albicapillus* 25cm, 10"

Large, long-tailed robin-chat, like Snowy-crowned but with *no rufous collar* and *more extensive white crown* usually heavily specked black, but black tips can wear to reveal greyish-white crown. Immature is similar but browner with pale tips on wing-coverts. Race in region is *omoensis.* **HH** Uncommon resident in SW highlands of Et, in dense forest undergrowth and thickets at 500–1000m. **Voice** Song is loud, fluty, complex and almost thrush-like, delivery slow and deliberate with marked pauses between phrases. Unlike close relatives, it uses little mimicry.

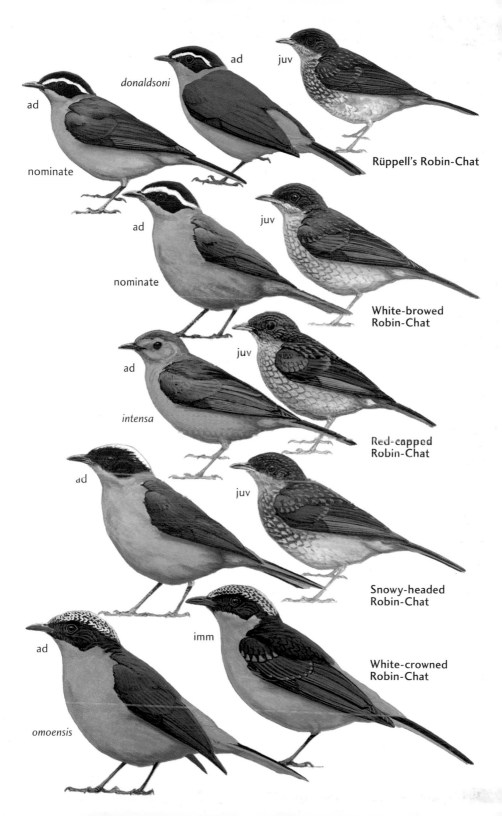

donaldsoni

ad

juv

ad

nominate

Rüppell's Robin-Chat

nominate

ad

juv

White-browed Robin-Chat

ad

juv

intensa

Red-capped Robin-Chat

ad

juv

Snowy-headed Robin-Chat

ad

imm

White-crowned Robin-Chat

omoensis

Common Nightingale *Luscinia megarhynchos* 16cm, 6.5"

An unstreaked rufous-brown chat with a *bright rufous rump and tail*. Differs from very similar Thrush Nightingale by *plain underparts* (not mottled) and *stronger contrast between rump and tail and rest of upperparts*. Three races occur, differing mainly in colour of upperparts: nominate (mainly found in west of region) is mostly warm rufous-brown above; *africana* (mainly in centre) is duller brown on back and wings; *golzii* (mainly coastal) is colder brown-grey above with rufous restricted to rump and tail, and a poorly defined supercilium; underparts paler than other races. All have dark eyes with narrow whitish eye-ring. Sexes alike. First-winter like adult but has pale tips on tertials and coverts. **HH** Common Palearctic passage migrant and winter visitor (Aug–Apr) but rare Er and NWSo; vagrant Dj and Soc. Frequents thickets, scrub, forest edge and cultivation up to 2100m. **Voice** Call is a loud harsh *tk-tk-trrrrrrk* (like running stick along fence), also a muffled *tuk tuk* in alarm and strong whistled *wheet* at dawn or as prelude to song. Song is a loud complex warble of mainly sweet notes, with pause between each sequence. **Note** Race *golzii* formerly called *hafizi*. [Alt: Rufous Nightingale]

Thrush Nightingale *Luscinia luscinia* 16cm, 6.5"

Very like Common Nightingale but generally duller rufous-brown above with *less contrasting rump and tail*. Dingy pale grey-brown below with *indistinct mottling across breast*, faint malar stripe and whiter throat; smudgy spots on sides of undertail-coverts diagnostic if present. Sexes alike. First-winter is greyer with pale tips on tertials and coverts. Sexes alike. **HH** Uncommon Palearctic migrant Sep–Nov and Mar–May, in similar range of habitats as Common Nightingale, up to 2000m, especially in Rift Valley. Vagrant Dj. **Voice** Two common calls (similar in Common Nightingale) are a whistled *weeep* and a harsh *takk*. Often sings with loud, rather strident musical refrain of sweet and harsh notes, which continues for long periods without pause (not as pure or disjointed as Common Nightingale). Lacks slow introductory whistles of Common Nightingale, but song ends with rising series of dry *tocky-tock-tock* notes. [Alt: Sprosser]

White-throated Robin *Irania gutturalis* 18cm, 7"

Adult male is boldly marked: blue-grey above with *all-black tail* contrasting with black-and-white head pattern and rich rufous-orange breast. Female is rather plain grey-brown above with blackish tail, whitish throat, scaly buff-and-grey breast, and flanks washed pale rufous-orange. First-winter is like female, but has browner wings and lightly spotted greater coverts. Black tail is characteristic feature when birds fly away into cover. Told from robin-chats by black tail and orange underwing-coverts. **HH** Frequent to common Palearctic migrant in thickets, dense bush and gullies up to 2300m in Er, Et and NWSo, Aug–Oct and Mar–Apr. Usually in drier habitats than nightingales. **Voice** May sing on spring passage: a loud musical warble, not unlike speeded-up version of Thrush Nightingale. Alarm is a throaty *trrrr* (similar to but quieter than Common Nightingale). [Alt: Irania]

Common Redstart *Phoenicurus phoenicurus* 14cm, 5.5"

Male in Jan–Apr is grey above with *white forehead, black face*, orange-red underparts and bright rufous tail with dark brown centre; in Oct–Dec has pale fringes on head and breast giving frosty, mottled appearance. Two races occur: nominate as described; male *samamisicus* usually has conspicuous *white wing-panel*. Female is grey-brown above with narrow pale eye-ring, buffy below with paler throat and buffy-orange breast; tail as male. Female *samamisicus* may show paler wing-panel. **HH** Common Palearctic passage migrant and winter visitor to Er, Et (except SE) from Oct–Apr, favouring wooded areas and thickets, from sea-level to 3000m. Rare in NW&SSo. Active, shivering tail regularly; often first recognised when it shows flash of rufous tail. **Voice** Usually silent; sometimes gives a soft *tik*.

Black Redstart *Phoenicurus ochruros* 14cm, 5.5"

Male of distinctive Central Asian race *phoenicuroides* similar to nominate Common Redstart but *lacks extensive white on forehead*, has darker upperparts and more extensive black breast. Tail pattern as in Common. First-winter male resembles female, which is darker and greyer than female Common, especially below. **HH** Uncommon to rare Palearctic winter visitor, Oct–May, to Er, NEt, Dj and NSo, mainly on rocky slopes and in wooded gorges from sea-level to 2000m. Perches upright and shivers tail regularly. Dark-bellied European forms do not occur in region. **Voice** Gives an irregular *tick*. Typical chat-like song unlikely in winter, but at times birds give a muffled warble, particularly when sheltering from midday heat.

Common
Nightingale

ad

nominate

ad

ufricana

ad

golzii

ad

Thrush Nightingale

♀

♂

White-throated
Robin

♀

nominate

♂

Common Redstart

♀

♂

samamisicus

Black
Redstart

♂

phoenicuroides

SCRUB ROBINS *Mostly similar-looking chats with rufous or black tails, tipped white on all except central feathers. Tails are frequently cocked, waved and spread. Colour of underparts, presence or absence of streaking and tail markings aid identification. Sexes alike. Immatures are mottled with buff and dark brown. Sometimes placed in genus Erythropygia (except Black Scrub Robin).*

Rufous Scrub Robin *Cercotrichas galactotes*   16cm, 6.5"

Brownish above with dark eye-stripe and long off-white supercilium, *rufous rump and tail broadly tipped black and white* (most visible when tail is spread), and *pale unstreaked underparts*. Sexes alike. Four races occur, varying slightly in size and colour of upperparts: resident *minor* (Er, NEt, NWSo) is warm pinkish-brown above with narrower black spots in tail, and *hamertoni* (endemic to SEEt and N&CSo) is darker and rather small; migrant *syriaca* is grey-brown above and *familiaris* is slightly paler and greyer (probably not separable in field). **HH** Resident populations are locally common in north and east; *syriaca* and *familiaris* are common and widespread Palearctic migrants and winter visitors, Sep–May, in dry bush country and wide variety of woodland and scrub up to 1500m. Feeds mainly on ground. **Voice** Migrants are usually silent, but may give a quiet hesitant *seeep*. Song is a sweet, thrush-like warbling. **Note** The two resident races are sometimes split as African Scrub Robin *C. minor*. [Alt: Rufous-tailed Scrub Robin, Rufous Bush Robin, Rufous Bush Chat]

White-browed Scrub Robin *Cercotrichas leucophrys*   15cm, 6"

Similar to Rufous Scrub Robin but always *lightly streaked on breast and flanks*, and *broad white edges to wing-coverts and inner secondaries form large white wing-patch*. Upperparts and tail similar to Rufous, but usually darker earth-brown on crown and mantle, with broader black subterminal tips on tail. Head pattern more striking, with white supercilium and submoustachial stripes contrasting with dark ear-coverts. Immature lacks supercilium and is more rufous above, with heavy scaling on upperparts and breast. Two races occur: *leucoptera* (C&SEt and NWSo) as described; *eluta* (SSo and SEEt) is slightly paler above. **HH** Common in wide variety of habitats (but not forest or barren desert) from sea-level to 1850m. Often keeps within cover unless singing, when displays repeatedly from bush tops. **Voice** An accomplished and persistent songster which varies locally and individually: usual song consists of loud phrases repeated over and over again with or without modification. **Note** The white-winged races in our region are sometimes considered to be a separate species: White-winged Scrub Robin *C. leucoptera*. [Alt: Red-backed Scrub Robin]

Bearded Scrub Robin *Cercotrichas quadrivirgata*   15cm, 6"

Rather plain olive-brown above with bold face pattern, *pale buffy-orange on breast and flanks*, white wing-flashes, warm rufous rump, and *blackish-brown tail with white tips*. Immature similar to adult but heavily scalloped above and below. **HH** Often shy and difficult to observe, keeping to thick cover in forest. In our region, confined to riverine woodland in SSo. **Voice** A persistent singer, particularly at dawn and dusk, with pleasant varied whistles; individuals often repeat favoured phrases. Alarm is a harsh *chrrrt*. [Alt: Eastern Bearded Scrub Robin]

Black Scrub Robin *Cercotrichas podobe*   21cm, 8"

Conspicuous, long-legged, highly distinctive scrub robin, mainly *sooty-black with long, graduated, white-tipped tail*, frequently cocked and waved, undertail-coverts tipped white forming prominent chevrons. In flight, wings show rufous panel. Immature is browner with narrower white tips on tail and all-black undertail-coverts. **HH** Common breeding resident in arid scrub and savanna with scattered bushes in Er, below 900m. Uncommon non-breeding visitor to NEEt, Dj and NWSo, from sea-level to 1800m, Sep–Mar. Mainly on ground. **Voice** Song is quite simple but more fluty and with stronger delivery than other scrub robins, including *swi-swi-swi swrrrr* (with a rattled finish).

Spotted Palm-Thrush *Cichladusa guttata*   17cm, 6.5"

Uniform brown or rich brown above with white supercilium, and rufous-brown rump and tail. Whitish below with *black malar stripes extending as spots across breast and as elongated streaks on flanks*. Sexes alike. Immature duller. Three similar races: nominate (SWEt), *intercalans* (SEt) and *rufipennis* (SEEt, SSo). White-browed Scrub Robin has much white in wing and black-and-white tipped tail. **HH** Common but shy resident in coastal thickets, wooded grasslands and semi-arid bush (but not palms) up to 1500m, feeding on ground near cover. **Voice** Characteristic voice of dry scrub; sings throughout day and by moonlight. Song almost thrush-like, fluttier than scrub robins, usually involving short repeated or alternating phrases with some mimicry. [Alt: Spotted Morning-Thrush]

Rufous Scrub Robin

ad

ad

syriaca

minor

juv

juv

ad

leucoptera

ad

White-browed Scrub Robin

Bearded Scrub Robin

ad

ad

Spotted
Palm-Thrush

Black Scrub Robin

STONECHATS Small, large-headed, short-tailed chats; Siberian and African are frequently united with extralimital European Stonechat S. (t.) rubicola as a single species: Common Stonechat S. torquatus. **WHEATEARS** are medium-sized chats, mostly with white or buffy rumps and an inverted black T on the tail. Mainly ground-dwelling in open country.

Siberian Stonechat Saxicola (torquatus) maura　　　　　　13cm, 5"

Breeding male (not usual in region) has black head and throat, chestnut on breast (variable in extent), white collar, white patches on wings and rump, and blackish tail. Non-breeding male is much duller, with *blackish face and throat*, pale collar and indistinct *buffy-white wing-patch*. Two races occur: commoner *variegatus* has extensive *white bases to black tail feathers* in all plumages; *armenicus* has less white at base of tail, and non-breeding male is slightly darker than *variegatus*. Females of both races are rather pale, streaked brown and buff above with *prominent buff supercilium*, indistinct white wing-stripe, and buffy-white throat contrasting slightly with pale rufous-brown breast. Immature is like dull female. **HH** Frequent to uncommon Palearctic winter visitor to Er, Et and Dj, Sep–Apr, from sea-level to 2400m; vagrant NWSo (one record) and Soc. Sits in open on fence posts, tree stumps and small bushes. **Voice** Mainly silent in region.

African Stonechat Saxicola (torquatus) torquatus　　　　13cm, 5"

Adult male of highland race *albofasciatus* is highly distinctive, entirely black and white. *White neck and wing-patches and extensive black throat and breast* are diagnostic. First-year male is similar but has chestnut and black on breast. Female is much darker than Siberian Stonechat. **HH** Locally common resident in open country in W&CEt, typically at 1800–3000m. Inhabits variety of habitats including moorland, grasslands, cultivation and marshy areas. **Voice** Attractive repeated short scratchy warbling song may be sung for long periods. **Note** Race *albofasciatus* may be worthy of consideration as separate species.

Whinchat Saxicola rubetra　　　　　　　　　　　　　　13cm, 5"

Breeding male has distinctive *long white supercilium and blackish ear-coverts*; washed buffy-orange below, with small white patches on wing-coverts and *white sides at base of tail*. Non-breeding male, female and first-winter resemble female Siberian Stonechat: best distinguished by *well-defined buffy supercilium and white base to outer tail*. **HH** Common Palearctic winter visitor to S&WEt and passage migrant in Er and Et, Sep–Apr, from sea-level to 2400m; commoner in spring. Scarce in NWSo. Sits on small bushes and trees within grasslands and cultivated areas. **Voice** Usually silent in winter.

Capped Wheatear Oenanthe pileata　　　　　　　　　　　17cm, 6.5"

Adult has narrow white band across forecrown, white supercilium, *white throat and (uniquely) broad black breast-band.* Immature like female Northern Wheatear but spotted buff above and washed yellow-brown with darker brown mottling below. **HH** Inhabits short grassy plains above 1400m in E Africa; in NE Africa, just a single old migrant record in SSo. Stands very upright, often on fence posts and other low perches. **Voice** Song mixes harsh and sweet notes in short bursts, often with mimicry, sometimes performed in low song-flight. Alarm call is a muffled *tik*.

Red-breasted Wheatear Oenanthe bottae　　　　　　　　16cm, 6.5"

Large, upright, highland wheatear with narrow creamy-white supercilium. Grey-brown above with *white chin and throat contrasting with rich rufous breast and belly.* Underwing-coverts cream. Broad black bar at end of tail. Sexes alike. **HH** Race *frenata* is common resident of montane grasslands and moorland in Et, at 950–3200m; rare in Er. Nominate *bottae* occupies SW Arabia and may occur as vagrant. **Voice** Song is short but loud and fluty. Frequently gives a throaty *chuk* whilst perched. [Alt: Botta's Wheatear]

Heuglin's Wheatear Oenanthe heuglini　　　　　　　　　14cm, 5.5"

Similar to Red-breasted Wheatear including dark eye-stripe and narrow whitish supercilium, but *distinctly smaller and darker brown above.* Underparts rich rufous-buff when fresh, fading to warm brown-olive; paler on throat and belly. Underwing-coverts pinkish-buff. Sexes alike. Female Northern has narrower tail-bar. **HH** Uncommon resident in NWEt; rare visitor to WEr. Perches on bushes in burnt grassland or on rocky hillsides, dropping to feed on ground; frequently waves tail. **Voice** Song is long series of jumbled notes and whistles, including much mimicry. Call is a hard *chack*. **Note** Formerly considered conspecific with Red-breasted Wheatear..

1st-summer ♂

variegatus

♂

♀

Siberian Stonechat

♀

armenicus

1st-year ♂

African Stonechat
albofasciatus

non-br ♂

br ♂

br ♀

♂

non-br ♀

Whinchat

imm

ad

frenata

Red-breasted Wheatear

ad

Capped Wheatear

ad

livingstonii

Heuglin's Wheatear

Isabelline Wheatear *Oenanthe isabellina*   17cm, 6.5"

Very like female Northern Wheatear but often *stands very upright* and is slightly larger, stronger-billed and generally paler with pearly-buff underparts. Supercilium is whiter in front of eye (whiter behind eye in female Northern). *Wings have broad buffy feather-edgings and in flight appear uniform with mantle;* dark alula usually conspicuous on closed wing. *Terminal tail-band is broader than in Northern;* tail appears half black and half white in flight. Sexes alike (unlike Northern). **HH** Common passage and winter visitor throughout up to 2500m, Aug–Apr, preferring dry country but can turn up in any open area. **Voice** Usually silent; song consists of a complex warble of scratchy, nasal twanging. Call is a harsh *tchak*.

Northern Wheatear *Oenanthe oenanthe*   15cm, 6"

Breeding male has grey crown, nape and mantle, broad black mask and black wings, and buffy throat and breast. Terminal tail-band broader than Pied and Black-eared Wheatears. Female and non-breeding male are earthy-brown above, with pale supercilium and buffy underparts. In flight *dark wings contrast strongly with paler brown mantle* and white rump. First-winter has buffy wing-edges like Isabelline Wheatear, but tail-band always narrower. Two similar races occur: nominate, as described; *libanotica* has whiter supercilium and is purer grey above and whiter below. **HH** Common and widespread passage migrant, wintering in SEt and SSo in wide range of more open habitats from sea-level to 3600m, Aug–May. Vagrant Soc. **Voice** Usually silent, but before departing may sing a mixture of rapid scratchy and sweet notes. Alarm call is a repeated *tchak*.

Pied Wheatear *Oenanthe pleschanka*   15cm, 6"

Breeding male has black on face, upper breast, mantle and wings, with *crown and nape white or silvery-grey* in fresh plumage and narrow black terminal tail-band (sometimes broad). Breeding female is cold earth-brown above with buffy supercilium and warmer cheeks. Fresh-plumaged birds in autumn are like female but dark grey-brown mantle is finely scaled and blackish wings have prominent pale fringes; males look dark-faced and pinkish-brown on breast. An uncommon white-throated form also occurs ('*vittata*'). **HH** Common passage migrant and winter visitor throughout, Sep–May, in wide range of habitats up to 2700m; often perches on small bushes. **Voice** Usually silent in region; song is a short sweet refrain interspersed with harsh *chak* notes.

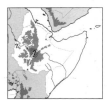

Cyprus Wheatear *Oenanthe cypriaca*   14cm, 5.5"

Very like Pied Wheatear but smaller and more compact with shorter primary projection. Breeding male has less white on crown and nape, *underparts are less white, tinged peachy,* and tail-band is usually broader. Sexes similar (unlike Pied). Non-breeding birds have *greyish crown and nape* with narrow whitish supercilium, rest of upperparts dark with fine scaling. Face and throat blackish, often with scaling on chin, and underparts are deep ochre-yellow (richer than Pied). **HH** Winter range unclear, but presumed to overlap with Pied in Et. Several records claimed but none fully acceptable. **Voice** Song is a series of hoarse notes, *bizz-bizz-bizz-bizz*, unlike other wheatears, but unlikely to be heard in region. **Note** Formerly treated as conspecific with Pied Wheatear.

Black-eared Wheatear *Oenanthe hispanica*   15cm, 6"

Breeding male has both pale- and black-throated forms. Pale-throated birds differ from '*vittata*' Pied Wheatear in having *whitish mantle tinged sandy-buff*, uniform with crown and nape. On black-throated form *black face-mask does not join black wings.* Usually more white in tail than any other wheatear in region. Female is virtually identical to female Pied but warmer above, brighter below. **HH** Race *melanoleuca* is fairly common winter visitor to Er and NEt, Sep–Mar, up to 3000m; vagrant NWSo (twice). Prefers acacia savanna, but also in rocky hills and cultivation. **Voice** Usually silent in region; song is short warbled refrains, lacking harsh scratchiness of other wheatears. Call is a descending whistle or a harsh *tchak*. **Note** The form concerned is sometimes split as a separate species.

Desert Wheatear *Oenanthe deserti*   15cm, 6"

Differs from all other wheatears in having *virtually all-black tail*, only showing white at very base. Adult male can be further identified by sandy mantle and white scapulars, and from black-throated form of Black-eared Wheatear by *black face-mask contiguous with wings.* Female grey-brown, paler than other female wheatears; wings extensively fringed white. First-winter male like female but with mottled dark face. **HH** Nominate *deserti* is common winter visitor to Er, NEt and NSo, Sep–Mar, in sandy areas and grassy plains up to 1200m; C Asian race *oreophila* recorded in Soc and SSo. **Voice** Song, not usually heard in region, is a plaintive, descending whistle of 2–4 notes, ending in a harsh trill. Calls include a drawn-out *seeeu*.

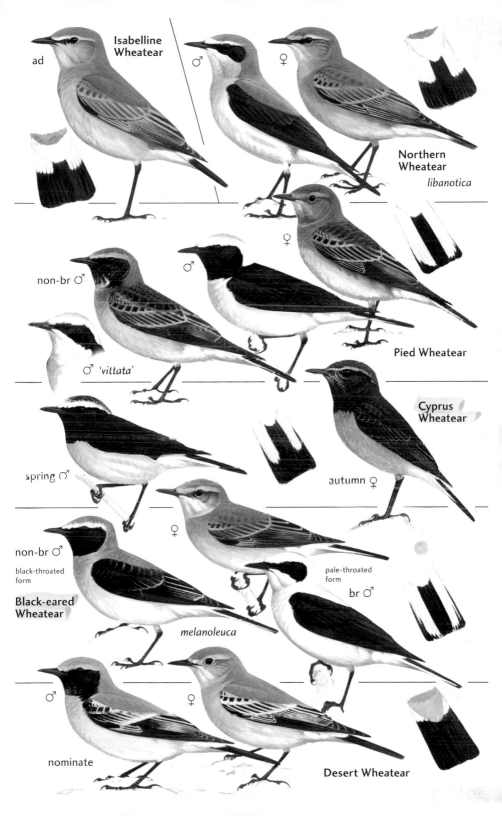

Isabelline Wheatear

ad

♂ ♀

Northern Wheatear

libanotica

♀

non-br ♂

♂

♀

♂ 'vittata'

Pied Wheatear

Cyprus Wheatear

spring ♂

autumn ♀

♀

non-br ♂

black-throated form

Black-eared Wheatear

melanoleuca

pale-throated form

br ♂

♂ ♀

nominate

Desert Wheatear

Somali Wheatear *Oenanthe phillipsi* 14cm, 5.5"

Adult male easily told from other wheatears by *grey crown and back* and *black throat and breast*. Remiges mainly black with white wing-coverts. Female similar to male but black of face and breast replaced by grey. Immature is browner above and black areas are mottled grey. **HH** ENDEMIC to EEt and NSo. Locally common resident in open areas and light bush, and especially newly burnt ground, at 200–2000m. Usually solitary or in pairs; generally confiding. **Voice** Two calls are a low, drawn-out whistle uttered repeatedly, and a buzzing sound. Song is fairly short, sweet and melodious, given from small tree.

White-crowned Black Wheatear *Oenanthe leucopyga* 15cm, 6"

Adult is mainly *black wheatear with white crown* and white vent and undertail-coverts. Tail is mainly white with black central feathers. Sexes alike. Immature like adult but has black crown. Hooded Wheatear has white belly. **HH** Nominate *leucopyga* is a local presumed resident in Er, NEt and Dj. Poorly marked race *ernesti* may occur in Er as non-breeding visitor. Inhabits rocky desert areas including human habitation. **Voice** Song consists of short series of slurred notes, first rising then falling towards end, *wer-wii wrrrrr wrrrrr*, sometimes ending with pair of thrush-like interrogatory notes.

Hooded Wheatear *Oenanthe monacha* 17cm, 7"

Adult male is large black-and-white wheatear with white crown, attenuated shape and *long bill*. Tail mostly white with black central feathers (like White-crowned Black, which has black belly and longer legs). Female is pale grey-brown, with same tail pattern as male but white replaced by warm buff. **HH** Vagrant to Dj (from coastal Sudan or Arabia), Apr 1984 and Feb 1986. In normal range, inhabits wild rocky areas in desert, occupying large territories and generally shy. Usually solitary or in pairs. **Voice** Song is a chatty series of notes with plenty of mimicry.

Abyssinian Black Wheatear *Oenanthe lugubris* 14cm, 5.5"

Variable species with mainly black and white plumage in males. Two races occur: male nominate *lugubris* (Er, Et, Dj) is all black except for *dirty brown crown* (streaked black) and white vent tinged orange-buff on undertail-coverts. *Rump and base of tail pale orange-buff* (not white). A white-bellied morph is frequent. Male of race *vauriei* (NSo) is like white-bellied morph of *lugubris* but has paler crown and less black on breast. Females are rather dark with heavy streaking; female *vauriei* is paler than *lugubris*. **HH** ENDEMIC. Common resident in Er, Et and Dj, inhabiting rocky country with bushes at 800–3000m. Occurs at 1800–2100 in NSo. **Voice** Likely to be similar to extralimital Schalow's Wheatear *O. schalowi* (may be conspecific with *O. lugubris*), which sings short bursts of identical muffled but sweet refrains. **Note** Sometimes treated as conspecific with **Mourning Wheatear** *O. lugens*. The *persica* race of Mourning winters in Sudan and could occur in Eritrea. Sexes are alike and resemble male *O. lugubris vauriei*, but crown is usually whiter and rump and base of tail are white (with no buff). [Alt: Abyssinian Wheatear]

Kurdish Wheatear *Oenanthe xanthoprymna* 14cm, 5.5"

Breeding male differs from all other wheatears in region by black face and throat *and rufous rump contrasting with white bases to outer tail*. Underwing-coverts black. Female is brownish-grey with indistinct supercilum and darker face; tail pattern as in male, but white bases sometimes buffish. **HH** Rare winter visitor from E Turkey and W Iran to NEr (once). Usually in arid, rocky habitats. **Voice** Song is a constant twittering of whistles and trills with some scratchy notes. Mainly silent in winter quarters. **Note** Formerly called Red-tailed Wheatear, but red-tailed form now split off (see below). [Alt: Kurdistan Wheatear; Chestnut-rumped Wheatear]

Red-tailed Wheatear *Oenanthe chrysopygia* 14cm, 5.5"

Adult is greyish-brown above with indistinct pale grey supercilium and sides of neck; *ear-coverts tinged rufous*. Tail pattern like Kurdish Wheatear, but *rump and base of tail entirely rufous*. Underwing-coverts silvery-white. *Sexes alike.* **HH** Uncommon winter visitor from Iran and Afghanistan to Er, Oct–Mar, in desert and semi-desert, up to 600m. Vagrant Et (twice) and Dj (once). **Voice** Mainly silent in winter quarters. **Note** Formerly treated as conspecific with Kurdish Wheatear (as Red-tailed Wheatear *O. xanthoprymna*). [Alt: Persian Wheatear; Rusty-tailed Wheatear]

White-crowned Black Wheatear

ad

imm

nom.

Somali Wheatear

♂

♀

Hooded Wheatear

♀

♂

♀

lugubris

lugubris
white-bellied morph

Abyssinian Black Wheatear

♂

♀

vauriei

Kurdish Wheatear

♀

xanthoprymna

♂

ad

Red-tailed Wheatear

chrysopygia

PLAIN CHATS Tame, subdued, dull-plumaged chats which frequently flick their wings while foraging or after landing. Sexes alike. Careful attention to subtle plumage features is needed, as well as to habitat and range.

Familiar Chat *Cercomela familiaris* 15cm, 6"

Rather uniform drab grey-brown chat with *rufous rump and outer tail; centre of tail and terminal band blackish, forming inverted T*. Ear-coverts tinged rufous; narrow white eye-ring. Throat and breast pale grey, whiter on belly. Immature is spotted buff above, mottled buff and dark brown below. Two similar races: *falkensteini* (NWEt) as described; *omoensis* (SWEt) slightly darker above, greyer below. **HH** Pairs are uncommon residents in open woodland and bush country, often in rocky areas, frequently in small trees (but also feed on ground), at 1100–2000m. Recently discovered in Er, at 2400–2500m. Frequently flicks wings and raises and lowers tail (unlike similar female Common Redstart which shivers its tail). **Voice** Sings from bush tops a tuneless scratchy warble incorporating its call, a repeated *wii cha-cha*. [Alt: Red-tailed Chat]

Brown-tailed Rock Chat *Cercomela scotocerca* 14cm, 5.5"

Similar to Familiar Chat, but *no rufous in plumage*. Ear-coverts slightly warm brown, but otherwise all drab dark brown above; paler below. Immature is like adult. Four disjunct races occur: nominate (Er, NEt) is greyish-brown above; *turkana* (SEt) slightly darker and larger; *spectatrix* (NEEt, NSo) much paler and greyer; *validior* (NESo) like *spectatrix* but with yellowish undertail-coverts. Differences from Sombre Rock Chat given below. Moorland Chat lives at higher altitudes and Blackstart has black tail. **HH** Uncommon, localised resident in rocky, semi-arid bushland at 900–2000m where it sits on bushes and drops to ground to feed, particularly in broken rocky areas. **Voice** Repeated wispy song begins *wip* followed immediately by burry rolling liquid *shrererererereep*.

Sombre Rock Chat *Cercomela dubia* 15cm, 6"

Rather featureless rock chat, slightly larger than Brown-tailed with stout bill and upright posture. Mainly dark brown above including tail. *Pale fringes on dark undertail-coverts create diagnostic pattern*. Overlaps with Blackstart and Brown-tailed Rock Chat: former is paler and has black tail, latter has whitish undertail-coverts. Some races of Brown-tailed are very similar to Sombre in coloration, but sympatric race is pale grey *spectatrix* which should not be confused. **HH** ENDEMIC. Very localised and poorly known, from upper Awash valley eastwards in NEEt; one old record from NWSo. Inhabits arid rocky areas with scattered bushes and lava fields at 750–1800m. **Voice** Song, given from prominent perch, is remarkably like Banded Martin but less rambling, comprising short series of rising-and-falling dry staccato *chip* notes, repeated monotonously. [Alt: Sombre Chat] **DD**

Moorland Chat *Cercomela sordida* 15cm, 6"

Dumpy, short-tailed, dark brown chat with *wheatear-like tail pattern*: white outer bases and black centre and terminal band forming an inverted T. Paler grey-brown below. Immature is lightly scaled above and speckled below. **HH** Nominate race is endemic to higlands of Er and Et. Common in high alpine grasslands and moorlands at 1800–3300m. Tame and inquisitive, hopping on ground and perching on low vegetation. **Voice** Song is a formless unattractive series of various sparrow-like chirps, interspersed with squeaks. [Alt: Alpine Chat; Hill Chat]

Blackstart *Cercomela melanura* 14cm, 5.5"

Readily told from other *Cercomela* chats by pale grey-brown upperparts and *all-black tail*. Underparts paler, creamy-white with pale greyish breast. Immature is browner. Two races occur: *lypura* (Er, NEEt) as described; *aussae* (Danakil Desert, Dj, NSo) darker and greyer. **HH** Common resident in dry rocky areas with scattered bushes at 600–1700m, perching on rocks, low vegetation or on ground. *Constantly fans tail and opens wings*. **Voice** Song is a throaty melodious short series of notes, repeated monotonously from prominent perch. Call is a single phrase of the song.

ad

imm

Familiar Chat

falkensteini

ad

ad

Brown-tailed Rock Chat

spectatrix

nominate

imm

Moorland Chat

ad

ad

Sombre Rock Chat

nominate

ad

Blackstart

lypura

ad

aussae

WHITE-WINGED CHATS *Medium-sized chats with variable white patches on crown, throat or wings. Frequently on the ground or singing from prominent perches. Usually in pairs or small groups.*

Mocking Cliff Chat *Thamnolaea cinnamomeiventris* 21cm, 8″

Adult male is an attractive *black and rufous chat with white shoulder-patch* and narrow whitish band across breast, dividing black and rufous colours. Adult female has similar basic pattern *without any white*. Immature is dull version of adult. Two races occur: male *albiscapulata* (Er, N&WEt) has black upper- and undertail-coverts, female is as dark as male but lacks white; male *subrufipennis* (SWEt) has rufous upper- and undertail-coverts, female much greyer (also lacking any white). **HH** Pairs are frequent and widespread in Er and Et at 1000–2800m. Inhabits rocky gorges and hillsides, occasionally associated with buildings. **Voice** Complex song, with much local variation, is long, rambling and rather thrush-like, but notes are spitted out and interspersed with sweet warblings and flourishes recalling song of White-throated Robin; frequently amplified by rocky gorge habitat. [Alt: Cliff Chat; formerly *Myrmecocichla*]

White-winged Cliff Chat *Thamnolaea semirufa* 21cm, 8″

Adult male is very like Mocking Cliff Chat but has *small white patch at base of primaries* rather than on shoulder, more obvious in flight. Female is mainly brownish-black with *white wing-patch*; belly and vent finely fringed buff or orange. Female Mocking Cliff Chat has entire belly and vent orange. Immature is black, profusely spotted buffy-orange above and below. **HH** ENDEMIC to Er and Et. Pairs are frequent to common in highlands, at 1500–2500m, in mountain gorges and on rocky slopes, as well as borders of forest; rare in Er. **Voice** Gives long series of attractive rising-and-falling warbled notes from prominent perch, very throaty in quality and sometimes sustained for long periods. [Alt: formerly *Myrmecocichla*]

Rüppell's Black Chat *Myrmecocichla melaena* 20cm, 8″

Large black chat with prominent white patches in wings in flight (invisible at rest). Sexes alike. White-fronted Black Chat is smaller with white on forehead in male and dusky-white on chin in female; it also occurs at lower altitudes and is more arboreal. **HH** ENDEMIC to Er and Et (but not in SE highlands). Uncommon but locally frequent. Inhabits ravines, gorges and cliffs, usually on bare rocks, at 1800–2800m (occasionally down to 1050m). Usually in pairs. **Voice** Common call is a loud dry throaty rasp. Song is an extension of this.

White-fronted Black Chat *Myrmecocichla albifrons* 16cm, 6″

Medium-sized black chat with *white on forehead* and silvery-white underwings. Adult male nominate race (Er, NEt) has *small white forehead;* male *pachyrhyncha* (SWEt) has more extensive white on forecrown. Adult female of both races is all-blackish but with greyish-white chin and throat; female *pachyrhyncha* usually has flecked greyish-white forehead. Immature is like dull adult but with some tawny mottling on wings and below. **HH** Uncommon in open bush and semi-arid country with rocks at 1050–1900m, often perching on small trees. Drops to ground to feed. **Voice** Call consists of repeated whistled downslurred *siuu*; song is a repeated rambling warble.

Bluethroat *Luscinia svecica* 14cm, 5.5″

Small, slim, long-legged chat, usually in damp habitats. Breeding male is unmistakable with prominent *white supercilium and blue throat*. Three races occur, males differing in throat pattern: nominate *svecica* has red spot on blue throat, *cyanecula* a white spot, and *magna* no spot. Non-breeding male is duller with buffy-white chin and upper throat, but retains much of its breast pattern. Female is like non-breeding male, but usually lacks blue and red on breast; white supercilium and gorget of black streaks always present. Both sexes in all plumages show *rusty-red sides to base of black tail*, most conspicuous in flight. **HH** Locally frequent to common Palearctic passage migrant and winter visitor to Er, Et and Soc, Sep–May, from sea-level to 2300m. Usually solitary and skulking in low rank vegetation and thickets in wetland habitats. Unobtrusive; flies close to ground when flushed, quickly dropping back into cover. **Voice** Migrants frequently give loud *tick* from cover; long rambling song not usually heard in region.

♂

♀ *subrufipennis*

♂

imm ♂

♂

Mocking Cliff Chat

♀

White-winged Cliff Chat

albiscapulata

♀

♂

ad

pachyrhyncha

Rüppell's Black Chat

White-fronted Black Chat

♀

imm/♀

♂

albifrons

Bluethroat

br ♂

br ♂

magna

nominate

Song Thrush *Turdus philomelos* 21 cm, 8″

Medium-sized thrush with *warm brown upperparts* and boldly spotted underparts, breast and flanks washed buff and in flight underwing-coverts orange-buff. Sexes alike. Groundscraper Thrush is larger, with longer bill, shorter tail, more upright stance and black facial marks (and usually found in open country). **HH** Frequent Palearctic winter visitor, Oct–Mar, to coastal areas of CEr in variable numbers; uncommon in NEt and Dj. May be found in any woodland or scrub habitat, and commonly in juniper up to 2500m, but migrants are shy and generally avoid open situations. **Voice** Only call likely to be heard in region is distinctive *tsip* given in flight. On breeding grounds gives a richly varied song.

Groundscraper Thrush *Psophocichla litsitsirupa* 22 cm, 8.5″

Distinctive thickset thrush with *upright stance and short tail*. Upperparts are brownish-grey, underparts boldly spotted with buffy wash on breast and flanks; *two vertical black stripes on face* diagnostic. In flight rufous bases to primaries appear as two pale buffy patches; yellow-buff underwing-coverts also conspicuous. Immature is finely spotted with buffy-white above. **HH** Race *simensis* is common in highlands of Er and Et at 1500–3400m, inhabiting grasslands, open woodland and moorland; usually terrestrial. **Voice** Song is loud, slow and very burry but quite melodious. Diagnostic call is a rapid hollow clicking. **Note** The three disjunct races in southern Africa are greyer-brown above and whiter below, preferring woodland to alpine moorlands.

ROCK THRUSHES *Three small or medium-sized thrushes of rocky areas or woodland, with long wings and short tails. Females of two species are scaly and quite unlike the males; female Little is similar to the male.*

Blue Rock Thrush *Monticola solitarius* 23 cm, 9″

Breeding male is *all dark blue-grey with blackish wings and tail* and rather *long bill*. Non-breeding male is duller with paler chin and bill. Adult female is dark grey-brown above and below, finely banded buff on underparts; shape and habitat are good clues to identity. Immature is similar to female. Two similar races winter in our region: nominate and *longirostris*. Females of latter are paler below with less barring. **HH** Frequent Palearctic winter visitor to Er, Et, Dj and NSo, Oct–Mar, from sea-level to 2400m. Favours mountain crags, rocky coasts, quarries and buildings, but may turn up in other habitats on migration. **Voice** Full song consists of short series of melodious notes from prominent perch; unlikely to be heard in region but migrants give subsong on arrival, and again before departure.

Common Rock Thrush *Monticola saxatilis* 20 cm, 8″

Breeding male has head, throat and upper mantle blue-grey with *white patch on back;* rest of underparts orange-red; *tail orange-red with dark central feathers*. Little Rock Thrush is smaller, without white back. Non-breeding male is *mottled and scaly all over with rufous tail* and some rust on flanks. Female and first-winter like non-breeding male, but generally browner, rufous limited mainly to tail, but lower underparts also washed pale rufous. **HH** Common and widespread Palearctic passage migrant and winter visitor, Sep–Apr, favouring open woodland and bush in winter but also rocky grasslands, cliffs and buildings, up to 2400m. Vagrant Soc. Often stands upright, looking shorter-tailed than other rock thrushes, and quivers tail like redstart. **Voice** Silent and unlikely to sing in region, but may utter a soft *tak*. [Alt: Rufous-tailed Rock Thrush]

Little Rock Thrush *Monticola rufocinereus* 15 cm, 6″

Considerably smaller, slimmer and longer-tailed than Common Rock Thrush, and like short-tailed robin-chat; quivers tail like redstart. Adult male is brownish-grey above, without white back of Common and with blue-grey head extending onto breast (only reaches throat in Common). Bold blackish *central tail feathers and tips form distinctive inverted T*. Female is duller and paler than male with whitish chin. Immature is spotted buff above, buff below with heavy blackish scales; tail like adult. **HH** Pairs are frequent to common residents in Er, Et and NSo, at 300–3000m, on rocky slopes and in broken hill country with some tree cover; often favour junipers and euphorbias. **Voice** Sings a simple, sweet thrush-like refrain from tops of small trees, ending each phrase with double *zi-zit*, rather like 'innit' at the end of a sentence.

ad

Groundscraper
Thrush

Song Thrush

nominate

simensis

♀

br ♂

non-br ♂

nominate

Blue Rock Thrush

br ♂

♀

♂

♀

Common
Rock Thrush

Little
Rock Thrush

nominate

TURDUS THRUSHES *are a well-known genus of larger thrushes: several are similar, but in the main have different ranges, habitat preferences and altitudinal limits. Sexes alike. Immatures have spotting on wing-coverts and breast.* **GROUND THRUSHES** *usually keep to thick cover within forest undergrowth; only one species in NE Africa.*

Mountain Thrush *Turdus (olivaceus) abyssinicus* 22cm, 8.5″

Adult is dark grey-brown above with *orange bill and narrow orange eye-ring*; grey-brown throat is streaked faintly with black. Breast grey-brown, belly and flanks rich rufous-orange extending right across lower breast; lower belly white. Immature is generally darker than adult with small buffy spots on wings, breast heavily spotted dark brown. **HH** Most common and widespread *Turdus* thrush in highlands of Er and Et, pairs occupying wide range of woodland habitats including forest edge, gardens and cultivation, at 1650–2500m. **Voice** Song consists of short typical thrush-like phrases followed by pause, each phrase ending with short series of repeated subdued notes, like an echo. **Note** Usually treated as conspecific with Olive Thrush *T. olivaceus* of southern Africa. [Alt: Northern Olive Thrush]

Somali Thrush *Turdus ludoviciae* 23cm, 9″

Very dark thrush. Head and breast of male are black, upperparts slate-grey, underparts paler grey, especially belly, *without any rufous*, but underwing-coverts are pale rufous (like Mountain Thrush); bill yellow. Female is similar but duller with less black on chin and throat, appearing to be diffusely streaked black. Immature is heavily spotted above and below. **HH** ENDEMIC to NSo. Locally common in juniper forests at 1300–2000m, but seriously threatened by habitat destruction. **Voice** Undescribed. **Note** Formerly considered conspecific with Olive Thrush *T. olivaceus* of southern Africa. [Alt: Somali Blackbird] **VU**

African Thrush *Turdus pelios* 22cm, 8.5″

Very like Mountain Thrush, but *paler with pale yellow-orange bill* and lightly and evenly streaked brown on buff throat. Breast is pale grey-brown with pale buff-orange flanks *not usually extending across lower breast* (rarely as faint wash). Two similar races occur: nominate (Er, N,C&EEt) and *centralis* (S&SWEt). **HH** Largely replaces Mountain Thrush in west, being common and widespread in forest edge, thickets, gardens and cultivation at 500–2000m. In areas of overlap, African is at lower altitudes. **Voice** More varied than Mountain Thrush, with *completely different structure of various repeated phrases, given for long periods without pause*, and no softer terminal calls. May mimic other birds.

Bare-eyed Thrush *Turdus tephronotus* 21cm, 8″

Grey above with orange bill, *diamond-shaped patch of bare orange-yellow skin around* eye, and white throat strongly streaked black; breast grey, lower breast and flanks rufous. **HH** Localised retiring resident of generally drier areas including coastal scrub, riverine vegetation and wooded bushland in SEt and SSo, from sea-level to 1600m. **Voice** Song is like Mountain Thrush but louder and slower, incorporating diagnostic rapid bubbly and peculiarly nasal *pi-pu pi-pu pi-pu*, also given as alarm.

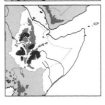

Abyssinian Ground Thrush *Zoothera piaggiae* 19cm, 7.5″

Striking montane thrush, with olive-brown upperparts, bright orange underparts, prominent *large white eye-ring and broad, double white wing-bars*. Forehead is usually dark rufous, bill black. Rump and tail more reddish-brown. In flight shows broad white bar on underwing. Immature has buffy streaks above and profuse black spotting below. **HH** Nominate race is widespread but shy in forested highlands in Et, at 1300–3300m, favouring juniper and *Podocarpus* forests. **Voice** Song like Mountain Thrush, but richer and flutier.

Red-tailed Ant-Thrush *Neocossyphus rufus* 22cm, 8.5″

Thrush-like bird with a rather small head and long tail; wings and tail rounded. *Mostly bright rufous* with slightly duller brown head and mantle, paler throat, and rufous-brown rump and tail (slightly darker in centre). Has typical thrush-like horizontal stance. Immature like adult but duller and unspotted. **HH** Shy and ground-dwelling in forest undergrowth, often following army ants. In our region, just one recent record from Boni Forest in SSo, presumably a wanderer from coastal forests in Kenya (nominate *rufus*). **Voice** Call is a ratchet-like *trrrt*, often followed by long falling whistle *fweeeeeee*.

Somali Thrush

ad

Mountain Thrush

juv

ad

abyssinicus

ad

ad

centralis

African Thrush

ad

Bare-eyed Thrush

ad

**Red-tailed
Ant-Thrush**

nominate

juv

ad

**Abyssinian
Ground Thrush**

nominate

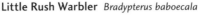

BRADYPTERUS *warblers are rather plain, skulking, brown warblers of marshes and dense forest undergrowth, some with streaking across the breast. They often first draw attention to themselves with their powerful songs, but remain hard to see. Sexes alike.*

Little Rush Warbler *Bradypterus baboecala* 14cm, 5.5"

Secretive dark brown warbler with broad rounded tail, pale supercilium and *short heavy streaks across breast*. Race *abyssinicus* (Et) has olive-brown upperparts and olive-tawny wash below; *sudanensis* (WEt) is similar but slightly smaller. **HH** Locally common but patchily distributed in swamps and marshes in Et at 750–2100m. Displays amongst reeds and sedges with loud burring wings. **Voice** Song is a high-pitched, almost hissing series of descending *tirrup* notes that accelerate to end in dying rattle (usually followed by a low aerial display of wing burring); call is a nasal *pink-pink*. [Alt: African Sedge Warbler]

Cinnamon Bracken Warbler *Bradypterus cinnamomeus* 15cm, 6"

Uniform *rufous-brown above*, with long buffy supercilium, white throat and centre of belly, and *rich cinnamon band across breast and flanks*. Tail long and slightly graduated. Immature is browner with yellowish supercilium, throat and belly, and olive brown on breast and flanks. **HH** Nominate race is locally common in undergrowth, at forest edge and in gardens in W and SE highlands of Et, at 1800–3600m. Creeps around in thick cover and is usually located by its loud song or by flash of rufous as it flies. **Voice** Typical loud song is an introductory *wii* followed by 3–6 identical explosive notes. Call is a nasal *pink*.

Bamboo Warbler *Bradypterus alfredi* 15cm, 6"

Dark brown above with short pale supercilium and rounded tail. White on throat shades into olive-brown breast; lower breast to vent white with *strong grey wash over sides of breast and flanks*. *Undertail-coverts barred brown-and-white*. Immature has yellowish wash on underparts, especially on undertail-coverts. **HH** Rare, skulking warbler of forest undergrowth, long grass and forest edge; in Et known only from three sites: Didessa (Shoa Prov.), Bulcha Forest (Sidamo Prov.) and Gambela, at 525–1260m; perhaps only an intra-tropical migrant. **Voice** Simple song is a repeated series of ten or so paired hollow notes *tik-er-tik-er-tik-er...* Short ticking call likened to Common Redstart.

Fan-tailed Grassbird *Schoenicola brevirostris* 15cm, 6"

Resembles dark-coloured, *short-billed* Eurasian Reed Warbler with a disproportionately heavy, *long, broad graduated black tail* (obvious in flight). Tail and long undertail-coverts broadly tipped whitish, giving barred effect from below. Immature washed pale-yellow below with shorter tail. **HH** Rare resident of dense grassland, moist bush and cultivation in W highlands of Et, with just four old records at 1500–2100m. Hard to see unless flushed from wet grass, but will sit on exposed grass stems in early mornings, and performs conspicuous flight display. **Voice** Song is a simple short, metallic piping *ping ping ping...* Alarm and contact notes are a sharp *tak-tak-tak...* [Alt: Broad-tailed Warbler]

Moustached Grass Warbler *Melocichla mentalis* 19cm, 7.5"

Large warbler, plain brown above with chestnut-washed forecrown, pale yellow eyes, and broad, blackish-brown rounded tail. Chin and throat white; rest of underparts cinnamon-buff. When seen well facial pattern distinct, with white supercilium and eye-ring *and narrow black malar streak*. Immature is like dull dark-eyed adult, with mottled breast and no malar streak. Race in Et is *amauroura*. **HH** Singles and pairs are locally common in savanna, woodland, rank grass and thick cover along streams in WEt at 750–1200m. Shy but vocal, singing frequently from prominent perches. **Voice** One of best songsters in rank herbage. Basic song begins with series of *tip tip tip...* breaking into varied and complex falling flourish, ending *tweedle-iddle-ee*. Also utters a nasal scolding *chahhchahhchahh...* [Alt: African Moustached Warbler]

sudanensis

Little Rush Warbler

abyssinicus

Cinnamon Bracken
Warbler

nominate

nominate

Bamboo Warbler

Moustached
Grass Warbler

umauroura

alexinae

Fan-tailed Grassbird

LOCUSTELLA warblers are shy with indistinct superciliary stripes, strongly graduated tails and very long undertail-coverts (which may be mottled or streaked) almost reaching the tip of the central tail feathers. ACROCEPHALUS warblers are a group of similar-looking plain warblers, with rather flat heads and rounded tails, and are invariably brown above and paler below. Size, overall tone, leg colour and range aid identification. Sexes alike.

River Warbler Locustella fluviatilis 14cm, 5.5″

Cold olive-brown and unstreaked above, with narrow supercilium and diffusely mottled breast, long and conspicuously pale-tipped undertail-coverts giving marbled effect. Tail broad and rounded. Legs pink. **HH** Uncommon Palearctic passage migrant in CEt (Rift Valley) at 1300–1700m, Sep–Nov and Apr–May; one record SSo (Nov). Shy and hard to see; inhabits thick scrub and undergrowth. **Voice** Rarely heard song is a protracted rattling zri-zri-zri-zri-zri... (like Yellow Bishop); call is a soft, irregularly repeated tak. [Alt: Eurasian River Warbler]

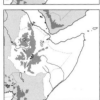

Savi's Warbler Locustella luscinioides 14cm, 5.5″

Unstreaked warm olive-brown above with indistinct supercilium, whitish throat and belly contrasting with unmarked deep buff breast and flanks; plain or only lightly mottled long buff undertail-coverts. Some birds show faint gorget of small spots around base of neck. Eurasian Reed Warbler (plate 148) lacks broad rounded tail and long undertail-coverts. Three similar races: nominate, as described; sarmatica slightly lighter; fusca more olive-grey above, whiter below. **HH** Locally common but elusive winter visitor to N&CEt and Er up to 2300m, Aug–May. Prefers damp habitats including reedbeds, swamps and rank grass; also in Salvadora thickets near permanent water. **Voice** Song is a fast, high-frequency reeling, rather insect-like and buzzing. Call is a single tchik.

Grasshopper Warbler Locustella naevia 13cm, 5″

Slim, skulking warbler that keeps low in cover or creeps on ground. Olive-brown above finely streaked dark brown on crown and more boldly on mantle, with weak supercilium, whitish below with finely streaked gorget; olive-brown uppertail-coverts and long pale undertail-coverts both have diffuse dark streaks. Immature is tinged yellow below. Sedge Warbler (plate 148) has broad buffy supercilium and unstreaked undertail-coverts. **HH** Uncommon Palearctic winter visitor (race straminea) in N&CEt, Sep–Apr, in low cover and herbaceous undergrowth at 400–2000m. Vagrant Er. Dives quickly into cover when disturbed. **Voice** Song is a high-pitched mechanical reeling, with individual notes more easily discernible than Savi's Warbler. Call is a short hard tic.

Great Reed Warbler Acrocephalus arundinaceus 19cm, 7.5″

Very large, warm brown above with distinct buffy supercilium, strong bill and long wings. Below whitish with strong tawny-buff wash on sides of breast and flanks. Legs usually pale brownish. Two races occur: nominate as described; zarudnyi paler and more olive above, whiter below. **HH** Mainly a Palearctic passage migrant, Sep–Nov and Apr–May, but small numbers winter in Et, up to 2150m. Inhabits rank vegetation, thickets and wetland areas. **Voice** Song is much slower than smaller Acrocephalus warblers, but still typical: a loud, very deep, scratchy croaking medley. Call is a single chakk.

Clamorous Reed Warbler Acrocephalus stentoreus 18cm, 7″

Almost as large as Great Reed Warbler, but with longer, narrower bill, longer tail and shorter, more rounded wings; supercilium narrower and less prominent. Structural differences most noticeable in flight. Coloration as in Great Reed, but often slightly darker below. Basra Reed is smaller and colder-toned. Two races probably occur: nominate, as described; brunnescens (status uncertain) is less warm above, whiter below. **HH** Locally common resident in mangroves of Er, Dj and NWSo. **Voice** Loud, deep song similar to Great Reed, but more melodious and higher-pitched, with short pauses.

Basra Reed Warbler Acrocephalus griseldis 16cm, 6″

Larger than Eurasian Reed Warbler (plate 148) but smaller and slimmer than Great Reed Warbler with distinctive long slim bill and long wings. Cold olive-brown above with obvious whitish supercilium above broad dark loral line, and dark tail; white below, faintly washed buff on sides of breast and flanks. Legs grey. Lesser Swamp Warbler (plate 148) has more rufescent tones and shorter wings. **HH** Locally common Palearctic passage migrant up to 1500m, mainly in Rift Valley, late Aug–early Dec, with small northbound spring passage in Apr. Occurs in marshy areas and damp thickets. Small numbers winter in SSo. **Voice** Song, heard prior to departure, is clearly like other Acrocephalus but coarse and tuneless, with rather similar notes like a protracted scolding. **EN**

River Warbler

Savi's Warbler

fusca

Grasshopper
Warbler

straminea

Great Reed
Warbler

nominate

Clamorous Reed
Warbler

brunnescens

Basra Reed
Warbler

Lesser Swamp Warbler *Acrocephalus gracilirostris* 15cm, 6"

Fairly large warbler, size of Basra Reed Warbler but with more rounded wings (shorter primary projection) and more rufescent plumage. Four races occur: all have short pale supercilium, *whitish throat contrasting with darker breast* and flanks, *dark grey legs* and longish thin bill. Race *jacksoni* (WEt) is greyish-brown above and below, with whiter belly; *parvus* (Rift Valley) olive-brown above with slightly rufous rump and greyish-brown on breast and flanks; *tsanae* (Lake Tana, NWEt) like *parvus* but greyer below; *leptorhynchus* (SSo and SEEt lowlands) reddish-brown above with brighter rufous rump, paler tawny-buff breast and flanks. **HH** Common resident of waterside vegetation, reedbeds and papyrus, with fragmented range in region up to 1850m. **Voice** Song loud, frequent and fluid, mixing melodious phrases with subdued chattering. Commonest calls include a rapid interrogatory see-sawing *wee-ter-ree-ter-ree-ter-reet*. [Alt: Cape Reed Warbler]

African Reed Warbler *Acrocephalus baeticatus* 13cm, 5"

Much smaller than Lesser Swamp Warbler; shorter-winged and much warmer buffy-brown than similar-looking Palearctic species. Two races occur: widespread *cinnamomeus* (W&CEt and SSo) is *pale warm-brown above* with short buffy supercilium, whitish throat and *warm buffy breast and flanks*; *avicenniae* (Er, NSo: mangroves) olive-brown above, tinged rusty on rump, creamy-white below. Legs grey-brown. **HH** Widespread but seldom common resident of marshes, reedbeds (particularly *Typha*) and rank vegetation from sea-level to 1800m. **Voice** Song much like Eurasian, but notes slower, clearer and smoother. **Note** May be conspecific with Eurasian Reed Warbler. Race *avicenniae* sometimes treated as separate species, Mangrove Warbler *A. avicenniae*, or as race of Eurasian Reed Warbler. [Alt: African Marsh Warbler]

Eurasian Reed Warbler *Acrocephalus scirpaceus* 14cm, 5.5"

In our area, race *fuscus* is grey-brown above, with grey-olive tones to head and nape, whitish underparts. Very like Marsh Warbler but with slightly rufous-washed rump and whiter underparts. Some individuals are warmer brown above with more russet tones to rump and whitish below with buffy-brown sides to breast and flanks (perhaps nominate birds?). In all birds *head appears flat-topped, not rounded*. Legs usually dark brownish. **HH** Widespread Palearctic passage migrant and winter visitor Aug–May, wintering mainly in and west of Rift Valley; rare in So; vagrant Soc. Inhabits thickets, bush, rank vegetation and cultivation. **Voice** Song typical of *Acrocephalus*, given for long periods without pause, most notes rather scratchy, twangy and unmusical. Alarm is repeated harsh burry *cherrr*. **Note** Race *fuscus* is sometimes considered specifically distinct as Caspian Reed Warbler *A. fuscus*.

Marsh Warbler *Acrocephalus palustris* 15cm, 6"

Very like Eurasian Reed Warbler, both having short pale supercilia and small eye-rings, but uniform cold olive-brown above and whitish below with buffy-yellow tinge, plumper with more rounded head and shorter bill. *Legs pale pinkish-brown* (can be dark on first-winter birds). **HH** Frequent to common Palearctic migrant, Aug–Dec, in variety of bush country and overgrown cultivation up to 2400m, mainly in and west of Rift Valley. Few records on spring passage in Et (Apr–May). **Voice** Rather quiet in NE Africa. Full song is rich and melodious but also scratchy, with much mimicry. Call is a soft *tuk*. [Alt: European Marsh Warbler]

Sedge Warbler *Acrocephalus schoenobaenus* 13cm, 5"

Streaked above with *distinctive bold creamy supercilium*, whitish below with buffy-rufous flanks. In flight, shows contrasting *plain rusty-orange rump* and dark tail. First-winter birds may show hint of pale crown-stripe. **HH** Common Palearctic passage migrant and winter visitor to reedbeds, marshes and lakeside vegetation up to 2500m, Sep–May. Winterers are most numerous in W&CEt, but there is a strong and widespread northerly passage in Apr–May. Vagrant Dj and Soc. **Voice** Often heard; typical song is subdued, sweeter and less scratchy than other small *Acrocephalus*. Call is a harsh rolling *chirrr*.

leptorhynchus

parvus

**Lesser Swamp
Warbler**

cinnamomeus

**African Reed
Warbler**

avicenniae

**Eurasian Reed
Warbler**

fuscus

Marsh Warbler

Sedge Warbler

Dark-capped Yellow Warbler *Chloropeta natalensis* 14cm, 5.5"

Bright resident warbler with characters of both *Acrocephalus* and *Hippolais*. Race *massaica* is olive-brown above with darker *blackish-brown crown* (rear may be slightly raised giving crested appearance) and entirely yellow below. Crown feathers often raised when singing, giving appearance of peaked crown and upright stance. Sexes alike. Immature is tawny-brown above and yellow washed tawny below. **HH** Pairs are frequent in W & SE highlands of Et, inhabiting undergrowth and dense vegetation, often near water, at 1200–2300m. **Voice** Varied song commonly begins with a few chips and continues with either a rather urgent *tp...wi-chi-wi-chi-wi-chi-wi-chi* or a nasal *weeeez*. [Alt: African Yellow Warbler]

HIPPOLAIS *warblers are fairly uniform in coloration, with flat-looking foreheads, short superciliary stripes and strong bills. Tails are square-ended with short undertail-coverts. Note size, overall tone, wing-panels and wing length, as well as behaviour such as tail flicking and waving. Sexes alike.*

Eastern Olivaceous Warbler *Hippolais pallida* 13cm, 5"

Widespread race *elaeica* from SE Europe and SW Asia is fairly uniform grey above, tinged olive (no wing-panel), with pale supercilium, and paler creamy-buff below. Outer tail feathers narrowly edged whitish (hard to see in field). Lower mandible pale yellowish-horn. Legs pinkish or brownish-grey. Nominate race (from Egypt) is browner and slightly smaller. Newly described resident race *alulensis* from NSo is smaller with more rounded wing, and more grey-brown above; very like Sykes's Warbler. **HH** Common winter visitor from sea-level to 1500m, Aug–May (most are *elaeica*). Restless, often pumping tail while calling; favours canopy of large acacias. Race *alulensis* inhabits mangroves. **Voice** Regularly calls a fairly harsh *chk*; often sings a soft *Acrocephalus*-like refrain.

Sykes's Warbler *Hippolais rama* 12cm, 5"

Very like Eastern Olivaeous Warbler, but has plainer secondaries, shorter primary projection and tends not to pump tail. Shorter-winged race *alulensis* of Eastern Olivaceous may not be separable in field. In hand, *rama* and *alulensis* may be separated on tail:wing ratio and wing formula. **HH** Breeds in C Asia and winters in India. Vagrant to Er (one specimen record in Nov). **Voice** Not heard in region. **Note** Formerly treated as conspecific with Booted Warbler *H. caligata*.

Upcher's Warbler *Hippolais languida* 14cm, 5.5"

Larger than Eastern Olivaceous and greyer above with whitish supercilium; duller white below with pale buff or buffish-grey flanks. Narrow white edges to *longer, much darker tail* are more easily seen (*tail constantly waved or even slightly fanned*). Wings are also darker with pale panel on secondaries when fresh, but less distinct than on Olive-tree. Lower mandible pinkish; legs pinkish-grey. **HH** Common Palearctic passage migrant, Aug–Oct and Apr–May, wintering in SEt and SSo. Inhabits dry bush country from sea-level to 1500m, tending to keep to cover. **Voice** Call is unlike Eastern Olivaceous, a soft nasal *chah-chah-chah...*, repeated rapidly and for long periods if agitated. *Acrocephalus*-like song is sometimes heard on winter quarters.

Olive-tree Warbler *Hippolais olivetorum* 17cm, 7"

Largest *Hippolais*, grey-brown above with narrow whitish supercilium, whitish below with variable pale-grey wash; notably long strong bill with *yellowish-horn base to lower mandible*. Long wings are darker than mantle and in fresh plumage pale-edged secondaries form pale panel. Tail is very dark with narrow white edges to outer feathers. Strong blue-grey legs. **HH** Rare Palearctic passage migrant or winter visitor, Aug–May, but probably under-recorded. **Voice** Call is a harsh *tak*; song, rarely heard, is *Acrocephalus*-like but deeper and more musical, not scratchy.

Icterine Warbler *Hippolais icterina* 13cm, 5"

Adult is greenish-olive above, yellow below, with prominent yellow supercilium. Long pointed wings show long primary projection (equal in length to tertials). Fresh-plumaged birds have yellow-edged secondaries forming *obvious wing-panel*, but first-winters arriving in Aug–Oct are much more washed out, often appearing dull greyish-green above and very pale yellow or mostly white below. Can resemble other *Hippolais* or even dull Willow Warbler, but long primary projection and lack of dark eye-line distinctive. Lower mandible pinkish. *Legs blue-grey.* **HH** Uncommon passage migrant in Er and Et, Sep–Oct and Apr–May, in acacia bush or woodland at 500–1600m; once in NWSo (May). **Voice** Rarely heard in region: song is an *Acrocephalus*-like but more musical rambling interspersed with sweeter, canary-like squeaks and chips. Call is a simple *tak*.

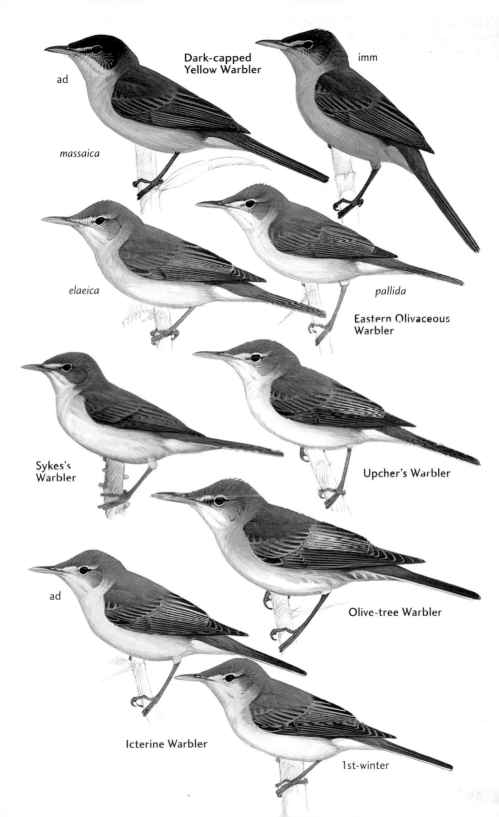

Dark-capped
Yellow Warbler

ad

imm

massaica

elaeica

pallida

Eastern Olivaceous
Warbler

Sykes's
Warbler

Upcher's Warbler

ad

Olive-tree Warbler

Icterine Warbler

1st-winter

CAMAROPTERAS AND WREN-WARBLERS A closely related and taxonomically confusing group of small warblers which are variously lumped and split across the continent. Camaropteras inhabit forest and more verdant habitats, while the all-dark wren-warbler prefers dry bush country. Both genera cock (and latter frequently fans) their tails. Sexes are alike.

Grey-backed Camaroptera *Camaroptera brachyura* 10cm, 4"

Small warbler with short cocked tail. Various races in Africa are either green-backed (sometimes considered separate species). The four races in our region are all of grey-backed *brevicaudata* group. All have grey or grey-brown head and mantle, with green wings and grey-brown tail. Underparts vary from grey to pale greyish-white. Immatures are variably washed yellow below. Races vary slightly in tone: *brevicaudata* (WEr, NWEt) has grey back, throat and breast, *abessinica* (Et except NW; Dj, NSo) darker above and more olive below, *insulata* (WEt: Ghere region) darker grey above and below, *erlangeri* (SSo) much whiter below. **HH** Common in undergrowth and lower levels of forest, thick bush, gardens and cultivation, from sea-level to 2600m. Shy but inquisitive. **Voice** Musically versatile but all calls are simple. Frequently heard is a very nasal pinched wheeze or bleat, *bzeeee*. Song is a loud whip-cracked *t'chk t'chk t'chk* and a nasal *wiwiwiwiwiwi...* [Alt: Bleating Warbler, Green-backed Camaroptera]

Grey Wren-Warbler *Calamonastes simplex* 13cm, 5"

All brownish-grey with long tail often cocked and waved. At close range may show slightly speckled throat and indistinct barring on belly. **HH** Common and widespread east of Rift Valley in acacia scrub and bushed savanna from near sea-level to 1700m. Usually seen slowly moving around low in bushes, or even on ground below them, but will move to tops of small trees when calling. **Voice** Song is an explosive repeated *chup, chup, chup* given for long periods at about once per second.

EREMOMELAS Active small warblers of the canopy and middle levels in a variety of forest, woodland and bush country. Usually found as pairs or small flocks, and often join mixed bird parties. Sexes are alike.

Green-backed Eremomela *Eremomela canescens* 11cm, 4.5"

Bright attractive warbler. In our area, race *abyssinica* is olive-green above, with well-defined grey crown and nape and *broad dark mask through eye, very white throat and upper breast* contrasting with lemon-yellow breast to vent. Eyes yellowish, legs bright orange-pink. Immature like adult but duller and paler. **HH** Uncommon to frequent in WEr and W&CEt, at 600–2000m. Usually in small flocks in open bush and woodlands, sometimes in canopy. **Voice** An effervescent rambling of excitable musical chips and churrs and louder *wi-chi-chit* phrases. **Note** Sometimes lumped with Senegal Eremomela as *E. pusilla*.

Yellow-bellied Eremomela *Eremomela icteropygialis* 10cm, 4"

Short-tailed species, adult grey above, whitish on throat and breast, and *bright yellow from breast or lower breast to vent*. Immature is variably washed olive above, and yellow on underparts is paler and often restricted to ventral area (very like Yellow-vented Eremomela). Race in NE Africa is *griseoflava*. **HH** Pairs are widespread in open woodland and bush country, mainly in lowland areas of Et and NWSo, up to 2000m. Often found in mixed-species flocks with white-eyes, penduline-tits and crombecs. **Voice** Rather crombec-like, but more penetrating; song is a variable rising-and-falling or rolling series of distinct notes, typically *t'tri-t'ri-t'tri*. A nasal contact note is also used in display.

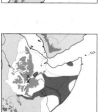

Yellow-vented Eremomela *Eremomela flavicrissalis* 9cm, 3.5"

Slightly smaller than Yellow-bellied Eremomela, with slenderer bill and very short tail; plumage almost identical but *pale yellow restricted to vent* (can be difficult to see). Legs grey or black. Immature has almost no yellow or faintest wash. Philippa's Crombec (plate 151) has more prominent mask, more extensive yellow wash below, and pinkish or reddish legs. Mouse-coloured Penduline-tit (plate 168) has shorter, conical bill and no yellow on vent. **HH** Common in dry bush and semi-desert country in So (except NW) and S&SEEt, up to 900m. **Voice** Song a loud, burry *ser-si-ser'si-sit*, scratchier and without variety of Yellow-bellied.

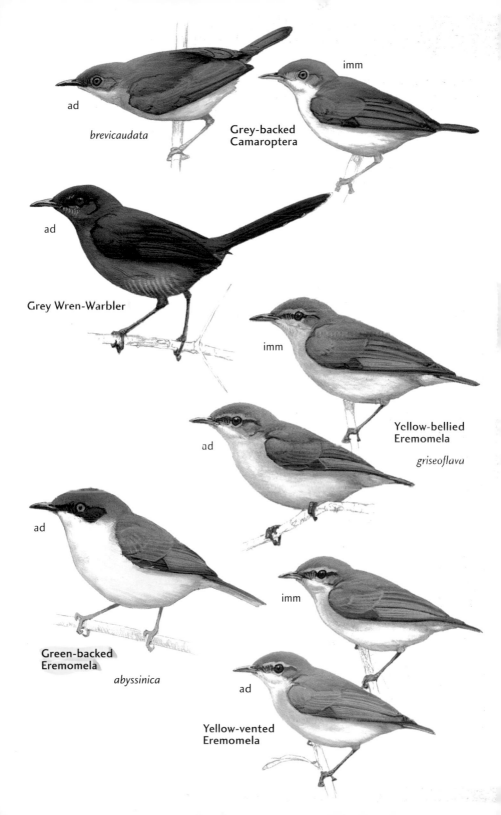

ad

brevicaudata

imm

**Grey-backed
Camaroptera**

ad

Grey Wren-Warbler

imm

**Yellow-bellied
Eremomela**

griseoflava

ad

ad

**Green-backed
Eremomela**

abyssinica

imm

ad

**Yellow-vented
Eremomela**

CROMBECS Very small warblers of bush and woodland with a tail-less appearance. All are very active, constantly foraging as they move from tree to tree. Solitary or in pairs, they often join mixed-species flocks. Sexes are alike.

Northern Crombec *Sylvietta brachyura*   8cm, 3"

Uniform grey or brownish-grey above, with *whitish chin and belly, dark eye-line*, and buffy-cinnamon underparts. Two distinctive races occur: nominate (WEr) has supercilium and throat tawny-buff, while *leucopsis* (EEr, Dj, Et, So) has *supercilium and throat whitish, giving pale-faced appearance*. Immature has buffy tips to wing-coverts. **HH** Common resident of woodland, gardens and dry bush country from sea-level to 2500m. **Voice** Usually a simple repeated phrase; eastern birds have a long sweet complex song like a *Sylvia* warbler, with serin-like phrases interjected.

Red-faced Crombec *Sylvietta whytii*   9cm, 3.5"

Slightly larger than Northern Crombec with similar grey or brownish-grey upperparts, but lacks pale-faced appearance, with *sides of face, throat and most of underparts plain cinnamon*. Race *loringi* in Et can be almost as pale as Northern below, but *lacks dusky eye-line so that colour of face extends above eye*. Immature has buffy tips to wing-coverts. **HH** Fairly common resident in C&SEt, in wide variety of woodland and bush country at 400–1800m. **Voice** Usually sings variations on a loud, repeated rolling *si-si-siu si-si-siu si-si-siu si-si-siu*.

Somali Crombec *Sylvietta isabellina*   10cm, 4"

Pale buffy-grey crombec with *long bill* and whitish superciliary stripes. *Very pale buffy-white below*, palest on throat. Immature similar, but lightly mottled on throat. Pale underparts and sunbird-like, slightly downcurved long bill distinguish it from all other crombecs in region. **HH** Locally common to uncommon in dry *Commiphora*/acacia bush country of S&EEt and NW&SSo, up to 1500m. **Voice** Song is a typical crombec-like *tichi tichi tichi ri-ti-chu*, last note lower. In flight gives a sharp *chik*. [Alt: Somali Long-billed Crombec]

Philippa's Crombec *Sylvietta philippae*   9cm, 3.5"

Small pale crombec reminiscent of an eremomela, with *short bill and dark face-mask*. Upperparts pure grey with narrow white supercilium. Chin and throat white, *rest of underparts pale yellow*, slightly duskier on breast and flanks. *Legs pinkish or reddish-brown*. No other crombecs have yellowish underparts, but Yellow-bellied and Yellow-vented Eremomelas (plate 150) can be confusingly similar; both eremomelas usually have brighter and more restricted yellow below, and grey legs. **HH** ENDEMIC resident in NW&WSo and adjoining parts of Et up to 950m; inhabits dense thickets in areas of semi-arid bush, often in rocky or red sandy soil areas. **Voice** Song is typical of genus, a repeated series of notes; main song is deep and throaty for a crombec, interspersed with dry introductory rattles. [Alt: Somali Short-billed Crombec] **DD**

Buff-bellied Warbler *Phyllolais pulchella*   10cm, 4"

Very small, slim pale warbler, uniform olive-brown or grey-brown above and pale creamy-yellow below, with very narrow, white-edged blackish tail. Pink lower mandible and legs obvious in field. Immature is more yellowish below, and mistakable for Willow Warbler; latter is larger with obvious supercilium and no white in tail. **HH** Singles, pairs or small groups are common in Er and Et (especially in Rift Valley) at 400–1900m; confined to acacias, busily foraging in canopy. **Voice** Noisy: parties constantly give a chittering *tit-tit-tit-tit-tit...* often breaking into a dry trill.

Northern Crombec

leucopsis

nominate

Red-faced Crombec

loringi

Somali Crombec

Philippa's Crombec

Buff-bellied Warbler

PHYLLOSCOPUS *WARBLERS* Phylloscopus *or leaf warblers are small, greenish, arboreal birds, with rather rounded heads, slim bills and slender legs. They are very active, flitting through the upper storey and canopy of trees. Some have yellow on the face or underparts. Sexes alike.*

Willow Warbler *Phylloscopus trochilus*   11 cm, 4.5"

Widespread race *acredula* is dull olive above and pale yellow below, with long pale yellow supercilium and indistinct dark line through eye. First-winter birds are greener above and have much more yellow below. Nominate *trochilus* also reported (mainly winter in W Africa); typically brighter, but many birds hard to assign to race. Eastern *yakutensis* should also occur: grey-brown above, greyish-white below (no olive or yellow tones) with whitish supercilium. In all races, *legs usually pale yellowish-brown*, but dark on some birds. Best told from Common Chiffchaff by song. **HH** Very common Palearctic passage migrant Sep–Nov and Mar–May in wide variety of bush and woodland from sea-level to 1800m (occasionally to 3300m); a few winter in W&CEt and SSo. Vagrant Soc. Usually at lower altitudes than Common Chiffchaff. **Voice** Song is a silvery descending cadence ending in a flourish; call is a short interrogatory *hooweet*.

Common Chiffchaff *Phylloscopus collybita*   11 cm, 4.5"

Very like Willow Warbler, but usually has *dark legs and shorter wings*, more rounded crown, supercilium less well marked and bill shorter and darker, but only safely distinguished in field by song. Downward flicks of tail distinctive. Two races occur: nominate is brownish-olive above, whitish or buffy below; *abietinus* (from N Europe) greyer above, whiter below. **HH** Common Palearctic winter visitor to Er, W&CEt, with smaller numbers in Dj and NSo, mainly to highland forest and forest edge at 2000–3300m, Oct–May. Vagrant Soc. **Voice** Usually located by song: its onomatopoeic *chiff-chiff-chaff-chiff-chaff...* is distinctive, heard from January to departure. Call is also an upslurred *hweet*, more monosyllabic than Willow Warbler.

Eastern Bonelli's Warbler *Phylloscopus orientalis*   11 cm, 4.5"

Similar to Willow Warbler and Common Chiffchaff, but greyer above, whiter below, supercilium and eye-stripe weaker, bill with pinkish lower mandible. Prominent *greenish-yellow edgings to wing-coverts and flight feathers* often form panel on secondaries. Sides of tail also edged greenish-yellow, but yellowish rump often concealed. Legs brown. **HH** Rare Palearctic winter visitor to Er and N&CEt with only a few records, Oct–Jan; possibly overlooked. **Voice** Call is a monosyllabic hard *chip*, song a high-pitched loose trill, similar to Wood Warbler. **Note** Formerly treated as conspecific with Western Bonelli's Warbler *P. bonelli.*

Wood Warbler *Phylloscopus sibilatrix*   12 cm, 5"

Larger than Willow Warbler and Common Chiffchaff and greener above, with longer wings and prominent, *brighter yellow supercilium, face and upper breast.* Very white below with rather short tail making undertail-coverts look long and creating a drawn-out look to rear end. Legs yellowish-brown. **HH** Rare Palearctic passage migrant in Er and Et, and uncommon winter visitor to SSo, Oct–Apr. Vagrant Soc. Inhabits forest and woodland, feeding in middle and higher levels of tall trees. **Voice** Usually silent, but song is an attractive descending silvery cadence that breaks into a dry trill, ending with or without a descending series of mournful pipings. Call is a monotone *hweeet.*

Brown Woodland Warbler *Phylloscopus umbrovirens*   11 cm, 4.5"

Much *browner than other leaf warblers* in our area, with *wings and tail edged green.* Three races occur: nominate (Er, N&CEt, NWSo) is olivaceous-brown above and washed brown below; *omoensis* (W&SEt) more greenish-brown above; *williamsi* (NSo) brighter than nominate, whiter below, with no green edges to wing-coverts. All have weak greyish or buffy supercilium. **HH** Locally common in many highland forests in Er, Et and NSo, at 1500–3700m. Generally solitary or in pairs, feeding in canopy or tall bushes. **Voice** Variable and complex song of sweet see-sawing notes followed by trills and flourishes, with very brief pause between each phrase.

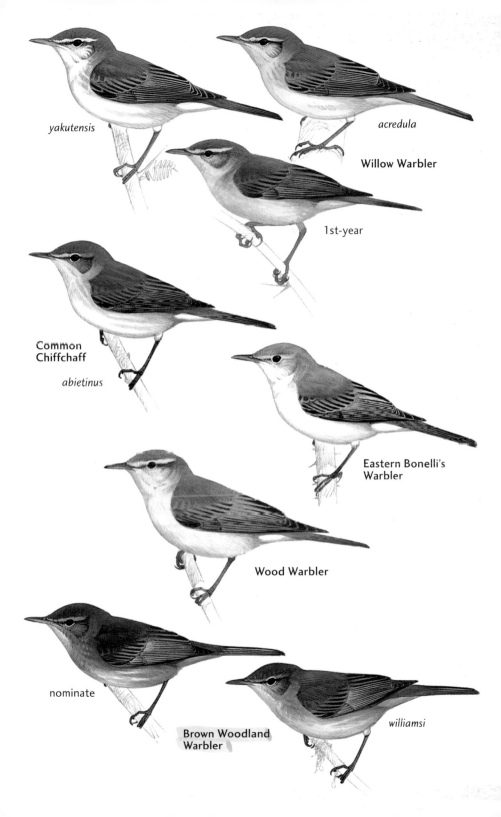

yakutensis

acredula

Willow Warbler

1st-year

**Common
Chiffchaff**

abietinus

**Eastern Bonelli's
Warbler**

Wood Warbler

nominate

**Brown Woodland
Warbler**

williamsi

SYLVIA WARBLERS A group of variable warblers with well-rounded heads, short strong bills and narrow square-ended tails (see also plates 159–160). Some are sexually dimorphic. Most species are winter visitors from the Palearctic, and only Arabian Warbler is resident in NE Africa.

Barred Warbler *Sylvia nisoria*   17cm, 7"

Large and rather long-tailed, grey or grey-brown above with narrow whitish wing-bars and variable degrees of barring below. Adult male is well barred below with *pale yellow eyes*. Adult female is browner above, less barred below. First-winter bird shows only hint of barring (often restricted to flanks and vent) and eyes are dark, resembling Garden Warbler, but Barred identified by larger size, longer tail and pale-tipped wing-coverts. First-winter Orphean Warbler is similar size but has dark ear-coverts contrasting with white throat. **HH** Common Palearctic passage migrant in Er and Et (mainly Rift Valley and WEt) Sep–Dec and Feb–Apr; occasional SSo. Occurs in thick cover in bush country from sea-level to 2400m. Both nominate and *merzbacheri* probably occur. **Voice** Contact call is a rapid *tektektektektektek*, and its seldom-heard song is a rich varied sweet warbling.

Lesser Whitethroat *Sylvia curruca*   13cm, 5"

Small grey-brown warbler with greyer head and white underparts. *Dark grey ear-coverts contrast with paler head and white throat.* Tail grey with white sides; *legs grey*. First-winter is browner and less well-marked. First-winter Orphean similar but notably larger and stronger-billed (adult greyer with pale eyes). Arabian also much larger and greyer, with much darker tail. Most other small *Sylvia* warblers have pale legs. Two races probably occur: nominate *curruca* as described, and *caucasica*, darker and greyer above and buffier below. **HH** Common Palearctic winter visitor to Er and N&CEt, Sep–May, in acacias and bush up to 2300m. Vagrant So and Soc. **Voice** Call is a loud *chik*, usually from cover. Subsong consists of subdued scratchy warble; full song, a rattling series of notes, unlikely in region.

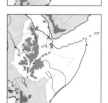

Desert Whitethroat *Sylvia minula*   12cm, 5"

Slightly smaller than Lesser Whitethroat with smaller bill and *paler, sandier-brown upperparts*. Ear-coverts darker than head, but less contrasting than on Lesser. **HH** Central Asian form, wintering in SW Asia; vagrant Soc (once). **Voice** Song is a churring *che-che-che-che-che*. **Note** Often treated as conspecific with Lesser Whitethroat. [Alt: Small Whitethroat, Desert Lesser Whitethroat]

Orphean Warbler *Sylvia hortensis*   16cm, 6.5"

Large, long-billed warbler with grey or grey-brown upperparts and large dark head. Adult male has *blackish ear-coverts contrasting slightly with dark grey head*, white throat and *pale eye*. Dark grey, square-ended tail has prominent white sides, and *undertail-coverts are diffusely spotted* (in race *crassirostris*). Legs dark grey. Adult female has paler head and more contrasting ear-coverts, recalling large Lesser Whitethroat. First-winter bird is duller, browner, dark-eyed and buffier below; large size and diffusely spotted undertail-coverts separate them from other *Sylvia* warblers. **HH** Locally frequent Palearctic winter visitor to Er and NEt, Nov–Mar, in acacia scrub and woodland up to 2100m. Vagrant Dj. **Voice** Call is a loud *chack*; song is similar to Garden Warbler, but stronger and broken into short series with marked pauses. **Note** Race in NE Africa is sometimes considered a separate species: Eastern Orphean Warbler *S. crassirostris*.

Arabian Warbler *Sylvia leucomelaena*   16cm, 6.5"

Large, dark-headed warbler, similar to Orphean but with shorter bill and wings and longer, more rounded *black tail with broad white tips* visible only on underside; undertail-coverts are unmarked. Adult male has blackish head with *dark eye and narrow white eye-ring*, white underparts often tinged pink on breast and flanks. Sexes similar, but female may show more contrasting dark ear-coverts and broken eye-ring. First-winter is browner above and buffier below, and lacks eye-ring. Two races occur: *blanfordi* (Er) as described; *somaliensis* (Dj, NSo) slightly browner above. **HH** Uncommon to frequent resident in acacia woodland and scrub, from sea-level to 1800m. Often perches upright and frequently flicks tail downwards. **Voice** Song is a loud melodious warble, but generally silent outside breeding season. Call is a loud *chack*. [Alt: Red Sea Warbler]

Barred Warbler

1st-winter

nominate

ad ♂

Lesser Whitethroat

ad

nominate

1st-winter

non-br

br

Desert Whitethroat

minula/halimondendri

1st-winter

Orphean Warbler

♂

crassirostris

ad

somaliensis

imm

Arabian Warbler

Common Whitethroat *Sylvia communis*   14cm, 5.5″

Adult male has greyish hood, narrow white eye-ring, *gleaming white throat, large rusty wing-panel*, pinkish breast and fairly long tail with narrow white edges. Female has brownish hood and is buffier below, but still shows rusty wing-panel. Legs pale pinkish-brown. First-winter is like female but dingier. Lesser Whitethroat is greyer with dark ear-coverts, lacks wing-panel. Four similar races occur: nominate and western *volgensis* from Europe, and eastern *volgensis*, *icterops* and *rubicola* from Asia. **HH** Common Palearctic passage migrant and winter visitor, Aug–May, wintering mainly in Er and Et; largely passage bird in So. Vagrant Soc. Occurs in wide variety of habitats, including woodland and dry scrub, from sea-level to 2400m. **Voice** Call is a dry *tek tek*; song in NE Africa is similar to Garden Warbler but more rambling and lacks the scratchy phrases of European birds.

Asian Desert Warbler *Sylvia nana*   12cm, 5″

Small, pale grey-brown warbler with white underparts, recalling pale female Common Whitethroat. *Mainly rusty tail with conspicuous white sides* diagnostic, showing well as bird flies away in low vegetation. *Eyes yellow* and legs pale yellowish. Sexes alike. Immature has dark eyes. **HH** Frequent winter visitor from Central Asia to coastal areas of Er, Dj and NWSo, Nov–Mar; also rarely inland in NEt. Favours open sandy plains with sparse scrub and coastal sand-dunes. **Voice** Call is a sharp *chik*, typical of *Sylvia*; song is a monotonous short warbled phrase, repeated for long periods.

Ménétriés's Warbler *Sylvia mystacea*   13cm, 5″

Adult male is small, pale grey warbler with blackish hood grading to paler grey nape, bordered below with white malar stripe. Tail red with white sides. Eye dark red with *narrow red orbital ring*. Underparts of nominate race (from NE Turkey and Caucasus) has *extensive pink wash, especially on throat and breast*; *rubescens* (from SE Turkey to SW Iran) is paler above and mainly whitish below with very slight pink tinge. Female is rather nondescript, browner above and buffy below, but shows red orbital ring. Both sexes most easily identified by *constant twitching of dark tail from side to side.* **HH** Common to uncommon Palearctic winter visitor to coastal plains of Er, NEEt, Dj and NWSo, Sep–Apr. Rare Soc. Inhabits low bushes and scrub, usually at low altitudes, but up to 1500m. **Voice** Call is a hard *tchak* or rattling *tcherrrr*. Song is a melodious warble interspersed with harsh chatters and rattles.

Subalpine Warbler *Sylvia cantillans*   12cm, 5″

Adult male of race *albistriata* (from SE Europe and W Turkey) is *blue-grey above, brick-red below with prominent white moustachial stripe*. Eyes pale brown with conspicuous red orbital ring; legs dull yellowish-brown. Female is much plainer with only light pinkish-buff wash on breast, but white moustachial usually evident; only likely to be confused with female Ménétriés's, but latter has darker, slightly longer tail frequently waved from side to side, and usually lacks pinkish on breast. **HH** Winters mainly in Sahel in low scrub and thickets. Hypothetical vagrant: Dj records withdrawn and Et record unconfirmed. **Voice** Call is a dry *chit*, sometimes repeated rapidly into a rattle. Song is typical of *Sylvia*, a throaty warble broken into short phrases.

Rüppell's Warbler *Sylvia rueppelli*   13cm, 5″

Adult male has *bold white moustachial stripe separating black throat from black head*, eye dark red with bold red orbital-ring, upperparts grey but wings with *strong white edgings on tertials and greater coverts*, underparts pale grey grading to whitish on belly. Non-breeding male has white chin and throat with dark spotting. Female is browner with no obvious moustachial but shows pale edgings on tertials and greater coverts; otherwise rather like female Ménétriés's, but latter waves tail from side to side and has less patterned wings. Lesser Whitethroat has dark mask and grey legs. **HH** Mainly winters in low scrub in Chad and Sudan; vagrant Dj (once, Mar 1984). Three unconfirmed records in Er and Et. **Voice** Calls consist of a harsh *chik* and sparrow-like 'chipping'. Song is a varied warble interspersed with clear whistled notes.

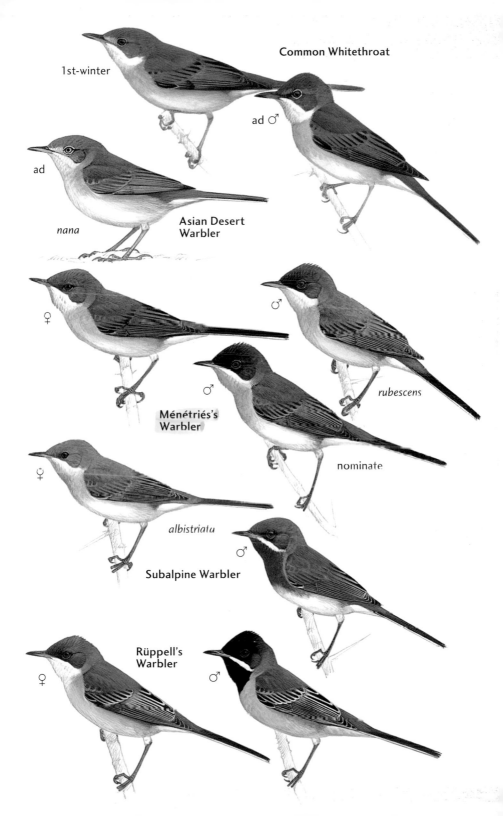

1st-winter

Common Whitethroat

ad ♂

ad

nana

Asian Desert Warbler

♀

♂

Ménétriés's Warbler

rubescens

♂

nominate

♀

albistriatu

Subalpine Warbler

♂

♀

Rüppell's Warbler

♂

Blackcap *Sylvia atricapilla*   14cm, 5.5"

Adult male is grey-brown above, paler grey below with striking *black cap*. Similar adult female is slightly browner above, buffier below with *cap bright rusty or reddish-brown*. First-winter similar to female but duller. Two races occur: nominate as described, *dammholzi* slightly paler and greyer. **HH** Common Palearctic winter visitor and passage migrant to Er and Et (uncommon in NSo), occurring in wide variety of habitats, Sep–May, including scrub and forest edge; wintering birds are mainly in highlands, up to 2700m. **Voice** Call is a hard, sometimes rapid *tak tak tak*; song is a scratchy, melodious warble often heard from January until departure.

Garden Warbler *Sylvia borin*   14cm, 5.5"

Rather uniform greyish-brown warbler with blue-grey neck patch, indistinct short buffy supercilium, narrow pale eye-ring and notable dark eye. Buffy-brown below with grey-brown legs. *Well-rounded head and short bill* distinguish it from similar *Hippolais* warblers. Two races probably occur: nominate as described, *woodwardi* slightly colder and greyer above, paler below. **HH** Common and widespread Palearctic passage migrant to Er and Et (rare NSo) in Sep–Nov and Mar–May. Occurs in variety of woodland, from forest edge to lush bush country and gardens, often near water, up to 3000m. **Voice** Song is a varied continuous warble like Blackcap, but lacks scratchiness and is more muffled and sweeter. Call is an abrupt repeated *teck*.

PARISOMAS *Active warblers which are constantly on the move in the canopy of acacia woodland. Formerly known as tit-flycatchers or tit-babblers, some recent authors treat them as Sylvia warblers. Sexes are alike.*

Banded Parisoma *Parisoma boehmi*   12cm, 5"

Adult is brownish-grey above with pale eyes, white wing-bars, *distinct black breast-band*, tawny-buff flanks and vent, and fairly long, white-edged dark tail. Immature is washed brownish above, with buffy wing-bars, and no black breast-band. Two races occur: *somalicum* (NWSo and adjacent Et), and *marsabit* (disjunct population in SEt) which is paler with greyer breast-band and paler flanks. **HH** Single birds or pairs are found in acacia country and open woodlands up to 1800m. **Voice** Attractive loud rolling and rattling song begins with a reeling fluid trill and continues *chip-chit-wurr-chewy-chewy-chewy*. Often a pair will call together and be answered by other parisomas.

Brown Parisoma *Parisoma lugens*   14cm, 5.5"

Rather uniform dull dark brown warbler with slightly paler grey-brown throat to breast, dingy white belly, and *narrow white edges and tips to tail*. Paler throat is usually finely mottled. Immature resembles adult. Two races occur with distinct habitat and altitude preferences: nominate (Et except Bale Mts) as described; race *griseiventris* (Bale Mts, Et) darker and more uniform above, and pale greyish below. **HH** Nominate birds inhabit open highland woodland with acacias and olive–juniper–*Podocarpus* forest at 1600–2700m. Race *griseiventris* favours moorlands with *Erica* at 3350–3700m. **Voice** Not as vocal as Banded Parisoma. Song is a complex, rambling slow and lazy warbling *swee-seet-s-swee-wee*, and monotonous loud *ch-wee ch'wee*. Contact call is a harsh *tchk*, often in pairs. **Note** The Bale race is sometimes considered a separate species: Bale Parisoma *P. griseiventris*.

HYLIOTAS *Small active warblers of the canopy, constantly moving around with a rather horizontal posture. Usually in pairs, but they also join mixed-species flocks. Immatures are duller than adults with buffy-fringed upperparts.*

Yellow-bellied Hyliota *Hyliota flavigaster*   11cm, 4.5"

Adult male is *glossy blue-black above with large white patch in wing*, and *underparts extensively washed rich tawny-yellow*, paler on belly. Adult female similar but dark-grey above with bluish wash on wings and tail. Similar to Semi-collared Flycatcher (plate 162) but latter has no yellow below and has more upright stance. **HH** Rather localised and uncommon in WEt at 750–1850m, where it favours canopy of leafy trees within open woodland or savanna. **Voice** Usual call is an explosive *swit-itt*, second note slightly lower than first, and song is a rapid twittering incorporating same notes. [Alt: Yellow-breasted Hyliota]

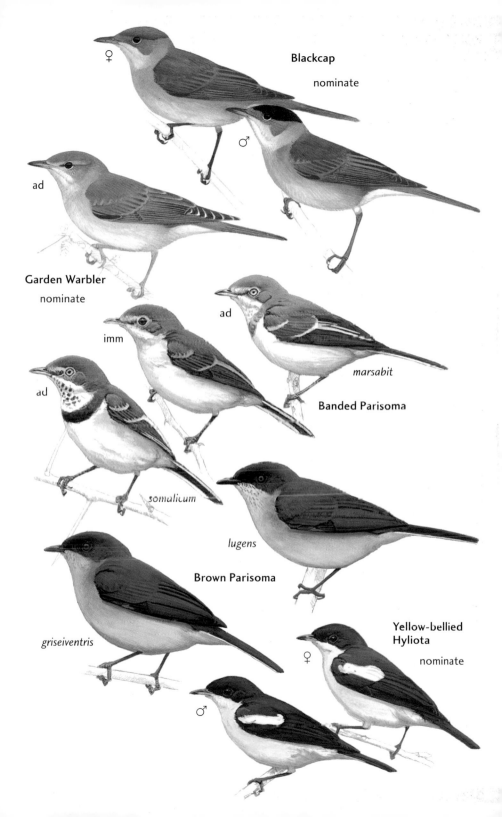

Blackcap

nominate

♀

♂

Garden Warbler

nominate

ad

imm

ad

marsabit

Banded Parisoma

ad

somalicum

lugens

Brown Parisoma

griseiventris

Yellow-bellied Hyliota

♀

nominate

♂

CISTICOLAS *One of Africa's most challenging groups of birds to identify. Males are up to 20% larger in some species. Most have the same plumage throughout the year ('perennial plumage'), but some have different breeding and non-breeding plumages, and in a few species the tail is considerably shorter in breeding plumage. Immatures are often yellowish below. Key features to look for include size, density of streaking, presence or absence of wing-panel, colour of crown, rump and tail, as well as voice and habitat. Most are found singly or in pairs, but may be numerous within suitable habitat.*

Pectoral-patch Cisticola *Cisticola brunnescens* 9cm, 3.5"

Small with very short blackish white-tipped tail and *no obviously contrasting coloured rump*. Breeding male has *unstreaked crown and blackish lores*, and often shows dark patch at side of breast. Non-breeding male and female have forecrown to tail evenly streaked, no loral spot and no breast-patch. Two races occur: nominate (Et except NW) as described; *wambera* (Wambera Plateau, NWEt) darker and more richly coloured: striped black-and-rufous above, rufous-buff below. **HH** Locally common in grassland and moorland in highlands of Er and Et (rare NWSo), at 1650–3000m. Feeds on ground, occasionally perching on grass stem; when disturbed flies short distance before dropping back into grass. **Voice** In high-level display repeats a soft *chht...chht....chht....*, often preceded by wing-click, before plummeting earthwards with accelerating *chht* notes ending abruptly on apparent impact, or continuing in low wavering flight over grass. Neither calls nor wing-snaps relate to changes of direction. Also utters a soft *tic*.

Zitting Cisticola *Cisticola juncidis* 10cm, 4"

Widespread race *uropygialis* is fairly evenly streaked above, with paler unstreaked nape-collar and buff lores; in flight shows *plain rufous-buff rump* and medium brown tail with dark subterminal spots and pale tips (tail is longer than most others in this group). Sexes similar; no non-breeding plumage. **HH** Locally common in Rift Valley with fragmented range elsewhere, up to 2300m; inhabits wide range of habitats including both damp and dry grasslands. **Voice** Cruises in a display-flight, calling *zit...zit...zit...* at top of each of series of undulations; never wing-snaps. [Alt: Fan-tailed Warbler]

Desert Cisticola *Cisticola aridulus* 10cm, 4"

Like Zitting Cisticola with *plain rufous-buff rump*, but slightly paler overall and longish tail much *blacker* with white tips. Race *lavendulae* (Er, Et, So) has greyish-white edgings on upperparts, giving greyer impression compared to Zitting, and is paler below. Pectoral-patch Cisticola has similar but shorter tail and lacks rufous rump. Sexes alike. Immature has white underparts. **HH** Locally common and widespread in short dry open grasslands (favouring arid habitats) from sea-level to 1400m. **Voice** Gives a high-pitched plaintive *p'ink... p'ink... p'ink...*, at half-second intervals, either from perch or in low display flight; usually a wing-snap with each note when singing in flight.

Socotra Cisticola *Cisticola haesitatus* 10cm, 4"

Very pale, washed-out cisticola; breeding adult is similar to Zitting but entirely grey and brown above, except for pale rufous rump, and largely lacking buff. Underparts mainly white with buffish wash on flanks and vent. Sexes alike. Non-breeding birds are more richly coloured. **HH** ENDEMIC to Soc, inhabiting sandy dunes and stony areas with sparse vegetation and tamarisk, from sea-level to 900m (where found in upland meadows). No other small cisticola on Socotra. **Voice** Song is series of *chip* notes repeated monotonously during display-flights, with notes becoming shorter and faster as song progresses. [Alt: Island Cisticola] **NT**

Black-backed Cisticola *Cisticola eximius* 10cm, 4"

Breeding male has *plain rich rufous crown and nape*, very heavily streaked back, rich rufous rump and short, very dark, pale-tipped tail; flanks washed rufous. Non-breeding male has heavily streaked crown separated from mantle by *rufous nape-collar*, and longer tail. Female has streaked crown at all times. **HH** Rare resident in both short and seasonally flooded grasslands in NWEt at 1800–2400m (sympatric Pectoral-patch is in drier habitats); one old record in Er. Stays mainly on ground and prefers to run from danger. **Voice** Displays like Pectoral-patch including wing-snapping, but song is a burry repeated phrase, *tlii-tlii-tlii tlu-tlu-tlu...* with some variation.

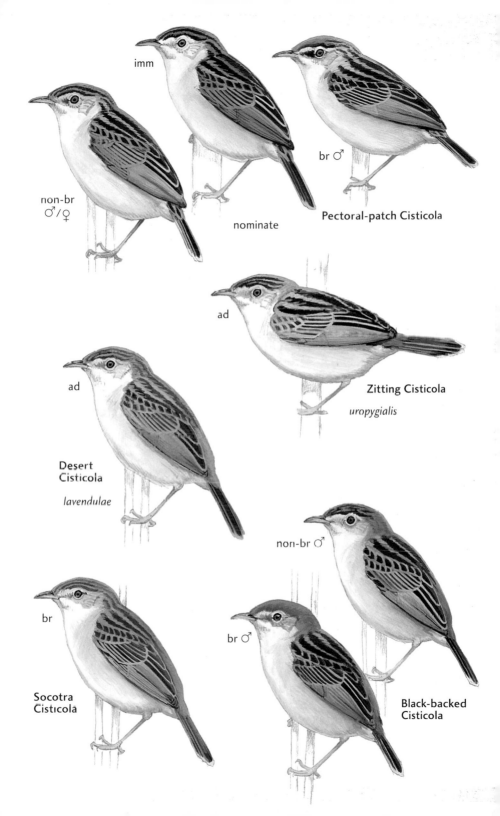

imm

non-br
♂/♀

nominate

br ♂

Pectoral-patch Cisticola

ad

ad

Zitting Cisticola

uropygialis

**Desert
Cisticola**

lavendulae

non-br ♂

br

br ♂

**Socotra
Cisticola**

**Black-backed
Cisticola**

Red-pate Cisticola *Cisticola ruficeps*   10cm, 4"

Slightly larger and longer-tailed than Tiny, with two different seasonal plumages. Breeding adult has *dull chestnut crown and nape, and plain slightly browner back*. Non-breeding adult has bright rufous crown and nape, heavily streaked back, and longer tail. Breeding adult may also show narrow white supercilium which is more obvious in non-breeding plumage. Immature is like non-breeding adult but duller and yellowish below. Two races occur: *mongalla* (SWEt) as described; *scotoptera* (NWEt, Er) slightly paler and greyer in breeding plumage, and less heavily streaked above in non-breeding plumage. **HH** Rare resident of dry bush country and wooded grasslands at 750–2300m. **Voice** Song is a ringing, penetrating and continuous piping *pi-pi-pi-pi...*

Tiny Cisticola *Cisticola nana*   9cm, 3.5"

Small short-tailed cisticola with *bright reddish crown, plain greyish-brown back* (may look very lightly streaked at close range), and buffy-white underparts; shows pale line in front of eye like Siffling Cisticola. Immature is mostly rufous above and buffy-yellow below. **HH** Pairs are frequent to common in SEt at 500–1800m, in *Commiphora* and acacia savanna, often in mixed bird parties. One old record in SSo. **Voice** Sings a rather prinia-like monotonous series of see-sawing notes or musical chittering from tops of trees and bushes. Gives a rapid set of *cht* notes in alarm.

Stout Cisticola *Cisticola robustus*   ♂ 14cm, 5.5"; ♀ 11cm, 4.5"

Distinctive large highland cisticola, with rufous crown thinly streaked black, *unstreaked tawny or rufous nape, and heavily streaked back*; rufous-buff fringes on flight feathers form indistinct wing-panel; tail blackish with obvious buffy-white tips (most noticeable in flight). Sexes similar but female markedly smaller. Immature is yellow below with some streaking on nape. Three races occur: nominate (N&CEt) as described but darker and more rufous in non-breeding plumage; *schraderi* (CEr and adjacent NEt) slightly paler; *omo* (SWEt) darker, with blacker crown and broader black streaking on upperparts. **HH** Pairs and groups are frequent in wooded grasslands with scattered bushes and dry bushy slopes at 1500–2850m. **Voice** Song is a long rising staccato rattle, very like Lesser Whitethroat, usually given from prominent perch. **Note** Nominate birds in Et have different song from birds in E Africa, and all three races in Et might better be regarded as a single separate species.

Croaking Cisticola *Cisticola natalensis*   14cm, 5.5"

Generally a large bulky cisticola with *thick, slightly decurved bill*. Streaked dark above on paler buffy-brown (including nape), *without bright rufous in plumage*; flight feathers fringed rufous, forming warm wing-panel. Tail brown with subterminal dark spots and white tips. Sexes similar but female is notably smaller. Two races occur: *inexpectatus* (Er, Et) has brighter non-breeding plumage; *argenteus* (SSo, SEt) has perennial plumage slightly paler than non-breeding *inexpectatus* with browner wing-panel. **HH** Pairs are uncommon but widespread in tall grasslands with scattered bushes at 750–3300m. **Voice** Unique among cisticolas, has a drawn-out nasal call terminating in short explosive note, *tk'weeeeeeee-chunk*, and a repeated see-sawing metallic *tink-tonk...*, first note higher.

Siffling Cisticola *Cisticola brachypterus*   11cm, 4.5"

Rather drab variable species (paler on lores with beady-eyed look), best told by song. Density of streaking above varies seasonally, being less distinct in breeding birds and heavier in non-breeding. Buffish below with whiter throat, tail dull brown with dark subterminal spots and white tips. Two races occur: *zedlitzi* (Er, Et) is tinged rufous on crown and wings; *reichenowi* (SSo) has slightly rustier crown and perennial plumage. Immature is yellow below. **HH** Frequent to common in bushed grasslands and open forest edge, often singing from tops of small trees, up to 2100m. **Voice** Quiet, high-pitched song varies locally, but is usually a repeated series of three or more sibilant descending notes, *si-si-siu si-si-siu...* [Alt: Short-winged Cisticola]

Foxy Cisticola *Cisticola troglodytes*   10cm, 4"

Adult is small, distinctive, short-tailed cisticola, uniquely entirely *plain bright rufous above* (including tail), *pale buff below* with paler throat and belly. Sexes alike. Immature is duller above and yellow below. **HH** Localised and generally uncommon in wooded grasslands at 750–1650m in WEt, where it creeps around in low bushes but flies to tree-tops when flushed. **Voice** Common call is a rapid series of harsh chat-like *tat-tat-tat-tat-...* and a *tiptiptiptip...* Rarely heard song is a long series of nasal chips and slurs.

non-br

scotoptera

Red-pate Cisticola

non-br

br

br

Tiny Cisticola

mongalla

imm

♀

nominate

♂

omo

br ♂

Stout Cisticola

non-br

Siffling Cisticola

zedlitzi

br

♂

♀

**Croaking
Cisticola**

inexpectatus

Foxy Cisticola

ferrugineus

Ethiopian Cisticola *Cisticola (galactotes) lugubris* 13cm, 5"

Breeding adult is typically boldly streaked black and grey on mantle, with *rufous-brown crown and obvious rufous wing-panel*; tail is greyish-brown with dark subterminal spots and white tips. Underparts rich buff. In non-breeding plumage, tail is longer and entire upperparts are brighter rufous, with prominent black streaks on crown. Immature is washed yellowish below. **HH** ENDEMIC to Er and Et. Common in reeds, sedges and rank vegetation in highlands, at 700–4000m. Usually near water, but also in highland grassland and savanna. **Voice** Varies from complex and musical 'winds' to much more simple trills, often with set of squeaky upslurs, *wiii wiii wiii...* **Note** Recently split from Rufous-winged Cisticola *C. galactotes* (= Winding Cisticola).

Coastal Cisticola *Cisticola (galactotes) haematocephala* 12cm, 5"

Like Ethiopian Cisticola but much duller on crown (sometimes with some diffuse streaking), with pale face, less distinct back-streaking, and *dull* rufous wing-panel. Sexes alike, and plumages similar all year. **HH** Locally common in wetland habitats in SSo, but also occurs in drier scrubby bush. **Voice** Call is a monotonous short raspy prinia-like trill. **Note** Recently split from Rufous-winged Cisticola *C. galactotes* (= Winding Cisticola).

Winding Cisticola *Cisticola (galactotes) marginatus* 12cm, 5"

Very like Ethiopian Cisticola but slightly smaller with brighter rufous crown in breeding plumage; less boldly streaked above, paler buff below. Almost identical to Ethiopian in non-breeding plumage. **HH** Common in lowlands of WEt, in rank grass, along streams and in marshy areas. **Voice** Call is like a ratcheting fishing-reel *rrrrrrrrrrrrrr.* **Note** Usually considered conspecific with Rufous-winged Cisticola *C. galactotes* of southern Africa.

Rattling Cisticola *Cisticola chiniana* 14cm, 5.5"

Familiar dry-country species with pale lores and no supercilium; *crown and nape lightly washed dull rufous and lightly streaked*, with medium-dense streaked back, and *no obvious rufous wing-panel*; tail brown with dark subterminal spots and whitish tips. Sexes alike; non-breeding birds brighter above. Immature is buffier above and washed yellowish below. Croaking Cisticola has much heavier bill. Ethiopian has much brighter crown and wing-panel. Most similar to Boran. **HH** Race *fricki* is common in much of Et and CEr in open bush and grassland at 600–2000m. Usually in cover near ground, but scolds and calls from bush tops. **Voice** Song is 3–5 squeaky downslurs followed by lower scolding rattle, *wiu-wiu-wiu-chuchuchuchuch.* Call note is a rather nasal tit-like *chht.*

Boran Cisticola *Cisticola bodessa* 14cm, 5.5"

Very like Rattling but *crown plain dull brown* (without rufous and virtually unstreaked), and back not as heavily streaked. Best told by voice. Two races occur: nominate (SEt) and darker *kaffensis* (Kaffa Prov., SWEt). **HH** Pairs are locally common, occurring on rocky hillsides with some bush and cover, usually at 900–1600m. Prefers thicker, lusher habitats than Rattling, and on steeper slopes, but both species occur together in some places. **Voice** Song is distinctive, fast and clear, commencing with *chik-chik-chik* followed by a liquid descending *chewewewewewewe.*

Singing Cisticola *Cisticola cantans* 14cm, 5.5"

Breeding adult has *rufous crown and wing-panel* contrasting with plain grey-brown back, and is buffy-white below washed grey on flanks. Lores dark. Non-breeding adult of nominate race (Er and Et) has dark streaks on upperparts. **HH** Fairly common in fairly dense vegetation at forest edge or in scrubby areas, around cultivation and in rank undergrowth, at 1800–2450m. **Voice** Despite name, song is very simple: typically male first delivers loud chips and then an explosive paired *whi-chip whi-chip...*, female joining in with dry raspy churrs or the same.

Red-faced Cisticola *Cisticola erythrops* 14cm, 5.5"

Like Singing Cisticola, but adult has *rusty wash extending over face and ear-coverts*, yellowish-brown crown and *no contrasting rufous wing-panel*; underparts rich rufous-buff. Immature is more rufous-brown above. Two races occur: *pyrrhomitra* (most of Et) and slightly paler *niloticus* (extreme WEt). **HH** Fairly common in luxuriant vegetation, often near streams or lakes, at 750–2100m. **Voice** Song is a loud complex rather rhythmic duet: generally male gives a nasal *zwink* and *chip-wee* notes and female utters rising piping squeaks, *hoo-hoo-hoo-wiwiwi.*

Ethiopian Cisticola

lugubris

imm

ad

Coastal Cisticola

haematocephala

br

Winding Cisticola

marginatus

ad

Singing Cisticola

br

nominate

non-br

Boran Cisticola

ad

Rattling Cisticola

fricki

ad

Red-faced Cisticola

pyrrhomitra

ad

Ashy Cisticola *Cisticola cinereolus*   13cm, 5″

Slim ashy-grey or grey-brown cisticola, uniformly and heavily streaked above and *no rufous* in plumage; brownish tail with dark subterminal spots and white tips. Two races, showing slight variation: nominate (NEEt and NSo) and *schillingsi* (SEt and SSo). Most sympatric cisticolas have some rufous on crown. Boran has rich brown unstreaked crown and Desert is much smaller. **HH** Locally common in dry bush country from sea-level to 2500m. **Voice** Song is a pretty liquid descending whistled refrain, *si-swi-si-swi-siwoo*. Calls are a pinched nasal *tsit* and *tseent*.

Socotra Warbler *Incana incana*   13cm, 5″

Small plain warbler with *distinctly long bill*, upperparts uniform greyish sandy-brown with *crown tinged rufous*. Graduated tail is darker brown with blackish subterminal bands and white tips visible from below. Underparts greyish-white. Sexes alike. Socotra Cisticola (plate 156), the only other warbler on Soc, is smaller and heavily streaked, with shorter bill. **HH** ENDEMIC to Soc, occupying dense low scrub in variety of habitats including coastal sand-dunes, in foothills and on higher mountain slopes up to 1400m. **Voice** Song is described as a quiet unmusical trill or spluttering series of identical notes. Call is a chattering or scolding *chip-chip, chip, chip-chip...* **Note** Sometimes placed in *Cisticola* but has similarities to *Prinia* or even *Sylvia*.

PRINIAS *Small active warblers, usually found in the undergrowth, which frequently cock and wave their long tails from side to side. Sexes alike.*

Tawny-flanked Prinia *Prinia subflava*   12cm, 5″

Typical birds are pale brown or grey-brown, with obvious pale supercilium, narrow dark eye-line, off-white throat and breast, and *belly and flanks washed pale tawny-buff*. Immature is washed yellowish below. Three races occur: nominate (W&CEt), *pallescens* (NWEt, WEr) and *melanorhyncha* (SSo), differing mainly in amount of grey or brown above. **HH** Pairs are common and widespread, usually active low down in all habitats except forest interior and arid areas, from sea-level to 3300m. **Voice** Simple unmusical song consists of rapid-fire *tititititititititit...* or rasping *zhertzhertzhert...* Also a buzzy scolding *jeee jeee...*

Pale Prinia *Prinia somalica*   11cm, 4.5″

Very like Tawny-flanked but generally paler, *whiter below* with no tawny wash on flanks. Immature is washed pale buff on breast and flanks. Two races occur: *erlangeri* (SEt, S&CSo) is pale greyish-brown above; nominate (NSo and adjacent Et) paler and sandier. **HH** Single birds and pairs inhabit dry bush country with or without grass cover, from sea-level to 1500m, preferring drier situations to Tawny-flanked where ranges overlap. **Voice** Song differs from Tawny-flanked in being a rattle of dry cricket-like notes lasting 4–5 secs, *zherzherzherzherzher...*

Graceful Prinia *Prinia gracilis*   14cm, 5.5″

Small, short-winged, long-tailed prinia with *fine streaking on crown* and more diffuse streaking on mantle. Cisticola-like, but frequently jerked and cocked long, *strongly graduated tail* typical of prinias. Black subterminal bars and white tips to rectrices show prominently on undertail. Sexes alike, but female has paler bill. Both Plain and Pale Prinias have obvious pale supercilium and are unstreaked. **HH** Race *carlo* is common resident in coastal areas of Er, Dj and NSo, also occurring inland along Awash valley in Et and on SESo coast. Inhabits wadis with tamarisks, *Suaeda* bushes on coastal flats, young mangroves and low thorn scrub, up to 400m. **Voice** Song is a monotonous series of disyllabic notes *zerwit'zerwit'zerwit'zerwit...* Call is a drawn-out rattling trill *trrrrrrt*.

Red-winged Warbler *Heliolais erythropterus*   14cm, 5.5″

Rather like a prinia, but lacks broad supercilium. Breeding adult of race *major* has *dark rufous wings* which contrast with rufescent olive-brown upperparts, darker rufous forehead, and white underparts (washed cinnamon on flanks and belly). Tail is long with blackish subterminal spots and white tips. Bill black. Non-breeding adult has tawnier crown and back, with brown upper and whitish lower mandible. Sexes alike. **HH** Singles and pairs are uncommon and local in long grass within open woodland in WEt, at 750–1800m. Often in undergrowth, but flies to tree-top if disturbed or displaying. **Voice** Varies locally, but song is always strident and based around a repeated sharp *chip* or nasal downslur; also a prinia-like *chtchtchtcht...*, *siusiusiusiu...*

Ashy Cisticola

ad

schillingsi

ad

Socotra Warbler

ad

imm

Tawny-flanked Prinia

ad

nominate

ad

Pale Prinia

Graceful Prinia

carlo

erlangeri

non-br

br

Red-winged Warbler

major

Cricket Warbler *Spiloptila clamans* 13cm, 5"

Distinctive pale warbler with *scaly black-and-white forehead and crown*, cinnamon mantle and prominent *black-and-white wing-coverts*. Fairly long, strongly graduated tail is grey with black subterminal bars and white tips. Underparts uniformly pale cream. Sexes similar, but female is shorter-tailed and less well-marked on crown; nape is sandy-cinnamon. Immature is duller with streaky crown. **HH** Formerly common resident in WEr, at 1000–1400m, in variety of savannas, but few recent records. Occurs singly or in pairs, sometimes in family groups, feeding actively in bushes or on ground. Tail is continually moved up and down or side to side. **Voice** Usual song is an insect-like slow musical trill; this is interspersed with a variety of chips and squeaks. [Alt: Scaly-fronted Warbler]

Red-fronted Warbler *Urorhipis rufifrons* 11cm, 4.5"

Small warbler with *variable amount of rufous on forecrown and crown*, smoky-grey back and whitish underparts. Long narrow white-tipped blackish tail is habitually *cocked and waved from side to side*. Two races occur: nominate (Er, NEEt, Dj, NWSo) has rufous on forehead only; *smithi* C&SEt, So except NW) has rufous extending onto crown, broad pale edges and tips to secondaries and wing-coverts. Immature lacks rufous on forecrown. **HH** Singles and pairs are fairly common in dry bush from sea-level to 1700m, endlessly seeking insects in low dry vegetation, rarely far above ground. **Voice** Lively song is a long varied medley of nasal buzzes and chips (each note repeated many times before next). Call is a harsh repeated nasal slur. [Alt: Red-fronted Apalis; formerly *Spiloptila rufifrons*]

APALISES Small, fairly long-tailed warblers usually found in pairs or small groups, actively moving through the foliage as they search for food.

Yellow-breasted Apalis *Apalis flavida* 13cm, 5"

Complex species with several races variously placed in two groups based on tail colour and voice. All forms are greenish above with varying amounts of grey on crown, and have *yellow across breast*; many also have *small black breast-spot*. Three races occur: *abyssinica* (SWEt highlands in mainly broadleaved forest) has grey crown and olive-green upperparts and tail. In semi-arid acacia scrub, *flavocincta* (SEt lowlands and SSo) has grey forehead, green crown, *brownish uppertail* (but outer two pairs yellowish, making it hard to see in field) and often lacks black breast-spot; and *viridiceps* (N&CSo and adjacent SEEt) has an almost entirely green crown, olive suffusion on breast and *brownish uppertail*. **HH** Pairs are common and widespread in variety of woodland, riverine forest, bush, gardens and cultivation from sea-level to 1950m. **Voice** Race *flavocincta* sings a monotonous dry rasping duet, male calling *krik-krik-krik...*, female accompanying with very quiet throaty growls. Green-tailed birds have slower, more distinctive rhythm like galloping horse, male calling *chirrit-chirrit-chirrit-...*, female accompanying with rising nasal *eek eek eek eek...* **Note** Races *viridiceps* and *flavocincta* are sometimes considered a separate species: Brown-tailed Apalis *A. viridiceps*.

Black-headed Apalis *Apalis melanocephala* 13cm, 5"

Black and white apalis with *largely black tail with white tips*. Male of nominate race (SSo) is very black above (especially on crown and face) with yellowish-brown eyes. Female is typically paler and more olivaceous-grey above. Both sexes are entirely white below. **HH** Locally fairly common resident in lower Jubba valley and Boni Forest in SSo. Usually in pairs in forest canopy and middle levels, frequently in mixed bird parties. **Voice** Song is a typical monotonous apalis-like chipping: a sibilant *tiree-tiree-tiree-tiree...* repeated 4–5 times and then again after a pause of varying length.

Cricket Warbler

imm

♂

Red-fronted Warbler

ad

ad

nominate

smithi

imm

Yellow-breasted Apalis

flavocincta

abyssinica

viridiceps

Black-headed Apalis

♂

♀

nominate

PLATE 161: *MELAENORNIS* AND *BRADORNIS* FLYCATCHERS

SLATY FLYCATCHER *A dark highland flycatcher, larger than most* Muscicapa *species and darker than* Bradornis. *Sexes alike.*

Abyssinian Slaty Flycatcher *Melaenornis chocolatinus* 16cm, 6"

Adult is nondescript grey-brown flycatcher with prominent *yellow eye*. Upperparts wholly dark brown with greyish tinge, underparts smoky-grey with buffy wash, paler on belly. Two races occur: nominate (most of range) and *reichenowi* (WEt), which has throat and breast greyer and slightly darker. Immature dark brown, spotted buff above and scaled below. Much darker above than Pale or Grey Flycatchers. **HH** ENDEMIC to Er and Et. Common in woodland and forest edge in highlands, often near streams, at 1800–3200m. Hunts in canopy and from lower branches. **Voice** Call is an insect-like loud rapid *si-si-si-si*.

BLACK FLYCATCHERS *Two similar flycatchers best identified by overall colour, song and range. These are typical flycatchers sitting quietly with an upright posture for long periods. Larger than most* Muscicapa. *Sexes alike. Also consider other black birds like cuckooshrikes (plate 133), boubous (plate 176-7) and drongos (plate 182).*

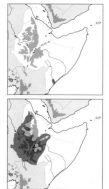

Southern Black Flycatcher *Melaenornis pammelaina* 18cm, 7"

Adult is very like Northern Black Flycatcher, but is *glossy blue-black* (not dull black); eye dark brown. Immature is dull black, spotted above with buff and scalloped below. For differences from Northern Black and other confusables see that species. **HH** A rare resident of lower Jubba riverine forest in SSo. **Voice** Song is very complex, sweet and warbler-like.

Northern Black Flycatcher *Melaenornis edolioides* 18cm, 7"

Two races occur: in Er and WEt the more widespread *lugubris* is totally *dull slate-black* with dark brown eyes, while in N&EEt *schistaceus* is dull grey-black. Immature is streaked tawny on crown, more heavily spotted tawny elsewhere. Similar drongos have red eyes, black boubous have horizontal posture, cuckooshrikes are restless and usually have obvious yellow gape. **HH** Widespread in much of Er and Et (not overlapping with Southern Black), occupying woodland, dry bush country and cultivated areas at 500–2100m. **Voice** Song is very different from Southern Black, rather slow and sibilant, with many drawn-out burry slurs and occasional soft nasal chips.

BRADORNIS *FLYCATCHERS A widespread pair of similar-looking, medium-sized flycatchers. Note presence or absence of crown- or breast-streaking, and consider voice and range. Sexes are alike. Immatures are spotted and streaked above with tawny or buff, and mottled below.*

African Grey Flycatcher *Bradornis microrhynchus* 14cm, 5.5"

Very like Pale Flycatcher but usually rather smaller and greyer: best told by grey-brown plumage with *fine blackish streaks on crown* and stronger contrast between pale throat and darker breast. Bill black. From Spotted Flycatcher by absence of breast-streaking. Three races occur: *neumanni* (SEt and C&SSo) as described, *pumilus* (C&EEt and NSo) larger, darker and browner, especially below; *burae* (extreme SSo) paler, greyer and smaller than *neumanni*. **HH** Pairs and family groups are common and widespread in dry bush and open wooded acacia country from near sea-level to 1600m; where ranges overlap, Pale occupies locally more verdant broadleaved habitat. **Voice** Commonly heard alarm is a rather nasal scraping *shree-shree*. Rarely heard song is a complex, variable and continuous warble with mostly harsh and scratchy notes. **Note** Formerly in genus *Melaenornis*.

Pale Flycatcher *Bradornis pallidus* 17cm, 6.5"

Six races occur, varying slightly in size and overall colour: all best separated from African Grey Flycatcher by uniform *brown crown with no streaking*, prominent tan edgings on primaries and horn base to lower mandible. Western and southern races are generally larger and browner; in SSo, *erlangeri* is smaller and more sandy-brown with striking sexual size dimorphism, and may be a separate species. **HH** Always in lusher, more wooded habitats than African Grey, from sea-level to 2100m. **Voice** Call is a spitting note, very like Yellow-spotted Petronia, and often followed by a scratchy *shrehh*. Rarely heard song is a harsh, rather unmusical warbled *treet-etreet-et-ti-cherr et-ti-cherr...* **Note** Formerly in genus *Melaenornis*. [Alt: Mouse-coloured Flycatcher]

Abyssinian Slaty Flycatcher

imm

ad

Southern Black Flycatcher

ad

Northern Black Flycatcher

ad

ad

African Grey Flycatcher

imm

imm

ad

neumanni

ad

Pale Flycatcher

parvus

ad

erlangeri

A widespread group of similar-looking flycatchers. Muscicapa are small or medium-sized typical flycatchers, sitting upright for long periods and then making short flights, or dropping to ground to take food. Note presence or absence of crown- or breast-streaking, and consider voice and range. Sexes alike. Immatures are spotted above and mottled below. The single species of migrant Ficedula in region has a distinctive black-and-white breeding male plumage, but most birds seen are brown and white.

African Dusky Flycatcher *Muscicapa adusta* 10cm, 4"

Small, rather dumpy flycatcher, uniform dark brown above, paler buff-brown below, with pale loral spot and creamy-whitish throat and belly; base of lower mandible yellowish. Familiar and widespread African species represented by race *minima* in our region. Readily told from other small brown flycatchers by small size and short-tailed appearance. **HH** Very common in highland forest, riverine woodland and gardens, at 1350–3000m. Typical flycatcher, making short flights and returning to favourite exposed perch. **Voice** Song is a high-pitched, continuous series of varied unmusical squeaks and hisses, sounding a little chat-like.

Ashy Flycatcher *Muscicapa caerulescens* 14cm, 5.5"

Slim flycatcher, plain ash-grey or blue-grey above with narrow dark line through eye, short whitish line from base of bill to above eye, and small indistinct broken eye-ring. Greyish-white below, paler on throat and belly. Very similar Lead-coloured Flycatcher (plate 163) has horizontal posture often with fanned, white-edged tail held over back. **HH** Fairly common presumed resident in forests of SSo, mostly in Boni Forest (race *cinereola*). Usually seen as 2–3 together, often in mixed bird parties, in canopy and middle levels of forest edge, clearings, and along well-wooded rivers. **Voice** Call is a descending series of spaced, harsh but musical chips, *trit tit tit it*, which may break into a flourish. Song is a sweet chat-like warble. [Alt: Blue-grey Flycatcher]

Gambaga Flycatcher *Muscicapa gambagae* 13cm, 5"

Slightly smaller than Spotted Flycatcher but larger than African Dusky with which it is frequently confused. Head rounded with plain forecrown, indistinctly streaked hindcrown, browner, more diffuse streaking on breast, and yellowish base to lower mandible. Closed wing only reaches base of tail. **HH** Uncommon solitary resident of dry bush and open wooded country in W&CEt, at 750–1700m; apparently fairly common in dry montane forest at 1800–1970m on Mt Wagar in NSo. Uncommon migrant Dj. Usually flicks wings when landing after short flights, like a *Ficedula* flycatcher. **Voice** Call consists of a repeated series of paired and single clicks, like snapping of dry twig, *t'lik t'lik...*, unlike anything by Spotted. Agitated birds give distinctive explosive *tik-tik* from exposed perch; rarely heard song is a sweet warble.

Spotted Flycatcher *Muscicapa striata* 14cm, 5.5"

Medium-sized slim grey-brown flycatcher, paler below with *streaked crown and breast* (sometimes obscure) and black bill. Hind-crown seems peaked, wings pointed and long, reaching halfway down tail. Two races occur: nominate and *neumanni*, latter paler above, whiter below. **HH** Common and widespread Palearctic passage migrant, Aug–Nov and Mar–May; may occur in any habitat from sea-level to 2500m. Vagrant Soc. **Voice** Song is not heard in region, but still quite vocal: call is a harsh *chick*.

Semi-collared Flycatcher *Ficedula semitorquata* 13cm, 5"

Breeding male has one or two small white patches on forecrown, *half-collar on hindneck*, and extensive white in wing including small white patch at base of primaries and white-tipped median coverts forming second wing-bar. *Open tail shows wheatear-like pattern, with much white in outertail bases.* Breeding female is grey-brown above, with variable but often paler rump; *white tips to median coverts form second wing-bar,* and white patch at base of primaries is intermediate in size between extralimital Collared and Pied Flycatchers. Non-breeding male is like female but much blacker on wings and tail; differs from non-breeding male Collared by distinct white tips to median coverts. First-year is like adult female but browner. **HH** Uncommon Palearctic passage migrant in Er and Et at 750–2400m, Aug–Oct, in various wooded habitats; scarce in spring (Apr). Usual confusion species, Collared and Pied Flycatchers, never recorded in our region. **Voice** Variously reported as an occasional sharp *eeet, eeep,* or *tec.* **NT**.

imm

ad

African Dusky Flycatcher

minima

imm

ad

Ashy Flycatcher

cinereola

imm

Gambaga Flycatcher

ad

ad

Spotted Flycatcher

♀

imm

♂

Semi-collared Flycatcher

MONARCH FLYCATCHERS *In our region, the monarchs (Monarchidae) are represented by a single species from each of three rather distinctive genera. The paradise flycatcher (Terpsiphone) is unmistakable with a long rufous or white tail. The crested flycatcher (Trochocercus) is a dark grey, black and white monarch with a long crest that may be erected when excited. It is restless and frequently fans its tail. Little Yellow Flycatcher (Erythrocercus) is a very small monarch with a rather warbler-like appearance. Sexes are alike.*

African Paradise Flycatcher *Terpsiphone viridis*   18cm, 7" (plus 18cm tail in ♂)

Highly variable with two distinct colour morphs, white and rufous, and many variations. Only race in our region is *ferreti*. Typical rufous adult male has slightly crested black or blue-black head merging into *grey underparts*, chestnut mantle, wings and tail with very long central tail feathers, belly and undertail-coverts greyish-buff. Typical white morph male has mantle, wings and tail white. Rufous birds with partially white wings and white central tail feathers are also common. Adult female and immatures of both sexes are like rufous male but with shorter tails. **HH** Single birds or pairs are common and widespread in forest, open woodland, gardens and bush from sea-level to 2600m. White birds are commoner in dry country. **Voice** Song is a loud, scratchy, nasal and cheerful warbling, sometimes breaking into a rhythmical *pi-pi-pi-pi pi-pi-pi-pi pi-pi*, falling very slightly in pitch towards end.

Blue-mantled Crested Flycatcher *Trochocercus cyanomelas*   13cm, 5"

Black-and-white crested flycatcher with white in wings and plain dark tail. Adult male has long pointed crest, glossy blue-black head and upper breast, dark blue-grey mantle, and white lower breast to vent. Eastern race *bivittatus* male has prominent white wing-patch. Female is grey above, with mottled grey-and-white breast and two narrow whitish wing-bars. Immature is like female but has buffy edges to wing-coverts. **HH** Locally common presumed resident in undergrowth and denser middle levels of riverine forest in SSo, mainly along Jubba river; often joins mixed-species flocks. **Voice** Vocal and noisy: usual call is several rising nasal scratchy slurs (similar to African Paradise Flycatcher), often followed by a run of rapid, pure, rather hollow bell-like notes, *wiu-pupupupupupupu....* [Alt: Blue-mantled Flycatcher]

Little Yellow Flycatcher *Erythrocercus holochlorus*   9cm, 3.5"

Plain yellowish-olive above with rather obvious dark eye (narrowly ringed yellow) and pink lower mandible, and bright yellow underparts. Immature is very similar, but slightly paler. **HH** An uncommon presumed resident in riverine forest in SSo, mainly along Jubba river and in Boni Forest. Occurs in high and middle canopy, often in mixed-species flocks, or low down along forest edges. **Voice** Noisy despite tiny size, with a complex, cheerful chittering song breaking into a silvery descending series of clear notes.

Lead-coloured Flycatcher *Myioparus plumbeus*   14cm, 5.5"

Blue- or ashy-grey above with blackish tail and *white outertail feathers*, greyish-white below. Only darker nominate race occurs in our region. Generally resembles Ashy Flycatcher (plate 162) but moves with horizontal posture, frequently waving and fanning tail over back. Immature is washed brownish above with small buffy wing-spots. **HH** Singles and pairs are widespread but local and generally uncommon in canopy of variety of woodland in W&CEt at 700–2400m. **Voice** Far-carrying song consists of long pure burry notes, starting with a long note, quickly followed by a shorter higher note of the same quality. [Alt: Fan-tailed Flycatcher, Grey Tit-Flycatcher]

Silverbird *Empidornis semipartitus*   18cm, 7"

Distinctive flycatcher, silvery-grey above, rufous-orange below. Sexes are alike. Immature is heavily spotted above with creamy-buff and black, and mottled and patched buff, brown and orange below. **HH** Pairs or single birds are uncommon in WEt, at 450–750m; type collected in NWEt at Gonder. Occurs in wooded acacia and bushed grassland and at edges of cultivation. Sits out in open and drops to feed on ground. **Voice** Infrequent song is sweetest of flycatchers: random short phrases with thrush-like pattern but chat-like delivery, *swi-sisi sir wi-wir...*

African Paradise
Flycatcher

ferreti

♀

♂

♂

white
morph

♀

imm

Blue-mantled
Crested Flycatcher

bivittatus

♂

Silverbird

ad

Little Yellow
Flycatcher

imm

ad

ad

Lead-coloured
Flycatcher

BATISES *Small, neat and boldly patterned black, white and grey birds with yellow eyes and black (adult male) or chestnut (female and immature) breast-bands. Usually found in pairs. Only three species in region but can be confusingly similar. Colour of crown, extent of supercilium, throat and breast markings, voice and range all aid identification.*

Pygmy Batis *Batis perkeo* 9cm, 3.5"

Small, rather short-tailed batis: adult male has grey crown and *only a short white supraloral stripe* (may be hard to see in field). Adult female has similar supraloral, rufous-tawny breast-band and white (or very faint buff) throat. **HH** Frequent to common in semi-arid *acacia* bush country in SEt and SSo up to 1350m. **Voice** Song is a loud, high, pure piping of identical notes, *hi hi hi...*, recalling Desert Cisticola.

Grey-headed Batis *Batis orientalis* 10cm, 4"

Adult male very like Black-headed Batis, but has paler grey crown and slightly broader breast-band; from smaller Pygmy Batis by long narrow white supercilium extending almost to white nuchal spot. Adult female has similar grey crown and supercilium, but breast-band fairly broad and chestnut. Two races occur: nominate (most of range and includes 'bella') has dark grey crown and mantle; *chadensis* (extreme WEt) is smaller. **HH** Frequent to common in acacia woodland and subdesert steppe throughout most lowland Er and Et, up to 2100m; also in Dj and N&SESo. **Voice** Song is a musical descending series of four notes, unlike any other batis in region. Female often accompanies with short whipcrack upslurs.

Black-headed Batis *Batis minor* 10cm, 4"

Two races occur in region: *erlangeri* in west and nominate *minor* in east. Crown colour is variable, usually blackish, but may be greyer (particularly on eastern birds, which can then be mistaken for Grey-headed Batis). Black-crowned birds are distinctive, but greyer-crowned birds cannot be safely identified. Both Black-headed and Grey-headed have long narrow white superciliary stripes. **HH** Ranges from sea-level to 2600m: *erlangeri* is widespread and locally common in variety of woodland and open bush in Er and Et; *minor* is fairly common in bush and woodland, mainly along Jubba and Shabeelle valleys in SSo. **Voice** Varies locally; song is a series of pure pipes on identical note, *hi-hi-hi-...*, at intervals of just more than one per second, sometimes followed by series of peculiar paired nasal downslurs. **Note** The two forms are sometimes considered separate species: Eastern Black-headed Batis *B. minor* and Western Black-headed Batis *B. erlangeri*.

WATTLE-EYES *Platysteira wattle-eyes are medium-sized, flycatcher-like and resemble batises. Both species have broad strong bills, conspicuous eye-wattles, and are named after the female plumage (the males of both species have white throats). Found in pairs, family groups or with mixed-species flocks, usually in forest.*

Brown-throated Wattle-eye *Platysteira cyanea* 13cm, 5"

Adults have *bright red wattle above eye and white wing-bar*. Male has white throat and black breast-band recalling batises; female is greyer above with dark chestnut-brown throat and upper breast. Immature also has wattle and is brownish-grey above with tawny-buff wing-bar, throat and breast. **HH** Race *aethiopica* is common and widespread in middle stratum and canopy of thick bush, woodlands and forest edge at 750–2400m, mainly west of Rift Valley. **Voice** A unique syncaphonic sound: usually three minor key descending notes precede a series of up to five descending minor key notes; some notes burry and scratchy. Female may give scratchier accompaniment. [Alt: Common Wattle-eye]

Black-throated Wattle-eye *Platysteira peltata* 13cm, 5"

Adult like Brown-throated Wattle-eye with bright red wattles above eye, but has *no white in wing*. Male has white throat and narrow black breast-band. Female has throat and breast black. Immature is browner above with tawny edges to wings, and buffy wash on throat. **HH** Fairly common presumed resident in Jubba riverine river in SSo. **Voice** Song is a monotonous repeated series of rhythmic scratchy notes followed by a nasal buzzy see-sawing *ch'ch'ch'... in-cherin-cherin-cherin-cherinch*, often in duet. [Alt: Wattle-eyed Flycatcher]

Pygmy Batis

♀

♂

Grey-headed Batis

♀

♂

Black-headed Batis

♀

♂

erlangeri

nominate ('bella')

imm

Brown-throated Wattle-eye

♂

♀

Black-throated Wattle-eye

♂

♀

imm

HILL BABBLER Solitary, small babbler, related to African Illadopsis species (none in Horn of Africa), but forages at middle levels rather than on the ground. Attractive fluty song is unlike other African babblers.

African Hill Babbler *Pseudoalcippe abyssinica*   13cm, 5"

Widespread nominate race has *grey head and breast*, reddish-brown upperparts, whitish belly and undertail-coverts, and brownish patch on flanks. Sexes alike. **HH** Singles and pairs are common in highland forest of Et, inhabiting tangled vines and undergrowth at 1300–3000m. **Voice** Sings a variety of repeated thrush-like rich fluty warbles, but notes are often slurred together. [Alt: Abyssinian Hill Babbler]

TURDOIDES BABBLERS These babblers typically occur in groups of 4–10 birds, moving together between patches of cover, and also feeding in open ground. Slim and unobtrusive chatterers make frequent contact with quiet high-pitched calls. The bulkier babblers are noisy birds, regularly giving a harsh loud babbling. Underparts pattern, eye colour and range aid identification. Sexes alike. Immatures are similar to adults but dark-eyed.

White-headed Babbler *Turdoides leucocephala*   23cm, 9"

Pale desert species with white head and mainly brown plumage. Pale tips of throat and breast feathers give scaly effect. Eye yellow. Differs from white-headed forms of White-rumped Babbler in paler plumage and *lack of white rump*. Immature has dusky-white head and dark eyes. **HH** Common in dense scrub in wadis and dry acacia woodland in WEr and NWEt, at 700–1400m. Noisy and inquistive, living in parties of up to 12 birds. **Voice** A continuous string of rattling *churr* notes, lasting for 30 secs or more.

White-rumped Babbler *Turdoides leucopygia*   25cm, 10"

Large variable highland babbler always with *white rump*. Five races occur in our region: *smithii* (NWSo to E&SEEt) prominently scaly with greyish-white face; nominate *leucopygia* (CEr to NEt) less scaly with whole head white; *limbata* (WEr to NWEt) like *smithii* but less scaly and with white forehead; *lacuum* (Rift Valley in CEt) like *smithii* but white of face confined to ear-coverts; *omoensis* (W&SWEt) like *lacuum* but lores and chin black. **HH** Near-endemic (range just extends into Sudan); frequent to common in highlands of Er, Et and NWSo, at 750–2700m. Inhabits dense scrub and bushes, light woodland and forest edge, in groups of 6–10 birds. **Voice** Long series of loud, raucous notes, sometimes ending querulously. Groups break into long rambling rattled series of notes; more musical than Scaly Babbler.

Scaly Babbler *Turdoides squamulata*   22cm, 8.5"

Dark grey-brown or olive-brown babbler, with *very dark ear-coverts* (in most populations), and pale fringes to the feathers of crown, throat and breast giving a scaly appearance; eyes orange. Rather variable with several disjunct populations. Nominate *squamulata* (extreme SSo) is all-dark; *jubaensis* (Jubba river, SSo and SEEt) is paler with a white chin; *carolinae* (Shabeelle river, SSo and SEEt) has white face. Other populations in Et may be undescribed races. Overlaps with White-rumped Babbler in Et, but distinguished by *uniform dark underparts* and *lack of white rump*. **HH** Groups are shy keeping to coastal bush and other thick cover within its restricted range; often along watercourses. **Voice** One of the most grating and toneless calls of any passerine, with a typical babbler pattern. Group keeps up continuous rasping noise that has a peculiar undulating quality. Single call is a *ti-yor ti-yor ti-yor...*

imm

ad

African Hill Babbler

ad

White-headed
Babbler

nominate

nominate

omoensis

limbula

smithii

White-rumped
Babbler

nominate

Scaly Babbler

carolinae

jubaensis

Brown Babbler *Turdoides plebejus*   22cm, 8.5"

Rather plain grey-brown babber with yellow eyes, *whitish lores and chin*, and pale tips to feathers of throat and breast. Immature is brown all over, paler below without pale tips on throat and breast, with brown eyes. **HH** Groups are frequent to locally common in SWEt (race *cinerea*) in bushed and wooded country at 700–1400m. **Voice** A very loud, raucous wooden-sounding chatter breaks into a scolding *k-tchah k-tchah k-tchah*.

Dusky Babbler *Turdoides tenebrosa*   23cm, 9"

Dark babbler with *black lores* and pale yellow or whitish eyes, crown slightly paler than rest of upperparts; chin whitish, throat to upper breast scaly, each feather with dark centre and pale fringe, rest of underparts plain dark brown. **HH** Uncommon in SWEt at 500–900m. Groups are rather shy and secretive keeping to dense cover, often near water, in bush or woodland. **Voice** Reported to call a hoarse *chow* and more nasal *what-cow...*

CHATTERERS *The three chatterers comprise a distinctive subgenus Argya. Fulvous and Rufous form a superspecies, and the former more correctly should be called Fulvous Chatterer.*

Fulvous Babbler *Turdoides fulva*   22cm, 8.5"

Large pale babbler, *sandy-brown above* with diffuse streaking, paler sandy-buff below with whitish throat. Eyes brown, legs greenish. NE African race *acaciae* has yellowish bill with dark tip. **HH** Uncommon resident in bushes and desert scrub in wadis and plains of coastal WEr, up to 300m; usually in groups of 5–6 birds. **Voice** Song is a series of fluty mournful descending whistles, the first longer and more drawn out, *peeeeooo, peeoo-peeoo-peeoo-peeoo-peeoo-peeoo*. Various calls include short *pwit* or *chitt* notes, and a metallic trill. [Alt: Fulvous Chatterer]

Rufous Chatterer *Turdoides rubiginosa*   19cm, 7.5"

Uniform brown above with very fine crown-streaks, pale yellow eyes, pale yellow or brownish bill and *bright russet-brown underparts*. Three races occur: nominate in most of Et; *bowdleri* (SEEt, SSo: Shabeelle river valley) larger; *heuglini* (SSo: Jubba river valley) darker with deeper rufous-brown underparts. **HH** Common and widespread in variety of dry bushed habitats and nearby riverine vegetation from sea-level to 1650m. **Voice** Calls are very unlike babblers, being quieter and higher-pitched: group members keep in contact with excited piercing squeaks. Song is similar, but many notes are downslurred, louder and purer with irregular chittering, and interspersed with louder downslurred *seeeu*.

Scaly Chatterer *Turdoides aylmeri*   22cm, 8.5"

Dull brown above, with *small mask of grey or pale blue skin* around yellowish eye, and rather long decurved pale horn bill. Throat and breast have scaly appearance. Two similar races occur: nominate (SEEt and So) and *boranensis* (SEt), slightly darker. **HH** Small groups are uncommon or locally common in thick bush country, particularly *Commiphora*, from sea-level to 1350m, usually in drier situations than Rufous Chatterer. **Voice** A high-pitched metallic, scraping and ratchet-like noise is usual call, often given excitably by all members of group.

CATBIRD *A distinctive endemic species in a monotypic genus. The affinities of this unique bird are unknown and it is currently grouped with the babblers. Its fine song is unlike other babblers and has been compared to nightingales. Sexes are alike.*

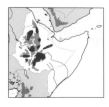

Abyssinian Catbird *Parophasma galinieri*   14cm, 5.5"

Uniformly grey, with black lores and whitish forehead. Wings and tail somewhat darker, and *belly and undertail-coverts bright orange-chestnut*. **HH** ENDEMIC to Et and unmistakable. Frequent to common in highlands of Et, inhabiting dense tangles and thickets in juniper and *Podocarpus* forest, at 1800–3600m. Sometimes found in wooded gardens in highland cities. **Voice** Song is a series of attractive fluty notes repeated without much variation, usually in duet; female answers with a long dry throaty rattle.

Brown Babbler

cinereus

Dusky Babbler

acaciae

Fulvous Babbler

nominate

Rufous Chatterer

heuglini

Scaly Chatterer

Abyssinian Catbird

TITS *A well-known family, tits are very active birds working their way along branches, gleaning leaves and buds, and often hanging upside-down. Found in pairs and small groups, they frequently join mixed-species feeding flocks. Sexes similar but females and immatures are duller than males; other differences in text.*

Northern Grey Tit *Parus thruppi*   11 cm, 4.5"

Boldly marked black, white and grey tit, with *large white cheek-patch encircled by glossy black cap, bib and collar.* Black bib extends as vertical black line down breast to belly. Two races occur: nominate (E&SEEt, NSo) and slightly paler *barakae* (SEt, SSo). **HH** Locally common in variety of dry bush country (particularly acacia), up to 1950m. **Voice** Calls and scolds are like other tits, but harsher with a more vibrating ratchet-like quality, *chrrrt-chah, chrrt chah-chah.* [Alt: Acacia Tit, Somali Tit]

White-winged Black Tit *Parus leucomelas*   14cm, 5.5"

Formerly considered conspecific with White-shouldered Tit and only reliably separated from it by *dark eyes.* Immature is duller with a creamy-buff wing-patch. **HH** Locally common in open woodland and moist bush country at 750–2300m in Er and Et, including Rift Valley and adjacent lowlands of W and SE Highlands. **Voice** Utters usual rasping calls, one sounding like Rattling Cisticola, but also has sweet thrush-like phrases quite unlike other tits in region (except White-shouldered). [Alt: Northern Black Tit]

White-shouldered Black Tit *Parus guineensis*   14cm, 5.5"

Very like White-winged Tit, but adults have *yellow eyes.* Immature is duller with grey or brown eyes and thus like immature White-winged. **HH** Fairly common in open woodland and moist bush in W&SWEt at 400–1600m. **Voice** A rather untit-like attractive and varied song with both bunting- and thrush-like qualities. **Note** Formerly lumped in White-winged Black Tit.

White-backed Black Tit *Parus leuconotus*   13cm, 5"

Small all-black tit with obvious *triangular whitish patch on back.* Juvenile similar but duller and browner; mantle with dusky brown mottling. Only confusion species is White-winged Black Tit which inhabits lower elevations and has white wing-patch instead of white on back. **HH** ENDEMIC to Er and Et. Pairs and small parties are fairly common in various wooded highland areas, including juniper, bamboo and giant heath, at 1800–3400m. **Voice** Attractive singer. Usual phrase has a metallic, rather starling-like quality, *twik-or wee-wee,* sometimes breaking into complex series of chips and warbles, more typical of genus but with fewer abrasive notes than relatives. [Alt: White-backed Tit]

CREEPER *The sole Afrotropical member of the Certhiidae, the Spotted Creeper has a curiously disjunct distribution in Africa, and the same species is also found in India (but African birds may be split as* S. salvadori *in future). It is sometimes placed in its own family, Salpornithidae.*

Spotted Creeper *Salpornis spilonotus*   15cm, 6"

Well-camouflaged mottled brown and white creeper with long decurved bill. Upperparts brown with profuse buff spotting and barring; underparts rufescent-buff with numerous cream spots. Race in region is *erlangeri.* **HH** Solitary birds or pairs are uncommon in open woodland in Rift Valley and highlands of Et, at 1800–2400m. Birds are very active, climbing up trunks or large limbs in canopy before swooping to bottom of another tree and working upwards again. Can be hard to see against lichen-covered branches and wrinkled bark. **Voice** Frequently heard call is a high-pitched *si si si si...*; song consists of different, very high-pitched toneless and rhythmical slurs, *si sisi siu siu seeu seeu.*

White-winged
Black Tit

Northern Grey Tit

nominate

White-shouldered
Black Tit

nominate

imm

ad

White-backed
Black Tit

Spotted Creeper

erlangeri

PENDULINE-TITS *Small, active tit-like birds with tiny pointed bills (almost conical), short tails and rather dull plumage. Solitary or in pairs, but also join mixed-species flocks. Sexes and immatures are alike.*

Sennar Penduline-tit *Anthoscopus punctifrons* 8.5cm, 3.25"

Tiny short-billed short-tailed bird of Sahel, *greenish above*, buffy-white below; forehead yellowish with conspicuous dark spotting. **HH** Uncommon and local in WEr, inhabiting acacias in desert or semi-desert, often in wadis, at 900–1050m. **Voice** Call is loud for size, a *siu-siu-siu-siu* alternating with a dry drawn-out rattled churr. Sometimes nasal helmetshrike-like notes are introduced.

Mouse-coloured Penduline-tit *Anthoscopus musculus* 8cm, 3"

Like Sennar Penduline-tit but grey-brown above and *very pale grey-brown below*. Immature Yellow-vented Eremomela (plate 150) has longer legs and finer bill. **HH** Widespread but never numerous in dry bushland east of Rift Valley in Et, and in NW&SSo, from near sea-level to 1650m. **Voice** Typical call is a repeated *si si si si si si si si si si* and more complex warbled series of high squeaky notes.

WHITE-EYES *Active small birds usually found in flocks. The species and many races are confusing, but markings on the underparts, size of eye-ring, and range aid identification. Sexes are alike. Identification can be problematic in areas of overlap.*

Montane White-eye *Zosterops poliogastrus* 11cm, 4.5"

Montane forest white-eye with black lores, greenish upperparts and *broad white eye-ring*. Two distinctive races occur: *kaffensis* (W&SWEt) is entirely yellow below apart from greenish flanks; nominate *poliogastrus* (Er, Et except W) has pale greyish breast and flanks and white belly; chin, throat and undertail-coverts remain yellow. **HH** Common in *highland* evergreen forest and forest edge, including isolated patches, gardens and cultivation, at 1350–3600m. **Voice** Call is a downslurred *seyuuu* and *piu*; song is a rising-and-falling series of slurred notes, rather mournful in quality. [Alt: Mountain White-eye, Broad-ringed White-eye]

Yellow White-eye *Zosterops senegalensis* 11cm, 4.5"

Typical birds are greenish-yellow above and bright yellow below (including flanks), with *narrow white eye-ring*. **HH** In our region, nominate race occurs in variety of habitats including forest, forest edge, gardens and cultivation in WEt at 750–1800m; rare in Er. Barely overlaps with yellow-bellied races of Montane and Abyssinian and can usually be separated on range and altitude. **Voice** Attractive songster; has a series of typical white-eye notes, some with a rather burry quality.

Abyssinian White-eye *Zosterops abyssinicus* 10cm, 4"

Small white-eye with *narrow white eye-ring* and often no yellow band on forehead. Lores usually show less black than Montane White-eye. Two distinct plumage-types occur: yellow-bellied and white-bellied. Race *jubaensis* (SEt and SSo) is very like Yellow White-eye (but does not overlap in range) with clear *pale yellow underparts*; yellowish-green upperparts are tinged greyish. Other races in region show bright yellow throat, *pale greyish breast and flanks with greyish-white belly*: nominate *abyssinicus* (Er and N&CEt) is greyish-green above with horn-brown bill; race *omoensis* (WEt) yellowish-green above with brown bill. Race *socotranus* (Soc and NSo), described on basis of blackish bill, brighter yellow throat and whiter underparts, included here with *abyssinicus* owing to much overlap. White-bellied races differ from nominate Montane White-eye by narrower eye-ring and preference for lower elevations, but eye-ring variable and some 'socotranus' can show broader eye-rings. **HH** Inhabits variety of woodland and scrub from sea-level to 2300m (up to 850m on Socotra), often in drier areas. Generally common throughout range. **Voice** Typical white-eye song is an excitable collection of random squeaks and descending slurs. Call is a burry descending *seeu*. [Alt: White-breasted White-eye]

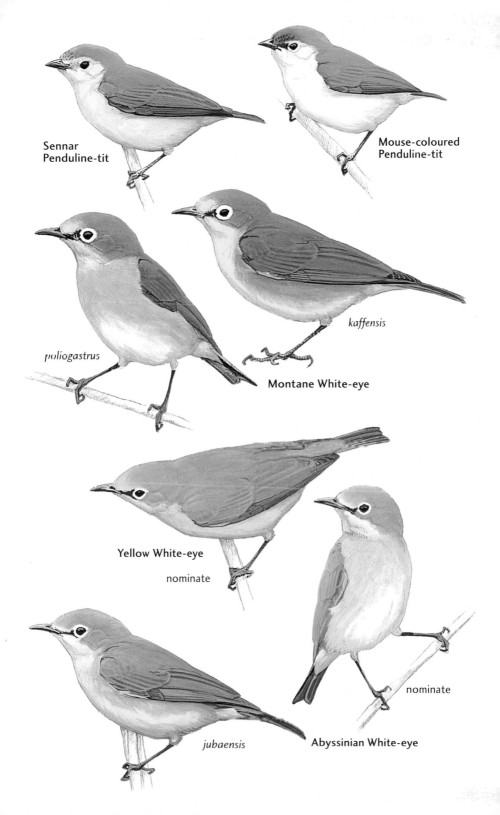

Sennar Penduline-tit

Mouse-coloured Penduline-tit

poliogastrus

kaffensis

Montane White-eye

Yellow White-eye

nominate

jubaensis

nominate

Abyssinian White-eye

Males of many sunbirds are characterised by their iridescent plumages and decurved bills. Some have long central tail feathers. Many have brightly coloured pectoral tufts which are hidden except when used in display. Females and immatures are typically dull olive or greyish, but may have distinctive eye-stripes, breast-streaking or tail colour. Non-breeding and immature males often have dark throats. Constantly on the move, they feed on nectar and insects, and can hover briefly. Song is typically fast and musically complex; distinctive calls are useful for identification.

LONG-TAILED SUNBIRDS *Males of these two larger species are readily identifiable.*

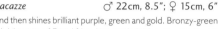

Tacazze Sunbird *Nectarinia tacazze*   ♂ 22cm, 8.5"; ♀ 15cm, 6"

Breeding male often looks very dark and then shines brilliant purple, green and gold. Bronzy-green head is like familiar Bronze Sunbird *N. kilimensis* of East Africa, but *purple back, wing-coverts and breast* distinctive. Rest of underparts sooty-black. Non-breeding male loses most iridescence. Adult female is dusky grey above, with long whitish supercilium, *dark lores, whitish malar stripe* and unstreaked paler grey below. Immature like female. **HH** Common in highland forest (including eucalyptus and acacia), cultivation, and gardens with flowering plants at 1800–3900m in Er and Et. **Voice** Call is a simple series of 4–5 notes given as a slow, deliberate descending series. Song is a loud, complex, rather liquid ramble centred on a few repeated notes.

Malachite Sunbird *Nectarinia famosa*   ♂ 24cm, 9.5"; ♀ 14cm, 5.5"

Breeding male is slim, *very bright, uniform electric emerald-green* sunbird with yellow pectoral tufts. Non-breeding male is like female but often retains some bright green on wings and rump. Adult female and immature are dusky-brown above, yellowish below, washed darker olive across breast. Immature male may have dark throat. Race in region is *cupreonitens.* **HH** Solitary birds or pairs are uncommon inhabitants of montane grasslands, moorlands and forest edges, at 1800–3000m, where they are particularly fond of *Kniphofia* and *Lobelia* flowers, occasionally moving to lower altitudes. **Voice** Call is a metallic, rather explosive *sit.* Song is *sit* note repeated and speeded up, before ending in a rattled descending flourish.

DARK SUNBIRDS *The males of these two shorter-tailed species look all-dark unless seen in good light.*

Copper Sunbird *Cinnyris cupreus*   13cm, 5"

Breeding male has *fiery-copper head, mantle and upper breast* with blacker wings and tail, and bright gold or red (depending on angle) shoulder. Non-breeding male is more like female but with a few random iridescent feathers. Female is olive-brown above with blackish tail, and dull yellow below. Immature is like female but with dark throat on immature male. **HH** Nominate race is locally common in WEt in lightly wooded areas, bush country, fringes of swamps and cultivation at 750–2700m. **Voice** One song is like a bouncing ball, *tit tit tit tit tttttttttt,* and there is a similar series that breaks into a twittering flourish. [Alt: Coppery Sunbird]

Amethyst Sunbird *Chalcomitra amethystina*   14cm, 5.5"

Adult male sometimes appears all black, but in good light shows small *iridescent blue-green cap and golden to claret throat-patch.* Small patch on bend of wing is iridescent fiery-amethyst. Adult female has narrow white supercilium and is streaked below: similar female Scarlet-chested Sunbird (plate 170) lacks supercilium and is mottled below. Immature is like female but with dark throat. **HH** Absent from most of region, but race *kalckreuthi* is uncommon resident in secondary woodland and forest edge along Jubba river in SSo. **Voice** Calls include scratchy chirps and a sweeter *seet.* Song is not unlike a small *Acrocephalus* in quality. [Alt: Black Sunbird]

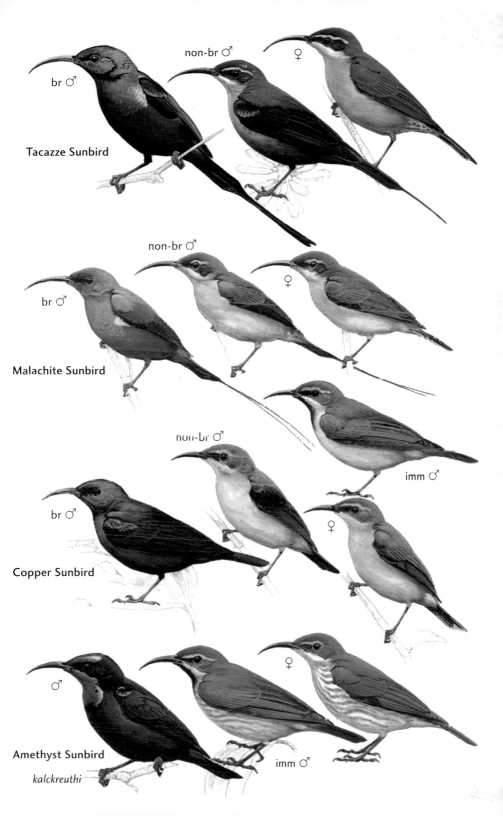

Tacazze Sunbird
br ♂
non-br ♂
♀

Malachite Sunbird
br ♂
non-br ♂
♀
imm ♂

Copper Sunbird
br ♂
non-br ♂
♀

Amethyst Sunbird
kalckreuthi
♂
♀
imm ♂

BLACK AND RED SUNBIRDS *Two very similar, fairly large, short-tailed species with striking black and red plumage in the males, and long curved bills; they are best separated by habitat, range and altitude.*

Scarlet-chested Sunbird *Chalcomitra senegalensis* 15cm, 6"

Adult male is very like Hunter's Sunbird with brilliant scarlet breast and small iridescent green cap. Most races have green throat, but race *proteus* (formerly *cruentata*) in our region has sooty-black chin and throat bordered by metallic green moustachial stripes (like Hunter's) but differs by *prominent blue barring on breast*. Adult female is dark brown above with no supercilium, and dirty yellowish-white below, mottled brown. Immature male is like female but with some dull red feathers on breast. Immature female is like female with blackish throat. **HH** Usually in pairs but sometimes present in large numbers in flowering trees. Inhabits wide variety of forest edge, wooded valleys, gardens and cultivation, up to 2400m. Common in Et, but absent from EEt and So. **Voice** Song is a short series of loud explosive notes, interspersed with monotonous, complex chips and scratchy notes.

Hunter's Sunbird *Chalcomitra hunteri* 15cm, 6"

Adult male is like Scarlet-chested Sunbird but usually blacker. Throat is black bordered with narrow iridescent green malar stripe (can be hard to see in field) and red breast lacks blue barring. Diagnostic *purple rump* and *small purple shoulder-patch* can be better field marks. Female and immature female are similar, but not as dark brown as female Scarlet-chested, and underparts are less yellowish. Immature male is like female but with red feathers on breast. **HH** Pairs and single birds are widespread in S&EEt and So (except NE), and locally fairly common in semi-arid bush country, up to 1350m. Often restless and shy. **Voice** Song is very different from Scarlet-chested: a fast energetic rolling warble.

SUNBIRDS WITH RED BREAST-BANDS *There are four species with red breast-bands in our region, two with short tails and two with long (see also plate 171). Males of all four have metallic green head, breast and upperparts.*

Beautiful Sunbird *Cinnyris pulchellus* ♂ 15cm, 6"; ♀ 11cm, 4.5"

Breeding male has *red centre to breast bordered by large yellow patches at sides*, and long narrow central tail feathers. Northern nominate birds (race in NE Africa) have green belly, while extralimital race *melanogastra* (mainly south of equator) is black-bellied. Non-breeding male is like female but with long central tail feathers and some iridescent green on wing-coverts. Female is greyish-olive above with short indistinct supercilium, plain pale yellow below. Immature is like female but immature male has black throat. **HH** Widespread and often common in semi-arid bush country, wooded grasslands and gardens in Rift Valley and lowlands of WEt and Er, at 400–1500m. **Voice** Call is a scrapy chattering. Song starts with chipping notes, then short musical warbles of chips and squeaks.

Olive-bellied Sunbird *Cinnyris chloropygius* 11cm, 4.5"

Adult male has *broad red breast-band* with yellow pectoral tufts usually concealed, green upper tail-coverts and *dark olive belly*. Adult female is dark olive above with short supercilium, paler yellowish-green below with indistinct streaking on breast and paler throat. Immature is duller and paler than female with dark throat and breast. **HH** Race *orphogaster* is rare resident in WEt at 1500m, inhabiting forest edge, moist bush and woodland. **Voice** Song is a dry rattle preceded by a rather tuneless warbled *trtrtrtr trilitrilitrilitrilit*.

Black-bellied Sunbird *Cinnyris nectarinioides* ♂ 13cm, 5"; ♀ 10cm, 4"

Adult male is like small Beautiful Sunbird with shorter tail, but with *complete red breast-band*. Race *erlangeri* (in NE Africa) lacks yellow pectoral tufts. Female is olive above, pale yellowish below, with olive streaks and sometimes a faint patch of orange-red in centre of breast. Immature is like female with blackish throat. **HH** Uncommon resident in S&SEEt and SSo in variety of riverine habitats in the Dawa, Jubba and Shabeelle valleys up to 900m; fond of flowering *Loranthus*. **Voice** Call is a loud dry repeated chipping. Song begins with rapid higher-pitched hissed *chit* notes turning to extraordinary complex flourish, recalling some weavers.

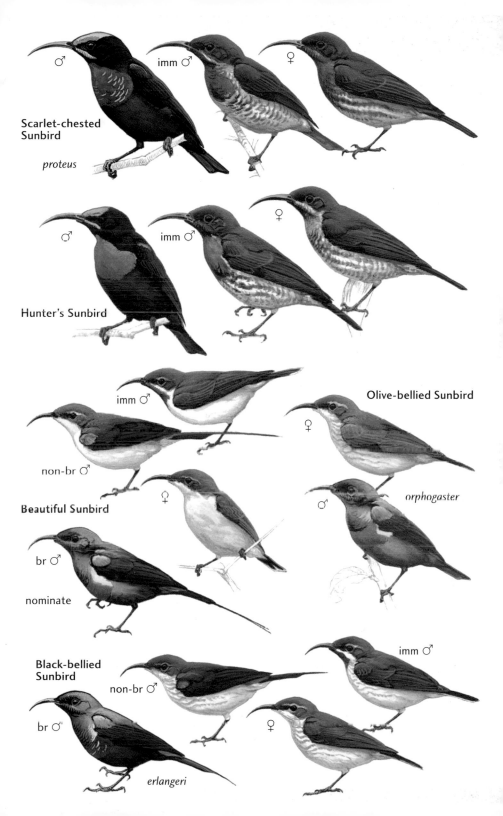

Scarlet-chested Sunbird

proteus

♂ imm ♂ ♀

Hunter's Sunbird

♂ imm ♂ ♀

Beautiful Sunbird

imm ♂

non-br ♂

♀

br ♂

nominate

Olive-bellied Sunbird

♀

♂

orphogaster

Black-bellied Sunbird

br ♂'

non-br ♂

imm ♂

♀

erlangeri

Shining Sunbird *Cinnyris habessinicus* 13cm, 5"

In good light adult male shows *small purple cap*, broad red breast-band sometimes narrowly bordered above and below with blue, and black belly. Adult female is mostly cold ash-grey, with long whitish supercilium and blackish tail, very narrowly edged white. Immature is like female with blackish throat. Three races occur: nominate (Er, N&CEt); *turkanae* (SEt, SWSo) with a broader breast-band; larger birds in NSo are sometimes separated as *alter*. **HH** Feeds on aloes and flowering acacias in semi-arid bush country and open woodland, up to 2000m. **Voice** Call is 4–5 distinct similar or rising-then-falling chips. Song is a rather monotonous but musical two-tone see-sawing like a slow trill.

SUNBIRDS WITH MAROON OR VIOLET BREAST-BANDS *This group of rather similar, fairly dark species all have maroon or violet breast-bands and short tails. All species were formerly placed in* Nectarinia.

Marico Sunbird *Cinnyris mariquensis* 12cm, 5"

Adult male has *broad maroon breast-band* bordered above with blue and no pectoral tufts. Crown is wholly green. Northern race *osiris* has black belly. Larger and longer-billed than similar Purple-banded. Female is greyish-brown above with narrow supercilium, yellowish below with dark streaking and paler throat. Immature is like female but has blackish throat and mottled breast. **HH** Common and widespread but patchy, in open woodland and bush country at 400–1850m. **Voice** Strong call is a rapid nasal chipping, often given in long complaining series. Song incorporates call with some loud sweet warbled chipping notes.

Purple-banded Sunbird *Cinnyris bifasciatus* 10cm, 4"

Breeding male of race *microrhynchus* (SSo) is very like Marico Sunbird but *slightly smaller and shorter-billed*. Female is grey-brown above with light supercilium and darker tail; underparts are pale yellowish, streaked dusky, with centre of throat olive. Immature is like female with dark throat. **HH** Favours woodland, thickets and coastal scrub in SSo (rare in SEEt), but precise range and status in So not known due to confusion with Tsavo Sunbird. Further confirmation of this species is needed for both So and Et. **Voice** Call is a distinctive *sip sip*. Song commences with call and breaks into complex musical rolling twitter.

Tsavo Sunbird *Cinnyris tsavoensis* 10cm, 4"

Almost identical to Purple-banded (with which it was formerly lumped), but male has slightly more decurved bill, purplish breast-band bordered below with *much narrower marooon band* (sometimes absent) and breast and belly shot with iridescent violet. Male also apparently lacks eclipse non-breeding plumage. Female is like female Purple-banded, but has pronounced white malar contrasting with pale grey throat and more uniform yellow underparts; usually paler-throated than female Purple-banded. Immature is like female with dark throat. **HH** Shows distinct preference for drier habitats including *Commiphora* and acacia scrub. In our region, only recorded in SSo where its precise distribution is unclear, but notably within Jubba valley. **Voice** Call is a soft *si*. Song is a long twittering trill with introductory *chip* notes. [Alt: Tsavo Purple-banded Sunbird]

Violet-breasted Sunbird *Cinnyris chalcomelas* 11cm, 4.5"

Larger than both Purple-banded and Tsavo Sunbirds (with which it overlaps), with longer bill and shorter tail. Adult male has e*xtensive iridescent violet from lower throat to breast*, and no maroon band below it; lacks pectoral tufts. Female is grey-brown above with light supercilium and darker tail; plain grey below with pale yellowish belly. Immature male like female with blackish throat. **HH** Locally fairly common in wide range of less arid, coastal bush country in SSo. **Voice** Call is reported as thin high hurried *tsewtsi-tse-tseep-sisisi-tsewtsi-tsi-tsi*. **Note** Formerly treated as a race of extralimital Pemba Sunbird *C. pembae*.

Shining Sunbird

♀

imm

♂

nominate

Marico Sunbird

osiris

♂

♀

Purple-banded Sunbird

microrhynchus

non-br ♂

br ♂

♀

♀

Tsavo Sunbird

♂

♀

♂

Violet-breasted Sunbird

RESTRICTED RANGE SUNBIRDS *Toha Sunbird, known only from Djibouti, is so distinctive that it may well be a new, undescribed species. The Socotra Sunbird is restricted to that island where it is the only sunbird.*

Toha Sunbird *Chalcomitra* sp.   c. 13cm, 5″

Male (possibly a non-breeding bird) showed distinctive metallic yellow-green crown; rest of upperparts uniform greyish-brown, tail blackish. Chin, throat and upper breast bright metallic green, bordered below with narrow black band. Rest of underparts white. Undertail-coverts with broad dark tips. Presumed female similar, but crown less metallic and lacked green chin to upper breast. Long pale yellow moustachial streak separated grey-brown cheeks from dappled brownish chin and throat. Rest of underparts dirty white dapppled with grey-brown. Presumed immature like female but showed distinct supercilium and paler underparts. **HH** Known only from a sight record of three birds together in Djibouti in 1985; as yet undescribed and may be a new species (*Bull. ABC* 5: 46-50; Fry *et al.* 2000). Found in secondary forest with acacia scrub at 180m. **Voice** Unknown.

Socotra Sunbird *Chalcomitra balfouri*   ♂ 13cm, 5″; ♀ 12 cm, 4.5″

Robust sunbird with stout bill and legs. Unique plumage of brown above and white below with *heavy scaling on breast.* Darker lores and ear-coverts contrast with long white submoustachial stripe and dark chin. Male has yellow pectoral tufts (not always visible). Sexes similar. **HH** ENDEMIC to Soc. Common resident in wooded areas and wadis, as well as on open, rocky hillsides with sparse trees or scrub, from sea-level to at least 1370m. Only sunbird on Socotra. **Voice** Song is a series of quick jangling notes, usually delivered in short bursts. Call is a squeaky, strident *zee*; alarm call is a repeated harsh grating *tchee-up* or *tchee.*

PLAIN OLIVE OR GREY SUNBIRDS *Rather plain species that lack iridescence, and which basically look like female sunbirds. Both were formerly placed in* Nectarinia. *Olive Sunbird is sometimes regarded as two species.*

Mouse-coloured Sunbird *Cyanomitra veroxii*   13cm, 5″

Like Olive Sunbird in structure but plumage is mostly *cold grey with darker tail.* At close range, shows oily-blue sheen on shoulder, very narrow black malar stripe, and *red pectoral tufts.* Sexes alike. Race in region is *fischeri.* **HH** Single birds or pairs inhabit woody thickets, coastal scrub and mangroves; only occurs in SSo where considered a rather rare resident. **Voice** Call is a harsh tuneless scratchy note. Song is an attractive simple refrain of well-emphasised rather indignant notes, *tu-ti-tu ti-tu-tu,* rising then falling. [Alt: Grey Sunbird]

Olive Sunbird *Cyanomitra olivacea*   ♂ 14cm, 5.5″; ♀ 12cm, 5″

Large, long-billed, all-olive sunbird variably paler below. Bill is black or with smidgen of orange at base of lower mandible. Plumage details often hard to see in forest interior. In western birds, male has *yellow pectoral tufts* (which may be hidden); female *lacks pectoral tufts* and can be identified by strong bill, uniform olive plumage and voice. In eastern birds, underparts less grey and tinged yellowish-olive; unlike western birds, *both sexes have yellow pectoral tufts.* Immature resembles adult. **HH** Race *ragazzii* is an uncommon resident in W&CEt at 1200–2450m; *changamwensis* is locally very common in riverine woodland along lower Jubba in SSo. Inhabits forest and dense woodlands at all levels, but usually fairly low and rarely in canopy. **Voice** A very noisy, musical sunbird: song usually consists of a descending series of separated explosive squeaks. Calls are dry raspy chips. **Note** The two disjunct populations are sometimes regarded as separate species: Eastern Olive Sunbird *C. olivacea* and Western Olive Sunbird *C. obscura.*

Eastern Violet-backed Sunbird *Anthreptes orientalis*   12cm, 5″

Adult male is violet-blue above with contrasting *turquoise-blue rump and shoulders* and white below (but looks black-and-white in poor light). Warbler-like adult female is brown above with *bold white supercilium* and iridescent dark blue tail; *entirely white below.* Bill fairly straight for a sunbird. Beware of pollen-stained individuals with orange throats, after feeding in aloes. Immature similar to female but may have faint yellow belly. **HH** Singles or pairs are common in semi-arid areas from sea-level to 1350m; they are particularly fond of acacia and *Commiphora* bush where aloes and *Loranthus* are plentiful. **Voice** Call is a scratchy complaining downslur, given irregularly when feeding or repeatedly when excited.

Toha Sunbird

♂

♀

imm ♂

Socotra
Sunbird

♂

Mouse-coloured
Sunbird

fischeri

ad

Olive Sunbird

♂

ad

changamwensis

ragazzii

♂

♀

Eastern
Violet-backed Sunbird

GREEN AND YELLOW SUNBIRDS *Some plumages of Variable Sunbird are confusable with Collared, although the larger size and longer, more decurved bill of the former is usually obvious; both have short tails. The males of the other two species in this group have elongated central tail feathers.*

Variable Sunbird *Cinnyris venustus*   11 cm, 4.5"

Two races occur, varying in belly colour on breeding male: in west *fazoqlensis* is yellow, and in east *albiventris* is white. Both races have *violet-blue throat and upper breast*. Pectoral tufts are either yellow or orange. Non-breeding male is like female with some iridescent feathers above. Adult and immature female are olive-brown above with blue-black tail, and plain yellow below, or white in *albiventris*. Immature male is like female with blackish throat. **HH** Common in wide range of wooded and bushed habitats from sea-level to 2600m, with yellow-bellied *fazoqlensis* mainly west of Rift Valley and *albiventris* to east. **Voice** Call is a harsh, rather nasal scraping note. Among wide variety of songs a *si-sit-swit chichichchi* is commonest. [Alt: Yellow-bellied Sunbird]

Collared Sunbird *Hedydipna collaris*   10cm, 4"

Adult male has upperparts, head, throat and *upper breast iridescent green*, latter bordered below with violet band (can be hard to see). Lower breast to vent bright yellow without pectoral tufts; *bill short*. Three races occur: *djamdjamensis* (SEt) has broader violet breast-band and is brighter yellow below; *garguensis* (extreme SWEt) is similar but has dusky flanks; *elachior* (extreme SEEt, SSo) has narrower breast-band and is paler yellow below. *Adult female has similar iridescent green upperparts*, but entire underparts are yellow. Immature is like dull, pale female. **HH** Pairs are common and widespread in wide range of fairly lush habitats in SEt and SSo, including forest, moist bush, gardens and coastal lowlands, up to 2400m. **Voice** Usual call is a repeated, slightly lisping, penetrating *seeyu seeyu seeyu...* Song is a repeated *si-si-sut seeu seeu seeu seeu seeu seeu...*

Pygmy Sunbird *Hedydipna platura*   ♂ 18cm, 7"; ♀ 9cm, 3.5"

Breeding male is like Collared Sunbird but with *very long, thin tail-streamers* and lacking violet band below green breast; upperparts iridescent bronzy-green, *uppertail-coverts violet*. Non-breeding male is like female with some iridescent feathers above (sometimes with streamers). Adult female is greyish-olive above, plain yellow below with whitish chin. Similar female Beautiful Sunbird is paler yellow below including chin. Immature is like female, with blackish throat on immature male (cf Nile Valley Sunbird). **HH** Occasional visitor to WEt with only four confirmed records, all in Gambela area. Inhabits semi-arid bush and wooded grasslands. **Voice** Call is a downslurred, very pinched *seea seea seea*. Song begins with these notes and continues with high-pitched series of hissed notes breaking into a flourish.

Nile Valley Sunbird *Hedydipna metallica*   ♂ 18cm, 7"; ♀ 9cm, 3.5"

Very like Pygmy Sunbird, differing in blue-green upperparts, *extensive violet on lower back, rump and uppertail-coverts*, and *violet band below green throat*. Males without tail-streamers may be confused with Collared Sunbird, but separated on range and habitat. Non-breeding male is like female with some iridescent feathers above (and sometimes with streamers). Female is very like female Pygmy, but has more prominent supercilium and is slightly paler. **HH** Common resident in Er, Dj, NEEt and (probably) NWSo; non-breeding visitor to NESo (Mar–May). Favours arid scrub and bushy areas, especially with acacias, up to 1200m. **Voice** Call is a loud nasal downslur. Song is a very complex series of twittering and maybe some mimicry, interspersed with the nasal call.

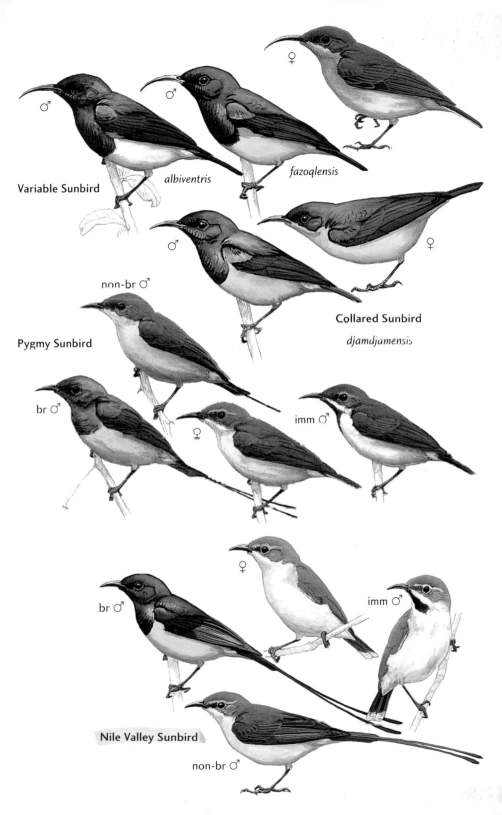

Variable Sunbird

♂

albiventris

♂

fazoqlensis

♀

♂

♀

non-br ♂

Pygmy Sunbird

Collared Sunbird

djamdjamensis

br ♂

♀

imm ♂

br ♂

♀

imm ♂

Nile Valley Sunbird

non-br ♂

PLATE 174: RESIDENT SHRIKES

RESIDENT SHRIKES Found singly or in small groups, Lanius shrikes are mostly conspicuous birds of open habitat. Plumages are bold patterns of black, white, grey and brown; several have long tails, and all have hook-tipped bills. Female fiscal shrikes have partly concealed chestnut flanks.

Common Fiscal *Lanius collaris* 23cm, 9"

Adult male is a slim, narrow-tailed shrike with white scapulars forming an obvious V across back, and grey rump. Tail is black with white outer edge and tips. Adult female is similar but with small chestnut flank-patch. Immature is much browner with fine barring both above and below. Race in region is *humeralis*. **HH** Singles and pairs are very common in highlands of Er and Et at 900–3000m, in open country with trees. **Voice** Simple song consists of repeated mournful burry downslurs. Distinct call is a repeated harsh grating *scherrrr*.

Taita Fiscal *Lanius dorsalis* 20cm, 8"

Adult male appears stocky and short-tailed with black crown and nape contrasting with pale grey back. Very like Somali Fiscal, but *secondaries are all black* (without white tips) and tail proportionately longer. Adult female has small chestnut flank-patch. Immature is dark grey-brown above and white below, all with fine barring. **HH** Single birds or pairs are widespread and fairly common in dry open grassland and bush country in lowlands of S&SEEt and SSo, up to 1500m. **Voice** Rarely heard song is a simple but very liquid and rhythmic *wi-tirir-chh, wi-tink-tink*, repeated monotously. Alarm is a nasal buzz.

Somali Fiscal *Lanius somalicus* 20cm, 8"

Slightly slimmer than very similar Taita Fiscal and best told by *white tips to secondaries* which appear as narrow white trailing edge to wing in flight. Sexes alike (female lacks chestnut on flanks, unlike other fiscals). Immature is like other fiscals with fine barring on grey-brown upperparts, and whitish underparts. **HH** Near-endemic, confined to Horn of Africa and adjacent northern Kenya. Single birds and pairs are widespread and fairly common in arid and semi-arid areas of Et and So, from sea-level to 1600m. **Voice** Rarely heard song is quite different from Taita Fiscal, having a scratchy rather than liquid quality, *wir-chi-ri-ri*, the rising notes repeated for long periods.

Long-tailed Fiscal *Lanius cabanisi* 31cm, 12"

Largest fiscal with *long broad all-black tail* and white rump. Black cap contrasts with dark grey back and scapulars; all other similar but smaller fiscals have white scapulars. Female shows some chestnut on flanks. Immature similar to other immature fiscals but larger. **HH** Common and sociable with groups of up to 10 birds interacting noisily in wooded grasslands, acacia country and coastal bush in SSo. **Voice** Groups call noisily together from tops of bushes, a lazy, liquid simple sequence of 3–5 notes mixed with a throaty *churr*.

Grey-backed Fiscal *Lanius excubitorius* 25cm, 10"

Adult male is large, bulky shrike with broad, black mask (across forecrown), grey upperparts and *large white patches at base of tail*. Adult female is similar but with small chestnut flank-patch. Immature is grey-brown above with much fine dusky barring. Two races occur: nominate (N&WEt) and larger *intercedens* (SCEt). **HH** Common resident in open woodland, acacia country and cultivated areas, often near water, at 500–2000m; occurs mainly west of Rift Valley. Small sociable groups are conspicuous and noisy, often gathering to display and wave their broad tails. **Voice** Several group members sing together a sequence of liquid but raspy descending slurred scraping notes. Call is a harsh *schaah*. **Note** Formerly *Lanius excubitoroides*.

imm

♂

imm

♀

Common Fiscal
humeralis

♂

Taita Fiscal

Somali Fiscal

imm

ad

♂

imm

Long-tailed Fiscal

♂

imm

Grey-backed Fiscal

nominate

MIGRANT SHRIKES *Six Palearctic species that winter in the Horn of Africa, although some populations of Southern Grey Shrike are resident in region (see also plate 176).*

Southern Grey Shrike *Lanius meridionalis*　　　　24cm, 9.5″

Large, grey-backed shrike with prominent face-mask. Longer-billed than Lesser Grey but without broad black band across forecrown, and with white on scapulars. Sexes alike. Four races may occur, differing in tone of grey upperparts, extent of white on wings, and tone of underparts. Resident race *aucheri* (Er, N&CEt, Dj and NSo) is mid-grey above, greyish-white below, with *narrow black frontal band*; *buryi* (probably scarce winter visitor to CEt and Dj from Yemen) is darker above, greyer below with less white on scapulars; *uncinatus* (Soc) is very like *aucheri* and now considered invalid; distinctive Central Asian migrant *pallidirostris* is much paler, with narrow white supercilium, whitish lores, no black frontal band and pale bill (usually with dark tip); also has longer primary projection than other races and is sometimes regarded as a separate species, Steppe Grey Shrike *L. pallidirostris*. Juveniles of all races are brownish-grey, with brown mask and buff-tipped wing-coverts and tertials. First-winter *aucheri* lacks narrow black frontal band; first-winter *pallidirostris* has paler face and more white in wing. **HH** Resident and winter visitor to open plains with scattered bushes and acacias, from sea-level to at least 2000m. Race *pallidirostris* prefers more arid sandy plains with *Suaeda*. Resident *aucheri* is frequent to common (but in coastal areas augmented by winter migrants); presence of *buryi* in winter requires confirmation; '*uncinatus*' is common resident on Soc. Race *pallidirostris* is frequent winter visitor to northern coastal areas and Rift Valley, Oct–Feb. **Voice** Call is a rising, abrasive *kwerrrr*. Song is a musical leisurely rambling medley of single notes, with some mimicry; recalls Long-tailed, Taita and Grey-backed Fiscals rather than Great Grey Shrike. **Note** Formerly treated as conspecific with Great Grey Shrike *L. excubitor*.

Lesser Grey Shrike *Lanius minor*　　　　21cm, 8″

Palearctic migrant mainly in spring when in very clean adult plumage with dove-grey upperparts, broad black face mask extending across forecrown, white throat and *pale pink breast*. Plumage pattern not dissimilar to larger Grey-backed Fiscal (plate 174). Non-breeding adult and first-year are whiter below and lack black on forecrown. **HH** Common passage migrant, Aug–Sep and Mar–May, appearing almost anywhere from sea-level to 2400m and sits conspicuously in open. **Voice** Frequent call is a sharp scolding *chek*, but otherwise rather quiet. Spring passage birds may sing a sweet *Acrocephalus*-like song with a strange throaty quality.

Woodchat Shrike *Lanius senator*　　　　18cm, 7″

Adult male is distinctive with black mask, *bright chestnut crown and nape*, and white scapulars. Adult female is similar but duller with more white on face. Race *niloticus* in our region (breeding in Asia Minor and Levant) has extensive white at base of tail and large white patch on primaries. First-winter has less defined mask and duller crown. Younger birds are grey-brown and scaly, reminiscent of juvenile Red-backed (plate 176), but told by pale scapulars. **HH** Fairly common Palearctic winter visitor, Sep–May, in open country and bush, up to 2400m. **Voice** Generally silent in region; sometimes a harsh *chhh chhh-chhh-chhh-chhhh*.

Masked Shrike *Lanius nubicus*　　　　17cm, 6.5″

Adult male is *black and white with pale apricot flanks*, unlike any other shrike. Adult female is similar but slightly paler and browner above. First-winter is mainly grey and white, with scaly fringes and pale-faced appearance; unlikely to be confused with other smaller migrant species which are all browner. **HH** Common Palearctic winter visitor, Sep–May, in bush and woodland with undergrowth from sea-level to 1600m (and up to 2400m on passage); now uncommon in NWSo. Birds are shy, sitting within canopy of acacia trees and then dropping to ground to feed. **Voice** Usually silent in region, but occasionally gives a harsh *tthek*.

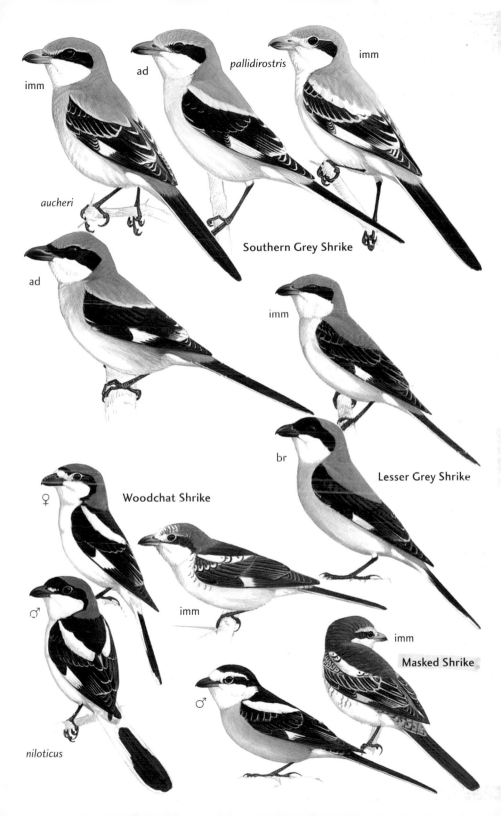

imm

ad

pallidirostris

imm

aucheri

Southern Grey Shrike

ad

imm

br

Lesser Grey Shrike

♀

Woodchat Shrike

imm

♂

imm

Masked Shrike

♂

niloticus

Red-backed Shrike *Lanius collurio*   18cm, 7"

Adult male is distinctive with blue-grey crown, neat black mask, chestnut wings, *blue-grey rump* and *black tail with white patches at base*. Two similar races occur, differing mainly in back colour: grey in *kobylini*, chestnut in nominate; a third race, *pallidifrons*, with paler forehead, is sometimes recognised. Female and first-winter birds are very like Isabelline, but best told by grey undertail and more heavily barred underparts. First-winter is more heavily barred above than similar-aged Isabelline. First-winter Woodchat (plate 175) is greyer and scalier, best told by pale scapulars. **HH** Palearctic loop migrant: autumn passage mainly in west of region, Aug–Nov; strong spring passage in east of region, Apr–May; vagrant Soc. A few birds overwinter in south. Favours bush country up to 2000m. **Voice** Call is a *tak* or *chack*, higher-pitched than Isabelline. Song before departure is rather sweet and *Sylvia*-like.

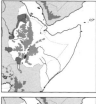

Isabelline Shrike *Lanius isabellinus*   18cm, 7"

Two races occur: adult male *phoenicuroides* is reddish-brown above, particularly bright on crown and tail; adult male nominate has crown and mantle uniform greyish-brown with rufous rump and tail. Both races have prominent black mask with narrow white supercilium. Female and first-winter birds are like Red-backed Shrike, but *tail is rufous both above and below*. First-winter is also more lightly barred above than similar-aged Red-backed. **HH** Common Palearctic winter visitor, occurring almost anywhere, Sep–Apr, but most numerous in open bush country from sea-level to 2400m. **Voice** Call is a harsh *chack* or quiet repeated *ch-ch-ch...* From February to departure, birds give a subdued *Sylvia*-like chatter. **Note** Race *phoenicuroides* is sometimes considered a separate species, Turkestan Shrike *L. phoenicuroides*. [Alt: Red-tailed Shrike]

Brubru *Nilaus afer*   13cm, 5"

Adult male is small black and white bush-shrike with *chestnut flanks* and *bold white supercilium*, vaguely recalling batis. Female is similar but more blackish-brown above, some showing dark streaks on throat. Immature is dark brown heavily mottled creamy-buff and white above, whitish with brown crescentic barring below. Two races occur: East of Rift Valley and in So, *minor* has broad white line in wings; west of Rift, nominate *afer* has rufous-buff in wings and narrower, darker chestnut stripe on flanks. Birds in C&NEEt have been separated (from *minor*) as *hilgerti*. **HH** Single birds or pairs are widespread, common and vocal in canopy of open woodlands and acacia country, up to 2100m. **Voice** Song (usually first sign of presence) is a loud, very burry, gently rising, rather telephone-like slur, *brrrrrrrp*; also has loud scraping notes.

LANIARIUS *BUSH-SHRIKES All are rather stocky and move actively, but slowly, with a horizontal posture. They frequently draw attention to themselves with loud, far-carrying, often duetted calls. Sexes alike unless otherwise mentioned.*

Black-headed Gonolek *Laniarius erythrogaster*   21cm, 8"

Adults are a striking *black and scarlet* with creamy-white eyes and buffy vent. Immature is blackish-brown above, pale dirty yellow below with extensive dark scaling and random red spotting. **HH** Common but rather shy resident of woodland, thickets, bush country and cultivation in WEt and WEr, up to 900m. Usually keeps low but ascends to canopy to call loudly. **Voice** Male makes loud, rather oriole-like note and female may answer with harsh ratchet-like *tchtchtchtchtch*.

Slate-coloured Boubou *Laniarius funebris*   19cm, 7.5"

Only black boubou of bush country: adult is *dull dark slate-grey*. Dark morph of Erlanger's Boubou (plate 177) is glossy black with different song. Immature is finely barred above and below with tawny and black. From drongos (plate 182) and black flycatchers (plate 161) by horizontal posture; from male cuckooshrikes (plate 133) by matt plumage. **HH** Common and widespread in semi-arid bush in Et and So; in moister woodland and evergreen scrub up to 1550m in Et, and down to sea-level in SSo. Invariably in pairs and rather shy, often on ground. **Voice** Duets: male mainly calls a loud *shhhhhhh* or loud clicking followed by *coco-weet*, the *weet* rising as an interrogatory slur. Also makes variety of nasal, gruff and reverberating calls accompanied antiphonally by female.

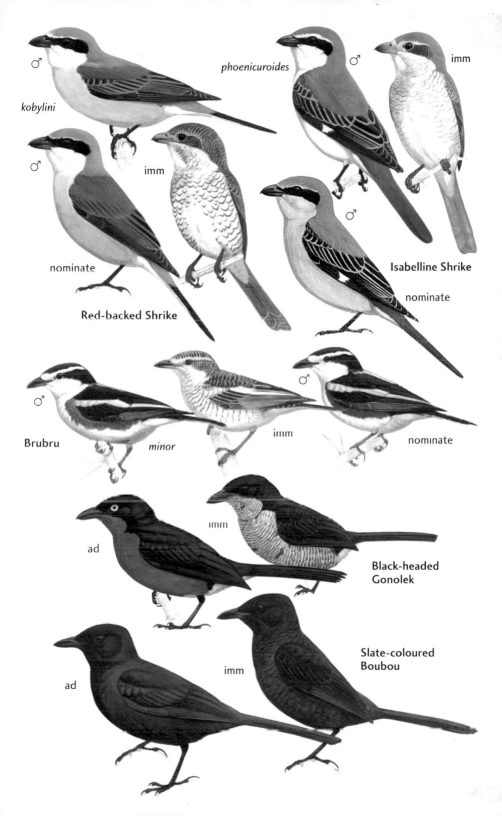

kobylini

♂

phoenicuroides

♂

imm

♂

imm

nominate

Red-backed Shrike

♂

Isabelline Shrike

nominate

♂

Brubru

minor

imm

nominate

imm

Black-headed
Gonolek

ad

ad

imm

Slate-coloured
Boubou

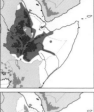

Ethiopian Boubou *Laniarius aethiopicus*   23cm, 9"

Black and white boubou tinged pink below with *long white bar on closed wing* but not extending onto secondaries as on extralimital Tropical Boubou *L. major*. Immature duller with buffy-white tips above and some barring below. Black-backed Puffback is smaller (see below). **HH** Common near-endemic in woodland undergrowth, thick bush and gardens from sea-level to 3000m in Er, Et and NWSo, but absent from hot lowlands in many areas. **Voice** Pairs usually give a very variable, melodious antiphonal duet, so well timed as to sound like one bird, e.g. *wii-hoo wii-hoo* or *wii-hoo-hoo-hoo-hoo*. Calls include a harsh *tchik* and coarse scolding. **Note** See page 388.

Erlanger's Boubou *Laniarius erlangeri*   20cm, 8"

Entirely black boubou glossed greenish (not bluish) above. A black-and-white morph ('*somaliensis*') is very like Ethiopian Boubou but paler pink below with only a *short white bar on median coverts*. Slate-coloured Boubou (plate 176) is matt slate-grey (not black) and prefers dry country. **HH** ENDEMIC. Common in thickets and woodland in SSo. Both morphs occur in Jubba valley; only black morph is in Shabeelle valley. **Voice** Reported to sound more like a gonolek than Ethiopian Boubou. **Note** See page 388.

East Coast Boubou *Laniarius sublacteus*   23cm, 9"

Adult is similar to Ethiopian Boubou but has *no white in wing at all*, and is pinkish-buff below; also has rare black morph, so far known only from coastal Kenya. Juvenile has no barring on underparts. **HH** In our region, only known from Boni Forest in extreme SSo. **Voice** Call is *uh-wheeee-yuk* and a gonolek-like *whee-yup whee-yup*. **Note** See page 388.

Red-naped Bush-shrike *Laniarius ruficeps*   18cm, 7"

Black, white and grey bush-shrike with *orange-red crown or nape*. Three races occur: nominate *ruficeps* (NWSo) has black forehead and rufous crown and nape; *rufinuchalis* (Et, SSo) has black forehead/crown and rufous nape; *kismayensis* (coastal lowlands of SSo) has entirely rufous crown. Female similar, but slightly duller with olive-grey back. Immature lacks rufous on crown. **HH** Retiring but sings in open from tops of bushes, keeping to thick cover in semi-arid *Commiphora* and acacia bush from sea-level to 1350m. **Voice** Male calls a nasal, burry, frog-like upslur, female answering with loud ratchet-like antiphonal notes or series of four identical descending ratchet-like rasps.

PUFFBACKS *A similar-looking group of small bush-shrikes: red eyes and pattern on scapulars and wings, as well as range, aid identification. Males display by puffing out long, loose back feathers and flying about calling loudly.*

Black-backed Puffback *Dryoscopus cubla*   17cm, 6.5"

Adult male of race *affinis* is black above with *pure white rump and scapulars*. Adult female has short white stripe in front of eye and greyer rump. All adults have *bright red eyes*. Immature is like female but duller above with buffy underparts. **HH** Pairs are fairly common in woodland and riverine forest in SSo. **Voice** Male calls a short click followed by rising upslurred whiplash note, female frequently answering with harsh paired *sssssshh sssssshh*. In display flight also gives a loud abrupt *chow-chow-chow-chow-chow-...*, up to ten times, and a rapid *tik-weeu- tik-weeu- tik-weeu...*

Northern Puffback *Dryoscopus gambensis*   18cm, 7"

Adult male is like male Black-backed, but *pale grey on scapulars and rump* with slightly heavier bill. Unlike race *affinis* of Black-backed, wings have pale edgings. Adult female is dark chocolate-brown above, creamy-white below. Eyes of both sexes are orange-red. Immature is like female but with buffy fringes above. **HH** Common and widespread in variety of woodland and dry acacia country in Er, Et and NWSo, at 500–1900m. **Voice** Calls are shorter, harder and more rapid than Black-backed; often calls *tik-teek* or *tik-tik-teek*, and in display flight a strident *chok-chok-chok-chok-chok*.

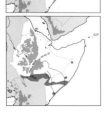

Pringle's Puffback *Dryoscopus pringlii*   14cm, 5.5"

Adult male is much smaller than other puffbacks, with *pale base to lower mandible* and pale grey scapulars and rump. Adult female and immature are pale grey-brown above with whitish loral spot, narrow white eye-ring, and pale, dirty white underparts. Eyes bright red. **HH** Uncommon and elusive in SEt and SSo up to 1350m. Restricted to semi-arid and arid bush, particularly in *Commiphora* and acacia woodland. **Voice** Male repeats a downslurred *cheow-cheow-cheow-cheow-* during display flight; female known to sing a subdued complex warble incorporating clicks and strange mewing sounds.

ad

ad

Ethiopian Boubou

black-and-white morph
'*somaliensis*'

ad

Erlanger's Boubou

black morph

ad

'Bulo Burti
Bush-shrike'
'*liberatus*' morph
(see note on p.388)

imm

**Red-naped
Bush-shrike**

ad

♂

sublacteus

**East Coast
Boubou**

rufinuchalis

♂

♂

kismayensis

**Black-backed
Puffback**

♀

♀

affinis

**Pringle's
Puffback**

♂

♂

erythreae

♀

Northern Puffback

TCHAGRAS Rather shy, grey-brown bush-shrikes with rufous wings and white-tipped tails, best identified by their distinctive head patterns. Inhabiting thick cover, they have slow movements, often feed on the ground and rarely ascend above eye-level. All display in flight, ascending on noisy vibrating wings and then descending into cover calling loudly.

Black-crowned Tchagra *Tchagra senegalus* 21 cm, 8"

Largest of region's tchagras, with strong bill, long tail, long buffy-white supercilium and *black crown*. Immature is duller with brown crown-stripe, often mottled black. Two similar races occur in region: *habessinicus* (Er, Et, Dj, NSo) and *orientalis* (SSo). **HH** Common and widespread from sea-level to 3000m, inhabiting cover within open woodland, bushed grasslands and dry country. **Voice** Song is a loud, far-carrying fluty and thrush-like whistling unlike any other tchagra. Calls include a wide variety of harsh hollow-sounding taks and churrs. [Alt: Black-headed Tchagra]

Three-streaked Tchagra *Tchagra jamesi* 17 cm, 6.5"

Small, slim tchagra with *three narrow black stripes on ashy-grey head, one through each eye and one over centre of crown*. Lacks prominent supercilium of Black-crowned. Immature is like adult but crown-stripe shorter. **HH** Uncommon to locally common in dense cover in dry bush and semi-desert country in S&EEt and most of So, mainly at low altitudes but up to 1600m in Et. Rather skulking and usually solitary, but may join mixed-species flocks. **Voice** Parachuting song-flight consists of series of descending, downslurred whistles, *tui tui tui tui tui...*

Marsh Tchagra *Tchagra minutus* 18 cm, 7"

Smallish, sexually dimorphic tchagra. *Male has solid black cap*, and *female has broad, buff-white supercilium*. In NE Africa, widespread nominate race has heavy black patches on scapulars and mantle, forming distinct black V. Immatures have crown mottled black and pale brown. Race in Et is nominate. **HH** Uncommon and thinly distributed in WEt, inhabiting rank vegetation along streams, tall wet grasslands with scattered bushes or trees, and edges of marshes at 1200–2100m; also inhabits cotton and coffee plantations in Et. **Voice** Displays, usually in flight, with bulbul-like, fairly harsh *swi'weet'weet'weer*. Calls are harsh scraping noises given slowly, or rapidly in alarm. **Note** Formerly *Bocagia minuta* or *Antichromus minutus* [Alt: Blackcap Bush-shrike]

Rosy-patched Bush-shrike *Rhodophoneus cruentus* 23 cm, 9"

Slender, long-legged, striking bush-shrike, with distinctive patches of brilliant crimson in plumage. Two races occur: n Er and NEt, nominate male is grey-brown above with whitish chin and *brilliant pink-carmine stripe from throat to lower breast*; in E&SEt and So, male *hilgerti* has richer upperparts tinged carmine, stronger supercilium, greyish ear-coverts, and red of throat and breast extends to chin. Both have bright pink backs and white corners to tail (most obvious in flight). Females have whitish throat edged with black gorget and bright pink breast-stripe. Immatures are duller than adults and pale-fringed above. **HH** Common in pairs and small groups in semi-arid bush country from sea-level to 2000m. Calls from open bush tops and frequently runs on ground. **Voice** Race *hilgerti* sings a loud far-carrying high-pitched metallic *peeee-yng*, dropping and fading at end and frequently given in duet, or sometimes with distant female replying with lower note. **Note** Formerly in genus *Telophorus*.

PLATE 177 (continued)

Note Ethiopian, Erlanger's and East Coast Boubous were formerly considered to be races of Tropical Boubou *L. aethiopicus*, but a recent molecular study (Nguembock et al. 2008) has shown that they are sufficiently distinct to be regarded as separate species. The remaining (extralimital) races of Tropical Boubou are now united as *L. major*.

Bulo Burti Bush-shrike In 1991 a single unsexed adult boubou was captured in disturbed acacia scrub at Bulo Burti in SSo (within range of black morph of *L. erlangeri*) and was kept in captivity for several months before being released in Balcad NR. It was described as a new species, Bulo Burti Bush-shrike *L. liberatus*, similar to Tropical Boubou but with long yellowish supercilium and yellow wash on breast. No further individuals have been found. Recent molecular work (Nguembock et al. 2008) shows that this bird is genetically almost identical to black morph *L. erlangeri* and should be regarded as a colour morph of Erlanger's Boubou (see plate 177).

Black-crowned Tchagra

ad

imm

♂ Three-streaked Tchagra

ad

nominate Marsh Tchagra

♀

imm

♂ nominate

Rosy-patched Bush-shrike

♀

♂ hilgerti

TELOPHORUS AND MALACONOTUS *BUSH-SHRIKES Stunning bush-shrikes of forest and bush country. Occurring singly or in pairs, they move stealthily through cover with a horizontal posture. Several attract attention to themselves with far-carrying whistled calls. Sexes similar.*

Sulphur-breasted Bush-shrike *Telophorus sulfureopectus* 17cm, 6.5"

Adult has *narrow yellow supercilium separating grey crown from black eye-mask.* Bright yellow below with broad wash of orange over breast. Immature is plain yellow below with whitish throat and no black on face. Similar Grey-headed Bush-shrike is much larger with yellow or orange eyes, huge thick bill and no black on face. Race in NE Africa is *similis.* **HH** Frequent to common in wide variety of woodland, thickets and acacia country in Et (especially Rift Valley) and SSo, up to 1850m and often in mixed-species flocks. **Voice** Varied song is repeated series of high bell-notes which fade at end, *whi-wi-whi-whi-whi-wherrr.* Also calls *pupupupu* and assortment of harsh scolds. **Note**: Formerly in genus *Malaconotus* or *Chlorophoneus.* [Alt: Orange-breasted Bush-shrike]

Four-coloured Bush-shrike *Telophorus quadricolor* 18cm, 7"

Adult male is easily told by *yellow-orange forecrown*, bright orange-red chin, throat and undertail-coverts, and broad black breast-band. Adult female is similar but slightly duller with narrower breast-band. Immature is dull green above and faintly barred yellowish-green below, with breast-band absent or broken. The race in the region is *nigricauda.* **HH** Pairs are secretive but call frequently from dense thickets and forest undergrowth in coastal lowlands; in our region, only reaches extreme SSo where a rare resident. **Voice** Typical call is an explosive, far-carrying, rhythmical *wik-a-wik-a-wik, wik*, but also utters strange short frog-like churrs in alarm. **Note** Formerly in genus *Malaconotus* or *Chlorophoneus.* Sometimes lumped in Gorgeous (or Perrin's) Bush-shrike *T. viridis* of C & S Africa.

Grey-headed Bush-shrike *Malaconotus blanchoti* 25cm, 10"

Large bulky grey-headed bush-shrike with *massive bill and yellow or orange eyes*, yellow below with variable rufous-orange wash across breast. Two races occur: in *catharoxanthus* (Er, N&WEt and NWSo) underparts are bright uniform yellow; *approximans* (S&EEt and So) has extensive rufous-orange wash across breast. Immature is paler with dark eyes. **HH** Widespread and frequent at forest edge, in woodland, thickets and acacia country from sea-level to 1800m, often in same areas as much smaller Sulphur-breasted Bush-shrike. **Voice** Usual call is a slowly repeated hollow whistle, either *whoo-whooik, whoo-whooik…* or either note repeated singly. Also makes loud clicks and a screeched *ereeek, ereeek, ereeek…*

NICATOR A fairly large olive-green bird with a large shrike-like bill and loud bubbling song. Its affinities are uncertain and it is placed by various authors with either greenbuls or bush-shrikes, but may merit elevation to its own family (together with two closely related extralimital species). Solitary unless breeding, it is a shy bird of the forest interior, active but slow, skulking around within cover. Its vibrant song and harsh contact calls can be heard throughout the day. Sexes and immatures look alike, but males are larger than females.

Eastern Nicator *Nicator gularis* 20–23cm, 8–9"

Adult is olive-green above with obvious creamy-yellow spots on wing-coverts and secondaries, and *grey-brown wash to crown and ear-coverts.* Washed grey-brown below, and whiter on belly with yellow vent. **HH** Fairly common but very hard to see in riverine forest, patches of woodland and other dense cover in lower Jubba and Boni Forest in SSo. **Voice** Highly vocal, invariably from dense cover, with loud song that starts hesitantly with *yu-ik-wit-wer-trrr* and bubbles into a jumbled *cho-chou-choou-chueeee.* Also gives a repeated sharp *tuk.* [Alt: Yellow-spotted Nicator]

Sulphur-breasted Bush-shrike

imm

ad

Four-coloured Bush-shrike

imm

ad

nigricauda

Grey-headed Bush-shrike

ad

catharoxanthus

ad

approximans

ad

Eastern Nicator

WHITE-CROWNED SHRIKE *Together with the closely related Southern White-crowned Shrike E. anguitimens, the two white-crowned shrikes may be more closely related to the true shrikes (Laniidae) than the helmetshrikes (Prionopidae). They perch conspicuously on bushes in open country and have a distinctive flight.*

Northern White-crowned Shrike *Eurocephalus rueppelli* 21 cm, 8″

Stocky and thick-necked with white crown, blackish eye-mask and dark brown wings and tail; *white rump conspicuous in flight.* Immature is finely barred above, with scaly brown crown, broad white nape and collar, and buffy-brown band across breast; *bill yellowish.* **HH** Singles or small flocks are common in bush country, mainly in and east of Rift Valley, from sea-level to 1600m, perching in small trees and flying down to ground to feed. Distinctive butterfly-like flight is interspesed with long glides. **Voice** Group frequently calls together with series of pinched nasal complaining notes and harsh chattering, and also make querulous loud squeaks in flight. [Alt: White-rumped Shrike]

HELMETSHRIKES *Helmetshrikes are active, social and vocal birds which travel slowly in loose flocks, often snapping their bills. Head and crest markings aid identification. Sexes are alike.*

White-crested Helmetshrike *Prionops plumatus* 18–23 cm, 7–9″

Common open country black-and-white helmetshrike. Three races occur: *concinnatus* (Er, N&WEt) and *cristatus* (C&SWEt including Rift Valley) are large with long curly white crests; closed wing of *cristatus* almost plain black, *concinnatus* with long white wing-stripe; in E&SEt and So, smaller *vinaceigularis* has straight white crest, no white in closed wing. All races have yellow eyes and rich yellow eye-wattles, and in flight show conspicuous white bar across primaries. Immatures are like adults but dingy, with dark eyes and no wattles. **HH** Widespread and locally common in open and riverine woodland and bush country from sea-level to 1800m. Invariably seen in small vocal groups, seemingly always on move. **Voice** Flocks frequently call long burry downslurred notes, *kirro, kirro, kirro,* often accompanied with bill-snaps and chattering. [Alt: White Helmetshrike]

Retz's Helmetshrike *Prionops retzii* 21 cm, 8″

Like Chestnut-fronted Helmetshrike but larger and *much blacker with curling black crest, bright red bill and eye wattles,* and yellow eyes. Immature is duller and browner with shorter crest. **HH** Very sociable; flocks of 10 or more are fairly common in variety of woodland in lower Jubba and Boni Forest in SSo (race *graculinus*), where often mix with Chestnut-fronted, invariably in canopy. **Voice** Mobile flocks give mixed assortment of strange burry, buzzy calls and loud descending sequence of piercing upslurred whistles, *tiyui-tiyui-tiyui-tiyu-tiyui-tiyui...,* accompanied by rasping notes and bill-snapping. [Alt: Red-billed Helmetshrike]

Chestnut-fronted Helmetshrike *Prionops scopifrons* 18 cm, 7″

Mostly grey-brown, darker on head and wings, with whitish vent and corners to tail. Forecrown has rectangular patch of *velcro-like chestnut bristles,* and eyes are yellow with blue-grey wattles. Immature is rather duller brown, lacks bristles on forecrown, and has dark eyes. **HH** In our region, race *kirki* is only found in Boni Forest in extreme SSo; groups of 10 or more birds are locally common in woodland and forest canopy, often in mixed-species flocks. **Voice** Very noisy; members of roving flocks giving frequent high-pitched upslurred trilled rattles *trrrrrrrrt trrrrrrrrrt;* song consists of these rattles mingled with tit-like whistles.

ad

vinaceigularis

ad

imm

Northern White-crowned Shrike

imm

ad

cristatus

ad

White-crested Helmetshrike

concinnatus

imm

ad

imm

ad

Retz's Helmetshrike

graculinus

Chestnut-fronted Helmetshrike

kirki

ORIOLES Bright yellow birds with black heads or eye-stripes and red bills. Two pairs of similar species occur in our region and are best identified by the colour of their wing edges and the upperside of the tail, and by range and habitat preferences. All immatures have dark bills.

African Golden Oriole *Oriolus auratus* 20cm, 8″

Adult male is only likely to be confused with Eurasian Golden Oriole, but has *longer black streak extending behind eye and broad yellow edges to most wing feathers.* Adult female is similar to male but is duller and washed olive above. Immature has dark bill, *greenish-yellow edges to wing-coverts* and pale yellow and whitish underparts with black streaks. **HH** Uncommon intra-tropical migrant to lowlands of W&SEt, at 750–1800m. In SSo, it is a rare migrant to Jubba valley and Boni Forest, Jul–Oct. All records are of northern nominate race. Inhabits forest, woodland, lush gardens and moist bush country. **Voice** Has rather forced but typical oriole-like song: *wee ah hah waah*, but also commonly gives a burry extended miaowing upslurred *nahararahhhhh*.

Eurasian Golden Oriole *Oriolus oriolus* 22cm, 8.5″

Adult male has *short black eye-stripe extending from base of bill to eye, and mostly black wings.* Adult female is highly variable, either like male, or with white from throat to vent, or like immature with red bill. Immature is olive-green above and streaky below with dark bill; differs from immature African Golden by having slightly darker, plainer wings. **HH** Common Palearctic passage migrant, Sep–Nov and Mar–May, in variety of wooded habitats. Can occur anywhere on passage, from sea-level to 1800m. Vagrant Soc. **Voice** Most frequently heard call is a harsh scolding miaowing *kree-er*, but may also give familiar fluty rolling *ori-ori-ori-ole* in Apr or May.

Black-headed Oriole *Oriolus larvatus* 20cm, 8″

Black-headed oriole with *upperside of central tail feathers olive-green*, greater coverts greenish-yellow, outer secondaries black edged whitish and inner secondaries black broadly edged yellow. Immature has head and breast streaked blackish or dark green. Two races occur: larger *rolleti* (SW&SEt) and more golden *reichenowi* (SSo). **HH** Race *rolleti* is common and widespread in woodlands, forest edge, gardens and bush country at 200–1800m, less common in eastern parts of range. In SSo race *reichenowi* is common resident in riverine forest and coastal woodlands. **Voice** Typically gives a hurried set of 4–6 mainly slurred notes lasting at c.2 secs: *tiau tor te wah (wee o)*, repeating same sequence monotonously, and at times mimicking other species softly. [Alt: Eastern Black-headed Oriole]

Abyssinian Oriole *Oriolus monacha* 23cm, 9″

Larger than Black-headed Oriole with more uniform wing pattern. Outer secondaries and outer greater coverts broadly edged grey (not white), forming *long grey panel on wing*; inner secondaries mainly yellowish-green. Black-headed has black, white and green. Sexes alike. Two races occur, differing in tail pattern. Nominate *monacha* (Er, NEt south to 10°N) has mainly olive and yellow tail, but *meneliki* (SEt) shows varying black on feather bases, making it rather like *rolleti* race of Black-headed. As latter two taxa are partly sympatric, careful attention to wing pattern is esssential. Immature is like adult but head is brownish-black, bill is black and throat is lightly mottled, lacking prominent breast-streaking of Black-headed. **HH** ENDEMIC to Er and Et. Fairly common highland forest species, occurring in woodlands and forest including juniper, at 600–3000m. Overlaps with Black-headed in parts of Et, but latter prefers more open habitats or forest edge and lower altitudes. **Voice** Song is much like other orioles, but phrases are more hurried and notes lack flutiness of other species in group. [Alt: Abyssinian Black-headed Oriole; Ethiopian Oriole]

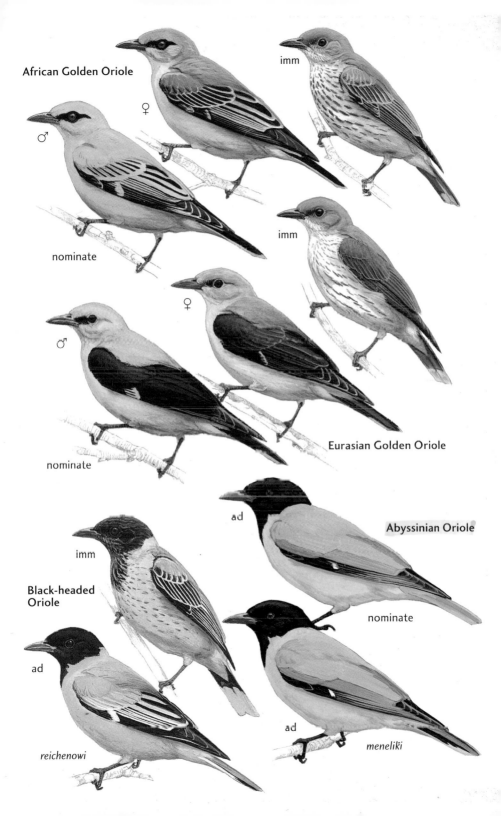

African Golden Oriole

♀

imm

♂

nominate

imm

♂

♀

nominate

Eurasian Golden Oriole

Abyssinian Oriole

ad

Black-headed
Oriole

imm

nominate

ad

ad

ad

reichenowi

meneliki

DRONGOS *Medium-sized black birds with hook-tipped bills and red or orange-red eyes. Best distinguished by tail shape, habitat, range and voice. They often sit still for long periods and then make feeding sallies. Upright posture similar to black flycatchers (plate 161), but drongos are easily separated by red eyes and thicker, shrike-like bills. Black boubous (plate 176-7) and cuckooshrikes (plate 133) are more active and move with a horizontal posture. Sexes are similar.*

Square-tailed Drongo *Dicrurus ludwigii*   19cm, 7.5"

Smaller than Fork-tailed Drongo, lacking pale wing-patches and, despite name, tail is not square but *less deeply forked*. Usually easily told from Fork-tailed by *forest habitat*. In race *muenzneri* (SSo) adult male has blue-green gloss on upperparts and much of underparts; female is less glossy and more blackish-grey below. Immature duller, with buffy speckling on wing-coverts and light barring below. **HH** Single birds or pairs are uncommon residents in riverine forest in lower Jubba in SSo. **Voice** Song consists of loud, rhythmical, rapidly delivered phrases. **Note** Race *muenzneri* is sometimes considered synonymous with *ludwigii*.

Fork-tailed Drongo *Dicrurus adsimilis*   25cm, 10"

Adult is glossy black (blue-black in good light) with *deeply forked tail* and red eye. Moulting birds can show strange-looking double-forked tails. Inner webs of flight feathers are ashy thus making wings look pale or silvery in flight. Immature has brown eyes, some buffy speckling on wings, fine buffy-grey and black barring below, and less deeply forked tail. Race in NE Africa is *divaricatus*. **HH** Singles and pairs are common and widespread throughout region, except in highlands and forest (also absent from parts of NESo); occupies wide range of habitats including open wooded country, semi-arid bush and cultivated areas from sea-level to 1800m. Perhaps most familiar bird of African savanna, frequently perching conspicuously. **Voice** Highly variable song is a long rambling and rather coarse mixture of nasal, twangy notes, none clear or pure; often mimics other species in song. Calls are rather harsh. [Alt: Common Drongo]

DISTINCTIVE CROWS *Stresemann's Bush-crow has been subject to much taxonomic debate and, although now placed with crows, it was thought to be more closely related to starlings (Sturnidae). It is restricted to a tiny range in southern Ethiopia. The Red-billed Chough is a distinctive Palearctic species with an isolated population in the highlands of Ethiopia.*

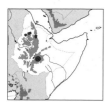

Stresemann's Bush-crow *Zavattariornis stresemanni*   30cm, 12"

Unmistakable, gregarious species confined to single small area in southern Ethiopia. Pale grey plumage with whiter face, chin and vent, black wings and tail, *bright cobalt-blue skin on lores and around eye*. A smaller bare buffy patch behind the eye is not always visible. Bill, eyes and legs are black. Sexes alike. **HH** ENDEMIC to SEt, occurring from just north of Yabelo to just south of Mega, at 1200–1800m, and common and conspicuous within this tiny range of less than 6000km². Sedentary cooperative breeder, but locally dispersive. Inhabits acacia savanna and scrubby grassland, foraging on ground, usually in small flocks. **Voice** Varied loud calls are similar in delivery and variety to a *Turdoides* babbler rather than any other corvid in Africa; described as a rapid *kaka*, and *kakakakakaka*. [Alt: Ethiopian Bush-crow] **EN**

Red-billed Chough *Pyrrhocorax pyrrhocorax*   40cm, 16"

Elegant, montane crow with glossy-black plumage and *red bill and legs*. No other corvid has red bill (juvenile Piapiac has shorter pink bill and is a lowland species). Bill is fairly long and strongly decurved. In flight, long, broad wings show deep 'fingers'. Sexes alike. Juvenile has shorter, orange-yellow bill and duller plumage. **HH** In our region, endemic race *baileyi* is restricted to Simien and Bale Mountains in Et, at 2700–4400m. Strongly gregarious and sociable; flocks feed on ground in open habitats such as rocky slopes, alpine meadows, grassy plateaux and even cultivated fields. Breeds on cliff ledges or in caves. Choughs are well known for their acrobatic flight. **Voice** A piercing and far-carrying *chee-ow* or *chi-ah* is commonly heard all year.

Square-tailed Drongo

♂

Fork-tailed Drongo

imm

ad

divaricatus

Stresemann's Bush-crow

ad

Red-billed Chough

ad

CROWS AND RAVENS *Large, strong and familiar black, grey and black, or black and white birds, with powerful flight and harsh voices. Easily identified by the extent of white in the plumage or, in the blacker species, by overall size and shape. Often unafraid of man, scavenging around villages and at rubbish dumps in towns and cities. Sexes are alike.*

Pied Crow *Corvus albus*   46cm, 18"

Boldly marked black and white crow; *white hind-collar extends around sides of neck and across breast* rendering it unmistakable. Immature is similar to adult, but duller. In a few areas in Et and So hybridises with Somali Crows leaving white parts speckled black. **HH** Pairs to large flocks are common and widespread, occurring in all but driest areas as well as towns and open country, from sea-level to at least 3000m. Mainly sedentary, but seasonal in SE Highlands of Et, and absent from EEt and much of So. Vagrant Soc. **Voice** Variable calls include both long and short 'caws' in flight, but while perched birds may utter a deeper call or quiet musical hollow *clork clork…*

House Crow *Corvus splendens*   40cm, 16"

Slim black crow with variable grey neck and breast, and longish, slightly decurved bill. Immature is duller than adult with brownish cast. Three races occur in Africa, differing in tone of grey areas. Racial distribution uncertain due to hybridisation: nominate birds are commonest, but *protegatus* (darkest grey birds) recorded in So, and *zugmayeri* (palest birds) also occurs. **HH** An introduced or self-established crow from Indian subcontinent now numerous and regarded as a serious pest along much of coast, where it destroys nests of smaller birds and competes with resident Pied Crow. **Voice** Very noisy, calling a short, hurried *kwaa kwaa…* [Alt: Indian House Crow]

Brown-necked Raven *Corvus ruficollis*   54cm, 21"

Large all-dark raven with (usually but not always) *brown head and nape*, only visible at close range. In flight, easily separated from similar-sized Fan-tailed Raven (plate 184) by obviously longer, slimmer tail which, on perched birds, extends beyond wing-tips. Generally considered monotypic over wide range in northern Africa and the Middle East, but shows marked individual variation in size. Isolated population on Socotra is consistently larger and may be distinct race. **HH** Occurs in arid desert and semi-desert regions, often near habitation. In our region, it is a rare resident in Er and vagrant in NWEt; also resident on Socotra up to 460m. Largely no overlap in range with Dwarf Raven. **Voice** A deep, harsh croak is common call, but also gives longer, more drawn-out *crrrarrr* or *crrra-waa*. Other calls include a soft *kruk-kruk-kruk* and loose throaty rattle.

Dwarf Raven *Corvus edithae*   46cm, 18"

Very similar to Brown-necked Raven but *distinctly smaller* with shorter, slimmer bill and slightly less graduated tail. Replaces Brown-necked in Horn of Africa and previously considered a race of it. Smaller than Fan-tailed Raven (plate 184) with much longer tail, and readily separated from Cape Rook by thicker bill and less glossy plumage. **HH** Singles and small flocks are common in deserts, semi-deserts and dry savannas in Er, Dj, So and Et (mainly east of Rift Valley), from sea-level to 2500m; largely replaced by Cape Rook in highlands of Ethiopia. In a few places, range of Somali Crow meets similar-sized Pied Crow, and distinct hybrids are well known. **Voice** Gives variety of 'caws' and *kwaar-kwaar* notes, plus throaty rolling *krrrrrrrr*. All calls are very like Pied Crow, but Dwarf Raven may be more raucous. [Alt: Somali Crow]

House Crow

Pied Crow

Brown-necked Raven

Dwarf Raven

hybrid
Pied Crow ×
Dwarf Raven

Cape Rook *Corvus capensis* 43cm, 17"

Slim-looking, all-black crow with noticeably *narrow bill* and lax throat (feathers appear shaggy). Adult may show bluish or purplish sheen in good light, but in worn plumage is often rather brown. Immature has dull brownish wash on head and underparts. Race throughout NE Africa is *kordofanensis*, smaller than nominate of southern Africa. **HH** Small flocks occur commonly in highlands of Et, Er and NSo, mainly favouring open country and farmland above 1800m, and up to 4100m in Et; an isolated population occurs at lower altitudes in coastal SSo. **Voice** In addition to typical crow-like 'caws' makes variety of strange throaty and liquid calls, notes tending to slur together: *kwah kworlik kworlik koh*. [Alt: Black Crow; Cape Crow]

Fan-tailed Raven *Corvus rhipidurus* 48cm, 19"

Rather stocky, glossy black crow with thick bill and short tail that stops well before wing-tips at rest. In flight, *tail looks very short and wings appear broad*, giving almost tail-less appearance. Head usually black (like body) but may be dark brown and thus like Brown-necked and Dwarf Ravens (plate 183), both of which have longer tail. Immature duller and browner than adult. Race in NE Africa is nominate. **HH** Singles and small flocks are common across most of Er, Et, Dj and NSo from near sea-level to 3600m in dry bush country with cliffs. **Voice** Typical calls are varied but rather high-pitched 'caws', but also has quiet subsong of sweet notes usually given from shade in heat of day.

Thick-billed Raven *Corvus crassirostris* 62cm, 24.5"

Very large black raven with *huge bill and prominent white patch on nape*. Massive bill is black tipped ivory, upper mandible with pronounced ridge on culmen. Sexes alike. Long wedge-shaped tail distinguishes it from smaller Fan-tailed Raven; at rest tip of tail reaches wing-tips. In flight, can look rather hornbill-like. Immature is browner than adult, and bill lacks ivory tip. **HH** ENDEMIC to Er and Et (except for two records across border in Sudan and another in NWSo). Occupies range of montane habitats, mainly at 1200–4200m. Singles or pairs are common around cliffs, grassland and moorland, but especially in cultivation throughout highlands. Uncommon to rare in Er. **Voice** Unlike other ravens of region, utters very deep, repeated gargled notes.

PIAPIAC *Monotypic, crow-like bird with long graduated tail, considered to be more closely related to jays than crows. Sexes alike.*

Piapiac *Ptilostomus afer* 36cm, 14"

Unusual, unmistakable crow; slender adult often *appears all black with long graduated tail* but at close range may show dull brown wings and tail edges. In flight pale grey-brown *translucent primaries* are visible. Bill is black in adult, bright pink with black tip in immature. Eyes violet-purple. **HH** Usually occurs in small flocks at 600–1500m in open country and near *Borassus* palms, associating with cattle or large game and running about catching disturbed insects. Mainly sedentary but subject to local movements. In our region only known from extreme SEEt (one record) plus several unconfirmed records in SWEt. **Voice** A noisy species, especially at dawn and dusk, when parties keep up a cacophony of loud squealing *skweeer* or *pee-ip* notes.

Cape Rook

Fan-tailed Raven

Thick-billed Raven

ad

Piapiac

ad

imm

OXPECKERS Endemic to Africa and related to starlings, the two species differ mainly in bill, eye, eye-wattle and rump colour. Often called tick birds, they are mainly seen feeding on large wild mammals or cattle. Flocks roost together in dead trees. Sexes are alike.

Red-billed Oxpecker *Buphagus erythrorhynchus* 20cm, 8"

Adult differs from Yellow-billed Oxpecker by *entirely red bill, red eye with bright yellow eye-ring, and plain brown rump* (uniform with back, wings and tail). Immature is like immature Yellow-billed but more uniform dark brown above and may show reddish base to bill. **HH** Common and widespread from sea-level to 3000m, wherever wild mammals and undipped cattle occur. Overlaps with Yellow-billed, but latter localised in NE Africa. **Voice** Calls are softer than Yellow-billed Oxpecker, a *ssshhhhhh* all given on one tone, and often accompanied with spitting notes and clicks, *tsik, tsik…*

Yellow-billed Oxpecker *Buphagus africanus* 22cm, 8.5"

Adult has bulbous, *bright yellow red-tipped bill and bright red eyes, and pale creamy-buff rump* that contrasts with darker back, wings and tail (obvious even at distance). Immature has bill and eyes dark brown and slightly less obvious pale rump. **HH** Highly fragmented range; formerly common in WEr and rare in NWEt up to 900m, but absent from most of our region. Typically occurs in small loose flocks, feeding around variety of large mammals. **Voice** Calls are harsh rasps, *rraaah*, given at rest and in flight.

STARLINGS In North-East Africa the nine genera of starlings are a diverse group, varying from the iridescent glossy starlings and largely similar red-winged group to the singularly beautiful Golden-breasted Starling. Sociable birds, they live mainly in small groups and may occur seasonally in large mixed species flocks. Sexes similar in many species.

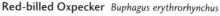

Golden-breasted Starling *Lamprotornis regius* 35cm, 14"

Stunningly beautiful starling: iridescent blue, green and purple above, with very long narrow graduated tail and *bright golden-yellow breast and belly*. Sexes are alike. Immature is much duller, with head, mantle and upper breast mainly dull olive-brown, and breast to vent pale yellow. **HH** Common in dry bush country in much of So, and in S&EEt, from near sea-level to 1200m. Usually in small flocks, restlessly moving through low bushes. **Voice** Calls are simple: a repeated, complaining downslurred *rranyh*. **Note** Sometimes placed in genus *Cosmopsarus*.

Stuhlmann's Starling *Poeoptera stuhlmanni* 19cm, 7.5"

Small starling with slender build. Adult male appears all black in field (blue-black in good light) with brown iris and very narrow pale yellow outer ring. Adult female is dark slate-grey with chestnut primaries, easily visible in flight. Immature is like dull female. Confusable with other red-winged starlings (plate 186), but latter larger and much stockier. **HH** Uncommon in canopy of highland forest in WEt, at 1700–2800m. **Voice** Flocks are very vocal, especially in flight when they give a simple but musical *tuweet…*

Rosy Starling *Pastor roseus* 21cm, 8"

Adult is unmistakable, with *pink and black plumage*. Size and shape like Common Starling. Breeding male has metallic purple and green sheen on head and wings, with long, drooping crest. Female is duller with shorter crest. Juvenile is similar to juvenile Common but paler with contrasting pale rump and yellowish bill. Immature Wattled Starling (plate 188) has darker wings and whitish rump. **HH** Central Asian species wintering in S Asia. Vagrant to our region with two recent records from Et, Mar–Apr. **Voice** Similar to Common Starling, but largely silent in winter. **Note** Formerly in genus *Sturnus*. [Alt: Rose-coloured Starling]

Common Starling *Sturnus vulgaris* 21cm, 8"

Compact dark starling with *long pointed yellow bill*. Appears black in breeding plumage, with glossy purple and green sheen. In winter adult is heavily speckled white and buff all over, with black bill. Legs pinkish. Sexes are alike. Juvenile is uniform grey-brown with paler throat, gradually acquiring spotty winter plumage. Distinctive shape in flight with triangular wings and short tail. **HH** Palearctic species that winters in N Africa; vagrant to Et, Dj and So (single records) and Soc (several records). **Voice** Calls consist of varied rasping slurs whilst song is a jumble of squeaks and chips. [Alt: European Starling]

imm

ad

**Red-billed
Oxpecker**

imm

ad

**Yellow-billed
Oxpecker**

ad

imm

Golden-breasted Starling

**Stuhlmann's
Starling**

ad

imm

♀

Rosy Starling

♂

**Common
Starling**

imm

♀

♂

ad

RED-WINGED STARLINGS *Superficially like Stuhlmann's Starling (plate 185), but larger and stockier, and both sexes have chestnut in the primaries. Most have long tails. At a distance, males look black or blue-black, often with a glossy blue-green sheen or streaking, and females are greyer on the head. Immatures are all like dull adults.*

Somali Starling *Onychognathus blythii* 35cm, 14"

Large and slender, *with long graduated tail that looks diamond-shaped in flight* (broadest point is one-third to halfway from base). Adult male is glossy black with greenish sheen on upperparts and tinged violet below. A male collected on Abd al Kuri in 1903 had an oily green sheen below and was described as race *creaghi* (further validation required). Adult female has *pale grey hood.* Immature similar to male but duller and shorter-tailed. Male Red-winged Starling has heavier bill and shorter, less graduated tail. Larger than Socotra Starling (both sexes) with longer, more graduated tail. Confusion most likely with Slender-billed, but note stronger bill of Somali and differences in tail shape. Pale grey, unmottled head and long tail distinguishes Somali from all other females. **HH** ENDEMIC to Horn of Africa. Singles or pairs inhabit rocky areas with trees or bushes as well as dry watercourses. Patchily distributed in Er, N&EEt, Dj and NSo, from sea-level to 3800m. Rather common on Soc. Presence in Bale Mts requires confirmation. Wanders widely outside breeding season. **Voice** Fluty, almost oriole-like notes are interspersed with squeaky calls. Flight call is a musical, high-pitched *pee-weep.*

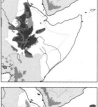

Red-winged Starling *Onychognathus morio* 31cm, 12"

Adult male is large blackish starling (shines blue-black in good light) with stout bill and *long pointed but not particularly well-graduated tail.* Adult female has greyer head and neck with some dark grey and violet streaking. Immature is similar but duller. Slender-billed has much slimmer bill, longer, more graduated tail and generally occurs at higher elevations. Race in NE Africa is *rueppellii.* **HH** Pairs and small flocks are common, usually near rocky hills or cliffs but also in towns, at 600–2400m, mainly in W and SE Highlands of Et. **Voice** Call is an attractive loud, oriole-like fluty note, *wi-tyuor,* either repeated when perched or as a single downslur in flight.

Socotra Starling *Onychognathus frater* 33cm, 13"

Glossy black starling with bluish-purple sheen. *Sexes are alike.* Smaller than Somali Starling with shorter, square-ended tail and longer, thinner bill. **HH** ENDEMIC to Soc, where local and uncommon in range of habitats from sea-level to 1500m. Generally shyer than Somali Starling, the only other red-winged species on Socotra. **Voice** Usual call is a pure, far-carrying whistle.

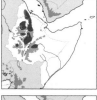

Slender-billed Starling *Onychognathus tenuirostris* 33cm, 13"

Similar to Red-winged Starling but slimmer with *well graduated tail and long slender bill.* Broadest point of tail is two-thirds from base (cf Somali Staling). Adult male has *deep violet-blue-black gloss.* Adult female is duller with scaly grey head and breast extending onto upperparts and underparts. Immature is like dull adult. **HH** Small flocks are locally common on cliffs, in rocky gorges (often near waterfalls), around highland forest and on alpine moorlands in Er and Et at 1800–3700m, but are not restricted to high elevations and wander widely. **Voice** Perched flocks give a loud but rather tuneless warble which may continue for long periods without pause. In flight flock members call harsh slurred notes, *teeeo* or *teeoo.*

White-billed Starling *Onychognathus albirostris* 30cm, 12"

Easily told from other red-winged starlings by *white bill and shorter, square-ended tail.* Male is glossy dark purple; female has grey hood. Immature is less glossy. **HH** ENDEMIC to Er and Et. Pairs or small flocks are locally common in highlands, mainly N and W of Rift Valley at 2300–3100m. Occurs on cliffs and rocky gorges, often near waterfalls. **Voice** Song is a repeated series of *twee-ww, twee-ee, twee-ee,* with no musical quality. Birds give chipping notes while feeding. Roosting birds utter a cacophonous roar when congregating in large numbers.

Bristle-crowned Starling *Onychognathus salvadorii* 42cm, 16.5"

Largest of red-winged starlings with *very long graduated tail and small spiky cushion of feathers on forecrown.* In good light, plumage shines glossy blue-black. Sexes similar, immatures are duller. **HH** Pairs and small flocks are uncommon or local in semi-arid, rocky country in Et and So, up to 1700m, often near cliffs and gathering to feed in *Salvadora* bushes. **Voice** Usual flight call is a loud, rising *swi-chit* or more subdued fluty *weeo,* which perched birds may develop into a long simple medley.

Somali Starling

Red-winged Starling

ad

Socotra Starling

Slender-billed Starling

White-billed Starling

Bristle-crowned Starling

ad

ad

GLOSSY STARLINGS These birds are characterised by their highly iridescent blue-green plumage and brightly coloured (often yellow) eyes. A difficult group, but their distinctive calls and ranges help with identification. Sexes are alike.

Lesser Blue-eared Starling *Lamprotornis chloropterus* 19cm, 7.5"

Very like Greater Blue-eared Starling but smaller, *smaller-billed* and shorter-tailed, with neater, more compact posture. Dark mask through eye is narrower and well-defined. Often looks very green, but this is not a reliable field character. Immature is dull sooty-brown on head and underparts with grey-brown eyes. **HH** Nominate race is locally common in open woodland and bush at 450–2500m in WEr and WEt, but also wanders to seasonally moist semi-arid areas. **Voice** Groups give continuous chattering consisting of a warbled, burry downslur mixed with explosive *swii* notes, latter also given in flight.

Greater Blue-eared Starling *Lamprotornis chalybaeus* 23cm, 9"

Iridescent blue-green plumage (including tail) with blue-black ear-coverts and conspicuous yellow eyes. Ear-coverts reflect light and give the illusion of changing colour, unlike Lesser Blue-eared Starling. Violet-blue or purplish on breast and belly. Immature is dark-eyed, uniform dull blue-black above and sooty-brown below. **HH** Most common and widespread member of this group, represented by race *cyaniventris* in NE Africa. Pairs and small flocks occur in wide variety of habitats including woodland, bush country, cultivation and gardens at 500–2400m in Er, Et and NWSo. **Voice** Song is a very complex, varied, somewhat drongo-like warble, incorporating harsh and sweet notes. Call is a nasal cat-like mew *myaaah*, often given in flight.

Splendid Starling *Lamprotornis splendidus* 28cm, 11"

Largest glossy blue starling and, in good light, a stunning bird: brilliant green and blue with golden reflections above, black wing-spots, and iridescent deep-purple, blue and coppery underparts. *Eyes are pale creamy-yellow.* Sexes similar, but female has bluer underparts. Immature is blackish below with random blue feathers. In flight birds appear distinctively front-heavy with longish tail, and wings look broad and make loud swishing. **HH** Small flocks are locally fairly common in tree-tops at forest edge and in forests at 1200–2000m in WEt. **Voice** Unusual, rather outrageous call combines mixture of explosive and variable gurgles, plops and creaks, *krrrau kiau ko-chock wiow wi-eee*; may be delivered as song for long periods. [Alt: Splendid Glossy Starling]

Rüppell's Starling *Lamprotornis purpuroptera* 31cm, 12"

Large, dark-looking, purplish-blue starling with *long graduated tail*, black mask and conspicuous *creamy-white eye*; lacks black wing-spots. Immature similar but duller and dark-eyed. Two races occur: nominate (C&SEt, SSo) and *aenecephalus* (WEr, NWEt), more violet with bluer wings and much longer tail. **HH** Pairs are common, wide-ranging, and often on ground in woodlands, bush country and around cultivation from sea-level to 2400m. **Voice** Song is a long complex loud warble with both harsh and sweet notes and mimicry. Calls include *swi-chew* and a slightly tremulous *kwerr*, given both perched and in flight. [Alt: Rüppell's Long-tailed Starling]

Black-bellied Starling *Lamprotornis corruscus* 18cm, 7"

Dark glossy starling, much smaller and slimmer than Rüppell's or Greater Blue-eared (only other species in range). Often shows dark purple and green gloss to head, mantle and upper breast. Rest of underparts are dark purplish-black *blending to black on belly and vent*. No black spots on wing-coverts; eyes bright orange with yellow inner ring. Immature is duller with sooty-black underparts. **HH** Usually in flocks; common in forest and coastal bush in SSo, mainly in Jubba valley and Boni Forest. Race concerned, *mandanus*, often considered synonym of nominate *corruscus*. **Voice** May call for long periods, often from perches within shade, a variety of short pinched notes interspersed with an oriole-like *wi-tchew*.

imm

ad

**Lesser
Blue-eared
Starling**

imm

ad

cyaniventris

**Greater
Blue-eared
Starling**

ad ♂

imm

Splendid Starling

imm

imm

ad

ad

Rüppell's Starling

nominate

**Black-bellied
Starling**

RUFOUS-BELLIED STARLINGS *Three similar-looking rufous-bellied starlings best identified by the presence or absence of white on the vent, and by the exact colour of the underparts and eyes. Sexes are alike.*

Chestnut-bellied Starling *Lamprotornis pulcher*   21 cm, 8"

Less iridescent than other rufous-bellied starlings, adult has *grey-brown head, white eyes and oily dark green breast* sharply demarcated from chestnut belly (but no white breast-band). Rest of plumage dull green, slightly bluer on tail. Shows pale buffy patch in wings in flight. Sexes alike. Immature is browner, showing some chestnut on belly and brown eyes. **HH** Small flocks are frequent to common in thornbush and savanna in WEr and NWEt, up to 2000m. Range does not overlap with other rufous-bellied starlings. **Voice** Song is a rarely heard rambling series of high-pitched trilling notes, quite unlike any other starling. Flight call is a high-pitched, downslurred trill, *trrreeeairrrr.*

Superb Starling *Lamprotornis superbus*   19 cm, 7.5"

Adult is separated by *creamy-white eyes, narrow white breast-band, white under wing-coverts, and white vent and undertail-coverts.* Immature is duller with dark eyes and no white breast-band; from immatures of other species by *white ventral area.* **HH** Small flocks are confiding, common and widespread in semi-arid country, open woodland, bushed grasslands, towns and gardens, from sea-level to 2100m. Absent from Er, Dj, N&WEt and extreme NESo. **Voice** Song is a long ramble of rising-and-falling skirls and squeals. In flight gives a purred *skrrrrrri.*

Shelley's Starling *Lamprotornis shelleyi*   19 cm, 7.5"

Adult is richer and darker than both Superb and Chestnut-bellied Starlings with *orange or orange-red eyes and very dark rufous belly.* Head, breast and upperparts largely glossy violet-blue. Immature has head and mantle dull ash-brown. **HH** Small flocks are generally frequent to common wanderers in dry bush country (especially *Commiphora*) from near sea-level to 2000m, and often associate with other rufous-bellied starlings. Apparently resident in much of Et, but breeding visitor to NSo, Apr–Sep, and non-breeding visitor to SSo. **Voice** Song is like Superb Starling but louder, harsher and broken into short phrases rather than a long continuous ramble. In flight gives a throaty *kurrikurrikurri.*

PALE STARLINGS *These two paler species are typical of bush and savanna, and can be easily separated by rump colour.*

Fischer's Starling *Lamprotornis fischeri*   19 cm, 7.5"

Adult is a rather distinctive ashy grey-brown starling with *paler crown, black lores, white eyes and white lower breast to belly.* Immature is browner with yellowish bill and dark eyes. In flight, told from Wattled Starling by grey-brown not white rump. **HH** Small flocks are very common in dry bush country in SSo, below 300m; also occurs around Dolo in SEEt. **Voice** Typical song is rather burry and monotonous with some notes repeated for long periods. A striking *krrrrrrikrrrrrikrrrrrri* is given in flight. **Note** Sometimes placed in genus *Spreo.*

Wattled Starling *Creatophora cinerea*   20 cm, 8"

Non-breeding male, female and immature are the most frequently encountered: all are *pale brown with darker wings and tail and whitish rump.* At close range, show small area of pale yellow skin around and behind dark eye. Greyer breeding male has extensive yellow and black skin and wattles on head. **HH** Flocks are highly mobile, common and widespread throughout region from sea-level to 2400m, often near cattle and plains game. Nomadic and migratory, seasonal movements are poorly understood; in SSo present only Aug–Dec. **Voice** Flocks create an unusual medley of squeals, squeaks and hisses, without no distinctive form or pattern.

Chestnut-bellied Starling
imm
ad

Superb Starling
imm
ad

Shelley's Starling
ad
imm

ad
Fischer's Starling

imm

br ♂
non-br ♂
Wattled Starling

BICOLOURED STARLINGS *Three distinctive starlings (in separate genera) with bold plumage patterns, especially in males. Easily identified if seen well. Female Violet-backed is completely different from the male and may be misidentified if not seen with males.*

Violet-backed Starling *Cinnyricinclus leucogaster* 17cm, 6.5"

Adult male has *entire upperparts, throat and upper breast brilliant fiery iridescent violet and plum,* with snowy white breast to vent; may appear black and white when backlit. Adult female is very different and almost pipit-like, mottled brown and blackish above, slightly rufous on head, and white below with numerous narrow brown streaks. Immature is like female. Three similar races occur: nominate (C&SEt, resident), *arabicus* (NEt, Er, Dj, NWSo, mainly Mar–Sep) and *verreauxi* (migrant to SEt, Apr–Nov). Female of race *arabicus* is slightly larger and plainer brown above, largely lacking buff fringes; male *verreauxi* has white base to outer tail feathers. **HH** Common throughout year (resident and migrant) mainly at 400–2500m, frequently in nomadic flocks around fruiting trees. Widespread in Er, Dj and Et, but absent from So except NW. **Voice** Song has no real pattern nor particularly sweet or harsh notes, but consists of rather rambling, slurred wails, *riariarowh*. [Alt: Plum-coloured Starling, Amethyst Starling]

Magpie Starling *Speculipastor bicolor* 19cm, 7.5"

Adult male is *black and white with brilliant red eyes,* in flight with obvious *white wing-patches.* Adult female has similar pattern and eye colour but is grey on head and upper breast. Immature is grey-brown above with dark eyes. **HH** Flocks are common and widespread in S&SEEt and So (except NE) from sea-level to 1200m. Although present most of year in SEt and SSo, subject to irregular nomadic movements; breeding visitor only to NSo (Apr–Jul). Inhabits semi-arid thornbush and savanna woodland, but also wanders to moist coastal woodlands in SSo. **Voice** Song is a jumble of harsh soft squeaks, resulting in an unmusical formless ramble. Alarm calls are harsh loud *ti-chuk chuk-chuk.*

Sharpe's Starling *Pholia sharpii* 17cm, 6.5"

Adult is dark blue-black above, *with white throat and upper breast merging to tawny-apricot on flanks and belly;* eyes are creamy-yellow. Sexes alike. Immature is duller above and dark-eyed, with small arrow-shaped spots on breast. **HH** Pairs or small flocks are generally uncommon in canopy of highland forest in S&WEt, at 1300–2900m, where often sit on exposed dead branches. **Voice** Song is an extraordinary refrain of very high tinkling, bell-like notes, rising and falling, then rising again, vaguely recalling Dark-backed Weaver and reminiscent of wind-chimes. Flight calls include high-pitched *spink* and *chin'k* notes. **Note** Formerly in genus *Cinnyricinclus.*

WHITE-CROWNED STARLING *Distinctive, short-tailed starling of open country. Gregarious at all times and typically forages on the ground. Sexes alike.*

White-crowned Starling *Spreo albicapillus* 27cm, 10.5"

Large white-crowned starling, brown with iridescent green sheen above, brown with white streaks below, and white *vent and undertail-coverts.* Eyes white, bill black. Sexes alike. Immature is much duller brown with less streaking below and black-tipped bright yellow bill. In flight, white wing-patches are obvious. Two races occur: nominate (SE&EEt, N&SWSo) and smaller *horrensis* (SEt). **HH** Small flocks are common in grasslands and savannas of SEt, and in semi-arid and desert country of EEt and NSo; often on ground around human habitation, from sea-level to 1600m. **Voice** Song consists of various long or short rising slurs with skirled quality, producing a querulous and soft sounding *krrrri-kuri-kuri-koyi.* Flight call is a burry *koyi.*

Violet-backed Starling

♀

nominate

♂

♀

arabicus

imm

♂

♀

Magpie Starling

ad

Sharpe's Starling

White-crowned Starling

imm

ad

nominate

SPARROWS *Well-known, small stubby-billed birds with predominantly brown and grey plumages, some with a small amount of black on the head. All frequently feed on the ground. Shelley's, Socotra and Abd al-Kuri were formerly regarded as part of a single species, Rufous Sparrow P. motitensis, while Parrot-billed and Swainson's were regarded as races of Grey-headed P. griseus. The two similar golden sparrows ecologically replace each other in the Sahel and Arabian regions. Sexes are alike in the Grey-headed group, but separation of females of other species requires care.*

Shelley's Rufous Sparrow *Passer shelleyi*　　　　　　　　14cm, 5.5"

Breeding male has distinctive head pattern with *black line through eye curving around ear-coverts, cinnamon supercilium* above it, and *dark eyes*. Crown and nape are grey, bib black. *Rufous rump* is most visible in flight. Female is duller and paler with grey (not black) throat. **HH** Rather local in E&SEt and NWSo in bushed grasslands, open woodland and cultivation, at 1150–1550m; partial to whistling thorns where they co-occur. **Voice** Birds give a fairly loud musical chipping, quite typical of genus. **Note** Formerly lumped in Rufous Sparrow *P. motitensis*.

Socotra Sparrow *Passer insularis*　　　　　　　　　　14cm, 5.5"

Adult male is like Shelley's Rufous Sparrow, but *lacks rufous on upperparts* including rump; rufous is confined to scapulars and long postocular supercilium, and is darker than on Shelley's. Underparts are washed dirty grey contrasting with white cheeks. Female is duller than male with smaller, paler bib; from female House Sparrow by richer coloration, black bill. **HH** ENDEMIC. Widespread in all habitats on Soc (where the only sparrow), from sea-level to 1200m. **Voice** Calls include dry chirping *chirrup, cheep, chee-cheep, chip* and *chlip*. **Note** Formerly lumped in Rufous Sparrow *P. motitensis*.

Abd al-Kuri Sparrow *Passer hemileucus*　　　　　　　　12cm, 5"

Normally regarded as race of Socotra Sparrow, the much *smaller* sparrow on neighbouring Abd al-Kuri has recently been judged a full species. Both sexes are paler and browner above, and *almost pure white below*. Adult male has *much smaller black bib* and prominent white tips to median coverts. Adult female has stronger supercilium behind eye and *no trace of bib*. **HH** ENDEMIC to Abd al-Kuri in Socotra archipelago. **Voice** Not known.

House Sparrow *Passer domesticus*　　　　　　　　　　14cm, 5.5"

Adult male differs from Shelley's Rufous Sparrow in having larger black bib, extensive dark chestnut on sides of nape, whiter cheeks and *grey rump*. Bill and eye dark. Non-breeding male has greyer nape, smaller grey freckled bib and yellowish bill. Adult female and immature are plainer and buffier than female Shelley's with short pale supercilium and yellowish bill. **HH** Has recently spread through Er up to 2300m (race *rufodorsalis*), probably from Sudan, and is well established in SSo (race *indicus*) after spreading from Kenya. Vagrants in NSo (race *niloticus*) were presumably ship-assisted. **Voice** Rather monotonous rapid rambling chirping, with some variation and rhythm, *trit treet trit tret tret...*

Somali Sparrow *Passer castanopterus*　　　　　　　　12cm, 5"

Breeding male has *bright chestnut crown and nape*, grey mantle and rump, black bib, and *yellow cheeks and underparts*. Non-breeding male has greyer crown and is generally paler. Adult female and immature are like female House Sparrow, but have longer, pale buffy supercilium and are washed pale yellow below. Two races occur: nominate *castanopterus* (EEt, NSo) as described; male *fulgens* (SWEt) brighter yellow below. **HH** Pairs and small flocks are common in arid and semi-arid country, open plains, tree-lined dry riverbeds, villages and rocky coasts, from sea-level to 1700m. Largely resident but wanders in non-breeding season. **Voice** Typical call is a rather loud monotonous upslurred chirping, *treeet, cheritt*.

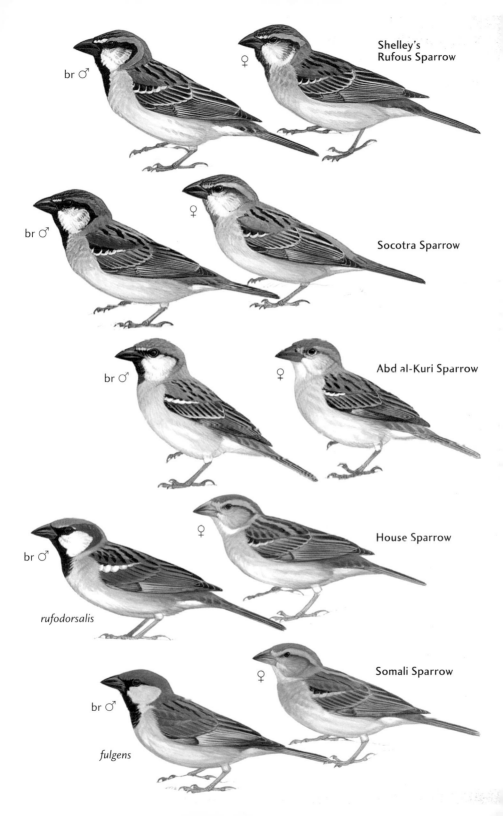

br ♂

♀

Shelley's
Rufous Sparrow

br ♂

♀

Socotra Sparrow

br ♂

♀

Abd al-Kuri Sparrow

br ♂

♀

House Sparrow

rufodorsalis

br ♂

♀

Somali Sparrow

fulgens

Northern Grey-headed Sparrow *Passer griseus* 15cm, 6"

Classic grey-headed sparrow: rufous-brown back contrasts with pale grey nape and crown, *whitish throat clearly separated from greyer breast and upper belly*, lower belly whitish. Immature browner with horn bill, no white wing-patch. **HH** Inhabits open bushland, savanna, light woodland and human settlements. Generally prefers higher rainfall areas than Parrot-billed Sparrow. In NE Africa, race *ugandae* occurs below 1200m in WEr, and in NWEt. **Voice** Song consists of typical sparrow-like chirping, either delivered slowly or more rapidly with see-saw effect *chup chep chup chep...*

Parrot-billed Sparrow *Passer gongonensis* 18cm, 7"

Largest and darkest member of group; *uniform grey below* (no white on chin), *with heavy rounded bill*. Dull brown mantle and back contrasts with rufous rump. Immature is browner with horn bill, no white wing-patch. **HH** Inhabits wide variety of semi-arid bush country and open wooded grassland in S&SEEt and SSo, from sea-level to 1500m; less fond of settlements than some other species, but does occur around Mogadishu. **Voice** Calls variable; higher-pitched, squeakier musical chirps than close relatives in continuous, rather monotonous ramble, *chip chip tt-tt chip chet treet...*, which may be rather sharp and explosive.

Swainson's Sparrow *Passer swainsonii* 16cm, 6"

Like Northern Grey-headed Sparrow but *dull brown back* contrasts with more rufous rump, head and underparts darker grey *with less contrasting white throat and some white on belly*. Parrot-billed is larger with much heavier bill. Immature is browner with horn bill, no white wing-patch. **HH** Near-endemic to Horn of Africa. Occupies most habitats except forest, including towns and villages. Common throughout most of Er, Et (except SE), Dj and NSo from sea-level to 3000m. **Voice** Chirping calls are similar to Northern Grey-headed.

Sudan Golden Sparrow *Passer luteus* 13cm, 5"

Breeding male is unmistakable with *lemon-yellow head and underparts and chestnut back*. Female is buff-brown above with some dark streaks and buff supercilium; chin and throat are pale yellow, rest of underparts buffish-white. Immature is like female but paler; young females lack yellow below and young males show variable amounts of yellow. **HH** Common breeding resident in Er and NEt below 400m, inhabiting arid bushland, dry woodland and semi-deserts. Highly gregarious and nomadic; invariably in large flocks outside breeding season. Eritrean population nearly reaches Dj border, almost meeting Arabian Golden Sparrow, recently spread to Dj from So. **Voice** Constant trilled chips and slurs are very like song of Chestnut Sparrow, and quite different from single chirps given by most members of genus.

Arabian Golden Sparrow *Passer euchlorus* 13cm, 5"

Breeding male is *golden-yellow above and below* (darker than Sudan Golden Sparrow) with white-edged black flight feathers and tail. Breeding female is greenish-grey above and pale yellowish below, especially from chin to breast. Non-breeding female and immature are grey-brown above and buffish-white below with yellow restricted to throat (Sudan Golden is buff-brown, rather than grey-brown). **HH** Arabian species occurring in our region in coastal areas in Dj and NWSo, up to 200m. Gregarious and mainly sedentary, but flocks sometimes wander outside breeding season. Range now almost meets Sudan Golden Sparrow in Dj. **Voice** Flocks utter constant twitter like House Sparrow.

Chestnut Sparrow *Passer eminibey* 11cm, 4.5"

Smallest sparrow in our region. Breeding male is *all deep chestnut* gradually blending to darker face with blackish wings and tail. Non-breeding male has fine buffy edges to feathers giving scaly appearance. Immature male is irregularly and boldly mottled chestnut and buff. Adult female is like typical female sparrow, but small size, pale chestnut supercilium and chestnut throat-patch (if present) aid identification. Plumage of breeding male suggests much larger Chestnut Weaver (plate 197) but latter has all-black head, red eyes and heavy bill. **HH** Locally common in wide variety of bushland and open woodland with good ground cover, mainly in Rift Valley of Et at 500–1900m. Rare visitor (or perhaps local resident) in SSo. Wanders widely, sometimes in large flocks, particularly after rains. **Voice** Song is a continuous series of varied trills, while flight call is *chup chup chup...*

Northern
Grey-headed
Sparrow

ad

ad

ugandae

Parrot-billed
Sparrow

♂

ad

Swainson's Sparrow

Sudan Golden Sparrow

♀

Arabian Golden
Sparrow

♀

♂

♀

br ♂

imm ♂

Chestnut Sparrow

PETRONIAS (ROCK SPARROWS) *Dull grey-brown sparrows with yellow throat-spots which are often extremely hard to see. Sometimes placed in genus Gymnoris. Pale Rockfinch was formerly considered to be a Petronia, but is now placed in a monotypic genus.*

Yellow-spotted Petronia *Petronia pyrgita* 15cm, 6"

Fairly uniform, pale grey-brown sparrow-like bird, typically with *yellow spot at base of throat* (but usually concealed). *Pale bill and eye-ring* are often more obvious than throat-spot. Sexes alike. Immature browner with buffy supercilium. Race in NE Africa is nominate. **HH** Singles and pairs are uncommon throughout most of region (but absent from WEt), inhabiting dry bush country and open woodland from near sea-level to 1800m. **Voice** Song is a repeated rising *t'chepor*. Call is an explosive dry *chirp*.

Bush Petronia *Petronia dentata* 13cm, 5"

Adult male is *smaller and browner* than Yellow-spotted with prominent pale throat and *rufous line extending from eye to behind ear-coverts*; yellow throat-spot is often concealed. Adult female is rather nondescript sparrow except for *long pale buffy supercilium*; from female House Sparrow by broader supercilium and well-defined white throat. Immature is like female but browner. **HH** Frequent to common in lowlands of N&WEt (including Rift Valley) and WEr, at 750–1800m. Presumed resident, but no records Jun–Oct. Inhabits variety of woodland and savanna, cultivation and sparsely vegetated hillsides. **Voice** Sings fast repeated phrases, including *triup-triup-triup*; rapid series of sparrow-like chirps recalls Grassland Pipit. Also gives a soft sparrow-like *chewee*.

Pale Rockfinch *Carpospiza brachydactyla* 14cm, 5.5"

Nondescript sparrow-like bird of uncertain affinities. Slim with *short swollen bill*, short tail and long wings. Plumage is *overall grey-buff with no obvious field marks*; lacks streaking on mantle. Other features include short pale supercilium, dark eyes, narrow white eye-ring, buffy malar stripe and two indistinct wing-bars. Bill dark grey when breeding, paler in winter; legs pinkish. Sexes alike. **HH** Gregarious Palearctic winter visitor, to Er, Dj and NEEt (to Awash NP), Nov–Mar; mainly in lowlands below 300m in Er, to 2400m in Et, in semi-desert, sparse bush, open coastal plains and rocky areas. **Voice** Song (not yet heard in Africa) is a high-pitched insect-like buzz, lasting 1–1.5 secs. Flight call is a liquid *pluip* or soft purr, recalling distant European Bee-eater. [Alt: Pale Rock Sparrow]

SPARROW-WEAVERS *Larger than the true Ploceus weavers, breeding in colonies with nests that are loosely woven balls of pale brown grasses, often with an entrance hole on both sides. Sexes and immatures are similar.*

White-browed Sparrow-Weaver *Plocepasser mahali* 17cm, 6.5"

Boldly marked, brown above with *broad white supercilium, white rump*, and two broad white wing-bars. Underparts white with dark smudges at sides of breast in northern race *melanorhynchus*. Birds in extreme SEEt and SSo are sometimes separated as race *propinquatus*. **HH** Very common in dry bush country (particularly acacia) and wooded grasslands up to 1800m in Et (mainly Rift Valley) and SSo. Highly sociable: small flocks found at nesting colonies all year. Feeds on ground; often tame. **Voice** Song is a musical chattering medley of chirps and throaty churrs given from nest or on ground.

Donaldson Smith's Sparrow-Weaver *Plocepasser donaldsoni* 17cm, 6.5"

Medium-brown above, finely mottled grey-brown, except for white rump. Whitish throat has *narrow black malar stripe* running below *buffy cheek* and extending back to side of neck; lightly mottled brownish below. **HH** Uncommon and local at a few sites in SEt and SSo, in semi-desert and open bush, generally preferring drier areas than White-browed Sparrow-Weaver; occurs from near sea-level to 900m. **Voice** Song is a scratchy rambling medley of chirrups and nasal skirls, usually delivered from nest.

Chestnut-crowned Sparrow-Weaver *Plocepasser superciliosus* 17cm, 6.5"

Slightly slimmer than other sparrow-weavers and rusty brown above with *chestnut crown and ear-coverts*. Bold face pattern has white superciliary stripe and black and white stripes on side of throat. Shows two white wing-bars, but rump concolorous with mantle. **HH** Pairs or small groups are locally common in dry bushland and woodland in WEr and N&WEt, at 600–2200m. It is less common and much more inconspicuous than other sparrow-weavers; often in rocky areas, quietly walking on ground or under bushes feeding. **Voice** Song is a very varied selection of twitters, trills and sweet canary-like notes. Contact call is a fast high-pitched *titititit titititit…*

ad

imm

nominate

Yellow-spotted Petronia

♂

Bush
Petronia

♀

Pale Rockfinch

ad

ad

White-browed
Sparrow-Weaver

Donaldson Smith's
Sparrow-Weaver

melanorhynchus

ad

Chestnut-crowned
Sparrow-Weaver

ad

Speckle-fronted Weaver *Sporopipes frontalis*   11 cm, 4.5"

Small weaver with rather sparrow-like appearance. Forecrown black speckled with white, nape chestnut, malar stripe black. Rest of plumage grey-brown above and pale greyish-white below. Sexes alike; immature slightly duller. Two races occur: nominate (WEr, NWEt) as described; *emini* (vagrant SSo) has darker grey mantle. **HH** Small flocks are common in Er but rare in Et, at 750–1900m. Feeds on ground in wooded grassland and semi-arid areas with bush cover. **Voice** Song is a rather pipit-like series of chips and trills. Flight and feeding call is a series of identical notes, *tsitsizizizizit...*

SOCIAL WEAVERS *Small, sociable weavers which occur in large flocks, often feeding together on the ground. Their nests are tightly woven balls of grass that hang from the very ends of the thinnest branches of large trees, often hundreds of pairs breeding together. Sexes are alike.*

Grey-capped Social Weaver *Pseudonigrita arnaudi*   11 cm, 4.5"

Small, brown, short-tailed weaver with contrasting *neat grey cap*. In flight shows *pale grey band across end of tail*. Northern nominate birds have brown backs. Immature has much browner cap than adult, hardly contrasting with mantle. Two races occur: nominate (SSo) as described, and *australoabyssinicus* (SEt) with a less contrasting grey cap. **HH** Locally common resident in SEt at 1200–1350m, but very rare in SSo, known from single site close to sea-level. Inhabits wide variety of bush and open wooded country including semi-arid areas. **Voice** Song and call are a series of high-pitched piercing squeaks, *tseer tseer...,* given for long periods.

Black-capped Social Weaver *Pseudonigrita cabanisi*   13 cm, 5"

Small attractive weaver with *black cap and tail* contrasting with brown back and wings, *white bill with greenish tinge*, and red eyes. White below with black streaks on flanks and belly (hard to see in field). Immature has brown crown. **HH** Locally common in two areas of SEt at 1200–1500m; in SSo only known from a few sites on Kenyan border. Flocks inhabit drier country than Grey-capped Social Weaver, including quite arid areas if large trees are present for breeding. **Voice** Gives a very sparrow-like mixture of chirps and skirls, and feeding birds keep up a constant chipping.

BUFFALO-WEAVERS *Large weavers with heavy bills. Bubalornis are mainly black and their nests are very large constructions of dead thorn branches. Dinemellia is distinctly orange-red, brown and white. Its nest is smaller, includes more grass, and often has some thorny branches attached to the outside. All occur in small flocks.*

White-headed Buffalo-Weaver *Dinemellia dinemelli*   18 cm, 7"

Very distinctive, particularly in flight, when white head, *bright orange-red rump* and large white wing-patches show clearly. Mantle and tail are brown in northern nominate race. Sexes alike. **HH** Common in acacia bush country and wooded grasslands from sea-level to 1900m in much of Et (east of Rift Valley) and So. Often seen on ground or calling loudly from nest trees. **Voice** Song and calls are slowly delivered, drawn out, and piercing nasal skirls which are variations of *skrieril skri-skril skrieril...*

Red-billed Buffalo-Weaver *Bubalornis niger*   22 cm, 8.5"

Adult male is *deep black with red bill* and variable small patches of white on sides of breast. In flight, wings look black, but from below can show white streaks at base of primaries. Adult female is browner, mottled brown and white below, with dull red bill. Immature is like female, but more grey-brown with heavy whitish mottling below; bill usually shows some pale red or orange colour. Race in NE Africa is *intermedius*. **HH** Common in dry bush country and wooded grasslands with acacias from near sea-level to 2000m, in Et (east of Rift Valley) and So (except NE). **Voice** Song is usually given from colonial nest by several members at same time., a mixture of nasal skirls *chn chn chn chrerlink chrerlink…* which may continue for long periods and grow more excited with arrival of female.

White-billed Buffalo-Weaver *Bubalornis albirostris*   23 cm, 9"

Breeding male is *black with greyish-white bill* and white streaks along flanks. In non-breeding plumage, bill is blackish with paler base. Adult female like male but bill black. Immature is dark brown above with brown and white mottled underparts, and blackish bill. **HH** Small parties and flocks are locally common in WEr and N&SWEt, from near sea-level to 1800m, favouring dry acacia country. **Voice** Song is similar to Red-billed but possibly more exuberant, varied and metallic.

Grey-capped Social Weaver

imm

Speckle-fronted Weaver

ad

ad

nominate

nominate

imm

ad

White-headed
Buffalo-Weaver

Black-capped Social Weaver

imm

Red-billed
Buffalo-Weaver

♂

intermedius

♀

imm

br ♂

White-billed
Buffalo-Weaver

BLACK AND YELLOW WEAVERS Ploceus *weavers all build tightly woven nests, varying from small onion-shapes to large round structures with long vertical entrance tunnels. Plates 194–197 illustrate some common and widespread species (plus some less common but similar looking ones). Careful attention to the exact shape of the face mask, eye colour and back pattern aids identification of the males.*

Village Weaver *Ploceus cucullatus*   17cm, 6.5"

Two distinct forms occur: breeding males of both are *large with red eyes, heavy-bills and extensive black hoods tapering to point on breast.* Race *abyssinicus* (Er and Et) has *black scapulars forming black V on yellow back,* with yellow nape and underparts; race *paroptus* (extreme SEt, SSo) has *yellow back evenly spotted black,* more black on crown and variable chestnut wash bordering black. All females have olive-streaked backs, yellow supercilia and yellow underparts when breeding. Non-breeding males and females have *greenish-yellow heads contrasting with either an olive or greyish dusky-streaked back,* yellow breast and whitish belly. **HH** Widespread and very common from sea-level to 2400m in wide range of habitats and human settlements. **Voice** When dangling below nests and flapping wings, males sustain constant chattering punctuated with higher-pitched squeaks, strange snoring churrs and short flourishes. [Alt: Black-headed Weaver, Spotted-backed Weaver]

Lesser Masked Weaver *Ploceus intermedius*   13cm, 5"

Breeding male has *creamy-white eyes* that stand out against black mask which extends over forecrown and is variably edged with chestnut wash; *legs pale blue-grey.* Bright yellow below with light chestnut wash. Similar Vitelline Masked Weaver lacks black on forecrown, has red eyes and pink or reddish legs. Non-breeding male and female have *pale eyes, blue-grey legs* and fairly strong yellow wash across breast. Immature has dark eyes. Race in NE Africa is nominate. **HH** Common in Et (mainly Rift Valley) and SSo, in bush country, woodland, cultivation and wide variety of vegetation near water, from sea-level to 1650m. **Voice** Song is very different from other masked weavers, consisting of an accelerating series of both nasal and liquid notes.

Vitelline Masked Weaver *Ploceus vitellinus*   13cm, 5"

Breeding male has *red eyes, pinkish-red legs and black mask extending below eye with only very narrow band above bill;* crown strongly washed chestnut. Lesser Masked Weaver has whitish eyes and black on forecrown. Speke's Weaver is pale-eyed with pale yellow crown. Non-breeding male and female have *red eyes, pink legs* and yellowish breast. Immature is browner than female, with dark eyes. Race in NE Africa is *uluensis.* **HH** Pairs are widespread in variety of bush and wooded habitats including semi-arid areas, from near sea-level to 1950m in SEt and NW&SSo. Usually solitary or in pairs, building distinctive onion-shaped nests with entrance hole at bottom. **Voice** Long rambling song is buzzy and scratchy, without musical flourishes. **Note** Formerly lumped in Southern Masked Weaver *P. velatus.*

Northern Masked Weaver *Ploceus taeniopterus*   13cm, 5"

Breeding male has *dark brown eyes and black mask extending from just behind eye and down to upper breast,* broadly edged chestnut-orange (almost blackish on forecrown). Non-breeding male and female have dark eyes and buffy breasts. Immature is similar, but with whitish eyes. Race in Et is nominate. **HH** Common but very local in S&WEt, at 550–1800m, inhabiting tall grassland (with acacias), reedbeds and swamps. **Voice** Hesitant song is somewhat jerky and terminal flourish is dry and unmusical.

Speke's Weaver *Ploceus spekei*   15cm, 6"

Fairly large, stocky weaver with heavy bill. Adult male has black mask extending from eye downwards, edged rufous on breast, an *all-yellow crown, and pale-yellowish eyes. Mantle is spangled yellow and black.* Female is dull olive-green above with broad streaking on mantle, very indistinct supercilium, and pale yellow throat and breast. Immature is like female, but more olive-brown. **HH** Patchy distribution in Et and So; uncommon in small flocks within open woodland, acacia country and around settlements from near sea-level to 2100m. **Voice** Breeding colonies keep up a constant chattering that lacks musical quality although individuals sing a nasal burry skirl which ends in a series of chattering notes.

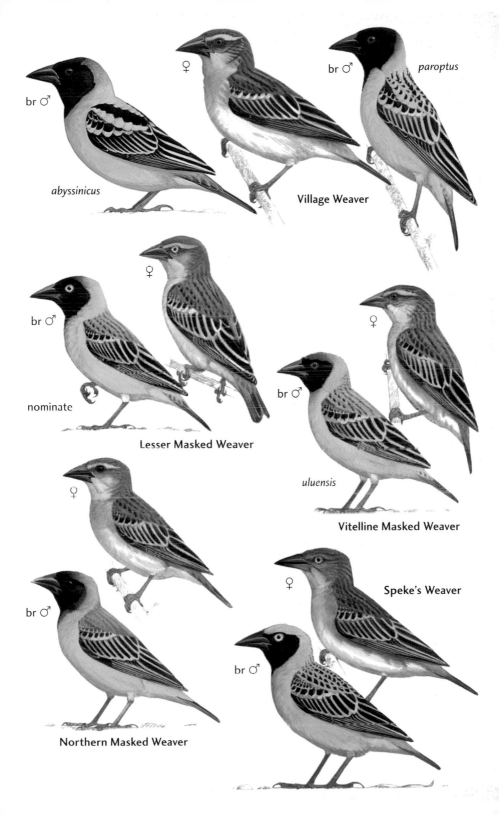

br ♂

abyssinicus

♀

br ♂

paroptus

Village Weaver

br ♂

♀

nominate

Lesser Masked Weaver

♀

br ♂

uluensis

Vitelline Masked Weaver

♀

Speke's Weaver

br ♂

♀

br ♂

Northern Masked Weaver

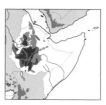

Spectacled Weaver *Ploceus ocularis*　　　14cm, 5.5"

Adult male is mostly yellow with *green back and wings, narrow black line through eye and broad black stripe down throat*. Eyes are very pale yellow, bill rather slender. Adult female is similar, but lacks black throat-stripe. No non-breeding plumage. Northern race *crocatus* lacks rufous wash to head. Immature is like dull female. **HH** Single birds and pairs are common in wide variety of habitats at 1200–1900m in W&SEt, including forest edge, woodland, bushed grasslands and overgrown cultivation. Most often seen slowly creeping about within cover. **Voice** Common and familiar call is 6–7 rapidly delivered, descending whistles *si si si si si si...* Song begins with this and breaks into complex musical buzzy flourish before ending with *cht* notes that fade away.

Black-necked Weaver *Ploceus nigricollis*　　　14cm, 5.5"

Adult male has narrow black eye-stripe and black throat-patch contrasting with yellow (or orange-yellow) head and underparts. Adult female has black extending over crown, yellow supercilium and black line through eye. In race *melanoxanthus* in our area, *both sexes are black above (including nape)* and have *red eyes*. No non-breeding plumage. Immature has pale brown bill and brown eyes. **HH** Widespread but never numerous; single birds and pairs occur in variety of lowland woodland and thick bush including semi-arid areas, in SWEt and SSo. from sea-level to 1500m. **Voice** Song is a rapid, short flourish, typical of weaver, but with strange liquid bubbling quality. Call is a spitting *chwit chwit chwit...*

Dark-backed Weaver *Ploceus bicolor*　　　15cm, 6"

White-billed, dark-headed forest weaver with red eyes, blackish upperparts and yellow breast to vent. In race *kersteni* in our region, mantle, wings and head are uniform black. Sexes alike. Immature duller with a pale throat. **HH** Common in riverine forests in SSo, especially along middle and lower Jubba; often works through middle stratum in pairs, small groups or mixed-species flocks. **Voice** Wonderfully distinct song typically starts with a few chips, buzzes or squeaks and continues musically with double nasal squeaks, rising-and-falling bell-like notes or rhythmic and rising *wi-wi wi-chuk-chuk wi-chuk*, randomly peppered with weird bleats, trumpets and squeaky hinge noises! [Alt: Forest Weaver]

Rüppell's Weaver *Ploceus galbula*　　　14cm 5.5"

Breeding male has small *chestnut mask extending across forehead* (can look blackish in some lights), *and orange-red eyes*. Crown, nape and underparts are bright yellow. Non-breeding male and female washed yellow above and on throat, and buffy across breast. Female is like female Vitelline Masked Weaver (plate 194) but eyes dark, not red. **HH** Common to locally abundant in Er, Dj, NSo and Et (mainly Rift Valley), from sea-level to 2400m. Inhabits coastal plains, arid savannas and cultivation. Gregarious; known for erratic wanderings. **Voice** Long, typical weaver-like series ends with drawn-out snore and distinctive metallic chitter.

Compact Weaver *Ploceus superciliosus*　　　12cm, 5"

Thickset, short-tailed weaver with heavy bill. Breeding male has yellow crown washed chestnut frontally, black mask, and *streaky olive-brown nape, back, wings and tail*. Breeding female is like breeding male but with dark crown and broad rusty-yellow supercilium. Non-breeding birds are browner above and buffy below, with dark brown crown, buff supercilium and dark brown eye-stripe. **HH** Pairs and small flocks are rather local in damp wooded grasslands, marshy areas and nearby cultivation, at 400–1200m in WEt. Often perches on tall grass stems. **Voice** Feeding parties give a buzzing twitter, also in flight. Song is similar but a little more varied and burry: *trrri-titi-trrrri-titi-tri*.

crocatus

♂ ♀

Spectacled Weaver

♀

♂

Black-necked Weaver

melanoxanthus

imm

Dark-backed Weaver

ad

kersteni

non-br ♂

br ♀

Rüppell's Weaver

br ♂

♀

br ♂

Compact Weaver

Little Weaver *Ploceus luteolus* 10cm, 4"

Distinctly *smaller* than other weavers. Breeding male has *lemon-yellow nape and underparts* (unlike orange-yellow of so many other weavers), and small black mask, with no chestnut edging, extending onto forehead. Back, wings and tail are greenish, eyes brown. Lesser Masked Weaver (plate 194) is larger with pale eyes. Non-breeding male and female are olive above with darker streaking, mostly yellow below, male with whiter belly. Immature is like pale female, but buffy and whiter below. Race in region is nominate. **HH** Single birds or pairs are common but not numerous in acacia bush country, open woodland and trees within farmland, at 400–1800m mainly west of Rift Valley. **Voice** Song is a typical weaver buzz breaking into a flourish, with rather nasal pinched quality; each set is often introduced by musical *sweetiswiswi*.

CHESTNUT-BELLIED WEAVERS *Two similar weavers, males differing mainly in the colour of the nape, mantle and underparts.*

Yellow-backed Weaver *Ploceus melanocephalus* 13cm, 5"

Breeding male has *black hood ending near rear of crown and lower nape yellow, forming distinct collar.* Eyes brown; *underparts rich chestnut with yellow restricted to belly.* Non-breeding male, female and immature are olive-brown above with dark streaking on mantle; yellowish supercilium, dull yellowish wash on throat and breast, and rest of underparts whitish; sometimes show pale greyish eyes. Race in region is *dimidiatus.* **HH** Frequent to common in WEr and NWEt, inhabiting wide range of vegetation usually near water at 500–1500m, including reedbeds, papyrus, moist thickets and farmland. **Voice** Breeding colonies maintain a squeaky chipping in which individuals are indiscernible. Song is quite buzzing, beginning with squeaky *si si si...* notes and continuing with weaver-like chatter and low nasal notes. [Alt: Black-headed Weaver]

Juba Weaver *Ploceus dichrocephalus* 13cm, 5"

Breeding male is like Yellow-backed Weaver, but *black on crown merges to blackish-chestnut on nape and sides of face* (sometimes wholly dark chestnut); *eyes reddish-brown.* Bright lemon-yellow back is unstreaked. Underparts washed chestnut; belly and undertail-coverts yellow. Non-breeding male, female and immature are similar to female Yellow-backed, but more yellow below with obvious bicoloured bill. **HH** Locally common near-endemic resident in riverine vegetation in SSo and SEt, from near sea-level to 1000m. **Voice** Rambling, rather unmusical, slightly swallow-like song includes varied squeaks, snores and buzzes. [Alt: Jubba Weaver, in accordance with modern Somali spelling of Jubba river]

GOLDEN WEAVERS *Yellow weavers with some orange or chestnut on the head; the exact extent of these marks and eye colour aid identification.*

Golden Palm Weaver *Ploceus bojeri* 14cm, 5.5"

Adult male is very bright yellow with *orange head and throat, dark brown eye* (often looks blackish), and black bill. Adult female is yellow above with indistinct streaking, uniform yellow below, and bicoloured bill. Immature is like dull pale female. **HH** Gregarious and common in SSo in coastal palms, wooded areas and gardens, as well as inland where it favours lowland riverine habitat in dry country. Two records from upper Jubba and Shabeelle rivers in SEEt. **Voice** Prolonged song is high-pitched and hissing. Call is an explosive, very metallic repeated *chwenk*.

African Golden Weaver *Ploceus subaureus* 14cm, 5.5"

Like Golden Palm Weaver, but breeding male is a little *duller orange on head, with pale red eyes* (not dark). Non-breeding male has olive wash to head. Breeding female like female Golden Palm, but has reddish eyes. Non-breeding female and immature are more boldly streaked above, with yellow breast and white belly. **HH** Inhabits coastal plains and lowland river valleys, preferring wetter habitats than Golden Palm. In our region, known from single record of male nest-building in SSo. **Voice** Song is rambling winding-up series of soft squeaky *tikotikotikotiko*, before breaking into set of complex flourishes, many with a canary-like quality. [Alt: Yellow Weaver; Eastern Golden Weaver]

br ♂

♀

Little Weaver

♀

br ♂

Yellow-backed Weaver

dimidiatus

♀

br ♂

Juba Weaver

♀

♂

Golden Palm Weaver

♀

African Golden Weaver

aureoflavus

br ♂

Baglafecht Weaver *Ploceus baglafecht* 15cm, 6"

Three races, previously regarded as separate species, occur. All *males in our region have yellow crowns and black masks*, females black or greenish crowns, and both sexes with *yellow or green wing-edgings and yellow eyes* (eyes browner in immature). Nominate male (Er and N&WEt) has greenish nape and upperparts, and yellow underparts sometimes fading to white on lower belly; male *reichenowi* (SEt) has nape and upperparts black, underparts all yellow; male *emini* (C&EEt) also has black nape and upperparts (with some green fringes) and yellow breast, but belly and undertail-coverts are white. Intermediate forms occur in contact zones, and non-breeding birds are greyer (except for seasonally unchanging *reichenowi*). Nominate female has whole head greenish (mask darker), female *reichenowi* and *emini* have whole head black (other features as males). Immatures are mostly like dull versions of females, but often more olive above. **HH** Pairs are very common and widespread in highlands of Er and Et at 1100–3000m, occupying forest edge, open woodland, marshes, cultivation and gardens. Nominate race is typical form in our region. **Voice** Usual song is a complex buzzing churr that breaks into a flourish, often then ending in another buzzy churr and punctuated by a loud *zwink zwink* (also given as call). There is little difference in dialect between races.

Chestnut Weaver *Ploceus rubiginosus* 15cm, 6"

Breeding male is distinctive with *clear-cut black head contrasting with all-dark chestnut back and underparts, and red eye*. Wings and tail blackish, edged buffy-brown or yellow. Similar Chestnut Sparrow (plate 191) is much smaller and has very dark brown face blending into chestnut on nape and throat. Non-breeding male, female and immature are browner than similar female-type weavers, the only *Ploceus* in region with no trace of yellow or green in plumage; streaked black above, and white below with broad, lightly streaked tawny-buff band across breast and down flanks. Race in region is nominate. **HH** Locally common resident or migrant in Er, Et and SSo, from sea-level to 1850m. Wanders widely, often appearing during rains in very large numbers. Highly colonial, building hundreds of nests together. Most frequent in dry woodland and bush country (particularly acacia). **Voice** Call is like other weavers. Song is unique with birds suddenly giving a very short dry fizzling call in bouts of general chattering.

Grosbeak Weaver *Amblyospiza albifrons* 17cm, 6.5"

Large stocky weaver with *very thick bill*. Adult male has variable plumage: in race *melanota* (W&CEt), head is brown contrasting with blacker mantle, wings, tail and underparts; in *unicolor* (SSo) males are all blackish-brown. All forms have *small white patch at base of primaries* and often *patch of white on forecrown*. Female and immature are brown above with no white in wing, heavily streaked brown and white below, and have huge yellowish-horn bill. **HH** Occurs singly or in small flocks in swamps, but also in forest edge, riverine bush and overgrown cultivation, from sea-level to 1800m. Always breeds over water: nest is a finely woven fibrous dome with entrance near top. **Voice** Song is a random mix of very harsh nasal skirls interspersed with loud rattles and softer twittering. [Alt: Thick-billed Weaver]

CUCKOO FINCH Previously considered a weaver, but is now thought to be more closely related to the whydahs. It is a brood parasite on cisticolas and prinias.

Cuckoo Finch *Anomalospiza imberbis* 11cm, 4.5"

Adult male is bright yellow on head and underparts with *very stubby black bill*, olive back and wings heavily streaked black (all suggesting a heavy-billed canary). Adult female is very like female Northern Red Bishop (plate 199) but with stubbier bill. Immature is tawny-brown above with some streaking, dull buff below. **HH** Localised and generally uncommon in wet grasslands with scattered bushes, open woodland and cultivated areas at 500–2100m. Fragmented range in Et includes Gambela, Lake Tana and Debre Zeit. **Voice** Flight call is a fast *tititit*. Song includes a *swi-sun-suit* with weaver-like quality and sometimes a long wheezy *vweeeeeoooooo*. [Alt: Parasitic Weaver]

imm

♀

non-br

br ♀

emini

♂

reichenowi

Baglafecht Weaver

br ♂

emini

br ♀

br ♂

nominate

♀

♀

br ♂

Chestnut Weaver

nominate

Grosbeak Weaver

♂

nominate

♀

Cuckoo Finch

melanota

QUELEAS Weaver-like birds which often congregate in large flocks. Males in breeding plumage pose no identification problems, but non-breeding males and females look very similar to each other, and also to several weavers, widowbirds and whydahs.

Red-billed Quelea *Quelea quelea*   12cm, 5"

Breeding male has *black mask* (not extending as band across forehead on race *aethiopica*) and *red bill*. Colour of crown and breast variable: pink, tawny-yellow or buff. Non-breeding male and female have streaky sparrow-like plumage with *whitish superciliary stripes and red bills*. Immature is similar, but with much duller, brownish-pink bill. Pin-tailed Whydah (plate 207) is similar in non-breeding plumage, but smaller and smaller-billed with much more boldly streaked head. **HH** Common, widespread, and sometimes abundant but seasonally migratory, so may be absent from apparently suitable areas for months at a time. Race *aethiopica* (including '*intermedia*') occurs throughout most of our area (except much of EEt and NSo) in bush country, grasslands and cultivation, up to 2650m. **Voice** Song is a medley of chipping mixed with mournful downslurs *seu seu seu seeeeu* and given from vicinity of nest. Roosting flocks keep up a continuous chipping that can be heard at considerable distance.

Red-headed Quelea *Quelea erythrops*   12cm, 5"

Breeding male is larger than Cardinal Quelea with longer bill and entire head (including nape) darker red with *variable black scalloping on throat*. Non-breeding male, female and immature are very like corresponding plumages of Cardinal, but throat is slightly whiter. **HH** Locally common at just a few sites in W&SWEt at 750–2000m, most regular in marshy areas and wet grassland, but also in open bush. **Voice** Song is a formless, tuneless, squealing chatter; birds give a chipping call in flight.

Cardinal Quelea *Quelea cardinalis*   11cm, 4.5"

Breeding male has most of head, throat and upper breast bright red. Nominate birds (in our region) have red extending onto upper nape. Non-breeding male and female have supercilium and throat washed yellowish, and dark brown bill. Immature is like female but throat is pale brown. **HH** Rare non-breeding visitor to W&SEt, with only few records, Jul–Oct. Favours rank grassy areas and marshland fringes, preferring drier areas than Red-headed. **Voice** Song is a series of chip notes which descend and accelerate before ending with nasal downslurred *sheeeeu*. Other chip calls are frequently heard from feeding flocks.

RED-HEADED WEAVER In the monotypic genus Anaplectes; it is often considered to be a link species between the yellow weavers and the black and red malimbes of W & C Africa.

Red-headed Weaver *Anaplectes rubriceps*   16cm, 6"

Two distinctive races occur: in widespread race *leuconotus* (mainly north of equator) breeding male has black mask, red primary panel and white breast to vent; in SSo (and adjacent coastal Kenya) localised race *jubaensis* is almost entirely red. Both have *waxy red bills*. Females of both races are *greyish-brown with distinctive orange-red bills and primary panels*. Non-breeding males are like females. Immatures are like females with yellow wash to head. **HH** Solitary birds or pairs are widespread and locally common in wide variety of woodlands, bush country, grasslands with scattered trees, and gardens. Race *leuconotus* occurs widely in Et and NWSo (but is rare in Er and NEt), at 750–2000m, while *jubaensis* is found in lowlands in SSo, mainly along Jubba river. **Voice** Song is a complex mix of high-pitched sizzling and chipping. Feeding birds give a smooth *chut*. **Note** Formerly *A. melanotis* or *Malimbus rubriceps*.

br ♂

aethiopica

Red-billed Quelea

non-br ♂

♀

br ♂

♀

Red-headed Quelea

♀

Cardinal Quelea

nominate

br ♂

♀

br ♂

Red-headed Weaver

br ♂

jubaensis

br ♂

leuconotus

BISHOPS Breeding males are shorter-tailed than widowbirds, with more extensive colour to the body plumage. Most bishops have a female-like non-breeding plumage and extreme care is needed in identifying these birds.

Yellow-crowned Bishop *Euplectes afer* 10cm, 4"

Very small, short-tailed, black and yellow bishop. Breeding male is much smaller than Yellow Bishop with obvious *bright yellow crown, mantle, rump and vent*. Two races occur: in highlands of Et, breeding male *strictus* has narrow black band on nape and all-black underparts; race *taha* (formerly *ladoensis*) (SWEt) has broader black band on nape and variable yellow feathering on sides of breast. Non-breeding male and female are whitish below with blackish streaking; *dark ear-coverts contrast with white face*. Immature similar, but buffier below. **HH** Uncommon resident and wanderer, sometimes occurring after rains in large numbers, in reedbeds, flooded grasslands and arable croplands at 500–3000m. **Voice** Song is a tuneless, monotonous dry chipping with slight variation, given perched and in flight.

Fire-fronted Bishop *Euplectes diadematus* 10cm, 4"

Breeding male is distinctive small bishop with *bright red spot on forecrown*, extensive yellow on lower back, rump and vent, and yellow and black-streaked mantle. Non-breeding male, female and immature are also small with *yellowish-edged primaries*; could be confused with non-breeding queleas – note bill-shape. **HH** Highly nomadic; may appear in large numbers after rains, preferring wet grassy areas and cultivation in coastal lowlands of SSo. **Voice** Makes a sizzling song similar to other small bishops.

Black Bishop *Euplectes gierowii* 15cm, 6"

Large black and red bishop. Breeding male of race *ansorgei* is thickset black bishop with *orange-red nape blending into yellowish upper back* and extending round sides of neck and across upper breast as narrow orange-red band. *Rump and uppertail-coverts black*. Similar Black-winged Red Bishop has entirely red crown. Non-breeding male, female and immature are dark and very heavily streaked black above (particularly male), with black spots at sides of breast; very similar to non-breeding/female Red-collared Widowbird (plate 200). **HH** Local but not uncommon in tall wet grasslands, scrub and cultivation in W&SWEt, at 500–2000m. **Voice** Very simple songs are either nasal slurs rapidly repeated in a short series, or a dry twittering.

Black-winged Red Bishop *Euplectes hordeaceus* 12cm, 5"

Larger than Northern Red Bishop with heavier bill and longer tail. In flight, breeding male shows *broad rounded black wings and tail. Red on crown extends (or almost) to bill*. In Et, race *craspedopterus* has whitish undertail-coverts. Non-breeding male, female and immature are larger than female Northern Red with stronger wash of tawny-brown across breast and flanks; very similar to non-breeding/female Red-collared Widowbird (plate 200). **HH** Locally common in WEt, inhabiting bushed grassland, woodland and cultivation at 750–1200m. **Voice** Song is an insect-like accelerated twittering *tititititrrrrrrr*, sometimes interspersed with high-pitched musical squeaking. [Alt: Black-winged Bishop, Fire-crowned Bishop]

Northern Red Bishop *Euplectes franciscanus* 11cm, 4.5"

Small red and black bishop; breeding male easily told from larger Black-winged by shape of black on head (*black crown and red chin* versus red crown and black chin). *Exceptionally long upper and lower tail-coverts hide all but very tip of brown tail*. Two races occur: in SEEt and SSo race *pusillus* may be orange and black rather than red and black of more widespread nominate. Non-breeding male, female and immature are small and streaky with buffy supercilium and whitish throat and belly. **HH** Locally common with fragmented range in Er, Et and So, inhabiting tall open or bushed grasslands, cultivation and marshes, from sea-level to 2300m; frequently in irrigated agricultural areas in Er. **Voice** Simple song is a tuneless dry chipping and trilling.

Yellow Bishop *Euplectes capensis* 15cm, 6"

Breeding male is rather stocky, short-tailed bishop with *bright yellow shoulders and rump*. Non-breeding male is like female, but has yellow on shoulders and rump. Adult female has typical female-like streaky plumage, but with dingy uniform olive-yellow rump. Immature is like female, but rump is brown with darker streaking. **HH** Usually solitary or in pairs but flocks outside breeding season; common and widespread in bushed grasslands, marshes and cultivation at 1800–3300m in highlands of Et (isolated endemic race *xanthomelas*). **Voice** Song reminiscent of widowbird, consisting of a high-pitched *sisisisisisi...* with notes interspersed with insect-like trills and chittering. [Alt: Yellow-rumped Widow]

br ♂   *strictus*

♀

Fire-fronted Bishop   ♀

br ♂

Yellow-crowned Bishop

taha display

♂

♀

br ♂   **Black-winged Red Bishop**

br ♂

craspedopterus

Black Bishop

ansorgei

br ♂

br ♂ display

br ♂   **Yellow Bishop**

♀

xanthomelas

♀

non-br ♂

Northern Red Bishop

nominate

WIDOWBIRDS *Males have distinctive breeding plumages, mostly with long tails and patches of red or yellow on their wings. Non-breeding males resemble females, but are larger, and some can be identified by coloured patches in their wings. Females are extremely difficult to identify; they are similar to female and non-breeding male bishops but generally have longer tails.*

Red-collared Widowbird   *Euplectes ardens*   ♂ 25cm, 10"; ♀ 13cm, 5"

Breeding male is unmistakable, with *long floppy tail* and all-black plumage except for *bright red crown, nape, sides of neck and collar.* Race in NE Africa is *laticauda*, shorter-tailed than races elsewhere in Africa. Non-breeding male becomes streaky like female but retains long tail and has some streaking on breast. Female and immature have yellowish supercilium and are rather plain below, similar to non-breeding Black-winged and Black Bishops. **HH** Gregarious, occurring commonly in highlands of Er and Et, at 750–3300m, in variety of vegetation including tall grass, wheat fields, overgrown cultivation and rank herbage. **Voice** In both display-flights and when perched, usual song is an insect-like *sisisisisisisisisi...*, intermixed with dry rasps and rustling sounds when excited. [Alt: Red-collared Widow]

Fan-tailed Widowbird   *Euplectes axillaris*   15cm, 6"

Breeding male is heavy, *short-tailed black widowbird,* with orange lesser coverts and cinnamon greater and primary coverts, and blue-grey bill; tail is only fan-shaped in display. Three races occur: *phoeniceus* (WEt) has orange and cinnamon shoulders; *traversii* (highlands of Et) is similar but slightly longer-tailed; *zanzibaricus* (SSo) is also similar but has dark spots on cinnamon wing-coverts and heavier bill. Non-breeding male is like female but with orange and cinnamon shoulders. Female and immature have typical streaky brown plumage, but with small area of pale rusty-brown at bend of wing. **HH** Common and widespread, favouring marshy areas and wet grasslands from sea-level to 2800m, but also found in drier habitats. Males often sit on reed tops making short display-flights; females more skulking. **Voice** In flight parties maintain a constant twittering. Song is usually heard in display-flight, a slightly variable insect-like trilling. [Alt: Red-shouldered Widow]

Yellow-mantled Widowbird   *Euplectes macroura*   ♂ 21cm, 8"; ♀ 14cm, 5.5"

Black and yellow widowbird with moderately long tail. In NE Africa breeding male of race *macrocercus* [Yellow-shouldered Widowbird] has *yellow restricted to shoulders.* Non-breeding male is like female but retains yellow shoulders. Females and immatures are typically streaky but may show yellow fringes at bend of wing. **HH** Flocks are locally common in moist grasslands, marshy areas and cultivation at 750–2500m in highlands of Er and Et, mainly west of Rift Valley. **Voice** Sings from perch a high-pitched, rapid twitter *tzip-tzip-tzip...* followed by a subdued nasal downslur, *weah.* [Alt: Yellow-backed Widow]

White-winged Widowbird   *Euplectes albonotatus*   ♂ 16cm, 6"; ♀ 12cm, 5"

Small widowbird with medium-length tail. In NE Africa, breeding male of race *eques* is black with *deep chestnut-brown shoulders,* prominent *white edges on primary and secondary coverts* and white bases to primaries (showing as *obvious white patches in flight*). Underwing white. Non-breeding male has streaky plumage but retains chestnut and white on wing. Female and immature may show hint of chestnut feather edgings at bend of wing. **HH** Small flocks are local and uncommon in moist grasslands and cultivation at 1100–2400m in highlands of Et. **Voice** Song is a repeated high-pitched insect-like buzzing, *sisisisisisisisisi,* interspersed with a dry rasping. Call is a repeated *twit twit,* similar to many other widowbirds. [Alt: White-winged Widow]

br ♂

♀

non-br ♂

Red-collared
Widowbird

laticauda

br ♂

♀

Fan-tailed
Widowbird

phoeniceus

non-br ♂

Yellow-mantled
Widowbird

macrocercus

♀

br ♂

non-br ♂

br ♂

♀

eques

White-winged
Widowbird

non-br ♂

PYTILIAS Brightly coloured waxbills found in pairs and small flocks in bush country and wooded grasslands, often on the ground, or low down in fairly thick cover. Extent of mask and wing colour aid identification.

Green-winged Pytilia *Pytilia melba*   14cm, 5.5"

Adult male has bill and face red, hind part of head grey, *mantle and wings green*, rump and tail red, and breast to vent barred and spotted dark grey (or olive-grey) and white. Four races occur: males differ in amount of red on face and breast-band colour. Race *citerior* (NWEt) has *entire face red* (including lores and extending back to eye) with a golden-yellow breast-band; *soudanensis* (most of Et and So) is similar but the red is more extensive, merging gradually into the greenish-yellow breast; *jessei* (Er, NEt) is like *soudanensis* but has *grey lores*; *'flavicaudata'* (Dj) also has grey lores, but *red of face, rump and tail replaced with golden-yellow*. Adult females are all similar, paler than males with grey heads (lacking any red), and well-barred underparts. Immatures are like dull females, but may have yellowish edges to wings—beware confusion with Orange-winged Pytilia. **HH** Uncommon but widespread in semi-arid acacia country, scrub and wooded grasslands, from sea-level to 1500m. **Voice** Usually sings quite loud persistent series of chips, squeaks and nasal notes, well imitated by Eastern Paradise Whydah. Call is a loud, series of identical notes, *spit-spit-spit*. **Note** Race *'flavicaudata'* is not technically named as no specimen was collected. It is so different from other races that it may be a separate species (Yellow-tailed Pytilia), or perhaps a genetic mutant of *P. melba*. [Alt: Melba Finch]

Orange-winged Pytilia *Pytilia afra*   11cm, 4.5"

Adult male is like larger Green-winged Pytilia, but has *smaller, rounder red mask extending well back behind eye, and orange-edged wings*; lores grey; belly olive with narrow white bars. Adult female is like male with orange wing-edgings, but no red on head. Immature is like drab female. **HH** Scarce in Rift Valley and SE Highlands of Et, inhabiting moist wooded grasslands, savannas and thickets at 950–1800m; often shy and elusive. **Voice** Song is simpler than Green-winged Pytilia, a monotonous series of chips and squeaks. [Alt: Golden-backed Pytilia]

Red-billed Pytilia *Pytilia lineata*   13cm, 5"

Adult male is *all medium dark-grey with crimson wings*, rump and tail, and *red bill*. Lower breast, belly and flanks finely barred white. Adult female is similar but washed grey-brown, with duller bill. Immature is duller and browner than adult with subdued areas of red. Lack of green separates all plumages from other pytilias, and lack of red face separates males. **HH** Fairly common near-endemic in wooded grasslands and bush country at 750–1800m in WEt and central highlands of Et. **Voice** After a few squeaky notes, calls a loud obtrusive machine-gun-like rattle *titititititititit*. **Note** Previously lumped with extralimital Red-winged Pytilia *P. phoenicoptera*, differing only in its red bill (ranges do not overlap).

TWINSPOTS Two brightly coloured waxbills in different genera. Rarely far from cover, they are usually found in pairs or groups feeding quietly on the ground or in low vegetation.

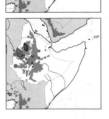

Peters's Twinspot *Hypargos niveoguttatus*   13cm, 5"

Adult male is mainly brown above with red rump and base of tail; rest of tail black. *Sides of face to breast red, lower breast to vent black with conspicuous white spots.* Adult female is like male, but more washed out, with greyer face, and buffy-orange sides to head and breast. Immature is dull brown with pale buffy face, dull red rump and black belly. **HH** In our region, only known from Boni Forest in extreme SSo, in undergrowth at forest edge (race *macrospilotus*). **Voice** Varied song is a complex mix of very high-pitched sibilant trills, mournful downslurs and single extended notes. Call is a distinctive *tit-tit*. [Alt: Red-throated Twinspot]

Green-backed Twinspot *Mandingoa nitidula*   10cm, 4"

Adult male is *mainly green twinspot with contrasting bright red mask* and black breast to vent well-spotted with white. Green-winged and Orange-winged Pytilias are larger and have barred bellies. Adult female is paler than male with *buffish-yellow mask*. Immature is mostly dull grey-green with paler area around eye. Race in region is *chubbi*. **HH** Local and rather uncommon in W&SEt, at 1200–1800m. Particularly shy; occurs in dense undergrowth and thick cover within forest, but also in canopy. **Voice** Song is a complex mix of very high-pitched canary-like phrases with variety of sibilant trills and slurs. Call is a high *zit-zit…*, given perched and in flight. [Alt: Green Twinspot]

♀ **Green-winged Pytilia**

♂ *soudanensis*

♂ *jessei*

♂ *citerior*

♂

♀ **Orange-winged Pytilia**

♀

Red-billed Pytilia

imm

♂

Green-backed Twinspot

chubbi

♂

♀

♂ *macrospilotus*

Peters's Twinspot

CORDON-BLEUS *Slim blue and brown waxbills usually found feeding on the ground in pairs or in small flocks. Head pattern identifies males; other plumages are often more difficult.*

Red-cheeked Cordon-bleu *Uraeginthus bengalus* 13 cm, 5"

Three races occur: all adult males are easily told by their *bright red cheek-patches* and brown crown. All adult females are brown above (except for blue rump and tail), but extent of blue on face and underparts varies: in Er and Et, nominate *bengalus* has most blue, extending over sides of face, neck, breast and flanks; in SWSo *brunneigularis* differs in having brown sides to face and neck; in extreme SSo *littoralis* has pale brownish cheeks. Immatures are like dull female. **HH** Very common and widespread in virtually all habitats except forest interior from sea-level to 2400m; absent from much of EEt and So. **Voice** Rhythmic but lazy song consists of 4–6 high-pitched lispy notes with last note lower, longer and more burry. Contact call is an often-repeated high-pitched *siii siii...*

Blue-capped Cordon-bleu *Uraeginthus cyanocephalus* 13 cm, 5"

Adult male has *entirely bright blue head*, breast and flanks, and *bright pink bill*. Adult female is like female Red-cheeked Cordon-bleu with brown on crown, but may show diagnostic *deep pinkish-red bill*. Immature is paler, with brownish breast and dark grey bill. **HH** Uncommon in semi-arid country in SSo and extreme SEt, mainly in lowlands; rather shy. **Voice** Complex and varied song has peculiar metallic twang,. Calls are stronger and less lispy than Red-cheeked Cordon-bleu, and retain metallic timbre.

Purple Grenadier *Uraeginthus ianthinogaster* 13 cm, 5"

Brightly coloured red-billed waxbill with long pointed tail: adult male has russet-brown head with blue face marks, *deep violet-blue breast to vent and rump*, and black tail. Adult female is similar above, but has pale blue or whitish incomplete eye-ring, and is paler russet brown below variably barred white on flanks. Immature is fairly uniform dull warm brown, with plain face, dark bill, blue rump and black tail. **HH** Common in S&EEt (mainly east of Rift Valley) and So (except NE), inhabiting open woodland, bush, cultivation and semi-arid areas from near sea-level to 1600m. **Voice** Song often starts with strong high trill which continues as rising metallic squeaking, *sit-t-sit sit siiiiiii*. Call is a metallic explosive *zeet*, sometimes repeated. **Note** Formerly in genus *Granatina*.

CRIMSONWINGS *Only one species of this distinctive genus in our region: an olive-green and red waxbill of the undergrowth in and around highland forest. Found mainly in pairs or small groups, it feeds in low cover and on the ground. Generally rather shy, it quickly flies into cover if disturbed.*

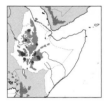

Abyssinian Crimsonwing *Cryptospiza salvadorii* 11 cm, 4.5"

Sexes are very similar with uniform greyish-olive head, and *dark crimson on back, wings and rump*. Olive-grey below with contrasting buffish chin and throat. Male has conspicuous pinkish-red eye-ring and some crimson on flanks. Immature has less red above and is washed brownish-olive. Race in NE Africa is nominate. **HH** Uncommon and elusive in undergrowth in montane forest, clearings and forest edge, at 1800–3000m in W and SE Highlands of Et. **Voice** Gives a high sibilant *tsit-tsit...* which can break into a rapid delivery of even higher-pitched notes.

Red-cheeked Cordon-bleu

nominate

Blue-capped Cordon-bleu

imm

Purple Grenadier

Abyssinian Crimsonwing

nominate

FIREFINCHES A similar group of small, red and brown waxbills. Different races complicate identification but they can be separated by attention to bill colour, extent of red in the plumage and presence or lack of black on the vent. Immatures are like dull, browner or paler versions of females. Many are hosts to the nest-parasitic indigobirds.

Red-billed Firefinch *Lagonosticta senegala*   10cm, 4"

Three races occur but limits are not well known: male of race *rhodopsis* (W&CEr and N&WEt) has red forehead and brown crown, with buffy-brown back; face and underparts pinkish-red, *lower belly and undertail-coverts greyish-buff.* Bill is pinkish-red on sides with grey culmen. Race *brunneiceps* (CEt, mainly above 1000m) is brighter above with brown crown with reddish sides. Race *somaliensis* (SEEt and NW&SSo) has reddish-brown crown and pale brown upperparts with pink wash. Females are largely brown with reddish on sides of face, red rump and duller bill. Both sexes may show small white spots at sides of breast. **HH** Commonest firefinch, from sea-level to 2500m, occupying wide range of habitats (including human settlements) and only really avoiding forest interiors and desert. **Voice** Varied song is mix of chip notes and rising upslurs, *chep chep de-zwizwi,* and also *chick-pea-pea-pea,* a song mimicked by Village Indigobird. Also gives a downslurred *seeu* both perched and in flight.

African Firefinch *Lagonosticta rubricata*   10cm, 4"

Adult male shows more contrasting upperparts than Red-billed Firefinch, with distinct *grey-brown mantle,* red rump and black tail; *underparts red with black belly and vent.* Bill is grey in both sexes. In widespread race *ugandae* female is largely brownish except for red rump, blackish tail, pink-washed underparts and black undertail-coverts. **HH** Uncommon and rather shy in highlands of Er and Et, often keeping to cover within woodland, thickets and overgrown cultivation, at 1200–2500m. **Voice** Song varies locally but typically consists of dry trills interspersed with bunting-like *suwee suwee suwee suwee* notes. Alarm call is a rather sharp *pit-pit-pit,* mimicked by Variable Indigobird. [Alt: Blue-billed Firefinch]

Bar-breasted Firefinch *Lagonosticta rufopicta*   10cm, 4"

Like Red-billed Firefinch with pink sides to bill, but *crown and nape are same earth-brown as mantle, and clearly separated from red face.* Underparts vinaceous-red; small white bars on breast, or sides of breast, highly variable and often hard to see; rump and base of tail red. Undertail-coverts buff. Sexes alike. Juvenile is grey-brown with vinous wash on breast. Race in Et is poorly marked *lateritia;* species sometimes regarded as monotypic. **HH** Locally common, favouring savanna in WEt as well as overgrown cultivation and lush vegetation near water, at 500–1800m. **Voice** Song is a mix of rising-and-falling chipping notes interspersed with short sibilant upslurs, *chip chip weee weeee...* Alarm call is a repeated metallic chip.

Jameson's Firefinch *Lagonosticta rhodopareia*   10cm, 4"

In Et nominate male is very like male African Firefinch, being *brown above and bright red on head and underparts;* also has black tail and vent and grey bill. Best distinctions are preference for drier habitats and rapid purring call. Female has *red lores,* brown crown and upperparts without pink wash, and is mostly orange-pink below with grey lower belly and some *blackish bars on vent.* **HH** Local and uncommon, mainly in dry bush country at 750–1300m in W&SEt, occurring at lower altitudes than African. **Voice** Song varies but is often a rather bunting-like *si..syee-syee-syee-syee-syee,* all on one pitch, and frequently interrupted by a *fast purring trill.*

Black-faced Firefinch *Lagonosticta larvata*   10cm, 4"

Adult male is atypical firefinch being greyer and darker with *black mask* and red rump and tail. Nominate race in our region is much darker than other races, with brownish-grey crown and upperparts, and pinkish-red collar and breast with small white spots on sides of breast. Belly and undertail-coverts black. Adult female is dark grey-brown above, with red rump and uppertail, and fulvous-brown underparts including vent. Bill in both sexes is dark grey. Black-cheeked Waxbill (plate 205) has longer tail, barred wings and no black on throat. **HH** Local and uncommon in tall grassland, thickets and open woodland at 750–1500m in W&NWEt. **Voice** Song consists of repeated phrases of 2–4 plaintive whistles, and call is a weak lisping *seesee.*

Red-billed Firefinch

♀

♂

brunneiceps

♀

African Firefinch

♂

ugandae

imm

ad

Bar-breasted Firefinch

luteritia

♀

Jameson's Firefinch

♂

nominate

♂

Black-faced Firefinch

nominate

♀

WAXBILLS A rather variable group of small estrildid finches, some of which congregate in large flocks. Sexes are similar.

Yellow-bellied Waxbill *Coccopygia quartinia*   10cm, 4"

Small and colourful but *pale-toned* waxbill, with pale grey head and upper breast, olive-green mantle and wings, red rump, blackish tail and *yellow belly*. Upper mandible black, lower mandible red. Immature similar, but paler with dark bill. **HH** Common at forest edge, in grasslands, scrub and around cultivation at 900–2750m in highlands of Er and Et (nominate race). **Voice** Song is a short series of slurred, whistled squeaks and nasal notes. Call is a high-pitched lispy *siii siii siii...* **Note** This species (and Swee Waxbill of southern Africa) was formerly in genus *Estrilda*. [Alt: East African Swee]

Common Waxbill *Estrilda astrild*   10cm, 4"

Commonest waxbill, *brown above including rump and tail*, and all finely barred, with bright red streak through eye, white cheeks, and waxy red bill. Pale brown below with variable pink wash, or red streak on belly. Two races occur: in Et, *peasei* suffused with rosy-pink below making belly-patch less distinct; in SSo, *minor* generally paler and pink below confined to belly-patch. Immature paler with blackish bill. **HH** Small to large flocks are locally common and widespread in grasslands, bush, cultivation and marshes, avoiding forest interior and lowland arid habitats, at 750–3000m. Race *minor* is uncommon in wet areas with lush vegetation in SSo. **Voice** Foraging birds usually keep in contact with irregular dry squeaks and chips. Song consists of a paired *tikatik-wheez tikatik-wheez*, with last note burry and upslurred.

Crimson-rumped Waxbill *Estrilda rhodopyga*   10cm, 4"

Like Common Waxbill with red streak through eye and finely barred brown upperparts, but has blackish bill, *crimson-red rump, and red edges to wing-coverts and tertials*. Underparts are buffy with pink restricted to undertail-coverts. Immature is plain brown, darker above than below, *lacks red eye-stripe* and has duller red rump. Two races occur: nominate (Er, NEt) as described, and overall darker *centralis* (C&SEt, NW&SSo) which has crimson undertail-coverts. **HH** Common resident in acacia woodland, thickets and damp grassland from sea-level to 1900m. **Voice** Song structure is similar to Common Waxbill, but notes are nasal and more clearly defined, consisting of musical chips forming regular rhythmic pattern, *wi-chi wi-chi wi chi-chi...* Calls include a low churr and nasal chipping in flight.

Black-rumped Waxbill *Estrilda troglodytes*   10cm, 4"

Like Common Waxbill but cleaner and pallid-looking with *jet-black rump and tail*, latter narrowly edged white. Bill and streak through eye red; faint barring above may be visible in good light. Very pale pinkish-buff below, whiter on throat. Immature is duller, with blackish bill and dark smudgy eye-stripe. **HH** Fairly common in WEr but rare in WEt, inhabiting both dry country and thicker vegetation near water, at 700–2100m. **Voice** Call is a loud, somewhat metallic chipping. Song is similar but more subdued, punctuated by long single upslurs, *soyiiiii...*

Abyssinian Waxbill *Estrilda (paludicola) ochrogaster*   10cm, 4"

Rather plain-looking waxbill with bright red bill, red rump and black tail. Race in region, *ochrogaster*, is almost endemic to Et and may be distinct species. Upperparts brownish, slightly greyer on head, lores and cheeks tinged yellow. Underparts *entirely yellowish-buff*, usually with a few pink feathers on belly. Immature generally paler with dark bill. **HH** Common to abundant near-endemic in WEt at 750–1800m, preferring lush habitats along streams, open woodland, marshes, wet grasslands and overgrown cultivation. **Voice** Song is a loud, energetic, rolling and rhythmic nasal series of chips and squeaks. Call is a short nasal downslurred *sieu*. **Note** Usually lumped with Fawn-breasted Waxbill *E. paludicola*, but plumage of *ochrogaster* is distinctive.

imm

ad

nominate

Yellow-bellied Waxbill

imm

Common Waxbill

peasei

imm

ad

**Crimson-rumped
Waxbill**

ad

centralis

Black-rumped Waxbill

imm

ad

ad

imm

ochrogaster

Abyssinian Waxbill

Black-cheeked Waxbill *Estrilda charmosyna* 11 cm, 4.5"

Distinctive dry-country waxbill with *black mask mainly confined to cheeks* (only very narrow black line crosses chin), upperparts pinkish-brown, and *underparts entirely pinkish-grey or pinkish-buff* in both sexes. Wings are strongly but finely barred black and white. Immature is less pink than adult. Only possible confusion species in NE Africa is Black-faced Firefinch (plate 203), which has shorter tail, plain wings, and black face and throat. **HH** Nominate race is uncommon in semi-arid bush country in Et (mainly east of Rift Valley) and NW&SSo up to 1800m. **Voice** Calls include a repeated dry chipping, short dry rattled trills and, for contact, a high-pitched nasal upslur.

Zebra Waxbill *Sporaeginthus subflavus* 9 cm, 3.5"

Very small bright waxbill. Adult male is olive-brown above with red eye-stripe and bill, red uppertail-coverts and blackish tail. Nominate race (in Et) is *bright orange-yellow on chin and throat; rest of underparts orange with barred flanks.* Adult female is duller and paler, without red eye-stripe. Immature is like pale, drab female with black bill and brown rump. **HH** Uncommon, often in small flocks, and very active inhabitant of reedbeds, marshy grassland and cultivated areas in highlands of WEt, at 750–2400m. **Voice** Most frequently heard calls are short repeated and complaining nasal downslurs, usually paired. Song mixes these notes with long descending rattled trills or a series of random metallic notes *tit tit tit tit…* [Alt: Orange-breasted Waxbill; *Amandava subflava*]

African Silverbill *Euodice cantans* 11 cm, 4.5"

Sandy-brown waxbill with blackish wings, rump and tail, buffy-white below, with rather large stubby blue-grey bill. Graduated tail is rather pointed. Immature similar but has browner tail. Race in region is *orientalis*. **HH** Uncommon to locally common in semi-arid bush and dry wooded grasslands throughout much of region, from sea-level to 2400m. **Voice** In flight gives a loud, harsh, hollow-sounding *tink-tink…*, but from perch may utter an extended dry rattle. **Note** Sometimes placed in genus *Lonchura*.

Grey-headed Silverbill *Odontospiza griseicapilla* 11 cm, 4.5"

Slightly larger than African Silverbill with *grey head,* white-speckled cheeks, pinkish-brown upperparts, *white rump* and blackish tail (shorter than African Silverbill). Adult is washed peachy-pink below. Immature is duller than adult without peachy-washed underparts or white spotting on cheeks. **HH** Uncommon and patchily distributed in SEt at 900–1300m, occurring in open wooded grasslands, bush and semi-arid acacia country; rare wanderer to SSo. **Voice** In flight utters soft downslurred mournful *seeu*. Song is a series of these notes which rise and fall and are occasionally mixed with sharp metallic notes. **Note** Sometimes placed in genus *Lonchura*.

QUAILFINCHES *Dumpy, short-tailed waxbills found in flocks on the ground. Often difficult to see until flushed. The many races in Africa are variously treated as one, two or three species.*

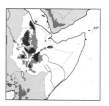

African Quailfinch *Ortygospiza fuscocrissa* 9 cm, 3.5"

Adult male is mostly grey-brown above (with blackish streaks), with blackish face and throat, *conspicuous white lines above and below lores,* white eye-ring and red bill; below, has a *tiny white chin-patch,* barred brown-and-white upper breast and flanks, and deep tawny lower breast and belly. *Shows small white corners to tail in flight.* Adult female is much duller, with dark upper mandible. Immature is like pale dull female. **HH** Nominate race is uncommon to common in short grasslands, ploughed fields and along barren lakeshores in Er, Et and NSo (once), at 1500–2700m. **Voice** When flushed individuals within flock utter burry metallic *tchink-tchink…* calls.

Black-faced Quailfinch *Ortygospiza atricollis* 9 cm, 3.5"

Very like African Quailfinch, but male *lacks distinct white loral lines and eye-ring* (but may sometimes show narrow line above lores and eye). Adult male has more extensive *black on forehead,* giving it a more black-faced appearance, contrasting with greyish ear-coverts. Mantle plain with only faint streaking. Breast is brighter rusty-orange, fading to tawny on belly. Female is paler with entire head greyish-brown. Immature is like female but duller with blackish bill. **HH** Recorded once in extreme WEt at 700m, but likely to be resident or a wanderer from Sudan. Race concerned is nominate (sometimes separated as '*ugandae*'). **Voice** Very like African Quailfinch. **Note** May be conspecific with African Quailfinch.

**Black-cheeked
Waxbill**

imm

imm

ad

ad

Zebra
Waxbill

nominate

nominate

ad

ad

Grey-headed
Silverbill

African Silverbill

orientalis

African
Quailfinch

♀

♂

fuscocrissa

Black-faced
Quailfinch

♂

♀

nominate

MANNIKINS *Four similar waxbills, also known as munias. All have blackish heads and barred flanks, but the overall size and mantle colour aid identification. They occur in small flocks, feeding in long grass and on the ground. Sexes are alike. Formerly placed in the genus* Lonchura.

Bronze Mannikin *Spermestes cucullata* 9cm, 3.5"

Small with *blackish head and breast* contrasting with *dull brown nape, mantle and wings.* In good light may show small glossy dark-green patch at shoulder. Lower breast to vent white. Race *scutata* (in Et) has brown barring on sides of breast. Bill is stubby with dark grey upper and pale grey lower mandible. Immature is plain buffy-brown with darker wings and tail. **HH** Commonest mannikin, widespread in all habitats except desert and forest interiors, at 750–2000m. **Voice** Song and calls consist of rapid delivery of rising-and-falling short burry chips, sometimes developing into a churr. Similar twittering is given in flight.

Black-and-white Mannikin *Spermestes bicolor* 9cm, 3.5"

Small, smart mannikin, *entirely black and white with no contrast between head and mantle. Flight feathers and rump are barred black and white* (plain on Bronze Mannikin) and bill is pale blue-grey. Immature is plain dull brown above, paler below with buffy flanks. **HH** Race *poensis* is locally common in S&WEt at forest edge, in lush thickets and around cultivation, at 1300–2700m. **Voice** Calls recall white-eye but consist of a little harsher, more mournful, whistled downslurs, *tsiu tsiu…*

Red-backed Mannikin *Spermestes (bicolor) nigriceps* 9cm, 3.5"

Very like Black-and-white Mannikin, with which it is often lumped, but *mantle, tertials and wing-coverts are chestnut-brown.* Flight feathers and rump are barred black and white (plain on Bronze Mannikin) and bill is pale blue-grey. Immature is washed warm brown on mantle. **HH** Apparently rare and local in riverine habitats in SSo, along Jubba valley and in Boni Forest. **Voice** Similar to Black-and-white Mannikin.

Magpie Mannikin *Spermestes fringilloides* 12cm, 5"

Largest mannikin, most like Bronze but with heavier dark grey and pale blue-grey bill. *Black on head extends over nape,* and upperparts warmer brown than Bronze; rump black and unbarred. Black smudges at sides of breast are large; black-and-white barred flanks may also have some rufous markings. Immature is dull brown above with paler mantle, buff underparts (brighter on flanks) and all-dark bill. **HH** Rare resident of forest edge, secondary growth and cultivation; only recorded at two sites in WEt, at 1200–1500m. **Voice** Calls are similar to Black-and-white Mannikin but louder with whistled downslurs longer and not so mournful, *tsiu rsii tsiu tsii…* [Alt: Pied Mannikin]

Cut-throat Finch *Amadina fasciata* 11cm, 4.5"

Adult male is very distinctive with *bright red crescent-shaped stripe like cut across throat,* otherwise all scaly grey-brown with a variably sized patch of chestnut on belly. Adult female is entirely barred and scaly, without red throat-stripe or chestnut on belly. Immature male shows hint of red throat-stripe. Two races occur: nominate (illustrated) extends into extreme NWEt and WEr; race *alexanderi* (widespread in Er, Et and So) is darker and browner, with bolder barring above; underparts more extensively barred and belly-patch smaller. **HH** Frequent to common, usually in flocks, mainly in semi-arid country but wanders erratically, occurring less frequently in farmland and at coast, from sea-level to 2100m. **Voice** Song consists of short abrupt phrases mixing nasal notes and squeaks. [Alt: Cut-throat]

Bronze Mannikin

scutata

ad

imm

Black-and-white Mannikin

imm

poensis

ad

ad

Red-backed Mannikin

imm

nigriceps

Cut-throat Finch

♀

♂

nominate

imm

ad

Magpie Mannikin

WHYDAHS *All whydahs except Pin-tailed are species-specific brood-parasites, laying their eggs in the nests of a particular waxbill (see text). Within our area, breeding males have long tails and distinctive plumages (except for the similar paradise whydahs). Non-breeding males and females are extremely similar to each other and also to the smaller indigobirds; careful attention to head pattern, bill and foot colour aids identification. All attain breeding plumage during the rains, when they display and perch prominently, but feed on the ground. Relative tail lengths are hard to judge if tail is not fully grown or is abraded.*

Eastern Paradise Whydah *Vidua paradisaea* ♂ 40cm, 16"; ♀ 13cm, 5"

Breeding male has striking buffy-yellow, chestnut and black plumage with *very long tapering tail*. Hind-collar is mostly golden-buff, and breast has extensive chestnut around black bib. Female has buffy crown-stripe bordered with black, pale-buff superciliary stripes, *two blackish crescents behind eye*, and usually blackish bill. Upperparts are heavily streaked blackish, sides of breast indistinctly streaked. Non-breeding male is like female, but head pattern is bolder, more black and white. Juvenile is plain grey-brown with paler belly. **HH** Fairly common and widespread in Et and So, with preference for semi-arid acacia country from sea-level to 2100m. In NE Africa, parasitic on red-lored race of Green-winged Pytilia *P. m. soudanensis*. **Voice** Amidst chattering, song consistently introduces chipping and squeaky nasal phrases resembling Green-winged Pytilia and Blue-capped Cordon-bleu. [Alt: Long-tailed Paradise Whydah]

Exclamatory Paradise Whydah *Vidua interjecta* ♂ 36cm, 14"; ♀ 13cm, 5"

Breeding male is similar to Eastern, but with *slightly shorter tail with broader vanes* (not tapering); collar is mostly chestnut, but less chestnut on breast, black bib slightly smaller. In flight male looks like flying exclamation mark (hence name). Female is like Eastern, but lacks crescents behind eye and has *reddish bill*, slightly browner upperparts and unstreaked breast. Non-breeding male is like female, but head pattern bolder, more black and white. Juvenile is plain grey-brown with paler belly. **HH** Known from several widely scattered localities in WEt at 750–2100m. Inhabits open woodland and rocky hillsides, within range of host, Red-billed Pytilia. **Voice** Presumably mimics songs and calls of Red-billed Pytilia. [Alt: Uelle Paradise Whydah]

Sahel Paradise Whydah *Vidua orientalis* ♂ 30cm, 12"; ♀ 13cm, 5"

Breeding male is like Eastern, but *tail much shorter and of moderate width*. Nominate race in region has golden-buff collar (like Eastern) and extensive chestnut on breast around black bib. Female is very like female Exclamatory, lacking crescents behind eye of Eastern, but *bill is grey*, not reddish. Non-breeding male is like female, but head pattern is bolder, more black and white. Juvenile is plain grey-brown with paler belly. **HH** Inhabits grassy acacia savanna and open woodlands in WEr and WEt at 800–1400m; in WEt occurs within range of Eastern. A single record west of Lake Tana at 2130m was probably a vagrant. Parasitic on Green-winged Pytilia, both with red-lored *citerior* and grey-lored *jessei*. **Voice** Harsh churrs and spitting notes similar to its host.

Pin-tailed Whydah *Vidua macroura* ♂ 31cm, 12"; ♀ 11cm, 4.5"

Breeding male has striking *black and white plumage*, red bill and *long narrow black tail*. Female has boldly patterned head and upperparts; bill is black when breeding, red when not. In flight may show white inner webs to outer tail feathers. Non-breeding male and immature are like female, but with bolder black and white head pattern and red bill. Juvenile is plain grey-brown with whitish throat and blackish bill. **HH** Commonest and most widespread whydah, inhabiting wide variety of woodland, bush country, cultivation and gardens in WEr, most of Et (except E) and NW&SSo, from sea-level to 2800m. It is not host-specific but parasitises several *Estrilda* waxbills including Common, Crimson-rumped, Black-rumped and Fawn-breasted. **Voice** Song is a relatively tuneless jumble of harsh squeaks and sparrow-like chirps that form a rhythmic pattern.

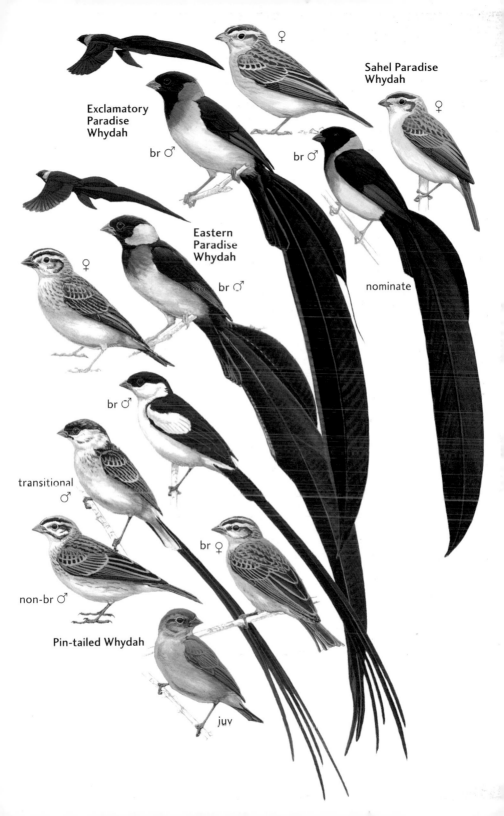

Exclamatory
Paradise
Whydah

br ♂

♀

Sahel Paradise
Whydah

♀

br ♂

nominate

Eastern
Paradise
Whydah

♀

br ♂

br ♂

transitional
♂

br ♀

non-br ♂

Pin-tailed Whydah

juv

Straw-tailed Whydah *Vidua fischeri*   ♂ 31cm, 12"; ♀ 10cm, 4"

Breeding male has unique buffy-yellow and black plumage, with red bill and feet, and *long thin straw-coloured tail*. Female is streaked brown above, with distinctive *plain rufous-tawny head, and reddish bill and feet*. Female Red-billed Quelea (plate 198) is similar but larger with more robust bill. Non-breeding male is like boldly marked female. Juvenile is plain rufous-brown with dark bill (similar to juvenile Purple Grenadier, the host species). **HH** Widespread in bush country and drier cultivated areas in Et (east of Rift Valley) and So (except NE), from sea-level to 1600m. **Voice** Attractive song has very lively, lark-like phrases, *si-si-sit swi si swit*, with bouts persisting for long periods.

Steel-blue Whydah *Vidua hypocherina*   ♂ 31cm, 12"; ♀ 10cm, 4"

Breeding male looks totally glossy blue-black in field with *white or greyish bill*. White flank-spot and white at sides of rump are usually concealed at rest, as are white underwing-coverts. Female and non-breeding male are very like several other female whydahs and indigobirds, but *bill is small and grey*, feet grey. Juvenile is plain brown with greyer cheeks (like juvenile Black-cheeked Waxbill, the host species). **HH** Rather uncommon in dry bush and bushed grassland in Et and So, from sea-level to 2100m. **Voice** Infrequently heard song is similar to Black-cheeked Waxbill, a lazy extended medley of varied dry chips and nasal notes.

INDIGOBIRDS Closely related to the whydahs, indigobirds also parasitise estrildid finches. Most are extremely difficult to identify. Breeding males are blackish with a blue, purple or green gloss. Bills and feet are varying combinations of red, pinkish or white. Each species is a brood-parasite on one particular species of finch. Males sing from prominent perches and are best identified by song. In addition to their own rapid chattering, they imitate their host species, particularly its alarm calls. Non-breeding males and females are boldly streaked brown above and buffy below, and many cannot be identified (even in the hand).

Village Indigobird *Vidua chalybeata*   10cm, 4"

Two races occur, differing in bill colour: breeding male *ultramarina* (Er and Et, mainly west of Rift Valley) has *purplish gloss, black wings and white bill*; *amauropteryx* (SSo) has *steel-blue gloss, browner wings and red bill*. Both races have red or pinkish-red feet. Female is much like other female indigobirds, but *amauropteryx* has orange bill. **HH** Most common and widespread indigobird occurring in wide variety of habitats from sea-level to 2400m, closely matching range of Red-billed Firefinch which it parasitises. **Voice** Males sing a two-tone *chick* followed by simple clear rising whistles *pea pea*, as well as *chick-pea-pea-pea* which may rise and fall. Pattern uttered frequently between phrases of its own chattering song. [Alt: Steelblue Widowfinch]

Barka Indigobird *Vidua larvaticola*   10cm, 4"

Breeding male is *black with blue or blue-green gloss*, pale purplish feet and white bill; primaries show contrasting brown panel. Female indistinguishable. **HH** Known only from a few records in W&NWEt at 500–1800m. Inhabits wooded savannas and grassland where it parasitises Black-faced Firefinch. **Voice** Very like song of host, *siu siu siu siu*, interspersed with chattering shared by other members of genus. [Alt: Baka Indigobird]

Wilson's Indigobird *Vidua wilsoni*   10cm, 4"

Breeding male is *black with purplish gloss*, pale purplish feet and white bill; primaries show contrasting brown panel. Female indistinguishable. **HH** Known only from Gambela, Wet, at 500m. Inhabits bushed grassland and overgrown cultivation where it parasitises Bar-breasted Firefinch. **Voice** Rapid squeaky series of rising-and-falling notes; extremely similar to song of host. [Alt: Pale-winged Indigobird]

Jambandu Indigobird *Vidua raricola*   10cm, 4"

Breeding male is *black with green gloss*, pinkish-grey feet and white bill; primaries show contrasting brown panel. Female indistinguishable. **HH** Known only from single record in WEt, but presumably resident there. Inhabits grassy wetlands and edges of cultivation where it parasitises Zebra Waxbill. **Voice** Unlike other indigobirds, gives series of spitting notes. Song is very varied with mixture of harsh and sweet notes combined into a long refrain. [Alt: Goldbreast Indigobird]

Straw-tailed Whydah

br ♂

♀

Village Indigobird

juv

♀

ultramarina

Steel-blue Whydah

♀

br ♂

juv

br ♂

amauropteryx

br ♂

Village Indigobird

ultramarina

Barka Indigobird

♂

♀

♂

Jambandu Indigobird

♂

♀

Wilson's Indigobird

CANARIES AND SEEDEATERS Small finches with mostly green and yellow, and/or brown and white plumage, with streaked upperparts. In North-East Africa the yellow-plumaged birds are called canaries and the browner species seedeaters.

Yellow-fronted Canary *Serinus mozambicus*   11cm, 4.5"

Adult male is quite distinctive with bright yellow forecrown extending back as well-marked superscilium. Narrow black line through eye and *strong black malar stripe* create well-marked face pattern. Bright yellow rump contrasts with streaked greenish mantle; underparts entirely plain bright yellow. Two similar races: *grotei* (W&SWEt) has broad frontal band; *gommaensis* (NW&CEt, Er) is darker with narrow frontal band. Female is similar but paler. Immature is much paler than adult with light streaking on sides of breast and flanks. **HH** Small flocks are common and widespread in open woodland, bush country and cultivation at 750–2150m. **Voice** A rather monotonous songster; refrain may continue for long periods, but is broken into short phrases, *si-yu sisi si yu*, with embellishments. [Alt: Yellow-eyed Canary]

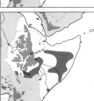

White-bellied Canary *Serinus dorsostriatus*   11cm, 4.5"

Adult male of race *maculicollis* has distinctive *white belly and vent* and *olive-green malar stripe*; also shows contrasting yellow rump in flight. Female also has *white belly* but is paler than male with variable streaking on breast and flanks. Immature like female but paler and buffier below. Yellow-fronted Canary has black malar and shorter tail. **HH** Common in drier areas than Yellow-fronted, usually in dry bush country of Et and So, from sea-level to 1800m. **Voice** Attractive song is high-pitched and sustained, but is broken into complex, slightly varying phrases which last c.5 secs.

Northern Grosbeak-Canary *Serinus donaldsoni*   15cm, 6"

Large canary with heavy pinkish bill. Adult male is dark olive-green above and distinctly streaked, with strong yellow superscilium, bright yellow below with streaked flanks *and white vent*. Female and immature have crown, nape, mantle and wings brown with darker streaking, and bright yellow rump, but are *off-white below with heavy brown streaking across breast and flanks*, resembling giant version of Reichenow's Seedeater (plate 210). **HH** Pairs or family groups are uncommon in semi-arid bush and desert country of Et and So, up to 1800m. **Voice** Varied calls include a rapid *seu-seu-seu-seu-seu-seu...*, same note repeated 10–20 times, *suweer* and an upslurred *tuweeer*.

Yellow-crowned Canary *Serinus flavivertex*   12cm, 5"

Slim, brightly coloured highland canary with longish tail. Adult male has *golden-yellow forecrown and two bright yellow wing-bars*, and obvious yellow rump in flight. Female is duller, with variable amount of white and dark streaking below. Immature is more buffy-brown with extensive streaking below. **HH** Often in flocks, nominate *flavivertex* is common at high altitudes in Er and Et at 1400–3500m, in cultivation, forest edge, woodland and moorlands. **Voice** In flight birds often give short rapid trill of about five quite low notes, *tirirrirrir*. Long rambling song has a strange tinny tone. **Note** Formerly lumped in Cape Canary *S. canicollis*.

African Citril *Serinus citrinelloides*   11cm, 4.5"

Adult male is easily told by *black face* and unstreaked bright yellow underparts; in endemic nominate race (in Er and Et) yellow superscilium is narrow. Some males have greyer faces but may be subadult. *Bill is rather straight and pointed* compared to other canaries. Female lacks black face and is mainly olive-green streaked blackish above, pale yellow with prominent streaking below, with indistinct yellowish superscilium. Immature is browner above and less yellow below with heavier streaking. **HH** Locally common in small flocks in highlands of Er and Et, occurring in evergreen and juniper forest, clearings, moist scrub, gardens and cultivated areas, mainly at 1200–2500m. **Voice** Song is very like Reichenow's Seedeater, but more pinched, slightly nasal and with series of diagnostic falling piped notes.

Southern Citril *Serinus hypostictus*   11cm, 4.5"

Very like African Citril, with which formerly considered conspecific. Adult male differs by *grey face*, weak superscilium (sometimes absent) and streaked underparts. Unlike African Citril, *sexes are alike*. Female African Citril is very similar but has whitish (not grey) chin. **HH** Several specimen records from WEt, but status uncertain (race is apparently nominate *hypostictus*, although *brittoni* of S Sudan and W Kenya is closer than known nominate populations); range overlaps with African Citril. **Voice** Song is similar to African Citril, but with more variation and more hurried delivery.

imm

♂

Yellow-fronted Canary

grotei

♂

White-bellied Canary

maculicollis

♀

Northern Grosbeak-Canary

♀

♂

♀

Yellow-crowned Canary

nominate

♂

♀

♂

ad

Southern Citril

nominate

African Citril

nominate

Black-headed Siskin *Serinus nigriceps* 12cm, 5"

Adult male is unmistakable with *black hood, yellow scapulars and prominent yellow wing-bars*; rest of wings blackish with pale fringes. Female lacks hood but has brownish-olive head and olive-green upperparts with diffuse dark streaking; from female African Citril and Yellow-crowned Canary by *lack of supercilium, more prominent wing-bars on darker wings* and less streaking below. Immature is like female but browner and more heavily streaked below. **HH** ENDEMIC to highlands of Et. Common to abundant in moorland, grassland and open forest, at 1800–3600m. **Voice** Very musical, constant metallic twitter interspersed randomly with chipped notes. Fairly similar to Yellow-crowned Canary but harsher and more irregular in delivery. [Alt: Ethiopian Siskin]

Reichenow's Seedeater *Serinus reichenowi* 11cm, 4.5"

Small *streaky brown seedeater with yellow rump*, whitish superciliary stripes and buff or whitish throat; yellow rump conspicuous in flight. Density of streaking below is variable. Sexes and immature are similar. Some birds in SEt have dark mottling on chin, recalling extralimital Black-throated Seedeater. **HH** Flocks are common and widespread in C&SEt, Dj and SSo in open woodland, dry bush country and cultivation, from sea-level to 2400m. **Voice** Typical canary song is loud and continuous with little variation, same notes and occasional trills being repeated for long periods. **Note** Formerly considered conspecific with Black-throated Seedeater *S. atrogularis*. [Alt: Yellow-rumped Seedeater]

White-throated Seedeater *Serinus xanthopygius* 11cm, 4.5"

Northern counterpart of Reichenow's Seedeater. Adult differs in greyer upperparts, indistinct supercilium and *white throat*. Rest of *underparts plain pale grey*, sometimes with faint diffuse streaking on breast. Sexes alike; immature similar. **HH** ENDEMIC to Er and Et. Locally common in highlands of Er and NEt (e.g. at Tississat Falls near Bahar Dar, Jemmu valley and Ankober escarpment) in dry open scrub, grassy areas and open forest at 900–2500m. **Voice** Simple song is a repeated high-pitched *weeo-chi-chi*, sometimes *wee-chi*, rather monotonous for *Serinus*. **Note** Formerly considered conspecific with Black-throated Seedeater *S. atrogularis*. [Alt: Yellow-rumped Seedeater]

Yellow-throated Seedeater *Serinus flavigula* 11cm, 4.5"

Slimmer and less dumpy than Reichenow's and White-throated Seedeaters, recalling small Yellow-spotted Petronia. Rather plain, greyish above, pale and unstreaked below. *Bright yellow rump* is conspicuous, *extending onto uppertail-covers*. *Pale yellow throat* is not always obvious. Sexes alike. **HH** ENDEMIC to Shoa Prov., Et. Rare and little known, confined to a few localities near foot of eastern escarpment of W Highlands, including Melka Ghebdu, Mt Fantalle and Awash NP, at 1300–1600m. Inhabits bushes and scrub on steep, rocky slopes. **Voice** Song is a monotonous *wheec-chi-weeet*; occasionally *wheee-chit*. Call is a very dry, repeated *ch-ch-ch-ch*. **EN**

Salvadori's Seedeater *Serinus xantholaemus* 11cm, 4.5"

Rather plain greyish seedeater with bright yellow rump, very like Yellow-throated. Differs in *more prominent yellow throat and upper breast with narrow black bar across it*, greyer face, and small pale spot on forehead. Sexes alike. **HH** ENDEMIC to Sidamo, NW Bale and NW Harar Provs, Et. Very uncommon in rocky gorges and acacia bush at 300–2000m. Key localities in SEt include Arero and Sof Omar. At Sof Omar inhabits mixed acacia and deciduous woodland in steep-sided valley. **Voice** Song is a slow musical warble, more bunting-like than a *Serinus*. **VU**

White-rumped Seedeater *Serinus leucopygius* 11cm, 4.5"

Like Reichenow's Seedeater, but more grey-brown, with *white rump* (not yellow) and *lacking obvious supercilium*. Underparts whitish with fine streaking on breast, and wings show two narrow wing-bars. Sexes alike. Immature more buffish and more heavily streaked below. **HH** Nominate *leucopygius* is locally common in dry bushed grassland and light woodland in WEr and WEt, at 600–2000m. A population in Rift Valley and Awash NP (c.10 sightings in 20 years) is of unknown race. **Voice** Sings for long periods without pause, notes smooth and rounded without scratchiness or hissed quality of some other canaries.

♂

♀

Black-headed Siskin

ad

Reichenow's
Seedeater

White-throated
Seedeater

ad

ad

Yellow-throated
Seedeater

White-rumped
Seedeater

ad

ad

nominate

Salvadori's Seedeater

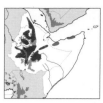

Brown-rumped Seedeater *Serinus tristriatus* 13cm, 5"

Small unstreaked seedeater of highlands, *dark grey-brown above with narrow whitish supercilium and white chin*; rest of underparts plain grey-brown. Sexes alike. Immature similar but with some streaking above and below. Race in Er and Et is nominate; *pallidior* (NSo) is paler and greyer, with faint streaking on mantle. **HH** ENDEMIC to Horn of Africa. Common in forest, juniper scrub and undergrowth in highlands of Er, Et and NSo, at 1050–3300m. Common in gardens in Addis Ababa. **Voice** Song is a monotonous repeated rambling series of squeaky sparrow-like chipping notes.

Streaky Seedeater *Serinus striolatus* 14cm, 5.5"

Widespread nominate race has bold facial pattern with well-defined creamy-white supercilium, *heavy streaking both above and below*, and variable greenish edges to primaries. Differs from Stripe-breasted by broad dark malar stripe and pale cheek-patch. Smaller Ankober Serin lacks supercilium. **HH** Common and widespread in highlands of Er and Et at 1500–4100m. Inhabits moorland heath, forest edge, rank vegetation, gardens and cultivation. **Voice** Song has rather forced thrush-like quality and often ends with soft rattle; sung in repeated short phrases or as an attractive continuous refrain. Cheerful call is a loud upslurred whistle, *siyuya*.

Stripe-breasted Seedeater *Serinus reichardi* 13cm, 5"

Race in Et, *striatipectus* (which may be separate species) is dark brown above, with long white superciliary stripe, brown sides to face, and *usually fairly heavily streaked underparts*. Differs from Streaky Seedeater in lack of malar stripe, and from Brown-rumped by streaked underparts. **HH** Uncommon to rare in highlands of Et at 1200–2000m, usually in pairs or small flocks on wooded escarpments. **Voice** Rather quiet but sings from tops of small trees when on territory; song often begins with *djee t'what* or *djee tu-waa* and continues with prolonged rambling which includes much mimicry. Call is interrogatory *siyuah*. **Note** Extralimital Streaky-headed Seedeater *S. gularis* might possibly occur in SEt; it is like Stripe-breasted but unstreaked below. [Alt: Reichard's Seedeater]

Socotra Golden-winged Grosbeak *Rhynchostruthus socotranus* 15cm, 6"

Unmistakable large-headed grosbeak with stout bill and short tail. Adult male has *sooty-black head with large white patch on ear-coverts*, and wings and tail have extensive golden-yellow. Female has browner head. Immature is heavily streaked with buffy-white patch on ear-coverts and less yellow in wings. **HH** ENDEMIC to Soc; locally common at 150–1400m, inhabiting rocky, scrub-covered hillsides. **Voice** Song is medley of thin musical notes, bubbly phrases and short twitters.

Somali Golden-winged Grosbeak *Rhynchostruthus louisae* 15cm, 6"

Adult male is very like Socotra form, but black on face restricted to forehead, lores and throat and white cheeks to narrow vertical band. Rest of *ear-coverts pale grey*; crown dark brown. Female has greyer head with black restricted to chin. **HH** ENDEMIC to NSo where uncommon from near sea-level to at least 1400m, inhabiting rocky areas with thorn bushes and euphorbias. **Voice** Unknown. **NT**

Ankober Serin *Carduelis ankoberensis* 12cm, 5"

Small brown seedeater, now considered a *Carduelis* finch rather than a serin. Upperparts brown with heavy streaking and ill-defined pale collar. Underparts buffy-brown with prominent streaking. *Lack of supercilium and pale spot below eye* distinctive. Sexes similar. **HH** ENDEMIC to Et, inhabiting high altitude cliff-tops and steep rocky slopes at 2600–4250m in N Shoa and N Gonder Provs. Gregarious, often in flocks. **Voice** Flocks give constant low twitter, much more reminiscent of Twite *C. flavirostris* than any *Serinus*. **Note** Formerly placed in *Serinus*. **VU**

Warsangli Linnet *Carduelis johannis* 13cm, 5"

Adult male unmistakable; mainly grey and white with black wings and tail, chestnut rump and *chestnut patch on flanks*. In flight, *white wing-patches* and chestnut and white rump are distinctive. Female is browner above, buffier below with duller flank-patch. Immature is boldly streaked but retains white wing-patch. **HH** ENDEMIC to NSo, inhabiting highland juniper forest and rocky euphorbia country at 1200–2300m. Local and uncommon, perhaps nomadic, and frequently perches on bare branches. **Voice** Song is a patternless series of serin-like notes. **Note** Formerly placed in *Acanthis*. **EN**

Brown-rumped Seedeater

ad

nominate

Streaky Seedeater

ad

nominate

Stripe-breasted Seedeater

ad

striatipectus

imm

Ankober Serin

ad

Socotra Golden-winged Grosbeak

♂

♂

Somali Golden-winged Grosbeak

♂

Warsangli Linnet

imm

Trumpeter Finch *Bucanetes githagineus* 12cm, 5"

Small, large-headed finch with *stubby bulbous bill, bright pink* in breeding male, yellowish-horn in female and immature. Adult male has grey head with pale eye-ring, and brown mantle; *rump and underparts strongly suffused pink*. Blackish wings and tail with prominent pink edges. Legs pinkish. Female and non-breeding male duller, with less pink and more brownish-grey. Immature lacks pink. **HH** Widespread in Sahara and Middle East, but in our region known only from Dj where rare and perhaps a non-breeding visitor; all records Dec–Mar. Race in Dj not known, but may be *crassirostris* of Arabia. **Voice** Song is an extraordinary long, drawn-out nasal buzzing note, like sound of toy trumpet, sometimes preceded with few short notes. Call is a loud sparrow-like chipping which breaks into nasal slurs.

BUNTINGS The African representatives of the Old World buntings are often colourful, with boldly marked heads; in NE Africa they are either rufous or golden-yellow below (see plate 213). Pairs or small flocks feed on the ground, but fly to cover when disturbed. They frequently sing from exposed perches. The three species on this plate are Palearctic winter visitors or vagrants.

Cinereous Bunting *Emberiza cineracea* 17cm, 7"

Rather large, long-tailed bunting with narrow yellow eye-ring and plain plumage. Two races occur: nominate male (from Turkey) is *mainly ashy-grey* with light streaking above, washed yellowish-olive on head, with *yellow submoustachial and throat*. Female is similar but duller and browner, with buffy-white throat. Immature is more streaked below. Male *semenowi* (from SW Iran) is much brighter, with olive breast-band and *rest of underparts mainly yellow*. Female *semenowi* is pale olive-yellow below (nominate female is greyish-brown and buffy-white below). **HH** Uncommon to rare winter visitor, Oct–Apr, to Er and Et, up to 1500m in dry rocky country with little vegetation, short grassland and cultivation. Both races occur, but most records are *semenowi*. **Voice** Silent in region. On breeding grounds song is a series of short, scratchy notes. Calls include a harsh *tsik* or *kyip*. **NT**

Ortolan Bunting *Emberiza hortulana* 16cm, 6.5"

Adult male has *olive-grey or grey-green head*, narrow yellowish eye-ring, pink bill, *and yellowish throat and submoustachial with olive-grey malar stripe*. Female is duller and paler with some brown streaking on head and breast. First-winter bird is even browner and more streaked above and below, but *pale eye-ring, pale submoustachial and stubby pink bill* are conspicuous; rump is grey-brown (more rufous on Cretzschmar's). *Broad areas of white on outer tail are obvious in flight* in all plumages. **HH** Fairly common winter visitor, Sep–May, to Er and Et from sea-level to 3300m. Frequents grassland, acacia savanna and cultivation, mainly in upland areas. Generally quiet and unobtrusive, occurring singly or in small flocks; feeds on ground. Vagrant Soc. **Voice** Song is a trilled series of ringing notes, rarely heard in NE Africa. Calls include a downslurred *seeoo* and short *tyip*, given in flight.

Cretzschmar's Bunting *Emberiza caesia* 15cm, 6"

Like Ortolan in all plumages but slightly smaller with *whitish eye-ring* and pink bill. Adult male has *blue-grey head* (with no olive wash), and *rufous-cinnamon throat and submoustachial*. Female is duller and similar to female Ortolan, but head greyer, throat and submoustachial rusty-buff (not yellowish). First-winter is very like first-winter Ortolan, but plumage tends to be rustier, especially on tertials and rump (latter earth-brown on Ortolan). **HH** Formerly a common winter visitor (Dec–Mar) to lowlands of Er, below 600m, but few recent records; usually at lower altitude and more coastal than Ortolan. Vagrant WEt and Dj. Occupies dry steppe and semi-desert habitats, including acacia savanna, coastal plains and dry hillsides; often in small flocks; highly terrestrial. **Voice** Silent in our region. On breeding grounds has very musical, mournful piped series of notes. Calls include a hard *jit* or liquid *tyeep*.

♀

♂

Trumpeter Finch

♂

imm

semenowi

♂

♀

Cinereous Bunting

♂

imm

Ortolan Bunting

nominate

♂

♀

Cretzschmar's Bunting

Socotra Bunting *Emberiza socotrana* 13cm, 5"

Small bunting with striped head, easily told from Cinnamon-breasted (only other bunting on Socotra) by *white underparts with rufous breast-band*. Adult male has bold black and white head pattern, pale brownish back with blackish streaks, and entirely rufous median and lesser coverts. Female is similar but breast-band is paler and head-stripes browner. **HH** ENDEMIC to Soc, mainly at 500–1500m, where uncommon to scarce. Inhabits dry rocky hillsides and steep precipices. May disperse altitudinally after breeding. **Voice** Song described as ringing and metallic whistled *hue-heee hu-hey*, or high thin whistle. **VU**

Cinnamon-breasted Bunting *Emberiza tahapisi* 15cm, 6"

Adult male is rufous with black streaking above, black and white striped head, *black throat, and rich cinnamon breast to vent*. Female is duller with subdued head pattern. Immature is plainer than female, with mostly brown-streaked head and duller brown underparts. Three similar races occur: nominate (C&SEt and NSo) as described; male *septemstriata* (Er and NEt) has throat mottled black and grey; *insularis* (Soc) is paler above and below with smaller bib; latter two now considered invalid, rendering all NE African birds nominate. **HH** Singles and pairs are widespread (sometimes common) residents of rocky areas (usually with some bare soil and trees or bush), from sea-level to 2800m. On Soc, locally common in mountains, at 100–850m. **Voice** Song is a monotonous repeated scratchy phrase of mainly falling notes, lasting c.2 secs, *si siri si stri*. [Alt: Cinnamon-breasted Rock Bunting]

Striolated Bunting *Emberiza striolata* 14cm, 5.5"

Adult male has bold black and white striped face pattern, but *crown, nape and upper breast are finely streaked pale grey, black and white*. Wing feathers are extensively edged with warm rufous and conspicuous in flight. Female and immature are largely brown (more rufous on wings), with paler buff-brown head pattern. Two races occur: nominate (Er, NEEt and NSo) as described; male *saturatior* (SWEt) has more subdued head pattern, grey (not black) facial stripes. **HH** Locally common, inhabiting rocky, arid and desert country from sea-level to 2000m. **Voice** Song is a series of short repeated phrases, *siti tiri tiri si tiou*, or similar variations. **Note** Formerly called House Bunting when united with N&W African races; the latter are now known as House Bunting *E. sahari*.

Golden-breasted Bunting *Emberiza flaviventris* 15cm, 6"

Adult male has white stripes both above and below eye, *lightly mottled or plain rufous-cinnamon mantle*, two white wing-bars, and grey rump. Bright golden yellow below with whitish flanks and belly. Female is duller. Immature is similar to female, but paler and duller, with more subdued brown and buff head pattern, and faint streaks on breast. **HH** Race *flavigaster* is fairly common in WEr and NEt at 750–2400m, in acacia woodland or bushed grassland. **Voice** Individual songs vary, but typically a series of 4–5 downslurs, *siu siu siu siu siu*, *chip-chip choo chip-chip choo* or *cheree cheree cheree cheree cheree*, all with high-pitched far-carrying quality. [Alt: African Golden-breasted Bunting]

Somali Bunting *Emberiza poliopleura* 15cm, 6"

Adult male is very like Golden-breasted Bunting but *chestnut-brown mantle is broadly edged pale buffy-grey*, creating very scaly appearance, and rump greyer. Female is duller. Immature is much paler with browner head pattern, prominent dark brown streaks across breast and only a hint of yellow below. **HH** Common and widespread in dry bush country in Et (east of Rift Valley) and So (except NE), from sea-level to 1800m; no overlap in range with Golden-breasted. **Voice** Songs are similar in form and pattern to Golden-breasted Bunting but are hurried, not relaxed, in delivery: *siu siu siu siu siu siu siu* and *swit swit swit chee t'choo t'choo t'choo*. Call is a distinctive piped upslurred *p'yuuu* given in flight or on perch. [Alt: Somali Golden-breasted Bunting]

Brown-rumped Bunting *Emberiza affinis* 14cm, 5.5"

Adult is very like Golden-breasted Bunting but has *broader white stripes on head, all-grey bill, no white wing-bars, brown rump and entirely yellow underparts including flanks*. Sexes alike. Immature similar but paler with chestnut head-stripes. Two races may occur: nominate (?NWEt) as described; *omoensis* (SW&SEt) with duller brown mantle and heavier streaking. **HH** Fairly common in open woodland and bushed grasslands at 750–1900m. **Voice** Song is a warbled deliberate scratchy *switirichiri switirichireerrr*. **Note** Formerly *Emberiza forbesi*.

Socotra Bunting

♂ ♀

Cinnamon-breasted
Bunting

♂ ♀

nominate

Striolated Bunting

♂ ♀

nominate

Golden-breasted
Bunting

♂ *fluvigaster* imm

Brown-rumped
Bunting

imm

nominate

♂

Somali Bunting

ad

CHECKLIST OF THE BIRDS OF THE HORN OF AFRICA

This checklist consists of all the species reliably recorded within the territories of Ethiopia, Eritrea, Djibouti, Somalia and Socotra (and their territorial waters) and is provided to present species in correct taxonomic sequence (the field guide occasionally deviates from this sequence for a variety of reasons – see page 16). A few hypothetical or unconfirmed species are included in the field guide and are marked with an asterisk (also listed in Appendix 2). Endemic and near-endemic species are listed in Appendix 1. This list is based on the checklist of African birds produced by the African Bird Club (ABC) and published on their website (www.africanbirdclub.org).

Ostriches STRUTHIONIDAE
Common Ostrich *Struthio camelus*
Somali Ostrich *Struthio molybdophanes*

Albatrosses DIOMEDEIDAE
Shy Albatross *Thalassarche cauta*

Petrels and shearwaters PROCELLARIIDAE
Southern Giant Petrel *Macronectes giganteus*
Cape Petrel *Daption capense*
Kerguelen Petrel *Aphrodroma brevirostris*
Atlantic Petrel *Pterodroma incerta*
Antarctic Prion *Pachyptila desolata*
Jouanin's Petrel *Bulweria fallax*
Streaked Shearwater *Calonectris leucomelas*
Wedge-tailed Shearwater *Puffinus pacificus*
Flesh-footed Shearwater *Puffinus carneipes*
Tropical Shearwater *Puffinus (lherminieri) bailloni*
Persian Shearwater *Puffinus (lherminieri) persicus*

Storm-petrels HYDROBATIDAE
Wilson's Storm-petrel *Oceanites oceanicus*
White-faced Storm-petrel *Pelagodroma marina*
Black-bellied Storm-petrel *Fregetta tropica*
White-bellied Storm-petrel *Fregetta grallaria*
Swinhoe's Storm-petrel *Oceanodroma monorhis*

Grebes PODICIPEDIDAE
Little Grebe *Tachybaptus ruficollis*
Great Crested Grebe *Podiceps cristatus*
Black-necked Grebe *Podiceps nigricollis*

Tropicbirds PHAETHONTIDAE
Red-billed Tropicbird *Phaethon aethereus*
*White-tailed Tropicbird *Phaethon lepturus*

Boobies SULIDAE
Masked Booby *Sula dactylatra*
Red-footed Booby *Sula sula*
Brown Booby *Sula leucogaster*

Cormorants PHALACROCORACIDAE
Great Cormorant *Phalacrocorax carbo*
Socotra Cormorant *Phalacrocorax nigrogularis*
Long-tailed Cormorant *Phalacrocorax africanus*

Darters ANHINGIDAE
African Darter *Anhinga rufa*

Pelicans PELECANIDAE
Great White Pelican *Pelecanus onocrotalus*
Pink-backed Pelican *Pelecanus rufescens*

Frigatebirds FREGATIDAE
Greater Frigatebird *Fregata minor*
Lesser Frigatebird *Fregata ariel*

Bitterns, herons and egrets ARDEIDAE
Eurasian Bittern *Botaurus stellaris*
Little Bittern *Ixobrychus minutus*
Yellow Bittern *Ixobrychus sinensis*
Dwarf Bittern *Ixobrychus sturmii*
White-backed Night Heron *Gorsachius leuconotus*
Black-crowned Night Heron *Nycticorax nycticorax*
Squacco Heron *Ardeola ralloides*
Madagascar Pond Heron *Ardeola idae*
Indian Pond Heron *Ardeola grayii*
Cattle Egret *Bubulcus ibis*
Striated Heron *Butorides striata*
Black Heron *Egretta ardesiaca*
Western Reef Egret *Egretta gularis*
Little Egret *Egretta garzetta*
Yellow-billed Egret *Egretta intermedia*
Great Egret *Egretta alba*
Purple Heron *Ardea purpurea*
Grey Heron *Ardea cinerea*
Black-headed Heron *Ardea melanocephala*
Goliath Heron *Ardea goliath*

Hamerkop SCOPIDAE
Hamerkop *Scopus umbretta*

Storks CICONIIDAE
Yellow-billed Stork *Mycteria ibis*
African Openbill *Anastomus lamelligerus*
Black Stork *Ciconia nigra*
Abdim's Stork *Ciconia abdimii*
Woolly-necked Stork *Ciconia episcopus*
White Stork *Ciconia ciconia*
Saddle-billed Stork *Ephippiorhynchus senegalensis*
Marabou Stork *Leptoptilos crumeniferus*

Shoebill BALAENICIPITIDAE
Shoebill *Balaeniceps rex*

Ibises and spoonbills THRESKIORNITHIDAE
Glossy Ibis *Plegadis falcinellus*
Hadada Ibis *Bostrychia hagedash*
Wattled Ibis *Bostrychia carunculata*
Sacred Ibis *Threskiornis aethiopicus*
Northern Bald Ibis *Geronticus eremita*
Eurasian Spoonbill *Platalea leucorodia*
African Spoonbill *Platalea alba*

Flamingos PHOENICOPTERIDAE
Greater Flamingo *Phoenicopterus ruber*
Lesser Flamingo *Phoeniconaias minor*

Ducks and geese ANATIDAE
Fulvous Whistling Duck *Dendrocygna bicolor*
White-faced Whistling Duck *Dendrocygna viduata*
White-backed Duck *Thalassornis leuconotus*
Greater White-fronted Goose *Anser albifrons*
Blue-winged Goose *Cyanochen cyanoptera*
Egyptian Goose *Alopochen aegyptiaca*
Ruddy Shelduck *Tadorna ferruginea*
Common Shelduck *Tadorna tadorna*
Spur-winged Goose *Plectropterus gambensis*
Knob-billed Duck *Sarkidiornis melanotos*
African Pygmy-goose *Nettapus auritus*
Cotton Pygmy-goose *Nettapus coromandelianus*
Eurasian Wigeon *Anas penelope*
Gadwall *Anas strepera*
Eurasian Teal *Anas crecca*
Cape Teal *Anas capensis*
Mallard *Anas platyrhynchos*
Yellow-billed Duck *Anas undulata*
African Black Duck *Anas sparsa*
Northern Pintail *Anas acuta*
Red-billed Duck *Anas erythrorhyncha*
Hottentot Teal *Anas hottentota*
Garganey *Anas querquedula*
Northern Shoveler *Anas clypeata*
Southern Pochard *Netta erythrophthalma*
Common Pochard *Aythya ferina*
Ferruginous Duck *Aythya nyroca*
Tufted Duck *Aythya fuligula*
Maccoa Duck *Oxyura maccoa*

Hawks, buzzards and eagles ACCIPITRIDAE
Osprey *Pandion haliaetus*
African Cuckoo-Hawk *Aviceda cuculoides*
European Honey-buzzard *Pernis apivorus*
Bat Hawk *Macheiramphus alcinus*
Black-shouldered Kite *Elanus caeruleus*

African Swallow-tailed Kite *Chelictinia riocourii*
Black Kite *Milvus migrans*
Yellow-billed Kite *Milvus (migrans) aegyptius*
African Fish-Eagle *Haliaeetus vocifer*
Lammergeier *Gypaetus barbatus*
Egyptian Vulture *Neophron percnopterus*
Hooded Vulture *Necrosyrtes monachus*
White-backed Vulture *Gyps africanus*
Rüppell's Vulture *Gyps rueppellii*
Griffon Vulture *Gyps fulvus*
Lappet-faced Vulture *Torgos tracheliotus*
White-headed Vulture *Trigonoceps occipitalis*
Short-toed Snake-Eagle *Circaetus gallicus*
*Beaudouin's Snake-Eagle *Circaetus beaudouini*
Black-chested Snake-Eagle *Circaetus pectoralis*
Brown Snake-Eagle *Circaetus cinereus*
Southern Banded Snake-Eagle *Circaetus fasciolatus*
Western Banded Snake-Eagle *Circaetus cinerascens*
Bateleur *Terathopius ecaudatus*
African Harrier-Hawk *Polyboroides typus*
Pallid Harrier *Circus macrourus*
Montagu's Harrier *Circus pygargus*
African Marsh Harrier *Circus ranivorus*
Western Marsh Harrier *Circus aeruginosus*
Gabar Goshawk *Micronisus gabar*
Dark Chanting Goshawk *Melierax metabates*
Eastern Chanting Goshawk *Melierax poliopterus*
African Goshawk *Accipiter tachiro*
Shikra *Accipiter badius*
Levant Sparrowhawk *Accipiter brevipes*
Little Sparrowhawk *Accipiter minullus*
Ovambo Sparrowhawk *Accipiter ovampensis*
Eurasian Sparrowhawk *Accipiter nisus*
Rufous-breasted Sparrowhawk *Accipiter rufiventris*
Great Sparrowhawk *Accipiter melanoleucus*
Grasshopper Buzzard *Butastur rufipennis*
Lizard Buzzard *Kaupifalco monogrammicus*
Common Buzzard *Buteo buteo*
Socotra Buzzard *Buteo sp.*
Mountain Buzzard *Buteo oreophilus*
Long-legged Buzzard *Buteo rufinus*
Red-necked Buzzard *Buteo auguralis*
Augur Buzzard *Buteo augur*
Archer's Buzzard *Buteo (augur) archeri*
Lesser Spotted Eagle *Aquila pomarina*
Greater Spotted Eagle *Aquila clanga*
Tawny Eagle *Aquila rapax*
Steppe Eagle *Aquila nipalensis*
Eastern Imperial Eagle *Aquila heliaca*
Golden Eagle *Aquila chrysaetos*

Verreaux's Eagle *Aquila verreauxii*
Wahlberg's Eagle *Aquila wahlbergi*
Bonelli's Eagle *Hieraaetus fasciatus*
African Hawk-Eagle *Hieraaetus spilogaster*
Booted Eagle *Hieraaetus pennatus*
Ayres's Hawk-Eagle *Hieraaetus ayresii*
Long-crested Eagle *Lophaetus occipitalis*
African Crowned Eagle *Stephanoaetus coronatus*
Martial Eagle *Polemaetus bellicosus*

Secretarybird SAGITTARIIDAE
Secretarybird *Sagittarius serpentarius*

Falcons FALCONIDAE
Pygmy Falcon *Polihierax semitorquatus*
Lesser Kestrel *Falco naumanni*
Common Kestrel *Falco tinnunculus*
Greater Kestrel *Falco rupicoloides*
Fox Kestrel *Falco alopex*
Grey Kestrel *Falco ardosiaceus*
Red-necked Falcon *Falco chicquera*
Red-footed Falcon *Falco vespertinus*
Amur Falcon *Falco amurensis*
Eleonora's Falcon *Falco eleonorae*
Sooty Falcon *Falco concolor*
Eurasian Hobby *Falco subbuteo*
African Hobby *Falco cuvierii*
Lanner Falcon *Falco biarmicus*
Saker Falcon *Falco cherrug*
Peregrine Falcon *Falco peregrinus*
Barbary Falcon *Falco pelegrinoides*
Taita Falcon *Falco fasciinucha*

Guineafowl NUMIDIDAE
Crested Guineafowl *Guttera pucherani*
Vulturine Guineafowl *Acryllium vulturinum*
Helmeted Guineafowl *Numida meleagris*

Quails and francolins PHASIANIDAE
Common Quail *Coturnix coturnix*
*Blue Quail *Coturnix adansonii*
Harlequin Quail *Coturnix delegorguei*
Stone Partridge *Ptilopachus petrosus*
Coqui Francolin *Peliperdix coqui*
Moorland Francolin *Scleroptila psilolaemus*
Orange River Francolin *Scleroptila levaillantoides*
Crested Francolin *Dendroperdix sephaena*
Scaly Francolin *Pternistis squamatus*
Clapperton's Francolin *Pternistis clappertoni*
Harwood's Francolin *Pternistis harwoodi*
Chestnut-naped Francolin *Pternistis castaneicollis*
Djibouti Francolin *Pternistis ochropectus*
Erckel's Francolin *Pternistis erckelii*

Yellow-necked Spurfowl *Pternistis leucoscepus*

Buttonquails TURNICIDAE
Quail-plover *Ortyxelos meiffrenii*
Common Buttonquail *Turnix sylvaticus*

Rails, crakes and gallinules RALLIDAE
Buff-spotted Flufftail *Sarothrura elegans*
Red-chested Flufftail *Sarothrura rufa*
White-winged Flufftail *Sarothrura ayresi*
African Crake *Crex egregia*
Corncrake *Crex crex*
Rouget's Rail *Rougetius rougetii*
Water Rail *Rallus aquaticus*
African Rail *Rallus caerulescens*
Little Crake *Porzana parva*
Baillon's Crake *Porzana pusilla*
Spotted Crake *Porzana porzana*
Black Crake *Amaurornis flavirostra*
Allen's Gallinule *Porphyrio alleni*
Purple Swamphen *Porphyrio porphyrio*
Common Moorhen *Gallinula chloropus*
Lesser Moorhen *Gallinula angulata*
Eurasian Coot *Fulica atra*
Red-knobbed Coot *Fulica cristata*

Cranes GRUIDAE
Common Crane *Grus grus*
Wattled Crane *Bugeranus carunculatus*
Demoiselle Crane *Anthropoides virgo*
Black Crowned Crane *Balearica pavonina*

Finfoot HELIORNITHIDAE
African Finfoot *Podica senegalensis*

Bustards OTIDIDAE
Denham's Bustard *Neotis denhami*
Heuglin's Bustard *Neotis heuglinii*
MacQueen's Bustard *Chlamydotis macqueenii*
Arabian Bustard *Ardeotis arabs*
Kori Bustard *Ardeotis kori*
Buff-crested Bustard *Lophotis gindiana*
Little Brown Bustard *Eupodotis humilis*
White-bellied Bustard *Eupodotis senegalensis*
Black-bellied Bustard *Lissotis melanogaster*
Hartlaub's Bustard *Lissotis hartlaubii*

Jacanas JACANIDAE
African Jacana *Actophilornis africanus*
Lesser Jacana *Microparra capensis*
Pheasant-tailed Jacana *Hydrophasianus chirurgus*

Painted-snipe ROSTRATULIDAE
Greater Painted-snipe *Rostratula benghalensis*

Crab-plover DROMADIDAE
Crab-plover *Dromas ardeola*

Oystercatchers HAEMATOPODIDAE
Eurasian Oystercatcher *Haematopus ostralegus*

Stilts and avocets RECURVIROSTRIDAE
Black-winged Stilt *Himantopus himantopus*
Pied Avocet *Recurvirostra avosetta*

Thick-knees BURHINIDAE
Stone-curlew *Burhinus oedicnemus*
Senegal Thick-knee *Burhinus senegalensis*
Water Thick-knee *Burhinus vermiculatus*
Spotted Thick-knee *Burhinus capensis*

Coursers and pratincoles GLAREOLIDAE
Egyptian Plover *Pluvianus aegyptius*
Cream-coloured Courser *Cursorius cursor*
Somali Courser *Cursorius somalensis*
Temminck's Courser *Cursorius temminckii*
Double-banded Courser *Rhinoptilus africanus*
Heuglin's Courser *Rhinoptilus cinctus*
Bronze-winged Courser *Rhinoptilus chalcopterus*
Collared Pratincole *Glareola pratincola*
Black-winged Pratincole *Glareola nordmanni*
Madagascar Pratincole *Glareola ocularis*
Rock Pratincole *Glareola nuchalis*

Plovers CHARADRIIDAE
Little Ringed Plover *Charadrius dubius*
Comon Ringed Plover *Charadrius hiaticula*
Kittlitz's Plover *Charadrius pecuarius*
Three-banded Plover *Charadrius tricollaris*
Kentish Plover *Charadrius alexandrinus*
White-fronted Plover *Charadrius marginatus*
Lesser Sand Plover *Charadrius mongolus*
Greater Sand Plover *Charadrius leschenaultii*
Caspian Plover *Charadrius asiaticus*
Pacific Golden Plover *Pluvialis fulva*
Grey Plover *Pluvialis squatarola*
African Wattled Plover *Vanellus senegallus*
Spot-breasted Plover *Vanellus melanocephalus*
Black-headed Plover *Vanellus tectus*
Spur-winged Plover *Vanellus spinosus*
Senegal Plover *Vanellus lugubris*
Black-winged Plover *Vanellus melanopterus*
Crowned Plover *Vanellus coronatus*
Sociable Plover *Vanellus gregarius*
White-tailed Plover *Vanellus leucurus*
Long-toed Plover *Vanellus crassirostris*
Northern Lapwing *Vanellus vanellus*

Sandpipers and allies SCOLOPACIDAE
Great Knot *Calidris tenuirostris*
Red Knot *Calidris canutus*
Sanderling *Calidris alba*
Red-necked Stint *Calidris ruficollis*
Little Stint *Calidris minuta*
Temminck's Stint *Calidris temminckii*
Long-toed Stint *Calidris subminuta*
Pectoral Sandpiper *Calidris melanotos*
Curlew Sandpiper *Calidris ferruginea*
Dunlin *Calidris alpina*
Broad-billed Sandpiper *Limicola falcinellus*
Ruff *Philomachus pugnax*
Jack Snipe *Lymnocryptes minimus*
Common Snipe *Gallinago gallinago*
African Snipe *Gallinago nigripennis*
Great Snipe *Gallinago media*
Pintail Snipe *Gallinago stenura*
Black-tailed Godwit *Limosa limosa*
Bar-tailed Godwit *Limosa lapponica*
Whimbrel *Numenius phaeopus*
Slender-billed Curlew *Numenius tenuirostris*
Eurasian Curlew *Numenius arquata*
Spotted Redshank *Tringa erythropus*
Common Redshank *Tringa totanus*
Marsh Sandpiper *Tringa stagnatilis*
Common Greenshank *Tringa nebularia*
Green Sandpiper *Tringa ochropus*
Wood Sandpiper *Tringa glareola*
Terek Sandpiper *Xenus cinereus*
Common Sandpiper *Actitis hypoleucos*
Ruddy Turnstone *Arenaria interpres*
Red-necked Phalarope *Phalaropus lobatus*
Grey Phalarope *Phalaropus fulicarius*

Skuas STERCORARIIDAE
Pomarine Skua *Stercorarius pomarinus*
Arctic Skua *Stercorarius parasiticus*
South Polar Skua *Catharacta maccormicki*
Subantarctic Skua *Catharacta antarctica*

Gulls LARIDAE
Sooty Gull *Larus hemprichii*
White-eyed Gull *Larus leucophthalmus*
Pallas's Gull *Larus ichthyaetus*
Grey-headed Gull *Larus cirrocephalus*
Black-headed Gull *Larus ridibundus*
Slender-billed Gull *Larus genei*
Lesser Black-backed Gull *Larus fuscus*
Heuglin's Gull *Larus (fuscus) heuglini*
Caspian Gull *Larus cachinnans*
Sabine's Gull *Xema sabini*

Terns STERNIDAE
Gull-billed Tern *Sterna nilotica*
Caspian Tern *Sterna caspia*
Greater Crested Tern *Sterna bergii*
Lesser Crested Tern *Sterna bengalensis*
Sandwich Tern *Sterna sandvicensis*
*Black-naped Tern *Sterna sumatrana*
Roseate Tern *Sterna dougallii*
Common Tern *Sterna hirundo*
Arctic Tern *Sterna paradisaea*
White-cheeked Tern *Sterna repressa*
Bridled Tern *Sterna anaethetus*
Sooty Tern *Sterna fuscata*
Little Tern *Sterna albifrons*
Saunders's Tern *Sterna saundersi*
Whiskered Tern *Chlidonias hybrida*
Black Tern *Chlidonias niger*
White-winged Tern *Chlidonias leucopterus*
Lesser Noddy *Anous tenuirostris*
Brown Noddy *Anous stolidus*

Skimmers RYNCHOPIDAE
African Skimmer *Rynchops flavirostris*

Sandgrouse PTEROCLIDAE
Chestnut-bellied Sandgrouse *Pterocles exustus*
Spotted Sandgrouse *Pterocles senegallus*
Black-faced Sandgrouse *Pterocles decoratus*
Lichtenstein's Sandgrouse *Pterocles lichtensteinii*
Four-banded Sandgrouse *Pterocles quadricinctus*
Yellow-throated Sandgrouse *Pterocles gutturalis*

Pigeons and doves COLUMBIDAE
African Green Pigeon *Treron calvus*
Bruce's Green Pigeon *Treron waalia*
Tambourine Dove *Turtur tympanistria*
Blue-spotted Wood Dove *Turtur afer*
Black-billed Wood Dove *Turtur abyssinicus*
Emerald-spotted Wood Dove *Turtur chalcospilos*
Namaqua Dove *Oena capensis*
Lemon Dove *Aplopelia larvata*
Eastern Bronze-naped Pigeon *Columba delegorguei*
African Olive Pigeon *Columba arquatrix*
Somali Pigeon *Columba oliviae*
Speckled Pigeon *Columba guinea*
White-collared Pigeon *Columba albitorques*
Rock Dove/Feral Pigeon *Columba livia*
Red-eyed Dove *Streptopelia semitorquata*
African Mourning Dove *Streptopelia decipiens*
Vinaceous Dove *Streptopelia vinacea*
Ring-necked Dove *Streptopelia capicola*
African Collared Dove *Streptopelia roseogrisea*

African White-winged Dove *Streptopelia reichenowi*
European Turtle Dove *Streptopelia turtur*
Dusky Turtle Dove *Streptopelia lugens*
Laughing Dove *Streptopelia senegalensis*

Parrots and lovebirds PSITTACIDAE
Meyer's Parrot *Poicephalus meyeri*
African Orange-bellied Parrot *Poicephalus rufiventris*
Yellow-fronted Parrot *Poicephalus flavifrons*
Red-headed Lovebird *Agapornis pullarius*
Black-winged Lovebird *Agapornis taranta*
Rose-ringed Parakeet *Psittacula krameri*

Turacos MUSOPHAGIDAE
Fischer's Turaco *Tauraco fischeri*
White-cheeked Turaco *Tauraco leucotis*
Prince Ruspoli's Turaco *Tauraco ruspolii*
Bare-faced Go-away-bird *Corythaixoides personatus*
White-bellied Go-away-bird *Corythaixoides leucogaster*
Eastern Grey Plantain-eater *Crinifer zonurus*

Cuckoos and coucals CUCULIDAE
Jacobin Cuckoo *Clamator jacobinus*
Levaillant's Cuckoo *Clamator levaillantii*
Great Spotted Cuckoo *Clamator glandarius*
Red-chested Cuckoo *Cuculus solitarius*
Black Cuckoo *Cuculus clamosus*
Common Cuckoo *Cuculus canorus*
African Cuckoo *Cuculus gularis*
Asian Lesser Cuckoo *Cuculus poliocephalus*
African Emerald Cuckoo *Chrysococcyx cupreus*
Klaas's Cuckoo *Chrysococcyx klaas*
Diederik Cuckoo *Chrysococcyx caprius*
Asian Koel *Eudynamys scolopaceus*
Yellowbill *Ceuthmochares aereus*
White-browed Coucal *Centropus superciliosus*
Black Coucal *Centropus grillii*
Senegal Coucal *Centropus senegalensis*
Blue-headed Coucal *Centropus monachus*

Barn owls TYTONIDAE
African Grass Owl *Tyto capensis*
Barn Owl *Tyto alba*

Typical owls STRIGIDAE
Socotra Scops Owl *Otus (sunia) socotranus*
Eurasian Scops Owl *Otus scops*
African Scops Owl *Otus senegalensis*
Northern White-faced Owl *Ptilopsis leucotis*
Desert Eagle-Owl *Bubo (bubo) ascalaphus*
Cape Eagle-Owl *Bubo capensis*
Greyish Eagle-Owl *Bubo cinerascens*
Verreaux's Eagle-Owl *Bubo lacteus*

Pel's Fishing Owl *Scotopelia peli*
Pearl-spotted Owlet *Glaucidium perlatum*
African Barred Owlet *Glaucidium capense*
Little Owl *Athene noctua*
African Wood Owl *Strix woodfordii*
Abyssinian Owl *Asio abyssinicus*
Short-eared Owl *Asio flammeus*
Marsh Owl *Asio capensis*

Nightjars CAPRIMULGIDAE
Swamp Nightjar *Caprimulgus natalensis*
Long-tailed Nightjar *Caprimulgus climacurus*
Slender-tailed Nightjar *Caprimulgus clarus*
Montane Nightjar *Caprimulgus poliocephalus*
Donaldson Smith's Nightjar *Caprimulgus donaldsoni*
Plain Nightjar *Caprimulgus inornatus*
Star-spotted Nightjar *Caprimulgus stellatus*
Nubian Nightjar *Caprimulgus nubicus*
Freckled Nightjar *Caprimulgus tristigma*
Egyptian Nightjar *Caprimulgus aegyptius*
Dusky Nightjar *Caprimulgus fraenatus*
European Nightjar *Caprimulgus europaeus*
Nechisar Nightjar *Caprimulgus solala*
Standard-winged Nightjar *Macrodipteryx longipennis*
Pennant-winged Nightjar *Macrodipteryx vexillarius*

Swifts APODIDAE
Himalayan Swiftlet *Aerodramus brevirostris*
Mottled Spinetail *Telacanthura ussheri*
Böhm's Spinetail *Neafrapus boehmi*
Scarce Swift *Schoutedenapus myoptilus*
African Palm Swift *Cypsiurus parvus*
*African Black Swift *Apus barbatus*
Forbes-Watson's Swift *Apus berliozi*
Pallid Swift *Apus pallidus*
Nyanza Swift *Apus niansae*
Common Swift *Apus apus*
White-rumped Swift *Apus caffer*
Horus Swift *Apus horus*
Little Swift *Apus affinis*
Mottled Swift *Tachymarptis aequatorialis*
Alpine Swift *Tachymarptis melba*

Mousebirds COLIIDAE
Blue-naped Mousebird *Urocolius macrourus*
Speckled Mousebird *Colius striatus*
White-headed Mousebird *Colius leucocephalus*

Trogons TROGONIDAE
Narina Trogon *Apaloderma narina*

Kingfishers ALCEDINIDAE
Brown-hooded Kingfisher *Halcyon albiventris*

Grey-headed Kingfisher *Halcyon leucocephala*
Blue-breasted Kingfisher *Halcyon malimbica*
Woodland Kingfisher *Halcyon senegalensis*
Mangrove Kingfisher *Halcyon senegaloides*
Striped Kingfisher *Halcyon chelicuti*
Collared Kingfisher *Todirhamphus chloris*
African Pygmy Kingfisher *Ceyx pictus*
Malachite Kingfisher *Alcedo cristata*
Common Kingfisher *Alcedo atthis*
Half-collared Kingfisher *Alcedo semitorquata*
Giant Kingfisher *Megaceryle maxima*
Pied Kingfisher *Ceryle rudis*

Bee-eaters MEROPIDAE
Little Bee-eater *Merops pusillus*
Blue-breasted Bee-eater *Merops (variegatus) lafresnayii*
Swallow-tailed Bee-eater *Merops hirundineus*
Red-throated Bee-eater *Merops bulocki*
Somali Bee-eater *Merops revoilii*
White-throated Bee-eater *Merops albicollis*
Little Green Bee-eater *Merops orientalis*
Blue-cheeked Bee-eater *Merops persicus*
Madagascar Bee-eater *Merops superciliosus*
European Bee-eater *Merops apiaster*
Northern Carmine Bee-eater *Merops nubicus*

Rollers CORACIIDAE
Rufous-crowned Roller *Coracias naevius*
Indian Roller *Coracias benghalensis*
Abyssinian Roller *Coracias abyssinicus*
European Roller *Coracias garrulus*
Lilac-breasted Roller *Coracias caudatus*
Broad-billed Roller *Eurystomus glaucurus*

Wood-hoopoes & scimitarbills PHOENICULIDAE
Green Wood-hoopoe *Phoeniculus purpureus*
Black-billed Wood-hoopoe *Phoeniculus somaliensis*
*Violet Wood-hoopoe *Phoeniculus damarensis*
Common Scimitarbill *Rhinopomastus cyanomelas*
Black Scimitarbill *Rhinopomastus aterrimus*
Abyssinian Scimitarbill *Rhinopomastus minor*

Hoopoes UPUPIDAE
Eurasian Hoopoe *Upupa epops*
African Hoopoe *Upupa (epops) africana*

Hornbills BUCEROTIDAE
Red-billed Hornbill *Tockus erythrorhynchus*
Eastern Yellow-billed Hornbill *Tockus flavirostris*
Von der Decken's Hornbill *Tockus deckeni*
Jackson's Hornbill *Tockus jacksoni*
Hemprich's Hornbill *Tockus hemprichii*
Crowned Hornbill *Tockus alboterminatus*

African Grey Hornbill *Tockus nasutus*
Silvery-cheeked Hornbill *Bycanistes brevis*

Ground-hornbills BUCORVIDAE
Abyssinian Ground-hornbill *Bucorvus abyssinicus*

Barbets and tinkerbirds CAPITONIDAE
Red-fronted Tinkerbird *Pogoniulus pusillus*
Yellow-fronted Tinkerbird *Pogoniulus chrysoconus*
Red fronted Barbet *Tricholaema diademata*
Black-throated Barbet *Tricholaema melanocephala*
Banded Barbet *Lybius undatus*
Vieillot's Barbet *Lybius vieilloti*
Black-billed Barbet *Lybius guifsobalito*
Brown-breasted Barbet *Lybius melanopterus*
Double-toothed Barbet *Lybius bidentatus*
Red-and-yellow Barbet *Trachyphonus erythrocephalus*
Yellow-breasted Barbet *Trachyphonus margaritatus*
d'Arnaud's Barbet *Trachyphonus darnaudii*

Honeyguides INDICATORIDAE
Green-backed Honeybird *Prodotiscus zambesiae*
Wahlberg's Honeybird *Prodotiscus regulus*
Scaly-throated Honeyguide *Indicator variegatus*
Greater Honeyguide *Indicator indicator*
Lesser Honeyguide *Indicator minor*

Woodpeckers and wrynecks PICIDAE
Eurasian Wryneck *Jynx torquilla*
Red-throated Wryneck *Jynx ruficollis*
Nubian Woodpecker *Campethera nubica*
Mombasa Woodpecker *Campethera mombassica*
Green-backed Woodpecker *Campethera cailliautii*
Abyssinian Woodpecker *Dendropicos abyssinicus*
Cardinal Woodpecker *Dendropicos fuscescens*
Bearded Woodpecker *Dendropicos namaquus*
Grey Woodpecker *Dendropicos goertae*
Grey-headed Woodpecker *Dendropicos spodocephalus*
Brown-backed Woodpecker *Picoides obsoletus*

Pittas PITTIDAE
African Pitta *Pitta angolensis*

Larks ALAUDIDAE
Singing Bush Lark *Mirafra cantillans*
White-tailed Lark *Mirafra albicauda*
Friedmann's Lark *Mirafra pulpa*
Rufous-naped Lark *Mirafra africana*
Red-winged Lark *Mirafra hypermetra*
Somali Lark *Mirafra somalica*
Ash's Lark *Mirafra ashi*
Flappet Lark *Mirafra rufocinnamomea*
Collared Lark *Mirafra collaris*
Foxy Lark *Mirafra (africanoides) alopex*

Gillett's Lark *Mirafra gilletti*
Pink-breasted Lark *Mirafra poecilosterna*
Archer's Lark *Heteromirafra archeri*
Sidamo Lark *Heteromirafra sidamoensis*
Greater Hoopoe-Lark *Alaemon alaudipes*
Lesser Hoopoe-Lark *Alaemon hamertoni*
Bimaculated Lark *Melanocorypha bimaculata*
Desert Lark *Ammomanes deserti*
Greater Short-toed Lark *Calandrella brachydactyla*
Blanford's Lark *Calandrella blanfordi*
Erlanger's Lark *Calandrella erlangeri*
Somali Short-toed Lark *Calandrella somalica*
Obbia Lark *Spizocorys obbiensis*
Masked Lark *Spizocorys personata*
Short-tailed Lark *Pseudalaemon fremantlii*
Crested Lark *Galerida cristata*
Thekla Lark *Galerida theklae*
Chestnut-backed Sparrow-Lark *Eremopterix leucotis*
Black-crowned Sparrow-Lark *Eremopterix nigriceps*
Chestnut-headed Sparrow-Lark *Eremopterix signatus*

Swallows and martins HIRUNDINIDAE
Black Saw-wing *Psalidoprocne pristoptera*
*White-headed Saw-wing *Psalidoprocne albiceps*
Plain Martin *Riparia paludicola*
Sand Martin *Riparia riparia*
Banded Martin *Riparia cincta*
Grey-rumped Swallow *Pseudhirundo griseopyga*
Mosque Swallow *Cecropis senegalensis*
Lesser Striped Swallow *Cecropis abyssinica*
Red-rumped Swallow *Cecropis daurica*
*Red Sea Cliff Swallow *Petrochelidon perdita*
Rock Martin *Ptyonoprogne fuligula*
Eurasian Crag Martin *Ptyonoprogne rupestris*
Wire-tailed Swallow *Hirundo smithii*
White-tailed Swallow *Hirundo megaensis*
Ethiopian Swallow *Hirundo aethiopica*
Red-chested Swallow *Hirundo lucida*
Barn Swallow *Hirundo rustica*
Common House Martin *Delichon urbicum*

Wagtails, pipits and longclaws MOTACILLIDAE
Yellow Wagtail *Motacilla flava*
Citrine Wagtail *Motacilla citreola*
Grey Wagtail *Motacilla cinerea*
Mountain Wagtail *Motacilla clara*
White Wagtail *Motacilla alba*
African Pied Wagtail *Motacilla aguimp*
Golden Pipit *Tmetothylacus tenellus*
Grassland Pipit *Anthus cinnamomeus*
Tawny Pipit *Anthus campestris*

Long-billed Pipit *Anthus similis*
Plain-backed Pipit *Anthus leucophrys*
Malindi Pipit *Anthus melindae*
Bush Pipit *Anthus caffer*
Tree Pipit *Anthus trivialis*
Red-throated Pipit *Anthus cervinus*
Abyssinian Longclaw *Macronyx flavicollis*
Pangani Longclaw *Macronyx aurantiigula*

Cuckooshrikes CAMPEPHAGIDAE
Red-shouldered Cuckooshrike *Campephaga phoenicea*
Black Cuckooshrike *Campephaga flava*
Grey Cuckooshrike *Coracina caesia*
White-breasted Cuckooshrike *Coracina pectoralis*

Bulbuls PYCNONOTIDAE
Sombre Greenbul *Andropadus importunus*
Yellow-bellied Greenbul *Chlorocichla flaviventris*
Yellow-throated Leaflove *Chlorocichla flavicollis*
Terrestrial Brownbul *Phyllastrephus terrestris*
Northern Brownbul *Phyllastrephus strepitans*
Fischer's Greenbul *Phyllastrephus fischeri*
Common Bulbul *Pycnonotus barbatus*

Nicators INCERTAE SEDIS
Eastern Nicator *Nicator gularis*

Hypocolius BOMBYCILLIDAE
Grey Hypocolius *Hypocolius ampelinus*

Thrushes and chats TURDIDAE
Thrush Nightingale *Luscinia luscinia*
Common Nightingale *Luscinia megarhynchos*
Bluethroat *Luscinia svecica*
White-throated Robin *Irania gutturalis*
Rüppell's Robin-Chat *Cossypha semirufa*
White-browed Robin-Chat *Cossypha heuglini*
Red-capped Robin-Chat *Cossypha natalensis*
Snowy-headed Robin-Chat *Cossypha niveicapilla*
White-crowned Robin-Chat *Cossypha albicapillus*
Spotted Palm-Thrush *Cichladusa guttata*
Bearded Scrub Robin *Cercotrichas quadrivirgata*
White-browed Scrub Robin *Cercotrichas leucophrys*
Rufous Scrub Robin *Cercotrichas galactotes*
Black Scrub Robin *Cercotrichas podobe*
Black Redstart *Phoenicurus ochruros*
Common Redstart *Phoenicurus phoenicurus*
Siberian Stonechat *Saxicola (torquatus) maura*
African Stonechat *Saxicola torquatus*
Whinchat *Saxicola rubetra*
White-crowned Black Wheatear *Oenanthe leucopyga*
Somali Wheatear *Oenanthe phillipsi*
Northern Wheatear *Oenanthe oenanthe*
Pied Wheatear *Oenanthe pleschanka*

*Cyprus Wheatear *Oenanthe cypriaca*
Black-eared Wheatear *Oenanthe hispanica*
Hooded Wheatear *Oenanthe monacha*
Abyssinian Black Wheatear *Oenanthe lugubris*
Kurdish Wheatear *Oenanthe xanthoprymna*
Red-tailed Wheatear *Oenanthe chrysopygia*
Desert Wheatear *Oenanthe deserti*
Capped Wheatear *Oenanthe pileata*
Red-breasted Wheatear *Oenanthe bottae*
Heuglin's Wheatear *Oenanthe heuglini*
Isabelline Wheatear *Oenanthe isabellina*
Familiar Chat *Cercomela familiaris*
Brown-tailed Rock Chat *Cercomela scotocerca*
Sombre Rock Chat *Cercomela dubia*
Blackstart *Cercomela melanura*
Moorland Chat *Cercomela sordida*
Rüppell's Black Chat *Myrmecocichla melaena*
White-fronted Black Chat *Myrmecocichla albifrons*
Mocking Cliff Chat *Thamnolaea cinnamomeiventris*
White-winged Cliff Chat *Thamnolaea semirufa*
Little Rock Thrush *Monticola rufocinereus*
Common Rock Thrush *Monticola saxatilis*
Blue Rock Thrush *Monticola solitarius*
Red-tailed Ant-Thrush *Neocossyphus rufus*
Abyssinian Ground Thrush *Zoothera piaggiae*
Groundscraper Thrush *Psophocichla litsitsirupa*
Mountain Thrush *Turdus (olivaceus) abyssinicus*
Somali Thrush *Turdus ludoviciae*
African Thrush *Turdus pelios*
Bare-eyed Thrush *Turdus tephronotus*
Song Thrush *Turdus philomelos*

Warblers SYLVIIDAE
Little Rush Warbler *Bradypterus baboecala*
Bamboo Warbler *Bradypterus alfredi*
Cinnamon Bracken Warbler *Bradypterus cinnamomeus*
Moustached Grass Warbler *Melocichla mentalis*
Fan-tailed Grassbird *Schoenicola brevirostris*
Grasshopper Warbler *Locustella naevia*
River Warbler *Locustella fluviatilis*
Savi's Warbler *Locustella luscinioides*
Sedge Warbler *Acrocephalus schoenobaenus*
Eurasian Reed Warbler *Acrocephalus scirpaceus*
African Reed Warbler *Acrocephalus baeticatus*
Marsh Warbler *Acrocephalus palustris*
Great Reed Warbler *Acrocephalus arundinaceus*
Basra Reed Warbler *Acrocephalus griseldis*
Clamorous Reed Warbler *Acrocephalus stentoreus*
Lesser Swamp Warbler *Acrocephalus gracilirostris*
Dark-capped Yellow Warbler *Chloropeta natalensis*

Eastern Olivaceous Warbler *Hippolais pallida*
Sykes's Warbler *Hippolais rama*
Upcher's Warbler *Hippolais languida*
Olive-tree Warbler *Hippolais olivetorum*
Icterine Warbler *Hippolais icterina*
Yellow-bellied Eremomela *Eremomela icteropygialis*
Yellow-vented Eremomela *Eremomela flavicrissalis*
Green-backed Eremomela *Eremomela canescens*
Northern Crombec *Sylvietta brachyura*
Red-faced Crombec *Sylvietta whytii*
Philippa's Crombec *Sylvietta philippae*
Somali Crombec *Sylvietta isabellina*
Willow Warbler *Phylloscopus trochilus*
Common Chiffchaff *Phylloscopus collybita*
Wood Warbler *Phylloscopus sibilatrix*
Eastern Bonelli's Warbler *Phylloscopus orientalis*
Brown Woodland Warbler *Phylloscopus umbrovirens*
Barred Warbler *Sylvia nisoria*
Orphean Warbler *Sylvia hortensis*
Arabian Warbler *Sylvia leucomelaena*
Garden Warbler *Sylvia borin*
Blackcap *Sylvia atricapilla*
Common Whitethroat *Sylvia communis*
Lesser Whitethroat *Sylvia curruca*
Desert Whitethroat *Sylvia (curruca) minula*
Asian Desert Warbler *Sylvia nana*
Rüppell's Warbler *Sylvia rueppelli*
Ménétriés's Warbler *Sylvia mystacea*
*Subalpine Warbler *Sylvia cantillans*
Brown Parisoma *Parisoma lugens*
Banded Parisoma *Parisoma boehmi*
Yellow-bellied Hyliota *Hyliota flavigaster*

Cisticolas and allies CISTICOLIDAE
Red-faced Cisticola *Cisticola erythrops*
Singing Cisticola *Cisticola cantans*
Rattling Cisticola *Cisticola chiniana*
Boran Cisticola *Cisticola bodessa*
Ashy Cisticola *Cisticola cinereolus*
Winding Cisticola *Cisticola (galactotes) marginatus*
Coastal Cisticola *Cisticola (galactotes) haematocephala*
Ethiopian Cisticola *Cisticola (galactotes) lugubris*
Stout Cisticola *Cisticola robustus*
Croaking Cisticola *Cisticola natalensis*
Red-pate Cisticola *Cisticola ruficeps*
Tiny Cisticola *Cisticola nana*
Siffling Cisticola *Cisticola brachypterus*
Foxy Cisticola *Cisticola troglodytes*
Zitting Cisticola *Cisticola juncidis*
Socotra Cisticola *Cisticola haesitatus*

Desert Cisticola *Cisticola aridulus*
Black-backed Cisticola *Cisticola eximius*
Pectoral-patch Cisticola *Cisticola brunnescens*
Socotra Warbler *Incana incana*
Tawny-flanked Prinia *Prinia subflava*
Pale Prinia *Prinia somalica*
Graceful Prinia *Prinia gracilis*
Red-winged Warbler *Heliolais erythropterus*
Red-fronted Warbler *Urorhipis rufifrons*
Cricket Warbler *Spiloptila clamans*
Buff-bellied Warbler *Phyllolais pulchella*
Yellow-breasted Apalis *Apalis flavida*
Black-headed Apalis *Apalis melanocephala*
Grey-backed Camaroptera *Camaroptera brachyura*
Grey Wren-Warbler *Calamonastes simplex*

Flycatchers MUSCICAPIDAE
Abyssinian Slaty Flycatcher *Melaenornis chocolatinus*
Northern Black Flycatcher *Melaenornis edolioides*
Southern Black Flycatcher *Melaenornis pammelaina*
Pale Flycatcher *Bradornis pallidus*
African Grey Flycatcher *Bradornis microrhynchus*
Silverbird *Empidornis semipartitus*
Spotted Flycatcher *Muscicapa striata*
Gambaga Flycatcher *Muscicapa gambagae*
Ashy Flycatcher *Muscicapa caerulescens*
African Dusky Flycatcher *Muscicapa adusta*
Lead-coloured Flycatcher *Myioparus plumbeus*
Semi-collared Flycatcher *Ficedula semitorquata*

Monarch flycatchers MONARCHIDAE
Little Yellow Flycatcher *Erythrocercus holochlorus*
Blue-mantled Crested Flycatcher *Trochocercus cyanomelas*
African Paradise Flycatcher *Terpsiphone viridis*

Wattle-eyes and batises PLATYSTEIRIDAE
Brown-throated Wattle-eye *Platysteira cyanea*
Black-throated Wattle-eye *Platysteira peltata*
Grey-headed Batis *Batis orientalis*
Black-headed Batis *Batis minor*
Pygmy Batis *Batis perkeo*

Babblers TIMALIIDAE
African Hill Babbler *Pseudoalcippe abyssinica*
Brown Babbler *Turdoides plebejus*
White-headed Babbler *Turdoides leucocephala*
Dusky Babbler *Turdoides tenebrosa*
White-rumped Babbler *Turdoides leucopygia*
Scaly Babbler *Turdoides squamulata*
Fulvous Babbler *Turdoides fulva*
Rufous Chatterer *Turdoides rubiginosa*
Scaly Chatterer *Turdoides aylmeri*

Abyssinian Catbird *Parophasma galinieri*

Tits PARIDAE
Northern Grey Tit *Parus thruppi*
White-backed Black Tit *Parus leuconotus*
White-winged Black Tit *Parus leucomelas*
White-shouldered Black Tit *Parus guineensis*

Penduline-tits REMIZIDAE
Sennar Penduline-tit *Anthoscopus punctifrons*
Mouse-coloured Penduline-tit *Anthoscopus musculus*

Treecreepers CERTHIIDAE
Spotted Creeper *Salpornis spilonotus*

Sunbirds NECTARINIIDAE
Eastern Violet-backed Sunbird *Anthreptes orientalis*
Olive Sunbird *Cyanomitra olivacea*
Mouse-coloured Sunbird *Cyanomitra veroxii*
Amethyst Sunbird *Chalcomitra amethystina*
Scarlet-chested Sunbird *Chalcomitra senegalensis*
Hunter's Sunbird *Chalcomitra hunteri*
Socotra Sunbird *Chalcomitra balfouri*
*Toha Sunbird *Chalcomitra* sp.
Tacazze Sunbird *Nectarinia tacazze*
Malachite Sunbird *Nectarinia famosa*
Collared Sunbird *Hedydipna collaris*
Pygmy Sunbird *Hedydipna platura*
Nile Valley Sunbird *Hedydipna metallica*
Olive-bellied Sunbird *Cinnyris chloropygius*
Beautiful Sunbird *Cinnyris pulchellus*
Marico Sunbird *Cinnyris mariquensis*
Black-bellied Sunbird *Cinnyris nectarinioides*
Purple-banded Sunbird *Cinnyris bifasciatus*
Tsavo Sunbird *Cinnyris tsavoensis*
Violet-breasted Sunbird *Cinnyris chalcomelas*
Shining Sunbird *Cinnyris habessinicus*
Variable Sunbird *Cinnyris venustus*
Copper Sunbird *Cinnyris cupreus*

White-eyes ZOSTEROPIDAE
Yellow White-eye *Zosterops senegalensis*
Abyssinian White-eye *Zosterops abyssinicus*
Montane White-eye *Zosterops poliogastrus*

Shrikes LANIIDAE
Common Fiscal *Lanius collaris*
Taita Fiscal *Lanius dorsalis*
Somali Fiscal *Lanius somalicus*
Long-tailed Fiscal *Lanius cabanisi*
Masked Shrike *Lanius nubicus*
Grey-backed Fiscal *Lanius excubitorius*
Lesser Grey Shrike *Lanius minor*
Southern Grey Shrike *Lanius meridionalis*

Isabelline Shrike *Lanius isabellinus*
Red-backed Shrike *Lanius collurio*
Woodchat Shrike *Lanius senator*
Northern White-crowned Shrike *Eurocephalus rueppelli*

Bush-shrikes MALACONOTIDAE
Grey-headed Bush-shrike *Malaconotus blanchoti*
Sulphur-breasted Bush-shrike *Telophorus sulfureopectus*
Four-coloured Bush-shrike *Telophorus quadricolor*
Rosy-patched Bush-shrike *Rhodophoneus cruentus*
Marsh Tchagra *Tchagra minutus*
Three-streaked Tchagra *Tchagra jamesi*
Black-crowned Tchagra *Tchagra senegalus*
Black-backed Puffback *Dryoscopus cubla*
Northern Puffback *Dryoscopus gambensis*
Pringle's Puffback *Dryoscopus pringlii*
Slate-coloured Boubou *Laniarius funebris*
Red-naped Bush-shrike *Laniarius ruficeps*
Ethiopian Boubou *Laniarius aethiopicus*
Erlanger's Boubou *Laniarius erlangeri*
East Coast Boubou *Laniarius sublacteus*
Black-headed Gonolek *Laniarius erythrogaster*
Brubru *Nilaus afer*

Helmetshrikes PRIONOPIDAE
White-crested Helmetshrike *Prionops plumatus*
Retz's Helmetshrike *Prionops retzii*
Chestnut-fronted Helmetshrike *Prionops scopifrons*

Orioles ORIOLIDAE
Black-headed Oriole *Oriolus larvatus*
Abyssinian Oriole *Oriolus monacha*
African Golden Oriole *Oriolus auratus*
Eurasian Golden Oriole *Oriolus oriolus*

Drongos DICRURIDAE
Square-tailed Drongo *Dicrurus ludwigii*
Fork-tailed Drongo *Dicrurus adsimilis*

Crows CORVIDAE
Cape Rook *Corvus capensis*
Brown-necked Raven *Corvus ruficollis*
Dwarf Raven *Corvus edithae*
Pied Crow *Corvus albus*
Fan-tailed Raven *Corvus rhipidurus*
Thick-billed Raven *Corvus crassirostris*
House Crow *Corvus splendens*
Piapiac *Ptilostomus afer*
Red-billed Chough *Pyrrhocorax pyrrhocorax*
Stresemann's Bush-crow *Zavattariornis stresemanni*

Starlings STURNIDAE
Stuhlmann's Starling *Poeoptera stuhlmanni*
Red-winged Starling *Onychognathus morio*

Somali Starling *Onychognathus blythii*
Socotra Starling *Onychognathus frater*
Bristle-crowned Starling *Onychognathus salvadorii*
White-billed Starling *Onychognathus albirostris*
Slender-billed Starling *Onychognathus tenuirostris*
Black-bellied Starling *Lamprotornis corruscus*
Greater Blue-eared Starling *Lamprotornis chalybaeus*
Lesser Blue-eared Starling *Lamprotornis chloropterus*
Splendid Starling *Lamprotornis splendidus*
Rüppell's Starling *Lamprotornis purpuroptera*
Golden-breasted Starling *Lamprotornis regius*
Shelley's Starling *Lamprotornis shelleyi*
Superb Starling *Lamprotornis superbus*
Chestnut-bellied Starling *Lamprotornis pulcher*
Fischer's Starling *Lamprotornis fischeri*
White-crowned Starling *Spreo albicapillus*
Magpie Starling *Speculipastor bicolor*
Sharpe's Starling *Pholia sharpii*
Violet-backed Starling *Cinnyricinclus leucogaster*
Wattled Starling *Creatophora cinerea*
Common Starling *Sturnus vulgaris*
Rosy Starling *Pastor roseus*
Yellow-billed Oxpecker *Buphagus africanus*
Red-billed Oxpecker *Buphagus erythrorhynchus*

Sparrows and petronias PASSERIDAE
Northern Grey-headed Sparrow *Passer griseus*
Swainson's Sparrow *Passer swainsonii*
Parrot-billed Sparrow *Passer gongonensis*
Shelley's Rufous Sparrow *Passer shelleyi*
Socotra Sparrow *Passer insularis*
Abd al-Kuri Sparrow *Passer hemileucus*
House Sparrow *Passer domesticus*
Somali Sparrow *Passer castanopterus*
Chestnut Sparrow *Passer eminibey*
Sudan Golden Sparrow *Passer luteus*
Arabian Golden Sparrow *Passer euchlorus*
Bush Petronia *Petronia dentata*
Yellow-spotted Petronia *Petronia pyrgita*
Pale Rockfinch *Carpospiza brachydactyla*

Weavers PLOCEIDAE
White-billed Buffalo-Weaver *Bubalornis albirostris*
Red-billed Buffalo-Weaver *Bubalornis niger*
White-headed Buffalo-Weaver *Dinemellia dinemelli*
White-browed Sparrow-Weaver *Plocepasser mahali*
Chestnut-crowned Sparrow-Weaver *Plocepasser superciliosus*
Donaldson Smith's Sparrow-Weaver *Plocepasser donaldsoni*
Speckle-fronted Weaver *Sporopipes frontalis*
Grey-capped Social Weaver *Pseudonigrita arnaudi*
Black-capped Social Weaver *Pseudonigrita cabanisi*

Red-headed Weaver *Anaplectes rubriceps*
Baglafecht Weaver *Ploceus baglafecht*
Little Weaver *Ploceus luteolus*
Black-necked Weaver *Ploceus nigricollis*
Spectacled Weaver *Ploceus ocularis*
African Golden Weaver *Ploceus subaureus*
Golden Palm Weaver *Ploceus bojeri*
Northern Masked Weaver *Ploceus taeniopterus*
Lesser Masked Weaver *Ploceus intermedius*
Vitelline Masked Weaver *Ploceus vitellinus*
Rüppell's Weaver *Ploceus galbula*
Speke's Weaver *Ploceus spekei*
Village Weaver *Ploceus cucullatus*
Juba Weaver *Ploceus dichrocephalus*
Yellow-backed Weaver *Ploceus melanocephalus*
Chestnut Weaver *Ploceus rubiginosus*
Dark-backed Weaver *Ploceus bicolor*
Compact Weaver *Ploceus superciliosus*
Grosbeak Weaver *Amblyospiza albifrons*
Cardinal Quelea *Quelea cardinalis*
Red-headed Quelea *Quelea erythrops*
Red-billed Quelea *Quelea quelea*
Northern Red Bishop *Euplectes franciscanus*
Black-winged Red Bishop *Euplectes hordeaceus*
Black Bishop *Euplectes gierowii*
Yellow-crowned Bishop *Euplectes afer*
Fire-fronted Bishop *Euplectes diadematus*
Yellow Bishop *Euplectes capensis*
White-winged Widowbird *Euplectes albonotatus*
Yellow-mantled Widowbird *Euplectes macroura*
Red-collared Widowbird *Euplectes ardens*
Fan-tailed Widowbird *Euplectes axillaris*

Waxbills ESTRILDIDAE
Green-backed Twinspot *Mandingoa nitidula*
Abyssinian Crimsonwing *Cryptospiza salvadorii*
Yellow-bellied Waxbill *Coccopygia quartinia*
Abyssinian Waxbill *Estrilda (paludicola) ochrogaster*
Crimson-rumped Waxbill *Estrilda rhodopyga*
Black-rumped Waxbill *Estrilda troglodytes*
Common Waxbill *Estrilda astrild*
Black-cheeked Waxbill *Estrilda charmosyna*
Red-cheeked Cordon-bleu *Uraeginthus bengalus*
Blue-capped Cordon-bleu *Uraeginthus cyanocephalus*
Purple Grenadier *Uraeginthus ianthinogaster*
Peters's Twinspot *Hypargos niveoguttatus*
Red-billed Pytilia *Pytilia lineata*
Green-winged Pytilia *Pytilia melba*
Orange-winged Pytilia *Pytilia afra*
Red-billed Firefinch *Lagonosticta senegala*

Bar-breasted Firefinch *Lagonosticta rufopicta*
Black-faced Firefinch *Lagonosticta larvata*
African Firefinch *Lagonosticta rubricata*
Jameson's Firefinch *Lagonosticta rhodopareia*
Cut-throat Finch *Amadina fasciata*
Black-faced Quailfinch *Ortygospiza atricollis*
African Quailfinch *Ortygospiza fuscocrissa*
Zebra Waxbill *Sporaeginthus subflavus*
Grey-headed Silverbill *Odontospiza griseicapilla*
Bronze Mannikin *Spermestes cucullata*
Black-and-white Mannikin *Spermestes bicolor*
Red-backed Mannikin *Spermestes (bicolor) nigriceps*
Magpie Mannikin *Spermestes fringilloides*
African Silverbill *Euodice cantans*

Whydahs and indigobirds VIDUIDAE
Cuckoo Finch *Anomalospiza imberbis*
Pin-tailed Whydah *Vidua macroura*
Sahel Paradise Whydah *Vidua orientalis*
Exclamatory Paradise Whydah *Vidua interjecta*
Eastern Paradise Whydah *Vidua paradisaea*
Steel-blue Whydah *Vidua hypocherina*
Straw-tailed Whydah *Vidua fischeri*
Village Indigobird *Vidua chalybeata*
Wilson's Indigobird *Vidua wilsoni*
Jambandu Indigobird *Vidua raricola*
Barka Indigobird *Vidua larvaticola*

Canaries and seedeaters FRINGILLIDAE
African Citril *Serinus citrinelloides*

Southern Citril *Serinus hypostictus*
White-rumped Seedeater *Serinus leucopygius*
Reichenow's Seedeater *Serinus reichenowi*
White-throated Seedeater *Serinus xanthopygius*
Yellow-fronted Canary *Serinus mozambicus*
White-bellied Canary *Serinus dorsostriatus*
Yellow-throated Seedeater *Serinus flavigula*
Salvadori's Seedeater *Serinus xantholaemus*
Northern Grosbeak-Canary *Serinus donaldsoni*
Streaky Seedeater *Serinus striolatus*
Stripe-breasted Seedeater *Serinus reichardi*
Brown-rumped Seedeater *Serinus tristriatus*
Yellow-crowned Canary *Serinus flavivertex*
Black-headed Siskin *Serinus nigriceps*
Socotra Golden-winged Grosbeak *Rhynchostruthus socotranus*
Somali Golden-winged Grosbeak *Rhynchostruthus louisae*
Warsangli Linnet *Carduelis johannis*
Ankober Serin *Carduelis ankoberensis*
Trumpeter Finch *Bucanetes githagineus*

Buntings EMBERIZIDAE
Golden-breasted Bunting *Emberiza flaviventris*
Somali Bunting *Emberiza poliopleura*
Brown-rumped Bunting *Emberiza affinis*
Cinnamon-breasted Bunting *Emberiza tahapisi*
Striolated Bunting *Emberiza striolata*
Socotra Bunting *Emberiza socotrana*
Cinereous Bunting *Emberiza cineracea*
Ortolan Bunting *Emberiza hortulana*
Cretzschmar's Bunting *Emberiza caesia*

Appendix 1
SPECIES ENDEMIC TO THE HORN OF AFRICA

		ET	ER	DJ	SO	SOC
Wattled Ibis	*Bostrychia carunculata*	X	X			
Blue-winged Goose	*Cyanochen cyanoptera*	X				
Socotra Buzzard	*Buteo* sp.					X
Archer's Buzzard	*Buteo (augur) archeri*				X	
Harwood's Francolin	*Pternistis harwoodi*	X				
*Chestnut-naped Francolin	*Pternistis castaneicollis*	X			X	
Djibouti Francolin	*Pternistis ochropectus*			X		
Rouget's Rail	*Rougetius rougetii*	X	X			
Little Brown Bustard	*Eupodotis humilis*	X			X	
Spot-breasted Plover	*Vanellus melanocephalus*	X				
Somali Pigeon	*Columba oliviae*				X	
White-collared Pigeon	*Columba albitorques*	X	X			
Yellow-fronted Parrot	*Poicephalus flavifrons*	X				
Black-winged Lovebird	*Agapornis taranta*	X	X			
Prince Ruspoli's Turaco	*Tauraco ruspolii*	X				
Socotra Scops Owl	*Otus (suniu) socotranus*					X
Nechisar Nightjar	*Caprimulgus solala*	X				
Banded Barbet	*Lybius undatus*	X	X			
Abyssinian Woodpecker	*Dendropicos abyssinicus*	X	X			
Somali Lark	*Mirafra somalica*				X	
Ash's Lark	*Mirafra ashi*				X	
Archer's Lark	*Heteromirafra archeri*				X	
Sidamo Lark	*Heteromirafra sidamoensis*	X				
Lesser Hoopoe-Lark	*Alaemon hamertoni*				X	
Erlanger's Lark	*Calandrella erlangeri*	X				
Obbia Lark	*Spizocorys obbiensis*				X	
White-tailed Swallow	*Hirundo megaensis*	X				
Abyssinian Longclaw	*Macronyx flavicollis*	X	?			
Somali Wheatear	*Oenanthe phillipsi*	X			X	
Abyssinian Black Wheatear	*Oenanthe lugubris*	X	X		X	
Sombre Rock Chat	*Cercomela dubia*	X			X	
Rüppell's Black Chat	*Myrmecocichla melaena*	X	X			

		ET	ER	DJ	SO	SOC
White-winged Cliff Chat	*Thamnolaea semirufa*	X	X			
Somali Thrush	*Turdus ludoviciae*				X	
Philippa's Crombec	*Sylvietta philippae*	X			X	
Ethiopian Cisticola	*Cisticola (galactotes) lugubris*	X	X			
Socotra Cisticola	*Cisticola haesitatus*					X
Socotra Warbler	*Incana incana*					X
Abyssinian Slaty Flycatcher	*Melaenornis chocolatinus*	X	X			
Abyssinian Catbird	*Parophasma galinieri*	X				
White-backed Black Tit	*Parus leuconotus*	X	X			
Socotra Sunbird	*Chalcomitra balfouri*					X
Erlanger's Boubou	*Laniarius erlangeri*				X	
Abyssinian Oriole	*Oriolus monacha*	X	X			
*Thick-billed Raven	*Corvus crassirostris*	X	X	V		
Stresemann's Bush-crow	*Zavattariornis stresemanni*	X				
Somali Starling	*Onychognathus blythii*	X	X	X	X	X
Socotra Starling	*Onychognathus frater*					X
White-billed Starling	*Onychognathus albirostris*	X	X			
Socotra Sparrow	*Passer insularis*					X
Abd al-Kuri Sparrow	*Passer hemileucus*					X
White-throated Seedeater	*Serinus xanthopygius*	X	X			
Yellow-throated Seedeater	*Serinus flavigula*	X				
Salvadori's Seedeater	*Serinus xantholaemus*	X				
Brown-rumped Seedeater	*Serinus tristriatus*	X	X		X	
Black-headed Siskin	*Serinus nigriceps*	X				
Socotra Golden-winged Grosbeak	*Rhynchostruthus socotranus*					X
Somali Golden-winged Grosbeak	*Rhynchostruthus louisae*				X	
Warsangli Linnet	*Carduelis johannis*				X	
Ankober Serin	*Carduelis ankoberensis*	X				
Socotra Bunting	*Emberiza socotrana*					X
TOTALS:	[Horn of Africa: 61]	39	18	2	20	11
Totals endemic to individual countries/region		15	0	1	11	10

Key: X = resident; x = status unknown (one old record only); V = vagrant; ? = uncertain
* Known also from recent sight records on the borders of the region, but treated as Horn of Africa endemics in this list.

NEAR-ENDEMICS

The following species are almost endemic to the Horn of Africa, with only very small ranges beyond the borders of the region.

	ET	ER	DJ	SO	SOC	Extralimital
Jouanin's Petrel *Bulweria fallax*		V	V	V	X	Oman
Erckel's Francolin *Pternistis erckelii*	X	X				Sudan
African White-winged Dove *Streptopelia reichenowi*	X			X		Kenya
White-cheeked Turaco *Tauraco leucotis*	X	X				Sudan
Forbes-Watson's Swift *Apus berliozi*				X	X	Kenya (NBr), Oman
Blue-breasted Bee-eater *Merops (variegatus) lafresnayii*	X	X				Sudan
Collared Lark *Mirafra collaris*	X			X		Kenya
Gillett's Lark *Mirafra gilletti*	X			X		Kenya
Somali Short-toed Lark *Calandrella somalica*	X			X		Kenya
Malindi Pipit *Anthus melindae*				X		Kenya
White-rumped Babbler *Turdoides leucopygia*	X	X		X		Sudan
Somali Fiscal *Lanius somalicus*	X		X	X		Kenya
Ethiopian Boubou *Laniarius aethiopicus*	X	X	X	X		Sudan, Kenya
Swainson's Sparrow *Passer swainsonii*	X	X	X	X		Sudan, Kenya
Juba Weaver *Ploceus dichrocephalus*	X			X		Kenya
Red-billed Pytilia *Pytilia lineata*	X					Sudan
Abyssinian Waxbill *Estrilda (paludicola) ochrogaster*	X					Sudan

Key: X = resident/breeding; V = vagrant; NBr = non-breeding visitor

Appendix 2:
HYPOTHETICAL SPECIES

a) Species requiring confirmation in the region, but included in the book

White-tailed Tropicbird – occurs offshore from Somalia
Beaudouin's Snake-Eagle – several recent records in Ethiopia; none fully acceptable
Blue Quail – several records in Ethiopia; none fully acceptable
Black-naped Tern – may occur in Somali waters
African Black Swift *Apus barbatus* – claimed Bale Mts in Dec 2006; confirmation required
Violet Wood-hoopoe – several records in Ethiopia; none fully acceptable
White-headed Saw-wing – several records in Ethiopia; none fully acceptable
Red Sea Cliff Swallow – extralimital (Sudan only) but may occur in region
Cyprus Wheatear – no confirmed records, but several claimed in Ethiopia and probably occurs
Subalpine Warbler – Djibouti records withdrawn, but could occur in region
Toha Sunbird *Chalcomitra* sp. – undescribed species, Djibouti

b) Species requiring confirmation in the region, but not included in the book

Cape Shoveler *Anas smithii* – two recent records not accepted (Ethiopia)
Blacksmith Plover *Vanellus armatus* – several recent unconfirmed reports (Ethiopia and Eritrea)
Asian Dowitcher *Limnodromus semipalmatus* – recent record not accepted (Ethiopia)
Lesser Yellowlegs *Tringa flavipes* – recent record not accepted (Ethiopia)
Armenian Gull *Larus armenicus* – claimed Feb 1998 without details (Eritrea)
Little Gull *Larus minutus* – flock of 60 at Lake Turkana in 1975 not accepted (Ethiopia)
Ross's Turaco *Musophaga rossae* – recent record; confirmation required (Ethiopia)
Hume's Owl *Strix butleri* – records now rejected (Socotra)
Meadow Pipit *Anthus pratensis* – several records; none acceptable (Ethiopia and Eritrea)
Arabian Babbler *Turdoides squameiceps* – recent record; confirmation required (Djibouti)
Mistle Thrush *Turdus viscivorus* – recent record; confirmation required (Djibouti)
Cassin's Grey Flycatcher *Muscicapa cassini* – record at Lake Zwai in Dec 2008; confirmation required (Ethiopia)
Pied Flycatcher *Ficedula hypoleuca* – recent record; confirmation required (Ethiopia)
Black-and-white Flycatcher *Bias musicus* – recent record; confirmation required (Somalia)
Bronze Sunbird *Nectarinia kilimensis* – records probably misidentified (Ethiopia)
Red-chested Sunbird *Cinnyris erythrocercus* – records probably misidentified (Ethiopia and Eritrea)

c) Species recorded within mapping squares of Eritrea, Ethiopia and Somalia, but across the border in countries outside the region – not included in the book

Sand Partridge *Ammoperdix heyi*	(Sudan)
Red-necked Spurfowl *Pternistis afer*	(Kenya)
Grey Crowned Crane *Balearica regulorum*	(Kenya)
Brown-headed Parrot *Poicephalus cryptoxanthus*	(Kenya)
Spotted Eagle-Owl *Bubo africanus*	(Kenya)
Fiery-necked Nightjar *Caprimulgus pectoralis*	(Kenya)
Black-shouldered Nightjar *Caprimulgus nigriscapularis*	(Sudan)
Rufous-rumped Lark *Pinarocorys erythropygia*	(Sudan)
Bar-tailed Lark *Ammomanes cinctura*	(Sudan)
Cinnamon Weaver *Ploceus badius*	(Sudan)

d) Species no longer considered valid – not included in the book

Degodi Lark *Mirafra degodiensis* (Collar *et al.* 2009)	(Ethiopia)
Bulo Burti Bush-shrike *Laniarius liberatus* (Nguembock *et al.* 2008)	(Somalia)

REFERENCES AND FURTHER READING

The following works were all consulted during the preparation of this guide, several of them extensively. They include some of the key sources of reference for birds of the region. The works marked with an asterisk are recommended in particular for more detailed information on plumages and distribution. Space has not permitted all our sources to be listed here, and many individual papers and notes consulted have been omitted. The journals Scopus, Bulletin of the African Bird Club, Sandgrouse, and the Bulletin of the British Ornithologists' Club are a rich source of material and highly recommended for further study.

Alström, P., Colston, P. and Lewington, I. (1991) A Field Guide to the Rare Birds of Britain and Europe. HarperCollins, London.

*Ash, J. S. and Miskell, J. E. (1998) Birds of Somalia. Pica Press, Sussex.

*Ash, J. and Atkins, J. (2009) Birds of Ethiopia and Eritrea. Christopher Helm, London.

BirdLife International (2000) Threatened Birds of the World. Lynx Edicions and BirdLife International, Barcelona and Cambridge.

*Brown, L. H., Urban, E. K. and Newman, K. (1982) The Birds of Africa: Volume 1. Academic Press, London.

Borrow, N. and Demey, R. (2004) Field Guide to the Birds of Western Africa. Christopher Helm, London.

Cheung, C. and DeVantier, L. (2006) Socotra: A Natural History of the Islands and their People. Odyssey Books and Guides, Hong Kong.

Cleere, N. and Nurney, D. (1998) Nightjars: A Guide to Nightjars and Related Nightbirds. Pica Press, Sussex.

Collar, N. J., Dingle, C., Gabremichael, M. N. and Spottiswoode, C. N. (2009) Taxonomic status of the Degodi Lark Mirafra degodiensis, with notes on the voice of Gillett's Lark M. gilletti. Bull. Brit. Orn. Club 129: 49–62.

del Hoyo et al. (eds) (1992-2008) Handbook of the Birds of the World. Volumes 1-13. Lynx Edicions, Barcelona.

Dickinson, E. C. (2003) The Howard and Moore Complete Checklist of the Birds of the World. Christopher Helm, London.

Dowsett, R. J. and Dowsett-Lemaire, F. (eds.) (1993) A Contribution to the Distribution and Taxonomy of Afrotropical and Malagasy Birds. Tauraco Press, Liège.

Dowsett, R. J. and Forbes-Watson, A. D. (1993) Checklist of the Birds of the Afrotropical and Malagasy Regions. Tauraco Press, Liège.

Ethiopian Wildlife and Natural History Society (1996) Important Bird Areas of Ethiopia: A First Inventory. Ethiopian Wildlife and Natural History Society, Addis Ababa.

Ferguson-Lees, I. J. and Christie, D. A. (2001) Raptors of the World. Christopher Helm, London.

Fishpool, L. D. C. and Evans M. I. (eds.) (2001) Important Bird Areas in Africa and Associated Islands: Priority Sites for Conservation. BirdLife International, Cambridge.

Francis, J. and Shirihai, H. (1999) Ethiopia: In search of endemic birds. Privately published.

*Fry, C. H., Keith, S. and Urban, E. K. (1988) The Birds of Africa. Volume 3. Academic Press, London.

*Fry, C. H., Keith, G. S. and Urban E. K. (2000) The Birds of Africa: Volume 6. Academic Press, London.

*Fry, C. H. and Keith, G. S. (2004) The Birds of Africa: Volume 7. Christopher Helm, London.

Gill, F. and Wright, M. (2006) Birds of the World: Recommended English Names. Christopher Helm, London.

Grimmett, R., Inskipp, C. and Inskipp, T. (1998) Birds of the Indian Subcontinent. Christopher Helm, London.

Keith, S., Urban, E. K. and Fry, C. H. (1992) The Birds of Africa Volume 4. Academic Press, London.

König, C. and Weick, F. (2008) Owls of the World, 2nd ed. Christopher Helm, London.

Mackworth-Praed, C. W. and Grant, C. H. B. (1957-60) Birds of Eastern and North Eastern Africa. Volumes 1 and 2. Longman, London and New York.

Madge, S. and McGowan, P. (2002) Pheasants, Partridges and Grouse. Christopher Helm, London.

Madge, S. C. and Redman, N. J. (1989) The existence of a form of cliff swallow Hirundo sp. in Ethiopia. Scopus 13: 126-129.

Malling Olsen, K. and Larsson, H. (1997) Skuas and Jaegers. Pica Press, Sussex.

Malling Olsen, K. and Larsson, H. (2004) Gulls of Europe, Asia and North America. Christopher Helm, London.

Mayaux, P., Bartholomé, E., Fritz, S. and Belward, A. (2004) A new land-cover map of Africa for the year 2000. *Journal of Biogeography* 31: 861-877.

Nguembock, B., Fjeldså, J., Couloux, A. and Pasquet, E. (2008) Phylogeny of *Laniarius*: molecular data reveal *L. liberatus* synonymous with *L. erlangeri* and 'plumage coloration' as unreliable morphological characters for defining species and species groups. *Molecular Phylogenetics and Evolution* 48: 396-407.

Nikolaus, G. (1987) Distribution atlas of Sudan's birds with notes on habitat and status. *Bonner Zoologische Monographien* 25: 1-322.

Nikolaus, G. (1989) Birds of south Sudan. *Scopus* Special Supplement 3: 1-124.

Onley, D. and Scofield, P. (2007) *Field Guide to the Albatrosses, Petrels and Shearwaters of the World.* Christopher Helm, London.

Rasmussen, P. C. and Anderton, J. C. (2005) *Birds of South Asia: The Ripley Guide.* Volumes 1 and 2. Smithsonian Institution and Lynx Edicions, Washington DC and Barcelona.

*Porter, R. F. (in prep.) Birds of Socotra. *Sandgrouse.*

Porter, R. F., Christensen, S. and Schiermacker-Hansen, P. (1996) *Field Guide to the Birds of the Middle East.* T & A D Poyser, London.

Porter, R. F. and Martins, R. P. (1996) Southern Yemen and Socotra: the report of the OSME survey in spring 1993. *Sandgrouse* 17.

Sibley, C. G. and Monroe, B. L. (1990) *Distribution and Taxonomy of the Birds of the World.* Yale University Press, New Haven and London.

Sinclair, I. and Ryan, P (2003) *Birds of Africa South of the Sahara.* Struik, Cape Town.

Smith, K. D. (1957) An annotated check-list of the birds of Eritrea. *Ibis* 99: 1-26, 307-337.

Stevenson, T. and Fanshawe, J. (2002) *Field Guide to the Birds of East Africa.* T & A D Poyser/Christopher Helm, London.

Svensson, L., Grant, P. J. Mullarney, K. and Zetterström, D. (1999) *Collins Bird Guide.* HarperCollins, London.

Taylor, B. (1998) *Rails: A Guide to the Rails, Crakes, Gallinules and Coots of the World.* Pica Press, Sussex.

Urban, E. K. and Brown, L. (1971) *A Checklist of the Birds of Ethiopia.* Haile Sellassie 1 University Press, Addis Ababa.

*Urban, E. K., Fry, C. H. and Keith S. (1986) *The Birds of Africa. Volume 2.* Academic Press, London.

*Urban, E. K., Fry, C. H. and Keith S. (1997) *The Birds of Africa. Volume 5.* Academic Press, London.

Vivero Pol, J. L. (2001) *A Guide to Endemic Birds of Ethiopia and Eritrea.* Shama Books, Addis Ababa.

Welch, H. and Welch, G. (1999) A report on the birds of Djibouti and the Bankoualé Palm *Livistona carinensis* Biodiversity Report no. 4. Ministère de l'Environnement, du Tourisme et de l'Artisanat, Direction de l'Environnement, Djibouti.

*Zimmerman, D. A., Turner, D. A. and Pearson, D. J. (1999) *Birds of Kenya and Northern Tanzania.* Christopher Helm, London.

INDEX

QUICK INDEX TO THE MAIN GROUPS OF BIRDS

Figures in **bold** refer to plate numbers